THE PAPERS OF

WOODROW WILSON

VOLUME 61

JUNE 18-JULY 25, 1919

SPONSORED BY THE WOODROW WILSON
FOUNDATION
AND PRINCETON UNIVERSITY

THE PAPERS OF

WOODROW

WILSON

ARTHUR S. LINK, *EDITOR*

DAVID W. HIRST, *SENIOR ASSOCIATE EDITOR*

JOHN E. LITTLE, *ASSOCIATE EDITOR*

MANFRED F. BOEMEKE, *ASSOCIATE EDITOR*

L. KATHLEEN AMON, *ASSISTANT EDITOR*

PHYLLIS MARCHAND, *INDEXER*

Volume 61
June 18-July 25, 1919

PRINCETON, NEW JERSEY
PRINCETON UNIVERSITY PRESS
1989

INTRODUCTION

THE opening of this volume, at June 18, 1919, finds Wilson on a whirlwind tour of Belgium, on which he sees at first hand the devastation of that victim of German aggression and of the fighting back and forth across its soil. Wilson greets Cardinal Mercier, the symbol of Belgian resistance, and he stands amidst the ruins of the library of the University of Louvain to receive an honorary degree from that institution as "the champion of the right." In speeches in Louvain and Brussels, Wilson hails Belgium for her fidelity to the cause of human freedom and reiterates American and Allied promises of prompt and full reparation and assistance in the reconstruction of the country.

Wilson returns to Paris to take up with his colleagues on the Council of Four the questions that remain to be solved before the treaty of peace with Germany can be signed. The first and most urgent of these is the completion of treaties with Poland, Rumania, and the successor states for the protection of ethnic and religious minorities, notably the Jewish people, in those countries. The Czechs gladly afford all guarantees, but the Rumanians are surly and defiant, while the Poles only grudgingly bow to the demands of the Supreme Council. Promises made in treaties signed under duress by the two latter countries render the future status of Jews in them problematic.

The Big Four continue to wrestle with a number of peripheral problems, such as the future of the Baltic provinces, the quicksand of Russia, clashing Italian and Yugoslav claims in Carinthia, the endless fighting between Poles and Ukrainians in eastern Galicia, and the fate of Turkey and the disposition of the provinces of the former Ottoman Empire. These problems remain unresolved when Wilson leaves Paris. In addition, Wilson, Lloyd George, and Clemenceau make another futile attempt to persuade the Italian government to yield its most pretentious claims in the Adriatic.

The main difficulty for Wilson and his colleagues during these last days of their deliberations is to find a German government that will sign the peace treaty. The government headed by Phillip Scheidemann resigns on June 20 rather than take the onus for accepting what it calls a *Diktat*. Then, on the next day, the Germans scuttle their fleet interned in the roadsteads of Scapa Flow in Scotland; a mob in Berlin burns captured French regimental flags due to be returned to Paris; and rumors sweep across western Europe of German plans to invade Poland and upset Allied terms of the settlement for the Polish-German frontiers. In spite of their indignation at the alleged German perfidy at Scapa Flow, Wilson, Lloyd George, and Clemenceau have no alternative but to accept what is a *fait accompli*; however, Clemenceau wants to occupy Essen in the center of the Ruhr in retaliation for the burning of the flags. Such talk becomes moot when the Big Four, forced to face the almost certain likelihood of a German refusal to sign the treaty, order Marshal Foch to prepare for a lightning thrust to Berlin. A great wave of relief sweeps over council chambers in Paris when the German National Assembly at Weimar votes on June 23 to yield to the Big Four's ultimatum, and a new government sends word that it will sign the treaty unconditionally.

The restoration of peace, for which the world has longed for five weary years, occurs with the signing of the treaty in the Hall of Mirrors in the Palace of Versailles (the very place in which the formation of the German Empire was proclaimed in 1871) in the afternoon of June 28. The simple ceremony that brings the war to an end is in stark contrast to the triumphal processions of Allied and American troops on the Champs Elysées, the clanging of bells, and the rejoicing of the crowds. Wilson, that same night, boards his train for Brest to return to the United States on the *George Washington*.

The return voyage provides a moment of leisure for Wilson, but there are signs that his mental strength has been strained beyond endurance. In his last days in Paris, he nearly creates an international incident by refusing to attend a dinner to be given in his honor by the President of the French Republic. Only an appeal by wise old Henry White persuades him to accept the invitation. On the *George Washington*, Wilson tries and fails to compose one of the most important speeches of his life—an address to the Senate to accompany his presentation of the treaty to that body. This is the first time that he has ever had difficulty in writing a state paper. He arrives in New York on July 8, responds gracefully to words of welcome in a speech in Carnegie Hall, and returns to Washington that night. Then, desperately mustering his intellectual resources, he writes the Senate speech but manages to complete it only hours before delivering it on July 10. It recalls America's contribution to the victory over the Central Powers, apotheosizes American soldiers as "crusaders" (but neglects to mention American seamen), reviews the peace settlement in very general terms, and ends by affirming that God Himself has led the American people to their destiny as leaders of the world. However, he fails utterly to answer senatorial critics of the treaty, who are objecting above all to the obligations which the United States would have to assume under the first article of that treaty, the Covenant of the

League of Nations. One loyal but cynical supporter of Wilson observes that the Senate wanted specific explanations, and Wilson entoned Longfellow's "Psalm of Life."

It is now obvious that the Senate's acceptance of the Versailles Treaty will depend upon Wilson's success in winning the support of about twenty Republican senators, called mild reservationists, who will consent to the ratification of that treaty only with reservations defining American obligations and protecting American interests under the Covenant. These reservations involve principally the right of member states to withdraw from the League, the jurisdiction of that body over such domestic matters as immigration and tariffs, explicit recognition of the Monroe Doctrine in the Covenant, and, most important, the obligations of the United States under Article X to go to war to protect the territorial integrity and political independence of member states. Actually, most of these senators ardently desire ratification of the treaty on these terms.

Wilson responds equivocally to this challenge—the greatest in his career as a legislative leader—to create a solid pro-League coalition and outmaneuver his opponent, Henry Cabot Lodge, chairman of the Foreign Relations Committee, who seems bent upon blocking American membership in the League of Nations. One stratagem fails very quickly—Wilson's attempt to establish the rule that amendments and reservations will have to be approved by a two-thirds vote of the Senate. Wilson seems to realize that he will have to accept some reservations. He thinks about going on a tour to appeal to the country to build support for ratification before dealing with the mild reservationists, but is dissuaded from this plan by Dr. Grayson, who warns that Wilson will probably not survive such a strenuous campaign. In his confusion and indecision, Wilson begins to hold a series of conferences with his potential Republican allies but offers no plan for his and their victory in the Senate. Then, on July 19, Wilson suffers what is most likely a small stroke. It disorients and disables him and, as this volume ends, Wilson is still without any strategy to assure ratification of the treaty. The outcome remains in suspense.

Publication of this volume brings to an end what we have called the Peace Conference Volumes, which began with Volume 53. We think that we have achieved the objectives that we announced for the Peace Conference Volumes in the Introduction to Volume 53, and we have nothing to add to what we said in that introduction about our editorial methods. However, we should reiterate that we did correct silently obvious errors and misspellings and occasionally added punctuation to the typescripts of the Hankey notes of the discussions of the Council of Ten and the Council of Four.

In the Peace Conference Volumes, as in all others in this series, we kept the focus on Wilson. However, since he was personally and directly involved in all decisions of the conference—important and unimportant—we think that we have brought together all materials essential for scholarly study of the Paris Peace Conference. In addition, the annotation of these volumes not only gives the broader historical context of the documents printed therein but also, through their cross references, provides a self-contained record beyond which only highly specialized scholars will need to go in order to understand the discussions and decisions of what was in fact the most complex international meeting in the history of the world.

"VERBATIM ET LITERATIM"

In earlier volumes of this series, we have said the following: "All documents are produced *verbatim et literatim*, with typographical and spelling errors corrected in square brackets only when necessary for clarity and ease of reading." The following essay explains our textual methods and review procedures.

We have never printed and do not intend to print critical, or corrected, versions of documents. We print them exactly as they are, with a few exceptions which we always note.

We never use the word *sic* except to denote the repetition of words in a document; in fact, we think that a succession of *sics* defaces a page. We usually repair words in square brackets when letters are missing. As we have said, we also repair words in square brackets for clarity and ease of reading. Our general rule is to do this when we, ourselves, cannot read the word without having to stop to puzzle out its meaning. Jumbled words and names misspelled beyond recognition of course have to be repaired. We correct the misspelling of names in documents in the footnotes identifying those persons.

However, when an old man writes to Wilson saying that he is glad to hear that Wilson is "comming" to Newark, or a semiliterate farmer from Texas writes phonetically, we see no reason to correct spellings in square brackets when the words are perfectly understandable. We do not correct Wilson's misspellings unless they are unreadable, except to supply in square brackets letters missing in words. For example, he consistently spelled "belligerent" as "belligerant." Nothing would be gained by correcting "belligerant" in square brackets.

We think that it is very important for several reasons to follow the rule of *verbatim et literatim*. Most important, a document has its own integrity and power, particularly when it is not written in perfect literary form. There is something very moving in seeing a Texas dirt farmer struggling to express his feelings in words, or a semiliterate former slave doing the same thing. Second, in Wilson's case it is essential to reproduce his errors in letters which he typed himself, since he usually typed badly when he was in an agitated state. Third, since style is the essence of the person, we would never correct grammar or make tenses consistent, as one correspondent has urged us to do. Fourth, we think it is very important that we print exact transcripts of Charles L. Swem's copies of Wilson's letters. Swem made many mistakes (we correct them in footnotes from a reading of his shorthand books), and Wilson let them pass. We thus have to assume that Wilson often did not read his letters before signing them, and this, we think, is a significant fact.

We think that our series would be worthless if we produced unreliable texts, and we go to considerable effort to make certain that the texts are authentic.

Our typists are highly skilled and proofread their transcripts carefully as soon as they have typed them. The Editor sight proofreads documents once he has assembled a volume and is setting its annotation. The Editors who write the notes read through the documents several times and are careful to check any anomalies. Then, once the manuscript volume has been completed and all notes checked, the Editor and Senior Associate Editor orally proofread the documents against the copy. They read every comma, dash, and character. They note every absence of punctuation. They study every nearly illegible word in written documents.

Once this process of "establishing the text" is completed, the manuscript volume goes to our editor at Princeton University Press, who checks the volume. The galley proofs are read against copy by the Press' proofreaders. We ourselves read the galley proofs three times. Our copyeditor gives them a sight reading against the manuscript copy to look for remaining typographical errors and to make sure that no line has been dropped. The Editor and Senior Associate Editor also sight read them against documents and copy. We then get the page proofs, which have been once more read against the manuscript copy at the Press. We check all changes three times. In addition, we get *revised* pages and check them twice.

This is not the end. The Editor, Senior Associate Editor, and Dr. Boemeke give a final reading to headings, description-location lines, and notes. Finally, our indexer of course reads the pages word by word. Before we return the pages to the Press, she brings in a list of queries, all of which are answered by reference to the documents.

Our rule in the Wilson Papers is that our tolerance of error is zero. No system and no person can be perfect. There may be errors in our volumes. However, we believe that we have done everything humanly possible to avoid error; the chance is remote that what looks at first glance like a typographical error is indeed an error.

We continue to be indebted to John Milton Cooper, Jr., William H. Harbaugh, Richard W. Leopold, and Betty Miller Unterberger for reading the manuscript of this volume and being helpful critics. As in the case of earlier peace conference volumes, Philippe-Roger Mantoux carefully reviewed our translation of his father's notes of the deliberations of the Council of Four. Alice Calaprice was the editor of this volume for Princeton University Press. Dr. Timothy Connelly of the staff of the National Historical Publications and Records Commission supplied copies from the National Archives of many documents printed in this volume. Finally, we welcome L. Kathleen Amon to the staff as the new Assistant Editor to succeed Denise Thompson.

THE EDITORS

Princeton, New Jersey
February 22, 1989

CONTENTS

The Papers, June 18-July 25, 1919
The Paris Peace Conference

Domestic Affairs

General Diplomatic, Military, and Naval Affairs

Personal Affairs

ILLUSTRATIONS

Following page 324

ABBREVIATIONS

A.C.N.P.	American Commission to Negotiate Peace
A.E.F.	American Expeditionary Forces
ALS	autograph letter signed
CC	carbon copy
CCL	carbon copy of letter
JD	Josephus Daniels
EAW	Ellen Axson Wilson
EMH	Edward Mandell House
FLP	Frank Lyon Polk
FR	*Papers Relating to the Foreign Relations of the United States*
FR 1919, Russia	*Papers Relating to the Foreign Relations of the United States, 1919, Russia*
GFC	Gilbert Fairchild Close
HCH	Herbert Clark Hoover
Hw, hw	handwritten, handwriting
HwLS	handwritten letter signed
JPT	Joseph Patrick Tumulty
MS, MSS	manuscript, manuscripts
NDB	Newton Diehl Baker
PPC	*Papers Relating to the Foreign Relations of the United States, The Paris Peace Conference, 1919*
RG	record group
RL	Robert Lansing
T	typed
TC	typed copy
TCL	typed copy of letter
THB	Tasker Howard Bliss
TI	typed initialed
TLS	typed letter signed
TNP	Thomas Nelson Page
TS	typed signed
WCR	William Cox Redfield
WGM	William Gibbs McAdoo
WHP	Walter Hines Page
WJB	William Jennings Bryan
WW	Woodrow Wilson
WWhw	Woodrow Wilson handwriting, handwritten
WWsh	Woodrow Wilson shorthand
WWT	Woodrow Wilson typed
WWTLS	Woodrow Wilson typed letter signed

ABBREVIATIONS FOR COLLECTIONS AND REPOSITORIES

Following the National Union Catalog of the Library of Congress

CaOOA	Public Archives Library, Ottawa
CSt-H	Hoover Institution on War, Revolution and Peace
CtY	Yale University

DLC	Library of Congress
DNA	National Archives
FFM-Ar	French Foreign Ministry Archives
MH-BA	Harvard University Graduate School of Business Administration
MiD	Detroit Public Library
NNC	Columbia University
NjP	Princeton University
PSC-P	Swarthmore College Peace Collection
SDR	State Department Records
VtU	University of Vermont
WP, DLC	Woodrow Wilson Papers, Library of Congress

SYMBOLS

[July 4, 1919]	publication date of published writing; also date of document when date is not part of text
[*July 25, 1919*]	composition date when publication date differs
[[July 9, 1919]]	delivery date of speech when publication date differs
* * * * * * *	text deleted by author of document
⟨ ⟩	text deleted by author of document and restored by Editors

THE PAPERS OF

WOODROW WILSON

VOLUME 61

JUNE 18-JULY 25, 1919

THE PAPERS OF
WOODROW WILSON

From the Diary of Dr. Grayson

Wednesday, June 18, 1919.

We[1] had breakfast on the train and arrived at Adinkerke at nine o'clock, where we found the King and Queen of Belgium[2] and the entire Belgian staff in waiting. The King and Queen had flown over to Adinkerke in an aeroplane, His Majesty being a speed maniac, as was thoroughly demonstrated to the satisfaction of every American in the party before we finally got back home to Paris.

There was the usual guard of honor lined up in front of the station and a long string of automobiles were in waiting. Originally, the Belgians had expected the President to remain with them for three days. This had been found impossible but they were determined that the program arranged for the three days should be carried out.

Entering the motor cars we left Adinkerke and started on a trip which covered by automobile more than 120 miles, and by rail another 100 miles. We started out over the main road towards the town of La Panne. The King and the President rode in an open motor car, while the Queen and Mrs. Wilson followed in a closed car directly behind. I was in the third car in a good position to collect the dust and to see just what was going on before we came to any particular spot but we went past everything so quickly that there was no chance to look when we were abreast of any matter of real interest.

Minister Brand Whitlock, accompanied by General Joostens of the Belgian Staff, also joined the party before we left.

The first stop that the party made was near Furnes, where the party alighted from the motor cars and inspected the locks of the famous Ypres Canal. It was by the use of these locks that the Belgians were able to flood the low territory of Flanders when the Germans made their famous effort to break through to the seas.

Returning to the cars the trip was resumed, passing through

---

[1] Accompanying President and Mrs. Wilson were Dr. Grayson, Vance C. McCormick, Bernard M. Baruch, Thomas W. Lamont, Herbert C. Hoover, Norman H. Davis, Charles L. Swem, Gilbert F. Close, General William Wright Harts, and Margaret Wilson.
[2] That is, Albert and Elisabeth, also Duchess of Bavaria.

Nieuport,[3] Pervyse, Dixmude and Houthulst Forest, where a stop was made for lunch.[4]

The trip was made at a speed that was never less than 35 miles an hour and averaged probably close to 50. The roads were very dusty. Most of the territory through which we passed was a complete waste, the armies having fought over and over it during the war. The towns had been leveled and only shattered semblances of buildings appeared on the horizon.

The luncheon stop had been arranged so that the President would see the wooded ridges where the Belgians finally turned back the German assault. A tent had been erected in the midst of a little clearing, just off the main roadway, and lunch was served in picnic fashion. Just a short distance away in the woods were the half-picked skeletons of a number of dead horses that had fallen victims to the shelling during the war, and the flies were as big as the normal bumble-bee at home. They bit right through heavy clothing and a more uncomfortable luncheon probably has never been enjoyed by a party.

During the luncheon the Queen, who is an expert photographer, insisted on photographing the party from every possible angle. She explained that she had collected several volumes of pictures, numbering many hundreds, which she personally had taken during the progress of the war.

Reentering the cars the trip was continued to Poelcapelle and to Ypres. The run from Poelcapelle to Ypres brought home to the entire party just what had happened during the war. This was the battlefield where the Canadian troops were practically annihilated, and at Ypres the Germans first used gas in shelling the Canadians, practically wiping out the crack Princess Pat's Light Infantry—the pride of the Dominion. As far as I could see, on either side of the road, was war wreckage—huge British tanks stood on end or lay shattered masses of steel, where they had been destroyed by German shell fire. Here and there the ground was dotted with the remains of shot-down airplanes; broken motor lorries were scattered in the dry sand. This ground was very dusty now, but during the entire time that it was being fought over it was a morass of mud.

---

[3] The party also stopped on the Yser River, two miles below Nieuport. This was the area where the British army had stopped the German advance on Calais in 1914. Wilson exclaimed to the King, "It is here, then—this immortal spot—where the fate of the world was played out." Brussels *La Libre Belgique*, June 19, 1919.

[4] In reply to a toast from the King, Wilson remarked as follows: "I am happy, on this first contact with my friends, the Belgians, in this Forest of Houthulst, where they showed in a supreme effort that they were strong enough to reconquer their Fatherland. The grandeur of sentiments that everyone must feel in such a place moves me to say to you once more what lively, profound, and sincere friendship I harbor for your country. I will carry away an unforgettable memory from this visit." *Ibid.*

In fact, it was explained that when anything—automobile or truck or munition lorry or even ambulances slipped off the road no effort was made to retrieve it; it was simply turned further over and gotten out of the way.

For miles along the road little clusters of graves could be seen—some German, some British, some Australian, some Canadian; in fact, every branch of the armies that had been fighting were represented by the crosses of the men who had left their bodies there.[5]

Arriving at Ypres the former Burgomaster of the town,[6] and the officials of the district, were in waiting. The President alighted from the car and was welcomed by the officials, who walked with him through the ruins, pointing out where the various historical structures had stood. The old Cathedral, which, before the war, was one of the noted landmarks of this section presented a fantastic appearance, one segment of the tower standing out in bold relief, with the rest of it just a crumbling mass of bricks and dust.[7] The noted Cloth Hall, which dated from the fifteenth century, was nothing but a memory—just a mound of broken stone standing where the structure had been. The Germans originally shelled the structure because the Canadians were using it for observation purposes. The Canadians after being driven out of the building completed the work of demolition by simply wiping the tower off the face of the earth. One great hall, to the right of the road on leaving Ypres, has been taken over by the Canadian government and a big sign upon it proclaimed that it was to be a memorial to those Canadian soldiers who had lost their lives while battling here, and that a suitable monument would later be erected here.

Leaving Ypres we motored at top speed through Menin, Roulers, Thourout, to the noted watering-place of Ostend. All along the road we passed hundreds of German prisoners, who were engaged in cleaning up the debris from the battlefields. They gazed curiously at the President's car but had no opportunity to see him because the King kept the machine moving at break-neck speed.

Instead of wearing the conventional garb, which ordinarily

[5] "Very impressing! Very impressing!" Wilson said, according to the English text in *ibid.*

[6] M. Colaert, acting Burgomaster of Ypres and a deputy from Ypres. After the presidential visit, Colaert told reporters that, in his conversation with Wilson, he had pleaded the cause that was dearest to him—the total reconstruction of his city. The Germans, Colaert said, liked ruins very much, but the people of Ypres did not like them at all. Wilson replied that he, also, hardly liked the preservation of ruins in the heart of localities called upon to live again. *Ibid.*

According to another report, Wilson listened attentively to Colaert and said: "These ruins will always be regarded as a monument of German barbarity and madness. One does not destroy such a city when there are no military reasons for doing so." Brussels *Le XXe Siècle,* June 20, 1919.

[7] Standing in front of the cloister of the cathedral, Wilson said: "It is a madness of destruction." Brussels *La Libre Belgique,* June 19, 1919.

would have been expected in these circumstances, the President was forced to wear a long linen duster to cover his clothes and protect them as much as possible from the dust. A golf cap had replaced the usual brightly polished silk hat. The King was in the uniform of a Field Marshal of the Belgian Army.

En route to Ostend the car carrying the Queen and Mrs. Wilson, and the car in which I was riding, took the wrong road and we were lost for some little time. The reason for this was that we were delayed from starting from the village of Thourout because a delegation of children were presenting the Queen and Mrs. Wilson with some bouquets of flowers, and the car with the King and the President had started not knowing that this was taking place. However, we managed to pick up the main party before Ostend was reached. We were given a warm reception at Ostend, where the people had gathered in large numbers in front of the Hôtel de Ville. The party passed down through the main thoroughfare in front of the famous Casino, around by way of the wharves, and thence to the Hôtel de Ville, where the King and the President and most of the members of the party alighted from the autos and went inside. The Burgomaster[8] made a short address of welcome, after which the President briefly told how glad he was to be able to make the trip.

Resuming the motor cars the trip was continued to Zeebrugge, which was the end of the motor journey. Zeebrugge naturally was a point of deep interest inasmuch as during the war it was utilized by the Germans as their submarine base, from which all of the undersea boats were sent out to prey upon shipping in the Atlantic lanes. It was at Zeebrugge that the British carried through what has been characterized as the best naval operation of the war. They sent a submarine into the mole loaded with dynamite and equipped as a depth bomb, timed to such an exactness that it exploded exactly as it was underneath the main bridge leading towards the Zeebrugge Canal; the bridge was blown up killing more than 300 Germans. It was also at Zeebrugge that the Cruiser Vindictive and a squadron of destroyers were run in and sunk so that they blocked the channel and made it impossible for the Germans to continue sending out their submarines through the canal. It was also at Zeebrugge that Captain Evans,[9] now the Port Commander of Zee-

[8] Dr. Moreaux, Acting Burgomaster. There is a brief account of Wilson's visit to Ostend in the Ostend *Le Carillon*, June 22, 1919.

[9] Capt. Edward Ratcliffe Garth Russell Evans, R.N., whose position at this time was actually Senior Naval Officer at Ostend. Grayson seems to have confused Evans' naval exploits with those of Capt. Alfred Francis Blakeney Carpenter, who was also present on this occasion. Carpenter, in command of an outmoded cruiser, *Vindictive*, not *Brussels*, had performed the feat described by Grayson during the famous British raid on Zeebrugge and Ostend in April 1918. Evans did not take part in the operation at all. See Arthur J. Marder, *From the Dread-*

brugge, ran the converted merchantman Brussels up against the concrete breakwater, demolished a section of the wall, and landed 400 men, who raided the German fortifications and caused great loss to the enemy. Captain Evans himself took charge of the party and escorted the President all over the fortifications. The President walked the entire length of the sea-wall, which was an enormous mass of concrete, having been constructed by the Germans at a very great cost. It bore all of the evidences of the various battles that had taken place in and about it. The President was very much interested in the recital of just what had taken place during the war.

Reentering the motors, the party was driven to the railroad station, where a special train was in waiting to bring us to Brussels. We arrived at Brussels at 9:30 in the evening to find the usual guard of honor lined up at the station and a good crowd along the streets between there and the Palace. The automobiles were quickly boarded, and we were escorted to the Palace, where the President and his immediate party were to be housed during their stay. The Palace in Brussels is one of the most magnificent structures in Europe. It was constructed by the late King Leopold, whose tastes were extremely luxurious, and who by reason of his Congo monopoly was the richest reigning monarch. He had spent money with a lavish hand and the structure not only is a delight to the eye but is one of the few modern buildings of its character in the world.

Gathered in the Palace to welcome the President were the chief officials, Cardinal Mercier, and members of the Belgian Cabinet. They were presented to the President, one by one, the King doing the introducing. While this was going on the crowd outside was cheering loudly demanding an opportunity to see the President. However, the King apparently had no intention of presenting the President to any one outside of the Palace walls and good-nights were speedily said, the King casually saying "good night," and leaving—all of the other guests departing forthwith. My attention, however, had been attracted to the size of the crowd and to its very evident desire to get at least a glimpse of the President before it dispersed. So I went to the President's bed-room and found him partially undressed. I told him of the circumstances, and he put on his coat, and the lights were turned on. As he moved over to the window the people recognized him and cheered, so he opened the window and stepped out upon a little balcony and made a brief but

nought to Scapa Flow: The Royal Navy in the Fisher Era, 1904-1919 (5 vols., London, 1961-70), V, 50-64.

touching address to the people below. In part the President said: "In coming personally I had merely followed my own heart and the heart of the people of America to Belgium." The crowd then dispersed and the President went to bed very tired as the result of the tremendous tax upon his resources by the day's strenuous program.

T MS (in possession of James Gordon Grayson and Cary T. Grayson, Jr.). About this diary, see n. 1 to the extract from it printed at Dec. 3, 1918, Vol. 53.

From Saad Zagloul[1]

Dear Sir: [Paris] June, 18, 1919.

I have the honour to acknowledge the receipt of your Confidential Secretary's letter of the 9th instant, in which he says that you have not had time to give an audience to one of my Colleagues and myself. We note with satisfaction that you do not exclude the hopes of a future interview.

We feel sure that you realize, Mr. President, the position in which you have been placed because of the role of International leadership which you have assumed.

We wish to impress upon you what would be the despair of the Egyptian people if their delegation failed to get even a hearing before the Exponent of International Right and Justice.

We do not believe you wish Egypt to be condemned unheard. And we do not feel that you can form a judgment on the Egyptian situation without giving a hearing to the Egyptians themselves.

We believe you purposely left open the possibility of a future audience with us, and we respectfully request that this be granted us as soon as possible, in order that history may reflect honour on you in this affair, as in all others connected with the Conference.

I have the honour to be Sir

Your humble and obedient servant.   Saad Zagloul

TLS (WP, DLC).
   [1] Egyptian nationalist leader, about whom see GFC to M. A. H. Kadi, March 20, 1919, n. 2, Vol. 56. Zagloul had come to Paris to plead Egypt's case for independence at the peace conference following his release from captivity in Malta on the orders of Gen. Allenby.

From Thomas Nelson Page
Personal

My dear Mr. President: Rome   June 18, 1919.

I want to thank you for your very kind letter,[1] and to say to you that it has relieved my mind very much. My whole desire in this matter has been to serve to the best of my ability yourself and the great principles for which you have stood and which you have championed so fearlessly.

I expect to arrive in Paris on Sunday afternoon, the twenty-second, should nothing happen to prevent my getting off on Saturday, and I hope very much that I may have the opportunity to see you either that evening or Monday to confer with you about the situation here.

I believe that I can render efficient service at home, possibly even more efficient than here now, and, therefore, I hope very much that I may be able to carry out my desire to join my wife and sail with her on the ship on which I have taken passage from Liverpool on the twenty-eighth. All particulars relating to my going may be left, I suppose, until I see you. Meantime, I want to say once more how highly I have appreciated your letter, as I have always appreciated your kindness to me. It has turned my most arduous duties into sincere pleasure.

Always, my dear Mr. President,
                    Yours most sincerely,   Thos Nelson Page

I can congratulate you on your choice of my successor.[2] I feel sure that he will do admirably. I hold him as you do in highest esteem.   T.N.P.

TLS (WP, DLC).
    [1] WW to TNP, June 14, 1919, Vol.60.
    [2] That is, Brand Whitlock.

From Joseph Patrick Tumulty

[The White House, June 18, 1919]

No. 196 Just a word for Ireland would help a great deal.
                    Tumulty.

T telegram (WP, DLC).

From Albert Sidney Burleson

Washington June 18-19

It is gratifying to be able to report that the attempted telegraphers strike has so far failed. Only two hundred seventy six of the forty thousand employees of the Western Union Co respected the order to strike. Certain newspapers, prompted by resentment growing out of the increase of the class postage rate, lent themselves to a grossly misleading propaganda, the effect of which was to encourage the spreading of the strike, but the public was not deceived and the telegraph traffic is now being handled without delay by both companies. The Senate has passed the resolution to return the wires forthwith. The House has not yet acted, but the House Committee reports a bill favoring an extension of the rates fixed during government control for a period that would safeguard the financial interest of the wire companies, which are cordially cooperating with me toward securing this end. I have taken all necessary steps to make prompt return to the various companies when the period of government control ends and it is a great satisfaction to me [to] assure you that I will be able to return these properties to the various owners with their operating organizations intact and without the values of these properties having been in the slightest impaired. The fear that this situation may have been the occasion of even slight worry to you has been the source of great distress to me. I feel you will believe me when I say that I would [not] have brought my troubles to you but for matter appearing in newspapers indicating that misleading information was being sent you. The American people watch with intense interest the great struggle you are making to safeguard the peace of the world and undoubtedly they are overwhelmingly in accord with what you are doing and only await the opportunity to make known their sympathy when you are ready to submit the fruits of your labors to the Senate of the United States. May God preserve and strengthen you.   Burleson

T telegram (WP, DLC).

From the Diary of Dr. Grayson

Thursday, June 19, 1919.

The President was forced to rise very early, and, after a hasty breakfast, the party entered automobiles for the trip to Charleroi. This trip had been arranged for the purpose of showing the President the ruined factories in that section which had been completely and systematically looted by the Germans. They had taken every piece of machinery out of all of these factories and had transferred them to German plants. Their work in looting was carried through with characteristic German thoroughness, the method being to card-index all of the machinery in all plants and to send catalogues to German manufacturers showing that this machinery was available and asking what particular pieces were needed to equip their plants. A good part of the machinery actually was taken into Germany, while train-loads were stopped as a result of the armistice and were still on the sidings along the railroad.

The trip to Charleroi carried the President past the historic battleground of Waterloo, and the roads were taken so that he went down on one side and returned on the other side of the famous monument. However, the President had little chance to see anything, as the trip was made at an even greater speed than that of yesterday, there being seldom a time when the speedometer was not close upon the 50 mark, and sometimes 60 was exceeded.

At Charleroi the President was met by the Burgomaster[1] and the city officials. Groups of children were around, all carrying flowers, which they presented to the President, the Queen and to Mrs. Wilson. Groups of children lined the road also on the way to Charleroi and tried to throw flowers at the President's car, but so great was the speed that before the flowers landed it was the third and fourth car that was opposite the thrower.

The President got back to the Palace at twelve o'clock, in time to wash and change his clothes. He then proceeded to the American Legation, where he was the host at a luncheon given in honor of the King and Queen. The President made a very brief but very effective address in proposing the health of the King and Queen.

As soon as the luncheon was over, the President received the members of the American colony in Belgium and, after them, a delegation of Belgian newspaper proprietors and correspondents.[2]

[1] Émile Devreux. Wilson and his party also visited the ruined "Usines de la Providence" at Marchienne-au-Pont, three miles from Charleroi.
[2] According to one report, Wilson said to this group: "I am happy to have the pleasure of your visit. I am sorry to learn that a certain number among you were not able to accompany me to Charleroi, but I want to tell you how I was profoundly impressed by my visit to the industrial region. It was a visible and tangible demonstration of what I imagined in advance. At Charleroi, I made a comparison between the state of that region and that which surrounds Pittsburgh, in the United States. I am reminded of the method and skill with which this evil work of the destruction of your industrial prosperity has been perpetrated. The impression that I gained has been so lively and so profound that I am happy that they have given me the opportunity of seeing for myself all that has been done there." Brussels Le XXᵉ Siècle, June 20, 1919.
From another report: "I am very happy to have your visit. I am very sorry that not all of you were able to go to Charleroi. I take this occasion to say to you how profoundly I was struck by this visit to the 'Usines de la Providence.' It was for me the visible and tangible demonstration of what I imagined in advance. In seeing the industrial area of

Leaving the Legation, we returned to the Palace and were driven in state to the Legislative Chamber, where the President was received by the Senate and the Chamber of Deputies in the Chamber Room. This was a most impressive function, probably the best of the entire trip. The Chamber itself is a high-ceilinged room, arranged in semi-circular form. To the left of the Speaker's stand a temporary throne had been constructed, with a wonderful canopy of scarlet velvet trimmed with gold above it. Here Mrs. Wilson and Miss Margaret Wilson sat with the Belgian Queen. They were escorted to their seats before the entrance of the President and the King. The seats on the floor were occupied by the Senators and Deputies, while their families occupied the boxes which towered in tiers in the rear of the room.

The President and the King were preceded into the Chamber by thirty Belgian officers escorting the standards of fifteen fighting Belgian regiments. These standards were massed at the rear of the Speaker's stand, with the escort standing at attention.

As the King and the President entered the room they were greeted with very warm applause. The address of welcome was made by the President of the Chamber of Deputies[3] speaking in Flemish. Then M. Hymans addressed the President in English. The President, responding, made a speech that probably pleased the audience more than any speech that they had heard in some time. Although the President spoke in English, it was apparent that two-thirds of the Legislative representatives understood what he was saying. This was demonstrated by the fact that they broke into applause time and time again in the middle of a sentence, which was filled with promise for Belgium's interest. Had they waited for him to conclude his sentences and stop as is usual with a practiced speaker, it would have been plain that they did not understand, but the very fact that their applause punctuated his address in exactly the same proportion as he spoke of promise for Belgium's future indicated that they knew just what he was saying

---

Charleroi, I thought that I could call to mind certain regions of my country, such as the one around Pittsburgh. At Marchienne, I was able to take account of the method and skill with which the Germans perpetrated their evil work. I felt there emotions so profound that I am happy that they gave me the opportunity to see for myself what the Germans have done." Brussels *Le Soir*, June 20, 1919.

Just before this meeting, Wilson received a delegation from the Belgian Socialist party. He then received a delegation from the National Political Committee. They presented a petition to Wilson asking for a complete revision of the Treaty of 1839. It requested the "restitution" to Belgium of the Dutch province of Limburg, freedom of navigation on the Meuse and its tributaries, and control of the mouth of the Scheldt. Wilson replied: "What you tell me is of the highest interest and will be examined, I promise you, in the most careful manner." Brussels *Le Soir*, June 20, 1919. See also Brussels *Le Peuple*, June 20, 1919, for a brief report on Wilson's meeting with the Socialist delegation.

to them. As soon as the President ended his speech he was escorted back through the building and across to the Senate Chamber. It was in this Senate Chamber that Edith Cavell,[4] the British martyred nurse, was court-martialed and condemned to death by the Germany military authorities. The seat which she occupied during the trial had been covered with flowers and the national colors, and it was stated that these flowers would be kept there perpetually as a memento of the heroism of the woman.

Leaving the Assembly Building the cars were reentered and the party proceeded to Malines, where Cardinal Mercier was in waiting to receive the President. The President had been very anxious to meet the Cardinal, whose action in defying the Germans during the entire period of German occupancy of Belgium had aroused the admiration of the entire world. The meeting between the two was touching in the extreme. Addressing the President, the Cardinal said that he was convinced that when the history of the war and the Peace Conference was finally written, it would be found that the peace arrived at would be referred to as the Wilsonian Peace. The President thanked the Cardinal for his complimentary reference. The President then made one of the most eloquent and touching speeches that I have ever heard, although it was only of about three minutes' duration.[5] He referred to the Cardinal as the shepherd who had watched over the welfare of his flock, despite the aggression and abuses at the hands of the Germans, and referred feelingly to the fact that the Cardinal at no time had deserted those who were looking to him for guidance. He declared that, owing to his heroic spirit and for the things that he had stood, the enemy had not dared to lay a hand upon or molest the Cardinal in any way.

The President inspected the Cathedral and then had tea in the Cardinal's apartment. During the time that the President was in Malines the wonderful chimes in the Cathedral tower were played by Jef Denyn.[6] He had arranged a program which commenced with Hail Columbia and which concluded with Brabançonne. The program is as follows:

Hail Columbia.

Old French Songs:

a. Chantons, je vous en prie, (1550).

[3] Prosper Antoine Joseph Marie Poullet.

[4] About whom, see the index references in Vol. 35 of this series.

[5] No text of Wilson's remarks seems to be extant. Grayson's paraphrase is fuller than those in the reports in the Belgian newspapers.

[6] Jef [Joseph Guillaume François] Denijn, not Denyn, master carillonneur of the Cathedral of Saint Rombant at Malines.

b. Plus ne suis ce que j'ai été, (1532) Cl. Marot[7]

6a Sonata—Val. Nicolai.[8]

Old Flemish Songs:

   a. 't Sneeuwwit vogeltje,
   b. 's Avonds als ik slapen ga,

Mijn Moederspraak, Peter Benoit.[9]

Praeludium, Jef Denyn.

Brabançonne.[10]

The cars were reentered and the party then proceeded to the Town Hall at Louvain, where the Burgomaster[11] and the officials of the city that was the scene of the first dastardly outrage of the Germans in the war were awaiting to welcome him. The President was given a very warm reception. It had been arranged by the University of Louvain to confer a degree upon the President while he was in the city. They had selected as the place to confer this degree the Library Building which the Germans had so ruthlessly burnt during the early days of the war in 1914. The President, accompanied by the Cardinal and by the King and other members of the party, walked from the Town Hall to the Library Building. Along the line were delegations of Belgian boy scouts, very picturesquely attired, while hundreds of children carrying bouquets of flowers crowded about the party and pelted the President and Mrs. Wilson with their flowers. Arriving at the Library Building, the party went into the room which was known as the Manuscript Room, in the center of which an altar had been erected. Lined up around the room were the monks of Louvain University. The Cardinal conferred the degree upon the President.[12] The scene was remarkable. There is no roof on the building at all, it having been burned off when the Germans fired the structure. The ruined, smoked walls were in sharp contrast to the new altar in the center of the room. In responding to the Cardinal's remarks in conferring the degree, the President bitterly arraigned the Germans for their destructive policy, especially for the wanton destruction that they had wrought in this historic building. He paid the highest tribute to education and declared that there had been absolutely no necessity for German ruthlessness in this particular case. He referred to the fact that the Germans had misused their education as a warning that

[7] Clément Marot, French poet of the sixteenth century.

[8] Valentino Nicolai, composer of unknown origin, active in London and Paris at various times between 1775 and 1798.

[9] Belgian composer (1834-1901).

[10] That is, *La Brabançonne*, the Belgian national anthem.

[11] M. Colins. Wilson's reply is printed below.

[12] Actually, Msgr. Paulin Ladeuze, Rector of the University of Louvain, conferred the degree upon Wilson. Wilson's remarks upon this occasion are printed below.

education also could be abused when the occasion demanded if the person was unscrupulous enough to do so.

The automobiles were reentered and the party returned immediately to Brussels, where a reception had been arranged for the President and the party at the Hôtel de Ville. This reception was presided over by Burgomaster Max.[13] In the square outside of the building an enormous crowd had gathered, made up chiefly of women and children, who cheered the President very loudly as he entered. The President was warmly received by the invited guests inside and Burgomaster Max feelingly referred to the part which America played in the war, and paid a high tribute to the President's efforts. The President responded in a brief address, in which he eulogized the Burgomaster as the highest type of a competent official.

Leaving the Hôtel de Ville, the President passed out through a large crowd of young school girls, who sang "Liberty Bells" and "America" in English.

Returning to the Palace, the President took part as the guest of honor at a state dinner given by the King and Queen. The dinner was served in a most sumptuous apartment. The silver set used is one of the most costly ever made and was presented by the late Queen Victoria to the late King Leopold of Belgium. There were more than 150 guests present.

The table was set in the form of a horse-shoe, and the decorations were elaborate in the extreme. The guests for the most part were in diplomatic costume, with their breasts covered with glittering decorations of every sort. Just before the dinner, the King sent for me and conferred upon me the decoration of the [blank].[14] He told me that he would esteem it as a high honor if I would wear it during the dinner, and, as there was nothing left for me to do but accept, I did so in as gracious a manner as possible.

Leaving the Palace, we were escorted to the station by the King and Queen and their suites. The President told the King that he would like very much to invite him to visit the United States, and he hoped that he would be able to come. He explained, however, that when Roosevelt was President, the latter had invited so many people to come to the United States in an official capacity that Congress objected to paying the bills and as a result passed a law that no one should be invited without their knowledge and consent. Therefore, the President explained he had to make his invitation more or less an informal one. The King told the President that he

[13] That is, Adolphe Eugène Jean Henri Max, about whom, see n. 3 to the extract from the Grayson Diary printed at June 17, 1919, Vol. 60.
[14] The Ordre de Léopold II.

hoped that he would be able to come to the United States, as he
has been very anxious to visit there.

We left Brussels at eleven o'clock. The President retired almost
as soon as the train passed out of the station. Just before I left him,
I asked him what his impressions were of the King and he said:
"He is every inch a man and a true democrat."

Remarks at a Luncheon[1]

19 June, 1919.

I want to express my pleasure not only to be in Belgium, but to
be personally associated with the King and Queen. We have found
them what all the world has told us they were—perfectly genuine,
perfectly delightful, and perfectly devoted to the interests of their
people; and not only so, but what is very rare just now, very just in
their judgments of the events of the past and of the events that are
now taking place.

I could not help expressing the opinion, which I did yesterday,
that that must arise from the fact that they had intimately associated themselves in life with their people. If you live with the talk-
ers, you get one impression. If you live with the liver, you get another impression. You come into contact with realities, and only
realities make you wise and just.

I want, with this very brief preface, in which I am speaking from
my heart, to propose the health and long life of His Majesty the
King and her Majesty the Queen.

T MS (WP, DLC).
    [1] Given in Wilson's honor at the American legation by Brand Whitlock. Numerous
dignitaries, including the King and Queen, were present.

An Address to the Belgian Parliament

19 June, 1919.

Your Majesty and gentlemen: It is with such profound emotion
that I express my deep appreciation of the generous welcome you[1]
have given me that I am not at all sure that I can find the words to
say what it is in my heart to say. Monsieur Hymans has recited to
you some of the things which America tried to do to show her profound friendship and sympathy with Belgium, but Mr. Hymans
was not able to testify, as I am, to the heart of America that was
back of her efforts; for America did not do those things merely because she conceived it her duty to do them, but because she re-

joiced in this way to show her real humanity and her real knowledge of the needs of an old and faithful friend. And these things, I hope, will be the dearer in your memory because of the spirit which was behind them. They were small in themselves. We often had the feeling that we were not doing as much as we could do. We knew all the time that we were not doing as much as we wanted to do, and it is this spirit, and not what was done, which deserves, I hope, to be remembered.

It is very delightful to find myself at last in Belgium. I have come at the first moment that I was relieved from imperative duty. I could not come for my own pleasure and in neglect of duty to a country, where I knew that I should meet men who had done their duty; where I knew I should meet a Sovereign who had constantly identified himself with the interests and the life of his people at every necessary sacrifice to himself; where I should be greeted by a Burgomaster who never allowed the enemy to thrust him aside and always asserted the majesty and authority of the municipality which he represented; where I should have the privilege of meeting a Cardinal who was the true shepherd of his flock, the majesty of whose spiritual authority awed even the unscrupulous enemy himself, who knew that they did not dare lay a hand upon this servant of God; and where I should have the privilege of grasping the hand of a General[2] who never surrendered, and on every hand should meet men who had known their duty and done it. I could not come to Belgium until I felt that I was released from my duty. I sought in this way to honor you by recognizing the spirit which I knew I should meet with here.

When I realize that at my back are the fighting standards of Belgium, it pleases me to think that I am in the presence of those who knew how to shed their blood as well as do their duty for their country. They need no encomium from me. I would rather turn for a moment with you to the significance of the place which Belgium bears in this contest which now, thank God, is ended. I came here because I wished to associate myself in counsel with the men who I knew had felt so deeply the pulse of this terrible struggle, and I wanted to come also because I realized, I believe, that Belgium and her part in the war is in one sense the key of the whole struggle, because the violation of Belgium was the call to duty which aroused the nations. The enemy committed many outrages in this war, gentlemen, but the initial outrage was the fundamental outrage of all. They, with an insolent indifference, violated the sacredness of treaties. They showed that they did not care for the honor of any pledge. They showed that they did not care for the independence of any nation, whether it had raised its hand against them or not, that they were ruthless in their determination to have their whim at their pleasure. Therefore, it was the violation of Belgium that wakened the world to the realization of the character of the struggle.

A very interesting thing came out of that struggle, which seems almost like an illogical consequence. One of the first things that the representatives of Belgium said to me after the war began was that they did not want their neutrality guaranteed. They did not want any neutrality. They wanted equality. Not because, as I understood them, their neutrality was insecure, but because their neutrality put them upon a different basis of action from other peoples. In their natural and proper pride, they desired to occupy a place that was not exceptional, but in the ranks of free peoples under all governments. I honored this instinct in them, and it was for that reason that the first time I had occasion to speak of what the war might accomplish for Belgium, I spoke of her winning a place of equality among the nations.

So Belgium has, so to say, once more come into her own through this deep valley of suffering through which she has gone. Not only that, but her cause has linked the governments of the civilized world together. They have realized their common duty. They have drawn together as if instinctively into a league of right. They have put the whole power of organized mankind behind the conception of justice, which is common to mankind. That is the significance, gentlemen, of the League of Nations.

The League of Nations is an inevitable consequence of this war. It is a league of right, and no thoughtful statesman who lets his thought run into the future could wish for a moment to slacken those bonds. His first thought would be to strengthen them and to perpetuate this combination of the great governments of the world for the maintenance of justice. The League of Nations is the child of this great war for right. It is the expression of those permanent resolutions which grew out of the temporary necessities of this great struggle, and any nation which declines to adhere to this Covenant deliberately turns away from the most telling appeal that has ever been made to its conscience and to its manhood. The nation that wishes to use the League of Nations for its convenience, and not for the service of the rest of the world, deliberately chooses to turn back to those bad days of selfish contest, when every nation thought first and always of itself and not of its neighbor, thought of its rights and forgot its duties, thought of its power and overlooked its responsibility. Those bad days, I hope, are gone, and the great moral power, backed if need be by the great physical power of the civilized nations of the world, will now stand firm for the maintenance of the fine partnership which we have thus inaugurated.

It cannot be otherwise. Perhaps the conscience of some chancelleries was asleep and the outrage of Germany awakened it. You cannot see one great nation violate every principle of right without beginning to know what the principles of right are and to love them, to despise those who violate them, and to form the firm resolve that such a violation shall now be punished and in the future prevented.

These are the feelings with which I have come to Belgium, and it has been my thought to propose to the Congress of the United States as a recognition, as a welcome of Belgium into her new state of complete independence, to raise the mission of the United States of America to Belgium to the rank of an Embassy and send an Ambassador. This is the rank which Belgium enjoys in our esteem. Why should she not enjoy it in form and in fact?

So, gentlemen, we turn to the future. Monsieur Hymans has spoken true terms of the necessities that lie ahead of Belgium and of many another nation that has come through this great war with suffering and with loss. We have shown Belgium, in the forms which he has been generous enough to recite, our friendship in the past. It is now our duty to organize our friendship along new lines. The Belgian people and the Belgian leaders need only the tools to restore their life. Their thoughts are not crushed. Their purposes are not obscured. Their plans are complete, and their knowledge of what is involved in industrial revival is complete.

What their friends must do is to see to it that Belgium gets the necessary priority with regard to obtaining raw materials, the necessary priority in obtaining the means to restore the machinery by which she can use these raw materials, and the credit by which she can bridge over the years during which it will be necessary for her to wait to begin again. These are not so much tasks for governments as they are tasks for thoughtful businessmen and financiers and those who are producers in other countries. It is a question of shipping also, but the shipping of the world will be relieved of its burdens of troops in a comparatively near future, and there will be new bottoms in which to carry the cargoes, and the cargoes ought readily to impel the master of the ship to steer for Belgian ports.

I believe, after having consulted many times with my very competent advisers in these matters, that an organized method of accomplishing these things can be found. It is a matter of almost daily discussion in Paris, and I believe that as we discuss it from day to day we come nearer and nearer to a workable solution and a practicable plan. I hope, not only, but I believe that such a plan

will be found, and you may be sure that America will be pleased, I
will not say more than any other friend of Belgium, but as much
as any other friend of Belgium if these plans are perfected and carried out.

Friendship, gentlemen, is a very practical matter. One thing that
I think I have grown weary of is sentiment that does not express
itself in action. How real the world has been made by this war!
How actual all its facts seem. How terrible the circumstances of its
life. And if we be friends, we must think of each other not only,
but we must act for each other. We must not only have a sentimental regard, but we must put that regard into actual deeds. There is
an old proverb which has no literary beauty, but it has a great deal
of significance: "The proof of the pudding is the eating thereof." It
is by that maxim that all friendships are to be judged. It is when a
friendship is put to the proof that its quality is found. So our business now is not to talk, but to act; is not so much to debate as to
resolve; is not so much to hesitate upon the plan as to perfect the
details of the plan, and at every turn to be sure that we think not
only of ourselves but of humanity.

For, gentlemen, the realities of this world are not discussed
around dinner tables. Do you realize for how small a percentage of
mankind it is possible to get anything to eat tomorrow if you do not
work today; how small a percentage of mankind can slacken their
physical and thoughtful effort for a moment and not find the
means of a subsistence fail them? Some men can take holidays.
Some men can relieve themselves from the burden of work, but
most men cannot, most women cannot, and the children wait upon
the men and women who work—work every day, work from the
dawn until the evening. These are the people we must think about.
They constitute the rank and file of mankind. They are the con-
stituents of statesmen, and statesmen must see to it that policies
are not now run along the lines of a national pride, but along the
lines of humanity, along lines of service, along those lines which
we have been taught are the real lines by the deep sufferings of
this war. This is the healing peace of which Monsieur Hymans el-
oquently spoke. You heal the nations by serving the nations, and
you serve them by thinking of mankind.

T MS (WP, DLC), with a few corrections from the text in the *Paris Herald*, June 20,
1919.
    [1] Poullet's and Hyman's speeches welcoming Wilson are printed in Brussels *La Libre
Belgique*, June 20, 1919, among other newspapers. There is an English-language digest
of Hyman's speech, a T MS, in WP, DLC. The full text of Wilson's speech is printed,
inter alia, in French in Brussels *La Nation Belge*, June 20, 1919, and Brussels *L'Indé-
pendance Belge*, June 20, 1919. The text in Brussels *La Libre Belgique*, June 20, 1919,
is an abridgement.
    [2] Lt. Gen. Gérard Mathieu Joseph-Georges Leman, who had defended the city of
Liège in August 1914 and spent most of the war as a prisoner in Germany.

Remarks at the City Hall of Louvain

Louvain, June 19, 1919.

Mr. Burgomaster: May I not say with what deep appreciation I have listened to your generous remarks,[1] and say that I know I am expressing not only my own feelings but the feelings of the people of the United States when I say that they will never forget your sufferings. We shall cherish with the deepest emotion the memories of the sufferings that came upon Louvain at the beginning of this war. As a man who has spent so many years at a university, you may be sure that I can testify to the feelings of the university men of the world at the wanton desecration of your university. I think, Sir, that what Louvain suffered was the first notification to the world in general of what the spirit of this war was on the part of the Germans, that Louvain will always stand with my own people, and, I am sure, with the other people of the world, as a symbol of undeserved suffering, as a symbol of war put to its wrong and terrible uses, as I trust the world may never see it again. It was the more distressing because the nation that committed this wrong was the nation that had pretended to stand for university development, for the development of those arts and sciences which should know no jealousy, much less the cruelties of international rivalries, and therefore it was with peculiar horror that the world noted the sufferings of this city. It is with peculiar feelings therefore that I greet you and receive this evidence of your friendship, which is unusually gratifying to me.

CC MS (WP, DLC).

[1] According to one report, Burgomaster Colins paid a moving tribute to Wilson and told him that the city had decided to name one of its main streets for him. Brussels *La Libre Belgique*, June 20, 1919.

A Greeting by Désiré Félicien François Joseph Cardinal Mercier

June 19th 1919.

Mr. President: During the past two years, the whole world has had its eyes constantly fixed on the great Nation, whose destiny was entrusted to your noble and wise guidance.

By the promptness with which America has recruited and equipped an army of over two million men; by the courage and the tenacity of her gallant sons on land and sea; by the inspiring sacrifice that led these soldiers and their chiefs to accept the unity of command of the French Generalissimo; America has brought the cause of civilisation to the ultimate and decisive Victory.

Since arrogant Germany has bowed her head and bent her

knees, now, more than ever, all hearts and eyes have been turned towards your eminent personality. The World's Peace, which we expect is going to be signed tomorrow, will largely be your work, and I would not be surprised if history gave it the name of the Wilsonian Peace.

We are, Mr. President, greatly honoured by the gracious visit which you are so kind as to make to our city of Malines, and to me, as the representative of the clergy and bishops of Belgium.

It will be the fulfilment of my dearest wish, to go to the United States to tell your countrymen, of my admiration and friendship, and to let them know how thankful I am for all they have done for my country.

I shall be especially proud to be able to visit Washington, in order that I may offer to you, Sir, to Madame and to Miss Wilson, whom I am most happy to greet here today, in the presence of our beloved King and Queen, public testimony of my great admiration and my eternal gratitude.[1]

I pray to God to bless you, Sir and your dear family, to bless your wonderful people, the great and noble Republic of the United States.

Long live President Wilson!

D. S. Card. Mercier, Arch. de Malines

TS MS (WP, DLC).
[1] Wilson, in part of his reply, said: "In the name of the American people, I can assure you that Your Eminence's visit to the United States will be marked by an enthusiastic reception." Brussels *Le XXᵉSiècle*, June 20, 1919.

Remarks at the University of Louvain

June 19, 1919.

I wish I could in some adequate manner, Sir,[1] express the profound emotions which this place and this scene excite in me. It is a very solemn thing for one who has been associated with university life to see the evidences of such acts as were capable of destroying a monument of scholarship and industry like this. It is one of the peculiar pains of this war, Sir, that a nation that had professed to devote itself to the highest studies, studies which ought to be elevated above all interested motives, should itself have been guilty of destroying the works of scholars. I cannot help feeling that for the time being, at any rate, it has put itself out of the brotherhood of scholars. Because there is a brotherhood of scholars. When it finds its true expression, it is the most generous brotherhood of all, because it expresses itself in the general ideas and concepts of humanity and of disinterested service which, after all, must sooner or later lift the levels of humanity. And so I shall never forget, Sir, the touching experience which you have permitted me to have today, of receiving an honorary degree from a great and ancient university amidst the ruins of a part of its establishment. I do not know how I shall be worthy of this honor, Sir. Apparently my years of scholarship have passed and strange fortunes have thrust upon me the role of actor in international scenes. But, after all, a man who has once served the things of the mind never willingly or entirely leaves that service. And I think it should be the ambition of all university men to show that their studies are not cloistered and selfish but that they are intended for the enlightenment of the world and that with enlightenment will come those permanent motives of service which cannot operate in the dark but must always operate where the light is full, and that underneath scholarship there should lie no selfish spirit of competition, no selfish spirit of envy, but always the generous spirit of cooperation. For unless there be a moral spirit underlying scholarship, it can be as hideously selfish as any other profession. Let us bind ourselves together then, Sir, in an international brotherhood of the mind which shall introduce into the products of the intellect also the fruits of the heart.

T MS (WP, DLC).
    [1] Msgr. Ladeuze had just conferred the degree of Doctor Honoris Causa upon Wilson and, while doing so, had said in part: "It is with deeply felt emotion that we salute here the former President of Princeton University and beg him to accept the diploma of Doctor Honoris Causa, which the faculty offers to the champion of the right." Brussels *La Libre Belgique*, June 20, 1919.

Remarks at the City Hall of Brussels

19 June, 1919.

Mr. Burgomaster: I feel highly honored to be received with such words from you, Sir,[1] speaking as the representative of this ancient municipality, with so many distinguished events associated with its sturdy independence and self-government. And I feel the more honored, Sir, because the whole world recognizes in you a worthy representative of this great municipality.

I think the reflection which comes uppermost in one's mind in thinking about this war is that no nation is conquered that is not conquered in its spirit; that an unconquerable spirit is the last word in politics; and that the unconquerable spirit lives particularly in those nations which are self-governed. The one thing that is indestructible in our time is the spirit of self-governed people. Therefore, it is inspiriting to me, and I think to all believers in self-government, to be welcomed by an ancient municipality like this, which represents in so distinguished a way the spirit and practice of self-government. I know something, Sir, of the history, the independence, the self-confidence, the proper self-confidence, of the municipalities of Belgium. I know how there has persisted into modern times something of that solidarity of the commune, something of that individuality of the municipality, which was characteristic of the Middle Ages and which brought the spirit of self-government through that dark period when nations had ceased to govern themselves, but when localities continued to assert their right of self-government. So that I feel welcomed today by those whom I would fain believe to be my friends and the friends of the American people, as the American people are certainly your friends.

They are your friends in a very deep and true sense. They understand what Belgian liberty signifies. They understand what Belgian suffering signifies. And it is, I believe, one of their deepest ambitions to satisfy the duty of friendship as towards the Belgian people. They have tried to do so in the past. It has been one of my pleasures on this trip to be accompanied by my distinguished fellow-countryman, Mr. Herbert Hoover, who I know has had Belgium written on his heart throughout this war, and whose pleasure it has been touching to see, as in going about the country we have seen, healthy children and robust men and women, whom he could properly believe were served by the food which came from America. I believe that I have the privilege of speaking his thoughts. One of the peculiarities of Mr. Hoover is that he is too modest to speak for himself, and therefore I am proud to share with him some of your welcome. I am accompanied by other colleagues with whom I have been in counsel throughout the war and whose thought, I can tell you, has been constantly upon the methods by which Belgium could be helped, whose thought is now upon that subject, whose hope is that some method will be worked out, as I had the privilege of saying to your Parliament today, by which systematic help can be rendered to Belgium.

So I feel peculiarly honored, in this ancient building of this ancient city, to be received at your hands, Sir, and I bring you the warm greeting of the people of America. I am sure I express their wish when I say, long live the prosperity of Brussels and of Belgium, and of her King and Queen.

T MS (WP, DLC).
[1] The text of Burgomaster Max's speech introducing Wilson is printed, *inter alia*, in Brussels *Le XXe Siècle*, June 20, 1919.

Remarks at a Dinner in the Royal Palace[1]

19 June, 1919.

Let me express, Sir, the very deep appreciation with which I have heard your remarks.[2] You truly say that I have come to Belgium to express my own deep personal interest and sympathy—sympathy with her sufferings and interest in her prosperity. But I would have no personal consequence if it were not my privilege for the time being to represent the people of the United States. What gives me confidence in expressing this sympathy and this interest is that I know in expressing those sentiments that I am expressing the feelings of the people of the United States. There has never been in the United States a more general and universal comprehension of sympathy with the affairs of another nation than that which the people of the United States have had for the affairs and the people of Belgium.

I have had the very great advantage of seeing the little that I have had time to see of the experiences of Belgium under your guidance, and I know how true it is, Sir, that you speak for your people. One of the delightful experiences of these last days has been to hear the acclaim from the heart which everywhere greeted *le Roi*. Their first cry was for their King, their second thought was the welcome of the stranger, and I was glad in my heart that it should be so, because I know that I was with a real statesman and a real ruler. No man has any power, Sir, except that which is given him by the things and the people he represents.

I have felt many points of sympathy between the people whom I have the pleasure of representing and the people whom you represent. They are a very democratic people, and it has been very delightful to find, Sir, that you are a true democrat. All real masters of the sentiments of the people are parts of the people, and one of the things that gives confidence in the future of Belgium is the consciousness that one has of the self-reliance and the indomitable spirit of her people. They need to have a friendly hand extended to them, but they do not need to have anybody take care of them. A people that is taken care of by its government is a people that its government will always have to take care of. But the people of Belgium, if I have caught any glimpse of their spirit and character, do not need to have anybody take care of them. They need, because of the catastrophes of this war, temporary assistance to get the means to take care of themselves, but the moment they have these means, then the rest of us will have to take care to see that they do not do the work they are addicted to do better than we do. The minute we cease to offer this assistance, they will become our generous and dangerous rivals, and for my part I believe I can say truthfully that the people of the United States want the people of Belgium to recover their power to be rivals, to be rivals in those fields in which they have for so long a time proved themselves masters.

It is, therefore, with a peculiar feeling of being among the people that I understand that I have found myself under your guidance, Sir, touching shoulders with the people of Belgium. Today when I went to the great destroyed plants of Charleroi, though most of the chimneys were smokeless, the whole region seemed like so many regions I am familiar with in my own country, and if the air had only been full of smoke, I should have felt entirely at home. The air was too clear to be natural in such a region; and yet I had the feeling that smoke was going to come in its old abundance from those chimneys and the world of industry was once more going to feel the pulse of Belgium, that vital pulse which no discouragement can restrain.

So it is with a heart full of genuine sympathy, of comradeship and of friendship, that I beg to drink to your health, Sir, and the Queen's, and to the long and abounding prosperity of the kingdom over which you preside.

T MS (WP, DLC).
　¹ A large gala affair. The list of guests, too numerous to be named here, is printed in Brussels *La Libre Belgique*, June 20, 1919.
　² Albert, King of the Belgians, Address, [June 19, 1919], T MS (WP, DLC). The King praised both the United States and Wilson for all that they had done for Belgium. He also asked that Wilson say to his countrymen that the Belgian people counted on the United States to repair the results of the sacrifices which Belgium had made "for that liberty dear to both." "The United States," he said, "has many ships and powerful economic resources. Our commerce looks toward you, and Belgium, anxious to see all its rights recognized, asks America's aid for its rebirth." The French text of the King's toast is printed, *inter alia*, in Brussels *La Libre Belgique*, June 20, 1919.

A Memorandum by Manley Ottmer Hudson

MEMORANDUM FOR THE PRESIDENT:　　　　　　　　　19 June, 1919

As a result of Mr. Paderewski's letter,¹ the Committee on New States is recommending the following changes in the Treaty with Poland:

1. That the Minority provisions be amendable with the consent of a majority, instead of all, of the Council of the League of Nations.

2. That the Principal Allied and Associated Powers, as well as Poland, should agree to accept such amendments.

3. That German Minorities should receive special protection only in that part of Poland which was formerly German.

4. That protection of the Jewish Sabbath should not involve any exemption from military service.

The French Delegate, Mr. Berthelot, would have favored an abandonment of the idea of a Treaty, and the substitution of a formal declaration by Poland voluntarily accepting certain obligations for the protection of her minorities.

This would necessitate the Council's receding from its decision, now publicly announced, to impose these obligations on the new States. This suggestion was stoutly opposed by Mr. Headlam Morley and myself.

All of the Committee agree that the separate Treaty with Poland must be signed when the Treaty of Peace with Germany is signed. It should, therefore, be ready for the possibility of the Germans' signing next week. The Poles ought to have the final draft several days in advance. This would necessitate immediate action by the Council, and I hope that will be possible.

Manley O. Hudson

TS MS (WP, DLC).
  [1] Printed as Appendix II to the minutes of the Council of Four, June 17, 1919, 4 p.m., Vol. 60.

Robert Lansing to Frank Lyon Polk

Paris, June 19, 1919.

2651. For your information.

Referring to Mission's Number 2562 of June 13, 1919, Treaty with Germany in final form released in full to press this afternoon for publication Friday morning, in accordance with decision by Council of Principal Allied and Associated Powers to publish at earliest possible date after release of German counter-proposals and reply thereto. Ten copies of proof copy, first print, of final treaty forwarded to you by courier this afternoon. Additional copies will be sent as soon as obtained. 2651 LANSING.   AMMISSION.

T telegram (SDR, RG 256, 185/52-A, DNA).

From William Monroe Trotter

Sir,   Paris, France, June 19th. 1919.

Failing to receive favorable response to my request for an audience with you,[1] I have the honor, in accordance with the instructions of the National Equal Rights League, to request you to present to the Council of the Five great powers the formal petition of

the National Colored World Democracy Congress of the National
Equal Rights[2] for the rights of democracy for citizens of color in
the Allied Nations respectively, copies of which I herewith enclose,
at the coming session of said Council.

Will you please have your secretary inform me of your decision
in this matter at your earliest convenience, as the immediate prospect of peace makes it vital to my mission to know your decision.

Respectfully submitted for the League

William Trotter, Secretary.

TLS (WP, DLC).
  [1] See W. M. Trotter to WW, June 12, 1919, and n. 1 thereto, Vol. 60.
  [2] What Trotter actually enclosed was a memorandum (T MS [WP, DLC]) setting forth
the history of the efforts of the National Equal Rights League and of its representative,
Trotter himself, to put before the peace conference its petition calling for the following
clause to be inserted in the Covenant of the League of Nations: "*Real Democracy for
World being avowed aim of nations establishing League of Nations high contracting
powers agree to grant their citizens respectively full liberty, rights of democracy, protection of life without distinction based on race, color or previous conditions.*"

Thomas Nelson Page to the American Mission

Rome June 19, 1919

388. Orlando's Cabinet fell on his motion that the Chamber go
into secret session, which was lost by 259 votes to 78. Orlando then
said he would resign at 6:00 p.m. First edition evening newspapers
heavily censored. Situation regarding new cabinet still obscure.

Italian newspapers are publishing long interviews with various
German politicians of old and new regime today. GIORNALE, June
19th, prints three column interview with Scheidemann, who, like
others, affirms German friendship for Italy and predicts close
union of the two democracies, German and Italian. The article is
significant of the strong pro-German tone which is being given
more and more to the Italian press. Its influence on public opinion
is clearly discernible.

I hear through good source that French troops being withdrawn
Fiume, also that England will withdraw hers.   Nelson Page

T telegram (WP, DLC).

From the Diary of Ray Stannard Baker

Friday the 20th [June 1919]

We returned this morning from the trip to Belgium—one of the
hardest I ever made—and one of the most interesting. I have not
time to begin to describe it here. Wednesday was devoted to an all
day motor ride over dusty & often badly broken roads through the

battle-fields & ruined cities of Flanders, including a most interesting visit to Zeebrugge harbor, where we were escorted by British
naval officers, who showed us how the gallant British naval contingent had blocked the harbor. At Nieuport & along the Yser canal
we covered the same territory that I visited less than a year ago in
the midst of the war. Then shells were singing overhead & it was
death to show one's head above the trenches. We arrived at Brussels Wednesday night about 9:30 & rode through crowded streets.
I was up half the night seeing that our communications were open
& the despatches of the correspondents moving properly.

Thursday—yesterday—was devoted to a paralyzing program of
trips, receptions, a big luncheon & a bigger dinner. Here is a program:

9 a.m. Depart for Charleroi to see factories from which the Germans stole the machinery.

12:30   Luncheon with Brand Whitlock.

1:30   Reception American colony at the Legation.

2:00   Reception of Belgians at Legation.

2:30   Great reception in the Chamber of Deputies, with a
speech by M. Hymans and a return by President Wilson (this
being the great speech of the day). The King, Queen & all the
members of the Belgian government & parliament were there. It
was a most interesting affair. We rode to the meeting in state in
our high hats & long coats & I was placed just behind the Queen
& Mrs. Wilson.

3:30 to 6:00 Trip to Louvain, where a degree was bestowed on
the President in the ruins of the university: then to Malines to call
on Cardinal Mercier.

6 pm. A reception at the Hôtel de Ville with a short speech by
the President.

7. pm Reception Diplomatic Corps at the Palace.

8:15 Grand Dinner at the Palace given by the King & Queen to
President & Mrs. Wilson. The President sat on the right of the
King, then the Queen, then the distinguished looking Cardinal
Mercier in his red gown & hat. On the left of the King sat Mrs.
Wilson. We entered between rows of red-clad flunkies & were relieved of our wraps but asked—such is the court custom—to carry
our hats: which was a nuisance. The dinner tables were profusely
decorated with roses & the gold court plate was displayed. It was a
simple enough dinner, very well served. The King, big, awkward,
handsome & boyish, looks the real monarch: and I lost my heart
outright to the little, sweet-faced Queen, who is as simple & unaffected as a schoolgirl. Cardinal Mercier was the most impressive
looking man, not excepting the King, who was present.

The King read, awkwardly & in a low, embarrassed voice, a

speech proposing the President's health: & the President responded—all of us standing. There was a most imposing array of guests in full diplomatic uniforms, bespangled with badges & gold braid. The vanity of old men!

We drove directly to the station from the banquet & took our train about 11 oclock.

Whitlock told me just before the train left that the President had completely won the Belgian people: and had he thought quite counteracted the effects of French propaganda. They nearly killed him with their strenuous program. They wanted to show him all their sores! They responded politely to his enthusiasm for the League of Nations & the reign of Right in the world: but when he spoke of giving Belgium help in credits, raw materials & new machinery, one could fairly *feel* the electric charge in the atmosphere: & there was a warmth in the response which left no doubt as to its complete sincerity.

Wilson made 5 speeches during the day—in addition to all of his other occupation—with one big one at the Chamber of Deputies. This latter was as perfect & artistic a performance of its kind as ever I heard in my life—and I am not alone in this judgment. He was appearing before one of the most critical & highly developed audiences—in its diplomatic sensitivity—in Europe. All small nations must more or less survive politically by their wits: & they develop therefore a singularly sharp sense of the finer shadings of political meaning. Wilson sensed it absolutely & without at any time being insincere, or slopping over. He said exactly the right things, referred with exactly the right emphasis to the right men.

One of the great sources of his power as an orator lies in [the] fact that the listener immediately dismisses the usual (though often unconscious) anxiety with which we so often listen to a speaker—fearful lest he fail for a word or blunder in an expression. One knows instinctively that in Wilson's case the medium will be perfect with complete mental attention, & he can therefore fasten upon what is said. For such speeches as these no leader in our generation, I believe, is Wilson's equal. The results are there in actual & definite influence upon the audience. One can feel it.

Hw MS (R. S. Baker Papers, DLC).

From the Diary of Edith Benham[1]

June 20, 1919

All questions of precedence being settled, we pulled slowly into Malines. All that day in every town the streets were lined with school children singing and waving flags. The old town was packed with people, and as we turned the corner we came on the lovely cathedral with an American flag floating from the spire. It was such a beautiful day, and the spontaneous applause, and the little children made a picture I shall always carry with me.

We drove slowly under the entrance to the Cardinal's Palace, and there stood the Cardinal in his black robes and with red facings, a tall stately figure, and his face as beautiful and spiritual as his pictures show. He has become such a symbol of unbeaten Belgium to us, and to see him there coming out of the sunshine, and the voices of the little Belgians of his town clustered around his Cathedral, into the dignity and calm of his fine old Palace, and seeing the man himself, so fine and so spiritual, made a tremendous call to the imagination. He led his guests slowly up a broad flight of stairs into a fine large room with the priests of his entourage, in black with red trimmings, and others in black. After a charming speech of welcome to which the P. responded, he led him around the room presenting him to the priests, and then the P. introduced him to the Americans. Then we went into another room, where the ceiling had been blown in by a bomb, and tea was served in some wonderful old cups. The windows were open and the chimes began to play. They are among the most famous in the world, and were played by a master. I walked over to the window to listen better and hear these old airs of the 15th and 16th centuries. I can't tell you how lovely they sounded, floating out from the old tower with the American flag over it. I could have stayed for an hour, but the procession started again, so we went down the hall and the old oak stairs to the motors, and on to Louvain.

Then more school children and flags as we drew up before a square at the old Hôtel de Ville. Inside we had children singing the Star Spangled Banner in English. The usual ceremonies of making the P. a citizen of the town were gone through, and speeches, and we started out to the ruins of the old University and Library on foot—rather a solemn procession, for the destruction of that place was one of the wanton barbarisms of the Germans, and the P. as a man of letters and loving the fruits of the mind, felt its loss keenly. The ecclesiastics who have it in charge are a very intelligent looking lot. The Count de Merode[2] told me they applied the torch to it as calmly as we would light a fire and as deliberately. It was his Alma Mater and that of so many of the men I met in Belgium. I can't do better than quote what the P. said to Dr. Axson about his trip: "Of all the incidents of my trip here and experiences, the one which will stand out among the clearest is receiving the degree at Louvain. Imagine a long room, the remains I think of a long hall, part of a building renewed with deliberate thoroughness. A space had been cleared and a red carpet spread. Some chairs of ceremony, and some plants, and overhead the sky, and in these most unusual circumstances I received my degree. In listening to the speech, and in making my reply, looking at the people who had climbed into all sorts of places in the ruins, I had the most curious sense of unreality, and it was hard to collect my thoughts to reply." I noticed that he looked up and down the walls as he spoke and not to the audience and the person he was addressing, unlike his custom.

T MS (Edith Benham Helm Papers, DLC).
  [1] About this diary, see n. 1 to the extract from it printed at Dec. 5, 1918, Vol. 53.
  [2] Jean de Merode, Grand Marshal of the Belgian Royal Court.

From the Diary of Dr. Grayson

Friday, June 20, 1919.

There were no incidents on the trip and Paris was reached at nine o'clock. The President and our party left the train, and we proceeded to the temporary White House, where we breakfasted.

At 11:00 o'clock the President came to the Hôtel Crillon, where the American Commissioners were in waiting. For more than an hour the President discussed with the Commissioners the various developments, and especially the situation in Germany, which had become extremely serious as a result of the differences of opinion between the various parties as to whether or not the treaty should be signed. The Scheidemann government was almost a unit in opposition to signing and there were many indications at this particular time that the war might have to be resumed. However, the President told the other Commissioners that he was satisfied that Germany would not resume the war, and that when the matter had finally been concluded it would be found that the peace terms would be accepted. The President spoke very frankly to his fellow-Commissioners and made it very plain to them that the slightest evidence of worry on their part at this particular crisis would very materially complicate the general situation.

After his conference with the American Commissioners, the President received reports from the Reparations experts, who had been working out the problems affecting Austria. He left the Crillon at 12:30 and returned to the temporary White House.

The President had lunch as usual, there being no guests, and after luncheon he devoted some time to working on a number of matters that had been sent to him.

During the entire time that the President had been in Belgium, he kept in close personal touch with everything that was developing in Paris, and he had the very latest word on the situation inside of Germany.

Today he sent the following message of appreciation of their hospitality to the King and Queen of Belgium:

"To His Majesty,
    King Albert of Belgium,
        Brussels.

Mrs. Wilson and I join in expressing to you and the Queen our very deep appreciation of your kindness to us, our great pleasure in having such an opportunity to know you, our admiration, and our cordial gratitude and good wishes.

Woodrow Wilson."[1]

It had been planned to hold a meeting of the Council of Three during the afternoon, but Lloyd George was confined to his bed as the result of a chill sustained during his visit to Verdun and the French front while we were in Belgium, so Clemenceau and the President held a brief conference with the economic [military] experts.[2]

In the late afternoon the President and Mrs. Wilson went for a ride through the Bois. There were no guests at dinner and the President retired early to recover as speedily as possible from the fatigue incurred through his strenuous Belgian experiences.

[1] There is a verbatim CC of this telegram, dated June 20, 1919, in WP, DLC, and an undated WWhw draft (written by the left hand) inserted in the Grayson Diary for this date.

[2] However, Wilson, Clemenceau, Balfour, and Sonnino met with Marshals Foch and Pétain and Generals Weygand, Bliss, Wilson, Robertson, and Cavallero at a special meeting at 5 p.m. at the French War Ministry to review plans for a military drive on Berlin and the occupation of Germany in the event that the German government refused to sign the treaty. Wilson said very little at this meeting but did join Clemenceau and Balfour in authorizing Foch to commence his advance into Germany in the event that the Germans refused to sign the treaty and the Armistice expired. The minutes of this meeting are printed in *PPC*, VI, 543-57, and Paul Mantoux, *Les Délibérations du Conseil des Quatre* (2 vols., Paris, 1955), II, 458-67.

From the Diary of Colonel House

June 20, 1919.

The President returned from Belgium this morning and had a meeting with all the Commissioners at eleven o'clock. At my suggestion, we first discussed the attitude we should take about the League of Nations. I thought we should take no part officially, but should advise unofficially until our Senate ratified the Treaty. This view met the approval of the President and the others and I shall

act accordingly. I have made it clear to all the newspaper correspondents that no appointments will be made on any of the commissions or [of] the League of Nations until after the Treaty has
been ratified.

We tentatively agreed that Lansing should return home with the
President or soon after, and that Polk should be substituted for
him. Our purpose in this was that Lansing should be in Washington at the earliest possible moment to explain to individual Senators something about our work here in Paris and the necessity for
early ratification. I furthered this as Lansing is anxious to return
and I not only wished to oblige him, but I know the President will
not do any missionary work himself further than making speeches
to a joint session of Congress, and perhaps throughout the country.
Then, too, I thought Polk needed a rest or, at least, a change from
Washington and that he could get it by coming here.

After the President left, Lansing wanted me to take the matter
up with him more urgently. I suggested that he prepare a cable
and let me have it and I would get the President to approve it. Why
he does not do this himself, I do not know. It indicates his timidity
when dealing with the President. One would think he would have
some hesitancy in approaching me in the matter, particularly since
there is so much talk about my being the real Secretary of State.

T MS (E. M. House Papers, CtY).

From the Diary of Ray Stannard Baker

Friday night [June 20, 1919]

I thought the President would be exhausted after the tremendous activities of the last two days: but when I saw him come to
the meeting of the Commission at the Crillon this morning, he was
wearing a new straw hat & looking as fit and alert as ever. He is a
wonder! I found him also this evening in excellent spirits. The
Four have been conferring with Foch & the generals regarding the
advance into Germany in case the Germans refuse to sign. But all
our news now is that they will sign. The Scheidemann government
has fallen[1] & we hear that Ertzberger is coming to sign the treaty.

The President hopes to sail next Wednesday (and I with him,
thank heaven!)

I spoke warmly of his speech at the Chamber of Deputies, and
he seemed pleased with the whole trip to Belgium. I told him that
Whitlock thought he had gone far toward correcting the impression left by French propaganda. He said that Whitlock said the
same thing to him.

I told him the story of the country Irishman who visited the Cathedral at Dublin for the first time. Well, said he when he had looked it over, "If this don't beat the devil." "That," said his companion, "is what was intended."

We talked about the Italian situation & I was able to tell him something about Nitti[2] who will probably be asked to form the next government. I met Nitti several times last fall at Rome. He is about the only Italian leader who has a modern outlook: knows well the great new economic & industrial forces. I suggested that he would be likely to try to get people's minds off from empty imperialistic dreams and try to get them interested in their own economic affairs: that he might offer some proposal to accept the allied settlement in the Adriatic for concessions in the way of ships, raw-materials & credits. The president smiled. "We would be interested in that," he said, "but not the British! They are nimble enough in making concessions of territory belonging to other people, but not in building up commercial rivals."

[1] Philipp Scheidemann, frustrated by the failure of his own Social Democratic party to support his stand against ratification of the peace treaty, announced the resignation of his cabinet to President Friedrich Ebert at about midnight on June 19-20. See Gordon A. Craig, *Germany, 1866-1945* (New York, 1978), pp. 425-26; Klaus Epstein, *Matthias Erzberger and the Dilemma of German Democracy* (Princeton, N. J., 1959), pp. 319-20; and Hagen Schulze, ed., *Das Kabinett Scheidemann, 13. Februar bis 20. Juni 1919* (Boppard am Rhein, 1971), pp. lxi-lxii.

[2] That is, Francesco Saverio Nitti, most recently Minister of the Treasury in the Orlando cabinet, October 1917-January 1919.

To Albert, King of the Belgians

Your Majesty: Paris, 20 June, 1919.

Mrs. Wilson and I have brought away with us from Belgium the most delightful recollections of the generous hospitality which you and the Queen showed us, and, what is better even than hospitality, the genuine kindness and friendship which we were made to feel by all your acts. We brought away also an impression of Belgium and her people and representatives which serves our thought in forming a just picture of her conditions and her difficulties. We want to express to you and to the Queen more fully than a telegram could express them, our deep sense of appreciation and our gratitude for your genuine kindness.

We unite in expressing our great appreciation of your kindness in presenting us with a complete file of "La Libre Belgique."[1] We realize the unique value of it and shall prize it for its own intrinsic worth and interest as well as for the added value it will have as an evidence of your generous kindness.

We join in very warm messages of friendship and in the hope that the times may rapidly brighten for you both and for your people, and that the future may turn out to have no difficulties in it which are not surmountable by the assistance of your friends, who I am sure are very numerous and who represent more countries than one.

With much regard,   Sincerely yours,   [Woodrow Wilson]

CCL (WP, DLC).
    ¹ A clandestine news sheet printed by Belgian resistance leaders during the German occupation. It appeared irregularly from February 1, 1915, to November 12, 1918. The underground *La Libre Belgique* is not to be confused with the Brussels daily, *La Libre Belgique*, which was founded in 1884.Oscar E. Millard, *Underground News: The Complete Story of the Secret Newspaper that Made War History* (New York, 1938).

To Robert Lansing

My dear Mr. Secretary: Paris, 20 June, 1919.

I am afraid I did not make my meaning clear in my earlier letter.¹ I meant to express the hope that you would take up with Baron Makino the question of the formulation and formal entrance into just such engagements as you suggested in your letter of June third; namely, the assurances and obligations which were orally assumed by Baron Makino and Viscount Chinda when they were in consultation with our little conference here with regard to the Shantung matter.

It will seem perfectly natural for us to take the initiative in this matter, through our own Secretary of State, because Baron Makino will understand without explication that the interests of the United States are very deeply involved, and it ought to be clear to him, as it is to me, that extended unrest in China, which will certainly ensue unless the most explicit reassurance is given, might not only immediately but for a long time to come disturb the peace of the East and might lead to very serious international complications.

I beg that you will take the whole matter up with him very earnestly, and I am sure you will know how to handle it, in view of your past discussions of kindred subjects, in a way which will be entirely without irritation to the Japanese.

Cordially and faithfully yours,   [Woodrow Wilson]

CCL (WP, DLC).
    ¹ See WW to RL, June 12, 1919 (first letter of that date), Vol. 60. Wilson was responding to RL to WW, June 16, 1919 (second letter of that date), *ibid.*

Two Telegrams to Samuel Gompers

Paris, June 20, 1919.

For Mr. Gompers stop Your message[1] came while I was in Belgium and reached me too late to make a full reply but as I indicated in an earlier message[2] comma while the labor provisions are somewhat weakened comma it is the opinion of friends of labor and my own opinion that they are not materially weakened and that they will constitute a most serviceable magna charta stop Will cable labor provisions but fear it will be too late for the convention.

Woodrow Wilson.

[1] S. Gompers to WW, June 17, 1919, Vol. 60.
[2] WW to JPT, May 3, 1919, Vol. 58.

[Paris] 20 June, 1919.

PRIORITY A 2671. For Samuel Gompers from the President.

Comparison between your draft Labor Convention as reported to the Plenary Conference,[1] and the labor provisions as they now appear in the Treaty of Peace shows the following categories of changes:

First, redraft of what is called in Commission's Report "Clauses for Insertion in Treaty of Peace" in actual Treaty they appear under the title "General Principles" and read as follows:

"The High Contracting Parties, recognising that the well-being, physical, moral and intellectual, of industrial wage-earners is of supreme international importance, have framed, in order to further this great end, the permanent machinery provided for in Section I and associated with that of the League of Nations.

They recognise that differences of climate, habits and customs, of economic opportunity and industrial tradition, make strict uniformity in the conditions of labour difficult of immediate attainment. But, holding as they do, that labour should not be regarded merely as an article of commerce, they think that there are methods and principles for regulating labour conditions which all industrial communities should endeavor to apply so far as their special circumstances will permit.

Among these methods and principles, the following seem to the High Contracting Parties to be of special and urgent importance:

First.—The guiding principle above enunciated that labour should not be regarded merely as a commodity or article of commerce.

Second.—The right of association for all lawful purposes by the employed as well as by the employers.

Third.—The payment to the employed of a wage adequate to maintain a reasonable standard of life as this is understood in their time and country.

Fourth.—The adoption of an eight-hours day or a forty-eight hours week as the standard to be aimed at where it has not already been attained.

Fifth.—The adoption of a weekly rest of at least twenty-four hours, which should include Sunday wherever practicable.

Sixth.—The abolition of child labour and the imposition of such limitations on the labour of young persons as shall permit the continuation of their education and assure their proper physical development.

Seventh.—The principle that men and women should receive equal remuneration for work of equal value.

Eighth.—The standard set by law in each country with respect to the conditions of labour should have due regard to the equitable economic treatment of all workers lawfully resident therein.

Ninth.—Each State should make provision for a system of inspection in which women should take part, in order to ensure the enforcement of the laws and regulations for the protection of the employed.

Without claiming that these methods and principles are either complete or final, the High Contracting Parties are of opinion that they are well fitted to guide the policy of the League of Nations; and that if adopted by the industrial communities who are members of the League, and safeguarded in practice by an adequate system of such inspection, they will confer lasting benefits upon the wage-earners of the world."

The second part of your Clause Seven has been transferred into the body of the Convention and now appears under Article 405 of the Treaty or under Clause 19 of your Report. I am convinced that except for changes in wording which do not affect the substance and spirit of these Clauses they remain the same.

Second, likewise your protocol to Article 19 has been transferred to body of Treaty under Article 405. The "Resolutions" adopted by the Commission do not appear in the Treaty, inasmuch as they were merely proposals of separate delegations and no part of the Report as unanimously adopted for incorporation in the Treaty.

Three, a number of changes of form have been made through the draft Convention to make it conform in phraseology with the Covenant of the League of Nations as redrafted by the League of Nations Commission: for example, the words "The High Contracting Parties" now reads "Members," and other similar unimportant changes.

Fourth, on April 11th at the Plenary Conference which adopted the Report of Labor Commission, Sir Robert Borden made the following remarks "This Convention is linked in many ways by its terms to the Covenant of the League of Nations, and I think it desirable to make it perfectly plain that the character of its membership and the method of adherence should be the same in the one case as in the other." He then offered the following resolution which was unanimously adopted by the Conference: "The Conference authorizes the Drafting Committee to make such amendments as may be necessary to have the Convention conform to the Covenant of the League of Nations in the character of its membership and in the method of adherence."

In pursuance of this resolution the following changes were made: Article One [of] your Commission Report, together with the first two Clauses of your Article 35, together with Article 36 have been combined as Article 387 of the Treaty to read "A permanent organization is hereby established for the promotion of the objects set forth in the Preamble.

The original Members of the League of Nations shall be the original members of this organization, and hereafter membership of the League of Nations shall carry with it membership in the said organization."

As you doubtless have in mind, these changes have the effect of giving the British Dominions and Colonies separate representation on the General Conference. When you give your final judgment upon the importance of these changes, I earnestly urge you to entertain the following considerations:

One: That Borden could not go back to the Canadian people who occupy a position of considerable importance in the industrial world and tell them that they were not entitled to representation on the General Labor Conference.

Two: that the changes did, in fact, bring the Labor Convention into harmony with the League of Nations Covenant.

Three: that the changes are not substantially important, inasmuch as every Labor Convention adopted by the Conference must be submitted to our Government for ratification. Thus the choice of acceptance or rejection lies in our own hands irrespective of the Constitution of the General Conference.

Four: that the problems of the chief British Colonies and Dominions are much more like our own than like Great Britain's, so that their representation will be a source of strength to our point of view rather than an embarrassment.

Five: that, in my opinion, the changes do not introduce any weakness or threat of weakness into the Labor provisions. They still stand, thanks to your efforts and guidance as one of the great progressive achievements of the Peace Conference, something from which peoples the world over may take courage and hope and confidence in a better future. I am sure that you will agree that nothing could be more fatal to these just aspirations than any fail-, ure to endorse these provisions. I count upon your support and sponsorship.   Ammission

T telegrams (WP, DLC).
    [1] For which, see H. M. Robinson to WW, March 24, 1919, and the notes and the Enclosure thereto, Vol. 56.

To Norman Hapgood

My dear Hapgood: Paris, 20 June, 1919.

Thank you for your very serviceable letter of June 15th about Russia.[1] I can say that it sums up my own impressions though they were much less definite than yours, because founded upon much less extended and more indefinite information. I shall try to keep in mind the whole aspect of the matter as you present it.

In unavoidable haste, with cordial regards,
                            Faithfully yours,   [Woodrow Wilson]

CCL (WP, DLC).
    [1] Insofar as we know, this letter is missing.

From Robert Lansing, with Enclosure

My dear Mr. President: Paris, 20 June 1919.

I enclose a copy of a telegram from the Department expressing its opinion that it is vital that the support which is to be given to Admiral Koltchak should be formulated and requesting some kind of a statement of the exact assistance which you are willing to give.

The Russian Political Conference[1] is also pressing for an answer regarding the sending to Koltchak of the Russian rifles in the United States.

Mr. McCormick agrees with the views expressed by the Department of State, and I will therefore be glad if you would tell me what answer I am to make to the Department on these two matters.

I am, my dear Mr. President,
                            Very sincerely yours,   Robert Lansing

TLS (WP, DLC).
    [1] About this group, see R. H. Lord to J. C. Grew, April 8, 1919, n. 1, Vol. 57.

E N C L O S U R E

Washington. June 16, 1919.

2315. For the Secretary of State and McCormick. Have suggested to Secretary of the Treasury that he ascertain from Kolchak just what supplies and support are needed and what can best be furnished by each of the powers who have undertaken to support him. The telegram sent you today from Mr. J. F. Stevens[1] discloses a very serious situation regarding the Czech army. Cannot some measures be formulated with the assistance of the Russian Conference at Paris or through the representatives of the Allies at Omsk for the early repatriation of the Czechs. Whatever is done it seems to us vital that the support which is to be given to Kolchak should be formulated now and given promptly. One of the difficulties in Siberia seems to be that of morale among the Czech and Russian troops. Some kind of statement of the exact supply to be given and the amount of it, financial, military and economic, followed by prompt and direct action would be very helpful. There is great difficulty in formulating any such concrete proposition in correspondence from here. As the heads of Governments concerned are now in Paris, it occurs to me they may be already talking in Paris in the directions I have indicated. The situation is so important that I would very much appreciate it if you would let me know just what is being done to meet it.   Phillips,   Acting.

T telegram (WP, DLC).
  [1] See W. Phillips to RL and V. C. McCormick, June 16, 1919 (first telegram of that date), Vol. 60.

From Douglas Wilson Johnson

Dear Mr. President: Paris, June 20, 1919.

Baron Sonnino has reported to the Council of Ministers that the Chiefs of Government decided, first to require the immediate and complete evacuation of the Klagenfurt basin by both Austrian and Jugo Slav troops; and later to determine (after asking and receiving the advice of the commission of four military experts on the ground) what steps should be taken for the maintenance of order in the basin.[1]

I am not sure whether this correctly represents the precise position taken by the Four, but desire to bring to the President's attention the following points:

There can be little doubt of the extreme anxiety of the Italians to secure military control of the basin and adjacent areas. The President is familiar with the varied and oft repeated efforts of the

Italian representatives to have a special status established for the Assling triangle, to give this triangle to Austria or to Italy, to have the northern exit of the Assling tunnel (in the Klagenfurt basin) excluded from the plebiscite area, to divide the basin on a north-south line and give the western half (including the tunnel) to Austria, and so on. Italian troops have already extended their military occupation around the northern side of the Klagenfurt basin by occupying the Villach-St. Veit railway, proclaiming that this action was taken pursuant to a decision of the Peace Conference. If such military occupation is further extended over the Klagenfurt basin, two most unfortunate results are likely to follow:

(a) a de facto situation would be created in which it might be practically impossible to prevent the Italians from forcing a decision favorable to their designs on the Assling tunnel exits.

(b) The Jugo Slavs in the southern half of the basin would find themselves under the military domination of the power which has employed repressive and unjust measures against their co-nationals on the Adriatic coast; and the proposed plebiscite would be vitiated because carried out under control of those who have, for selfish reasons, worked untiringly to have all or parts of the Jugo Slav area assigned definitely to Austria, and who would have every reason to favor pro-Austrians as against pro-Jugo Slavs in order to influence the result of the plebiscite.

If the basin is immediately evacuated by Austrian and Jugo Slav troops, it is difficult to see how Italian occupation can be prevented. If Italian troops do not occupy the area at once on pretext of the disorders which are certain to follow evacuation, the Conference will itself be forced to send in troops; and Italian troops are the most readily available, if not the only troops which it will be practicable to assign for this service. Thus events would force the issue which the Italians are so anxious to bring about.

In view of the difficulties of the situation, I respectfully submit for the President's consideration the following three propositions:

1. The ideal solution of the Klagenfurt problem would be complete evacuation of the basin by Austrian and Jugo Slav troops, with concurrent occupation by American, British or French troops. I am advised, however, that this is not a practicable solution.

2. If "1" is impracticable, the nearest approach to the objects which the Four have in view (cessation of hostilities and a fair plebiscite in the basin) will be secured by placing both Austrian and Jugo Slav troops in the basin under control of an inter-Allied Commission, which commission will require all Jugo Slav troops to retire south of the line separating areas "A" and "B" on the President's map, and all Austrian troops to retire north of that line; both

bodies of troops to be reduced to the dimensions necessary for the preservation of order, and to act to that end under inter-Allied control. Both bodies of troops to be replaced as rapidly as possible by a police force locally recruited.

3. Under no circumstances should Italian occupation of the basin be permitted.

4. I have submitted the above propositions to Mr. Tardieu* and to Sir Eyre Crowe, and they are in entire agreement with them.

Respectfully submitted,   Douglas Johnson.

* Since speaking with Mr. Tardieu yesterday, I have slightly changed the form of proposition 2, and have been unable to see Mr. Tardieu again, to see if he approves present form. Mr. Aubert[2] has seen it and thinks Mr. Tardieu would approve.

TLS (WP, DLC).
   [1] See Minute 3 of the minutes of the Council of Foreign Ministers, June 18, 1919, and the notes of the same group, June 19, 1919, printed in *PPC*, IV, 834-37 and 842-45, respectively. For the decision of the Council of Four on this subject, see Minute 9 of the minutes of that body printed at June 17, 1919, 4 p.m., Vol. 60.
   [2] About whom, see n. 1 to the extract from the House Diary printed at Dec. 17, 1918, Vol. 53.

From Henry Morgenthau

My dear Mr President!   Paris June 20. 1919

Some of my friends have informed me that there is grave danger that the Polish treaty—which they regard as the key to all the treaties affecting the status and rights of the Jews—will not be signed simultaneously with the German treaty. They fear that then it may never be signed in its present shape, and minorities will again be exposed to the tyranny and injustice of majorities.

We all consider your successful efforts on behalf of minorities one of the outstanding forward steps of the Peace Conference & we all hope and pray that it will not be defeated at the last moment. We look to you to prevent it.

With kindest personal regards

Yours Very Cordially   Henry Morgenthau

ALS (WP, DLC).

From Henry Churchill King and Charles Richard Crane

Jerusalem June 20, 1919.

For President Wilson.

Probably at no time has race feeling been so sensitive as just now. People in large bodies especially armed forces should move as little as possible and even then only with great care and on advice from competent officials in area affected. Careless descent of Greeks on Smyrna has produced distress reacting all over this coast where there was deep believing [belief] in our own declaration as well as in those of British Government and French Government made November 9[1] on right of people to self determination. Here older population both Moslem and Christian take united and most hostile attitude towards any extent of Jewish immigration or towards any effort to establish Jewish sovereignty over them. We doubt if any British Government or American official here believes that it is possible to carry out Zionist program except through support of large army. Signed King. Crane.

T telegram (SDR, RG 256, 867N.00/91, DNA).
[1] See R. Cecil to C. A. de R. Barclay, Oct. 31, 1918, n. 2, Vol. 51.

From the Diary of Dr. Grayson

Saturday, June 21, 1919.

The President went for a drive immediately after breakfast and returned to the temporary White House in time to meet with the Council of Three, which were taking up the question of the frontiers of Poland and Ukrainia. Lloyd George had not recovered from his illness and his place was taken by Mr. Balfour.

I was pleased during the morning when I received a message from Lloyd George asking me to come over to his house and look him over and prescribe for him. There was a very personal feeling for my feeling of satisfaction in this connection. When the President was taken ill several weeks ago, and I was compelled to keep him in bed for a week, Lloyd George took occasion later on to say that he (Lloyd George) had also been sick but that as he had no doctor he had recovered in two days, while the President, with a physician always available, had required more than a week to get back on the job. When I entered Lloyd George's room he looked at me with his usual quizzical smile and said: "I want to apologize to you for something I said once; you remember what it was." To this I replied, "Yes, I realize that very well, and this is certainly a day of great victory for me." Lloyd George then said: "Yes it is. I apologize for what I said. I think it will be fine to let by-gones be by-gones.

In any event, I must ask for your professional services." I then examined the British Premier and gave him the medicine which he required to break up his condition.

The Italian situation has now developed into a very serious one. While we were in Belgium Orlando had gone back to Rome, to be present at the opening session of the Italian Parliament. As soon as he began to talk he asked that all discussion on the matters affecting the Peace Conference be held in a secret session. The Socialists objected, and Orlando, in order to line up the opposition, and feeling confident that he had a majority of the Parliament, declared that the government would stand or fall on the proposition of a secret session, and insisted on a vote being taken. When the vote was taken it was adverse to the government and Orlando immediately submitted his resignation. Word of this development had reached the President on his return to Paris, but it was not until today that the full details made themselves felt in the deliberations of the Peace Conference. It was announced that Signor Nitti might be asked to reorganize the Cabinet, and in the meanwhile Foreign Minister Sonnino received instructions from the Italian government to continue and to act as the chief of the delegation until a new commission could be named. The Italian Foreign Minister sat in at today's session of the Council, which was devoted entirely to settling up the Polish problems.

At the close of the afternoon session the President went for a motor ride, returning to the house in time for dinner. The dinner was the usual family affair, and after dinner the President played Canfield before retiring.

From the Diary of Colonel House

June 21, 1919.

After lunch I gave Sir William Orpen a final sitting.[1] The President was there when I arrived. I talked to him for the last fifteen minutes of his sitting. Orpen has got a good portrait of him though not a flattering one. His hair is seldom as ruffled as Orpen has it. Before the President left I got him to approve the cable Lansing had drafted to send Polk about taking his place in Paris. I attach a copy of this cable. Orpen thanked me for having persuaded the President to sit for him. He declared, and with truth, that unless I had intervened he would not have been able to have finished the portrait except from a photograph.

[1] Sir William's portrait of Wilson is reproduced in Vol. 60. We have been unable to discover the location of Sir William's portrait of House.

From Edward Mandell House

Dear Governor: Paris, June 21, 1919.

Here is a cable which Lansing has prepared for your approval.[1]

The great essential now is to have the Treaty ratified with the Covenant, and I believe that Lansing in his quiet way could influence many Senators. Bliss and White could keep things going here and I would always be nearby in case of need.

Affectionately yours,   E. M. House

Okeh   W.W.

TLS (E. M. House Papers, CtY).
[1] This telegram is missing in SDR, RG 256, and in other collections. However, House describes the telegram's preparation and content in the extract from his diary printed at June 20, 1919.

Hankey's Notes of a Meeting of the Council of Four[1]

President Wilson's House,
C.F.77.   Paris, June 21, 1919, 12:30 p.m.

1. With reference to C.F.74,[2] Minute 2, the Council had before them a letter from M. Berthelot, dated June 19th, addressed to Sir Maurice Hankey containing the remarks of the Commission on New States (Appendix I) on M. Paderewski's letter of June 15th, 1919.

(After President Wilson had read a summary of the letter, it was approved.

The Commission on New States was authorised, in consultation with the Drafting Committee, to embody the changes proposed in their letter in a final text of a Treaty with Poland. The Commission was also instructed to prepare for the consideration of the Council, the draft of a letter forwarding the text of the Treaty to the Polish Delegation.)

(At Mr. Headlam-Morley's request, the Commission was also authorised to consider the nature of alterations required in the draft Treaty with Poland in order to provide that in all except the primary schools Jewish children should be instructed in the Polish, and not in the Yiddish language, thereby avoiding the risk of encouraging the use of Yiddish as one of the national languages for a part of the population of Poland.)

2. With reference to C.F.74, Minute 4, the Council had before them a letter from M. Berthelot, the Chairman of the Commission

[1] The complete text of these minutes is printed in PPC, VI, 569-74.
[2] See the minutes of the Council of Four printed at June 17, 1919, 4 p.m., Vol. 60.

on New States, suggesting that the points referred to the Commission at the instance of M. Sonnino on June 17th. were outside the competence of the Commission, and should be referred to the Council of Ministers of Foreign Affairs with their legal and technical experts, which had considered the political clauses relating to Italy in the Austrian Treaty. (Appendix II.)[3]

(The proposal of the Commission on New States was agreed to and Sir Maurice Hankey was instructed to acquaint the Secretary-General.)

3. Sir Maurice Hankey drew attention to a letter from M. Berthelot, dated June 16th. 1919,[4] dealing with the following questions:

(1) Clauses of a technical nature regarding the scale of tariffs for traffic towards the Adriatic intended for insertion in the Treaties for Czecho-Slovakia and Yugo-Slavia.

(2) Suggestions from the Italian Delegation with regard to the restitution of works of art carried off during the war, and removed to territory belonging to the New States. (Appendix.)[5]

(3) Concerning Financial Clauses relating to Poland proposed by the French Delegation.

(The Council postponed the discussion of this letter.)
(The Meeting then adjourned.)

APPENDIX I TO C.F.77.

M.293. Peace Conference, Secretariat-General.

Quai d'Orsay,
My dear Friend and Colleague,   Paris, June 19th 1919.

You have been good enough to transmit to the Commission on New States the copy of a Memorandum from M. Paderewski containing his objections to the draft Treaty between the Principal Allied and Associated Powers and Poland, which has been prepared by the Committee. The Supreme Council has sent this Memorandum to the Committee with instructions "to consider the objections raised by M. Paderewski and to seek whether some of these objections could not be met."

In conformity with these instructions the Committee on the New States has considered M. Paderewski's Memorandum. They have at once noted that except for some special points such as the provisions relating to the Jews and the lack of reciprocity as to the

---

[3] Printed in *PPC*, VI, 574.
[4] Printed in *ibid.*, pp. 593-98, as Appendix V to the minutes of the Council of Four, June 21, 1919, 3:45 p.m.
[5] Printed in *PPC*, VI, 596.

guarantees accorded to German Minorities in Poland, none of the
articles in the proposed Treaty is made the subject of an investigation which would serve to suggest modifications which it might
be desired to make in the text.

In reality the entire memorandum of the Polish First Minister
can be summed up as an opposition in principle to the conclusion
of a special treaty containing the solemn undertaking of Poland to
the Allies to guarantee the rights of racial linguistic and religious
minorities.

M. Paderewski objects both to pledging his country in this matter to the Powers and to accepting the jurisdiction of the League
of Nations on any eventual violation of the agreement. It would
therefore be in vain to attempt to satisfy him by modifying the particular articles of the Treaty. The difference is fundamental.

The Supreme Council alone has the authority to decide if it is
desirable to impose on the Polish Government what both the Diet
and its own opinion would desire to reject as an infringement of
the sovereignty of Poland.

The Commission on New States, so far as they are concerned,
can only comply with the decision of the Council of the Powers
which has been twice published, both by the insertion of Article 93
in the Treaty with Germany and by the maintenance of the principle embodied in this Article notwithstanding the observations
made at the Plenary Session by the representatives of the small
Powers. It is moreover too late to alter the Treaty with Germany.

An investigation of M. Paderewski's Memorandum calls for the
following observations: It is in harmony with the practice of public
law in Europe to insert in Treaties concluded with New States on
the occasion of their recognition a certain number of guarantees
(as has already been done in former times for Greece, Rumania,
Serbia); Poland can the less refuse to conform in that she owes her
liberation entirely to the efforts and sacrifices of the Powers.

The establishment of the League of Nations of which Poland is
a part, moreover removes as a consequence all interference of a
foreign Power in her internal affairs, for it assumes to her the guarantee of an impartial examination by the Court of Justice of the
League of Nations, i.e. by an Assembly which is judicial and not
political.

If to this is added that questions will be brought before the Court
by a State which is a member of the Council of the League and not
by the direct appeal of the Minorities, it will be recognised that
every precaution has been taken to conciliate both the sentiment
and meet the interests of the States.

The Polish Government declares itself in general ready of itself to grant the most complete guarantees of liberty and equality to all citizens without distinction of race, religion or language; there is then complete harmony on the fundamental matter between the Powers and Poland.

Three questions however are made the subject of special reserves:

(1) The special guarantees accorded to the Jews in Articles 10 and 12.

(2) The absence of reciprocity in the protection of German Minorities in Poland and Polish Minorities in Germany.

(3) Finally the interference in the fundamental laws of the Polish Constitution which results from the general application of the provisions of Article 1.

(1) M. Paderewski is of opinion that by giving to the Jews special privileges in regard to education and language, they will be placed outside the national community and difficulties will be created which it would be desirable to avoid. To this argument it can be replied that the immense majority of the Jews in Poland demand precise guarantees, and that the information as to the present situation of the Jews in Poland and the attitude towards them seems to justify special provisions; these provisions have besides been most carefully arranged in order to leave the Jewish institutions under public control and absolutely to avoid forming them into a separate national community. The Committee is prepared, in order to meet the suggestions, to modify the terms of Article 12 which, according to M. Paderewski, might justify the Jews in refusing public service in the army. It is for the Supreme Council to decide whether it is possible to go further and suppress the two articles referring to the Jews who, in that case, would only get the benefits given by the more general guarantees to all Minorities.

(2) With regard to the absence of reciprocity of the guarantees given to the Germans and the Poles, the Committee must point out that there will remain very few groups of Poles in Germany (apart from the miners in Westphalia who are foreign workers occupied in this district and not minorities definitely established) while more than 800,000 Germans will be incorporated in the Polish state. As the Allied Powers have assumed this responsibility, they are bound to assure to the latter the indispensable guarantees.

If the Committee had known at an earlier date that a plebiscite would be arranged in Upper Silesia, they would have asked for the insertion in the Treaty with Germany of a clause protecting Polish minorities; but even on the hypothesis that the plebiscite would result in the retention of a Polish population under the sovereignty of Germany, it would be the obvious interest of Germany to grant them the indispensable guarantees and the Powers would certainly be able to get an undertaking when the time came.

(3) Finally, the Committee, in order to meet in every possible manner the objections of M. Paderewski, in conformity with the instructions of the Supreme Council, suggest that the draft Treaty be modified in the five following points: the Drafting Committee might be instructed in concert with the Commission to draft the necessary articles.

(a) The three first lines of Article 1 should be made applicable only to Articles 2-8 i.e. to the exclusion of the special articles 9, 10 and 12.

(b) In the two last lines of Article 1 the words "the majority of the Council of the League of Nations" should be substituted for "the League of Nations."

(c) The Allied and Associated Powers would undertake to accept any modification determined upon by the majority of the Council of the League of Nations.

(d) Article 9 would be altered so as to limit the privileges provided in this article to former nationals of the State to which the territories transferred to Poland had previously belonged.

(e) Article 12 would be altered as indicated above in regard to military service.

These are the conclusions to which the Committee of the New States has come after a careful examination of M. Paderewski's memorandum.

I should be obliged if you would have the goodness to bring them before the Council of the Principal Allied and Associated Powers and request them to give us their instructions in view of the urgency of a final drafting of the Treaty with Poland, the signature to which ought apparently to be coincident with that of the Treaty with Germany.   Berthelot.

T MS (SDR, RG 256, 180.03401/77, DNA).

Hankey's Notes of a Meeting of the Council of Four[1]

President Wilson's House,

C.F.79.   Paris, June 21, 1919, 3:45 p.m.

1. The Council had before them a Note by the Committee on Roumanian and Jugo-Slav Affairs, giving its opinion on three letters from M. Vesnitch, two of which were dated June 7th and one dated June 9th[2] (Appendix I).

[1] The complete text of these minutes is printed in PPC, VI, 581-99.
[2] M. R. Vesnić to G. Clemenceau, June 7 (two letters) and 9, 1919, TCL (WP, DLC).

PRESIDENT WILSON pointed out that three points were raised:

(1) The majority of the Commission were agreed that during a plebiscite the Jugo-Slavs should occupy Zone A, and the Austrians should occupy Zone B. The Italian Delegation, however, dissented from this view.

(2) In regard to the spaces of time to elapse between the coming into force of the Treaty and the holding of the plebiscite, the majority of the Commission preferred three months, but the Italian Delegation preferred from six to eighteen months.

(3) The date of the qualification of those who would have the right to vote. The majority of the Commission favoured the vote being given to residents in the Klagenfurt Basin since 1905, but the Italian Delegation wished to bring it to August, 1914.

His personal view corresponded with that of the majority of the Commission on all points.

M. SONNINO, in regard to the first point, said that he thought it might jeopardise the liberty of the plebiscite if the Klagenfurt basin were occupied by the troops of the interested parties. To secure an absolutely free vote it would be better to provide in some other way, for instance, by means of Allied troops under the direction of the Commission.

PRESIDENT WILSON pointed out that in any case the Commission would be there to secure fair play.

M. SONNINO said that the presence of troops would hamper the liberty of the vote. He would prefer a local police force.

Reverting then to the question of the armistice, he said he had understood that the intention of the Principal Allied and Associated Powers was to confirm the telegram of 31st May, demanding complete evacuation of the Klagenfurt Basin. The first telegram, he pointed out, had reached Belgrade on June 3rd, notwithstanding which the Jugo-Slavs had continued to advance. An Italian Officer who had come from Vienna had tried to get into touch with the representatives of the two armies. He was able to get into touch with the Slavs, but was prevented from getting into touch with the Austrians. Consequently, on the eve of June 6th, the Austrians had been compelled to sign a sort of an armistice. Then, an order had come from the Austrian Government refusing to ratify the armistice as concluded, and which provided for the occupation of Klagenfurt by the Slavs. He understood that the Council had wished to repeat to Belgrade and Vienna the orders to withdraw troops from the whole basin. The other Foreign Ministers, however, had not interpreted the decision of the Council in the same sense, and had thought it would be better for the troops of the two forces to occupy the two plebiscite zones. If his colleagues thought it would be easier and that a more sincere result would be obtained by the presence of the Austrian and Jugo-Slav troops, he would have nothing to say.

PRESIDENT WILSON pointed out that the Principal Allied and Associated Powers would appoint the Commission, which would know whether there was interference by the troops. If they discovered that there was, they would have to make other arrangements.

M. SONNINO said it would be difficult for the Commission to know exactly whether pressure was being exerted by the troops or not.

PRESIDENT WILSON asked if, in M. Sonnino's judgment, an entire evacuation would now be safe.

M. SONNINO suggested that a local police force should be arranged for.

PRESIDENT WILSON asked, if this proved inadequate, what would happen.

M. SONNINO said he would consult the military advisers on the spot. He had suggested this at the Council, and had understood President Wilson to reply that the military men should inform them what was to be done.

PRESIDENT WILSON said that he had understood that the military advisers on the spot were only to report the cessation of hostilities.

M. SONNINO suggested that the military advisers might now be asked to report.

PRESIDENT WILSON said that news had reached the Council that Italian troops were moving towards Klagenfurt.

M. SONNINO said he had no news of this, but, if so, it was done by the orders of the Commission of Military Officers on the spot.

PRESIDENT WILSON said that the Commission of Military Officers had no authority, and no right to give such an order. If they had done so, it would be a dangerous extension of their functions.

M. CLEMENCEAU said that his information was that an Italian officer had said that he came in the name of the Peace Conference to authorise their action.

M. SONNINO said that when the Italian representative in Vienna first heard of the telegram of the 31st May, he had referred the matter to the armies; then the four Allied Military Officers on the spot, having heard of what had been decided, insisted with the Heads of the armies on their retiring. If they had taken on themselves to order Italian troops into Klagenfurt, he knew nothing of it.

COLONEL PARIANI[3] said there was no information to this effect.

M. TARDIEU said that the Commission had been impressed by the

---

[3] Col. Alberto Pariani, member of the Italian general staff and a technical expert on military questions in the Italian delegation.

consideration that it would be better now for the armies to adopt as the limits of military occupation their future military frontier. The Commission had accordingly reported in this sense in their remarks on M. Vesnitch's letters. The most simple plan was to take the purple line on President Wilson's map as the limit between the Austrians and Yugo-Slavians. This accorded with the views of all the Foreign Ministers except Baron Sonnino.

PRESIDENT WILSON said that the matter was really simpler than what appeared from this discussion. The premise on which the Commission had proceeded was that it was not safe to clear all the troops out of the Klagenfurt area: they assumed that some steadying force was necessary. If this view was accepted, the Council had only to decide what the force should consist of. There was no mixed Allied force in the neighborhood. The only possible Allied Force was the Italian force, but, as the Italian claims conflicted with the Yugo-Slavs in this part of the world, it might cause trouble to introduce Italians. Consequently, there was no alternative but to choose Austrians in the "B" area and Yugo-Slavs in the "A" area.

M. TARDIEU said that if the purple line did not exist, he could understand the plea for total evacuation of the area, but, if it was agreed to take the purple line as the boundary between the two plebiscite areas, he could not understand what objection there was to using it as the armistice line.

PRESIDENT WILSON said that he understood that Baron Sonnino was prepared to waive his objections if his colleagues were all agreed.

M. SONNINO said his point of view was that it was predetermining the plebiscite.

PRESIDENT WILSON said that the Commission could clearly object to any abuse of their position by the Military.

MR. BALFOUR suggested that it should be laid down that the Commission was to be the controlling power of the forces.

M. TARDIEU pointed out that this was already in the report on the Vesnitch letters.

PRESIDENT WILSON suggested the following formula:

"Both bodies of troops to be reduced to the dimensions necessary for the observation of order, and to act to that end under Inter-Allied control. Both bodies of troops to be replaced as rapidly as possible by a police force locally recruited."

(This was accepted, and it was agreed that the Commission should be instructed to insert words to this effect in their draft.)

The Council then discussed the third question mentioned by President Wilson, namely, as to the date of qualification of persons to vote.

M. TARDIEU explained that the majority of the Commission had based their proposal for 1905 on the belief that at that time a systematic introduction of a German element into the Klagenfurt Basin had commenced.

M. SONNINO said that possibly there had been a predominance of Austrian immigration at that time, but he could not see the argument for choosing the particular year 1905. According to the facts as stated to him, before that date there had been a systematic and arranged Slovene immigration. He could not see why, because M. Vesnitch said that after that date there had been an Austrian immigration, this date should be fixed. Surely the proper date to take was immediately before the war. The pre-war population was the one that ought to determine the sovereignty under which it should exist. He did not see how that principle could properly be departed from.

PRESIDENT WILSON said that Dr Seymour informed him that a new railway had been opened in 1907, after which there had been a great influx of German workmen. Also, after 1907, there had been a change in the school administration.

M. TARDIEU said that many special reasons had been given, but there was also a general reason, namely, that after the annexation of Bosnia and Herzegovina, the Austrian Government had directed itself to anti-Slovene organisation. If he himself had to give a date, he would choose 1909 rather than 1905.

M. SONNINO said that all these dates were artificial. The only proper persons to vote were those who had inhabited the district immediately before the war. That was the only date to take. Otherwise, it would be better to have no plebiscite at all.

PRESIDENT WILSON said that this was not a new precedent. In the narrow neck of Poland there had been a belt of German-inhabited territory, deliberately created by the Germans to separate the Poles.

M. SONNINO said that in that case there had been German laws and funds voted in the budget to Germanise Poland.

PRESIDENT WILSON said there had been a somewhat similar policy after the annexation of Bosnia and Herzegovina.

M. SONNINO said it had only been a very general policy. If workmen had been introduced, they remained just as much citizens as anyone else.

PRESIDENT WILSON said that in all previous cases there had been a qualifying period of residence, and the date immediately before the war had never been chosen.

M. SONNINO said that this was no argument for adopting M. Vesnitch's date.

PRESIDENT WILSON then suggested 1912 as the date.

M. SONNINO accepted, and the proposal was adopted.

The Council then discussed the period which should elapse after the coming into force of the Treaty of Peace before the plebiscite took place.

M. SONNINO said he would accept the views of the majority of the Commission that it should take place after three months.

The following decisions were reached:

1. In regard to the armistice, that the forces of the Kingdom of the Serbs, Croats and Slovenes and of the Austrian Republic should be withdrawn south and north of the purple line on President Wilson's map.

M. Tardieu undertook to draft a telegram in this sense, to be sent by the President of the Conference to the Governments of the Kingdom of the Serbs, Croats and Slovenes and of the Austrian Republic.

2. That a copy of this telegram should be communicated to the Officers representing the Allied and Associated Powers in the Klagenfurt area.

3. That the Committee on Roumanian and Jugo-Slav Affairs should proceed to draw up the articles for the Treaty of Peace with Austria relating to the plebiscite in the Klagenfurt area and connected questions on the following bases:

(a) With a view to the plebiscite, that Austrian troops in the "A" area, and troops of the Kingdom of the Serbs, Croats and Slovenes in the "B" area, should be reduced to the dimensions necessary for the observation of order, and should act to that end under Inter-Allied control. Both bodies of troops should be replaced as rapidly as possible by a police force locally recruited.

(b) That the plebiscite should be held within three months of the coming into force of the Treaty of Peace with Austria, in the zone "A," and, in the event of this vote being given in favour of union with the Kingdom of the Serbs, Croats and Slovenes, a plebiscite should be held within three weeks from that date in the "B" zone.

(c) That the International Commission should consist of four permanent members representing respectively the United States of America, the British Empire, France and Italy. When dealing with matters affecting the "B" area, there should be added an Austrian representative, and when dealing with matters in the "A" area, there should be added a Jugo-Slav representative.

(d) That persons should be qualified to vote who had resided in the district since January 1st, 1912. In other respects, the proposals of the Commission in their letter of June 18th, 1919, were approved.

4. That the Commission should be authorised to communicate

their completed draft direct to the Drafting Committee, who should have authority to prepare the necessary clauses on this basis without further instructions from the Council of the Principal Allied and Associated Powers.

(The Members of the Committee on Roumanian and Jugo-Slav Affairs withdrew at this point.)

2. The Council had before them a Report from the Commission on the International Regime of Ports, Waterways and Railways, dated June 18th, 1919 (Appendix II),[4] recommending the insertion of an additional article in the Treaty of Peace with Austria concerning freedom of transit for telegraphic correspondence and telephonic communications.

(The Article was approved and initialled by the representatives of the Five Principal Allied and Associated Powers. Sir Maurice Hankey was instructed to forward it to the Secretary-General for the Drafting Committee.)

3. The Council had under consideration a Note from the Superior Blockade Council containing a proposed agreement by Austria regarding Trade with Hungary and Germany. (Appendix III.)[5]

(The Note was approved and initialled by the representatives of the Governments of the United States of America, the British Empire, France and Italy, the representative of Japan not initialling it, as he said that Japan was not concerned. Sir Maurice Hankey was instructed to forward this to the Secretary-General for the information of the Drafting Committee.)

4. The Council had under consideration a Note prepared by the Council of Foreign Ministers, dated May 24th, 1919, in regard to the Roumanian frontiers in territories which were included in the former Austro-Hungarian Empire. (Appendix IV.)[6]

(The Note was approved and initialled by the representatives of the Five Principal Allied and Associated Powers.

Sir Maurice Hankey was instructed to communicate the Note to the Secretary-General for the information of the Drafting Committee.)

5. The Council had under consideration a letter, dated June 16th, 1919, addressed to Sir Maurice Hankey by M. Berthelot on behalf of the Commission on New States. (Appendix V.)[7]

(It was agreed:

1. That the document attached to the letter headed "Proposals concerning Traffic in the Adriatic" together with Annex I, should be referred to the Commission on the International Regime of Ports, Waterways and Railways.

[4] Printed in *PPC*, VI, 589-90.   [5] Printed in *ibid.*, pp. 590-91.
[6] Printed in *ibid.*, pp. 591-93.
[7] This Appendix and its Annexes are printed in *ibid.*, pp. 593-98.

2. That the proposal of the Italian Delegation to submit a clause relating to the restitution of works of art carried off during the war and removed to territory belonging to New States should be referred to the Reparations Commission.

3. That the proposed Financial Clauses relating to Poland suggested by the French Delegation and attached as Annex II to M. Berthelot's letter, should be referred to the Financial Commission.

Sir Maurice Hankey was instructed to communicate this decision to the Secretary-General for the necessary action.)

6. M. LOUCHEUR, who entered towards the end of this meeting, reported that good progress was being made with the completion of the Reparation and Finance Clauses for the Austrian Treaty. He hoped that the report would be ready for consideration by Monday afternoon or Tuesday.

7. During the meeting, a message was received from the British Admiralty to the effect that a number of German ships had been sunk by the maintenance crews on board.[8]

8. M. CLEMENCEAU reported that, after personal consultation with President Wilson and Mr. Lloyd George, he had taken the action recommended by the Military Representatives in their report on the Transfer of the 4th Polish Division from the Bukovina to Poland. (Appendix VI.)[9]

(At this point, the Drafting Committee were introduced for the consideration of the Note prepared by them in reply to the German Delegation. This discussion is recorded as a separate meeting.)

APPENDIX I TO C.F. 79.

NOTE ADDRESSED TO THE SUPREME COUNCIL OF THE ALLIES
BY THE COMMITTEE ON RUMANIAN AND YUGOSLAV AFFAIRS.

June 18th 1919.

The Commission has been asked by a letter from Sir Maurice Hankey to give its opinion on two letters from Mr. Vesnitch dated June 7th.

The Committee could not meet before June 18th, because sev-

[8] Following detailed plans made weeks in advance, Vice Adm. Ludwig von Reuter, commander of the German High Seas Fleet interned at Scapa Flow, a sea basin in the Orkney Islands off the northern coast of Scotland, at approximately 11:20 a.m. on June 21 gave a flag signal to the German crews maintaining the ships to scuttle them by opening their seacocks. Under the terms of the Armistice, no British guards had been placed on the vessels. Most of the British naval squadron assigned to guard the German fleet was on maneuvers in the North Sea. By the time the British ships were alerted and had returned to Scapa Flow in midafternoon, most of the German warships had sunk. Fifteen of the sixteen capital ships went down; one was beached by the British. Four light cruisers sank; four others were beached. Of fifty destroyers, thirty-two sank, fourteen were beached, and four were kept afloat. See Marder, *From the Dreadnought to Scapa Flow*, V, 270-93, and Dan van der Vat, *The Grand Scuttle: The Sinking of the German Fleet at Scapa Flow in 1919* (London, 1982).
[9] Printed in PPC, VI, 599.

eral of its members were also on the Committee for the revision of the Reply to the German Delegation.

The opinion of the Committee is as follows:

1) Mr. Vesnitch's two letters of June 7th, (completed by a third dated June 9th), suggest methods of procedure for giving effect to a proposal for a solution set forth in principle in a letter of June 6th, which was to the following effect:

"Assignment of Zone A to the Serbo-Croato-Slovene State; but the right of the inhabitants is acknowledged to express, by a plebiscite, within three, or at most six months, their desire that this territory should be placed under Austrian sovereignty.

Assignment of Zone B to Austria, but, vice versa, the same right is reserved to the inhabitants of the territory in favour of the Kingdom of the Serbs, Croats and Slovenes."

The Committee approves this suggestion in its broad lines, it being understood that the two zones shall be placed under the control of the International Commission.

2) As regards Paragraph 1 of the letter of June 7th, the Committee unanimously recommends that the space of time provided for in Paragraph 1 should begin from "January 1st, 1919," instead of "the coming into force of the present Treaty."

The United States, British and French Delegations recommend that the proposals of Mr. Vesnitch, contained in Paragraphs B and C, should be approved.

The Italian Delegation accepts Paragraph B, but demands that, in Paragraph C, the words "from August 1st, 1914" should be substituted for the words "at a date previous to January 1st, 1905."

3) As regards Paragraph 2 of Mr. Vesnitch's letter, the Committee proposes an International Commission of seven Members, viz., five appointed by the principal Allied and Associated Powers, one by the Serbo-Croato-Slovene State, and one by the Republic of Austria.

4) As regards Paragraph 3 of Mr. Vesnitch's letter, the United States, British and French Delegations propose that the plebiscite in Zone A should take place three months after the coming into force of the Treaty.

The Italian Delegation demands, as in the case of Upper Silesia, a period of from six months at the least, to eighteen months at the most.

As regards the date of the plebiscite in Zone B, Mr. Vesnitch's proposals have been unanimously approved.

5) As regards Paragraph 4 of Mr. Vesnitch's letter, the Committee unanimously recommends the maintenance, for Zone A of the

limits marked on the map known as "President Wilson's," that is to say, the exclusion of the district of Miesthal.

T MS (SDR, RG 256, 180.03401/79, DNA).

Hankey's Notes of a Meeting of the Council of Four[1]

President Wilson's House,
C.F.78.   Paris, June 21, 1919, 4:00 p.m.

1. The Council had before them a letter addressed by Marshal Foch to the President of the Council on the 18th June, 1919, No. 3051, (Appendix I.)[2] raising the following two questions.
    (1) Whether the United States of America would be represented on the Commission of Control for Military Clauses.
    (2) Whether Belgium should be entitled to be represented on this Commission.

PRESIDENT WILSON said he much regretted it would not be possible for him to make any appointments of United States' officers to the Commission before the ratification of the Treaty. As soon as the Treaty of Peace was ratified by the Government of the United States however he would be prepared to make appointments.

MR. BALFOUR suggested that it was not a matter of great moment, provided that the United States Government had means of knowing what was being done by their associates. They could do this by attaching liaison officers to the various Missions.

(It was agreed
    (i) That M. Clemenceau should reply to Marshal Foch;
        (a) That the United States of America would not be represented on the Commission of Control for the Military Clauses until after the ratification by her of the Treaty of Peace with Germany.
        (b) That he was inviting Belgium to be represented on the Commission.
    (ii) That the President of the Council should send a communication to the Belgian Government inviting them to nominate a representative on the Commission).

2. The Council had before them a Report of the Commission of Prisoners of War on the Commission and Sub-Commissions for the Repatriation of Prisoners of War under the Treaties of Peace.

M. CLEMENCEAU asked that the subject might be postponed as he wished to examine the Report.

3. MR. BALFOUR read a draft letter to the Turkish Government[3] which he had prepared at the request of the Council of Ten, made

at a short unrecorded meeting after the hearing of the Turkish Delegation on Tuesday, June 17th.[4] (Appendix II.)

The draft letter was approved. He (Mr. Balfour) said that although this fully represented his own views, there were some people who did not share these. He mentioned in particular Mr. Montagu, the Secretary of State for India, who had sent him a long memorandum of criticisms.[5] Mr. Montagu, however, represented an entirely different school of policy, and was strongly opposed to the removal of the Turks from Constantinople.

M. SONNINO pointed out that the Memorandum did not attack Moslems but only the Ottomans.

PRESIDENT WILSON said he had these points in his mind throughout the reading of the Memorandum, and he could not find anything against the Moslems. It was merely an indictment against the Turkish rule. He subscribed to the letter with great satisfaction.

The Memorandum was unanimously agreed to, subject to authority being given to Mr. Balfour to make such drafting alterations as he might consider desirable, and subject to a reservation which Mr. Balfour (particularly in view of Mr. Montagu's objections) asked for; namely, that the reply should not be dispatched until it had been approved by Mr. Lloyd George.

(It was agreed that when Mr. Lloyd George had given his assent, the letter should be signed by M. Clemenceau on behalf of the Council, and sent to the Turkish Delegation.)

4. During the meeting M. CLEMENCEAU received a dispatch to the effect that M. Nitti and M. Tittoni were forming a Government in Rome.

At this point the Council adjourned to the upstairs room for a discussion with experts in regard to Klagenfurt and Carinthia, which is recorded as a separate meeting.

T MS (SDR, RG 256, 180.03401/78, DNA).

[1] The complete text of these minutes is printed in PPC, VI, 575-80.

[2] Printed in ibid., p. 577.

[3] A. J. Balfour, "DRAFT ANSWER TO THE TURKS," June 19, 1919, T MS (SDR, RG 256, 180.03401/78, DNA), printed in PPC, VI, 577-80. Balfour's draft flatly denied the contention of the Turkish delegation that the Ottoman Empire should be preserved in its territorial integrity, both because the Turkish people should not be blamed for the sins of their wartime government and because of the alleged good record of Turkish rule over subject peoples. Every nation, Balfour replied, had to be judged by the government which ruled over it at a given time. Moreover, history proved conclusively that Turks were totally unfit to rule over subject peoples, whether Christian or Moslem. In fact the subject peoples would do much better both culturally and economically if freed from the burden of Turkish rule.

[4] The minutes of the Council of Ten of June 17, at which the Turkish spokesman read a long statement, are printed in PPC, IV, 508-12. For a summary, see the extract from the Grayson Diary printed at June 17, 1919, Vol. 60.

[5] "MR MONTAGU'S COMMENTS ON MR BALFOUR'S REPLY TO THE TURKS AND MR BALFOUR'S REMARKS THEREON," n.d., T MS (WP, DLC).

From Albert, King of the Belgians

[Brussels, June 21, 1919]

The Queen and I are very grateful for your most kind telegram. It was for us a great pleasure to receive you as well as Misses and Miss Wilson. My countrymen with us appreciate highly the visit of the illustrious President of the United States.   Albert.

T telegram (WP, DLC).

From John Joseph Pershing

Personal.

Dear Mr. President: Paris, June 21, 1919.

Referring to our conversation some time since regarding the possible forward movement of the Allied Forces, for which it was understood detailed instructions would be given by the Council to the Allied Commander-in-Chief, permit me to request a copy of these instructions, or so much thereof as may be expedient, with any special orders you may wish carried out, in order that I may transmit them to Lieutenant General Liggett, commanding our forces on the Rhine for his guidance.

General instructions have been given by the Allied Commander-in-Chief directing this forward movement, should Germany refuse to sign the treaty, and our troops are now in readiness.

Believe me, with great respect,

Cordially yours,   John J. Pershing.

TLS (WP, DLC).

From Herbert Clark Hoover

Dear Mr. President: Paris, 21 June 1919.

Before the present Joint Councils of the Heads of States dissolve by your departure, I wish to lay before you earnestly what appears to me (after Peace) the greatest outstanding situation in the world insistent for solution, and that is Russia. Nor do I wish to approach it from any point of view other than purely its economic phases.

Sooner or later the Bolshevik Government will fall of its own weight or it will have swung sufficiently right to be absorbed in a properly representative government. Already about one-half of the area of the old Russian Empire is under non-Bolshevik influences.

No government of any character can stand in this country without an economic reorganization. Such reorganization primarily revolves on two positive facto[r]s, first, currency, and second, transportation. Even the governments of Koltchak and Denikin are both likely to fail at any moment, due to the practical break-down in the distribution of commodities. There is in both of these areas not only ample foodstuffs for their populations but an actual surplus and yet there is here actual starvation.

I attach one single telegram[1] out of a host as indicating the character of the situation, and in this special case of the Donetz Basin there is ample wheat not 500 miles distant if there were some form of currency in which the population could have confidence, and transportation with which to expect exchange of coal for wheat. This is only typical of many other instances.

By and large, there can be no hope of any form of stable government unless these two primary things can be solved. It is already the defeat of Bolshevism and will be the defeat of any government that takes its place. The re-establishment of currency, transportation, the stimulation of production, and the normal flow of distribution, is sheerly a matter of some sort of economic dictatorship, backed by sufficiently large financial and moral support of the Allied Governments. These appropriations would need to be expended fundamentally in commodities and railway rolling stock for import into Russia and for the establishment of a currency. I do not believe that the sum involved is extraordinarily large if such an economic dictatorship could have command of the resources already in Russia.

Furthermore, it appears to me that some such an economic commission, if placed upon an economic and not a political basis, could if conducted with wisdom, keep itself free from conflicting political currents and allow a rational development of self-government in Russia. I have no idea that such self-government can develop over night in a nation totally inexperienced and without tradition, but there can be no foundation on which such government can emerge so long as populations are mad from starvation and unemployment and the lack of the very necessities of life.

This matter becomes of immediate importance if America is to have any hand in the matter, as the resources and organization at our disposal come to an end either upon the signing of Peace with Germany, or, alternatively, on the first of July with the expiration of the Acts with which you are familiar.

I wish to add one suggestion to you in organization of such a commission. It is utterly impossible that it could be organized on the basis of any Inter-Allied Commission with all the conflicting financial and trade interest that lies therein. It is necessary to set up one government as the economic mandatory, with the support of the other governments, and to set up some one man as the head of such a commission, who should choose his own staff for the great administration that will be involved. Such a staff could with judgment be composed of representatives of each nationality, but they must be definitely responsible to the head of such a commission and not independently responsible to different governments.

Faithfully yours,   Herbert Hoover[2]

TLS (SDR, RG 256, 861.00/786, DNA).
[1] Commander Galbraith to HCH, received June 20, 1919, T telegram (SDR, RG 59, 861.00/786, DNA).
[2] For Wilson's oral answer to this letter, see the extract from the Diary of Vance C. McCormick printed at June 23, 1919.

From Louis Marshall

Dear Mr. President: Paris, June 21, 1919.

It is only because of my deep concern in the fate of the Jews and other Minorities of Eastern Europe that I venture to intrude upon you. It is rumored that because of adverse agitation by the New States a tendency has developed within the past two days, in certain directions, to relax the principle announced in Article 93 of the German Treaty, relating to Minorities, confirmed though it has been during the present week, in the response of the Allied and Associated Powers to the objections of Germany,—and although several times reiterated in the draft of the Austrian Treaty. It is inconceivable that such a course can be seriously contemplated. Your repeated utterances have demonstrated that the maintenance of peace in these lands depends on the protection of the Minorities who dwell there.

It is, however, more confidently reported that even if in theory the principle may be formally adopted, in practice, as exemplified by vital changes in the Convention with Poland as heretofore formulated by the Commission on New States which have been suggested, it will be deprived of all value. This would, in effect, be as disastrous as the abandonment of the principle itself.

The following propositions are deemed essential:

I.—That the obligation of the New States to the racial, religious and linguistic minorities be recognized as of international concern;

II.—That jurisdiction over any infraction of them be conferred on the League of Nations and the Permanent Court of International Justice when created;

III.—That the several rights guaranteed by [be] incorporated in the Constitution of the New States as a bill of rights;

IV.—That these rights as formulated be unamendable without the concurrence of the League of Nations;

V.—That citizenship be defined in clear and unambiguous terms operating automatically;

VI.—That the civil, religious, political rights conferred, including equality before the law, freedom from discrimination and the protection of life, liberty and property be set forth in the time-honored terms of our American Constitution;

VII.—That language rights; immunity from enforced desecration of the Sabbath; the right of the Minorities to maintain their own schools and religious and charitable institutions and to receive from the public treasury toward their support a proportionate share of the funds to be raised for such purposes by State, Departmental or Municipal budgets be secured.

VIII.—That all existing or future laws, regulations or practices inconsistent with the foregoing be deemed of no effect.

The omission of any of these terms would cripple and weaken the entire plan, which, if adopted, would constitute the Charter of Freedom of the peoples of Europe.

It is assumed that if these rights are to be granted it can only be effectively done if the Convention with Poland is executed concurrently with the German Treaty, pursuant to which Poland is put in the enjoyment of the great sovereign powers, which constitute the consideration for the Convention. Otherwise performance of the obligation of Article 93 of the German Treaty might easily be evaded or delayed for a protracted period replete with controversy.

Pardon my anxiety, Mr. President, but with the responsibility resting upon me as the Chairman of the Jewish Delegations of America and Eastern Europe of securing emancipation in fact, for the ten millions of my brethren, who, virtually still in bondage, regard the action about to be taken as their last hope of attaining for themselves and their children those human rights that for many weary and sorrow-laden centuries have been withheld from them, I cannot fail at this fateful moment, in their behalf to ask you to whom their hearts go forth, to bring them solace.

Cordially and gratefully yours,   Louis Marshall

TLS (WP, DLC).

From the Diary of Ray Stannard Baker

Saturday June 21 [1919]

This day has been full of the electricity of expectation—with constantly growing assurance that Germany will sign. We hear that new governments are being formed both in Germany & in Italy.

I found the President this evening quite sanguine. The Council had spent the day answering 12 minor queries of the German government regarding the treaty. I asked the President if he intended to go to the opening exercises of the Pershing stadium to-morrow (Sunday). He has a record as a Presbyterian as a strict observer of Sabbath rest.

"Do you think the American people would like to have me do this?" he asked. Grayson at once broke in jokingly: "*You're* a Presbyterian, aren't you?" "Yes," I replied, "but I don't work very hard at it" The President will not go.

I had a long & very interesting talk to-day with Secretary Lansing—while he drew pencilled heads with his left hand on a block of paper. He told me about his struggle to get the South and Central American delegates admitted to the Versailles conference in which the German treaty was presented. He wrote 2 letters to the President strongly urging this courtesy—& the President took it up in the Council of Four. Lloyd George was absolutely opposed to the admission of any but "effective belligerents" but finally consented to admit China & Siam.[1] No doubt because they were in the sphere of British influence. The President told Lansing it was the best he could do, that the other two would consent to no more invitation[s]—except Brazil, which was regarded as an "effective belligerent." At the plenary session on the day before the treaty was presented Lansing leaned over (he sits next the President) and renewed his argument. The President finally turned to Clemenceau & said that the American delegation strongly favored the admission of the South & Central American delegates. Clemenceau made some non-commital reply & looked up at the ceiling in a way he has when he is opposed to a proposal but does not want to argue it. At this point Lansing leaned over & said,

"Monsieur Clemenceau the American delegation not only favors the admission of the delegates from South & Central America, but will feel offended & resentful unless they are admitted. Delegates from small nations in other parts of the world to say nothing of delegates from the colonies of Great Britain are admitted. Why not the American delegates?"

Clemenceau referred the question to Lloyd-George & after a moment's whispered conversation said to Lansing: "All right. I have no objection."

"And they will be invited?"

"Yes."

But Lansing, still skeptical, told Harrison[2] to go personally to all the South & Central American delegates & tell them to be there, whether they received invitations or not. They were there! And not one of *them had received an invitation.* Neither the French nor the British wanted them present.

[1] About this controversy, see the minutes of the Council of Four printed at May 6, 1919, 11 a.m., Vol. 58.
[2] That is, Leland Harrison, one of the secretaries of the A.C.N.P.

From Joseph Patrick Tumulty

[The White House, June 21, 1919]

No. 206 The fight against the League on Knox Resolution[1] faces utter collapse. Root and Hays[2] here advising Republican leaders. I learned that Root is advising Republicans to vote for the League, with reservations.[3] He is advising Republicans to concentrate their forces upon a resolution of ratification, which would contain specific reservations on the Monroe Doctrine, immigration, tariff and other purely American questions. I believe that this is the course the Republicans will finally adopt. A confidant of Mr. Taft's yesterday wanted to know from me what your attitude was in this matter, saying that Mr. Taft might favor this reservation plan. I told him I had no knowledge on the subject. It is a thing that you might consider. To me it looks like cowardice. The American Federation of Labor adopted resolution favoring the League of Nations by a vote of 29,750 against 420. Andrew Furuseth led the fight against it. The resolution supporting the League contained a reservation in favor of home rule for Ireland.   Tumulty.

T telegram (WP, DLC).
[1] See JPT to WW, June 10, 1919, Vol. 60.
[2] That is, Will H(arrison) Hays, chairman of the Republican National Committee.
[3] Elihu Root had set forth his current strategy for Republicans in regard to the League of Nations in a letter to Henry Cabot Lodge on June 19, 1919. "I should be glad," he began, "to see the peace terms and the League of Nations covenant separated, as proposed in the resolution offered by Senator Knox, so that the latter could be considered by the people of the country without coercion from the necessities of a speedy peace." He then referred Lodge to his earlier letter on the subject addressed to Hays on March 29, 1919 (for Root's views at that time, see the index references to him in Vol. 56 of this series). The changes in the Covenant made since that date were, in Root's opinion, "very inadequate and unsatisfactory."
"Nothing has been done," he said, "to provide for the re-establishment and strengthening of a system of arbitration or judicial decision upon questions of legal right. Nothing has been done toward providing for the revision or development of international law. In these respects, principles maintained by the United States without variation for half a century are still ignored, and we are left with a program which rests the hope of the

world for future peace in a government of men and not of laws, following the dictates of expediency, and not of right. Nothing has been done to limit the vast and incalculable obligation which Article X. of the covenant undertakes to impose upon each member of the League to preserve against external aggression the territorial integrity and political independence of all members of the League all over the world.

"The clause authorizing withdrawal from the League on two years' notice leaves a doubt whether a mere charge that we had not performed some international obligation would not put it in the power of the Council to take jurisdiction of the charge as a disputed question and keep us in the League indefinitely against our will.

"The clause which has been inserted regarding the Monroe Doctrine is erroneous in its description of the doctrine and ambiguous in meaning. Other purely American questions, as, for example, questions relating to immigration, are protected only by a clause apparently empowering the Council to determine whether such questions are solely within the domestic jurisdiction of the United States. I do not think that in these respects the United States is sufficiently protected against most injurious results, which are wholly unnecessary for the establishment and maintenance of this League of Nations.

"On the other hand, it still remains that there is in the covenant a great deal of high value that the world ought not to lose. The arrangement to make conferences of the Powers automatic when there is danger of war; provisions for joint action, as, of course, by representatives of the nations concerned in matters affecting common interests; the agreement for delay in case of serious disputes, with opportunity to bring the public opinion of the world to bear on the disputants, and to induce cool and deliberate judgment; the recognition of racial and popular rights to the freedom of local self-government; and the plan, indispensable in some form, for setting up Governments in the vast regions deprived by the war of the autocratic rule which has maintained order—all those ought not be lost, if that can possibly be avoided. The condition of Europe requires prompt action. Industry has not revived there. Its revival requires raw materials. To obtain these credit is necessary, and for this there must be security for the fruits of enterprise, and for this there must be peace. Satan is finding evil work for idle hands to do in Europe—evil work that affects the whole world, including the United States.

"Under these circumstances, what ought to be done?

"I am clear that, if the covenant has to be considered with the peace terms included, the Senate ought to include in its resolution of consent to the ratification an expression of such reservations and understandings as will cure, so far as possible, the defects which I have pointed out. You will probably be unable to do anything now about the system of arbitration and the development of international law. You can, however, put into the resolution of consent a reservation refusing to agree to Article X. and I think you should do so; you can clarify the meaning of the withdrawal article, and you can also include in your resolution the substance of the third amendment which I proposed in my letter to Mr. Hays, of March 29, relating to purely American questions, and I think you should do so. These clauses of the resolution shape themselves in my own mind as follows:

"The Senate of the United States advises and consents to the ratification of the said treaty with the following reservations and understandings to be made a part of the instrument of ratification, viz.:

"(1.) In advising and consenting to the ratification of the said treaty, the Senate reserves and excludes from its consent the tenth article of the covenant for the League of Nations, as to which the Senate refuses its consent.

"(2.) The Senate consents to the ratification of the said treaty reserving Article X. aforesaid with the understanding that whenever two years' notice of withdrawal from the League of Nations shall have been given, as provided in Article I., no claim, charge, or finding that international obligations or obligations under the covenant have not been fulfilled, will be deemed to render the two years' notice ineffectual or to keep the power giving the notice in the League after the expiration of the time specified in the notice.

"(3.) Inasmuch as, in agreeing to become a member of the League of Nations, the United States of America is moved by no interest or wish to intrude upon or interfere with the political policy or international administration of any foreign State, and by no existing or anticipated dangers in the affairs of the American continents, but accedes to the wish of the European States that it shall join its power to theirs for the preservation of general peace, the Senate consents to the ratification of the said treaty, excepting Article X. aforesaid, with the understanding that nothing therein contained shall be construed to imply a relinquishment by the United States of America of its traditional attitude toward purely American questions, or to require the submission of its policy regarding questions which it deems to be purely American questions to the decision or recommendation of other Powers.

"This reservation and these expressions of understanding are in accordance with long-established precedent in the making of treaties. When included in the instrument of ratification they will not require a reopening of negotiation, but if none of the other signatories expressly objects to the ratification with such limitations, the treaty stands as limited as between the United States and the other Powers."

Root followed these recommendations with a lengthy justification of them. He concluded by returning to the subjects of arbitration and the development of international law. "I think," he wrote, "that when the Senate consents to the ratification of the treaty with some such reservations as I have indicated, it ought also to adopt a separate resolution not a part of the action upon the treaty, but, practically at the same time, formally requesting the President, without any avoidable delay, to open negotiations with the other Powers for the re-establishment and strengthening of a system of arbitration for the disposition of international disputes upon questions of right, and for periodical meetings of representatives of all the Powers for the revision and development of international law." Printed in the *New York Times*, June 22, 1919, and in many other newspapers on that date; also printed in a slightly garbled version in *Cong. Record*, 66th Cong., 1st sess., pp. 1549-50. About Root's letter to Hays of March 29, 1919, see the Enclosure printed with WW to EMH, March 31, 1919, Vol. 56, and D. H. Miller to G. Auchincloss, June 26, 1919, and the notes thereto. Root's letter to Hays is printed in *Cong. Record*, 66th Cong., 1st sess., pp. 1546-49.

About the drafting, purpose, and significance of Root's letter to Lodge of June 19, 1919, see Lloyd E. Ambrosius, *Woodrow Wilson and the American Diplomatic Tradition: The Treaty Fight in Perspective* (Cambridge, New York, etc., 1987), pp. 148-49; Richard W. Leopold, *Elihu Root and the Conservative Tradition* (Boston, 1954), pp. 138-39; and Philip C. Jessup, *Elihu Root* (2 vols., New York, 1938), II, 399-402.

From Thomas William Lamont

Dear Mr. Wilson: Paris, June 21, 1919.

In the hope that on Monday the Germans will give an indication that they intend to sign the Treaty, I am, with your permission, planning to sail for home some time next week.

The unfinished matters relating to Austro-Hungary, Bulgaria and Turkey are so far advanced that certainly my presence is not needed here. I am joining with all my associates in certain specific recommendations as to personnel for certain of the Commissions that have come under our particular eye.

Furthermore, Morrow told me in that cable a fortnight ago,[1] he thought that I could be of some service at home in giving to various Republican Senators a more correct view of the situation over here and of the work which you have accomplished, and which, as you must let me tell you, commands my admiration.

If, in connection with any features of the campaign at home you would like to give me your views before my departure, I should be most happy. What little service I may have been able to render on this side, I am anxious to supplement on the other, in connection with the Treaty and the League of Nations. I depore an attempt on the part of certain Republicans to make a Party issue of a matter in which everyone should be first for America and for the world.

With great respect, my dear Mr. President, I am,

                        Faithfully yours,   Thomas W. Lamont

TLS (WP, DLC).
[1] See the Enclosure printed with T. W. Lamont to WW, June 5, 1919, Vol. 60.

From the Diary of Dr. Grayson

Sunday, June 22, 1919.

The President slept quite late this morning. I received a letter from Clemenceau enclosing a communication that the French had received from the German delegates at Versailles, and I took it to the President in his room. This note was signed by the German Premier and declared that Germany was prepared to accept the treaty in full if the Allied governments would eliminate from it the demand that the Kaiser and other German officials should be handed over for trial for their violations of international law, and also that the Allies eliminate from the treaty the admission by Germany that she actually was entirely responsible for the war. The President read the note and said to me: "Germany does not want to accept responsibility for the war alone. We do not charge Germany alone. It is Germany and her allies." He made this remark while in the hall in the presence of Mr. Bainbridge Colby and Mr. Charles H. Grasty, who had come to see me.

The President took only a short ride today. He was expecting communications from Lloyd George and Clemenceau concerning the German situation. At three o'clock he left the house for a ride through the Park, and at five o'clock he went to Lloyd George's house. Clemenceau had preceded him. The meeting was held in Lloyd George's apartment because of his illness. This meeting lasted until 8:30, causing the President to be an hour and half late for dinner. He ate his dinner in a hurry and returned to Lloyd George's for a meeting at 9:00 o'clock. I accompanied him. While at this meeting the President prepared the reply of the Council to the latest German request, which reply was afterwards signed by Clemenceau as Chairman of the Peace Conference and forwarded directly to Von Haniel[1] at Versailles. The President dictated this statement to Lloyd George's secretary. It was afterwards sent over to the temporary While House, and the President on discovering several typographical errors made the corrections in pencil and turned it over to me to give out to the newspapers through the press bureau. The reply was as follows:[2]

[1] That is, Edgar Karl Alfons Haniel von Haimhausen.
[2] Here follows the text of the statement printed as Appendix II to the minutes of the Council of Four printed at June 22, 1919, 9 p.m.

From the Diary of Ray Stannard Baker

Sunday [June] 22nd [1919].

This has been a hair-trigger day from the news point of view. This morning we put out under great pressure for time the German note of June 20th, with the allied reply. About 7 o'clock I got word from the French foreign office that there was still another German note (or *four* of them) in which the Germans agreed to sign with two reservations—(1) accepting the moral responsibility for the war, & (2) delivering over for punishment the guilty men.

I found that the Four were meeting with Lloyd-George, who has been ill, & I went over about 9 to see the President who had stopped for dinner & was just going back to the meeting. The President described the exact situation & said he would gladly accede to the Germans' request but felt himself bound by his agreement with his associates & that the only course seemed to be to send an absolute ultimatum to the Germans requiring a positive answer at the time set. Half an hour later Admiral Grayson brought this reply to me & still later I sent my orderly over to Sir Maurice Hankey for the text of the final German notes. We issued both notes & reply before 11 pm & had them all on the cables before midnight.

Hankey's Notes of a Meeting of the Council of Four[1]

Mr. Lloyd George's Residence,
C.F.80A.   Paris, June 22, 1919, 7:15 p.m.

1. The Council had before it the following Notes from the German Delegation dated June 22nd,—No. 68[2] and No. 70,[3] which was brought to the Meeting by Colonel Henri[4] direct from Versailles and which ends with the following declaration:

"The Government of the German Republic accordingly gives the declaration of its consent as required by the Note of June 16th, 1919, in the following form:

'The Government of the German Republic is ready to sign the Treaty of Peace without, however, recognising thereby that the German people was the author of the war and without undertaking any responsibility for delivering persons in accordance with Articles 227 to 230 of the Treaty of Peace.' "

N.B. All the above Notes will be found as Appendices to the following Meeting, namely, C.F.81.

After Colonel Henri and M. Mantoux had read a rough translation of the last-named Note, MR LLOYD GEORGE and PRESIDENT WILSON expressed the view that an immediate answer should be sent, refusing any alteration in the Treaty.

PRESIDENT WILSON then read the following draft reply:[5]

"The Allied and Associated Powers have considered the Note of the German Delegation of even date, and, in view of the shortness of the time remaining, feel it their duty to reply at once.

Of the time within which the German Government must make their final decision as to the signature of the Treaty, less than 24 hours remain.

The Allied and Associated Government have given the fullest consideration to all of the representations hitherto made by the German Government with regard to the Treaty, have replied with complete frankness, and have made such concessions as they thought it just to make; and the present Note of the German Delegation presents no arguments or consideration not already examined.

The Allied and Associated Powers therefore feel constrained to say that the time for discussion has passed. They can accept or acknowledge no *exception* or reservation, and must require of the German representatives an unequivocal decision as to their purpose to sign and accept as a whole, or not to sign and accept, the Treaty as finally formulated."

M. CLEMENCEAU suggested to add the following words: "After the signature, the Allied and Associated Powers must hold Germany responsible for the execution of every stipulation of the Treaty."

PRESIDENT WILSON said it had been suggested to him to substitute the word "qualification" for "exception" in his draft.

(This was agreed to.)

(It was agreed to summon a Meeting of the full Council of the Principal Allied and Associated Powers at 9 p.m. and submit the draft reply as amended above, for its consideration.[6])

2. (It was agreed that Mr Balfour should be asked to draft a letter to the German Delegation, calling attention to the sinking of the German ships in the Orkneys, which, whether or not it was a technical breach of the armistice, was unquestionably a breach of faith for which the German Government must be held responsible. Warning should be given that the Allied and Associated Powers were considering the matter, and reserved their right to take such action as they thought necessary.) (Sir Maurice Hankey was instructed to ask Mr Balfour to take this matter up.)

T MS (SDR, RG 256, 180.03401/80½, DNA).
   [1] The complete text of these minutes is printed in *PPC*, VI, 605-606.
   [2] E. K. A. Haniel von Haimhausen to G. Clemenceau, TCL (SDR, RG 256, 180.03401/81, DNA), printed in *PPC*, VI, 608. Haniel's letter embodied copies of his credentials authorizing him to hand to Clemenceau the German reply printed as Appendix I, referred to in n. 3 below, and to negotiate with the peace conference about it.
   [3] Printed as Appendix I to the following document.

. 4 Actually, Lt. Col. Marie Joseph Léon Augustin Henry, liaison between the Council of Four and the German delegation.
5 There is a WWsh "first sketch," as Wilson called it, of this reply in WP, DLC.
6 Printed as Appendix II to the following document.

Hankey's Notes of a Meeting of the Council of Four[1]

Mr. Lloyd George's Residence,

C.F.81.   Paris, June 22, 1919, 9:00 p.m.

1. M. SONNINO accepted the draft reply.

BARON MAKINO, after reading both documents, accepted the draft reply, which was signed by M. Clemenceau, and transmitted.

(The letter was then signed by M. Clemenceau, and dispatched by Colonel Henri to Versailles.)

(It was agreed to publish the letter and the reply in the morning newspapers of Monday, June 23rd.)

2. MR BALFOUR said that he had prepared a draft letter to the Germans, but had sent it to Mr Hurst to check certain points of law and fact.

(It was agreed to postpone consideration of this matter until the following morning.)

[Appendix I]

CONFIDENTIAL

W.C.P.1046   TRANSLATION OF GERMAN NOTE

No. 70.   GERMAN PEACE DELEGATION

Mr. President: Versailles. June 22nd. 1919.

The Imperial Minister of Foreign Affairs has instructed me to communicate the following to Your Excellency:

"The Government of the German Republic has, from the moment when the Peace Conditions of the Allied and Associated Governments were made known to it, left no doubt to subsist as to the fact that the Government, in harmony with the whole German people, must regard these conditions as being in sharp contrast with the principle which was accepted by the Allied and Associated Powers on the one hand, and Germany on the other hand, as being binding in accordance with the law of nations for the peace before the conclusion of the armistice.

"Relying upon this principle of justice which was agreed upon between the parties to the negotiations, and assisted by a clear exposition of conditions in Germany, the Government has left no

. 1 The complete text of these minutes is printed in *PPC*, VI, 607-12.

stone unturned in order to arrive at direct verbal exchange of opinions, and thus to obtain some mitigation of the unbearably harsh conditions which might render it possible for the Government of the German Republic to sign the Treaty of Peace without reservations, and to guarantee its execution.

"These endeavours of the Government of the German Republic, which were undertaken in the interest of the peace of the world, and the reconciliation of peoples, have failed owing to rigorous insistence on the conditions of peace. Far-reaching counter-proposals of the German Delegation have only in certain points received any acceptance. The concessions made only reduce the severity of the conditions in a small degree. The Allied and Associated Governments have, in an ultimatum which expires on June 23rd, confronted the Government of the German Republic with the decision either to sign the Treaty of Peace presented by them or to refuse to sign. In the latter case a completely defenceless people has been threatened with the forcible imposition of the conditions of peace already presented and with the increase of the heavy burdens.

"The German people does not wish for the resumption of the bloody war, it honestly wishes for a lasting peace. In view of the attitude of the Allied and Associated Governments, the German people has no other force in its hands save to appeal to the eternally inalienable right to an independent life which belongs to the German people as to all peoples. The Government of the German Republic can lend no support to this sacred right of the German people by the application of force. The Government can only hope for support through the conscience of mankind. No people, including those of the Allied and Associated Powers, could expect the German people to agree with thorough conviction to an instrument of peace, whereby living members of the very body of the German people are to be cut off without consultation of the population concerned, whereby the dignity of the German State is to be permanently impaired, and whereby unendurable economic and financial burdens are to be laid upon the German people.

"The German Government has received passionate expressions of opinion from the population in the districts to be cut off in the East, to the effect that they (the population) will oppose themselves to the separation of these districts which have for the greater part been German for many centuries by all means they possess. The German Government therefore finds itself compelled to decline all responsibility for any difficulties which may arise from the resistance of the inhabitants against their separation from Germany.

"If the Government of the German Republic is nevertheless ready to sign the conditions of the Allies with the above-mentioned reservation, yet this is not done of its free will. The Government of the German Republic solemnly declares that its attitude is to be understood in the sense that it yields to force, being resolved to spare the German people, whose sufferings are unspeakable, a new war, the shattering of its national unity by further occupation of German territories, terrible famine for women and children, and mercilessly prolonged retention of the prisoners of war. The German people expects in view of the grievous burdens which it is to take upon itself that all German military and civilian prisoners beginning on July 1, and thereafter in uninterrupted succession, and within a short period shall be restored. Germany gave back her enemies' prisoners of war within two months.

"The Government of the German Republic engages to fulfil the conditions of peace imposed upon Germany. It desires, however, in this solemn moment to express itself with unreserved clearness, in order to meet in advance any accusation of untruthfulness that may now or later be made against Germany. The conditions imposed exceed the measure of that which Germany can in fact perform. The Government of the German Republic therefore feels itself bound to announce that it makes all reservations and declines all responsibility as regards the consequences which may be threatened against Germany when, as is bound to happen, the impossibility of carrying out the conditions comes to light even though German capacity to fulfil is stretched to the utmost.

"Germany further lays the greatest emphasis on the declaration that she cannot accept Article 231[2] of the Treaty of Peace which requires Germany to admit herself to be the sole and only author of the war, and does not cover this article by her signature. It consequently follows without further argument that Germany must also decline to recognise that the burdens should be placed upon her on the score of the responsibility for the war which has unjustly been laid at her door.

"Likewise, it is equally impossible for a German to reconcile it with his dignity and honour to accept and execute Articles 227 to 230, by which Germany is required to give up to the Allied and Associated Powers for trial individuals among the German people who are accused by the Allied and Associated Powers of the breach

[2] That is, the so-called War Guilt clause, which reads as follows:
"The Allied and Associated Governments affirm and Germany accepts the responsibility of Germany and her Allies for causing all the loss and damage to which the Allied and Associated Governments and their nationals have been subjected as a consequence of the war imposed upon them by the aggression of Germany and her allies."

of international laws and of committing acts contrary to the customs of war.

"Further, the Government of the German Republic makes a distinct protest against the taking away of all the colonial possessions of Germany, and against the reasons given therefor which permanently deny to Germany fitness for colonial activity, although the contrary is clearly established and irrefutable evidence to this effect is contained in the Observations of the German Peace Delegation on the Conditions of Peace.[3]

"The Government of the German Republic assumes that it is in accordance with the desires of the Allied and Associated Governments that it has spoken openly, both as regards what concerns its goodwill and also as regards its reservations. Therefore, in view of the condition of constraint into which the German people are forced by the requirements of the Allies—a condition of constraint such as has never been inflicted on any people in any manner more crushing and more disastrous in its consequences—and relying on the express undertaking of the Allied and Associated Governments in their memorandum of June 16, 1919,[4] the German Government believes itself to be entitled to address the following modest request to the Allied and Associated Governments in the expectation that the Allied and Associated Governments will consider the following declaration as an integral portion of the Treaty:

'Within two years counting from the day when the Treaty is signed, the Allied and Associated Governments will submit the present Treaty to the High Council of the Powers, as constituted by the League of Nations according to Article 4, for the purpose of subsequent examination. Before this High Council the German plenipotentiaries are to enjoy the same rights and privileges as the representatives of the other contracting Powers of the present Treaty. This Council shall decide in regard to those conditions of the present Treaty which impair the rights of self-determination of the German people, and also in regard to the stipulation whereby the free economic development of Germany on a footing of equal rights is impeded.'

The Government of the German Republic accordingly gives the declaration of its consent, as required by the Note of June 16th, 1919, in the following form:

[3] Again, for the "Observations of the German Delegation on the Conditions of Peace," see Count Brockdorff-Rantzau to G. Clemenceau, May 29, 1919, and n. 1 thereto, Vol. 59.

[4] Again, G. Clemenceau to Brockdorff-Rantzau, June 16, 1919, printed in PPC, VI, 926-96. For the drafting of this document, see the relevant references in the Index to Vol. 60 under Paris Peace Conference and Philip Kerr.

'The Government of the German Republic is ready to sign the Treaty of Peace without, however, recognising thereby that the German people was the author of the War, and without undertaking any responsibility for delivering persons in accordance with Articles 227 to 230 of the Treaty of Peace.'

Weimar, June 21st, 1919.
(Signed) Bauer.[5]
President of the
Imperial Ministry."

Accept, Mr. President, the expression of my distinguished consideration.   (Signed)   von Haniel.

[Appendix II]

CONFIDENTIAL.

W.C.P.1051.

REPLY TO GERMAN NOTE OF 22ND. JUNE, 1919.

(See W.C.P.1046.)

(Approved by the Council of the Principal Allied and Associated Powers on June 22nd. 1919.)

The Allied and Associated Powers have considered the Note of the German Delegation of even date and in view of the shortness of the time remaining feel it their duty to reply at once. Of the time within which the German Government must make their final decision as to the signature of the Treaty less than 24 hours remain. The Allied and Associated Governments have given the fullest consideration to all of the representations hitherto made by the German Government with regard to the Treaty, have replied with complete frankness and have made such concessions as they thought it just to make; and the present Note of the German Delegation presents no arguments or considerations not already examined. The Allied and Associated Powers therefore feel constrained to say that the time for discussion has passed. They can accept or acknowledge no qualification or reservation and must require of the German representatives an unequivocal decision as to their purpose to sign and accept as a whole or not to sign and accept, the Treaty as finally formulated.

After the signature the Allied and Associated Powers must hold

[5] Gustav Adolf Bauer, Social Democratic leader and former Minister of Labor, who had become Chancellor in the new coalition government of the Social Democratic and Center parties, formed on June 21 to replace the Scheidemann cabinet. The principal objective in the formation of the new regime had been to secure ratification of the peace treaty by the National Assembly. Matthias Erzberger, a leading advocate of ratification, became Finance Minister and Vice Chancellor in the new government. See Epstein, *Matthias Erzberger*, pp. 320-21.

Germany responsible for the execution of every stipulation of the Treaty.
Paris.
June 22nd. 1919.

T MS (SDR, RG 256, 180.03401/81, DNA).

From Thomas Nelson Page

My dear Mr. President: [Paris] Sunday, June 22d [1919]
    I have arrived and hope very much you can spare me a little time tomorrow—Monday—to talk about the Italian situation and certain things relating thereto. I know that you are dreadfully pressed, but you will I feel sure excuse my thus adding to your burden in view of the importance of this matter.
            Always most sincerely yours,   Thos Nelson Page

ALS (WP, DLC).

From the Diary of Dr. Grayson

Monday, June 23, 1919.
    During the night word was received in Paris that the German government had fallen and that a new government had been organized. The word was telephoned to me from the French Foreign Office, and requests were made that the President be awakened and informed of the developments. But I refused to allow this, realizing that he needed all of his rest for the strenuous day that was in front of him. Early in the morning the French Foreign Office called me and stated that Mr. Clemenceau wanted a meeting held at the earliest possible moment. As Lloyd George was still ill it was decided that the meeting should be held in his apartment, and the President went there immediately after breakfast, reaching there before 9:00 o'clock. Clemenceau followed a few seconds later and brought with him the copy of the note received from the German government during the night.[1] This note stated that the German government was very anxious to sign but that it had not had time to settle upon the details. It asked for forty-eight hours additional time in which to reply to the Allied ultimatum. Dr. Bauer, the new German Premier, declared that the new Cabinet had been formed with the greatest difficulty and that after it had been formed the National Assembly adopted a vote of confidence in the Cabinet by a large majority and directed it to proceed to sign the Peace Treaty. Bauer declared that his government would have to communicate

with the Assembly at least once more before it could select delegates and authorize them to sign.

The Council of Three spent very little time in arriving at its decision, and the following note was sent to Dr. Bauer:

"Mr. President: The Allied and Associated Governments have the honor to acknowledge receipt of your communication dated June 23d. After full consideration of your request they regret that it is impossible for them to prolong the time already granted to Your Excellency to inform them as to your decision in regard to the signature of the treaty without reservation of any kind."

The meeting at Lloyd George's house lasted only thirty minutes, and the President returned to the temporary White House, and the Council of Three resumed its deliberations, with Mr. Balfour sitting as the representative of the British Government, and with Baron Sonnino in Orlando's place. The Austrian Treaty was under consideration.

There were no guests for luncheon. The President did not go for his usual ride after lunch but remained at the temporary White House waiting for word from Weimar.

The Council of Three reassembled in the afternoon and continued their discussion of the Italian situation. Meanwhile, tension throughout Paris became very acute. The time limit which had been granted Germany to agree to sign was due to expire at seven o'clock. Simultaneously, the armistice was to end if acceptance was not forthcoming. All along the line of the Rhine, the American, British and French Armies were waiting expectantly, ready to resume the conflict. The crowds in the streets of Paris were very great and everyone was waiting. At 4:55 in the afternoon, when the general sentiment had swung over to the belief that the acceptance would not be forthcoming, Secretary-General Dutasta, of the Peace Commission, was called on the phone by Colonel Henry at Versailles. Colonel Henry stated that he had been directed by Von Haniel, Acting Chief of the German Peace Delegation, to notify the Allied government that Germany had decided to accept. This word was immediately communicated to the Council of Three, and, later, to the representatives of the press and flashed throughout the world. The tense situation relaxed instantly. Everywhere pandemonium broke loose—crowds gathered and cheered that the war was won.

As soon as the Council of Three received word that Germany had accepted, the meeting adjourned. The President, who had been indoors all day, at once went for a ride, and we started for the Hôtel Wagram, intending to pick up Dr. Axson, the President's brother-in-law, and take him with us. We were forced to proceed very slowly down the Champs Élysées, which was crowded with spectators, who cheered the President again and again. At the Hôtel Wagram a large crowd gathered and applauded while we waited for Dr. Axson. When we started off we had gone only a few yards when the crowd stopped the car and an old man stepped forward and said to the President: "Mr. President, I want to thank you for peace."

The President returned to the house for dinner, and shortly afterwards received a copy of the final reply of the German government, which was dated at Versailles, and which stated that the Minister of Foreign Affairs of Germany had instructed Von Haniel to communicate to the Allied Governments the following message: . . .[2]

After reading the communication the President went to bed.

[1] Printed as Appendix I to the following document.
[2] E. K. A. Haniel von Haimhausen to G. Clemenceau, June 23, 1919, TCL (SDR, RG 256, 180.03401/88, DNA), printed in *PPC*, VI, 644. The message reads as follows: "The Government of the German Republic has seen with consternation from the last communication of the Allied and Associated Governments, that the latter are resolved to wrest from Germany by sheer force even the acceptance of those conditions of peace which, though devoid of material significance, pursue the object of taking away its honour from the German people. The honour of the German people will remain untouched by any act of violence. The German people, after the frightful sufferings of the last few years, lacks all means of defending its honour by external action. Yielding to overwhelming force, but without on that account abandoning its view in regard to the unheard of injustice of the conditions of peace, the Government of the German Republic therefore declares that it is ready to accept and sign the conditions of peace imposed by the Allied and Associated Governments."

Hankey's Notes of a Meeting of the Council of Four[1]

Mr. Lloyd George's Residence,
C.F.82.   Paris, June 23, 1919, 9:00 a.m.

1. The Council had before them Note No. 85 from the German Peace Delegation dated June 23rd, 1919 (Appendix I), which had been distributed to the Heads of Government by the Secretary-General between 6:0 and 7:0 a.m.

MR LLOYD GEORGE said that after carefully considering the matter he felt that the sinking of the German ships in the Orkneys weighed principally with him against granting the German request for an extension of the armistice for 48 hours. There was no doubt that the sinking of these ships was a breach of faith. If bridges were blown up, and loss of life caused, and military operations hampered by these or similar measures, the public would say that this was the reason for which time had been granted. Consequently, he was inclined to reply with a refusal, mentioning the sinking of the German ships.

PRESIDENT WILSON said that if he was assured that he was dealing with honourable men, or even with ordinary men, he would be willing to give not 48, but 24, hours. However, he shared Mr Lloyd George's suspicions to the full, and did not trust the Germans. He would like to know, however, whether it was correct that the direct telephonic line between Versailles and the German Government was broken. If they could not communicate with their Government until the evening, it might make a difference.

M. CLEMENCEAU said they could obtain immediate communication by telephone.

PRESIDENT WILSON said that he had just been reading the German authorisation given to Von Haniel. He observed that he was given full powers to hand over the reply of the Imperial Government to the Note of the President of the Peace Conference of the 16th inst. to afford explanations, to receive counter-explanations, and to conduct negotiations, but he had no powers to sign.

M. CLEMENCEAU said that so far as he was concerned, he was in favour of refusing the German request.

PRESIDENT WILSON said that in that case he would not say anything about the sinking of ships at the Orkneys. He would rather not mention a matter about which the full circumstances were not yet known.

MR LLOYD GEORGE said there was no doubt about the sinking of the ships, and that they had been sunk by the Germans themselves. A possible excuse was that the German Government was so disorganised, that individuals were acting on their own initiative without higher authority. This, however, was a reason against granting an extension of time.

PRESIDENT WILSON said that the case for the bad faith of the Germans was so overwhelming that there was no necessity to cite specific instances. It was a fact, however, that the German Government had been formed to sign the Treaty.

BARON MAKINO pointed out that the National Assembly had passed a vote of confidence in the new Imperial Ministry by 236 votes to 89, with 63 abstentions, and had made no reserves. (See Note No. 76.)[2]

MR LLOYD GEORGE said he had just received Mr Balfour's view, which was in favour of refusal. He took the view that we could trust no German officer, and that in the case of the ships in the Orkneys, they had conspired together to break the armistice.

PRESIDENT WILSON pointed out that the German Admiral was reported to have said that he was ordered to sink the ships on the termination of the armistice.

MR LLOYD GEORGE said that what influenced Mr Balfour was that the Germans could not be trusted.

PRESIDENT WILSON said that nevertheless he thought there was no need to make specific mention of the sinking of the ships.

MR LLOYD GEORGE considered that it was only important from a political point of view.

BARON MAKINO said that the principal object was to get the Germans to sign. He suggested that possibly it might make it more difficult for the Germans to sign if we insisted on their giving their answer this very evening.

M. CLEMENCEAU said that the great object and the greatest difficulty was to make the Germans honour their signature.

M. SONNINO suggested that the military authorities ought to be consulted.

MR LLOYD GEORGE said he had already consulted the British Military Authorities, who had no doubt at all that it would be a great mistake to give any extension of time. He recalled what had been stated at the Conference of Generals on the previous Friday that the soldiers had already been sleeping in the open air for five nights, and were exposed to considerable hardships.

M. CLEMENCEAU thought that there was no doubt about military opinion.

MR LLOYD GEORGE urged the importance of politeness in the reply. He pointed out that history was apt to judge these matters by the actual terms of the letter. He recalled how Bismarck's communications had been scrutinised from this point of view.

(After some further discussion, it was agreed to send the reply in Appendix II.)

APPENDIX I TO C.F.82.

Confidential.
W.C.P.1052.
GERMAN PEACE DELEGATION
No. 85.

Mr. President,   Versailles, June 23, 1919.

The Minister for Foreign Affairs instructs me to beg the Allied and Associated Governments to prolong for 48 hours the time limit for answering Your Excellency's note communicated yesterday evening, and likewise the time limit for answering the note of June 16, 1919.

It was only on Saturday, after great difficulties, that a new Cabinet was formed which, unlike its predecessor, could come to an agreement to declare its willingness to sign the Treaty as regards nearly all its provisions. The National Assembly has expressed its confidence in this Cabinet by a large majority of votes. The answer only arrived here just before midnight, as the direct wire from Versailles to Weimar was out of order. The Government must come into contact anew with the National Assembly, in order to take the grievous decision which is still required of it in such a manner as it can only be taken in accordance with democratic principles and with the internal situation in Germany.

Accept, Mr. President, the assurance of my distinguished consideration. (signed)   von Haniel

APPENDIX II TO C.F.82.

CONFIDENTIAL.   EXTENSION OF TIME LIMIT.
W.C.P. 1052A.
REPLY TO GERMAN NOTE OF JUNE 23RD, 1919.
(Ref. W.C.P.1052.)
(Approved by the Council of the Allied and Associated Powers on June 23rd, 1919.)

Monsieur le Président:

The Allied and Associated Governments beg to acknowledge the receipt of your communication of June 23. After full consideration of your request they regret that it is not possible to extend the time already granted to your Excellency to make known your decision relative to the signature of the Treaty without any reservation.

(Signed.)   G. Clemenceau.

T MS (SDR, RG 256, 180.03401/82, DNA).
  [1] The complete text of these minutes is printed in *PPC*, VI, 613-16.
  [2] E.K.A. Haniel von Haimhausen to G. Clemenceau, June 22, 1919, TCL (SDR, RG 256, 180.03401/81, DNA), printed in *PPC*, VI, 611.

Hankey's Notes of a Meeting of the Council of Four[1]

President Wilson's House,
C.F.83.   Paris, June 23, 1919, 11 a.m.

1. With reference to C.F.78, Minute 3, MR. LLOYD GEORGE said that he fully approved of Mr. Balfour's draft letter,[2] subject to two slight alterations in the following sense: (1) to show that, when referring to Ottomans, the letter referred only to Ottoman Turks, and (2) to ensure that we were not committed in any way to re-

  [1] The full text of these minutes is printed in *PPC*, VI, 617-22.
  [2] See n. 3 to the minutes of the Council of Four printed at June 21, 1919, 4 p.m.

moving the Turks from Constantinople. Mr. Montagu had obtained the impression that the letter did commit us to this.

MR. BALFOUR said that the letter was only intended to give a hint of this possibility.

PRESIDENT WILSON agreed that such a hint might be useful.

(Mr. Balfour was authorised to make the necessary modifications to meet Mr. Lloyd George's views after which the letter would be communicated to M. Clemenceau for despatch.)

2. MR. BALFOUR said that, on the previous evening, he had been asked to draft for the consideration of the Council a letter to the German Delegation dealing with the question of the sinking of the German Ships. He had actually prepared a draft but had come to the conclusion, after examining the facts, that it was not worth considering at this point. He was advised that the sinking of the ships by the Germans was not in the narrow technical sense a breach of the letter of the Armistice. The breach was rather one against general military law than the Armistice. We now knew that this action was a deliberate act of the German Admiral, who had been under the impression that the Armistice expired at noon on Saturday, and he thought, on the expiration of the Armistice, he had a right to commit an act of war.

(At this point Admiral Hope, Admiral Ronarc'h, Admiral Grassi, M. Fromageot, M. Weiss, Mr. Hurst and M. Loucheur were introduced.)[3]

PRESIDENT WILSON asked Admiral Hope to describe exactly what had occurred, in order to establish the facts.

ADMIRAL HOPE stated that at noon on Saturday the German ships had hoisted the German flag and the crews had commenced to abandon ship. They had not been permitted to have many boats and many of the crews consequently jumped overboard in lifebelts. British guard boats were at once ordered to the scene and directed the German boats to stop. Some of them had not done so and had been fired on. The German Admiral left his flagship in a trawler and reported that the sea-cocks had been opened. He also reported that he was under the impression that the Armistice had ended at noon and therefore he was not breaking its terms.

In reply to MR. LLOYD GEORGE, he said that it was not, he believed, correct that new crews had been substituted for the original crews. Some men had been sent back to Germany and the total

[3] Those not previously identified in this series were Vice Adm. Pierre Alexis Marie Antoine Ronarc'h, Chief of the French Naval General Staff, and André Weiss, legal adviser to the French Ministry of Foreign Affairs and a technical adviser in the French delegation.

numbers had been reduced, but, so far as he was aware, no new men had been brought in. Attempts had been made to tow the ships to the shore and three light cruisers and, he believed, eighteen destroyers had been beached. One battleship, the Baden, one of the latest German dreadnoughts, (the flagship), as well as four destroyers, still remained afloat. Some of the beached ships should be recoverable.

M. CLEMENCEAU suggested that, having heard the facts from Admiral Hope, the international lawyers should be heard next.

MR. BALFOUR said that there was apparently nothing specific in the Armistice against the sinking of these ships, but he understood it was in contradiction to the general principles governing armistices.

M. FROMAGEOT, asked for his opinion, read the following extract from Article XXIII of the Terms of Armistice:

"Les navires de guerre de surface allemandes que seront désignés par les Alliés et les États-Unis seront immédiatement désarmés puis internés dans des ports neutres, ou, à leur défaut, dans les ports alliés désignés par les Alliés et les États-Unis.

Ils y demeureront sous la surveillance des Alliés et des États-Unis—des détachements des gardes étant seuls laissés à bord."

From the use of the word "demeureront," he drew the meaning that nothing was to be changed. Consequently, the sinking of the ships implied an infraction of the Armistice. It was also stated that only guard and maintenance parties were to be left on board. These parties were intended to maintain the ships and not to sink them.

MR. HURST said that he had very little to add to what M. Fromageot had stated. Two points, however, occurred to him. In the official version of the Armistice, which he had in his hand, it was stated that the French text is the official one, the English and German texts being translations. On this point, the French text was much clearer. The fact that the German Admiral thought that he was entitled to sink the ships because the Armistice had expired had, in fact, no justification. The Armistice would not, in fact, terminate with the signature of the Peace nor before the ratification. Hence, his view was that there was no justification for the Admiral's action.

M. CLEMENCEAU said that this was very important.

M. SONNINO said that evidently the German Admiral's opinion that he was entitled to do it because he thought the Armistice had expired favoured our thesis that he was not entitled to do it during the Armistice.

MR. BALFOUR pointed out that the German Admiral may have

thought that signature to the Armistice had been refused, in which case he would be correct in assuming that hostilities had re-commenced.

M. CLEMENCEAU said that it was not an affair of ours what the Admiral had thought. We only had to consider the facts.

MR. BALFOUR said the next question was as to whether, apart from the damages we might demand from the German Government, the German Admiral could be tried, for example, by court-martial.

M. CLEMENCEAU asked under whose orders the German Admiral had been. Was he under the British Admiralty?

MR. LLOYD GEORGE replied that he was not; he was merely under the surveillance of the British Admiral.

MR. HURST said that there were principles laid down in the Regulations under the Laws and Customs of War on Land which were equally applicable to naval war, from which he quoted the following:

"*Article 40.* Any serious violation of the Armistice by one of the parties gives the other party the right to denounce it, and even, in case of urgency, to re-commence hostilities at once.

"*Article 41.* A violation of the Armistice by individuals acting on their own initiative only confers the right of demanding the punishment of the offenders and, if necessary, indemnity for the losses sustained."

M. WEISS said that Article 3 of the Laws and Customs of War on Land would apply to this case, namely:

"A belligerent party which violates the provisions of the said Regulations shall, if the case demands, be liable to make compensation. It shall be responsible for all acts committed by persons forming part of its armed forces."

There was no doubt that, under this provision, a Government was responsible for the actions of its agents and officers. The responsibility of the German Government, therefore, could not be doubted. In reply to the question as to the Court under which the German Admiral should be tried, he said it was a subject for negotiation.

MR. BALFOUR suggested that the Articles quoted were not quite consistent. Article 41 of the Regulations suggested that the individual was responsible, whereas Article 3 said that the Government was responsible. M. Weiss used the argument that because the German Admiral had committed this act, the German Government were responsible.

M. CLEMENCEAU said that there appeared to him to be no contradiction between the two texts. The Admiral might be personally responsible, but the damages for which reparation or indemnity might be claimed would not be levied on his private property but on the German Government. Therefore, each of the articles had its own effect. If the personal responsibility was the greater, Article 41 would apply. If compensation were the more important, Article 3 would apply. What he proposed was that the international lawyers should be asked to present a text, establishing the theory of jurisprudence on which action was to be taken, but the political decision as to the punishment of the Admiral or reparation from the German Government would rest with the Heads of Governments.

MR. BALFOUR suggested, since it was no use asking for reparation from the Germans in the form of money, as we had already demanded in the Treaty all the money that they could furnish, the Admirals should consider whether reparation should be demanded in the way of ships.

ADMIRAL HOPE said that the Germans had only been left a few old battleships and light cruisers.

(It was agreed that, before the 4 o'clock meeting, the following reports should be furnished:

1. *By the International Lawyers*, who should prepare a text stating the theory of jurisprudence on which action could be taken.
2. *By the Admirals* stating whether reparation could be furnished by the surrender of German ships.)

3. MR. BALFOUR said that he had also been asked to prepare a draft letter to the German Delegation on the subject of their contravention of the Terms of Armistice in the Baltic Provinces. He understood, however, that the demand to the Germans to withdraw from the Baltic Provinces had been made so recently[4] that the Allies had not yet a case against the Germans.

MR. HURST then read a summary of the demands made to the Germans. On June 10th, General Gough had given orders to General von der Goltz[5] for certain withdrawals. On June 14th, Helsingfors intercepted the following message:

"General von der Goltz takes orders only from his German superiors and rejects General Gough's orders to local forces."

Meanwhile, on June 12th,[6] the Council of the Principal Allied and Associated Powers had decided that Marshal Foch should order the Germans:

---

[4] See the minutes of the Council of Four printed at June 13, 1919, 11 a.m., Vol. 60.
[5] Lt. Gen. Sir Hubert de la Poer Gough, a member of the Inter-Allied Military Mission to the Baltic region and Gen. Gustav Adolf Joachim Rüdiger, Count von der Goltz, German governor and commander of German troops in the Baltic region.
[6] Actually, June 13. See n. 4 above.

(a) to stop all future advance Northwards towards Esthonia;
(b) to evacuate Libau and Windau at once and to complete the
       evacuation of all territory which before the war formed part
       of Russia, with the least possible delay, in accordance with
       Article 12 of the Armistice Terms.

This decision was not communicated to General Nudant at Spa
until June 18th. Consequently, the action was only four days old
and the Germans could not yet be accused of a breach of the Armistice.

PRESIDENT WILSON said that it ought to be borne in mind that
the Germans had altered the gauge of the railways in the Baltic
Provinces from the Russian to the German gauge and had put in
their rolling stock. One consequence of the evacuation of the German Army would be the withdrawal of this rolling stock, which
would affect the food distribution and inflict great privations on the
civil population. Mr. Hoover, who informed him of this, added that
the Germans claimed this rolling stock as their own.

MR. BALFOUR suggested that part of the rolling stock might be
taken as compensation for the ships.

M. CLEMENCEAU suggested that the Baltic Provinces, who would
benefit, ought to pay for the rolling stock.

PRESIDENT WILSON said that the Allies had no means of compelling the Germans to leave the rolling stock. Consequently, it must
be remembered that entire withdrawal meant the starvation of the
people in the Baltic Provinces.

(Mr. Hudson[7] entered at this point.)

MR. BALFOUR said he would ask General Gough and such other
sources of information that were open to him for information on
this point.

MR. LLOYD GEORGE suggested that the Allied and Associated
Powers ought to ascertain the views of the Letts and Lithuanians.
It was possible that they would prefer to risk the privations rather
than not get rid of the Germans. He understood that their representatives were in Paris.

PRESIDENT WILSON said he was informed by Mr. Hudson that a
provision in the Treaty of Peace compelled the Germans to leave
half the rolling stock in the Baltic Provinces. He suggested that the
question should be referred to the Baltic Commission in Paris.

(This was accepted. It was agreed to invite the Baltic Commission to report to the Council of the Principal Allied and Associated Powers on the effect which the evacuation of the Baltic

[7] That is, Manley Ottmer Hudson.

Provinces by Germany would have on the food supplies of these regions, taking into consideration the fact that the Germans have altered the gauge of the railways from the Russian to the German gauge and would withdraw a part of their rolling stock. The Commission should be authorised to consult the representatives of the Baltic Provinces in Paris. Mr. Hudson undertook to communicate this decision at once to the Baltic Commission.) (The Allied Admirals and the International lawyers withdrew at this point.)

T MS (SDR, RG 256, 180.03401/83, DNA).

Hankey's Notes of a Meeting of the Council of Four[1]

President Wilson's House,
C.F.85.   Paris, June 23, 1919, 12:10 p.m.

1. The Council had before them the draft, prepared by the Committee on New States, of the covering letter to be addressed to M. Paderewski in transmitting to him the Treaty to be signed by Poland, under Article 93 of the Treaty of Peace with Germany, which had been prepared in accordance with a decision taken on June 21st, C.F.77, Minute 1, (Appendix I).

MR LLOYD GEORGE raised the question of the language to be employed in the Jewish schools in Poland. He thought that M. Paderewski's criticisms in this respect had force. In the United States of America or in Great Britain, for example, the religious idiosyncracies of particular sects were given some latitude, but were fitted into the educational system of the country. It was a question, however, whether the Jews ought to be allowed separate schools in Poland.

MR HEADLAM-MORLEY said that under the stipulations of the Treaty, the schools for Jews in the Polish State were to be administered by Committees of Jews.

MR LLOYD GEORGE asked if that gave them more power than under the system in force in the United Kingdom, where Roman Catholics and Jews supervised their schools, but the general system and curriculum was part of the education of the country and under the State.

MR HEADLAM-MORLEY said that the system in the Treaty had been deliberately arranged so that the education should remain under the Polish State, though the management of the schools

[1] The complete text of these minutes is printed in *PPC*, VI, 624-34.

would be under persons of the Jewish faith. This point was explained in the covering letter.

MR HUDSON said that the principles adopted in the Treaty were very elastic so as to leave the schools under the general control of the State.

MR LLOYD GEORGE asked who would arrange the curriculum.

MR HEADLAM-MORLEY said that the State would be in a position to lay it down.

MR LLOYD GEORGE said that this was not M. Paderewski's reading of the Treaty.

MR HUDSON suggested that the draft letter might be amplified to make it quite clear to M. Paderewski.

MR HEADLAM-MORLEY said he had suggested that the word "persons" should be substituted for "Committees" in regard to the schools, the object being that people were apt to be frightened by the use of the word "Committee." His colleagues, however, had not agreed in this. In their latest draft, the Commission had cut out all reference to a Central Polish Committee, and had substituted the word "Committees."

MR BALFOUR pointed out that in the United Kingdom a Roman Catholic school was a local Roman Catholic school. No such provision was made here. Under this Treaty there might be a great Central Jewish Committee in Warsaw.

MR HEADLAM-MORLEY said that alterations had been inserted to meet this.

MR BALFOUR suggested that in Article 10 the word "local" should be added before "Committee."

(This was agreed to.)

MR LLOYD GEORGE asked if it should not be made clear that Yiddish should not be taught. There was no objection to Hebrew, which was a recognised language, but he did not think that Yiddish ought to be taught.

PRESIDENT WILSON pointed out that Yiddish was a spoken language in many parts of the world, including the United States. The Polish Government ought not to be in a different position towards it from other countries.

MR HEADLAM-MORLEY said that the Commission were informed that in the case of very small children, no other language but Yiddish could be used. They spoke Yiddish in their homes, and, when they first came to the school, they knew no other language. It ought not to be used, however, when the children were older.

MR LLOYD GEORGE asked what was done in New York?

PRESIDENT WILSON said that teachers were appointed, who understood Yiddish, and they gave their instruction in Yiddish.

MR LLOYD GEORGE said that there was all the difference between giving instruction in Yiddish and teaching the Yiddish language. Every effort ought to be made to merge the Jews of Poland in Polish nationality, just as the Jews in Great Britain or France became merged in British or French nationality. He was told there was an active movement to keep the Jews not merely as a separate religion, but as a separate race.

PRESIDENT WILSON pointed out that in this case we were not dealing with Great Britain or France or the United States, where the Jewish population knew that they were governed on the same principles as the other subjects of the State. If the Polish State would adopt the same principles, it would help matters.

MR HEADLAM-MORLEY said that in Poland there was an extremely aggressive Jewish national movement.

MR LLOYD GEORGE read the following resolution, which had been adopted on Saturday (C.F.77, Minute 1):

"The Commission was also authorised to consider the nature of alterations required in the draft Treaty with Poland, in order to provide that in all except the primary schools, Jewish children should be instructed in the Polish and not in the Yiddish language, thereby avoiding the risk of encouraging the use of Yiddish as one of the national languages for a part of the population of Poland."
He thought that that went rather too far, as it suggested that the children would be taught Yiddish in the primary schools.

PRESIDENT WILSON read the following extract from Article 9 of the draft Polish Treaty:

"Poland will provide in the public educational establishments in towns and districts, in which a considerable proportion of Polish nationals of other than Polish speech are residents, reasonable facilities for ensuring that instruction shall be given to the children of such Polish nationals in their own language."
He proposed to add after the word "public" the word "primary."

MR HEADLAM-MORLEY pointed out that that would enable the Germans to be instructed in the German language. The majority of the Committee, he said, thought that the decision on Saturday applied only to Yiddish children. Germans in the transferred districts could be taught in the German language, but they would have no Committee as the Jews would have. In the case of the Jews, Yiddish might be used in the primary schools as a medium of instruction, but not in secondary schools. The majority of the Committee thought that it was not fair to ask the Polish Government to devote funds for secondary instruction in the Yiddish language. The American Delegation, however, had dissented from this view.

PRESIDENT WILSON read the following extract from a memorandum giving the view of the American Delegation:[2]

"2. In pursuance of his suggestion to the Supreme Council on Saturday, Mr Headlam-Morley wants to add to Article 10, concerning the Jews' control of their own schools, a statement that

'Nothing in this article shall prevent the Polish Government from making obligatory the use of Polish as the ordinary medium of instruction in the higher schools.'

This addition goes beyond my understanding of his suggestion on Saturday. It is strongly opposed by the American Jews here. I have opposed it for the following reasons:

(a) It would encourage the Poles to forbid Yiddish instruction in Jewish superior schools, thereby greatly diminishing the value of Article 10.

(b) Since the Jewish schools are to be "subject to the general control of the State," the Polish Government is not forbidden by the articles as they stand to regulate the languages to be used in them.

(c) The articles as they stand leave the Polish Government free to require that all college and university instruction should be in Polish.

(d) The unity of the Polish State, so far as languages in schools are concerned, is already sufficiently protected by the provision that the teaching of Polish may be made obligatory."

It was not a question, he said, of whether children should be taught Polish, but whether it should be used as the sole medium of instruction in all but primary schools.

MR HEADLAM-MORLEY said that the view of the majority of the Commission was that, as the children came from homes where Yiddish only was spoken, it must be the medium of instruction in the first instance.

M. SONNINO asked why the teaching of Yiddish should be prohibited.

MR HEADLAM-MORLEY said it was not prohibited. The only question was how much the Polish Government was to be forced to do in the way of providing facilities for the use of Yiddish in the schools.

MR LLOYD GEORGE said that he was not in favour of imposing as an international obligation on the Polish Government the teaching of Yiddish. He would only assent to its use as a medium of instruction in primary schools.

M. SONNINO asked whether, supposing Poland prohibited the teaching of Yiddish, would not this be inflicting the hardship

[2] The Editors have been unable to find this memorandum by Manley O. Hudson in various collections and files.

which it was desired to avoid? The Jews would then either have to teach Yiddish at home, or maintain special schools for it.

MR HEADLAM-MORLEY said that the Jewish movement in Poland was not with the object of promoting a religious movement, but a separate Jewish nationalism. A Jewish friend of his, who had just returned from Poland, had told him that there was an increasing use of Yiddish in the streets.

(After some further discussion, it was agreed:

1. With regard to the use of languages other than Polish, the Polish Government should be given a free hand in all schools except primary schools. But, in those cases where there was a considerable minority, as provided in Article 9 and 10 of the draft Treaty with Poland, of children of Polish citizens speaking a language other than Polish, facilities should be given for them to receive instruction in the primary schools through the medium of their own language. The Commission on New States were authorised, in conjunction with the Drafting Committee, to make the necessary modifications in the draft Treaty with Poland.

2. The draft letter to the Polish Delegation submitted by the Committee was approved, subject to a re-drafting of the passage dealing with schools, in accordance with the above decision.)

2. MR BALFOUR urged that the term "persons of Jewish faith" should be used instead of Jews in the Treaty of Poland. He was strongly in favour of only giving privileges to Jews on the ground that they were of Jewish religion and not because they were of Jewish faith.

M. SONNINO pointed out that if a Jew became a Christian, he would then not receive the protection.

(Mr Headlam-Morley and Mr Hudson withdrew.)

(M. Tardieu, Captain Johnson, Mr Leeper, Colonel Pariani and Captain de St. Quentin were introduced.[3])

3. M. TARDIEU explained a difficulty that had arisen in the Commission on Roumanian and Yugo-Slav Affairs in regard to the reference that had been given to it on June 21st. In the Treaty with Austria, certain frontiers had been drawn subject to a reservation that the Principal Allied and Associated Powers reserve the right to define the plebiscite area in the Klagenfurt district. The frontiers given to Austria in the Treaty included a small section of the district now proposed for the Klagenfurt plebiscite. The Italian Dele-

---

[3] That is, Maj. Douglas Wilson Johnson; Alexander Wigram Leeper; Col. Alberto Pariani; and Capt. René Doynel de Saint-Quentin, a member of the secretariat of the French delegation.

gation urged that the frontiers granted to Austria should be maintained, and that the portion affected should be excluded from the plebiscite district. The majority of the Commission, however, maintained that the right to draw the plebiscite area justified the Allied and Associated Powers in including the whole area as now proposed.

M. SONNINO urged that Austria had provisionally been given a certain line, with a possible expectation of obtaining something more. It was not fair to Austria to alter this line. The implication to the Austrians was that for the moment they must content themselves with that line with a possibility of getting something more.

M. TARDIEU pointed out that the ultimate result might be a considerable improvement in the situation from Austria's point of view.

(After some discussion, it was agreed that no change should be made in the plebiscite area as already drawn.)

Appendix I to C.F.85.

DRAFT of the covering letter to be addressed to M. Paderewski in transmitting to him the Treaty to be signed by Poland under Article 93 of the Treaty of Peace with Germany.

Sir,   Paris, June, 1919.

On behalf of the Supreme Council of the Principal Allied and Associated Powers, I have the honour to communicate to you herewith in its final form the text of the Treaty which, in accordance with Article 93 of the Treaty of Peace with Germany, Poland will be asked to sign on the occasion of the confirmation of her recognition as an independent state and of the transference to her of the territories included in the former German Empire which are assigned to her by the said Treaty. The principal provisions were communicated to the Polish Delegation in Paris on the * * * May, and were subsequently communicated direct to the Polish Government through the French Minister at Warsaw. The Council have since had the advantage of the suggestions which you were good enough to convey to them in your Memorandum of June 16 [15],[4] and as the results of a study of these suggestions, modifications have been introduced in the text of the Treaty. The Council believe that it will be found that by these modifications the principal points to which attention was drawn in your Memorandum have, in so far as they relate to specific provisions of the treaty, been adequately covered.

In formally communicating to you the final decision of the Principal Allied and Associated Powers in this matter, I should desire

[4] It is printed as Appendix II to the minutes of the Council of Four printed at June 17, 1919, 4 p.m., Vol. 60.

to take this opportunity of explaining in a more formal manner than has hitherto been done the considerations by which the Principal Allied and Associated Powers have been guided in dealing with this matter.

I. In the first place, I would point out that this Treaty does not constitute any fresh departure. It has for long been the established procedure of the public law of Europe that when a State is created, or even when large accessions of territory are made to an established State, the joint and formal recognition by the Great Powers should be accompanied by the requirement that such State should, in the form of a binding international Convention, undertake to comply with certain principles of government. This principle, for which there are numerous other precedents, received the most explicit sanction when at the last great Assembly of European Powers, the Congress of Berlin, the sovereignty and independence of Serbia, Montenegro and Rumania was recognised. It is desirable to recall the words used on this occasion by the British, French, Italian and German Plenipotentiaries, as recorded in the Protocol of June 28, 1878:

"Lord Salisbury recognises the independence of Serbia but is of opinion that it would be desirable to stipulate in the Principality the great principle of religious liberty. * * *

"Mr. Waddington believes that it is important to take advantage of this solemn opportunity to cause the principles of religious liberty to be affirmed by the representatives of Europe. His Excellency adds that Serbia, who claims to enter the European family on the same basis as other States, must previously recognise the principles which are the basis of social organisation in all States of Europe and accept them as a necessary condition of the favour which she asks for. * * *

"Prince Bismarck, associating himself with the French proposal, declares that the assent of Germany is always assured to any motion favourable to religious liberty.

"Count de Launay says that in the name of Italy he desires to adhere to the principle of religious liberty which forms one of the essential bases of the institutions in his country and that he associates himself with the declarations made on this subject by Germany, France, and Great Britain.

"Count Andrassy expresses himself to the same effect, and the Ottoman Plenipotentiaries raise no objection.

"Prince Bismarck, after having summed up the results of the vote, declares that Germany admits the independence of Serbia, but on condition that religious liberty will be recognised in the Principality. His Serene Highness adds that the Drafting Committee, when they formulate this decision, will affirm the connection established by the Conference between the proclamation of Serbian independence and the recognition of religious liberty."

2. The principal Allied and Associated Powers are of opinion that they would be false to the responsibility which rests upon them if on this occasion they departed from what has become an established tradition. In this connection I must also recall to your consideration the fact that it is to the endeavours and sacrifices of the Powers in whose name I am addressing you that the Polish nation owes the recovery of its independence. It is by their decision that Polish sovereignty is being re-established over the territories in question and that the inhabitants of these territories are being incorporated in the Polish nation. It is on the guarantee of these Powers that for the future Poland will to a large extent depend for the secure possession of these territories. There rests, therefore, upon these Powers an obligation, which they cannot evade, to secure in the most permanent and solemn form guarantees for certain essential rights, which will afford the inhabitants the necessary protection whatever changes may take place in the internal constitution of the Polish State.

It is in accordance with this obligation that clause 93 was inserted in the Treaty of Peace with Germany. This clause relates only to Poland, but a similar clause applies the same principles to Czecho-Slovakia, and other clauses have been inserted in the Treaty of Peace with Austria and will be inserted in those with Hungary and with Bulgaria, under which similar obligations will be undertaken by other States which under those treaties receive large accessions of territory.

The consideration of these facts will be sufficient to show that by the requirement addressed to Poland at the time when it receives, in the most solemn manner, the joint recognition of the re-establishment of its sovereignty and independence, and when large accessions of territory are being assigned to it, no doubt is thrown upon the sincerity of the desire of the Polish Government and the Polish nation to maintain the general principles of justice and liberty. Any such doubt would be far from the intention of the Principal Allied and Associated Powers.

3. It is indeed true that the new Treaty differs in form from earlier Conventions dealing with similar matters. The change of form is a necessary consequence and an essential part of the new system of international relations which is now being built up by the establishment of the League of Nations. Under the older system the guarantee for the execution of similar provisions was vested in

the Great Powers. Experience has shown that this was in practice ineffective, and it was also open to the criticism that it might give to the Great Powers, either individually or in combination, a right to interfere in the internal constitution of the States affected which could be used for political purposes. Under the new system the guarantee is entrusted to the League of Nations. The clauses dealing with this guarantee have been carefully drafted so as to make it clear that Poland will not be in any way under the tutelage of those Powers who are signatories to the Treaty.

I should desire moreover to point out to you that provision has been inserted in the Treaty by which disputes arising out of its provisions may be brought before the Court of the League of Nations. In this way differences which might arise will be removed from the political sphere and placed in the hands of a judicial court, and it is hoped that thereby an impartial decision will be facilitated, while at the same time any danger of political interference by the Powers in the internal affairs of Poland will be avoided.

4. The particular provisions to which Poland and the other States will be asked to adhere differ to some extent from those which were imposed on the new States at the Congress of Berlin. But the obligation imposed upon new States seeking recognition have at all times varied with the particular circumstances. The Kingdom of the United Netherlands in 1815 formally undertook precise obligations with regard to the Belgian provinces at that time annexed to the Kingdom which formed an important restriction on the unlimited exercise of its sovereignty; it was determined at the establishment of the Kingdom of Greece that the Government of that State should take a particular form, viz: it should be both monarchical and constitutional; when Thessaly was annexed to Greece, it was stipulated that the lives, property, honour, religion and customs of those of the inhabitants of the localities ceded to Greece who remained under the Hellenic administration should be scrupulously respected; and that they should enjoy exactly the same civil and political rights as Hellenic subjects of origin. In addition, very precise stipulations were inserted safeguarding the interests of the Mohammedan population of these territories.

The situation with which the Powers have now to deal is new, and experience has shown that new provisions are necessary. The territories now being transferred both to Poland and to other States inevitably include a large population speaking languages and belonging to races different to that of the people with whom they will be incorporated. Unfortunately the races have been estranged by long years of bitter hostility. It is believed that these populations will be more easily reconciled to their new position if they know from the very beginning thay have assured protection and adequate guarantees against any danger of unjust treatment or oppression. The very knowledge that this guarantee exists will, it is hoped, materially help the reconciliation which all desire, and will indeed do much to prevent the necessity of its enforcement.

5. To turn to the individual clauses of the present Treaty. Clauses 2-5 are designed to ensure that all the genuine residents in the territories now transferred to Polish sovereignty shall in fact be assured of the full privileges of citizenship. Article 6 guarantees to all inhabitants those elementary rights which are as a matter of fact secured in every civilised State. Articles 7 and 8, which are in accordance with precedent, provide against any discrimination against those Polish citizens who by their religion, their language or their race differ from the large mass of the Polish population. It is understood that far from raising any objection to the matter of these articles, the Polish Government have already of their own accord declared their firm intention of basing their institutions on the cardinal principles enunciated therein.

The following Articles are of rather a different nature in that they provide more special privileges to certain groups of these minorities. In the final revision of these Articles, the Powers have been impressed by the suggestions made in your Memorandum of June 16th and the articles have in consequence been subjected to some material modifications. In the final text of the Treaty it has been made clear that the special privileges accorded in Article 9 are extended to Polish citizens of German speech only in such parts of Poland as are, by the Treaty with Germany, transferred from Germany to Poland. Germans in other parts of Poland will be unable under this article to claim to avail themselves of these privileges. They will therefore in this matter be dependent solely on the generosity of the Polish Government and will in fact be in the same position as German citizens of Polish speech in Germany.

6. Clauses 10 and 12 deal specifically with the Jewish citizens of Poland. The information at the disposal of the Principal Allied and Associated Powers as to the existing relations between the Jews and the other Polish citizens unfortunately compels them to recognise that special protection is necessary for the former. These clauses have been limited to the minimum which seems necessary under the circumstances of the present day, viz: the provisions for the maintenance of Jewish schools and the protection of the Jews in the religious observance of their Sabbath. It is believed that they will not create any obstacle to the political unity of Poland; they do not constitute any recognition of the Jews as a separate political community within the Polish State. The educational provisions

contain nothing beyond what is in fact provided in the educational institutions of many highly organised modern States. There is nothing inconsistent with the sovereignty of the State in recognising and supporting schools in which children shall be brought up in the religous influences to which they are accustomed in their home. Ample safeguards against any use of non-Polish languages to encourage a spirit of national separation have been provided in the express acknowledgment that the provisions of this Treaty do not prevent the Polish State from making instruction in the Polish language obligatory in all its schools and educational institutions.

7. The economic clauses contained in Chapter II of the Treaty have been drafted with the view of facilitating the establishment of equitable commercial relations between independent Poland and the other Allied and Associated Powers. They include provisions for reciprocal diplomatic and consular representation, for freedom of transit and for the adhesion of the Polish Government to certain international conventions.

In these clauses the Principal Allied and Associated Powers have not been actuated by any desire to secure for themselves special commercial advantages. It will be observed that the rights accorded to them by these clauses are extended equally to all States who are members of the League of Nations. Some of the provisions are of a transitional character and have been introduced only with the necessary object of bridging over the short interval which must elapse before general regulations can be established by Poland herself or by commercial treaties or general conventions approved by the League of Nations.

In conclusion, I am to express on behalf of the Allied and Associated Powers the very sincere satisfaction which they feel at the re-establishment of Poland as an independent State. They cordially welcome the Polish nation on its re-entry into the family of nations. They recall the great services which the ancient kingdom of Poland rendered to Europe both in public affairs and by its contributions to the progress of civilisation which is the common work of all civilised nations. They believe that the voice of Poland will add to the wisdom of their common deliberations in the cause of peace and harmony and that its influence will be used to further the spirit of liberty and justice, both in internal and external affairs, and that thereby they will help in the work of reconciliation between the nations which, with the conclusion of peace, will be the common task of humanity.

The Treaty, by which Poland at the same time solemnly declares before the world her determination to maintain the principles of justice, liberty, and toleration, which were the guiding spirit of the ancient Kingdom of Poland, and receives in its most explicit and binding form the confirmation of her restoration to the family of independent Nations, will be signed by Poland and by the Principal Allied and Associated Powers on the occasion of, and at the same time as, the signature of the Treaty of Peace with Germany.

T MS (SDR, RG 256, 180.03401/85, DNA).

Mantoux's Notes of a Meeting of the Council of Four

June 23, 1919, 4 p.m.

Messrs. Davis, Loucheur, Tardieu, and Taussig are introduced.

Mr. Balfour reports:

1. A dispatch intercepted from the Weimar government to the German delegation in Versailles: the Allies having decided to employ the most extreme violence to force Germany to accept conditions without material importance, but which tend to besmirch the honor of Germany, and the German people no longer having the means to defend themselves, the government declares itself prepared to sign. The German delegation must await confirmation of this message before transmitting it to the Allied and Associated Powers.

2. A telegram seized by the Polish authorities and addressed to two German generals, to organize local resistance against the cession of German territories to Poland. This resistance will be disavowed by the German government, but it will do what is necessary to support it.

3. A note from General Dupont,[1] reporting that, in Berlin, French flags which, according to the treaty, should have been restored to France, were carried off and burned publicly.

Lloyd George. There is German honor; truly, this is not a civilized nation that we have to deal with.

Lloyd George. Mr. Winston Churchill will come before long to speak to you about the repatriation of the Czechs by way of Archangel. They demand, in Bohemia, the instant return of the Czech troops from Russia. Mr. Winston Churchill is especially concerned to establish, if that is possible, communications between Admiral Kolchak and Archangel, and the Czech troops on the route of evacuation could help with that. But for that, they must be replaced, along the Trans-Siberian, by Japanese and American troops. I ask you to reflect about this question.

[1] That is, Gen. Charles Joseph Dupont.

Hankey. I must point out to you that I have found in the naval clauses of the Armistice one article—Article 31—that forbids all destruction of ships or naval matériel by the Germans before evacuation, surrender, or restitution.

Clemenceau. Article 31 is magnificent; why didn't our jurists notice it?

Lloyd George. When can we sign? Not tomorrow, in any case.

Clemenceau. It is impossible; Wednesday at the earliest.

Lloyd George. For tomorrow, all our plenipotentiaries could not be in Paris.

Wilson. I had hoped to leave tomorrow evening for Brest.

Lloyd George. The experts refer to us Article 41 [49] of the treaty with Austria, which relates to private property. I am told that this arrangement, as it has been drafted, constitutes an injustice.

Taussig. According to the first draft, all enemy property in the territories detached from Austria could be expropriated and liquidated. The new draft[2] limits this arrangement to properties of the Crown and merchant tonnage.

Lloyd George. I believed that we had already taken that decision.

Wilson. Yes, but this is the draft which corresponds to the decision taken. It is only justice. This text must be communicated to the powers concerned.

Davis. It is necessary to do it without delay, for the expropriations have already begun.

Loucheur: I submit to you a report of the commission which you charged with examining—along with the states whose territories, in whole or in part, belonged to the Austro-Hungarian Monarchy— the distribution of war costs and reparations.[3]

As far as reparations are concerned, the Yugoslav and Rumanian delegations do not seem inclined to accept our proposals. They prefer to await the estimate which will be made by the Reparation Commission.

As far as the contribution of these states to the expenses of the war of liberation is concerned, we proposed that each of them pay in a sum equivalent to 20 per cent of the Austro-Hungarian war loans invested in its territory. There is no difficulty there. I hope that an agreement will be reached on that basis today.

As far as reparations are concerned, must the solution we proposed be insisted upon? The states concerned are making extrav-

[2] Printed in PPC, VI, 637.

[3] According to Hankey's minutes (PPC, VI, 638-40), Loucheur was giving an oral report to the Council of Four. The Commission on Reparation Clauses in the Treaties with Austria, Hungary, and Bulgaria had met periodically since May 23, 1919, to discuss whether the new states should have a claim to reparations and whether they should be liable for contributions to the cost of the war.

agant demands. Serbia, for example, instead of the balance of 500 million francs which we offer her, is asking for five billion. For myself, I propose to leave to the Reparation Commission the task of fixing the sum: the difference between the sum thus determined and the 20 per cent of war loans that must be paid to us will be entered either to the debit or the credit of each of these states.

Lloyd George. Let us suppose that Serbia, on account of the acquisition of the territories forming with her Yugoslavia, be debited with a sum of one hundred million pounds, and that, moreover, the Reparation Commission estimates that Serbia has the right to 150 million pounds; the difference, that is to say fifty million pounds, would be paid to Serbia. Is that right?

Loucheur. Not exactly. The question is more complicated, because the reparations will be payable in gold, while the amount of the contribution of each country will be calculated in the currency of this country.

Lloyd George. In short, they will pay almost nothing and receive everything.

Loucheur. That is what I think.

Lloyd George. That is what you recommend?

Loucheur. For Serbia and Rumania, I am obliged to do it. For the Poles and the Czechoslovaks, the problem does not arise in the same terms, and, in my opinion, it would have to be treated differently; we would have to impose on them the payment of their contribution in bonds of external debt.

Lloyd George. Will you give the states you speak of all that they ask without imposing on them charges on account of the territories that they are acquiring?

Loucheur. They will carry in any case the prewar debt and the war debt accruing to these territories.

Lloyd George. In any case, their debt to the Allies would have to go before their obligations toward bearers of bonds of the Austrian or Hungarian debt.

Loucheur. Take Serbia, for example. Because of the financial clauses of the treaty, she must take her part of the Austro-Hungarian prewar debt. She will also bear part of the war debt. If we ask her besides to pay us a certain sum on account of the money that we paid for her liberation, she could answer that she has already paid her share of the costs of the war, and the only result would be that we would crush her. The same reasoning applies to Rumania.

If I have a different opinion concerning Poland and Czechoslovakia, it is that, for the one as for the other, the expenses of the war have been almost nil. As a consequence, they can make us a payment.

Lloyd George. What I cannot understand is this. M. Loucheur

considers it settled that Rumania and Yugoslavia must carry their part of the Austro-Hungarian war debt. If that is so, Poland, for the territories which she is acquiring, should carry a part of Germany's war debt. The situation would be exactly the same.

Davis. It was decided that Austria proper would be liberated from the part of her prewar debt corresponding to the detached territories, and, moreover, that each of those countries would contribute to the costs of the war of liberation. It is in execution of the second part of that decision that we are requesting of the states concerned a sum equivalent to 20 or 25 per cent of war loans invested in their territory. We tried to balance, on the one hand, the contribution that these states owe us, and on the other, the reparations to which they have a right. They are not prepared to accept it, because we cannot reach an agreement with them on the figures.

Lloyd George. In any case, if the Reparation Commission is left with the task of determining what will be due to each of these states, it must hold out for a 20 or 25 per cent contribution. I really hope that we will deduct nothing from this. When the claims of each of these countries have been verified, this figure will be put on one side, and on the other the 25 per cent which they must pay us, and they will receive the difference, if there is any. I hope that we will not budge from that conclusion.

The experts withdraw.

The members of the Drafting Committee are introduced.

Clemenceau. Our attention has just been called to Article 31 of the Armistice Agreement, which forbids to the Germans any destruction of warships.

Fromageot. We know that article; but we did not believe that we had the power to invoke it because, in our opinion, it applies to ships before they have left German ports.

Reading of a first draft of a note to be addressed to Germany, drawn up by the Drafting Committee.

Lloyd George. What do you have to say about the application of Article 31?

Hurst. Your legal advisers do not believe that Article 31 applies to the case at hand.[4] In any case, there is doubt, and we do not want to use, in the name of the Allied and Associated Governments an argument which could appear doubtful. In fact, that article appears to be attached to a group of stipulations different from those which concern us. The destruction in question took place after the surrender of German warships. We believe that this article applies to destructions which might have taken place before the execution of the Armistice Agreement.

4 The written opinion of the legal advisers is printed in PPC, VI, 641-42.

Lloyd George. In my opinion, Article 31 responds to the present situation exactly. It is said there that any destruction is forbidden before evacuation, surrender, or restitution. After the end of the Armistice, we can only keep these ships—that is surrender—or give them up—that is restitution. Article 31 says: there will be no destruction before one or the other has taken place; the preceding article of the Armistice relates precisely to interned vessels.

Wilson. I understand the argument of our jurists. The article says that no destruction must take place before evacuation, surrender, or restitution. The word "before" governs the entire sentence.

Lloyd George. The word restitution cannot apply to anything at all in the Armistice; it can apply only to restitution in execution of the peace treaty.

Clemenceau. I cannot accept the theory of the jurists. No Frenchman will admit that one could make no use of Article 31. The experts in international law have given their opinion. That is very good; the governments must consult them, but it is up to them to decide.

Balfour. In any case, if we have arguments which, in the opinion of the jurists, are valid, can it do the least harm to add another which, according to them, is less conclusive?

Sonnino. I believe that in that Article 31 it was not a matter of restitution of German warships to Germany, but, on the contrary, restitution by Germany of ships that had been taken from us and which they were forbidden to destroy.

Clemenceau. That is not my opinion. Three cases are anticipated. First evacuation, that is the departure of German warships for the place where they were to be interned. Then two eventualities can take place: surrender or restitution. In one case or the other, the Germans do not have the right to destroy their vessels. If the text does not mean that, I do not know what it means. Above the commentaries of the jurists, there is a supreme authority, that of common sense.

Wilson. The meaning of the word "evacuation" does not seem so clear to me.

Clemenceau. To evacuate is to empty a place. A warship that leaves a port evacuates it.

Wilson. I will call to your attention that Article 31 applies to cases anticipated by the preceding articles, that is Articles 29 and 30.

Balfour. It is pointless to settle the question out of hand. All that is important is to punish the guilty and to obtain the reparations due us. Our legal advisers tell us that, even without invoking Article 31, we have the right to take sanctions; as for reparations, it has already been indicated that the only possible thing is a new cession of enemy vessels.

At 5:40 p.m., M. Dutasta, Secretary General of the Conference, brings the note from the German delegation announcing the unconditional acceptance of the treaty by the German government.[5]

Mantoux, II, 491-96.
    [5] For which, see n. 2 to the extract from the Grayson Diary printed at June 23, 1919.

To Thomas William Lamont

My dear Lamont: Paris, June 23, 1919.

Thank you for your letter of Saturday.[1] Much as I hate to see you go and to see your influence lost on this side of the water, I cannot say that I do not think you are justified in going, and I am certain that you will render a very material service to the country by your influence on the other side. I am sure that some of those who are opposing the Treaty and the Covenant are not, in fact, fully informed as to the situation and the necessity for the United States to assume a real leadership in affaire [affairs] at this turning-point in the history of nations.

The service you can render in clarifying the situation will, I am sure, be very great, and also in convincing the opponents of the League that it is not within our power now to enter or not to enter the politics of the world. Our only choice is to enter it with advantage and as a leader, or to enter it by compulsion of circumstances and at disadvantages from time to time, as a nation that stands outside the common councils.

I do not know that there is any particular counsel that I can give you. I have found that our thoughts run along the same line, and apparently this is the psychological moment to strengthen the tide which now seems to be turning against opposition to the Treaty in any part.

With warmest regards,
            Cordially and sincerely yours,   Woodrow Wilson

TLS (T. W. Lamont Papers, MH-BA).
    [1] T. W. Lamont to WW, June 21, 1919.

From Robert Lansing and Others

My dear Mr. President: Paris June 23rd, 1919

We are transmitting to you herewith a copy of a memorandum which has been received from Dr. Westermann, the Commission Expert on Near Eastern Affairs, in which he requests replies to certain questions which require solution and we shall be glad to receive an expression of your views regarding these matters.[1]

Faithfully yours,   Robert Lansing
Henry White
Tasker H. Bliss.

TLS (WP, DLC).
[1] For the memorandum with Wilson's replies, see the Enclosure printed with GFC to RL, June 24, 1919.

From Brand Whitlock

Dear Mr. President: Brussels 23d June, 1919.

I am sending to you by the courier today, in the hope that it will reach you before you leave Paris, a copy of my book on Belgium.[1] It is the English edition, and I feel like apologizing for the paper on which it is printed, but it is the best the publisher could get in England in these parlous times.

It will please you, I am sure, to know that your visit has produced the happiest effect here. You quite captured the Belgian heart, and on all sides we have most enthusiastic evidences of the pride and the pleasure that everyone has in you and in your coming. Your remarkable addresses made a deep impression, intensified by the fact that they were improvisations. They were published in all the newspapers, but, even so, I am translating them, and shall have them printed in a pamphlet for distribution, so that their message may endure.[2]

The indications this morning are that you will be returning home in a day or so, in the triumph of a peace to which history will give your name. We who have so long followed you are very proud of your great achievement and very grateful for all that you have done for humanity. In the midst of all your mighty labour and great sacrifice, in the pain that wilful misunderstanding and reckless and disloyal opposition may have caused you, there is the consolation that the vision which you, alone of all those who have borne the heavy responsibilities of these years of anguish, have had,—a vision of a better order and a richer common life,—is about to be realized.

I can not find words, without trespassing too much upon your precious moments, to tell you of all that your visit meant to me. Those two days, hurried and crowded, and all too short, were to me an inspiration. The various scenes flash before me with the distinctness of pictures in the cinema: the luncheon in the forest of Houthoulst, the stories about Dr. Jowett,[3] and Their Majesties, I fancy, a little vague as to just who Dr. Jowett could have been! And that strange, beautiful ceremony at Louvain, when the degree was conferred in the midst of the ruins of the University,—! How I wish that I might have the privilege of seeing and speaking with you oftener! We here feel that we have a prophet in the house.

And now you turn your face homeward, to that dear, far off land, where, as one of Ibsen's characters says, "a freer air blows over the people." Our hopes and our affections go with you. Bon voyage, then, and with my homage to Mrs. Wilson and my compliment to Miss Margaret,

I beg you to believe me, dear Mr. President,

Ever faithfully and devotedly yours,   Brand Whitlock

TLS (WP, DLC).
 [1] Brand Whitlock, *Belgium Under the German Occupation: A Personal Narrative* (2 vols., London, 1919). These volumes are in the Wilson Library, DLC.
 [2] The Editors have found no evidence that Whitlock ever carried out this project.
 [3] Benjamin Jowett (1817-1893), Master of Balliol College and Regius Professor of Greek at Oxford University.

From Paul Hymans

Dear Mr. President,   Paris, le 23d Juin 1919

May I beg to remind you of the urgent necessity for Belgium to obtain before your departure the agreement of the United States, France and Great Britain to the financial settlement (priority of 500.000.000$—cancellation of the War Debt—per disposal of the marks)

Also the question of the mandates in German East Africa, concerning which an arrangement between Great Britain and Belgium now exists, must be settled and ratified.

You will no doubt understand my deep anxiety to obtain before you have left Paris a definite and satisfactory solution to these questions, and I trust I may rely upon your most friendly intervention to that effect.

Believe me, dear Mr President,

Your's respectfully   Hymans

ALS (WP, DLC).

From Edward Mandell House

Dear Governor: [Paris] 23 June, 1919.

Lord Robert Cecil has just telephoned from London to say that he is greatly concerned lest the Conference should break up before some explicit and forceful statement has been made and some definite action has been taken with regard to the mandatory policy of the Allied and Associated Powers.

I feel with Lord Robert that perhaps one of the chief duties of the Peace Conference will be left undone unless some authoritative statement is made at once concerning the mandatory system. As I visualize it, there should be a clear and ringing statement of general principle, which should set forth the objects which we intend that the mandatory system shall accomplish. It might further be stated that a Commission has been nominated to study the form which these mandates will take, and as soon as they have drafted the best forms for the three different classes of mandate which they can produce, they will be made public and criticism will be invited just as it was invited with regard to the Covenant of the League. Lastly, it might be stated that these forms of mandate, reconsidered in the light of criticism, will be presented to the Executive Council of the League at its first meeting. I am convinced of the great necessity of adopting this policy and of actually appointing such a Commission to be composed of the representatives of the United States, France, Great Britain, Italy and Japan before your departure.   Affectionately yours,   [E. M. House]

TCL (WP, DLC).

From Edward Mandell House, with Enclosure

Dear Governor: Paris, 23 June, 1919.

The morning after the Peace Treaty with Germany has been signed the Daily Mail wishes to publish comments on the Treaty by President Poincare, M. Clemenceau and yourself and they have asked me to ask you if you will be good enough to give them a short statement.

I have drafted the enclosed which seems to me to be appropriate. I suggest that you authorize me to give this to them. Generally speaking they have supported you during the Conference and I believe that your giving them this would be a graceful acknowledgement of this support.

Affectionately yours,   E. M. House

TLS (WP, DLC).

E N C L O S U R E[1]

By the terms of the Treaty ⟨of Peace⟩, the greatest possible measure of compensation has been provided for those peoples whose
homes and lives were wrecked by the storm of war, and security
has been given them that this storm shall ⟨never⟩ *not* rise again. In
so far as we came together to ensure these things, the work of the
Conference is finished.

But in a larger sense, its work begins today. In answer to an
unmistakable appeal a League of Nations has been constituted and
a Covenant has been drawn which shows the way to international
understanding and to peace. We stand at the cross-roads, however,
and the way is only pointed out. Those who saw through the travail
of war the vision of a world made secure for mankind must *now*
consecrate their lives to its realization.

T MS (WP, DLC).
  [1] Words in angle brackets deleted by Wilson; words in italics added by him. However,
Wilson further revised House's draft and wrote the statement for the *Daily Mail* which
is printed as the following document. It appeared in the *Daily Mail* on June 30, 1919.

A Statement

[June 23, 1919]

Many things crowd into the mind to be said about the Peace
Treaty, but the thought that stands at the front of all others is that,
by the terms of the Treaty, the greatest possible measure of compensation has been provided for those peoples whose homes and
lives were wrecked by the storm of war, and security has been
given them that this storm shall not rise again. In so far as we
came together to ensure these things, the work of the Conference
is finished.

But in a larger sense, its work begins today. In answer to an
unmistakable appeal a League of Nations has been constituted and
a Covenant has been drawn which shows the way to international
understanding and to peace. We stand at the cross-roads, however,
and the way is only pointed out. Those who saw through the travail
of war the vision of a world made secure for mankind must now
consecrate their lives to its realization.

CC MS (WP, DLC).

Peter Augustus Jay[1] to the American Mission

Rome   June 23d, 1919

396A. Nitti[2] coalition cabinet, which will be sworn in today, contains representatives of all parties from left to Conservative right, but has strong Giolittist color.[3] Schanzer, Treasury, and Tedesco, Finance,[4] are Giolittists, Nava[5] represents Catholic party, Tittoni, Rossi, Chimienti, Visocchi,[6] belong to conservative side of parliament, Dacomo, Baccelli and Mortara[7] are of the left and there are two radicals DeVito, Giolittist, and Pantano.[8] Dante Ferraris[9] is prominent industrialist. On the whole Ministry is representative and seems pledged to insist on Italian claims at Paris. Section of press and *public* state it is not without pro-German tendencies. MESSAGGERO, which is said to represent Nitti's ideas, says his work will be the "Moral and economic restoration of the Country." It says Nitti's cabinet is not predominantly Giolittist. GIORNALE says new ministry is against current of public feeling, and that Nitti was not in unison with nation in tragic hours of war.

Yesterday street orators addressed meetings in many parts of Rome demanding that new ministry take decisive action upon Italy's claims. References to Germany were cheered. I hear there was some anti-American talk.

Chief interest centers in new delegation to Paris headed by Tittoni, who insisted that Senator Scialoja,[10] leader of patriotic League, should be one of the delegates. Others of Mission are probably Marconi, Imperiali and Maggiorino Ferraris,[11] a well known economist. Appointments will be officially made later today, and TIEMPO says Mission will leave for Paris in two days. I am informed on good authority that delegation will urge immediate settlement of Adriatic question, and will demand large concessions in Asia Minor, including Italian protectorate for greater part of Anatolia, and some kind of mandate for Armenia, Georgia, and Azerbaijan republics. Same authority states Tittoni is determined to take strong stand with Tardieu project[12] as minimum for Fiume. Marquis Theodoli[13] informs me confidentially he will be either under Secretary for Foreign Affairs or for colonies. If latter some Italian Ambassador will take under Secretaryship of Foreign Affairs, a trained man being necessary there.   Jay

T telegram (WP, DLC).
    [1] Counselor and Chargé d'Affaires of the American embassy in Rome.
    [2] That is, Francesco Saverio Nitti.
    [3] That is, Giovanni Giolitti. Giolitti is usually characterized as a "liberal," that is, mildly leftist for Italy at this time.
    [4] Carlo Schanzer and Francesco Tedesco.
    [5] Cesare Nava, Minister of Liberated Territories.
    [6] Tommaso Tittoni, Minister of Foreign Affairs; Luigi Rossi, Minister of Colonies; Pie-

tro Chimienti, Minister of Posts and Telegraphs; and Achille Visocchi, Minister of Agriculture.

7 Ugo Da Como, Minister of Military Assistance and War Pensions; Alfredo Baccelli, Minister of Public Instruction; and Ludovico Mortara, Minister of Justice.

8 Roberto De Vito, Minister of Railways and Maritime Transport, and Edoardo Pantano, Minister of Public Works.

9 Minister of Industry, Commerce, and Labor.

10 That is, Vittorio Scialoja.

11 Guglielmo Marconi, the inventor of wireless telegraphy, active at this time on various diplomatic missions for the Italian government; Marquis Guglielmo Imperiali; and Maggiorino Ferraris, lawyer, publicist, and member of the Italian Senate. As it turned out, the new Italian delegation to the peace conference consisted of Tittoni, Scialoja, Imperiali, Ferraris, and Silvio Crespi. Imperiali and Crespi were in Paris and, together with Sonnino, signed the German peace treaty on June 28. Tittoni attended a meeting of the newly created Council of Heads of Delegations on July 1.

12 That is, the Tardieu plan, for which, see Appendix I to the minutes of the Council of Four printed at May 28, 1919, 11 a.m., Vol. 59.

13 Marquis Alberto Theodoli, who became Undersecretary for Colonies in the Nitti government.

From the Diary of Vance Criswell McCormick

June 23 (Monday) [1919]

At 2.45 went to keep appointment at "White House." Discussed with President his understanding as to meaning of the Kolchak correspondence.[1] He said the papers had interpreted it as being a recognition of the Kolchak Government, which it was not, but only making certain conditions under which they would continue to send supplies and munitions to the anti-Bolshevist forces. I argued the difficulty of furnishing money unless you could recognize some governmental obligation, particularly in Siberia for railroad development. He agreed with me the importance of telling Congress the whole story and said he would appeal for funds upon his return, as he also recognized the opportunity of a great constructive program in aiding Russia through Siberian road and keeping open door by preventing Japan from creating sphere of influence and monopolizing Siberia, which will also jeopardize Chinese interests.

He asked me to prepare a cable for him stating reasons why Roland Morris should go to Omsk, which I had advocated; also plan for financing Siberian road.

Just as I was going out Herbert Hoover was coming in and he asked me to remain. We discussed the question of maintaining Supreme Economic Council after signing of peace treaty.[2] President agreed with us it should be abolished and agreed he would have to go to the U.S. to talk with Department heads before discussing any new Inter-Allied organizations. We all discussed Russia; President said in answer to Hoover's statement[3] that Russia could not rehabilitate itself without economic aid, which should be given without political interference; that it was impossible for an Inter Allied body to give such aid without getting mixed up in politics to some extent, which is true, considering who Allies are. The President further said the Russian people must solve their own problems without outside interference and that Europe had made a great mistake when they attempted to interfere in the French Revolution. He said it seems hard on the present Russian generation, but in the long run it means less distress for Russia, and I believe he is right.

He told us of his having turned down the request of the Germans for forty-eight hours more time to consider Treaty and said in three hours we will know the answer, it then being nearly 4.00 o'clock.

He said the French and British were wildly excited about the sinking of the German ships and he had spent the entire morning trying to hold down Lloyd George and Clemenceau to reason, as they were figuring what else they could get out of the Germans in payment for their loss, and he said most confidentially that the British and himself were relieved by the sinking of the ships of a most embarrassing question, as the French wanted some of the German ships for their own navy.

Printed copy (V. C. McCormick Papers, CtY).
  [1] For the correspondence between Admiral Kolchak and the Big Four, see Appendix I to the minutes of the Council of Four printed at May 27, 1919, 4 p.m., Vol. 59; A. V. Kolchak to G. Clemenceau, June 4, 1919, Vol. 60; and the extract from the Grayson Diary printed at June 12, 1919, *ibid*.
  [2] About this matter, see HCH to WW, June 27, 1919, and its Enclosure.
  [3] See HCH to WW, June 21, 1919.

From the Diary of Colonel House

June 23, 1919

The other day when the President was here, Bliss and I suggested, as an argument in favor of the League of Nations, that war in future would become so atrocious that it might lead to the death of civilization. We thought the ingenuity of man would be directed toward every form of destruction. The President took the contrary view. He believed this war had been so terrible that it would restrain such efforts in future wars. Bliss and I argued with him that if two nations went to war and the balance of the world remained neutral, this might be true, but if all the world became involved, there would be no bystanders to see fair play, therefore warfare would be unrestrained in every sense and would be terrible in its consequences. We could not get him to see it as we did. Lansing and White mildly agreed with Bliss and myself.

The President has some peculiar quirks. This is one of them.

The fact that he could not be persuaded to believe in heavy battle-ships and fast cruisers during war was another. He has not many, but occasionally he astonishes one.

Yesterday Clemenceau asked whether I was really going away soon, and when I told him I was, he expressed regret and hoped Lan[s]ing would not be left in charge. He spoke of him as being "impossible" and intimated that he intended to speak to the President. Lansing has done everything to antagonize most of the people in the Conference. He has made a specialty of the French, the Belgians and the Japanese.

And this reminds me, when the President was here the other day, he spoke of Clemenceau with much kindness and compared him favorably to Lloyd George. He complained that Lloyd George's eloquence caused great waste of time, George having a liking for it. When the President was telling this, it occurred to me that there were others. For instance, our Commission meetings practically amount to a talking fest by the President.

Wallace and Jusserand were among my early morning callers. They came about the dinner President Poincaré wishes to give to President Wilson and which he absolutely refuses to accept.[1] It

[1] Wilson's behavior in this business, which subsequent documents will bring to its conclusion, was uncharacteristic, not to say bizarre, and can only be viewed as additional evidence of the effects of his illness in April and early May, about which see the Appendix in Volume 58.

In this connection, we print here an extract from an undated memoir by Irwin Hood (Ike) Hoover, White House head usher, "The Facts about President Wilson's Illness," Hw MS (I. H. Hoover Papers, DLC), which we should have noted or quoted in our "Editors' Commentary" in the Appendix in Volume 58 concerning Wilson's health at Paris.

"There has been so much guessing on this subject and I have about read it all that I am prompted to record the facts as they presented themselves at the time. The guessers have many times hit close to the mark but none just seem to have the correct information to make a truly historical record. Those in a position to know, and there are but few, seem disinclined to tell the truth or if they do, it is so meager or purposely misguiding as to loose [lose] its candid value.

"The fact is there is but one person in all the world who could tell the exact story and her lips seem sealed for reasons which many have professed to know and many others have tried to guess. The one person, Mrs. Woodrow Wilson the second, is the fountain source from which all information of necessity had its beginning. However I shall record what I know about it in the light of opportunities to observe and see and hear right at the time and on the premises.

"It has been said that President Wilson was always, more or less, a sick man. I saw nothing of the kind during the six and a half years I served under him, prior to this last illness. On the contrary he was an exceptionally robust man. Much more so even than his appearance would prompt one to believe. He was heavy set, muscular and courageous. An unusually robust chest, short limbs and a good feeder. He did have a little twitching in one eye but it was hardly notic[e]able. I do not believe it would be discovered if your attention were not called to it. I only noticed it myself after some one had spoken to me about it and was looking for it. Without his glasses it could be noticed all the more and I used to watch for it when he would take his glasses off to clean them.

"He was a man who took excellent care of himself. He knew how to work and when to work and how to rest. Most unusual, especially in the latter. He could lay down any time of the day, banish all thoughts from his mind and go off to sleep in a few minutes. Likewise when he went to sleep he could wake up just about when he would plan for.

bids fair to become an international episode. Wallace and Jusserand, having utterly failed to move the President, appealed to me. The President has become stubborn, and when Jusserand called, he refused to see him although Jusserand sent word by Grayson that he had a personal message for [from] the President of France. The matter has become so serious that Poincaré called a meeting of the Council of State in which Jusserand, Clemenceau, Pichon and others took part. Poincaré wrote a memorandum which he evidently intended for Jusserand to bring to me.

He never had to be called when he would get up early in the morning to go for golf. Four and five oclock were not unusual hours for him to be ready to start without a suggestion from any source as to the time. He prided himself on these two faculties [faculties] and I have often heard him proudly discuss them.

"So it was in this relatively satisfactory condition he left for Europe. The writer was one of the few who personally accompanied him. When he started out I believe he was tired but surely not sick.

"In Europe there were trying times for him. It was so different from what he had been passing thru the previous five or six years. Here he was certainly the whole show. At the beginning at least such was the case. The responsibility seemed something awful. I was by his side for 12 or 14 hours every day. As long as he worked, I worked. My hours were his hours. There was no let up, all days were alike. He was so intent it was a positive burden to try to keep up with him. The others of us in the party wanted to see Europe and especially Paris but our opportunities were limited on account of the intenseness and confinement of the President. But the day came when he wavered. The load was to[o] much. Some saw it from one angle, some from another. He went to bed ostensibly with a cold but I believe to this day, if he had the benefit of a real doctor at that time he would have been saved the terrible ordeal that came after or at least it might have been postponed indefinately. When he got on his feet again he was a different man.

"Even while laying in bed he manifested peculiarities one of which was to control the use of all the automobiles to strictly official purposes, when previously he had been so liberal in his suggestions and his solicitudes that all connected with his immediate party should have the benefit of this possible diversion in lieu of the fact of the hours we were working &c.

"But when he got on his feet his peculiar ideas were even more pronounced. He now became obsessed that every French employe about the place was in the position of a spy in the French Government. Nothing we could say could disabuse his mind of this thought and there was not one of us, including the secret service men but who knew absolutely that he was wrong. He insisted they all understood English while as a matter of fact there was just one of them in the more than two dozen about the place who understood a single word of English. We knew from experience, and even after the President's suggestion, we tried them out from every angle of approach, all to no avail. The President was adamant and nothing could change him. About this time he also took on a peculiar notion of his personal responsibility for all the property in the furnished palace he was occupying. He raised quite a fuss on two remembered occassions when he noticed articles of furniture had been removed. Upon investigation, for no one else had noticed the moving proposition, it was learned the custodian of the property for the French owner had seen fit to do a little rearranging.

"From the President, whom we all knew so well, these were very funny doings and we could but measure, at least some of us did, that there must be an unusual nervousness or something queer happening in the mind of the President.

"But one thing was certain, he was never the same after this little spell of sickness, socalled cold, by the doctor attending."

About Wilson's rearrangement of the furniture, see the extract from the Grayson Diary printed at May 1, 1919, Vol. 58, and the extract from the R. S. Baker Diary printed at May 17, 1919, Vol. 59. For evidence, contrary to Hoover's on the alleged spies, see the extracts from the Benham Diary printed at April 18 and 19, 1919, Vol. 57, and at May 17, 1919, Vol. 59, and the extract from the Grayson Diary printed at April 8, 1919, Vol. 57.

The President's attitude is an affront to France and will be so considered unless I can move him to reconsider his decision. He has made every sort of foolish excuse to Jusserand, such as "I am leaving immediately after the peace is signed and would not have time to partake of a dinner, since the train is to leave at nine o'clock in the evening." Jusserand send [sent] word that French officials were running the French trains and that the President's special train would not leave until after the dinner was over, and even not until the coffee and cigars were finished. He added that when he and Madame Jusserand went to Brest to meet the President they had dined with me at a large dinner party and had ample time to catch the train.

I had Jusserand and Wallace wait in my study while I went into another room to call up Grayson to find how matters stood. Grayson was not disposed to speak to the President further. He evidently wanted "to stand from under." I asked if Mrs. Wilson was there. He undertook to find out and reported that she was not in. This I think was untrue and she, too, evidently wished to avoid the controversy.

The President came to the Crillon around twelve o'clock and we had it out in great shape. He said he had no notion of eating with Poincaré, that he would choke if he sat at the table with him. I replied that if I were in his place I would go to dinner and choke. He looked at me but made no reply. I am glad he did not, as it probably would not have been pleasant. I called his attention to the fact that Poincaré was representing the French people and that he, the President, had been a guest of the Nation for nearly six months. He said it made no difference, that he would not eat with him; that Poincaré was "no good" and had tried to make trouble by sending a message to the Italian people, showing that he was in sympathy with them and out of sympathy with him, Wilson.[2] He went on to say that he had not come to the Crillon to discuss such an unimportant matter as eating with "that fellow Poincaré, not to mention, Madame Poincaré." He wished our opinion regarding a matter that had just come up between Lloyd George, Clemenceau and himself.

Clemenceau is angry with the Germans, first, about the sinking of the German battle fleet at Scapa Flow, second, because of the burning of the French flags which Germany, under the Treaty, would be compelled to return to France. What he wishes to do is to send a note to the Germans immediately protesting against these

[2] For Poincaré's message and the controversy over it, see the minutes of the Council of Four printed at May 1, 1919, 11 a.m., Vol. 58.

acts, and then, *after the Treaty is signed*, move Allied troops into Essen as a punitive measure.

General Bliss and I took the lead against such action. My advice was to not even send a protest, much less consent to the occupation of Essen. The great thing was to have the Treaty signed. After that was done, if it was thought wise, a protest might be sent Germany concerning the two incidents mentioned, preferably though, laying the blame to the old government and expressing a hope that the new Government would carry out in good faith the terms of the Treaty. My opinion was there would be lawless acts of this nature for some months, but after that, Germany would get down to a real understanding of the situation and try to fulfill her obligations, so far as she was able. I was surprised to hear the President express a desire to evade the matter until after he had gone and leave us with the question to settle.

When he had finished this, I went back to the Poincaré invitation and was not surprised to find signs of weakening. He insisted, though, he had not received a regular invitation; that Jusserand had merely called and asked what time would be convenient. In reply to this, both White and I told him that this was the only form in which an invitation could be brought to him. He insisted then that Poincaré was merely trying to get himself out of a hole and that he did not intend to help him. He said, "why does he not come to me direct instead of sending House, Lansing, White and Jusserand to help him out?" Both White and I tried to explain that what Poincaré had done was entirely regular and the only way it could be done. I suggested if he wished a regular invitation I would see that he got it in short order. This stirred him, and he expressed a hope that none of us would take further action, that if we did, it would be a reflection upon his attitude, and would show that we considered he was in the wrong. My feeling is that he will succumb and accept the hospitality offered.

Wallace came in the afternoon and it was agreed that Jusserand should make another effort tomorrow. I believe it will be successful.

To Joseph Patrick Tumulty

Paris, June 23, 1919.

My clear conviction is that the adoption of the Treaty by the Senate with reservations would put the United States as clearly out of the concert of nations as a rejection.[1] We ought either to go in or to stay out. To stay out would be fatal to the influence and even to the commercial prospects of the United States, and to go in would give her the leadership of the world. Reservations would either mean nothing or postpone the conclusion of peace, so far as America is concerned, until every other principal nation concerned in the Treaty had found out by negotiation what the reservations practically meant and whether they could associate themselves with the United States on the terms of the reservations or not. Moreover, changes in the Treaty seem to me to belong to the powers of negotiation which belong to the President and that I would be at liberty to withdraw the treaty if I did not approve of the ratifications. (Paragraph.)

I do not think it would be wise for me to wait here for the appropriation bills. I hope to sail on the 25th or 26th and suggest that you consider the plan of sending a vessel to meet me.

Woodrow Wilson.

T telegram (WP, DLC).
[1] Wilson was replying to JPT to WW, June 21, 1919.

Two Telegrams from Joseph Patrick Tumulty

[The White House] June 23 [1919]
No. 208. Your conclusions concerning reservations in ratification would make fine statement. The country would stand back of you in this. Can I use it in this way, or can I at least furnish copies to Senator Hitchcock and Mr. Taft? If you allow me to make public use of it, may I change "leadership of the world" too "a notable place in the affairs of the world"? This in order to avoid possibility of hurting feelings of other nations. Now is the time to issue statement of this kind as Lodge has practically withdrawn Knox Resolution and opponents seem to be concentrating on "reservations."

Tumulty.

The White House, June 23, 1919.
No. 209. Income tax matter has been arranged.[1]   Tumulty.

T telegrams (WP, DLC).
[1] About this matter, see JPT to WW, June 6, 1919 (first telegram of that date), and WW to R. Bolling, June 9, 1919, both in Vol. 60.

From the Diary of Dr. Grayson

Tuesday, June 24, 1919.
After breakfast Tay Pay O'Connor, the Irish statesman and author,[1] called for a moment to pay his respects to the President. He said that he did not want to take up his time, and told me that he

did not know whether it would be wise for the President to see him
or not, but that he simply had wanted to express to him his thanks
and his appreciation for what the President was doing in the interest of peace. The President was engaged, and it was impossible for
him to receive Mr. O'Connor, but Mr. O'Connor was well satisfied.
I put him in the President's car and sent him back to his hotel. He
was accompanied by a Mr. McGuire.[2] As Mr. O'Connor entered the
car he turned to McGuire and said: "Suppose the Sinn Feiners
could see me now." He seemed to be well pleased and the episode
of the car amused him.

The President met with the Council of Three, Lloyd George
being present again for the first time. The President told me afterward that the British Premier was extremely warm in his praises
of me and of appreciation for what I had done. The President said:
"He spoke very affectionately of you to the Council."

As the Council of Three was breaking up from the morning session, I went into the room with my pen in hand to get Clemenceau
to sign a picture of the Big Four. He took me to one side and told
me that he had signed an order directing that I be awarded with
the decoration of Commander of the Legion of Honor. I was not
only surprised but I really was shocked, as this was someting that
I did not desire and would not like to be placed in the position of
either accepting or having to refuse. It was not that I had any particular feeling other than my general feeling of opposition to decorations generally. The President had heard what Clemenceau told
me, and I asked him what I should do in the matter. he said: "By
all means, you should accept it. In the first place, you should accept it because I believe you deserve it. In the second place, if you
do not accept it your motives are apt to be misconstrued and there
is a possibility that some one would believe that you declined it at
my instigation, which might be embarrassing in existing circumstances."

Mr. and Mrs. Dumont,[3] the American Consul at Florence, Italy,
and Mr. Henry White were luncheon guests. The Dumonts were
extremely bitter against the Italian people generally, and especially
against those with whom they have recently had dealings since the
President refused to allow Italy to gobble the whole of Dalmatia.
Mr. Dumont stated that the only thing that he could say about the
Italians was that if the negroes of the South had white skins they
would be perfectly comparable to the Italians generally. He said
that he was completely disgusted with the manner in which the
Red Cross and Y.M.C.A. workers had allowed the Italians to treat
them. They had submitted to ill-treatment and indignities and had
failed to report them simply because they wanted to remain in that

section of Italy, and they knew if they directed attention to the actual facts they would be ordered out by the State Department.

At two o'clock the President asked me to accompany him to Versailles. As soon as we arrived there we were met by Mr. Balfour, who took Lloyd George's place. The object was to look over the arrangements made for the ceremony in connection with the signing of the treaty. After looking over the Hall of Mirrors and finding out how much space was available for the representatives of the press and officials, the President said: "We should admit some ladies. I would like to have Mrs. Wilson and my daughter witness the ceremony." Mr. Clemenceau turned around and said: "Very well, that settles it. We will have the ladies present. Furthermore, I think it is nice to have them. If we did not have them present (winking his eye at the President) Mr. Balfour would not come." Mr. Balfour, who was standing by, joined in the laughter.

After the arrangements had been completed, Mr. Balfour read a note which had been received from Germany saying that it would be impossible for the delegates to be present before Friday. The German authorities seemed to treat lightly the matter as to who would come. Whereupon the President said that if they tried to send office boys or messengers he was in favor of the Council of Three insisting on having representative men sent, and not take any foolishness from them.

Clemenceau conducted the President around the Palace personally and showed him the points of interest. He took him into the Senate room and pointed out the seat which Victor Hugo occupied. Then pointing to the Rostrum, he said: "There is where I made my maiden speech in 1871—47 years ago." Passing through the various chambers and rooms, he showed the President the bed-room of Louis XIV. Mr. Balfour remarked that the bed faced the windows, which was something he disliked owing to the morning light. It was arranged like his bed here in Paris, which also faced the light, and which was a bad arrangement.

Going through another room, we faced a number of mirrors, so placed that you could see yourself at several angles. Clemenceau turned and said to the President and Mr. Balfour: "If you were to embrace one lady in this room, and then look in the mirrors, you would think that you had your arms around several ladies." The President told him the story of a lady who was being kissed and who thought no one was present. Presently a little voice said: "Auntie, kiss me too." She replied to her young niece by saying: "Eleanor, you are speaking incorrect English; you should say: 'Kiss me twice.' " Both Clemenceau and Balfour laughed very heartily, the former saying: "She was a lady of experience."

When the President walked out of the Palace a large crowd had gathered and they cheered: "Wilson and Clemenceau."

Returning from Versailles the Council of Three reconvened and continued their conferences. The President urged his colleagues to expedite as much as possible all arrangements for the signing so that it could be disposed of without delay. The Council also considered a report which had been received dealing with the destruction of the German Fleet interned at Scapa Flow, which had been scuttled through the action of the German crews in opening the sea-cocks in the ships.

After dinner tonight Ambassador Jusserand came to the temporary White House to see the President. The President, however, was too busy to receive the Ambassador and told me to ascertain his mission. Jusserand informed me that the President of France was arranging a formal dinner to be held on Thursday night, and that he wished the President to attend as the guest of honor. I got in touch with the President and he told me that he simply could not go. He pointed out that there was still a possibility of the signing of the Treaty on Friday afternoon, and he intended starting back for the United States the moment the signatures were affixed. He said that if he went to the dinner it would take up too much of his time, pointing out that if the dinner was held on the day of the signing, before he would be able to get through with the soup, it would be time to start for the train. As a matter of fact, the President did not want to go to the dinner at all.

Poincaré had said a number of nasty things about the President during the latter's sojourn here, and the President had no desire to accept any hospitality whatever at his hands. However, the demand that Poincaré entertain the President at dinner was generally from the people of France, and it would be hard for the French President to explain why this had not been done. Although I had said nothing to Jusserand about our knowledge of the fact that Poincaré had spoken disrespectfully of the President, the Ambassador emphasized again and again to me that Poincaré thought a great deal of the President and had always spoken in the highest of terms of him. To my mind this was another clear case of a "guilty conscience being its own accuser."

[1] About whom, see WHP to WW, Sept. 3, 1917, n. 2, Vol. 44.
[2] Unidentified.
[3] Frederick Theodore Frelinghuysen Du Mont and Mary Wolfe Du Mont.

To Paul Hymans

My dear Mr. Hymans: Paris, 24 June, 1919.

I have your letter of the 23rd of June and you may be sure that I have not forgotten the priority agreement with regard to Belgium. I do not know why it has been delayed but we are trying now to get it signed by all the members of our little conference.

Sincerely yours,   [Woodrow Wilson]

CCL (WP, DLC).

Hankey's Notes of a Meeting of the Council of Four[1]

President Wilson's House, Paris,
C.F.89   June 24, 1919, 11 a.m.

1. The Council had before them proposals relating to Belgian claims for priority in reparation payments, which had already been approved by financial experts.

The following documents were approved:

(1) An agreement between the Governments of the United States of America, Great Britain, France, and Italy. This document was signed by the representatives of the four Governments. (Appendix I.)

(2) An annex prepared as an illustration of the method of applying the foregoing provisions. This document was initialled by the representatives of the four Governments. (Appendix II.)

(3) A letter to M. Hymans which was signed by M. Clemenceau, President Wilson, and Mr. Lloyd George. (Appendix III.)

M. LOUCHEUR took custody of the originals of the first two documents, and undertook to prepare a letter for M. Clemenceau's signature covering their despatch to the Belgian Delegation. He also took custody of the third document to dispatch it to the Belgian Delegation.

APPENDIX I TO C.F.89.

WHEREAS, Article 237 of the Conditions of Peace with Germany provides, among other things, that the payments to be made by Germany, by way of reparation, will be divided by the Allied and Associated Governments in proportions which have been determined upon by them in advance and on a basis of general equity and of the rights of each; and

WHEREAS, it is deemed equitable that after the priority accorded by Article 235, in respect of the expenses of the Armies of Occupation and payments for the supply of Germany, a certain priority should be granted to Belgium in respect of the payments made by Germany by way of reparation;

NOW, THEREFORE, the undersigned, in the name of their respective Governments, agree that out of the first cash received from Germany, in respect of reparation, Belgium shall receive, on account of the reparation payments to which she is entitled the equivalent of 2,500,000,000 gold francs.

For the purposes of the foregoing there shall be reckoned as cash:

(1) Currency received by the Reparation Commission;

(2) The proceeds of the sale by the said Commission of negotiable instruments or securities received from Germany;

(3) The value of deliveries and reparation in kind made by Germany pursuant to the provisions of the Conditions of Peace and debited to the Allied and Associated Governments. This last item shall not be taken into account before May 1, 1921.

It is understood that the restitutions contemplated by Article 238 of the Treaty will not be taken into consideration.

Irrespective of this priority of 2,500,000,000 francs, Belgium will participate in the proportion which will be accorded to her in the division of the first payments and the subsequent divisions contemplated by Article 237 above referred to.

Beginning with May 1, 1921, the above mentioned sum of 2,500,000,000 francs will be amortized at the rate of one-thirtieth per year out of Belgium's share in each of the subsequent payments made by Germany. If, however, Germany should complete payment of its debt in less than thirty years, such amortization will be accelerated so that it will conclude coincidentally with the final settlement of Germany.

The Annex attached hereto will serve as an illustration of the method of applying the foregoing provisions.

(Signed) G. CLEMENCEAU.

WOODROW WILSON.

D. LLOYD GEORGE.

S. SONNINO.

APPENDIX II TO C.F.89

ANNEX.

Let us assume that Germany pays up to May 1, 1921, in addition to sums which will be applied to its supply of food and raw materials and to the expenses of the Armies of Occupation, the total sum of 13 milliards of francs applicable to reparations. Let us suppose that this sum has been paid as follows:

In cash or securities converted into cash, 1½ milliards.

In different deliveries. 11½ miliards.

Let us further assume that Belgium's share is fixed at 7%, for example. On the foregoing hypothesis Belgium will be entitled:

(1) To receive the cash, that is, 1½ milliards.

(2) On May 1, 1921, each of the interested Powers, having been debited with the total amount of deliveries in kind received by it, payment will be made to Belgium out of the common fund of 1 milliard of the 11½ milliards mentioned above.

Out of the balance of 10½ milliards, Belgium will be entitled to 7%, that is to say, 735 millions.

If Belgium has received in kind 1,200,000,000 she should pay into the common funds the difference between this sum and the share of the 735 millions to which she is entitled, that is to say, 465 millions.

After 1921, for instance in 1922, if Germany has paid in that year 10 milliards and Belgium has received in kind 300 millions, its account will stand as follows:

Received in kind, 300 millions ------------------------- 300,000,000
Amortization payment on the priority of
$2\frac{1}{2}$ milliards --- 83,330,000
Total --- 383,330,000

Amount due to Belgium 700 millions, from which are to be deducted the above 383,330,000; balance due from the common fund to Belgium, 316,670,000.

G.C.
W.W.
D. Li. G.
S.S.

M. Hymans,
Ministre des Affaires Etrangères,
Hôtel Lotti, Paris
Sir,   Paris, June 16, 1919.

The Reparation Clauses of the draft Treaty of Peace with Germany obligate Germany to make reimbursement of all sums which Belgium has borrowed from the Allied and Associated Governments up to November 11, 1918, on account of the violation by Germany of the Treaty of 1839. As evidence of such an obligation Germany is to make a special issue of bonds to be delivered to the Reparation Commission.

Each of the undersigned will recommend to the appropriate governmental agency of his Government that, upon the delivery to the Reparation Commission of such bonds, his Government accept an amount thereof corresponding to the sums which Belgium has borrowed from his Government since the war and up to November 11, 1918, together with interest at 5% unless already included in such sums, in satisfaction of Belgium's obligation on account of such loans, which obligation of Belgium's shall thereupon be cancelled.

We are, dear Mr. Minister   Very truly yours,

(Signed)   G. CLEMENCEAU.

"   WOODROW WILSON.

"   D. LLOYD GEORGE.

T MS (SDR, RG 256, 180.03401/89, DNA).
[1] The complete text of these minutes is printed in *PPC*, VI, 645-48.

Hankey's Notes of a Meeting of the Council of Four[1]

President Wilson's House, Paris,

C.F.90.   June 24, 1919, 11:15 a.m.

1. MR. LLOYD GEORGE said he had received a long report from the British Admiralty regarding the sinking of the German ships at Scapa Flow. The case for the British Admiralty was that, at the time of the Armistice, the French and British naval representatives had pressed for the surrender of the German Fleet. Admiral Benson, however, had urged very strongly that surrender should not be demanded and that the Armistice should not be risked for this purpose. Marshal Foch had supported Admiral Benson very strongly. He had said that he did not wish to risk the lives of good soldiers for bad ships which had never fought a decisive battle. The Supreme War Council, consisting of the Prime Ministers and of Colonel House, had over-ruled the French and British Admiralties and unanimously agreed to ask only for the internment of the German ships and only for the surrender of certain submarines. It had been decided originally that the German ships to be interned should be interned in a neutral port. On further examination, it had been realised that this was impossible and the Allied Naval Council had chosen Scapa Flow as a suitable spot for the concentration of the German ships under surveillance. Then came the question of determining what kind of surveillance could be exercised. The British Admiralty had come to the conclusion that none but German crews could be put on board, as the removal of the German personnel would have been a breach of the Armistice. All that could be done was to exercise general surveillance over the fleet. He had seen the instructions issued by the British Admiralty. He quoted certain passages of these instructions. The latest report

[1] The complete text of these minutes is printed in *PPC*, VI, 649-54.

was that the 'Baden' and 'Hindenburg' had been saved or could be salvaged. There were, therefore, two capital ships available. He wished to add that Baron Makino had just informed him that the Japanese Admiralty did not consider the British Admiralty in any way to blame.

M. CLEMENCEAU then handed in the opinion of the French Admiralty. (Appendix I.)[2]

MR. LLOYD GEORGE said that, as Admiral Hope had pointed out, if the original intention of interning the ships in a neutral port had been adhered to, it would not have been possible to place Allied crews on board.

PRESIDENT WILSON said that Admiral Benson, who had been present at the discussions at the Armistice time, had, unfortunately, gone home. His substitute at present was Admiral Knapp. At Mr. Lloyd George's request, he had obtained his opinion on the point. (Appendix II.)[3]

ADMIRAL HOPE explained that the British Admiralty could not have demanded the complete removal of the German crews. This would have been equivalent to a surrender of the German ships. With any German personnel on board, it was impossible to safeguard the ships completely. Very large parties would have been required to take charge of every compartment in each ship and this could not have been done consistently with the retention of any German crews on board.

PRESIDENT WILSON said that he trusted Admiral Hope would not think he had expressed any opinion on the subject. All he had done was to furnish Admiral Knapp's personal views in compliance with Mr. Lloyd George's request. The chief interest of the Council was to see what ought to be done. He thought it was clear that the German Admiral could be held responsible and punished. It also seemed clear that the German Government could be held responsible, but what profit could be derived from the responsibility of the German Government was not so clear. The object of the Allies could not be to renew the war but to obtain some reparation, placing them in the same situation as if the fleet had not been sunk. He assumed that enough German ships remained to make the contemplated distribution, with the exception of the share due to the British Navy. This share being, of course, a very large one, could

---

[2] It is printed in *ibid.*, p. 653. Vice Admiral Ronarc'h argued that his understanding of the pertinent clause of the Armistice Agreement was that the interned German ships would be guarded by the Royal Navy by guards on board those ships.

[3] It is printed in *ibid.*, p. 654. Rear Admiral Knapp agreed with the opinion of the French Admiralty and observed that "the naval authorities of the United States would have felt themselves at liberty to have placed guards on board every one of the interned German naval vessels."

not be furnished, but he thought that there was perhaps enough to compensate the weaker navies.

MR. LLOYD GEORGE observed that there were two first class ships, one a battleship and one a battle-cruiser.

M. CLEMENCEAU said that he wished to make a few observations. First, as to the question of right. According to the legal advisers, Germany had violated the Armistice. On the previous day, the application of Article XXXI of the Armistice had been discussed. It seemed clear to him that it did apply, and, in addressing the Germans, he thought that advantage should be taken of that article. There was, further, an anticipated violation of the Peace Conditions and this must be taken into consideration. If this were all, the stories told by the Germany Admiral that he believed, on the strength of a newspaper, that the Armistice was over, might be alleged in defence of the act. This, however, was merely an instance of German mendacity. There was further evidence of the deliberate intention of the Germans to violate not only the Armistice but the Conditions of Peace in anticipation. French flags which, under the Peace Terms, were to be restored had been burned in Berlin. This incident had been deeply felt in France both by Parliament and people. There was, moreover, a telegram seized by the Polish authorities to the effect that an insurrection was to be organised in Upper Silesia. The movement would be disavowed officially but aided unofficially in every possible manner. Von Haniel had warned the Conference that there would be an insurrection against the Polish clauses.[4] There was a clause in the Treaty requiring the withdrawal of the German troops from Upper Silesia within 14 days after the ratification of the Treaty. It had been hard enough to get the Treaty signed, but this evidence showed that there would be even greater difficulty in obtaining its execution. He proposed, if there were no objections on the part of his colleagues, to have this intercepted telegram published in the Press to show the Germans we were awake to their intentions.

As to reparation, he was told that there might be enough ships to indemnify the French Navy. He could make no judgment on this. In regard to responsibility, he left the matter entirely in Mr. Lloyd George's hands, but he wished to say that material reparation was not enough. He now formally made a demand that reparation be exacted for the burning of the French flags, an act certainly done by order like the sinking of the ships. The question arose as to what form this reparation should take. He would not

---

[4] See Appendix I to the minutes of the Council of Four printed at June 22, 1919, 9 p.m.

ask for money. Money could only be obtained at the expense of France and her Allies. He would take ships, if he could get them, but even that was not enough. He wished, by a striking act, to show that the Allies did not mean to tolerate the conduct evidenced by the burning of the flags, the sinking of the ships and the plot against Poland. It must be remembered that it was difficult to bring aid to the Poles and the forts of Dantzig would be able to repel a naval attack. It was quite evident that the Germans meant to violate the Treaty which they were to sign in two days. No one who was not deaf and blind to evidence could doubt it. He regretted that President Wilson was shortly to leave, but he recognised the urgency of his business in America. The American flag, however, would remain side by side with those of the Allies. He desired that a military act be accomplished, showing the will of the Allies quite clearly not to submit to any fradulent breach of the Treaty by Germany. He did not wish this act to precede the signing of the Treaty, and, for the present, all he would ask was that a note be sent referring to the incident at Scapa Flow and to the burning of the flags and stating that reparation for these acts would be required. The note should further state that the Allies were aware of what Germany was plotting in Silesia and that precautions would be taken to prevent the execution of the plot. He would not mention that reparation or what precautions would be taken. That was all he would say for the present, with the object of establishing the position of the Allies and their right to act. But he would state what he had in mind very clearly.

He thought the Allies should take possession of Essen. M. Loucheur, whom he had asked to come, informed him that Essen was still at the present time making armaments. It was the most powerful centre of munition production in Germany. He had no intention of keeping Essen, but only of preventing supplies being made there to munition the attack on Poland. There could, in the nature of the case, be no military opposition to the operation. It would show the Germans quite clearly that their game was up. The Germans would yield and public opinion, which had supported the Allies throughout the war, would be satisfied. Failing this, there was a fear that the Germans would, one by one, get back every concession they had made. This would result in the necessity of re-mobilising to engage in definite acts of war. He recognised that it was necessary to act prudently for the time being, in order not to jeopardise the signature of the Peace, but it must be made clear to the enemy that Allied will would prevail.

PRESIDENT WILSON asked whether M. Clemenceau would allow the discussion of this proposal to be deferred until the afternoon?

MR. LLOYD GEORGE joined in this request.

MR. BALFOUR asked if he understood M. Clemenceau aright in thinking that his proposal was to write a letter at once or on the following day, regarding the sinking of the ships, the burning of the flags and the plot against Poland.

PRESIDENT WILSON interpolated a question. He asked whether M. Clemenceau had corroborated the last.

M. CLEMENCEAU said that he would produce full evidence.

MR. BALFOUR, continuing, asked whether the letter would state that those acts violated the Armistice and therefore gave rise to a claim for reparation.

M. CLEMENCEAU observed that the case of the flags and of the ships went together and gave rise to a claim for reparation. As regards Poland, a case would be made out. Reparation was not in question in regard to that.

MR. BALFOUR said that the proposal would be then to continue the arrangements for the signature of the Peace, whether the German answer to this letter came before the signature or after. If he understood M. Clemenceau's intention, he would prefer it to come after. Then, if the answer were unsatisfactory, which in all probability would be the case, the Allies would have to take action, and the action proposed by M. Clemenceau was to occupy Essen.

M. CLEMENCEAU said that Mr. Balfour had quite understood his policy. Of course, it would be necessary to hear Marshal Foch regarding the execution of the plan. He wished to add that he had no intention of keeping Essen for any length of time and would, of course, give it up as soon as the Polish difficulty had been cleared up.

T MS (SDR, RG 256, 180.03401/90, DNA).

Gilbert Fairchild Close to Robert Lansing, with Enclosure

My dear Mr. Secretary: Paris, 24 June, 1919.

The President asks me to return to you the enclosed memorandum which you sent him with your letter of June 23rd upon which he has indicated his answers to the questions asked by Dr. Westermann.[1]   Sincerely yours,   [Gilbert F. Close]

CCL (WP, DLC).
[1] Close wrote in Wilson's replies by hand; they are printed in bold face in the following document.

ENCLOSURE

21 June 1919.

To Commissioners Robert Lansing, Henry White, E. M. House,
    Tasker H. Bliss.

From: W. L. Westermann.

One of the papers of this morning states that President Wilson may leave for the United States next Wednesday. We take the liberty of suggesting that the Commissioners obtain from the President before his departure, his views as to United States policy regarding the following problems of the Near East:

1. Will the United States be a signatory to the treaty with Turkey? **Yes (?)**

2. Has any decision been made as to the granting of Asia Minor territory in sovereignty to Greece, or is this still an open question? **Yes.**

3. If Greece is to have this territory, what is to be the area of Greek sovereignty? **Almost as defined by the experts—Americans dissenting.**

4. Is it the President's desire, as expressed in Article XII of his speech of Jan. 8, 1918, that the sovereignty of Turkey will remain unimpaired, or does the President hope to see Anatolian Turkey placed under a mandate? **Yes.**

5. Is Anatolian Turkey to be treated as a whole, or divided under some form of sector scheme, or placed under a combined international control? **As a whole**

6. If Anatolian Turkey is to be treated as a whole and placed under the guidance of France or some other European power, what is to be done in regard to the 15,000 Italian troops now said to be occupying the southwestern section of Asia Minor? **Try to induce them to leave**

7. Does the reported occupation of Transcaucasia by Italian troops mean that there is an intention to grant the mandate over this area to Italy? **Yes, but Am. has not assented.**

8. Is Armenia, in the treaty with Turkey, to be distinctly marked off as a separate state? **Yes.**

9. Does the President hope to separate Russian Armenia from the old Russian Empire and incorporate it in a possible new Armenia, or do the terms of the agreement with Admiral Koltchak preclude this?

10. Is Cilicia, with the port of Mersina, to be included in the New Armenia? **Part of it.**

11. In regard to Palestine, is the United States committed to the Balfour declaration? **Yes.**

12. Is the desire of the Arab national leaders for independence, under European guidance, to be supported, or are the Arab provinces to be dealt with under the mandatory form of control? **Mandate.**
13. If the latter plan is to be adopted, are these provinces to be treated as a unit, or divided between France and Great Britain as mandataries? **As a unit, if advice of U. S. is taken.**
(Notes returned by Gilbert Close.)

T MS (E. M. House Papers, CtY).

To Richard William Martin[1]

My dear Mr. Martin: Paris, 24 June, 1919.

The time of my leaving France is approaching and I do not want to go away without saying something about the services which M. Auguste Alphonse Barthelemy, Captain and Adjutant Major of the Republican Guard, has rendered as the overseer of our household here on the Place des Etats Unis. He has been unremitting in his attention to duty and has won our confidence and admiration. I have learned to feel a great dependence upon him and it is a pleasure to have an opportunity to praise his ability, diligence, intelligence and watchfulness over our interests.

                    Sincerely yours,   [Woodrow Wilson]

CCL (WP, DLC).
    [1] To repeat, chief of protocol in the French Foreign Ministry.

To the Most Reverend Paulin Ladeuze

My dear Mr. Rector: Paris, 24 June, 1919.

I think that one of the most poignant memories of my whole visit to Europe will center about that little ceremony in the ruins of the library of the University of Louvain. I was unable at the time to give adequate expression to the emotions which that occasion excited, and perhaps it is never possible to put into words the thoughts and feelings which spring out of such a scene, but I hope that you and your colleagues of the University realized the profound emotions and the deep appreciation with which I received the honors of the University in such circumstances.

                    Cordially and sincerely yours,   [Woodrow Wilson]

CCL (WP, DLC).

To Désiré Félicien François Joseph Cardinal Mercier

My dear Cardinal Mercier: Paris, 24 June, 1919.

This is just a line to tell you how much I enjoyed the privilege of meeting you and to tell you how much I valued the opportunity to tell you what we were thinking of you and of Belgium in America. May not these few lines convey to you my warm friendship and admiration?

Cordially and sincerely yours,   [Woodrow Wilson]

CCL (WP, DLC).

To Robert Lansing

My dear Lansing: Paris, 24 June, 1919.

I have your letter of the 20th of June conveying the wish of the State Department that the kind of support which is to be given to Admiral Kolchak should be as soon as possible formulated. I had a long talk with McCormick about this yesterday and answered the questions, as well as I could, which he put to me. What I said to him would serve better to answer Polk's questions than anything that I could formulate off-hand.

Cordially and faithfully yours,   [Woodrow Wilson]

CCL (WP, DLC).

From Vance Criswell McCormick, with Enclosure

My dear Mr. President: Paris. June 24, 1919.

I am enclosing herewith a cablegram for Polk, which you asked me to prepare for you yesterday, in regard to sending Roland Morris to Omsk.

If this meets with your approval, I will have it sent at once.

Very sincerely yours,   Vance C McCormick

TLS (WP, DLC).

E N C L O S U R E

From the President for Polk: June 24, 1919.

In view of the fact that the joint action taken here by the Supreme Council with reference to Kolchak still leaves open the question of his formal recognition and the extent and nature of support which should be given him, I believe it will be useful to have Ambassador Morris proceed to Omsk as had earlier been planned. I therefore request that you direct him to proceed to Omsk at the earliest practicable date.

The purposes which I desire to have accomplished by his visit and which you may communicate to him are, in the first instance, to secure such first-hand information and personal impressions as will aid us in the formulation of our Siberian policy. I also feel that the personal contact of Morris at this time with Kolchak, and especially with those who surround him, will afford an excellent opportunity to get a first hand impression of their real spirit and purposes, and to impress these persons with the policy and viewpoint of the Administration, which, I am confident, Morris can admirably express.

I am also desirous that Ambassador Morris should so utilize his visit to Omsk as to impress upon the Japanese Government our great interest in the Siberian situation and our intention to adopt a definite policy which will include the "open door" to Russia, free from Japanese domination.

You will please instruct Morris in his dealings with the Omsk Government to be guided by the spirit of the communication of the Supreme Council to Kolchak. This, while not involving any present recognition of Kolchak, leaves us free to take a sympathetic interest in Kolchak's organization and activities.[1]

CC MS (WP, DLC).

[1] This was sent, verbatim, as RL to FLP, No. 2859, June 28, 1919, T telegram (SDR, RG 59, 123M 832/29, DNA). It was relayed to Morris in W. Phillips to R. S. Morris, June 30, 1919, T telegram (SDR, RG 59, 123M 832/29a, DNA).

From Edward Mandell House

Dear Governor: Paris, June 24, 1919.

Professor James T. Shotwell, who had been attached to the American Commission as Chief of the Historical Section, is shortly going back to the United States in order to work out plans for the Labor Conference to be held in Washington next October.

As you know, he has been particularly devoted to labor matters during the Conference. After Gompers left he acted in his place on the commission which drafted the Labor Convention. In this, as in many other ways, he has rendered extremely valuable service, and there has been no one connected with our Mission in Paris who has been so helpful in such matters.

During the time he is in the United States it is possible that questions may arise upon which he will need to ask your judgment. You may be sure that he will not disturb you unless it is absolutely necessary; but in case he should need your advice and judgment I trust that you will give it to him.

Affectionately yours,   E. M. House

TLS (WP, DLC).

From Henry White

PERSONAL

Dear Mr. President: Paris 24 June 1919

I have been giving careful consideration to what you have just been saying to us about the French President's invitation; and the more I think of it, the more convinced I am that your acceptance thereof will be merely an act of recognition by you of the hospitality of the French nation, through its President; whereas its refusal, in view of the fact that you have been this nation's guest for so many months, will be resented as a national affront.

I feel sure that the personality of the President, his relations with you or yours with him, will have no bearing whatever upon the public mind, and as the sympathies of our own people are so strongly pro-French, I cannot but think that they will share the feeling of resentment experienced here.

I feel strongly, therefore, that the relations between France and the United States should not be jeopardized by any incident which can possibly be avoided, especially in view of the effect which such a situation would produce upon the German national mind at this very critical moment.

Under these circumstances, I venture, dear Mr. President, to express the opinion—and I should be wanting in friendship to you if I failed to do so—that the invitation should be accepted; an opinion which I know is fully shared by our three colleagues.

Yours very sincerely,   Henry White

TLS (WP, DLC).

From Jean Jules Jusserand

Dear Mr. President   Paris June 24 1919

I was sorry to have to call yesterday at an inconvenient hour when, as I understand only too well, it was impossible for you, owing to work and fatigue, to receive me.

I reported this morning to President Poincaré what Admiral Grayson told me on your behalf, and how material difficulties would prevent you from being present at the contemplated dinner in honor of yourself and the delegates at the Peace Conference on the day of the signature.

The President asked me to say to you that nothing is further from his thought than to ask you at an inconvenient date: he gives up therefore the idea of a dinner on the day of the signing of the peace, and expresses the hope that you will kindly accept his invitation for the day before: according to present probabilities the signature would take place on friday (several German and Italian plenipotentiaries have not yet arrived); the dinner might be in that case, if agreeable to you, on thursday.

It would give the head of the French Republic very great pleasure to have this occasion to express his sentiments toward the allies and especially toward you who have played such a leading part in the great work of the world peace, and your compatriots whose help in the crisis was so powerful and timely.

Hoping that this invitation may meet your conveniences, I beg you to believe me, dear Mr. President

Very sincerely and respectfully yours   Jusserand

ALS (WP, DLC).

From Herbert Clark Hoover

Dear Mr. President: [Paris] June 24th, 1919.

Since speaking to you yesterday, I have reconsidered the matter as to closing my career as Food Administrator.

The Food Administration is in fact ended, except in the sense that the Relief of Europe represents its final phase. In this sense I think if you approve, I will remain in office until I get home with this last phase completed.   Faithfully yours,   Herbert Hoover

Approved
Woodrow Wilson

TLS (Hoover Archives, CSt-H).

From the Diary of Vance Criswell McCormick

June 24 (Tuesday) [1919]

We began to plan for home and the closing up of our work here, and we are wondering now whether the Commission and President will let us go or make us stay for the completion of the Austria-Hungary treaty.

I attended a meeting of the Blockade Council to plan for dissolving it and to make arrangements to cancel all neutral agreements at the signing of peace. We did not complete our work, so arranged for last meeting for next day. I was instructed to try to get a definite answer from Heads of States as to the date of signing and date of pulling down the blockade.

I caught the President at the Crillon after meeting with the Commissioners and asked him to bring up the question at the next meeting of the "Chiefs." He said he thought it bad policy to do so, as Clemenceau was in such a rage at the action of the Germans in sinking the fleet and lowering the flags that he was having great difficulty in preventing him from making war again on the Germans, and that this was the wrong time to submit the question of removing the blockade.

I lunched with Bainbridge Colby, who gave me the inside of many matters concerning the Shipping Board. I cannot understand how Hurley has held on as long as he has and why the President does not see through him. We are riding for a fall soon if he stays in office much longer.

Just before lunch I had a talk with Lansing, who told me he might go home and let Polk come to take his place, as he said Frank had broken down and must be relieved, and he thought the trip might be helpful. He said the State Department was being badly broken up, as Phillips wanted to go and other changes were contemplated and he ought to be home to make his plans for the future. He asked me what I thought of getting Roland Morris to take Frank Polk's place. I told him he could not get a better man, but doubted if he would accept. He wondered if Frank would take Belgium, as Whitlock was going to Italy. I told him when we got home that I would be on call at Harrisburg if anything turned up in which I could help upon any of the hangovers of the war, and would be glad to run down if he needed me. He seemed very grateful and I am afraid he will need help after Polk goes.

I notice now all the Mission conferences are held in Lansing's office and not in House's as early in the conference, and the Colonel is not permitted to monopolize the "Chief" as much as he and Gordon[1] would like.

[1] That is, Gordon Auchincloss.

From the Diary of Edith Benham

June 24, 1919

The great excitement of the day was the Treaty signing. About six Mrs. W. saw a French officer jump out of a motor before it came to a stop, and dash up the street pavement into the house. Then the P. came down a few minutes after, from the Conference, to tell her the Germans had agreed to sign. After a little while pandemonium broke loose, sirens moaning and guns being fired and the church bells ringing. Before dinner my office force said the maids had kissed all of them in the hall. This didn't seem a complaint. The garage had been making merry in the back yard, making fiendish noises with motor engines and horns. At dinner we had champagne glasses at our plates, and when the P. started to drink I asked if he would let us drink to "The greatest man in the world and the greatest peace made by him." He is so modest he never seems to think much of himself, but the rest all drank heartily to it. Then he raised his glass and drank, "To the Peace, an enduring Peace, a Peace under the League of Nations." Mrs. W. and he drove down to the Crillon after dinner, where he had quite an ovation. The people waited for some time for him to come and then formed a lane for him to drive through.

Tasker Howard Bliss to Eleanora Anderson Bliss

My dear Nellie: Paris.   June 24, 1919

Your letter of June 9 has just come, and I return the envelope you enclosed with my autograph. Yesterday morning at 10 o'clock the President sent for me and asked me to prepare for him the draught of certain instructions to be given by the Council of Four to the Allied Commander in Chief in case the Germans refused to sign the treaty, with the resulting advance of the Armies into Germany. When I finished it in the afternoon, I telephoned to have an interview with him. He said that the Council was just going into an important conference that would last till late in the evening and he would send word later when to come. But about 6:45 the guns at the Invalides began to boom and I knew that the word must have come that the Germans would sign. But this morning there are signs that the fat may all go into the fire again. The French are all wrought up over the sinking of the German ships at Scapa Flow. They regarded a good part of these ships as a sure increase to their own fleet. They may begin a series of notes to Berlin on the subject and then no one can tell when the treaty will be signed. The President says that if they sign he will immediately return to Washington and leave the rest of us here. The Austrian treaty has not yet been agreed on. And as yet there is no government in Hungary that can be trusted to sign a treaty. But the President wants us also to participate in the discussions on the treaties with Bulgaria and Turkey even though *we* (the Americans) may not sign those treaties. We did not declare war on Turkey and Bulgaria and I do not see how we can make a treaty of peace with them. Your last letter says that you are beginning to have hot weather in Washington. Here we *had* several very warm days but it has turned quite cool again. The summer has been very dry, quite unlike last year when we had constant rain.

Later. I have just been with the other Commissioners drawing up a letter to the President on a very important subject which I do not like to mention in a letter which might go astray.[1] He is certainly a most extraordinary man. Ambassador Jusserand described him to me a few days ago as a man who, had he lived a couple of centuries ago, would have been the *greatest tyrant in the world, because he does not seem to have the slightest conception that he can ever be wrong*. Therefore, there are times when his associates want to have their views *on record*. That is why we wrote the letter I spoke of. Now I must send this to the courier-office.

TCL (T. H. Bliss Papers, DLC).
  [1] H. White to WW, June 24, 1919, just printed.

A Translation of a Letter from Eduard Beneš and Karel Kramář

Mr. President: [Paris, June 24, 1919]

Following the liberation of our country in the month of November last, the Tcheque University of Prague took a solemn decision by which it conferred on you the title of the Doctor of the University of Prague. The University wishes by this solemn decision to render homage to your great work accomplished during the war to make right and justice triumphant and to establish new basis for general welfare in the new world of the future. The University wishes at the same time to humbly manifest to you the gratefulness of the Tchecoslovaque nation for the assistance which you were good enough to loan it for this fight for its liberation from the yoke of strangers.

The University of Prague has asked the Tchecoslovaque Delegation to announce this decision to you and to transmit to you the diploma of "Doctor of the Tcheque University of Prague." We are happy to be able to fulfill this wish and we assure you, Mr. President, that we are in accord with the manifestation of the ancient and glorious University of the capital of our new state.

We permit ourselves, Mr. President, to renew the assurances of our high consideration.   Eduard Beneš
Karel Kramář

T MS (WP, DLC).

To Joseph Patrick Tumulty

Paris, 24 June, 1919.

I am quite willing that you should make public use of my cable[1] to you about reservations by the Senate in regard to the treaty, with this change in the sentence to which you call attention: quote and to go in would give her a leading place in the affairs of the world end quote, omitting also the last sentence about changes belonging to the power to negotiate treaties.   Woodrow Wilson

T telegram (WP, DLC).
[1] See WW to JPT, June 23, 1919, and JPT to WW, June 23, 1919 (first telegram of that date).

From Edward Mandell House, with Enclosure

Dear Governor: Paris, 24 June 1919.

I enclose a telegram just received from Oscar Strauss and David Miller, which I think will interest you.
Affectionately yours,   E. M. House

TLS (WP, DLC).

E N C L O S U R E

[Washington, June 23, 1919]

107. For Auchincloss from Straus and Miller.

Knox resolution has been practically abandoned and no vote of any kind in the Senate likely before President returns. Root letter[1] has immediate effect of grouping majority of Republicans in one viewpoint, though extremists like Borah are not reconciled, and some others like McCumber are firm for ratification, but letter has this advantage: that it practically limits field of debate to points made by Root. We consider the letter adroitly put and requires answer. [blank]s serious its chief weakness is that as to Article X it is contrary to Root letter of March 29th.[2] Also we think serves to put matter over till President returns.   Polk, Acting.

T telegram (WP, DLC).
    [1] That is, Root's letter of June 19, 1919, to Senator Lodge, about which, see JPT to WW, June 21, 1919, n. 3.
    [2] That is, Root's letter to Will H. Hays, for a digest of which, see the Enclosure printed with WW to EMH, March 31, 1919, vol. 56; also D. H. Miller to G. Auchincloss, June 26, 1919, and the notes thereto.

From Samuel Gompers

Washington. June 24, 1919.

2396. For the President, from Samuel Gompers.

"Thank you for your comprehensive messages.[1] They were received just in time to be submitted to our Convention. I am instructed by the Convention and take pleasure in advising you that the Convention by a vote of 29,909 to 120 indorsed the principles of the League of Nations."   Polk,   Acting.

T telegram (WP, DLC).
    [1] WW to S. Gompers, June 20, 1919 (two telegrams).

From the Diary of Dr. Grayson

Wednesday, June 25, 1919.

It had been expected that the German Peace Delegation would be announced from Weimar during the night and that arrangements could be made for their reception today. However, when the Council of Four went into session this morning no word whatever had been received. There was a general feeling of distrust against the Germans, and the questions of what should be done were taken under consideration.

While the Council of Three was in session, a representative of the French Government came to see me and told me that he had been directed to refund the money that had been paid out by us to defray the expenses of the special trains which we had had for the trips in France.[1] I told him, however, that this was entirely out of the question. The visit was an illuminating one, since it showed how public sentiment in France was again swinging very rapidly back in favor of the President. The politicians, with the aid of the subsidized French press, had been able to carry on a bitter campaign against the President and to poison the minds of many people with stories that he was not giving France a square deal. However, truth always prevails, and it was now beginning to prevail, as the people of France saw for themselves that it was the President and no other person who had been able to keep the varied diverse interests aligned and maintain the solid front that had forced the German General Assembly to accept the peace terms.

After dinner tonight the President received the final drafts of the Austrian reparations report and studied them for a time before going to bed.

¹ About this matter, see the extract from the Diary of Edith Benham printed at March 31, 1919; WW to RL, April 1, 1919 (second letter of that date); and RL to WW, April 2, 1919 (first letter of that date), all in Vol. 56; and GFC to RL, April 15, 1919 (second letter of that date), and the extract from the Grayson Diary printed at April 8, 1919, both in Vol. 57.

Hankey's Notes of a Meeting of the Council of Four[1]

President Wilson's House, Paris

C.F.91.   June 25, 1919, 11 a.m.

1. The Rhine Convention.   (Captain Portier[2] was present during this discussion.)

M. CLEMENCEAU read the following letter from the German Delegation:

Mr. President,   "Versailles, June 24th, 1919.

In accordance with instructions received from the Imperial Minister of Foreign Affairs, I have the honour to enquire from the Allied and Associated Governments when the negotiations can begin on the subject of an agreement relating to the occupied Rhenish territories.   (Signed)   VON HANIEL."

SIR MAURICE HANKEY, at M. Clemenceau's request, read the pertinent Article of the Treaty of Peace with Germany, namely, Article 432.

"All matters relating to the occupation and not provided for by the present Treaty shall be regulated by subsequent agreements which Germany hereby undertakes to observe."

MR. LLOYD GEORGE said he would take no risks and would insist on the Germans signing without any discussion.

PRESIDENT WILSON and M. SONNINO agreed.

M. MANTOUX, at M. Clemenceau's request, then read the follow-

¹ The complete text of these minutes is printed in PPC, VI, 655-68.
² André Léon Marie Portier, Secretary of the Committee for the Coordination of the Replies to the German Counter Proposition, which the Council of Four had established on June 12, 1919.

ing draft of a letter prepared by the Secretary-General of the Peace Conference:

"Monsieur le Président,

In acknowledging the receipt of your letter of June 24 with reference to the agreement as to the military occupation of the territories of the Rhine, I have the honour to remind you that under Article 432 of the conditions of peace, now accepted by the German Government, Germany is bound thereby to accept the terms of this agreement.

There is therefore no need to open negotiations on the subject and the instrument in question must be signed under the same conditions as the Treaty."

M. CLEMENCEAU suggested that in the last line the words "under the same conditions" should be deleted, and there should be substituted the words "at the same time."

(This was agreed to, and Capt. Portier was asked to prepare a text for M. Clemenceau's signature.)

CAPTAIN PORTIER, on his return, stated that M. Fromageot did not like the use of the words "at the same time." His objection was on the ground that Article 432 spoke of "subsequent agreements," whereas if signed at the same time, it would be a "simultaneous agreement."

(It was agreed to ignore this objection and M. Clemenceau signed the letter, which was despatched to the German Delegation.)

2. The Sinking of the German Fleet at Scapa Flow.

PRESIDENT WILSON read the Report furnished by the Allied Admirals (Appendix I).[3]

M. CLEMENCEAU said that for reasons he had already given, he could not confine himself to a purely naval point of view. The action of the Germans in sinking their ships at Scapa Flow must be considered in connection with the information as to their intentions in Poland, which was confirmed from many quarters.

MR. LLOYD GEORGE commented on the fact that the information from Poland had been published in the newspapers without any explanation being asked for from the Germans.

M. CLEMENCEAU said it was useless to ask for explanations, as the Germans would only say that we had falsified the document. His view was that nothing should be done to delay the signature of

[3] This was a report on the warships left to Germany under the preliminary peace treaty. The admirals concluded that, if a measure of punishment for the scuttling of the German warships at Scapa Flow was required, all the remaining German warships should be surrendered to the Allies. However, they went on, such punishment would be "totally inadequate," and they suggested that the Council of Four might consider other compensation, mainly in the form of merchant tonnage. See *PPC*, VI, 664-68.

Peace. All he would do today was to write to the Germans on the questions of the sinking of the ships and the burning of the flags. The Polish affair would grow in a day or two, and give ample reasons for action.

MR. LLOYD GEORGE thought it would be much better to take action to stop the development on the Polish front. The Germans now know that the Allies were aware that the movement there was not spontaneous, and could probably be stopped.

M. CLEMENCEAU agreed that it was worth trying.

PRESIDENT WILSON recalled that an alleged letter from Erzberger,[4] which had been alluded to before at the Council, had turned out to be false. It had been traced to Polish sources. While he had the utmost confidence in M. Paderewski (Mr. Lloyd George said he also had this confidence), he suspected Polish sources of information. Consequently, he would like to have confirmation of the information as to German intentions on the Eastern front from other sources, before taking action.

M. CLEMENCEAU said that he was thinking of sending an officer today to Warsaw to photograph the intercepted document.

MR. LLOYD GEORGE pointed out that all that had been done up to the present was to publish it in the "Matin." We ought to write to the Germans and say that this document had come into our hands, and to inform them that if the information should prove correct, the Germans would be held responsible.

M. SONNINO agreed, provided that the signature of the Treaty of Peace was not retarded.

M. CLEMENCEAU said he had received a despatch from Poland to the effect that the Polish Government were doing their best to prevent the peasants in Upper Silesia from being goaded into a rising against the Germans.

MR. LLOYD GEORGE said that riots must be expected, though he did not anticipate serious fighting. The German Government ought to be told that they would be held responsible.

M. CLEMENCEAU offered to bring all papers on the subject to the afternoon meeting.

PRESIDENT WILSON said that the sinking of the German ships at Scapa Flow had been a constant subject in his thoughts. The more he considered the matter, the more doubtful he felt. On the previous day he had met his four colleagues of the American Delegation, in order to learn their views. Mr. Lansing, who was a very experienced international lawyer, said he seriously doubted whether the German Government could be held responsible for

4 About this matter, see n. 12 to the minutes of the Council of Four printed at June 2, 1919, 4 p.m., Vol. 60.

something that had happened outside their jurisdiction. If the ships had been sunk on the High Seas, or in a German Port, his doubts would be removed, but he very much doubted whether the German Government could be held responsible in International Law for what had happened in Scapa Flow. About the responsibility of the German Admiral, he had no doubt. The Allied and Associated Powers were now about to make Peace. They were dealing with a people of such a character that this new act made no difference to our knowledge of it. Difficulties of this kind would often occur in connection with the carrying out of the Treaty. The Germans would be tricky and would perhaps often destroy things that they had undertaken to return, alleging that the destruction had been perpetrated by irresponsible persons over whom they had no control. Hence, it was necessary to face the issue as to whether if they did so, we were prepared to renew the war. All we could say at present was that the sinking of these ships was a violation of the Armistice. If we treated it as a violation of the Armistice, it would lead to an outbreak of war. He recalled that the Armistice continued in operation until the ratification of Peace by Germany and three of the Principal Allied and Associated Powers. Until these ratifications were deposited, the Armistice would prevail. To take any military action was to abrogate the Armistice and to create a state of war while we were awaiting ratification. It would be a very serious step after we had signed the Treaty of Peace, thus to abrogate the Armistice and renew the war.

M. CLEMENCEAU suggested that it would not be the Allies who renewed it.

PRESIDENT WILSON pointed out that if action was taken by the Allies, they would have to sweep the Armistice aside and there would be a state of war.

M. CLEMENCEAU did not agree in this. He pointed out that in the paper by the legal advisers, the action of the Germans gave the right to proceed to such further measures as the Allied and Associated Powers might deem appropriate.

MR. LLOYD GEORGE did not consider this would entitle them to occupy a city which was left to Germany under the terms of the Treaty of Peace, which had been signed.

M. CLEMENCEAU said that if something was not done, it would be taken in France as a great recoil and a surrender of victory.

M. SONNINO said that if action was taken *after* signing, it would be regarded as an act of violation of the Armistice undertaken by the Allies.

M. CLEMENCEAU said that there were two questions; one of International Law, and one of policy. As regards the first, the Council had all agreed yesterday that the action of the Germans constituted a violation of the Armistice. His own opinion was unchanged. The Allies were free to take note of it, or to say nothing about it, or to say it was an excellent thing, but they could not say it was not a violation of the Armistice. In his view, they were either forced to act, or otherwise to find some further means of protest. It was impossible for them to do otherwise. No Parliament in France would tolerate inaction. France alone had suffered from this action. Coming to the question of policy, President Wilson said he was not prepared to renew the war. The losses of the French had been greater than those of their Allies. In all quarters, demobilization was demanded. In the lobby, on the previous day, many Deputies had spoken to him of this. Consequently, he had no desire to re-open the war. But there was a great and supreme political interest at stake which prevailed over these considerations. Germany had shown every possible proof of bad faith at every point. She had committed a number of violations of the Armistice. Germany was not now in a position to resist, but if the Allies were to wait each time and take no action, the day would come when Germany would violate the Treaty of Peace, when the Allies were no longer together and when the soldiers had all been demobilized. Hence, in his view, this was the psychological moment at which to say that we insisted on proper reparation. To take action now would have a very great influence on the future doings of Germany. If this opportunity was lost, he begged President Wilson to remember that the Treaty would be in great danger.

MR. LLOYD GEORGE said he was most reluctant to intervene in this discussion. Although the British Admiralty had made the strongest possible protest against interning instead of surrendering the German Fleet, nevertheless, the ships had been sunk in a British Port and under British care. This was the reason of his reluctance. He had consulted such of his colleagues as were in Paris, and they were quite clear as to their views. It was not a question as to whether to allow flagrant violation of the Armistice by Germany to pass without protest, or for not exacting punishment or compensation. That was not the point. The real point was that the form of compensation should have some relation to the offence. Hence, the question arose as to whether in compensation for the sinking of the ships, the Allies were entitled to seize a town after the signature of Peace. This offence had taken place last Saturday. The Treaty would be signed a week later. In the meanwhile, the Treaty contained a precise definition of the areas of occupation. In these circumstances, to occupy other territory would be a little bit tricky.

If Essen was to be occupied, the Allies ought to do so now. The only reason we did not do so was because we were afraid the Germans would not sign. This was admitted in these conversations, and this was the reason why it was proposed not to tell them. At the present time the whole feeling of the world was against Germany, and their action at Scapa Flow, and more especially in burning the French flags, had accentuated this feeling. The burning of the flags was felt to be a wanton insult. But to get the Germans to sign, knowing perfectly well that after their signature we did not intend to adhere to the letter of the Treaty, but proposed to advance further into Germany, would outrage the sense of decent people. The position of British public opinion was different from that of the French, and he did not want to have trouble with it. The Germans were old enemies of the French, and were the enemies of the British for the first time. Although British public opinion had been solid to march to Berlin if the Germans would not sign, nevertheless, it must not be forgotten that there was some feeling against the Treaty, including a considerable feeling amongst intellectuals. He instanced Lord Robert Cecil and the two Archbishops.[5] What he wanted to avoid was causing a feeling that the Allies were not exacting justice, but were trampling on the fallen foe. Hence, he begged his colleagues not to advance into Germany after Peace had been signed.

M. CLEMENCEAU, interrupting, said that the French troops would never advance without the consent of their Allies.

MR. LLOYD GEORGE said that M. Clemenceau asked what was to be done. Would we allow the incident to pass? Certainly not, but whatever was done must be announced before the signature of peace. He would take the risk of that. First he would punish those who were responsible, and this would apply not only to the German Admiral, who should be court-martialled, but to those persons who had destroyed the flags, who should be put in the same category as the other Germans to be tried.

Secondly, he thought that the Allied and Associated Powers were entitled to relevant compensation. If some action of the same kind had taken place on land, no-one would ever dream of asking for compensation on the sea. The punishment must fit the crime, and consequently must be Naval. Two German ships of the first class had been saved, namely the battle-ship "Baden" and the battle-

<hr>

[5] That is, the Most Rev. Randall Thomas Davidson, Archbishop of Canterbury and Primate of All England, and the Most Rev. Cosmo Gordon Lang, Archbishop of York and Primate of England. About the wave of feeling against the alleged harshness of the treaty then sweeping over the United Kingdom, see A. Lentin, *Lloyd George, Woodrow Wilson and the Guilt of Germany: An Essay in the Pre-History of Appeasement* (Baton Rouge, La., 1984), pp. 132-54.

cruiser "Hindenburg," which he supposed was better than any battle-cruiser the British Navy had. He would say at once that as those
ships had been sunk in British ports, subject to the consent of his
colleagues, France must have first claim to them. To show the importance of battle-cruisers, he recalled that he had had a conversation during the war with Admiral Sims, who had pointed out that
in 1921 the Germans would have had a superiority in battle-cruisers, a superiority which could have been countered only by obtaining battle-cruisers from Japan. If the Germans had had a superiority of one battle-cruiser it would have been extremely difficult to
bring their fleet to action. In addition to the "Hindenburg" and the
"Baden," some light cruisers had been beached at Scapa, and he
would say at once that so far as the British Empire was concerned,
he waived all claim to them and would allow France to have them,
subject to the consent of his colleagues.

PRESIDENT WILSON interpolated that, for his part, he agreed.

MR. LLOYD GEORGE said that as regards the rest of the German
fleet, the report of the Admirals showed that it was of two categories. The first category consisted of some very useful light cruisers. Great Britain did not require these, and if France wished to
have them, he would support her claim. As regards the second category, they were said not to be of much value, but he recalled that
during the war old material had often proved to be useful. He did
not know what more he could offer. In regard to the flags, it was
more difficult to provide for compensation. He begged, however,
that France would on no account act alone in occupying some city.

M. CLEMENCEAU said he would not do so without the agreement
of the Allies.

MR. LLOYD GEORGE said that nothing could be more fatal. He did
not anticipate real trouble with Germany for at least ten years.

M. CLEMENCEAU thought he was wrong, and that trouble might
come at once.

MR. LLOYD GEORGE said that even if it were in five years, it was
just as important that the Allies should hold together.

He felt himself to be in the position of a supplicant, handicapped
by what had happened in a British port, but nevertheless he hoped
that France would not insist on any action being taken as a act of
retaliation after the signature of peace.

(M. Clemenceau withdrew at this point to speak to M. Fromageot, and on his return,)

MR. LLOYD GEORGE said that the British Government would give
up all claim to the German destroyers at Scapa Flow.

PRESIDENT WILSON said he would give expression to the fear that
had been in his mind for many weeks. So far as he could recall,

the Treaty of Peace only gave one method of securing compulsion on Germany for its execution, namely that the period of occupation could be extended by the Council of the League of Nations. He had asked himself, supposing Germany acts in bad faith and does not fulfil the Treaty what could we do? In his view, any exercise of force would be an act of war and the whole Treaty would be at an end. Everyone agreed that the action of the Germans at Scapa Flow had been a breach of the Armistice. But if we were to retaliate the Armistice would be off, and the war would be on.

MR. LLOYD GEORGE said that the action taken by the Germans on Saturday had been an act of war.

PRESIDENT WILSON said he thought the best plan was that proposed by Mr. Lloyd George, namely, to write to the Germans and tell them that the act of the German Admiral was a breach of the Armistice, and that he would be tried. Also that the Allies felt it right to demand that the German Government should make restitution as far as possible. We could not get more than Mr. Lloyd George had proposed, because the Germans had no more ships. He thought, however, that we ought to avoid military action or anything that would give the impression that we were renewing the war.

M. CLEMENCEAU said he had tried his best to agree with his colleagues, and he hoped that they would try to do something to agree with him. He had asked M. Fromageot whether the occupation of Essen would be a renewal of the war, and M. Fromageot had replied that it looked very much like it. It would be an act of reprisal. He would, therefore, let this drop, though he still thought, himself, that it was the best thing to do and that this fact would be especially decisive on the Polish question. There were three questions: first, the juridical question as to whether the Germans had broken the Armistice, and the Council were all agreed on this. Secondly, the question of punishment of the Admiral. They were agreed on this also. The third was the question of reparation in kind and in amount. He would acknowledge that if adequate reparation could be made in kind, this would be the best solution, but it was not easy to arrange and he did not think it was possible. He asked himself, however, whether France could not demand some of the mercantile marine left to Germany. M. Bérenger[6] had written him yesterday and said he ought to ask for some petroleum ships. He thought something might be done in this direction. He considered Mr. Lloyd George's proposals as to warships satisfactory in proportion to their number. Perhaps some others could be salved. His

---

[6] Victor-Henry Bérenger, Senator of Guadeloupe and General Commissioner for Petroleum.

idea to-day was to send the Germans a letter based on the text of the report from the Legal Advisers. He would accept this report subject to the few corrections as the basis of the letter to the Germans but would add a paragraph about the burning of the flags. He would add that the Allies would demand reparation as soon as the investigations they were making allowed them to do so. To-day he did not wish to go further than this. A remark of President Wilson's had put into his mind the thought that it might be useful to add a warning that if the Germans continued in this war it would be necessary for the Allies to consider the prolongation of the military occupation. This would make them think a good deal, and would be a certain compensation for public opinion in France. In the meanwhile, the naval experts should be asked to give further information about oil vessels and the merchant fleet. Consequently, he thought he was not so far from what President Wilson had proposed.

PRESIDENT WILSON then read the report by the Legal Advisers. (Appendix II.)[7]

It was agreed to adopt this as the basis of a letter to the German Delegation, subject to the following modifications:

In the following sentence:

"The destruction of these ships, instead of their preservation as has been provided, constituted at once a violation of the Armistice, the destruction of the pledge handed over, and an act of insubordination towards the Allied and Associated Powers,"

It was agreed to substitute the words "Gross breach of good faith, (felonie)" for "insubordination."

In Paragraph 3 it was agreed to insert the last sentence, beginning "As regards the question whether * * *" as an allusion to Article 31 of the Armistice Convention of November 11th, 1918, in some such terms as the following: "According to the principles acknowledged in Article 31 of the Armistice of November 11, 1918."

PRESIDENT WILSON said he would accept it provisionally, although he did not believe Article 31 was applicable.

M. SONNINO pointed out that even if the Article was not directly applicable, the principle might be applicable.

At the end of the first sentence of Para. 4, M. CLEMENCEAU suggested to add, after the word "appropriate," the following words: "as reparation for the loss caused."

(This was agreed to.)

M. CLEMENCEAU suggested an addition at the end of the memorandum in some such terms as the following:

---

[7] About which, see n. 4 to the minutes of the Council of Four printed at June 23, 1919, 4 p.m.

"The fact of sinking the German Fleet not only constitutes by itself a breach of the Armistice, but the burning of French flags in Berlin, taken in conjunction with it, constitutes a deliberate and systematic breach of the Articles of the Treaty of Peace. Consequently, the Allied and Associated Powers take official cognisance of these acts of breach of faith, and as soon as they have investigated all the circumstances of the act, they will demand the necessary reparation."

PRESIDENT WILSON proposed that an English and French speaking person should be nominated by the Council to draft a letter to the Germans on the above basis. He proposed that the final sentence should be put in some such manner as the following:

"These articles are in effect a breach of the terms of the Treaty in anticipation, and inevitably create an impression that shakes the confidence of the Allied and Associated Powers in the good faith of the Germans, and makes it necessary to warn them of the consequences."

M. CLEMENCEAU urged that the prolongation of the period of occupation should be specifically referred to.

PRESIDENT WILSON suggested some such phrase as the following:

"Makes it necessary to suggest the probable necessity of resorting to the means provided for in the Treaty of Peace."

He thought, however, it would be advisable to leave the matter to the Drafting Committee.

(It was agreed that Mr. Balfour and M. Loucheur should prepare a letter to the Germans, based on the above discussion.)

M. Loucheur, accompanied by Mr. Hurst and M. Fromageot, entered the room to receive instructions from M. Clemenceau.

MR. LLOYD GEORGE undertook to communicate with Mr. Balfour.

3. Arrangements for Signing the Treaty.

M. CLEMENCEAU said that the Germans would arrive on Friday morning, but their credentials would first have to be checked.

MR. LLOYD GEORGE said that he had been informed that a telegram received on the previous day by the German Delegation had caused great hilarity. It was rumoured that the Germans were sending some persons of minor importance to sign the Treaty. He recalled that they had attempted the same thing in connection with the Armistice, and suggested that an immediate demand should be made to them to state who their delegates would be.

M. CLEMENCEAU sent for M. Dutasta and instructed him to make this demand immediately to the Germans.

4. Polish Treaty.

The following resolution was approved and initialled by the five

Heads of Governments, and given to Captain Portier, who accompanied the Secretary-General:

"The Secretary-General of the Peace Conference is instructed to make the necessary arrangements for the signature of the Treaty with Poland not later than the signature of the Treaty of Peace with Germany."

T MS (SDR, RG 256, 180.03401/91, DNA).

Hankey's and Mantoux's Notes of a Meeting of the Council of Four[1]

President Wilson's House, Paris,
C.F.92.   June 25, 1919, 4 p.m.

1. (M. Dutasta, Secretary-General of the Peace Conference, was introduced.)

M. DUTASTA, said that he had seen von Haniel, who told him he had telegraphed twice to Berlin asking who the German representatives would be and when they were due to arrive, but had received no answer. Von Haniel had added that the German Government had removed from Weimar to Berlin and that their first Cabinet Council in Berlin was to be held this morning. On the conclusion of that, he expected an answer. M. Dutasta had asked him to communicate again and he had promised to do so immediately. According to von Haniel, the German Government was encountering great difficulty in finding persons ready to sign the Treaty. He had made von Haniel understand that an answer was expected this evening, or tomorrow at the latest.

M. CLEMENCEAU instructed M. Dutasta to proceed to Versailles tomorrow morning at 9 a.m. unless he had heard in the meanwhile from Colonel Henri.

2. Shipping for the French Colonies.

M. MANTOUX said that M. Tardieu was in attendance to obtain a decision of principle on a point connected with the desire of the French Government to be allowed to buy or to borrow United States ships for communication with the French Colonies, for which France had a great insufficiency of shipping.

M. CLEMENCEAU said the question should first be sent to experts.

(It was agreed, on President Wilson's suggestion:

That M. Tardieu should arrange for a joint memorandum to be prepared by the experts of the Allied and Associated Powers.)

3. Ratification of the Treaty of Peace.

[1] The complete text of Hankey's minutes is printed in *PPC*, VI, 669-96.

M. CLEMENCEAU, in reply to Mr. Lloyd George, said it was his intention to hand the Treaty of Peace to Parliament as soon as possible after the signature. He would not make any explanatory speech and the next step would be for the examination of the Treaty by the Commissions of the Chamber and Senate. He did not expect to make his own statement until after the various Commissions had reported, perhaps not for three weeks.

PRESIDENT WILSON said that he, himself, would leave Paris immediately after the signature of the Treaty. As soon as he arrived in the United States, he would take the Treaty to Congress.

M. CLEMENCEAU thought there were advantages in President Wilson making the first speech on the subject.

PRESIDENT WILSON said that, in his country, questions would then be asked as to why other Governments had done nothing.

MR. LLOYD GEORGE said the he could fit in his speech about the same time as President Wilson's, although he was anxious to be away for the second and third weeks after his arrival in England.

M. SONNINO said that the responsibility would be with the new Italian Government, but he thought there was little doubt they would proceed as rapidly as possible. In view of the necessity of reports by Commissions, probably a fortnight or so would elapse before the Treaty could be ratified.

4. Penalties and Prisoners.

MR. LLOYD GEORGE brought forward a proposal he had received from Sir Ernest Pollock, the English Solicitor-General, suggesting that, in the light of the experience gained at Scapa Flow and the burning of French flags, steps should be taken to make the execution of Clauses 214 to 224 (Repatriation of Prisoners) and Clauses 227 to 230 (Penalties) interdependent. (Appendix I.)[2]

(It was generally agreed that this suggestion was a useful one and should be taken note of, but that no immediate decision should be taken for its adoption.)

5. Trial of the Kaiser.

MR. LLOYD GEORGE suggested to his colleagues that the Trial of the Kaiser should take place in some Allied country removed from those where resentment at the Kaiser was naturally the most acute. He suggested that either Great Britain or the United States of America would be the most advantageous from this point of view.

PRESIDENT WILSON suggested that the Trial of the Kaiser should not take place in any great city.

M. CLEMENCEAU said he would like to consult his colleagues on the subject and would give a reply on the following day.

[2] Printed in *ibid.*, p. 679.

6. MR. LLOYD GEORGE read the attached note from Admiral Hope regarding the disposition of unsurrendered German and Austrian surface ships and submarines. (Appendix II.)[3]

SIR MAURICE HANKEY pointed out that a report had already been furnished by the Allied Admirals in regard to submarines, Admiral de Bon having made a minority report.

(It was agreed that:

The Allied Admirals should be asked to prepare a report advising the Council of the Principal Allied and Associated Powers as to what course they now recommend on all three heads.)

7. M. CLEMENCEAU adverted to the point he had raised at the morning meeting, namely, that France should be compensated for the loss she had incurred by the sinking of German ships at Scapa Flow, by being given some of the remaining German merchant ships and particularly oil tankers.

(It was agreed:

That a Commission, composed as follows:

Mr. Baruch for the United States of America,
Mr. Hipwood[4] (or representative) for the
British Empire,
M. Monet[5] (or representative) for France,
M. Crespi (or representative) for Italy, and
A Japanese representative to be nominated
by Baron Makino,

should meet to consider the possibility of exacting from Germany some reparation for the sinking of warships at Scapa Flow in the form of further merchant ships, special consideration being given to the case of oil tank vessels.)

8. PRESIDENT WILSON read the following questions presented by the Superior Blockade Council:

1. Does the Supreme Council, in view of the authorisation given by the Weimar Assembly to the German Delegates, desire that all restrictions upon trade with Germany shall be rescinded immediately upon the signature of the Treaty of Peace by the German Delegation?

2. If not, upon what date shall these restrictions be rescinded?

3. When is the German Delegation expected to sign? If the Supreme Council desires that the blockade restrictions shall be raised upon the signature of the Treaty by the German Delegates and if the signature is likely to take place on Saturday, it is de-

[3] Printed in *ibid.*, p. 680.
[4] That is, Charles Hipwood, Assistant Secretary of the Board of Trade and an adviser on economic questions in the British delegation.
[5] That is, Jean Omer Marie Gabriel Monnet, French representative on the Allied Maritime Transport Council.

sirable that the Blockade Council should be so informed today. At least two days are required in which to terminate the present restrictions.

At M. CLEMENCEAU's request the following note prepared by M. Mantoux, was read:

"Provision ought to be made for the eventuality of the German Government signing the Treaty of Peace, but delaying its ratification in the hope to embarrass the Allies and to take advantage of any incidents that might arise.

In 1871, it was stipulated by Art. 3 of the Preliminaries of Peace that the German troops were to evacuate Paris and the forts on the left bank of the Seine immediately after the act of ratification. Much to the surprise of the Germans, the Preliminaries, which had been signed on February 26th, 1871, were ratified by the Bordeaux Assembly as soon as March 1st, and the exchange of ratifications took place at Versailles the day after. Paris was evacuated at once, after less than two days of occupation, and the triumphal entry of William I, which had been prepared for March 3rd, was cancelled.

It may be useful today to remind the Germans of the fact that the blockade shall cease at the same moment as the state of war, and that legally what brings the state of war to an end is the exchange of ratifications. But for the sake of humanity, the Allied and Associated Governments may concede that as soon as they have been officially notified of the ratification of the treaty by the National Assembly of Germany the blockade shall be raised.

Such a declaration would encourage Germany to ratify the Treaty without delay, without fixing a narrow time limit to the debates in the representative Assemblies of the Allied and Associated countries."

MR. LLOYD GEORGE said that this seemed reasonable.

PRESIDENT WILSON reminded his colleagues of his reluctance to make women and children suffer for matters over which they exercised no influence. Nevertheless, the course proposed seemed the best in the circumstances.

M. CLEMENCEAU said that in the Rhine provinces there was little hardship.

PRESIDENT WILSON said that in the interior of Germany Mr. Hoover reported great shortage.

(It was agreed:

That the Blockade should cease on the same date as the ratification of the Treaty of Peace, as provided for at the end of the Treaty.)[6]

_____

[6] At about this point, the following exchange occurred:

9. MR. LLOYD GEORGE suggested that a special Committee should be set up to consider the working out of the various measures for putting the Treaty of Peace with Germany into effect.

(The proposal was accepted in principle, and it was agreed that the members should be designated on the following day.)

10. With reference to C.F.83,[7] Minute 3, the Council had before them a report by the Commission on Baltic affairs on the question submitted to it by the Council on the 23rd June, as to the effect which the evacuation of the Baltic Provinces by Germany would have on the food supplies in this region, in the event of the removal of the rolling stock by the Germans. (Appendix III.)

PRESIDENT WILSON after reading the report aloud, suggested that the second proposal of the Commission should be adopted, but he considered that the first proposal to take advantage of Article 375 of the Treaty of Peace with Germany was not feasible. He suggested that Marshal Foch should be asked to take the necessary action through the Armistice Commission.

(It was agreed that a copy of the Memorandum by the Baltic Commission should be sent to Marshal Foch, who should be asked to demand from the Germans that when evacuating the Baltic provinces they should leave behind the German railway material now in these provinces as part of the railway material which Germany was bound to deliver to the Allies in accordance with the terms of Clause VII of the Armistice of November 11, 1918, and which has not yet been delivered. The railway material so left would legally be the property of the Allied and Associated Powers and not of the Baltic States.

It was further agreed that it was to the interest of the Allied Powers to secure the restoration as soon as possible in the Baltic Provinces of the Russian gauge on the railways in view of the closer economic connections of these provinces with Russia than with Germany.)

11. The Council had before them a report from the Commission on Baltic Affairs, covering the recommendation made by the United States, British and French representatives at Libau. (Appendix IV.)

PRESIDENT WILSON, after reading the Report and enclosure aloud, remarked that the programme unhappily was not one that was practicable.

"Clemenceau (to Wilson). I am satisfied. You see I am not so difficult to deal with.
"Wilson. You never were.
"Clemenceau. It is what some people have reproach[ed] to me.
"Wilson. No matter for reproach. It is an admirable thing."
Written on the back of Mantoux's notes for this meeting (Hw MS in possession of Jacques Mantoux).
[7] The minutes of the Council of Four printed at June 23, 1919, 11 a.m.

MR. LLOYD GEORGE commented on the fact that peoples fighting for their liberties wanted to have even their soldiers paid by the Allies.

PRESIDENT WILSON said that probably they had no resources for paying them themselves.

MR. LLOYD GEORGE read a telegram from the British Commission at Helsingfors in regard to the complicated position that had arisen involving fighting betweeen Esthonians and Latvians.

(In the course of a short discussion it was pointed out

1. That a military mission of the Allied & Associated Powers under General Gough has already been sent to the Baltic Provinces.

2. That Marshal Foch has already ordered the Germans to evacuate the Baltic Provinces under the terms of the Armistice of November 11, 1918.

3. That the Council has sanctioned supplies being given to the Baltic Provinces, and that General Gough has been asked to advise as to what these supplies should consist of, as a preliminary to arrangements being made as to who was to give the supplies.

It was agreed that no further financial assistance to the Baltic Provinces could be at present given.)

12. Following on the remarks he had made at the morning meeting, C.F.91,[8] Minute 2,

MR. LLOYD GEORGE proposed the text of a note to the German Delegation in regard to their intrigues on the Eastern frontier.

After the note had been read and a few suggestions made, it was approved and signed by M. Clemenceau on behalf of the Allied and Associated Powers in the attached form. (Appendix V.)

(It was agreed that the letter and the enclosure should be published.)

13. MR. LLOYD GEORGE said that the present military position in Russia was that Koltchak's thrust, intended eventually to reach Moscow had failed. The intention had been as a first step to unite at Kotlas with the forces based at Archangel. The Bolshevists there had driven Koltchak's army back. Meanwhile, in the south Denikin had inflicted a severe defeat on Koltchak (?) The Don Cossacks had risen, and had taken 50,000 prisoners and 300 guns from the Bolshevists, and were now just outside Tsaritzen. Hence the latest information was that Koltchak was doing badly but that Denikin had routed his adversaries.

14. MR. LLOYD GEORGE said he had received a note from Mr. Churchill (Appendix VI) submitting a proposal for cooperation of the Czecho-Slovak troops in Siberia with the right wing of Admiral

[8] That is, the minutes of the preceding meeting.

Koltchak's army, and requesting that the matter might be dealt with as one of extreme urgency.

(It was agreed that the question should be referred to the military representatives of the Supreme War Council at Versailles, a Japanese and Czecho-Slovak military representative being added for the purpose.)

15. M. CLEMENCEAU said that he had received a letter from the Chinese Delegation stating that they would sign the Treaty of Peace with Germany, with a reservation relating to Shantung. He had replied that they must either sign the Treaty with the intention of abiding by it or not sign. They were just as much bound to honour their signature as the Germans were.

PRESIDENT WILSON said that Mr Lansing had spoken to him of this, and had said that any sovereign Power could make reservations in signing.

M. CLEMENCEAU reminded President Wilson that when the Roumanian and the Serb-Croat-Slovene Delegations had spoken of signing with reservations, they had been asked to say what they intended by this. A Treaty which was signed with reservations was not a Treaty.

MR LLOYD GEORGE pointed out that the Italians had said they made certain reservations, but they would sign the German Treaty without any reservation.

BARON MAKINO said that the Japanese Delegation had objected to many of the decisions of Commissions, but had bowed to the decision of the majority. The Treaty would have no effect if anyone could make reservations.

PRESIDENT WILSON suggested that someone should be asked to enquire from the Chinese Delegation what was reserved and what was intended by their reservation. If it was merely a protest, they were entitled to make this. He understood the Chinese Delegation were acting under specific instructions from their Government.

M. CLEMENCEAU instructed Captain Portier to ask M. Pichon to see a representative of the Chinese Delegation and to enquire the subjects on which they were making reservations, and whether their reservation amounted to more than a protest.

(Captain Portier telephoned this decision immediately to the Quai d'Orsay.)

16. MR LLOYD GEORGE asked that the question of Turkey might be considered. President Wilson would shortly be leaving. It was unreasonable to maintain a state of war with Turkey for the next two months. Would it not be possible, he asked, to agree on some Peace Terms which would put Turkey out of her misery, outlining the frontiers of Turkey, but leaving the final dispositions of the ter-

ritory that had not to remain Turkish until it was known whether the United States would accept a mandate.

PRESIDENT WILSON agreed that the final dispositions of Turkey ought not to be left for two months. His colleagues knew his mind on the subject, and could discuss the future arrangements of Turkey. He suggested that the portions which Turkey was to lose might be cut off and the Treaty might provide that she should accept the dispositions of the Allied and Associated Powers in regard to them, just as had been done in the case of Austria.

M. CLEMENCEAU pointed out that this involved the question of Constantinople.

PRESIDENT WILSON said that the amputations would involve Mesopotamia, Syria and Armenia. The Allied troops would remain there to keep order until the final settlement between the Allied and Associated Powers.

MR LLOYD GEORGE asked what would be done about Armenia. There were no Allied troops there. Turkey at present had some responsibility for the maintenace of order. If Armenia was cut off from Turkey, the Turkish troops would be withdrawn, and the Armenians would be left at the mercy of the Kurds. It would involve putting in some garrisons.

M. CLEMENCEAU asked what would be done about the Italians in Asia-Minor.

PRESIDENT WILSON said that this would not concern the Turks. He thought some formula might be worked out.

MR LLOYD GEORGE said that the district in question either belonged to the Turks or it did not. If it did, the Turk would say: "What are the Italians doing here?", and the Allies could only reply that the Italian occupation had been made without their knowledge or consent.

M. SONNINO demurred to this statement.

PRESIDENT WILSON said that his proposal in regard to Turkey would be to cut off all that Turkey was to give up; and to oblige Turkey to accept any conditions with regard to over-sight or direction which the Allied and Associated Governments might agree to. His present view was that a mandate over Turkey would be a mistake, but he thought some Power ought to have a firm hand. Constantinople and the Straits should be left as a neutral strip for the present, and it was already in Allied occupation. He would make the Sultan and his Government move out of Constantinople and he would say what was ceded to the Allied and Associated Powers. He was only arguing now as to what could be legally settled as a basis for a Treaty, and he was not attempting to decide an ultimate settlement. He only proposed an arrangement similar to what was being made in the case of Austria.

MR LLOYD GEORGE pointed out that this involved the question of whether the Turk was to go out of Constantinople.

PRESIDENT WILSON said that so far as his judgment was concerned, that was decided. He had studied the question of the Turks in Europe for a long time, and every year confirmed his opinion that they ought to be cleared out.

17. MR. LLOYD GEORGE said he had received a telegram from Feisal in regard to the United States Mission[9] complaining of a breach of faith that the Commission was not an Allied Commission. Feisal had interpreted a telegram that General Allenby had sent him, as suggesting that Great Britain would take a mandate for Syria if no other Power would do so. At his request, Mr Balfour had drafted a telegram to General Allenby stating in the most specific terms that in no circumstances would Great Britain take this mandate, and calling his attention to Mr Lloyd George's statement on this subject made at an earlier Meeting in General Allenby's presence.

18. PRESIDENT WILSON said that the hour was approaching when some demand would have to be made to Holland in regard to the surrender of the Kaiser. He was anxious that the demand should be made in such a form as would relieve Holland of any appearance of breach of hospitality.

MR. LLOYD GEORGE pointed out that a new principle was involved in this Treaty. A great crime had been perpetrated against the nations of the world. It had taken five years to bring this question to fruition, and the Allies could not afford to allow Holland to stand in the way.

PRESIDENT WILSON agreed that Holland was morally obliged to surrender the Kaiser, but he wished to make it as easy for her as possible.

M. CLEMENCEAU said he would be surprised if Holland objected.

(It was agreed that Mr Lansing, who had acted as Chairman on the Commission on Responsibilities, should be asked to draft for the consideration of the Council, a despatch to the Dutch Government. President Wilson undertook to inform Mr Lansing.)

19. The Council took formal note of the attached Note prepared for them by the Drafting Committee. (Appendix VII.)[10]

20. The Council approved the attached Note to the Polish Government submitted by the Council of Foreign Ministers, (Appendix VIII).

[9] That is, the King-Crane Commission. Faisal's telegram is missing in the British Foreign Office Archives. The two other telegrams mentioned in this paragraph are printed in E. L. Woodward and Rohan Butler, eds., *Documents on British Foreign Policy, 1919-1939*, First Series, Vol. IV (London, 1952), pp. 276, 298-99.
[10] Printed in PPC, VI, 686. It informed the Council of Four that a list of all errata in the treaty of peace with Germany had been sent to the German delegation.

The following Note was signed by the four Heads of Governments:

"25 Juin, 1919.

GOUVERNEMENT POLONAIS, VARSOVIE.

En vue de garantir les personnes et les biens de la population paisible de Galicie orientale contre les dangers que leur font courir les bandes bolchévistes, le Conseil Suprême des Puissances alliées et associées a décidé d'autoriser les forces de la République Polonaise à poursuivre leurs opérations jusqu'à la rivière Zbruck.

Cette autorisation ne préjuge en rien les décisions que le Conseil Suprême prendra ultérieurement pour régler le statut politique de la Galicie."

(The Note was signed by the representatives of the Five Powers, and was communicated by Captain Portier to a messenger who had brought it from the Council of Foreign Ministers.)

21. With reference to C.F.83,[11] Minute 1, the Council agreed that the final text of the Note to the Turkish Government, together with the document read by the Turkish Delegation to the Council of Ten,[12] should be published after it had been sent to the Turks. (Appendix IX.)[13]

22. The Council had before them the Note from the Turkish Delegation dated June 23rd, which was read aloud by President Wilson. (Appendix X.)[14]

(It was generally agreed that the document was not a very serious one.)

MR LLOYD GEORGE asked that before a reply was sent, a full discussion on the Turkish question should take place. It would be a great advantage if a short, sharp Peace with Turkey could be decided on while the Turkish Delegation were still in Paris.

M. CLEMENCEAU said he was not very hopeful of reaching a result.

(The proposal was agreed to.)

§ Mantoux's notes:

Reading of the memorandum from the Turkish delegation "on the new organization of the Ottoman Empire":

(Summary.) Despite the interests and traditions of friendship which it bears toward the western powers, Turkey was led into a disastrous war. Memory glorifies the past of Turkey, recalling that

---

[11] The minutes of the Council of Four printed at June 23, 1919, 11 a.m.
[12] About which, see n. 4 to the minutes of the Council of Four printed at June 21, 1919, 4 p.m.
[13] It is identical with Balfour's draft of this note summarized in n. 3, *ibid.*
[14] Printed in *PPC*, VI, 691-94. Mantoux summarizes it below.

she knew how to form and administer a great empire, that in it she respected the existence of all religious communities, and that she entered on to the path of reform as soon as she came into contact with the West. Turkey only desires to continue her advance toward progress.

The problems of the Ottoman Empire divide themselves into three parts: (1) in Thrace; (2) in Asia Minor; (3) in Arabia.

1. Thrace. To assure a lasting peace, it is important that Adrianople be better protected against eventual attacks. The Turks are, moreover, in the majority in western Thrace—today Bulgarian. Turkey requests that her frontier be moved forward as far as the Kara-Su, which flows into the sea across from the island of Thasos.

2. All of Asia Minor, as well as the neighboring islands of the coast, must remain Turkish. If the Armenian Republic of Erivan— former Russian Armenia—is recognized by the Allied and Associated Powers, its frontier can be determined by a common agreement, and all facilities will be given to the Armenians of the Ottoman Empire who wish to establish themselves on its territory. Just and equitable treatment will be assured to all minorities inside the Ottoman Empire.

3. The Arab countries will receive large administrative autonomy, under the sovereignty of the Sultan, who will name their governors, a special regime being provided for Mecca. The Turkish flag will fly over all these regions, justice will be rendered in the name of the Sultan, and currency printed with his effigy.

From the time of the signature of the treaty, the Allied troops will be withdrawn from Ottoman Territories, except where, by common agreement, it would be recognized that their presence is necessary to maintain order. Further, the Ottoman government declares itself ready to settle definitively, in the most amicable spirit, the legal status of Egypt and the island of Cyprus.

The peoples of the Ottoman Empire will not accept the division of their territories, nor the establishment of a system of mandates. All are attached to the Ottoman government, and the latter receives protests from everywhere in favor of the unity and independence of the Empire.

Lloyd George. That delegation and its memorandum are good jokes.

Wilson. I have never seen anything more stupid.

Lloyd George. It is the best proof of the complete political incapacity of the Turks. They have always placed men of other races at the head of their government.

Wilson. Is it necessary to reply to a document of this kind?

Lloyd George. Our reply is already made by Mr. Balfour's letter.

I propose to acknowledge receipt of this memorandum and to say to the Turkish delegation: "You can go home."

Wilson. Besides, the Turks only came here to explan their views. We are not bound to answer them.

Clemenceau. We must reply as a formality. Is it necessary to see them?

Lloyd George. In any case, they must be dismissed in one way or another. I propose to devote a morning in the near future to the discussion of the Turkish question. We will see if we can arrive at a solution, and, in that case, there could be reason to inform the Turkish delegates.

Wilson. The solution which we will reach has nothing to do with these three ridiculous people.

Lloyd George. If we could only make peace summarily and finish with it.

Clemenceau. I really fear that that is not possible. §

23. (It was agreed that, if possible, the questions of Reparation and Finance in the Austrian Treaty, which were at present the result of negotiation with the New States formerly forming part of the Austro-Hungarian Empire, should be considered on the morrow.)

24. Sinking of German Ships.

The Council had before them a draft letter to the German Delegation prepared by Mr Balfour and M. Loucheur, with the assistance of M. Fromageot and Mr Hurst.

(The letter was approved with the substitution in the seventh paragraph of the word "justification" for the word "explanation" (Appendix XI.)

(It was agreed that the letter should be sent to the Germans immediately, and published in the newspapers on Thursday, June 26th.)

25. MR LLOYD GEORGE insisted on the importance of settling the form of the Mandates.

PRESIDENT WILSON agreed, but said he wished to read the question up.

APPENDIX III TO C.F.92.

Report of the Commission on Baltic Affairs.

The Commission on Baltic Affairs has considered the question submitted to it by the Council of the Principal Allied and Associated Powers on the 23rd June on the effect which the evacuation of the Baltic Provinces by Germany would have on the food supplies in this region in the event of the removal of the rolling stock by the Germans.

The Commission are unanimous in the opinion that it is indispensable to prevent this removal. There does not, however, appear to be in the text of the Armistice any article specially applicable to this case. The Commission considers that advantage might usefully be taken of Article 375 of the Treaty of Peace with Germany. They consider that from the moment at which Germany has declared her intention of signing the Treaty the Allied Powers are in a position at once to inform her of their intention to make use of this Article in order to secure the movements of troops, transport and material and the supply of relief in the Baltic Provinces.

The result of such a notification will be that in the event of Germany removing rolling stock, even if the ratification of the Treaty is postponed for some days, this removal will forthwith constitute a formal violation of the Treaty comparable to certain other actions of the Germans, such as the destruction of the German Fleet at Scapa Flow, and of the flags to be surrendered to France. Germany could be called to account for this violation of the Treaty. In order to facilitate the retention of the material, which is of great importance, the possibility might be considered of reckoning this material as part of that which Germany was bound to deliver to the Allies in accordance with the clauses of the Armistice and which has not yet been delivered. In this way the material would be delivered in the east instead of the west and would be at once available on the spot. It should at the same time be noted that legally this material would be the property of the Allies and not of the Baltic States.

The Commission further consider that it is to the interest of the Allied Powers to secure the restoration as soon as possible in the Baltic Provinces of the Russian gauge on the railways in view of the closer economic connexions of these provinces with Russia than with Germany.

For this reason the proposed solution would be provisional and would not exclude the speedy and final restoration to the Allied and Associated Powers of the material left in this district.
25th June, 1919.

APPENDIX IV TO C.F.92.

Recommendation by Commission on Baltic Affairs.

The Commission on Baltic Affairs submits herewith to the Supreme Council of the Principal Allied and Associated Powers the text of a recommendation made by the French, British and American representatives at Libau, and communicated to the Commission by the American representative who has been sent from Libau as spokesman of the Allied representatives.

The supreme importance for a future peace of Europe that Germany should not obtain a permanent hold on the Baltic Provinces through which she would open the door to getting a predominant influence in Russia appears to the Commission to be beyond question. It is proved by various papers communicated to the Commission and by information received from the representatives of the Allied and Associated Governments on the spot that this is clearly the ultimate aim of her present policy and actions in the Baltic Provinces. On the other hand, the Bolshevik danger is equally serious. In these circumstances the Commission, while feeling that the enclosed recommendation, which includes the suggestion of a credit, is beyond their competence, feel it their duty to draw the earnest attention of the Council to the situation as explained therein, and to endorse the view expressed as to the necessity of providing immediate financial assistance if any policy is to be adopted which can give any hope of eradicating German domination in the Baltic Provinces, and meet the danger of Bolshevism breaking through to the Baltic and Scandinavia.

JUNE 24th, 1919.

In view of the extremely critical position in the Baltic Provinces, the British and American Political representatives, with the British and French Commodores here, have to-day agreed on the following statement:

"No question is more vital than the arrest of the movement of Prussia towards the North and East. At the same time the Bolshevik danger must not be under-estimated. The greatest immediate danger lies in the clash north of Riga, between troops, especially Letts, moving South from Esthonia and Germans and Balts moving North from Riga. Provided that the Associated Governments are in a position to enforce their demands, the Germans should be required, under penalty, of which the execution should immediately follow upon non-compliance, to refrain absolutely from advancing further northwards in the district north of Riga. In the absence of the Allied Military Mission, we feel otherwise unable to recommend the exact measures by which the advance of Prussian forces in the Baltic Provinces should be checked and their withdrawal secured.

"The first need of the situation is the arrival of the Allied Military Mission. It is, however, requested that the political representatives of America, France and Great Britain in the Baltic Provinces may be authorised to make a united statement immediately. It is suggested that the statement should as nearly as possible take the following form:

" 'An Inter-Allied Military Mission, under command of a British General, will reach the Baltic Provinces immediately. Arms, equipment, instructors and pay will be provided for local forces, and for volunteers who may be raised from external sources, in so far as this may be determined by the head of the military mission, to be necessary for the protection of the Provinces against Bolshevism or for other purposes of defence. The local distribution of such supplies will depend upon the loyal acceptance by the forces named of the general direction of the head of the Inter-Allied Military Mission in their fight against Bolshevism, their methods of recruitment and their relations between each other and with the German and Polish forces.

" 'A loan will be granted immediately to Lithuania and Esthonia respectively for civil purposes, on condition that the provisional Governments concerned will undertake to lay before the political representatives of the Associated Governments in their countries, their proposals for the use of the money thus raised, and that no such proposal is carried out without their approval. On such an arrangement being concluded the blockade of Lithuania would be raised. It is intended that this loan should in particular be used for the provision of the materials required for the restoration of industry and agriculture and the reduction of unemployment. A loan on similar terms will be granted to Latvia as soon as a provisional coalition Government has been formed, which, in the opinion of the political representatives of the Associated Governments in Latvia, is truly representative of the inhabitants of the country. On such an arrangement being concluded, the blockade of Latvia will also be raised.' "

This statement was agreed to by:

Commodore Duff,[15] R.N. Senior British Naval Officer, Libau.

Commodore Brisson,[16] Senior French Naval Officer in the Baltic.

Lt. Colonel Warwick Greene, U.S.A. Chief of American Mission.[17]

Lt. Colonel Tallents, Chief of British Economic Mission.[18]

Libau, June 7, 1919

APPENDIX V TO C.F.92.

LETTER FROM THE ALLIED AND ASSOCIATED POWERS
TO THE GERMAN DELEGATES.

M. le Président,

The Allied and Associated Powers feel it necessary to direct the attention of the German Government to the fact that the Polish authorities have come into possession of the attached official Ger-

[15] Arthur Allen Morison Duff.
[16] The Editors have been unable to find his given name or names.
[17] To Finland, Estonia, Latvia, and Lithuania.
[18] Stephen George Tallents.

man despatch[19] which states that while the German Government mean to sign the Peace, they intend to give unofficial support by all the means in their power to local movements of resistance to the establishment of Polish authority in the territories allotted to Poland in Posen, and in East and West Prussia, and to the occupation of Upper Silesia by the Allied and Associated Powers. In view of this information the Allied and Associated Powers think it necessary to inform the German Government that they will hold them strictly responsible for seeing that, at the time indicated in the Treaty, all troops and all officials indicated by the Allied Commission, are withdrawn, and that in the event of local disturbances in resistance to the Treaty no support or assistance to the insurgents is allowed to pass across the new frontier into Poland.

(Signed)   G. CLEMENCEAU.

June 25th, 1919.

APPENDIX VI TO C.F.92.
MEMORANDUM BY MR WINSTON CHURCHILL.

The recent reverses sustained by Admiral Koltchak's forces have led to the consideration of the various means which might be employed with a view to restoring the situation on the front held by the Siberian armies. One possible course is the re-employment on the front of a portion of the Czecho-Slovak troops now distributed along the Trans-Siberian Railway.

As the result of an interchange of views between the Secretary of State for War[20] and Dr. Benes, the following definite proposal is put forward for consideration, and attention is drawn to the fact that should the plan be approved, it is necessary that orders for its execution should be issued with the least possible delay, so that the project can be carried through to completion before the port of Archangel becomes ice-bound.

II. The scheme is as follows:

The Allied and Associated Governments should inform the Government of the Czecho-Slovak Republic that they are prepared to accept responsibility for the repatriation of all the Czecho-Slovak troops now in Siberia on the following basis:

(a) 30,000 men should take part in an operation on the right wing of Admiral Koltchak's army with a view to establishing a junction with the Archangel forces by advancing via Viatka and Kotlas to Archangel, whence they will be repatriated before the end of the current year.

(b) The remainder of the Czecho-Slovak troops to be moved

[19] This document does not accompany the minutes.
[20] That is, Churchill.

gradually to Vladivostok and to be embarked for Europe early in 1920, the 5,000 men already at Vladivostok to be shipped as soon as possible.

III. Action on the above lines offers several very considerable advantages:

(a) The effecting of a junction between Admiral Koltchak's armies and the Archangel forces during the period when it is anticipated that the British will be in occupation of Kotlas.

(b) The consequential establishment of the Russian forces and Government in North Russia on a self-supporting basis after the withdrawal of the Allied units.

(c) The relief of the dangerous situation now developing in Central Siberia through the presence of the discontented Czecho-Slovak troops.

(d) The strengthening of the Czecho-Slovak Government at Prague by the return of the troops from Siberia.

IV. Dr. Benes has been consulted with regard to the proposal and believes that his government would view it favourably provided that they were furnished with definite assurances as to the time and method of repatriating all the Czecho-Slovak troops now in Siberia.

V. It is necessary to take into account the fact that the morale of these troops has been seriously impaired by their long stay in Siberia, and it is clear that the project can only be proceeded with on the assumption that the prospect of repatriation will restore the morale of the elements destined for Archangel sufficiently to enable them to take part in operations against the Bolsheviks.

VI. It should be recognised from the outset that, owing to the lateness of the season, there is ground for doubt as to whether the Czecho-Slovak troops advancing by Viatka are likely to reach Archangel in time for repatriation before the winter 1919, as is shown by the following rough estimates of time and space:

It is estimated that 30,000 troops could not be concentrated in the region of Perm before the middle of August.

The distance from Perm to Viatka as the crow flies is 250 miles, and as it is probable that the troops would have to fight their way throughout this distance, the operation would almost certainly not be completed under five weeks, even making full allowances for the nature of the fighting likely to occur.

From Viatka to Kotlas is another 220 miles, and although it is possible that very little opposition would be met with between these two places, the railway would almost certainly be destroyed by the Bolsheviks, and at least three weeks should be allowed for the completion of this part of the movement.

Thus, assuming that all went well, the Czecho-Slovaks would

reach the Dvina at Kotlas about the middle of October. The port of Archangel is closed by ice about the middle of November, but in ordinary seasons can be kept open by ice-breakers for another month.

It will be seen from the above that the possibility of the troops reaching Archangel too late for repatriation before the winter must be faced, but this consideration is out-weighed by the great advantages which are offered by the proposal as set forth in Paragraph 3.

VII. If the proposal is accepted by the Allied and Associated Powers, action appears to be necessary as follows:

(a) To obtain the consent of the Czecho-Slovak Government, and that that Government should transmit the necessary orders to the Czecho-Slovak troops in Siberia, explaining clearly what is proposed, in the manner best calculated to secure their immediate compliance.

(b) That the French Government should make the necessary communication to General Janin,[21] who should arrange for

(c) Admiral Koltchak to organise an advance on Viatka of the right flank of General Gayda's[22] army after being re-inforced by the Czecho-Slovaks, who, after reaching Viatka, would be pushed through to Kotlas and thence to Archangel.

(d) Sanction to be communicated to General Ironside[23] for the occupation of Kotlas by British and Russian troops during July and August so as to relieve pressure on General Gayda and stretch out a hand towards the returning Czecho-Slovak troops.

(e) An agreement to be reached between the Powers concerned as to the taking over of the sector of the Siberian railway at present guarded by the Czecho-Slovaks by either Japanese or American forces or by both conjointly.

(f) Great Britain to provide ships at Archangel during October and November for all Czecho-Slovak troops returning via Archangel.

(g) The United States to arrange for the repatriation of the remainder from Vladivostok, such repatriation to begin at the earliest possible date.

As soon as the approval of the Czecho-Slovak Government is obtained as in (a), steps should be taken simultaneously to give effect to the remaining items indicated above.

June 24, 1919.

---

[21] That is, Maurice (Pierre Thiébaut Charles Maurice) Janin.
[22] That is, Rudolf Gajda (Gaida).
[23] That is, William Edmund Ironside, commander of Allied forces in North Russia.

APPENDIX VIII TO C.F.92.
NOTE BY MR. BALFOUR.

The question referred to the Foreign Ministers by the "Four," on the subject of Eastern Galicia, differs in some very important respects from other problems connected with the frontier arrangements in Eastern Europe.

We have got, if possible, to find a plan which will:

1. Satisfy the immediate Military necessity of resisting the Bolshevist invasion of Galicia; and

2. Avoid compromising the future interests of the Ruthenian majority who now inhabit Eastern Galicia. These two objects seem at first sight inconsistent, for the only troops which we have at our disposal for resisting the Bolshevists in this region are the Poles; and if the Poles are given complete Military freedom—as from a Military point of view they certainly ought to be—their occupation of the country may compromise the political future of this district. The Ruthenian majority is backward, illiterate, and at present quite incapable of standing alone. The urban and educated classes are largely Polish, and when not Polish are Jewish. The whole country is utterly disorganised. There is, or was, (for some slight improvement seems to have taken place), a most embittered feeling between the Poles and the Ruthenians, and it is manifestly impossible at the moment to determine the character of public opinion by a plebiscite, or other similar methods. If the Polish Military occupation be permanent, it is hard to see how this state of things will find a remedy.

The best suggestion I can make is the following: Appoint as soon as may be a High Commissioner for Eastern Galicia under the League of Nations, as proposed in plan II.a. of the Report of the Polish Commission. He must be instructed, while the Bolshevist peril lasts, to work in harmony with the Poles, and to facilitate the use of Polish troops as Military necessity may require.

The Poles, on the other hand, must be informed that their Military occupation of Eastern Galicia is a temporary one, and can only be allowed to last as long as the needs of common defence against the invading Bolshevism renders this proceeding necessary, and that of this the High Commissioner must be the judge. The Ruthenians must be told that, though the Poles are temporarily in occupation of their country, they are acting under the directions of the League of Nations, and that the Ruthenians will be given a full opportunity of determining by plebiscite, within limits to be fixed by the League of Nations, what their future status is to be.

This opportunity will be given them as soon as tranquillity is restored, and there is some chance of a fair vote being taken.

I do not know whether the Poles would accept this plan, though I think they might be induced to do so. Its advantages are that:

1. It provides for the defence of Galicia against the Bolshevists, which seems all important, both in the interests of the Ruthenians themselves, and of the security of Eastern Europe.

2. It combines with this a policy of self-determination, to be exercised as soon as circumstances permit.

No other plan that I have been able to think of combines those two advantages, both of which seem essential to any satisfactory policy for dealing with this embarrassing problem. (Intd). A.J.B. Paris, June 18th, 1919.

APPENDIX XI TO C.F.92.

W.C.P.-1069.

LETTER FROM THE ALLIED AND ASSOCIATED POWERS
TO THE GERMAN DELEGATION.

Monsieur le Président: June 25, 1919.

The terms of the Armistice signed by Germany on the 11th November, 1918, provided as follows:

"*Article XXIII.* The German surface warships which shall be specified by the Allies and the United States shall forthwith be disarmed and thereafter interned in neutral ports, or, failing them, in the Allied ports designated by the Allies and the United States. They shall there remain under the supervision of the Allies and the United States, only care and maintenance parties being left on board."

On June 21, the German warships which had been handed over to the Allied and Associated Powers and were at anchor in the roadstead at Scapa Flow, with the German care and maintenance parties on board as provided in the Armistice, were sunk by these parties under the orders of the German Admiral in command.

According to the information which has been collected and transmitted by the British Admiralty the German admiral in command of these parties of the German naval forces has alleged that he acted in the belief that the Armistice expired on June 21st at mid-day, and consequently in his opinion the destruction in question was no violation of its terms.

In law, Germany by signing the terms of Article 23 set out above entered into an undertaking that the ships handed over by her should remain in the ports indicated by the Allied and Associated Powers and that care and maintenance parties should be left on board with such instructions and under such orders as would ensure that the Armistice should be observed.

The sinking of these ships instead of their preservation as had been provided for, and in breach of the undertaking embodied in Article 31 of the Armistice against all acts of destruction, constituted at once a violation of the Armistice, the destruction of the pledge handed over, and an act of gross bad faith towards the Allied and Associated Powers.

The Admiral in command of the care and maintenance parties belonging to the German Naval forces has, while recognising that the act was a breach of the Armistice, attempted to justify it by alleging his belief that the Armistice had come to an end.

This alleged justification is not well founded as, under the communication addressed to the German Delegation by the Allied and Associated Powers on the 16th June, 1919, the Armistice would only terminate on refusal to sign the peace, or, if no answer were returned, on the 23rd June at 7 o'clock.

According to International law, as embodied particularly in Articles 40 and 41 of the Regulations annexed to the Fourth Hague Convention of 1907, every serious violation of the Armistice by one of the parties gives the other party the right to denounce it and even in case of urgency to recommence hostilities at once. A violation of the terms of the Armistice by individuals acting on their own initiative only confers the right of demanding the punishment of the offenders and, if necessary, indemnity for the losses sustained. It will therefore be open to the Allied and Associated Powers to bring before military tribunals the persons responsible for these acts of destruction so that the appropriate penalties may be imposed. Furthermore, the incident gives the Allied and Associated Powers a right to reparation for the loss caused and in consequence a right to proceed to such further measures as the said Powers may deem appropriate.

Lastly, the sinking of the German fleet is not only a violation of the Armistice, but can only be regarded by the Allied and Associated Powers as a deliberate breach in advance of the conditions of peace communicated to Germany and now accepted by her. Furthermore, the incident is not an isolated act. The burning or permission for the burning of the French flags which Germany was to restore, constitutes another deliberate breach in advance of these same conditions.

In consequence, the Allied and Associated Powers declare that they take note of these signal acts of bad faith, and that when the investigations have been completed into all the circumstances, they will exact the necessary reparation. It is evident that any repetition of acts like these must have a very unfortunate effect upon the future operation of the Treaty which the Germans are about to sign. They have made complaint of the 15 years' period of occupation which the Treaty contemplates. They have made complaint that admission to the League of Nations may be too long deferred. How can Germany put forward such claims if she encourages or permits deliberate violations of her written engagements? She cannot complain should the Allies use to the full the powers conferred on them by Treaty, particularly by Article 429, if she on her side deliberately violates its provisions.   (Sd)   G. Clemenceau.

T MS (SDR, RG 256, 180.03401/92, DNA); Mantoux, II, 519-21.

To Robert Lansing, with Enclosure

My dear Lansing: Paris, 25 June, 1919.

I am sending you the memorandum which I promised you and my other colleagues I would dictate with regard to the basis upon which we are to discuss the Adriatic question with the new Italian delegates to the Peace Conference, and along with this I am taking the liberty of sending you, rather than taking them away with me, the bundle of papers and maps which I have accumulated from one source and another, referring directly or indirectly to the Adriatic question. Perhaps you can have them classified and will find them serviceable. In the book-cover you will find some very interesting statistics which a group of Jugo-Slavs brought me with regard to plebiscites taken in Dalmatia and on the neighboring islands,[1] the items of which they professed themselves ready to prove in any way that they were called upon to prove them.
        Cordially and faithfully yours,   [Woodrow Wilson]

TLS (SDR, RG 256, 186. 3411/640, DNA).
  [1] See N. P. Pašić to WW, June 8, 1919, Vol. 60.

E N C L O S U R E

MEMORANDUM WITH REGARD TO THE ADRIATIC QUESTION

25 June, 1919.

First: There can be no profit in our covering again the field of discussion which we went over so often with Signor Orlando and Baron Sonnino. Our position has remained exactly the same throughout all the discussions, because though we have the most cordial good will towards Italy and the most sincere desire to meet her wishes in every possible way, we do not feel at liberty to depart, in respect of the territory, from the principles which have been followed throughout all the other settlements in which we have taken part.

Second: There is no longer any use in insisting upon the Treaty of London, because the United States is now an essential guarantor of all the settlements made, and no action of Great Britain or France could be effective without her. There is no means except that of the general settlement by which any territories could be handed over to Italy.

Third: Fiume can in no circumstances go to Italy. It must serve the uses and necessities of the several States behind it to the North and East, and can do so in our judgment only as a free state. It may be advantageous that this free state should have a territory including the islands of Cherso and Veglia and running upon the mainland up the so-called American Line along the crests of the Alps from the foot of the Istrian peninsula to the point of junction between the American and the London Lines, and with an Eastern line extended a little way beyond Fiume, as indicated on the last map submitted to Signor Orlando. (I think Major Johnson can easily draw this line. It is a modification of that proposed by M. Tardieu in the compromise which he proposed.) Within this state Fiume might be permitted to enjoy so great a degree of autonomy as she enjoyed under Hungary, but no more. This free state should be under the League of Nations, represented by a resident Commissioner, and at the end of a period of five years it should be left open to the choice of the Council of the League of Nations whether a plebiscite should be taken as to the ultimate sovereignty over its territories.

Fourth: Any territory east of the American line other than that of the free state thus defined may be conceded to Italy which she can get by plebiscite under the superintendence of the League of Nations, except that it is doubtful whether a single small locality like Zara should be ceded to Italy; and in such a case, should the citizens of Zara wish it, the only solution possible upon principle would be to make of Zara itself a free city with the proper connections of free intercourse with the Jugo-Slavic State. Self-determination must be accepted as the basis of any transfer of territory and population.

It should be carefully provided with regard to the free state of Fiume that it should be freely open and upon equal terms for residence to the populations about it, and that private capital should have equal opportunities of investment there, no matter what nationality supplied the capital, and that the facilities of the port should be open upon the most equal and favorable terms to the hinterland.[1]

T MS (SDR, RG 256, 186. 3411/640, DNA).
[1] There is a WWsh outline of this memorandum in the C. L. Swem Coll., NjP.

Two Letters to Robert Lansing

My dear Lansing: Paris, June 25, 1919.

I have your important letter of yesterday about the Austrian frontier[1] and mean to study it carefully with a desire to form a clear judgment and, wherever possible, remove future causes of difficulty. I must admit that much of the matter I have not had time to really study, and therefore I cannot form a present judgment with any degree of confidence.

Cordially and sincerely yours,   [Woodrow Wilson]

[1] This letter is missing in all collections and archives. However, as Wilson's letter shows, it was about the Austrian frontier and, most particularly, the Sudetenland. Moreover, Lansing summarizes it well in RL to WW, June 30, 1919; see also WW to RL, July 2, 1919.

My dear Lansing: Paris, June 25, 1919.

I would be very much obliged if you would have the enclosure[1] forwarded to Polk. I think that we should omit no step by which we can get nearer to the situation in Siberia and know more clearly what we are about.

Cordially and sincerely yours,   [Woodrow Wilson]

CCL (WP, DLC).
[1] The Enclosure printed with V. C. McCormick to WW, June 24, 1919. It was forwarded to Polk in RL to FLP, No. 2859, June 28, 1919, T telegram (SDR, RG 59, 123M 832/29, DNA). This message was in turn sent to Morris in W. Phillips to R. S. Morris, June 30, 1919, T telegram (SDR, RG 59, 123M 832/29a, DNA).

To Brand Whitlock

My dear Whitlock: Paris, June 25, 1919.

Your letter of June 23rd has quite filled my heart because of its generosity and all the evidence it gives of your friendship and approval. If it gives me more credit than is due me—and it does give me vastly more—I accept it with the deepest feeling of gratitude because I know that in it your heart speaks, and I will not hold your judgment responsible. Nothing could be more delightful to me, struggling here through the difficulties of the hour, than to receive such assurances from one whom I affectionately esteem and admire and whose approval means a vast deal to me.

The little hurried visit to Belgium will, I think, remain in my mind also as the most vivid impression which I shall carry away from Europe. I enjoyed it and felt inspired by it and it was a constant pleasure to be associated with Mrs. Whitlock[1] and you.

Thank you for remembering to send me your book on Belgium.

I shall read it and I shall know how to value it, because I know how straight you have seen into the heart of the country which you have served with so remarkable a devotion and a success.

Mrs. Wilson and my daughter join me in sending you the warmest greetings and most affectionate regard.

Cordially and sincerely yours,   [Woodrow Wilson]

CCL (WP, DLC).
¹ That is, Ella Brainerd Whitlock.

To Jean Jules Jusserand

My dear Mr. Ambassador: [Paris] 25 June, 1919.

I have your note of today. I have just learned this afternoon what I now find repeated in your note, that there is no probability—perhaps I should say possibility—of the signing of the Peace before Friday. This sets me at liberty to accept an invitation from the President of the Republic for the evening of Thursday, and I hope that you will convey to him my appreciation of his hospitable intentions.

Very sincerely yours,   [Woodrow Wilson]

CCL (WP, DLC).

To Herbert Clark Hoover, with Enclosure

My dear Hoover: Paris, 25 June, 1919.

What you propose in the enclosed letter, which I take the liberty of returning with this answer, meets with my entire approval, and I am glad that you thought of so interesting and serviceable a scheme.

Cordially and sincerely yours,   Woodrow Wilson

ENCLOSURE

From Herbert Clark Hoover

Dear Mr. President: Paris, 24 June 1919.

Before you leave I would like to know if I could have your informal approval to the following:

In addition to food activities, I am under a "mandatory" given to me by the Supreme War Council, a sort of a Receiver for the whole of the railways in the Austrian Empire, and I likewise enjoy the same "high" office in respect to the coal mines of the Austrian Empire and Poland. There [these?] very great matters have been carried with indeed great ability by the corps of American officers whom I have had in charge in these countries. As the result of their success in maintaining economic life in this area of political dissension we enjoy a great deal of prestige with all the six or eight different governments that nest around Southeastern Europe. At some moment after the signing of peace it will be necessary for us to withdraw all of these services. What these countries will want above all things will be some kind of economic inter-arrangement among themselves as to railway management, coal distribution, customs conventions, the common working of their telegraph and telephone systems, etc. I therefore have the notion that the opportunity may arise when I can go into this area and call a convention of economic delegates representing these different governments at some central point under my chairmanship, and on the ground that we were about to withdraw we should set up the preliminaries of their necessary co-operation. On this basis I have the feeling that I might produce substantial results in the solution of these vital problems.

I do not want to undertake these things without at least your approval. On the basis of simply arranging for withdrawal of our organization we will avoid jealousies of the other great governments and will, I am convinced, be able to perform a service that cannot otherwise be accomplished.

Faithfully yours,   Herbert Hoover

TLS (Hoover Archives, CSt-H).

From Tasker Howard Bliss

Dear Mr. President: Paris 25 June 1919

Before his departure from Paris on Sunday night, General Pershing asked me to obtain from you your decision as to the strength of the American force that would remain in occupation in German territory after the signature of the Treaty of Peace.

General Pershing informs me that you said to him (as you had already said to me) that under an agreement that you and Mr. Lloyd George had made with Mr. Clemenceau you would retain here, at the most, one American regiment. General Pershing desires to add to this regiment the necessary hospital and sanitary service and such other auxiliary services as are necessary to make the regiment independent of French resources. All American officers consider this to be very important. Especially is it necessary that we should have our own hospital and sanitary service, because if sick American soldiers have to be taken care of in French hospitals there will be bitter complaint just as there was when, for some time after our entrance into the war, we had to depend upon the French for this service.

I recommend that you authorize General Pershing to organize this regiment according to his best judgment so as to insure its contentment on what will doubtless prove to be disagreeable duty.

General Pershing also thinks that a general officer should be left in command of this organization. He thinks that nothing but the presence of an American general officer will prevent the regiment from being handled in about the same way that our single regiment in Italy was handled, and also our single regiment at Archangel,—that is to say, in a way which caused a feeling of bitterness and resentment among our officers and men.

I concur in General Pershing's views, and I suggest that, if you also approve them, you give General Pershing formal instructions to the effect that one regiment, together with the necessary auxiliary services, with a general officer to be selected by him in command, is the force that you will leave in France after the signature of peace, and that you authorize the return of the remaining forces to the United States. I am informed that transports are accumulating in Brest because the retention of the five divisions which we now have on the Rhine, together with the large number of S.O.S.[1] men, is preventing them from loading with troops and returning home.   Cordially yours,   Tasker H. Bliss.

    Approved
        Woodrow Wilson

TLS (T. H. Bliss Papers, DLC).
   [1] That is, Services of Supply.

From Stanley Kuhl Hornbeck

Confidential.

To the Commissioners,   [Paris] June 25, 1919.

During the course of the Peace Conference, officials of certain countries have repeatedly shown themselves indifferent to, if not deliberately arrayed against the rights, interests and susceptibilities of certain of what are collectively referred to as the "smaller countries."

A conspicuous instance of an attempt at an arbitrary ruling with apparently deliberate intent to humiliate certain delegations and to emphasize the distinction between states of greater and those of less prestige was seen in the preparation of the original list of the nations which were to be admitted at the ceremony of the presentation of the Treaty to the German delegation. That attempt failed because the matter was brought to the attention of the American Commission and the American Commission refused to countenance the contemplated procedure.

At the present moment an attempt is apparently being made quietly to force the Chinese delegation into choosing between signing the Treaty without reservations or not signing it at all. The adoption of either of these alternatives would be embarrassing to the delegation and probably to the disadvantage of China. The Far Eastern Division is informed by the Minister Koo, Chinese plenipotentiary, that he has been informed by the Secretary of the Conference, "speaking for the President of the Council," who in turn "is speaking for the Council," that in the signing of the Treaty the making of a reservation will not be allowed.[1]

In doubt as to whether any action on the point in question has been taken by the Council, and believing that such a ruling would be contrary to the principles and policies of the American Commission, I have the honor to bring this subject to the attention of the Commissioners and to suggest that it be given immediate consideration. I beg to suggest that the American Commission resolve not to countenance such a ruling and that it inform the Chinese delegation that, if the matter is brought to a test, the American delegation will support the Chinese in their contention for the right to enter a reservation.

Whatever may be the decision of the American delegation, I believe it only right that the Chinese should at this time be informed as to what they may or may not expect.

Respectfully submitted by   Stanley K Hornbeck

TLS (R. Lansing Papers, DLC).
 [1] Hornbeck enclosed a T memorandum, dated June 25, 1919 (R. Lansing Papers, DLC), from the Chinese delegation but presumably written by Koo. This memorandum stated that the Secretary General of the Peace Conference had informed the Chinese delegation that it would not be permitted to sign the treaty with any reservations whatsoever, and that this decision applied to all delegations. The memorandum further said that the Chinese government had instructed its delegates to sign the treaty with a reservation to the articles concerning Shantung Province (for the text of which, see the Enclosure printed with V. K. W. Koo to WW, June 27, 1919) and that the Chinese delegation earnestly solicited the good offices of the American delegation in this matter. In addition, Hornbeck, in a handwritten note also enclosed in the letter printed above, pointed out that Koo had particularly requested that the memorandum be considered confidential.

Robert Lansing and Vance Criswell McCormick
to Frank Lyon Polk

25 June, 1919.

2794. For Polk from Lansing and McCormick. Your 2343, June 19, 5 p.m.[1] McCormick has spoken to the President regarding Russian situation. He stated that the telegram to Koltchak does not imply political recognition at the present time by any of the Associated Governments but merely offers of assistance in so far as each Government's policy and legislation may permit. The absence of formal recognition will in our case prevent us from extending credit as suggested in your 2363, June 20, 8 p.m.[2] but anything for which they can devise means of payment may now be furnished the Koltchak forces. On his return the President intends to take up with Congress the entire question of economic support for Russia and particularly that pertaining to the Siberian railroad. He expects to send further Military instructions to General Graves.

The President expressed his regret at the interpretation given by the press to the telegram sent by the Associated Governments to Admiral Koltchak[3] as he feared that such interpretation might give rise to false hopes. 2794   Ammission

T telegram (WP, DLC).
[1] Printed in *FR 1919, Russia*, pp. 381–82. It reads as follows:
"Is Department to understand that acceptance of Kolchak's reply merely means continuation of present relations with Kolchak Government or does it convey *de facto* recognition and further and open extension of support along all lines available?
"Press reports from Paris leave public in doubt on this question. Secretary of War anxious to know whether he should change instructions to General Graves."
[2] Printed in *ibid.*, p. 383. In this telegram, Polk pointed out that Congress had recently authorized the Secretary of the Treasury to establish credits with the United States for foreign governments engaged in war with enemies of the United States, to enable them to purchase available property owned directly or indirectly by the United States. Polk continued:
"Does this offer any prospect of extending credit to Kolchak Government which repudiated treaty of Brest-Litovsk and now holds German and Austrian soldiers as prisoners of war? I understand the Omsk Government hopes to purchase in the United States materials, other than munitions, amounting to $164,000,000. I also have a proposal from Mr. [Samuel Matthews] Vauclain [president of the Baldwin Locomotive Works] to devise means to turn over to Russia 200 locomotives taken over by the War Department, which can now be returned and easily changed to Russian gauge, provided means of payment or credit be devised."
[3] The text of which is printed in the entry from the Grayson Diary printed at June 12, 1919, Vol. 60.

From the Diary of Colonel House

June 25, 1919.

Baruch and Thoman [Thomas] Nelson Page were early morning callers. Page came to discuss the Italian situation prior to his departure for the United States. He goes home to resign and Brand Whitlock is slated to take his place. I am glad the President appointed Whitlock. I had no idea he would take it. He is a fine character.

Baruch wished to tell me what a success he has been at the Peace Conference and how much he has accomplished for our country. I was glad he mentioned it. Otherwise it might have been overlooked.

Hugh Gibson followed Page and Baruch. When I turned Gibson over to Brandeis and Frankfurter yesterday I did it for the purpose of having him give them an idea of the Jewish situation in Poland. I coached him in advance and told him he ought to let the Jews know they were making a mistake by putting out false reports about Jewish massacres. Gibson tells me that the purpose of these reports is to help Zionism. He has had a long talk with Morganthau [Morgenthau] who has no sympathy with the Zionist point of view.

Frankfurter had the temerity to tell Gibson that the Jews had almost determined to keep him, Gibson, from being confirmed by the Senate because of what he termed, his anti-Jewish feeling.

This afternoon, White, Bliss, and I went to Versailles to see the arrangements for the signing of the peace. The French are decorating everywhere and are trying to make it an elaborate ceremony. They will make us rediculous [ridiculous] if they are not careful, because the Germans may send only one man to sign and that man of no consequence.

That President came to the Crillon and the entire Commission was photographed. I had a few words with the President concerning the appointment of Root to formulate plans for a[n] international court under the League of Nations. In the event Root did not accept, I suggested Wickersham[1] as an alternative since it seems wise to appoint a republican.

Speaking of the President reminds me that he completely capitulated as far as the Poincaré dinner was concerned. When he left the Crillon yesterday he sent a note to Jusserand naming tomorrow, Thursday, as the time he would be glad to accept an invitation for the dinner. The invitations were issued immediately and we received ours this morning.

This afternoon I received among other people, a delegation from Lemburg. They came to present their case to the Conference. Wallace, of course, was here, but I was so crowded that I could only give him a few minutes standing.

The British are trying to lay the blame for the sinking of the German ships upon us. They claim they wished to have the ships "surrend[er]ed" instead of "interned" but that we insisted upon internment. As a matter of fact, the British Navy did want them surrendered. Benson advocated internment and George, Clemenceau, Orlando, Foch and I thought it might imperil the chances for the Armistice if we demanded surrender, and we therefore thought it wise to intern them.

At the Armistice proceedings Foch made the remark that he would not give one French soldier's life for all the German ships afloat, and that to demand surrender might mean a continuance of the war and the loss of many lives. The reason the point is being raised is that the British Navy claim if the ships had been surrend[er]ed, they would have put their own crews on board, but since they were interned, it was necessary, under the terms of the Armistice, to leave the Germans in charge—hence the sinking.

Our Navy people, with whom I have talked, do not agree with this view.

Going back to the President and the Poincaré dinner, the episode was a revelation to everyone excepting myself of something in his character which had not been seen before. It accounted to them for his many enemies. Although he finally goes to the dinner, Poincaré will never forgive his having forced upon him such an unpleasant situation.

[1] That is, George Woodward Wickersham, Attorney General in the Taft Administration.

From the Diary of Ray Stannard Baker

Wednesday night [June 25, 1919]

The Four spent a large part of the day discussing the Scapa Flow sinking of the German fleet & in agreeing on a note to the Germans regarding it—a futile note! They also chided the Germans in another note—equally futile!—regarding a supposed plan for attacking Poland, based upon very doubtful information from Polish sources. More note writing—while the Germans hang fire in sending their delegation to sign the treaty. It is all bad business! The President told me about it this evening: he is impatient & disgusted.

Mrs. Wilson told me the story of the President's seal ring, about which we have all been curious—the one which he is to use when he signs the treaty. She said that when they were married the State of California sent them a nugget of gold out of which it was suggested that a wedding ring be made. This they had done, & Mrs. Wilson is wearing it. Out of the gold that remained a signet ring was made for the President. When a design was asked for he wrote his name in full—Woodrow Wilson—in shorthand & combined the two characters in a monogram which looks like an Arabic inscription & this is the seal which will be used on the treaty (if ever they get to the signing of it!)

From the Diary of Edith Benham

June 25, 1919

The great excitement today has been over a dinner the Poincares wanted to give. First, it was to be the night after peace was signed. The P. declined flat-footed, giving as an excuse that he would get on board the train too early. He dislikes the Ps very much, as P. has done everything he could to work against him since he had been here. Then the Ps said they would put the dinner ahead until Thursday, the 26th. Still the P. refused. All day yesterday there were delegations here to implore him to go. Wallace and Bliss came twice—no result. Jusserand came in the evening and the P. wouldn't see him. Poor Dr. Grayson saw all these people and had to listen to their wails. Col. House tried to see Mrs. W. and she wouldn't see him, for she was aiding the P. in his obstinacy. It was just one of the mulish attacks they get so often.

However, all is well and the P. says he will go. He always capitulates handsomely when he is sure he is wrong, and nothing could have been more lovable than the way he spoke to Mr. White. To quote his own language at luncheon today, "It didn't need your note to me to make me realize what I knew when I was talking to you, that you were right, for I knew I was wrong," and he added it was a question of personal dislike and he "seemed to have endangered the peace of Europe." Tonight in speaking of it he said Mr. White decided him, and not the serious faces of his colleagues, "for Mr. White is so thoughtful of me, and always tries to spare me in every way, and when I saw how grave and serious he was I decided to go." It must have made a fearful commotion. There is now some discussion of a reception at the Hotel de Ville, which he doesn't want to accept, and said he can't as he had told the Poincares he would board the train as soon as peace was signed. In the discussion, out of which I kept, Mrs. W. turned to me and asked if I thought they ought to go. I said, "Yes, if they put the reception at five." The P. said he loved his own country, but it is terrible to have to love another country as he has to love France!

From Edward Mandell House, with Enclosure

Dear Governor: Paris, 25 June 1919.

I enclose a telegram which I received from Miller, and which I am sure you will find interesting.

Affectionately yours,   E. M. House

TLS (WP, DLC).

ENCLOSURE

[Washington] June 23 [1919]

109. For Auchincloss from Miller.

The chief point of attack made in Root letter[1] is against Article X as to which he says in part: "It is an independent and indefinite alliance which may involve the parties to it in war against powers which have in every respect complied with the provisions of the League of peace. It was not included in General Smuts' plan,[2] the provisions of which have been reproduced almost textually in the League Covenant, and it stands upon its own footing as an independent alliance for the preservation of the status quo."

He says further, that people of the United States would later be unwilling to keep the agreement; that dissension and hatred would arise among our own citizens if we intervened against their friends for no cause of our own, and that Washington advised us to keep out of the quarrels of Europeans, but intimated that he might favor an agreement to support France if attacked. Article X has become a center of objection and it is undoubted that the attitude of many supporters of the League—Democrats and Republicans—are lukewarm as to this Article. Others like Straus, for example, regard it as essential. Contrast Root's earlier letter, published in NEW YORK TIMES March 31st, in which he supported Article X,[3] advising the addition of a clause permitting a withdrawal from its obligations after five years on one year's notice.

The first reservation advised by Root is really an amendment striking out Article X and it is doubtful if that procedure is proper but this will be examined. The third reservation advised by Root is to cover his objections to what he deems the insufficient amendments regarding Monroe Doctrine and American questions like immigration. This third goes to extreme lengths and would invite similar reservations by other powers.

The foregoing are the principal points which I think the President will have to answer as Root letter has, in my opinion, changed the situation so that debate will be on particular clauses of Covenant and not on question of value of League of Nations generally and of Covenant as a whole. Root letter also, I think, has ended attempt at amendments as such ancillary effort by Lodge, et al, will be for ratification with reservations. It is highly advisable that we ratify without reservation as is expressly required of neutrals who accede by Article One. Am preparing memorandum of answer to Root's points of which I shall cable a summary if you wish. Root's other point is as to withdrawal and in effect is that last twenty-three words of Article One create ambiguity. My own opinion is that this is not important but we might perhaps meet the objection by an agreement that after ratification we would propose an amendment to strike out or qualify these words, particularly in view of Article Twenty-six providing another case of [cause for?] withdrawal.   Polk, Acting

T telegram (WP, DLC).
  [1] About which, see JPT to WW, June 21, 1919, n. 3.
  [2] For which, see the memorandum printed at Dec. 26, 1918, Vol. 53.
  [3] About which, see the Enclosure printed with WW to EMH, March 31, 1919, Vol. 56; also JPT to WW, June 21, 1919, n. 3.

Six Telegrams from Joseph Patrick Tumulty

[The White House] June 25 [1919]

No. 210 McAdoo thinks if you are going to arrive at New York without greeting of some kind, it would be misunderstood. He suggests that you permit a citizens' welcome. I told him of Hyland-Hearst danger.[1] He said that would be obviated; that no speech would be asked of you, but simply some word of thanks in appreciation of welcome would be all that would be necessary. I think you ought to consider this matter as soon as possible.

                                                        Tumulty.

  [1] This so-called danger, which had been the subject of several earlier telegrams from Tumulty, was that Mayor John Francis Hylan of New York and William Randolph Hearst, both bitter opponents of Wilson and the League of Nations, would lead the delegation to greet Wilson upon his arrival in New York harbor.

[The White House] June 25 [1919]

No. 211 General Maurice, in wonderful article in New York Times on League of Nations,[1] says about Ireland, "One obvious need to complete the process of bringing all nations together is that we should show that we know what America did in the war, but there is another obvious need, which presents greater difficulties. We must have a policy in regard to Ireland, which we can explain to the American people. At present Ireland threatens to reopen all the rifts which comradeship in the war is closing."

The New York Evening Post of last night prints the following editorial, "Self-government for the Irish people, short of independence, is a right and a necessity, and it is a satisfaction that once more a movement is under way for the establishment of Ireland on the basis which logic and history have determined—a dominion on an equal footing with the other dominions under the British Crown."

Frankly, this represents the opinion of the average man in America, without regard to race or religion. The arrival of De Valera in America[2] is going to intensify the feeling and Republicans will take full advantage. Now that the League of Nations is on its feet, we should take the lead in this matter. It would do more toward bringing about a real comradeship between England and America than anything that could happen. I think the situation in Africa, India, and the seriousness of the situation in Canada, will inevitably force England to consider all these matters. It is in anticipation of this that I am anxious to have you play a leading part in this situation. It would do much to make the League of Nations a living, vital force in the affairs of the world. There are no boundary lines between free people any more.   Tumulty.

[1] Maj. Gen. Sir Frederick Barton Maurice, "Anxiety in England over League Fight. Maurice Tells of Fear of Its Effect on Anglo-American Friendship. Other Obstacles Serious. General Says Mutual Recognition of Countries' Part in War Would Help Clear Air," *New York Times*, June 25, 1919. The passage quoted by Tumulty actually reads as follows:

"One of the things most wanted today to complete the process of bringing our nations together is that we should show what America did in the war.

"This is a simple matter. But there is another obvious need, which presents the greatest difficulties: we must have a policy in regard to Ireland which we can explain to the American people. At present Ireland threatens to reopen all the rifts which comradeship in the war is closing."

[2] Eamon De Valera had arrived secretly and illegally in New York on about June 11, 1919, but had remained in hiding for the next two weeks. Although there had been earlier reports that he was in America, De Valera's presence was not officially announced until June 23. At a press conference on that day, De Valera stated that he had come to the United States to seek support for the recognition of the Irish Republic. However, as it turned out, his most immediate task and the primary purpose of his mission was to raise money for the administration of his government and the conduct of the escalating guerrilla war with Great Britain. To that end, De Valera and the Irish-American leaders eventually worked out a plan to sell up to $10 million worth of bond certificates, to be exchanged for bonds after the recognition of the Irish Republic. De Valera stayed in the United States until December 1920 and addressed countless public meetings throughout the country, spoke to state legislatures, city councils, chambers of commerce, and labor congresses, and was welcomed by United States senators and congressmen, state governors, the mayors of America's largest cities, civic and labor leaders, and the Roman Catholic hierarchy in the United States. He received honorary degrees from several American colleges and universities and was granted the freedom of the City of New York. For detailed accounts, see Patrick McCartan, *With De Valera in America* (New York, 1932); Katherine O'Doherty, *Assignment: America. De Valera's Mission to the United States* (New York, 1957); and Alan J. Ward, *Ireland and Anglo-American Relations, 1899-1921* (London, 1969), pp. 214-36.

[The White House] June 25 [1919]

No. 212 Officials of many municipalities throughout East in quandary to know what to do with reference to liquor licenses. Therefore, pressure great here for action with reference to raising ban. They have accepted following statement in your message with reference to this matter[1] as a promise that something definite would be done, "The demobilization of the military forces of the nation has progressed to such a point that it seems to me entirely safe now to remove the ban upon the manufacture and sale of wines, beers, etc."

If any action is to be taken, a statement should be made now. Will not the signing of peace be the opportunity for you to declare that demobilization is accomplished and that the object of the law having been satisfied, namely, the conservation of manpower, you would lift the ban by issuing a proclamation? I will confer with the Attorney General about the matter if you wish me to.

Tumulty.

[1] In his special message to Congress printed at May 20, 1919, Vol. 59.

The White House, 25 June 1919.

213 Suggest you prepare message of congratulation to American people to be released on signing of Treaty PERIOD My idea is to make the day one of national rejoicing COMMA a sort of peace jubilee with resolutions in Congress closing the Departments.

Tumulty

Washington June 26 [25] 1919

Two hundred and fifteen Am not giving out your statement about reservations until I confer with Hitchcock and other friends period It would be well to allow matter to be handled from this side period   Tumulty

[The White House] June 25 [1919]

No. 217 Conferred with Senators Swanson, Hitchcock, Pittman and Robinson about proposed statement on reservations. They think publication at this time unwise owing to new developments. Present indications are that the Republicans will make an effort to put through joint resolution, which proposes to have Congress declare a state of peace between Germany and the United States unconditionally. It also instructs the Executive to withdraw troops from Europe.[1] Committee considered resolution today without action, but may report the same Monday.

Will do nothing with statement and will await future developments.   Tumulty.

T telegrams (WP, DLC).
[1] Senator Albert B. Fall had introduced a resolution to this effect on June 23, 1919.

Joseph Patrick Tumulty to Edward Mandell House

The White House, 25 June 1919.

The New York Evening Post of last night prints following editorial QUOTE Self-government for the Irish people COMMA short of independence COMMA is a right and a necessity and it is a satisfaction that once more a movement is under way for the establishment of Ireland on the basis which logic and history have determined DASH a Dominion on an equal footing with the other Dominions under the British crown UNQUOTE If the President could make statement along line of foregoing COMMA it would go a long way toward solving the question PERIOD Nobody can exaggerate the depth of feeling throughout America on this question for the American people are looking to the President for at least a suggestion. I don't think it would be the part of wisdom for him to suggest a plan of solution but if he could make a statement embodying the thought in the Evening Post editorial, it would strengthen the League of Nations.

Tumulty

T telegram (WP, DLC).

Albert Sidney Burleson to Joseph Patrick Tumulty, with Enclosure

My dear Mr. Secretary: Washington June 25, 1919.

I am sending you herewith a note from Senator Swanson which I regard as extremely important. I concur thoroughly in the suggestions made by him. The President's ability to bring about the adoption of the peace treaty will depend on whether sufficient strength is developed in the Senate to amend it. There are two, possibly three, Republicans who will vote against any amendments. We will lose one, and maybe two, Democrats. If this is the situation amendments to the treaty will be defeated, in which event, in my opinion, there is no doubt about its final adoption.

Respectfully yours,   A. S. Burleson

Please cable this with Sen. Swansons note. A.S.B.

TLS (WP, DLC).

Claude Augustus Swanson to Albert Sidney Burleson

Dear Burleson: Washington, D.C. June 25th, 1919.

The President should first deliver his address to the Senate in Congress fully concerning the treaty and league. He should do this early on return. Let this permeate the country. He should not speak in the country until two or three weeks after this. To do otherwise would leave the impression he is appealing to the country over the Senate. This impression should not be created immediately. This speech with several weeks for consideration by country would do more good than to commence at once speaking through the country. Many Senators agree with me.

Swanson

TCL (WP, DLC).

William Monroe Trotter to Gilbert Fairchild Close

Dear Sir,   Paris, June 25, 1919.

I thank you for your answer to my letter asking whether the President would grant me an audience. I have your letter of the 21st instant saying that you will bring my letter of the 19th to the attention of the President, as well as yours of the 24th stating the same as to my letter of the 21st.

As the end is so near, will you do me the very great favor of informing the President that my mission makes it very important and necessary that I know whether he has, or whether he will present the petition of the National Equal Rights League to the Council of Four and ascertain the facts and let me know just as quickly as possible ere all is concluded. Again thanking you I am

Respectfully for the League   William Trotter, Secretary.

ALS (WP, DLC).

From the Diary of Dr. Grayson

Thursday, June 26, 1919.

There was still no word from Germany regarding the make-up of the German Peace Plenipotentiaries when the Big Four conference began today. The President had arisen early and worked for a time in his study before his colleagues arrived. Shortly after they went into session Secretary-General Dutasta was communicated with and he was directed to proceed to Versailles at once and to request from Von Haniel a statement regarding the intentions of the German government. Meanwhile, notification had been sent to the Armies on the Rhine and to the various other forces that were to be invoked not to relax any of their preparations. The failure of Germany to name delegates had created a situation that was distinctly and decidedly a serious one. However, when Dutasta reached Versailles he was told by Von Haniel that he had been notified a delegation had been named, headed by Hermann Müller, the new Foreign Minister, and that they would come to Paris in time to sign the treaty on Saturday afternoon. The Council, as soon as this word was received, made arrangements to have the credentials of the German delegates brought from Versailles to the Foreign Office for examination early tomorrow morning in order that nothing might intervene to delay the signing. The Council also received a protest from the Danish Government against certain regulations concerning the plebiscite that was to be planned in Schleswig.

There were no luncheon guests, and after lunch the President went for a long ride, I accompanying him. We rode around the outside of the Longchamps Race-track, and as we were passing it I said to the President: "Don't you think you are too good a Presbyterian to start on a voyage by sailing from Brest on Sunday? Don't you think you ought to wait and begin the trip on Monday?" The President looked at me and quizzically smiling said: "Don't you mean that the Grand Prix is to be run on Sunday and that you want to see it? I am not as green as I look." The President was really amused by my naive suggestion.

We returned to the house in time for the meeting of the Council of Four, which had before it Paderewski. The Polish Premier again repeated his request for "protection" for Poland. He declared that the Germans in Upper Silesia were doing everything they could to goad the Poles into taking military measures in order that they could retaliate, and then throw the blame upon the Poles. The Council decided to refer all of Paderewski's statements and his appeal to the Supreme Military Council and ask that body for a recommendation.

Because of the fact that the signing had been deferred until Saturday, the President found himself in the position where he had to accept the invitation to attend the state banquet which had been arranged by President Poincaré. The banquet was intended to celebrate the conclusion of the first part of the work of the Peace Conference, and it was served in the long state apartment which had been added to the Élysée Palace in the time of President Carnot.[1] The state dinner service of Sévres porcelain was used, some of the pieces of which are declared to be absolutely priceless. President

Wilson sat on the right of President Poincaré, with Mrs. Wilson on his left. Madame Poincaré[2] sat on the right of the President, with Mr. Lloyd George next to her. All of the plenipotentiaries to the Peace Conference who were in Paris had been invited to the banquet, as well as the Ministers and the principal official personages of France. There were 300 guests present. President Poincaré proposed a toast to the President, and the President replied extemporaneously.

[1] Marie François Sadi Carnot (1837-1894), fourth President of the Third Republic, 1887-1894.
[2] That is, Henriette Benucci Poincaré.

From the Diary of Edith Benham

June 26, 1919

Tonight was the grand dinner at the Elysee Palace for the Peace Delegates. The P. had a copy of Poincare's speech and reading it over the night before said he never hated anything so much as answering it, and going there. However, he was ready on time. Margaret, Dr. G and I went ahead, and just after we got there the P. and Mrs. W. arrived. The Garde Republicaine, drawn up in the courtyard, rolled out their salute on their kettle drums. Poincare's aides and old Gen. Leorat,[1] the P.'s aide, went to meet them, and at the doorway to the right came the Poincares, who had already greeted the guests. She would be so pretty if she was only less fretful looking, and would smile oftener. We were ushered into a small room where there were five large armchairs, not for them to sit on, for they stood all the time, but just to show they could if they wanted. The faithful William Martin was on hand to arrange all this and he placed Mme. Poincare, President P., the P. and Mrs. W. and Margaret, this last to the scandal of Mr. White, who said, "Daughters do not exist officially, and it was a great mistake having her go to Belgium, but these people know no better."

The first to start the procession was old Dubost,[2] President of the Senate. He is a stiff old gentleman with fine clacking false teeth and a pleated shirt front which seemed to match them. Then came Deschanel,[3] President of the Chamber of Deputies, and his wife.[4] Then everyone came as he wanted. With the aides I stood behind the royal arm chairs, an ordinary chair with arms having been provided for me to show I was a lesser bird. It was a wonderful place to see the crowd file by, for the dinner was an immense one, over 200. The Chief Delegates were there, and all the Ambassadors and Ministers of all the Allied countries, and lots of French officials.

The gowns were beautiful, but very few good looking women. The state dining room into which we filed is a wonderful place at night, with the beautiful hangings on the tapestries. It had been aired since we had the luncheon there on landing, and seemed free of the four years war stuffiness. The two Ps sat together and Mrs. W. on Poincare's left. Beside her she had Sonnino, looking very sulky. The new Italian Delegate, the Marquis Imperiali (Ambassador to London) and his handsome wife.[5] (Sonnino is a curious combination of Jewish, Scotch and Italian ancestry.) The prettiest woman was Mrs. House.[6] She is an old one, but very, very pretty. There were certainly all colors, for we had Liberia and the French Congo. Poor Mr. Venizelos was between the darky[7] and a Chinaman. Mrs. W. asked me if I didn't think the P.'s reply to Poincare's speech was stilted, and I did. It was a hard thing and old Mr. White said sympathetically he hadn't realized all he was letting him in for, as he had to say so much about France. I thought he got around the subject very cleverly. After dinner I saw the little Baroness Chinda,[8] who was in Washington when he was Ambassador. They are now in London and we saw them last winter. She is a delightful little person, speaking English very well. After a decent interval, the P. and Mrs. W. made their goodbyes, and the Poincares took them as far as the hall. So ended that lesson.

[1] Anne Henri Joseph Leorat.
[2] Henri Antoine Dubost.
[3] That is, Paul Eugène Louis Deschanel.
[4] Germaine Brice Deschanel.
[5] Maria Giovanna dei Principi Colonna, daughter of Eduardo Colonna, Prince of Summonte.
[6] That is, Loulie Hunter House.
[7] Charles Dunbar Burgess King, Secretary of State of Liberia.
[8] Iwako Chinda, second daughter of Itsuro Yamanaka.

After-Dinner Remarks

June 26, 1919

Mr. President: I thank you most sincerely for the words that you have uttered.[1] I cannot pretend, Sir, that the prospect of going home is not very delightful to me, but I can say with the greatest sincerity that the prospect of leaving France is very painful to me. I have received a peculiarly generous welcome here, and it has been pleasing for me to feel that that welcome was intended, not so much for myself as for the people whom I represented. And the people of France know how to give a welcome that makes a man's heart glad. They have a spontaneity about them, a simplicity of friendship which is altogether delightful.

I feel that my stay here, Sir, has enlightened both my heart and my mind. It has enabled me personally to see the evidences of the suffering and sacrifices of France. It has enabled me to come into personal touch with the leaders of the French people and, through the medium of intercourse with them, understand better, I hope, than I understood before, the motives, the ambitions and the principles which actuate this great nation. It has, therefore, been to me a lesson in the roots of friendship, in those things which make the intercourse of nations profitable and serviceable for the rest of mankind.

Sometimes the work of the conference has seemed to go very slowly indeed, sometimes it has seemed as if there were unnecessary obstacles to agreement, but as the weeks have lengthened I have seemed to see the profit that came out of that. Quick conclusions would not have produced that intimate knowledge of each other's minds which I think has come out of these daily conferences. We have been constantly in the presence of each other's minds and motives and characters, and the comradeships which are based upon that sort of knowledge are sure to be very much more intelligent, not only, but to breed a much more intimate sympathy and comprehension than could otherwise be created. These six months have been months which have woven new fibers of connection between the hearts of our peoples. And something more than friendship and intimate sympathy has come out of this intercourse.

Friendship is a very great thing. Intimacy is a very enlightening thing. But friendship may end with sentiment. A new thing that has happened is that we have translated our common principles and our common purposes into a common plan. When we part, we are not going to part with a finished work, but with a work one portion of which is finished and the other portion of which is only begun. We have finished the formulation of the peace, but we have begun a plan of cooperation which I believe will broaden and strengthen as the years go by. So that this grip of the hand that we have taken now will not be relaxed. We shall continue to be comrades. We shall continue to be coworkers in tasks which, because they are common, will weave out of our sentiments a common conception of duty and a common conception of the rights of men of every race and of every clime. If it be true that that has been accomplished, it is a very great thing.

As I go away from these scenes, I think I shall realize that I have been present at one of the most vital things that has happened in the history of nations. Nations have formed contracts with each other before, but they have never formed partnerships. They have

associated themselves temporarily, but they have never before associated themselves permanently. The wrong that was done in the
waging of this war was a great wrong, but it wakened the world to
a great moral necessity of seeing that it was necessary that men
should band themselves together in order that such a wrong
should never be perpetrated again. Merely to beat a nation that was
wrong once is not enough. There must follow the warning to all
other nations that would do like things that they in turn will be
vanquished and shamed if they attempt a dishonorable purpose.

You can see, therefore, Sir, with what deep feelings those of us
who must now for a little while turn away from France shall leave
your shores; and though the ocean is broad, it will seem very narrow in the future. It will be easier to understand each other than it
ever was before, and with the constant intercourse of cooperation,
the understanding will strengthen into action, and action will itself
educate alike our purpose and our thought. So, Sir, in saying good-
bye to France, I am only saying a sort of physical goodbye, not a
spiritual goodbye. I shall retain in my heart always the warm feelings which the generous treatment of this great people has gener-
ated in my heart; and I wish in my turn, Sir, to propose, as you
have proposed, the continued and increasing friendship of the two
nations, the safety and prosperity of France, the closer and closer
communion of free peoples, and the strengthening of every influence which instructs the mind and the purpose of humanity.

T MS (WP, DLC).
¹ There is an Hw MS, dated June 26, 1919, of Poincaré's introductory remarks in WP,
DLC. Poincaré made only a few personal references to Wilson and spent most of his
time talking about the importance of close Franco-American collaboration in preserving
the future peace of Europe.

Hankey's Notes of a Meeting of the Council of Four¹

President Wilson's House, Paris,
C.F.93.   June 26, 1919, 11 a.m.

I. MR. LLOYD GEORGE announced his intention of making a protest against some of the statements made in public speeches by
Signor Tittoni, the new Italian Minister of Foreign Affairs. His protest would be made in particular against the reference to the agreement of St. Jean de Maurienne and to statements about African
Colonies.²

¹ The complete text of these minutes is printed in PPC, VI, 697-709.
² About the agreement of St. Jean de Maurienne, see n. 13 to the minutes of the
Council of Four printed at May 6, 1919, 11 a.m., Vol. 58. Tittoni had spoken on these
matters most recently in an address to the Italian Senate on June 25. He was notably
ambiguous about Italian claims to Fiume and stated that, in conducting negotiations in

M. SONNINO, in reply to a question by Mr. Lloyd George, said that the proper medium for communicating such a protest would be through the British Ambassador in Rome.[3]

2. M. DUTASTA said that he had during the morning seen Herr von Haniel who informed him that the Germans had already nominated two of their plenipotentiaries, namely

Herr Müller, the new Minister of Foreign Affairs, and Herr Giesberts, the new Postmaster-General.

The third member would probably be Herr Leinert, the Chairman of the Prussian National Assembly. The German plenipotentiaries were due to arrive on Saturday morning early by the ordinary train, to which special carriages would be attached. Herr von Haniel had spoken to him as to the verification of the credentials and he had replied by proposing that it should take place at 10 a.m. on Saturday, June 28th. Von Haniel had agreed, and had undertaken to wire to the Germans accordingly. Later, von Haniel had spoken of the need of verifying the text of the copy of the Treaty of Peace to which the signatures were to be appended, in order to ensure that it was identical with the 200 copies that had been sent to the German Delegation. He had replied that this would be a long operation. Von Haniel had agreed, and had said that the German Government would be willing to give up this formality if the Allied and Associated Powers would guarantee that the text to be signed was the same in every particular as the 200 copies.

MR. LLOYD GEORGE recalled that a global list of amendments had been sent and that it was important the Germans should realise that those were included.

(It was agreed that the President of the Conference should give the German Delegation the assurance they desired.)

M. Clemenceau instructed M. Dutasta to prepare the necessary letter.

(It was further agreed that the signature of the Treaty of Peace should take place at 3 p.m. on Saturday, June 28th, and that the verification of credentials should take place at 10 a.m. on the same date.)

3. Affixing of Seals to the Treaty of Peace

M. DUTASTA said that von Haniel had wished to know whether M. Clemenceau proposed to make a speech. He had said that he could give no official reply, but unofficially he was sure that M.

Paris, he would rely upon the justice of the Italian cause and the mutual friendship and interest of Italy and her allies which, he remarked, were much more important than "the cavilling interpretations which may be attached to treaties." *New York Times* and London *Times*, both June 27, 1919.

[3] That is, Sir Rennell Rodd.

Clemenceau had no such intention, and that the ceremony would be confined to the formality of signature. Herr von Haniel had then asked about affixing seals.

It was agreed:

(1) That the seals of the representatives of the Allied and Associated Powers should be affixed to the Treaty of Peace at the Office of the Secretary-General, Quai d'Orsay, on Friday, June 27th, at 2 p.m.

(2) That the Secretary-General should arrange with the Secretaries of the various Delegations to bring the seals at that hour.

(3) That the seals of the German Delegates should be affixed to the Treaty on Saturday morning at the meeting held to verify credentials.

4. M. CLEMENCEAU stated that the French Government proposed to hold a review of troops on July 14th, when the representatives of the Army would march under the Arc de Triomphe, down the Champs Élysées and thence to the Place de l'Opéra. He hoped that General Pershing and General Sir William Robertson would be able to march with the French Generals at the Head of the procession and that the American, British and Italian contingents would be furnished. He also asked that any Japanese Military representatives in Paris might take part. He made a special appeal that naval contingents might in addition be available.

PRESIDENT WILSON, MR. LLOYD GEORGE, M. SONNINO and BARON MAKINO agreed to give the necessary instructions to the United States, British, Italian and Japanese Military and Naval Authorities.

5. M. CLEMENCEAU handed to M. Mantoux, in French, the following document, which M. Mantoux read in English. (French text, Appendix I.)[4]

"The German Government possesses information according to which the populations of the territories in the East, which, according to the conditions of the Treaty, are to be separated from Germany, have doubts and erroneous views as to the date of the cession of these territories; the same applies to the local authorities and Military Chiefs. In order to prevent misunderstandings and disagreeable incidents, it seems desirable in the interests of the two Parties, to notify the interested circles without delay, of the fact that the Treaty of Peace will not come into force from the signature, but only at the moment provided in the definite stipulations of the Treaty, and that until then the present situa-

[4] Not printed.

tion is maintained. For the territories in question which are on our side of the line of demarcation, the necessary action has already been taken on Germany's part.

The Allied and Associated Governments are asked, so far as concerns the territories situated on their side of the line of demarcation, to take as soon as possible the proper steps."

MR. LLOYD GEORGE said that this was the letter of a man who did not wish to see trouble.

PRESIDENT WILSON thought it a perfectly reasonable request. He supposed that by "line of demarcation" was meant "the Armistice line."

M. CLEMENCEAU said he did not understand exactly what the Germans wanted done.

PRESIDENT WILSON said it was for us to let the people on the other side of the Armistice line know what had been arranged.

MR. LLOYD GEORGE suggested that the document should be referred in the first instance to the Legal Advisers for their views.

(This was agreed to.)

6. Holland and delivery of the Kaiser. Flight of the Crown Prince.[5]

With reference to C.F.92,[6] Minute 18,

PRESIDENT WILSON read a letter he had received from Mr. Lansing covering a draft of a communication to the Government of the Netherlands. (Appendix II.)

MR. LLOYD GEORGE said he thought that this was a very able document. He questioned, however, whether it would be advisable to postpone sending this document until the ratification of the Treaty of Peace. He said he had received information that morning (as he had notified his Colleagues on arrival) that the Crown Prince had fled from Holland, and had been identified driving to the East in a motor car in company with a German Staff Officer. He presumed that the Crown Prince's flight was for mischief. The fact that he had gone with a Staff Officer gave the impression that there was some conspiracy. He had seen in the newspapers that an attempt was being made by the Military party in Germany to upset the Treaty of Peace. This made him wonder whether it was safe to leave the Kaiser in Holland. He had often thought that action ought to have been taken before in this matter.

PRESIDENT WILSON questioned whether action could be taken before ratification.

[5] Friedrich Wilhelm Viktor August Ernst. The newspapers on June 26 and 27, 1919, reported that he had escaped from Holland into Germany. However, they soon reported that he was still in Holland.

[6] See the minutes of the Council of Four printed at June 25, 1919, 4 p.m.

MR. LLOYD GEORGE suggested that action could be taken on the ground of public safety. If the Kaiser reached Germany a dangerous situation might arise, and war might be facilitated.

PRESIDENT WILSON said he did not dispute this. He was only seeking for the legal basis for action.

M. CLEMENCEAU said that the demand could be based on the escape of the Crown Prince and the danger of renewing the war if the Kaiser escaped.

PRESIDENT WILSON suggested that it would be sufficient to approach Holland at once with urgent representations, begging them that the Kaiser should not be allowed to leave the country. At present the Crown Prince and the Kaiser both had the right to leave the country if they wished, but in view of the signature of the Treaty of Peace he thought that Holland would have the right to refuse their departure.

MR. LLOYD GEORGE said that he would put the matter on the ground of the inflammable state of Germany: the escape of the Crown Prince: and the danger to the peace of the world if the Kaiser reached Germany.

M. CLEMENCEAU suggested that Mr. Balfour should be asked to draft a despatch to the Dutch Government.

It was agreed:

(1) That Mr. Balfour should be asked to draft a despatch to the Dutch Government, asking them to take precautions to prevent the departure of the Kaiser.

(2) That Mr. Lansing's despatch to the Government of the Netherlands requiring the Dutch Government to hand over the Kaiser should be approved for use when the occasion arose.

BARON MAKINO reserved his assent to this despatch until he had had an opportunity to study it more closely.

7. With reference to C.F.92, Minute 5,

M. CLEMENCEAU again asked that time might be given to him before he gave his final assent to the trial of the Kaiser in England.

8. Blockade of Hungary.

The Council had before them a proposal which had been forwarded to President Wilson by Mr. McCormick[7] recommending that:

After the Béla Kun Government of Hungary has withdrawn its military forces within the line fixed by the Allied and Associated Powers;

---

[7] This document does not accompany Hankey's minutes. It is also missing in WP, DLC.

And after the Béla Kun Government of Hungary has suspended military operations against the surrounding States as specified by the Allied and Associated Powers;

The Blockade of Hungary be raised in the same manner as has been done for German Austria, to permit shipments of food, raw materials, animal products, manufactured articles and all ordinary commodities, excluding, however, all implements of war, gold, securities or other values which would reduce the power of Hungary to complete such reparations as may be imposed upon her.

(It was agreed that the Superior Blockade Council should be authorized to carry out this recommendation as soon as they are notified by the Allied and Associated Powers that Hungary has actually complied with the requirements of the Principal Allied and Associated Powers.)

9. M. CLEMENCEAU communicated the attached letter which he had received from Béla Kun (Appendix III)[8] stating that the Roumanian Army had not conformed to the formal request of the Peace Conference to put an end to all bloodshed.

It was agreed:

That the telegram should be sent to General Bliss, who should be asked if Béla Kun's statement in regard to the attitude of the Roumanians were correct.

10. Klagenfurt.

M. MANTOUX read a despatch from the Military Representative in Paris of the Serbo-Croat-Slovene State addressed to Marshal Foch (Appendix IV)[9] indicating that Italian units had attacked Jugoslav units and occupied certain districts in the region of Tarvis.

M. SONNINO said he knew nothing about any action in the region of Tarvis. All he knew was that at an earlier date some Italian troops on the invitation of the four Military representatives of the Allies had advanced in the region of Villach. If he was given a copy he undertook to make enquiry.

M. Clemenceau instructed Capt. Portier to send him a copy.

11. With reference to C.F.92, Minute 14, MR. LLOYD GEORGE said he had received a letter from Dr. Beneš.

(It was agreed that this letter should be circulated both to the Military Representatives of the Supreme War Council at Versailles and to the Members of the Council (Appendix V.))

12. MR. LLOYD GEORGE pointed out that a question of shipping the Czecho-Slovak forces from Vladivostock was raised by the above letter. He asked that President Wilson and Baron Makino

[8] It is printed in PPC, VI, 706-707.
[9] Printed in ibid., p. 707.

respectively would enquire as to whether any United States shipping or Japanese shipping was available for this purpose.

PRESIDENT WILSON said that most of the United States shipping had been taken away from the Pacific Coast and he doubted whether much could be done. He agreed however to make enquiries.

BARON MAKINO said that a similar enquiry had been made by the Roumanian Government who wished to repatriate Hungarian prisoners in Siberia and natives of the districts which were being transferred to Roumania. He undertook to make enquiries.

13. With reference to C.F.92, Minute 9, it was agreed: That the Committee proposed on the previous day should be set up to enquire how far steps have already been taken by the Allied and Associated Powers to carry out the various provisions of the Treaty of Peace with Germany and to make recommendations as to such further measures as should be adopted for this purpose.

M. Clemenceau nominated M. Tardieu to represent the French Government; President Wilson said that Mr. Lansing should be asked to nominate a representative of the United States of America; M. Sonnino undertook to nominate an Italian Representative; Baron Makino undertook to nominate a Japanese Representative and Mr. Lloyd George undertook to nominate a British Representative.

14. (It was agreed that the Military Representatives of the Supreme War Council at Versailles, with whom should be associated Belgian and Japanese Military Representatives as well as Naval and Air Representatives of the five Principal Allied and Associated Powers, should work out for the consideration of the Council all details of the Interallied Military, Naval and Aerial Supervisory Commissions of Control to be set up to ensure execution by Germany of the Military, Naval and Aerial clauses in the Treaty of Peace.)

15. (It was agreed that a proposal by the Admirals of the Allied and Associated Powers that the Commission to supervise the destruction of the fortifications, etc. of Heligoland, should be a Sub-Commission of the Naval Interallied Commission of Control, should also be referred to the Military Representatives as above.)

16. SIR MAURICE HANKEY drew attention to the Report that had been furnished by the Prisoners of War Commission as to the measures to be adopted for the fulfilment of the terms of the Treaty of Peace in regard to Prisoners of War.

M. CLEMENCEAU asked that the subject should be reserved for the present.

M. MANTOUX at M. Clemenceau's request, read a telegram from General Dupont on the subject of Polish prisoners in Germany.

PRESIDENT WILSON pointed out that no steps could be taken for the repatriation of Polish prisoners until after the ratification of the Treaty of Peace.

17. PRESIDENT WILSON said that the only forms of mandate that he had seen were some that had been prepared by Lord Robert Cecil.[10]

MR. LLOYD GEORGE said that he would circulate Lord Milner's proposals on the subject.[11]

18. SIR MAURICE HANKEY said that he and Captain Portier had made enquiries and had ascertained that the Reparation Commission had failed to secure an agreement with the states acquiring territory formerly part of the Austrian Empire in regard to the reparation and financial clauses.

A further Meeting was to be held at 11 o'clock that morning.

19. (It was agreed that the letter to M. Paderewski[12] that had accompanied the Polish Treaty should not be published until the signature of the Treaty.)

20. SIR MAURICE HANKEY handed round a document relating to the size of the Army of Occupation on the Rhine for consideration at an early date.

NOTE. It has since been ascertained that the document handed round was incomplete. The complete document will be circulated.

21. M. CLEMENCEAU said that he thought the Council ought to hear the views of Marshal Foch as to what action should be taken if trouble should arise on the Eastern Frontier of Germany in connection with the Treaty of Peace. The Allied and Associated Powers had the duty to help the Poles to defend themselves if attacked, but it was a very difficult thing to do as if the Germans opposed, it would not even be possible to send any supplies through Dantzig.

(After a short discussion it was agreed that the Military Representatives of the Supreme War Council at Versailles should be asked to consider the following questions:

(1) In the event of trouble in the area ceded by the Treaty of Peace with Germany to Poland, what would they advise as to how the Allied and Associated Powers could best assist the Poles to establish their authority.

(2) The composition and size of the Army of Occupation of the

[10] See R. Cecil to EMH, May 24, 1919, Vol. 59.
[11] Printed as Enclosure I with WW to EMH, June 27, 1919.
[12] See Appendix I to the minutes of the Council of Four printed at June 23, 1919, 12:10 p.m.

Plebiscite area in Upper Silesia, and the method of occupation of this area.)

(The Meeting then adjourned.)

APPENDIX II TO C.F.93.

The Secretary of State of the United States of America.

My dear Mr. President,   Hôtel de Crillon, Paris. June 26th, 1919.

Enclosed please find a proposed draft of a request to the Government of the Netherlands for the surrender of the ex-German Emperor to the Principal Allied and Associated Governments.

As the Netherlands Government is not a party to the Treaty it was necessary to quote the text of Article 227 so as to inform it of its existence.

In the next place it seemed advisable to state that all the signatories (necessarily including Germany) had agreed to this action and then to ask for the surrender. It is next stated and most clear that the offense is moral and that even if political the submission to a court makes it judicial. The authority for this last statement is that of the Supreme Court in the well known and leading case of Rhode Island vs Massachusetts (12 Peters Reports 657, 737) decided in 1838. I did not quote it but in such an important matter it is well to have an unimpeachable authority.

You will observe that the time and place of delivery are not specified. These are perhaps best stated indefinitely at present. The Treaty must be ratified before it is binding and the "place" must be agreed on. Perhaps it would be proper to say within a month after the deposit of ratifications of the Treaty. Perhaps the ex-Emperor should be delivered to the country in which he is to be tried. These are however matters that can be settled later. England has seemed to be most eager for the ex-Emperor's surrender and trial and he might therefore be handed over to authorised agents of that country.

Finally the request, in the form of a Memorandum, might properly be delivered with a brief covering note by the French to the Netherlands as the Conference meets in Paris, the Treaty is to be signed at Versailles, ratifications deposited in Paris so that France acts as a general mandatory of the Powers in all matters pertaining to the Conference. It will be noted that the customary phrase "international comity" is omitted owing to the large number of powers concerned which goes further than mere comity could possibly go.

In the hope that the Draft may serve the purpose for which it has been prepared, I am

Faithfully yours,   (Signed) ROBERT LANSING.

The President,
PARIS.

ANNEX TO THE APPENDIX II TO C.F.93.
DRAFT OF COMMUNICATION TO THE GOVERNMENT OF THE
NETHERLANDS.

The Governments of the United States of America, the British Empire, France, Italy and Japan have the honour to call the attention of the Netherlands Government to Article 227 of the Treaty of Peace, signed at Versailles, the * * * day of June 1919, to which the twenty-seven Allied and Associated Powers and Germany are Signatory and Contracting Parties.

Article 227 is thus worded:

"The Allied and Associated Powers publicly arraign William II of Hohenzollern, formerly German Emperor, for a supreme offence against international morality and the sanctity of Treaties.

"A special tribunal will be constituted to try the accused, thereby assuring him the guarantees essential to the right of defence. It will be composed of five judges, one appointed by each of the following Powers: namely the United States of America, Great Britain, France, Italy and Japan.

"In its decision the tribunal will be guided by the highest motives of international policy, with a view to vindicating the solemn obligations of international undertakings and the validity of international morality. It will be its duty to fix the punishment which it considers should be imposed.

"The Allied and Associated Powers will address a request to the Government of the Netherlands for the surrender to them of the ex-Emperor in order that he may be put on trial."

Persons residing in Germany against whom judicial proceedings are to be taken by the Allied and Associated Powers will be delivered to them in accordance with the terms of Article 228 of the Treaty of Peace. If the ex-Emperor had remained in Germany he would have been delivered to them by the Government of that country upon the request of the Allied and Associated Powers. As, however, he is temporarily residing in the Netherlands the Principal Allied and Associated Powers, acting in their own behalf and in behalf of all the signatories of the Treaty of Peace and in accordance with its terms, have the honour respectfully to request the Government of the Netherlands to deliver to them the ex-Emperor at a time and place to be later specified to be proceeded against in the manner provided in Article 227 of the Treaty.

The Principal Allied and Associated Governments respectfully call the attention of the Netherlands Government to the fact that the delivery of the ex-Emperor is requested "for a supreme offence against international morality and the sanctity of Treaties"; that proceedings against the ex-Emperor are before a special tribunal in which the accused is to have "the guarantees essential to the right of defence"; that the decision is to be "guided by the highest motives of international policy," and that the punishment to be inflicted upon the accused, should he be found guilty of the offence with which he is charged, is to be fixed by the Tribunal "with a view to vindicating the solemn obligations of international undertakings and the validity of international morality."

The Principal Allied and Associated Powers further call the attention of the Government of the Netherlands to the well established principle of universal application that even if the offence with which the ex-Emperor is charged were to be considered political at the date of its commission the agreement of the nations to submit it and its submission to a judicial tribunal, thus transferring it from the political to the judicial forum, make that judicial which would have otherwise been political.

The Principal Allied and Associated Powers will be happy to receive the assurance of the Government of the Netherlands that it will take the necessary measures to comply with the present request.

W.C.P.1063   APPENDIX V TO C.F.93

Monsieur le Ministre,   PARIS, 23rd June, 1919.

Further to the conversation which I had the honour of having with you yesterday, I beg to set forth my point of view with regard to the question of our army in Siberia and its transport to Bohemia, whilst stating that in view of the present situation in Bohemia, I express my point of view subject to that of my colleagues in the Prague Government and of the President of the Republic.

(1) Our soldiers in Siberia have already suffered so intensely that their one desire is to return home as soon as possible. That is the reason actuating them at present, and all action undertaken should be looked at from this point of view.

(2) Would it be possible to consider the transport of our troops from Siberia by two routes, either via Vladivostock or via Perm, Viatka and Archangel? The latter route would probably be the shortest and quickest.

(3) This second route, however, might probably cause our soldiers to come once more into conflict with the Bolsheviki and to fight by the side of Admiral Kolchak's troops. This would be very serious for us in view of the political situation in Bohemia, and of the general state of affairs among our soldiers in Siberia.

(4) It would perhaps be possible to send part of our soldiers (about 20,000) via Vladivostok, and to make the others understand that they would travel more rapidly via Perm, Viatka and Archangel (30,000). I do not, however, conceal from myself the great difficulties which would confront our soldiers. If these 30,000 soldiers were sent to the North, not with the idea that they were to fight against the Bolsheviki and to support Admiral Kolchak's policy, but merely to be taken home after having joined the English troops operating in North Russia, we might have a chance of success.

(5) All this, however, would be subject to the preparation of public opinion in Bohemia, and to the state of mind of our soldiers in Siberia. I will not conceal that our public opinion in Bohemia and our soldiers in Siberia have not at present any very great faith in this enterprise. In any case, it would be necessary to demonstrate either to our public opinion in Bohemia or to our soldiers themselves that they were being looked after, and that those available and ready were going to be immediately transported from Vladivostok. A very detailed plan would have to be drawn up for the purpose, the Czecho-Slovak Government would have to be given the assurance that the Allies were preparing such-and-such a number of ships for such-and-such a date, and that they intended to complete the transport of our troops before the end of this year. If our public and our soldiers were further informed—as you informed me—that without the use of these two routes the transport of our troops could not be completed for two years, our public opinion and our soldiers in Siberia might perhaps accept the plan which you explained to me.

(6) I consider it essential to draw up an exact programme, to set forth the two above possibilities therein, and to give precise assurances to our Government, as also to draw up a mutual agreement wherein precise details should be set forth as to the conditions and time of return of our troops. If I had such a programme in my possession and could submit some precise assurances to my Government, we could probably arrive at a successful result.

I would ask you, therefore, if you consider it possible and advisable, to let me have details as to such programme or as to the assurances and conditions under which this operation would be effected. I would hope to obtain the consent of the Prague Government very quickly.

With apologies for a slight delay in sending this letter, I beg, etc.

(Signed)   DR. EDVARD BENEŠ.

T MS (SDR, RG 256, 180.03401/93, DNA).

Mantoux's Notes of a Meeting of the Council of Four

June 26, 1919, 11 a.m.

M. Dutasta is introduced.

Dutasta. I have just seen Von Haniel; the German government has named its plenipotentiaries, the list of whom will be completed today. The two names transmitted to me are those of Herr Hermann Müller, Minister of Foreign Affairs, and Herr Giesberts, Minister of Posts and Telegraphs. A third delegate will undoubtedly join them: that will be Herr Leinert, President of the Prussian Assembly.

These delegates are to arrive Saturday at dawn, by ordinary train. Von Haniel questioned me about the verification of the credentials. I told him that, in my opinion, that could be done Saturday morning at 10 o'clock. He telegraphed in that sense to Berlin. Under these conditions, the signing could take place Saturday afternoon, at 3 o'clock.

Von Haniel said to me again: "We want to verify the text of the copy which the German plenipotentiaries will sign." I answered him that that would take a very long time. He told me that he had thought of that, and that the Germans were prepared to renounce this right if the Allied and Associated Governments will give them a declaration attesting that the text of the authentic copy of the treaty is indeed identical on every point to that of the 200 copies which were sent to Germany. That declaration would have to be made by a letter from the President of the Conference.

Clemenceau. Do you consent?

Sonnino. Could we not give the Germans two copies of the treaty today?

Dutasta. There is only one diplomatic document, and two days would be needed to collate it.

Clemenceau. Do you agree to send the letter in question?

(Assent.)

Dutasta. Von Haniel asked if the President of the Conference would make a speech. I said to him that I could not reply officially, but unofficially I could tell him no.

I must draw your attention to the question of seals, which will take much time to affix. Since the Germans are only three, I would propose that their seals be affixed by them at the very moment of the signing.

Clemenceau. For the other seals, the best thing is to have them affixed in advance.

Wilson. We only have to give the seals to the secretaries of our respective delegations.

Clemenceau. We could proceed to that operation tomorrow at 2 o'clock. But could the seals of the Germans not be affixed Saturday morning? The presence of ours will reassure them.

Dutasta. Von Haniel delivered to me, moreover, a note about Poland. I transmit it to you.

M. Dutasta withdraws.

Clemenceau. On July 14, we will have a solemn parade of the troops. Our intention is to invite General Robertson, Marshal Haig, General Pershing, and General Diaz to participate in it. We would like to see there as many English and American soldiers as you can send, and also, naturally, Italian soldiers. I believe that Japan can only send us officers. Of course, the sailors must not be forgotten.

(Assent.)

Lloyd George. I have interesting news from Holland. The Crown Prince fled eastward by automobile, with a staff officer. That augurs nothing good.

Clemenceau. He did not leave to do nothing.

Lloyd George. I am told that he is not as stupid as he seems, and that he is even rather crafty.

Wilson. From the military point of view, he played a ridiculous role.

Reading of the German note concerning Poland, brought by M. Dutasta:

The German government asks that the populations on both sides of the line of demarcation be warned by Germany and by the Allies, respectively, of the moment when the cession of territories will be made. In any case, the latter can only take place after the ratifications of the treaty.

Lloyd George. This is not too bad. It seems that the German government is rather striving to prevent misunderstandings. But attention must be paid to the manner in which we reply to them, and I propose to send this question to our committee of jurists.

(Assent.)

Wilson. Since we are speaking of jurists, I must tell you that I consulted Mr. Lansing on the subject of Holland. In his opinion, we must notify her of our intention to claim the Kaiser, indicating that he is wanted for a moral crime rather than a political one. The place and time when he will be handed over will be fixed only after ratification of the treaty. This notification must be addressed to Holland by France, in the name of the conference. I submit to you the draft of the letter that Mr. Lansing has drawn up.

Lloyd George (after reading). I think that it is an excellent draft.

Clemenceau. That is also my opinion.

Lloyd George. But can we really wait to send this letter to Holland? The Crown Prince has already fled, not because he fears being indicted before us, but undoubtedly because he wants to attempt some political enterprise. He left with a staff officer, and, at this very moment, appeals are being sent to Berlin and different parts of Prussia for the army to revolt against the treaty. The Crown Prince is rather dangerous; but the Emperor would be much more so because of the prestige that he had in Germany.

Wilson. You cannot appeal to Holland before the treaty is signed.

Lloyd George. We can invoke reasons of international public safety. Here is a man who was a kind of demigod in his country; we must not forget the power that he can still have over the imagination of his people.

Wilson. At bottom, I agree with you. I think that Holland will find no excuse to refuse to hand over the Kaiser after the signing of the treaty. But today, she can resist you.

Lloyd George. I think that the Kaiser and his son are preparing a dirty trick against us.

Wilson. Then we must address Holland now, showing her that she must not permit the Kaiser to cross the frontier. From the strictly legal point of view, he has the right to go where he wishes.

Lloyd George. I would indicate clearly the political reason of our action, the signs that disturb us, and the danger of a civil war in Germany, which could be the prologue to a resumption of hostilities. The Dutch must commit themselves either to keeping the Kaiser, or to delivering him without delay.

The drafting of a note along these lines is decided.

Wilson. M. Beneš announces to us that hostilities between Czechoslovak and Hungarian troops were halted on June 24. Mr. McCormick calls to my attention that, from the cessation of hostilities, the blockade must be lifted for Hungary, or at least relaxed, as for Germany after the Armistice.

Clemenceau. I received a telegram from Béla Kun a few days ago; he asked for guarantees, of which the first was the recognition of his Republic of Soviets. I did not reply. Today, he complains that the Rumanians are renewing hostilities, after they were stopped on the Hungarian side.

Reading of the telegram from Béla Kun.

Clemenceau. I propose to send this to General Bliss for verification of the facts.

Wilson. What the Hungarian government says does not seem unreasonable.

Clemenceau. No, but the facts must be verified.

Lloyd George. On the other hand, we cannot say that we will never recognize a government of soviets. However flawed this kind of government may be, it is—all in all—more representative than was that of the Czar.

Clemenceau. That recognition would present real dangers here.

Lloyd George. It is necessary that our justice be impartial. We have taken a decision; if the Rumanians violate it, we must hold them responsible.

Clemenceau. The Hungarians complain about the Rumanians; but if we listen to the Rumanians, we will conclude that it is the Hungarians who are violating the agreement.

Reading of a note from General Pešić, in which the Yugoslavs complain of a movement of Italian troops on Tarvis.

Wilson. Is Baron Sonnino informed?

Sonnino. I know nothing; I did not know that there was fighting in that area. I will find out.

Lloyd George. I received a letter from M. Beneš about the plan relating to Czechoslovak troops in Russia. M. Beneš is not very hot for Mr. Winston Churchill's scheme; he says that, if we can give him a firm promise to withdraw these troops, he will submit the plan to his parliament. One part of the Czechoslovak troops will have to be embarked at Vladivostok; but only America could take charge of them. Does she have the necessary tonnage?

Wilson. I do not believe so. According to the last news, we had very few ships in the Pacific.

Lloyd George. See if you can transport twenty or thirty thousand Czechs.

Wilson. I fear that this is impossible.

Makino. Where are these Czech troops at present?

Lloyd George. In Siberia. If we do not evacuate them, we will have great difficulties with the Czechs. Could Japan undertake to transport them?

Makino. I will find out. We have already received a request from Transylvanian prisoners in Siberia, who also wish that we help to repatriate them.

Lloyd George. Then we will ask President Wilson and Baron Makino to inform us about the tonnage which their countries could furnish respectively.

Nomination of the members of the commission charged with preparing the execution of the treaty of peace with Germany: Mr. Clement Jones (British Empire) and M. Tardieu (France) are designated; the American and Italian members will be designated later.

Hankey. Your military advisers ask to be authorized to continue the preparatory work of the commission for the control of armaments in Germany.

Reading of a draft decision: Marshal Foch will be charged with forming a commission to prepare in detail the organization of the permanent commission which must control the execution of the military clauses of the treaty.

Lloyd George. Why Marshal Foch? Should this matter not belong to the Supreme War Council of Versailles?

Clemenceau. Certainly.

Lloyd George. I prefer the Supreme War Council, because there the control of the civilian authority makes itself better felt.

Clemenceau. It is to the organization in Versailles that this task must be entrusted.

Hankey. There is also the question of the measures to be taken for execution of the treaty where Heligoland is concerned.

Lloyd George. Let us refer that also to the Supreme War Council.

Hankey. I have to submit to you yet another note on the subject of the release of German prisoners.

Clemenceau. I propose to wait for a while before putting the treaty into execution. In a telegram about Poland, General Dupont warned me that the German prisoners of war that we send back to Germany will be immediately employed in fighting against the Poles.

Lloyd George. There is much to be said in favor of a suggestion of Sir Ernest Pollock, consisting of tying the liberation of German prisoners of war to the handing over of the culprits whom we intend to put on trial.

Clemenceau. According to certain information, we also know that the Germans are still holding prisoner two or three hundred French, English, and others. I am of the opinion that the Germans should begin by handing them over to us.

Lloyd George. Could we not take up the question of the mandate system?

Wilson. The only plan which has been delivered to me was drafted by Lord Robert Cecil, with amendments presented by the American experts; he proposes a provisional understanding on the different kinds of mandates; after our provisional decision, the plan would be published, and we would see what criticism would be made of it.

Lloyd George. Lord Milner has prepared a text which I have not yet read.

Wilson. I would like to receive it and to have the time to examine it. Did Lord Milner prepare this plan alone?

Lloyd George. No, with the representatives of the Dominions.

Wilson. I will call to your attention that the preparation of this plan belongs to the League of Nations.

Lloyd George. All that we are doing is presenting proposals. We could not have them drafted by a man more competent than our Colonial Secretary. Lord Robert Cecil does not have precise ideas on that question. The Ministers of the Dominions and their advisers are precisely the men most capable of anticipating difficulties and advising the means of getting around them.

Hankey. I have M. Paderewski's letter and the reply that you have made to it. Publication of them has been decided; is it not your intention that it take place only after the publication of the treaty?

(Assent.)

Presentation of a report of the Supreme War Council on the total strength of the army of occupation.

Clemenceau. I must consult Marshal Pétain about that. I therefore request adjournment.

Lloyd George. Do you want to take up the Turkish question this afternoon? We could take a general glance at it.

Wilson. Agreed.

Clemenceau. There is one point on which I believe Marshal Foch much be questioned; what will we do if something happens concerning Poland?

Lloyd George. If only small local movements develop in Poland, we must do nothing. But I believe that that cannot fail to happen, even without any outside encouragement from Germany.

Clemenceau. I do not believe that these encouragements will be lacking.

Wilson. What exactly is your concern?

Clemenceau. It is a matter of knowing how we will help the Poles, if they are attacked by the Germans.

Lloyd George. Of course, we must support the treaty.

Wilson. Then we would ask Marshal Foch: "In case of a conflict in the western part of Poland, what aid can we bring to the Poles?"

Lloyd George. In my opinion, unless the Poles are attacked from outside, they must begin by defending their liberty themselves.

Clemenceau. What would we do to aid them? The other day you admitted that we could not pass through Danzig.

Lloyd George. Excuse me; once the peace is signed, we have the right to demand passage through Danzig to aid the Poles. If Germany prevented us, we would find ourselves again in a state of war with her.

I propose to put the question first to the Supreme War Council and to formulate it in the following terms: "If there is a conflict in the territories ceded to Poland by the treaty, how does the council think that we should help the Poles to establish their authority over those regions?"

This first question is completely different from the one which would arise for the region of the plebiscite; there, if Germany refuses to withdraw her troops in conformity with the treaty, that means war. The question I would ask would be the following: "What measures are proposed to us for the occupation of the region where the plebiscite is to take place? What forces should we employ there? What should their strength be? What should be the occupation arrangement?"

Clemenceau. But we must anticipate what might happen before the occupation begins.

Lloyd George. If the Germans refuse to evacuate the territories that they must evacuate according to the treaty, it means war. Then we have the right to advance our troops from the bank of the Rhine. What we must avoid is committing ourselves to acts of war if Germany does not violate her commitments.

Mantoux, II, 522-29.

Hankey's Notes of a Meeting of the Council of Four[1]

Mr. Lloyd George's Residence, Paris,
C.F.93A.   June 26, 1919, 4 p.m.

1. M. CLEMENCEAU said that M. Wellington Koo had informed him that the Chinese Delegation would make a protest in order to satisfy public opinion in China. This would be done only in the hope that later on the clauses in the Treaty relating to Shantung would be revised. He wished to ask his Colleagues whether they thought the protest should be made before or after the signature of the Treaty. For his part, he would prefer that it should be after.

MR. LLOYD GEORGE agreed.

M. CLEMENCEAU pointed out that otherwise Roumania might be encouraged to follow suit.

MR. LLOYD GEORGE said that it might even set a bad example to the Germans.

(It was agreed that M. Clemenceau should ask M. Pichon to request the Chinese Government to make their formal protest at the very last possible moment.)

[1] The complete text of these minutes is printed in PPC, VI, 710-15.

2. With reference to C.F.93,[2] Minute 6, the attached telegram drafted by Mr. Balfour was agreed to (Appendix I).[3]

(M. Clemenceau undertook to despatch it to the Dutch Government on behalf of the Conference.)

3. M. CLEMENCEAU said that he had allocated 15 places in the Hall at Versailles for French soldiers, who had specially distinguished themselves in the war, to witness the signature of the Treaty of Peace, and he would be glad to offer the same facilities to the British and American Governments.

MR. LLOYD GEORGE and PRESIDENT WILSON thanked M. Clemenceau for his offer,which they accepted.

4. MR. LLOYD GEORGE asked what reply was to be given to the Turks.

PRESIDENT WILSON observed that Mr. Balfour had already made a reply.

MR. LLOYD GEORGE said that this was not his meaning. He wished to know whether the Turks were to be allowed to go or whether they were to be asked to meet the Representatives of the Powers, or should they be sent a letter suggesting that they should go home and return later on when summoned.

PRESIDENT WILSON expressed the opinion that it would be better to let them go. They had exhibited complete absence of common sense and a total misunderstanding of the West. They had imagined that the Conference knew no history and was ready to swallow enormous falsehoods.

MR. LLOYD GEORGE observed that this was Turkish Diplomacy.

PRESIDENT WILSON remarked that no promise had been made to reply to what they might say.

M. CLEMENCEAU agreed that they had only asked for a hearing.

PRESIDENT WILSON said that the Conference had given them sufficient attention. They had been treated favourably. They had been asked to come to the Conference and all they had wished to say had been listened to. They had been better treated in this respect than the Austrians.

MR. LLOYD GEORGE said that the question he had alluded to on the previous day was whether it was expedient to try and make Peace with Turkey without coming to a decision on the question of Mandates.

PRESIDENT WILSON said that he had reflected on this subject. It might be possible to tell the Turks that they must abandon their

[2] That is, Hankey's minutes of the previous meeting.
[3] It is printed with one minor change as Appendix II to the minutes of the Council of Four printed at June 27, 1919, 12 noon.

possessions in Europe and in certain specified territories in Asia, or else they might be told "Your territory will be bounded as follows—Turkey must renounce all rights over territories outside this boundary and accept in advance the disposal of these areas to be made by the Allied and Associated Powers." Furthermore, "Turkey must accept in certain Departments of State—Finance, Police, supervision of the Coasts—the assistance of a Power, hereafter to be designated." This appeared to him to be practicable and settlement of all other questions could be adjourned.

MR. LLOYD GEORGE said that this proposal was practicable if it be decided at once to take Constantinople from the Turks.

PRESIDENT WILSON observed that Constantinople was not a Turkish City, other races there were in the majority.

MR. LLOYD GEORGE said this amounted to a final expulsion of the Turks from Europe.

M. CLEMENCEAU said that he had an objection to make. If this solution were proposed to the Turks, they would refuse and would remain where they were. There was nothing ready to enforce immediate execution. What could the Allied and Associated Powers do? The whole of this question could only be settled at one time. For his part he agreed that Constantinople should not remain Turkish. The capture of Constantinople by the Turks had been, when it occurred, a very great event which had shaken up all Europe. Since then Europe had made every effort to maintain the Turks there.

PRESIDENT WILSON said doubtless because no successor could be found for them.

MR. LLOYD GEORGE said it was chiefly by reason of the fear of Russia.

M. CLEMENCEAU asked what immediate solution was in view. Constantinople had been offered to President Wilson, but he did not seem anxious to accept it.

PRESIDENT WILSON said he would take the proposal to the Powers but for the situation brought about by Italian action. Italians had continued to land troops in Asia Minor. M. Tittoni no doubt would cause these troops to advance still further. Conflicts were to be feared. What Italy aimed at was to obtain a position such that she could not be evicted without hostilities. Should she continue this Policy, she would place herself outside the law. A great Nation which behaved in this manner lost all its rights. The problem of Asia Minor would be easily settled if Italy were not concerned.

MR. LLOYD GEORGE thought it would be safer to say that Asia Minor would be "easier to settle."

M. CLEMENCEAU agreed and pointed out that there would still be ticklish problems. He reminded the meeting that the Indian Mohammedans had protested against any division of Turkish Asia.[4]

MR. LLOYD GEORGE said that they meant Anatolia.

M. CLEMENCEAU pointed out that the Greeks were in Smyrna and were extending up to Aidin. This was part of Anatolia. There was a considerable Turkish population in Smyrna itself. He was making no protest, merely drawing attention to facts. As to the Italians, they had seized ports and had stayed there in spite of clear warnings, they had advanced inland and were continuing to penetrate. He did not think that they would withdraw if asked to by the Council. Mr. Tittoni now said "Smyrna was promised to us." This meant "Italy is a great nation which might perhaps make concessions. It will not leave Smyrna to others except for compensation." He asked what was to be done.

PRESIDENT WILSON expressed the opinion that the Italian Government would not last. It would come to Paris and make claims which would not be accepted. These claims would be categorically refused and the Italian Government would be forced to withdraw.

M. CLEMENCEAU said that he was inclined to refuse discussion of Asiatic questions with the Italians for the present. He would say to them "We are now making Peace with Austria and we cannot allow negotiations to be suspended. The first question we must settle is that of the Adriatic."

PRESIDENT WILSON said that he agreed.

M. CLEMENCEAU said that any haste in dealing with the Turkish question would be dangerous. For instance, there was the French view. France had a disagreement with Great Britain. He did not wish to raise this question until Peace with Germany had been signed. Fortunately, public opinion was not for the time being exerting any pressure. This was a piece of good luck. If, unfortunately, this question got entangled with European questions, he was much afraid of what might be said and done by certain persons devoid of self control. If the Conference could reach satisfactory solutions of more important problems, public opinion would be greatly appeased and subsequent discussions would be rendered easier.

PRESIDENT WILSON said that for the time being all he proposed was to fix the frontiers of Turkey.

M. CLEMENCEAU said that was all that could be done and that as no immediate means of execution existed, the result would be deplorable.

---

[4] See the extract from the Grayson Diary printed at May 17, 1919, n. 1, Vol. 59.

MR. LLOYD GEORGE said that the Italian danger in Asia Minor was a matter of deep concern to him. The Italians were advancing straight before them and seizing in the interior everything that suited them. Great Britain had no ambition in this region, but he feared what the effect might be in Mussulman Countries. This concerned Great Britain in Egypt and in India and France in North Africa. M. Tittoni said that what Italy desired in Asia was mining concessions, but the Italians were now seizing everything that might be of use to them.

PRESIDENT WILSON observed that what they wanted was things it would be impossible for them to obtain under a mandate.

MR. LLOYD GEORGE observed that Italy alone among the Powers had not demobilised. She was afraid to do so out of fear of internal disorder. She had her troops and she was sending them to Asia Minor, to the Caucasus, and wherever she wished.

PRESIDENT WILSON said that he had reason to anticipate a period of famine in the Caucasus, when British troops were withdrawn, by reason of a momentary influx of population. This was a problem to which his attention had been drawn and which must be borne in mind. As to the Italians, he thought they should be asked clearly to state whether they remained in the Entente or not. If they did, they must take part with their Allies in the negotiations with Turkey and do nothing independently.

MR. LLOYD GEORGE pointed out that even according to the agreement of Saint Jean de Maurienne, the Italians had no right to the forcible occupation of all the places they had seized.

PRESIDENT WILSON said that he could not go back and tell the United States Senate "Here is a Treaty re-establishing Peace," if Italy were left a free hand. It would be on the contrary a treaty preparing war and could not be guaranteed by the Powers.

M. CLEMENCEAU said that as far as he was concerned, he would put the question to the Italians as clearly as possible. Fiume was at the present time administered in the name of the King of Italy. The local Government had lately asked the French General to expel the Serbians. The General had refused. The Italians had then expelled them themselves. The town was surrounded by barbed wire. This was a state of war. Was this the intention of the Treaty of London? The Italians were breaking their word there and everywhere else.

PRESIDENT WILSON said that they justified their presence in Fiume on the pretext that the Armistice granted them the right of advancing to re-establish order.

M. CLEMENCEAU said that they had gone so far in the last few days as to ask France for a small bit of French territory in the

County of Nice to improve their frontier which according to them was ill-drawn.

MR. LLOYD GEORGE observed that this was madness.

T MS (SDR, RG 256, 180.03401/93½, DNA).

Mantoux's Notes of a Meeting of the Council of Four

June 26, 1919, 4 p.m.

Clemenceau. Mr. Wellington Koo announced to me that the Chinese delegation will raise a protest, which is necessary to satisfy public opinion in China, but only in the hope of a later revision of the clauses of the treaty relative to Shantung. Must this letter of protest be written before or after the signing of the treaty? For myself, I would prefer that it be written after.

Lloyd George. Certainly.

Clemenceau. Otherwise, that could encourage Rumania to do as much.

Lloyd George. We must also be on guard on the side of the Germans.

Wilson. We have M. Tittoni's first statements and the letter he addressed to Mr. Lloyd George. If he comes here in the frame of mind he indicates, he would do as well to remain in Rome.

Lloyd George. He will not begin by attacking the question of the Adriatic. He will first try to obtain a solution favorable to Italy in the colonial field, and, once strengthened from that side, he will present us with his note for the Adriatic.

Lloyd George. What do we reply to the Turks?

Wilson. Mr. Balfour has already replied.

Lloyd George. Yes, but that is not what I mean. Do we permit the Turks to leave? Do we summon them? Or send them a letter to tell them: "Go home, you will return when we summon you"?

Wilson. It is better to let them leave. They have given proof of an absolute lack of common sense or a complete misunderstanding of the West. They believed we would not know a word of history, and they have presented us with enormous lies.

Lloyd George. That is Turkish diplomacy.

Wilson. We did not promise to respond to what they might say to us.

Clemenceau. In fact, they only asked to be heard.

Wilson. I believe that we granted them enough attention. We treated them courteously. We invited them to come see us, and we heard all that they wanted to tell us. We did not do as much for the Austrians.

Lloyd George. The question that I already asked yesterday is this: would the best thing not be to try to make peace with Turkey without settling now the question of the mandates?

Wilson. I thought about that. We could say to them: "You are abandoning your possessions in Europe and such and such territories in Asia." Or better still: "Your territory will be delimited as follows, and Turkey renounces all rights over territories located outside that limit, accepting in advance the disposition of it which will be made by the Allied and Associated Powers. In addition, Turkey accepts, for certain departments of her administration—finances, police, coastal surveillance—the assistance of a power which will be designated later."

This seems practicable and postpones the settlement of all other questions.

Lloyd George. It is practicable, if you decide now to take Constantinople from the Turks.

Wilson. In fact, Constantinople is not a Turkish city; the other peoples are in the majority.

Lloyd George. That is to expel the Turks once and for all from Europe.

Clemenceau. Here is my objection. If we put the question to them, they will answer no and remain where they are. Now, we have nothing ready for immediate execution. What will we do? You can settle all these questions only at the same time.

For my part, I am of the opinion that it is not necessary that Constantinople remain with the Turks. The capture of Constantinople by the Turks was in its time a very great event that shook all of Europe. Since then, Europe has done all it could to leave the Turks in Constantinople.

Wilson. That is no doubt because one did not know how to replace them.

Lloyd George. That is especially because one feared Russia then.

Clemenceau. What solution do you have for tomorrow? Constantinople has been offered to President Wilson; he does not seem to have decided to accept it.

Wilson. I will submit the proposal to the Senate of the United States.

Clemenceau. With the chance that it will be accepted?

Wilson. I think that it will be.

Clemenceau. I would like that. The presence of America in Constantinople would have a calming effect on the entire situation in the East.

Wilson. What will help in having this proposal accepted in America is that it is not a matter of business, in the financial and commercial sense of the word. Constantinople ceases to be the center of a great empire. Its only importance is that it commands the Straits, and we would go there only to guard them, in the interest of all nations. That will not involve us in European politics—of which America would be most frightened.

Clemenceau. Would you occupy Constantinople only?

Wilson. No, but the Straits, with a strip of territory surrounding the entire area.

Clemenceau. Would the forts be occupied by American soldiers?

Wilson. The Straits must be fortified in such a way as to make an attack on them impossible.

Clemenceau. That solution satisfies me. But it does not resolve the other questions, and you know that some of them are very delicate. I sense around me feelings that could become dangerous if they were not treated with caution.

Wilson. This morning, I saw M. Vénisélos. I told him that the difficulties which embarrass us in Asia Minor do not come from a divergence of opinion among our three countries, but from the situation created by the action of Italy; she has not ceased to make landings and to send troops to Asia Minor. M. Tittoni will no doubt push his troops forward. A collision is to be feared. What Italy wants is to take such a position that one will not be able to chase her out of it without opening hostilities. If she pursues this policy, she will by that put herself beyond the law. A great nation which acts in this way thus loses all its rights. The problem of Asia Minor would be easy to settle if Italy was not involved.

Lloyd George. Say: "Would be *easier* to settle."

Clemenceau. That is the word; delicate problems would still remain. The Moslems of India, when they came here, did they not protest against any division of Asiatic Turkey?

Lloyd George. Only against the division of Anatolia.

Clemenceau. The Greeks are in Smyrna and extend as far as Aidin; it is a part of Anatolia. Even in Smyrna, there is a large Turkish population. I do not protest, but I state the fact.

As for the Italians, they have seized ports; they have remained there despite our formal warnings; they have pushed into the interior and do not cease to penetrate it. I do not believe that they will leave at a word from us. M. Tittoni says today: "You promised us Smyrna." That means: "We are a great nation, and we can perhaps make concessions; but we will leave Smyrna to others only with compensation." What are we to do?

Wilson. This government will not last; for it will come here to present unacceptable claims, to which we can only answer no. Then it will be forced to resign.

Clemenceau. I favor refusing to discuss the questions of Asia with the Italians at present. I would say to them: "We are making peace with Austria, and we cannot leave that negotiation in suspense. The first question to settle is that of the Adriatic."

Wilson. I agree with you.

Clemenceau. Moreover, I believe it is dangerous to hurry concerning the Turkish question. Let us take it from the French point of view. We have a difference with England. I do not want to raise the question as long as the peace with Germany is not signed. Very happily, public opinion is not pressing us; we are offered a rare opportunity. If, unhappily, this question came to be involved with European questions, I greatly fear what some people who lack a cool head might say and do. If we have reached satisfactory solutions for other more important problems, that will bring great satisfaction to public opinion and make the discussions which will follow much easier.

Wilson. I am only proposing for the moment to fix the frontiers of Turkey.

Clemenceau. We will be obliged to leave it at that without means of immediate execution, and the result will be deplorable.

Lloyd George. The Italian danger in Asia Minor concerns me greatly. The Italians are advancing straight ahead, seizing everywhere in the interior of the country what suits them. England has no design on that region; but I fear the repercussions in the Moslem countries. That concerns us in Egypt and India, and that concerns France in North Africa.

M. Tittoni says that what Italy desires in Asia is, above all, mining concessions. But now, the Italians are grabbing everything that is of value to them.

Wilson. They want what would be impossible for them to obtain under the mandate system.

Lloyd George. I will call to your attention that Italy, alone among us, has not demobilized. She fears doing it, because her government fears disorder at home. So she has troops, and she is sending them to Asia Minor, to the Caucasus, everywhere she wishes.

Wilson. In the Caucasus, when the English troops are relieved, I fear a famine caused by the momentary influx of mouths to feed. This is a problem pointed out to me, and which we must take care of. As for the Italians, they must be told clearly: "Are you in the Entente or not? If you are, you must participate at the same time as the Allies in the negotiations with Turkey and do nothing apart from them."

Lloyd George. Even according to the agreement of Saint Jean de Maurienne, they would not have the right to occupy in force all these localities, as they are doing.

Wilson. I cannot go and say to the Senate of the United States:

"Here is a treaty which reestablishes the peace" if we leave Italy a free hand. On the contrary, that would be a treaty preparing for war, and we could not give it our guarantee.

Clemenceau. For myself, I would ask them the question as frankly as possible. Do you know that Fiume is today administered in the name of the King of Italy? The local government recently asked our general to expel the Serbians. He refused twice. Then the Italians expelled them themselves. The city is surrounded by barbed wire; it is a state of war. Is that what is called the execution of the Treaty of London? The Italians are violating their word there and everywhere else besides.

Wilson. The pretext which they invoke to justify their presence in Fiume is the right which the armistice gave them to advance in order to reestablish order.

Clemenceau. Do you know that these last few days they have gone as far as asking us for a small piece of French territory in the County of Nice, to improve the frontier which, it seems, is poorly drawn?

Lloyd George. It is madness.

Reading of the telegram addressed by the British government to the Emir Faisal.[1]

Reading of the letter addressed to the government of the Netherlands to protest against the departure of the Crown Prince, and to ask that government to prevent the Emperor of Germany from leaving its territory; the return of the Kaiser to Germany could only aid the recovery of the military party which ruined this country and put Europe in danger. To permit the Kaiser to return to Germany would be an outrage against all nations.

Clemenceau. I think that letter must be published.

Lloyd George. Yes, but not before the Dutch government has had time to take its precautions. The Kaiser must not be warned before it. I propose that publication take place only on Satuday. (Assent.)

Lloyd George. Will you see M. Pichon about the telegram to be sent to M. Tittoni?

Clemenceau. Yes.

Wilson. Are we in agreement about speaking very frankly to the Italians?

Lloyd George. The unfortunate thing is that neither you nor I will be still here when M. Tittoni arrives.

Wilson. What we can do is to prepare now a note in which I

---

[1] About this matter, see the minutes of the Council of Four printed at June 25, 1919, 4 p.m., and n. 9 thereto.

would say, first, that, by their action in Fiume, the Italians have violated the Treaty of London, and that they can not invoke it hereafter.

Lloyd George. I thought that we would only speak to them of Asia Minor.

Wilson. In Asia, they have acted without taking account of the very clear protests and formal warnings given their government. They must act with the Entente or against it. If they stay with us, they must evacuate Asia Minor and Fiume. Before talking with them, we must receive positive proof of their good will.

Clemenceau. What they will do is to turn directly toward Vienna and Berlin.

Wilson. In that way they would give us the right to do what we like toward them.

Lloyd George. The Germans will no longer have confidence in Italy, given the manner in which she abandoned them.

Wilson. An Italian statesman said to me: "We were in the Triple Alliance when, in 1914, we heard vague rumors about the conflict between Austria and Serbia. We asked our allies questions. They denied their intention to resort to force and were still denying it two hours before the fait accompli." This shows the lack of regard with which the Germans were already treating Italy at that time, when they were powerful and victorious.

Lloyd George. Italy is at the mercy of the maritime powers.

Wilson. Yes, but no one of us dreams of attacking her.

Lloyd George. The two principal railway lines of the peninsula run along the coast. Any threat from the sea would be grave for Italy.

Wilson. What is tragic in the situation is that we are friends of Italy, we want to be such, and it is she who makes that friendship impossible. It is a miserable tragedy.

Clemenceau. For myself, I cannot say that the Treaty of London no longer exists. I can say: "You are violating it yourselves now in Fiume, and it is the very existence of the treaty you are threatening."

Lloyd George. England's position is the same as France's. Mr. Balfour could draft our common note.

Wilson. I hope that you will seize the favorable occasion to rid yourselves of a treaty which, speaking in all conscience, I have never considered continued to bind you.

Lloyd George. We must take into account the critical moment when Italy joined us, and the 500,000 dead which the war cost her.

Clemenceau. Do not take that figure too literally.

Wilson. The truth is that Italy went to the highest bidder.

Lloyd George. That is a harsh word; but I fear that there is truth in it.

Wilson. During this conference, Italy was uninterested in everything that did not directly affect her. She took no active part in our deliberations.

Lloyd George. I went through the entire war, and, unfortunately, I always saw Italy try to do as little as possible. France, England— and the United States, when she joined us later—threw themselves into the battle without holding back, and with all their hearts. Italy always measured with care what she gave.

Wilson. The problem, today, is how to save Italy from those who are leading her and who are driving her to ruin.

Clemenceau. I greatly fear that they represent the Italian people fairly well.

Lloyd George. Our Ambassador, Sir Rennell Rodd, wrote us that M. Tittoni, in a conversation, said to him that "the question of Fiume would be easier to resolve if Italy could obtain satisfaction in other directions. The new government cannot go to Paris only for a renunciation. That could only compel it to resign, with the most serious consequences." The best way of preventing Italy from turning again to Germany is to show the Italian people that the Allies are her best friends.

Clemenceau. Thiers[2] anticipated all that. He made I don't know how many speeches on the dangers which would result from Italian unification.

Lloyd George. Can Mr. Balfour not take charge of drafting the note?

Clemenceau. Let him write it bluntly.

Lloyd George. He will be sarcastic, in his usual way.

Clemenceau. That is not sufficient, he must appear very forceful.

Mr. Balfour is introduced.

Sir Maurice Hankey reads aloud the protest raised by the American, English, and French governments on May 17, 1919, against the Italian landings in Asia Minor.[3] In the same meeting, to Baron Sonnino, who asked if the status quo could be accepted, President Wilson responded that he could not sanction the maintenance of Italian troops at points where they ought not to be.

Wilson. If Italy continues to advance in Asia, we could only ask her the question clearly: are you with us or against us?

Balfour. Do you not believe that the new government will try to turn over a new leaf?

---

[2] Louis Adolphe Thiers, first President of the Third Republic, 1871-1873.
[3] About which, see the Appendix to the minutes of the Council of Four printed at May 17, 1919, 4:15 p.m., Vol. 59.

Lloyd George. You see the first manifestation of its sentiment.

Balfour. Baron Sonnino is an honest man, but extremely obstinate, and his head is full of imperialistic ideas. He believes in nearly all the principles that we reject, and it is impossible to make him abandon positions which he has taken. M. Tittoni is a much less reliable man, but more flexible.

Lloyd George. Read the telegram from Sir Rennell Rodd; there you will see that the Italians want mines in Asia Minor.

Balfour. Without encroaching upon Turkish sovereignty, we can recognize the right of the Italians to priority for concessions in such or such a region. If they accept that, we can say to them: "Are you going to break with us to obtain, in the Adriatic, what has no true value?" I believe that then we could work things out.

Clemenceau. I do not believe it. According to my information, M. Tittoni will come to say to us: "Here are my proposals; if you do not accept them, I return to Rome."

Wilson. M. Tittoni is inclined to take up questions at the point where M. Orlando left off, and, if we do not accept what he demands, he will leave. I remember that M. Orlando told me that Italian soldiers in Fiume would not withdraw, even if one gave them the order to do so. He added that his son, who is in Fiume among these soldiers, would do the same.

Lloyd George. I do not picture things in that way. M. Tittoni will purr like a cat. He will carefully avoid everything that could give rise to a conflict and will compel us to admit him into our councils without abandoning any of his pretentions. The best thing is to ask the question quickly and plainly.

Wilson. He has shown his hand. He has said that, if concessions are made to him in other regions, he will not insist as much on the Adriatic. But he will, in any case, demand Fiume. I do not see what rights the Italians have in Asia.

Balfour. The unfortunate thing is that the Treaty of London, in fact, recognizes certain rights of the Italians in Asia and Africa. For it promises them compensation if England and France make acquisitions in the Mediterranean region.

Lloyd George. That does not give them the right to occupy the province of Adalia before the distribution of mandates has taken place.

Mr. Balfour reads aloud the article referred to in the Treaty of London.

Wilson. The case anticipated is that of a partition of the Ottoman Empire.

Clemenceau. This partition has not yet taken place.

Wilson. There will be no partition. The territories of the Ottoman Empire will not be distributed among us like properties; they will be administered, for the good of their peoples, according to the system of mandates. This is not a partition. In addition, it is not a matter of a partition between France and England; these territories will be placed by the treaty at the disposal of the principal Allied and Associated Powers. No solution is possible without an agreement among ourselves. Under these conditions, Italy must accept that the entire question be reexamined.

Balfour. The Italians will say: "If France sees her influence increase in the Mediterranean, whatever form it takes, our influence must increase proportionately." If any of us takes possession of territories, Italy will demand that she be given a sphere of influence, such as France will have in Syria.

Clemenceau. But France does not have one now.

Balfour. I am speaking of the final solution.

Lloyd George. The question is to know what we shall say immediately to M. Tittoni. I propose to say to him: "Even if you have the right to a sphere of influence, that does not mean that you have the right to occupy territories militarily. You have not waited for the discussion of the fate of the Ottoman territories, nor for the settling of boundaries of regions under mandate; you have sent troops where you wanted to, not when it was a matter of fighting the Turks, but to occupy ports and mines. We must protest against this attempt to force our hand."

Wilson. Today, if we wish to settle the affairs of Asia, we will be obliged to make Italian troops evacuate these territories. It is an unbelievable situation.

Balfour. If you begin to enumerate what the Italians can be reproached for, their present conduct in Hungary must not be forgotten. There is much to say about that.

Lloyd George. I am not proposing to enter into all these questions, but to tell them that they must not be in Asia Minor or Fiume today contrary to our decisions.

Wilson. Their presence in Fiume is contrary to the Treaty of London.

Balfour. Let us say to them: "You must withdraw your troops from all localities to which they have been sent in spite of our protest."

Wilson. Their presence in Fiume and their presence in Asia Minor make the settlement of the Asiatic questions impossible.

Clemenceau. I have a reservation to make about Fiume. For, if there are Italian troops there, they are alongside French and British troops. It is true we have sent our soldiers there, because the Italians were already there.

Wilson. Are you sure that royal decrees have been promulgated in Fiume?

Clemenceau. That is a certain fact.

Balfour. I would not like to speak about the Treaty of London any more than strictly necessary. I have every possible aversion to this treaty. But, if we reproach the Italians too much for not conforming to it, they will say to us: "Very well! In this case, we demand of you nothing more or less than the execution of the Treaty of London."

Clemenceau. Then they would have to abandon Fiume, and they know that, for his own part, President Wilson would not accept the application of the Treaty of London.

Balfour. Yes, but that would be a way of casting responsibility on us—on the signatory powers of this treaty.

Wilson. It is necessary to refuse to talk with them so long as their troops are where they do not have the right to be.

Balfour. In the letter that we addressed to the Rumanians and the Serbians about Hungary, we told them that "occupation grants rights." Baron Sonnino was there, and he said "ditto."

Mr. Balfour is charged with drafting the note that will be presented to the Italian government.[4]

Mantoux, II, 530-40.

[4] It is printed as Appendix I to the minutes of the Council of Four, June 28, 1919, 6 p.m.

From David Lloyd George

My dear Mr. President,   Paris. 26th June 1919.

I refrained from answering your letter of the 3rd May[1] before, as I thought it best to await the Report of the Committee which was set up to examine the possible methods of re-establishing more normal economic and financial conditions in Europe,[2] as the scheme which I submitted to you did not seem feasible from the American point of view. The Report of the Committee is a very interesting and valuable survey of the present economic and financial condition of the various States of Europe. It fully confirms the view which I previously formed that it is of the utmost importance to deal in some drastic manner with the situation. But it is unable to recommend any proposals which it regards as adequate to deal with the whole European situation.

In this letter I do not propose to discuss the Report of the Committee, but to comment on certain observations in your letter. You state that whenever the American representatives pointed out to the other Delegations that the plans they proposed would deprive Germany of the means of making any appreciable reparation payments they were accused of being pro-German. I must point out, however, that while the American representatives greatly criticised the total amount of the proposed indemnity, they did not, as far as I remember, oppose the initial payment of one thousand million pounds within the first two years; which was accepted as a more or less agreed figure from the start. Yet the force of the criticism in your letter entirely turns on the inadvisability of exacting this sum.

Further, while I am fully alive to the difficulties which will confront Germany in the payment of reparation I cannot shut my eyes to the difficulties which confront the Allies. After all it is not a question of deciding what amount can usefully be imposed on Germany by way of penalty for her crimes in plotting and starting the war; it is a question of compelling her to relieve, to the utmost of her power, the intolerable burden which she has imposed upon her neighbours. I would like to remind you in particular of what my own country, with a population of 45,000,000 has to bear in this respect. The estaimted [estimated] cost of the war to the United Kingdom from the first August 1914 to the 31st March 1919 is £8,543,000,000. This sum has been met as follows:

By borrowing	£6,860,000,000
By increased taxation	£1,566,000,000
By increased postal revenue or miscellaneous receipts not derived from taxes	£ 34,000,000
	£8,460,000,000
By cash contributions of Governments overseas	£ 83,000,000
	£8,543,000,000

Of the total sum raised to pay for the war, £1,349,000,000 has been raised in Allied and neutral countries and in the Dominions. On the other hand, we have advanced £1,570,000,000 to our Allies and Dominions to enable them to prosecute the war. What this means may be seen from the fact that at the outbreak of war the debt on the population of the United Kingdom amounted to £14 a head; it now amounts to over £160 a head.

These figures show that not only have the population of the United Kingdom an enormously heavy internal debt to bear on account of the war, but that they owe very large sums to other nations abroad. A very large part of the debts they incurred abroad were to pay for munitions and supplies purchased from the United States before America entered the war. On the other hand, it is very doubtful whether it will recover all or nearly all of the moneys it has lent abroad. I need only point to its debts from Russia as evidence on this point.

I think I have said enough to make it clear to you that if the British Delegation has pressed that Germany should pay reparation to the utmost of which she is capable, and if, at the same time, it puts forward proposals for the rehabilitation of the general credit of Europe, including Germany, through the financial cooperation of the civilised nations, it does so because it has already bled itself white for the sake of the Allies. It asks for nothing which it [is] impossible, but it does claim that it has the right to ask its colleagues of the Peace Conference both to compel Germany to pay whatever she is capable of paying and to place their own credit unreservedly at the disposal of the nations for the regeneration of the world as Great Britain placed hers unreservedly at the service of the Allies in order to save the freedom of the world.

There is another point I should like to make clear. The immediate problem is largely one of financing the process of purchasing raw materials abroad and exporting them to Europe to be worked up into manufactured goods. Europe cannot do its own financing. Nor can Great Britain help in this process. Before the war Great Britain had a surplus of exportable capital of £200,000,000 a year, which enabled her to finance a great deal of the export business from the Dominions of the British Empire, India, China and so forth. To-day not only has she no surplus, but largely because she disposed of her foreign securities to pay for American munitions in the early years of the war, she has not at the moment the capital with which to purchase her own domestic imports. The responsibility for the reconstruction of the world, therefore, depends in an exceptional measure upon the United States, for the United States is the only country in the world which is exceedingly prosperous and is not overburdened, in proportion to her resources and population, by external or internal debts.

I earnestly trust, therefore, that you will be able to find some way of really assisting the financial needs of the world. If Great Britain could shoulder any considerable share of the responsibility she would do so. As she cannot the responsibility must rest principally on the shoulders of the United States.

Ever sincerely,   D Lloyd George

TLS (WP, DLC).
    [1] Actually, WW to D. Lloyd George, May 5, 1919, Vol. 58.
    [2] About this report, see n. 11 to the minutes of the Council of Four printed at June 2, 1919, 4 p.m., Vol. 60.

From Tasker Howard Bliss

Dear Mr. President: Paris 26 June 1919

General Thwaites,[1] the representative in Paris of the British Chief of the Imperial General Staff, has come to see me with a

statement from General Maynard,[2] the British general commanding the Allied forces at Murmansk.

As you know, the American forces are withdrawing from North
Russia and by this time must be pretty well away from there. But,
at the urgent request of the British, the two companies of American railway troops that formed part of our force were permitted to
stay three or four weeks after the departure of the American infantry, provided they volunteered to do so.

It seems, from all reports including those from the British, that
these two companies of railway troops are composed of a very superior quality of men and the British have the greatest confidence
in them. General Maynard now says that he apprehends a serious
disaster if he cannot count upon these two companies, who are
handling the Murmansk railway, until September 1. They guarantee to have them embarked for home by that date.

The situation there is most embarrassing for us. Of course, it
would be a horrible thing for us if a disaster should happen to our
British associates and it could be fairly charged to our withdrawal.
Could we not say to our General Richardson[3] on the spot that, *provided these two companies volunteer to stay*, and *provided the
British guarantee to have them embarked by September 1 next*, he
can retain them for that length of time under those conditions.

The British declare most solemnly that the entire expedition will
be out by September next but that the services of these railway
troops are necessary to effect the withdrawal without disaster, in
the face of hostile pressure.

I think that, in view of these repeated declarations, and provided
it be an entirely voluntary act on the part of our railway troops, your
action in letting the troops stay could not be liable to criticism. At
any rate, after careful reflection, I assume the responsibility of recommending that you do so.

Cordially yours,   Tasker H. Bliss[4]

TLS (WP, DLC).
  [1] That is, Maj. Gen. William Thwaites, also Director of Military Intelligence of the
War Office.
  [2] Brig. Gen. Sir Charles Clarkson Martin Maynard.
  [3] That is, Wilds Preston Richardson.
  [4] Bliss' covering note to this letter, dated June 26, 1919 (TI MS, WP, DLC), reads as
follows:
  "If the President approves the attached letter, would it be well to have Mr. Lloyd
George attach a declaration, in the name of the British Government, as to the necessity
of the proposed action with respect to the two American railway companies, and his
definite agreement as to their withdrawal not later than September 1st next?   T.H.B."

From Douglas Wilson Johnson, with Enclosure

Dear Mr. President: Paris, June 26, 1919.

It would greatly help me to contribute my part toward carrying out the President's wishes in regard to further negotiations over the Adriatic problem, if I could know more accurately the President's present opinion on certain phases of that difficult question. To this end I have stated in the accompanying memorandum, somewhat fully, my conception of what our future policy should be, and beyond what limits we should definitely refuse to modify, even under combined pressure of our British, French and Italian friends, the position already taken by the President.

Would the President be willing to indicate in how far I have succeeded in expressing his own views, and in what respects he intends that a different policy should be pursued? If the President prefers to give his counsel orally, would he be good enough to give me an appointment before his departure for America?

I understand, of course, that responsibility for directing our policy will be delegated by the President to the competent authorities; and I request for my guidance only such expressions of the President's opinions as he deems it appropriate to make.

I am, my dear Mr. President,

Your obedient servant,   Douglas Johnson.

TLS (WP, DLC).

E N C L O S U R E

Suggested Policy in Re. Adriatic Problem.

1. The effort to find a solution acceptable to both sides should be continued with the new Italian Government. To this end the Jugo Slavs should be urged to make further substantial concessions. But care should be taken to avoid assuming an attitude which would enable the Jugo Slavs to say that the President had abandoned his high stand in favor of a just decision, or that America had renounced her role as the champion of equal justice for great and small peoples and had joined with others in forcing an immoral and indefensible solution upon them.

2. In no case should America agree, without Jugo Slav consent, to alienating from Jugo Slavia the Jugo Slav territory of the Assling triangle; to further concessions east of the "American line" than those represented in the free state proposition as outlined in the President's "Suggested Basis for Settlement of the Adriatic Question" of June 7th,[1] paragraphs 2nd to 5th, inclusive; to further

concessions as to Zara and Sebenico than those set forth in the 8th paragraph of the same memorandum, except that Sebenico might be made a free port under Jugo Slav sovereignty.

3. As regards the islands, the American representatives could accept as defensible the definite assignment to Italy, over Jugo Slav protest, of the Lussin group (on ethnic grounds) and the Lissa and Pelagosa groups (on strategic grounds); and could, if necessary, concede Italy's right to fortify these islands and use them as naval bases, trusting to the League of Nations to protect Jugo Slavia against undue aggression. American [America] should not be a party to forcing the alienation of other Jugo Slav islands from Jugo Slav sovereignty. As regards the concession of other islands indicated in the 6th paragraph of the President's memorandum of June 7th, the American position might be that this suggested basis of settlement was rejected by the Italians, and in any case was never submitted to the Jugo Slavs for their acceptance or rejection. Hence it has no more force than the many other projects which have failed of acceptance; while the conceding to Italy of the right to fortify the Lussin group and the Lissa and Pelagosa groups gives her greater security and meets her strategic arguments far more fully than would the assignment to her of additional islands with the provision (as in the President's memorandum) that none of the islands should be fortified. (Possession of the islands opposite Zara by Italy would have serious consequences. The whole economic life of the Dalmatian coast and the islands depends upon the coast-wise traffic carried on by small vessels which follow the protected inland waterways between the islands, to their port of discharge at Fiume. This is one of the two most important trade routes in the Jugo Slav Kingdom. It would be most unfortunate to place the entire central sector of this route in Italian hands, to force all traffic from the larger and more populous of the Dalmatian islands to pass through Italian territorial waters to reach its destination, and to give to Italy a portion of the small ports and products upon which this coastwise trade subsists. This would mean endless friction in time of peace, and the isolation of the whole southern Dalmatian region in the event of war.)

4. With the coming of a new Italian Government pledged, particularly to look to the economic interests of Italy, a special effort should be made to secure for Italy additional economic advantages which, without imposing injustice on others, could be accepted by the new government as being something of more substantial value than the barren rocks of the Dalmatian islands. England and France should be urged to facilitate such a solution for the problem created through their acceptance of the Treaty of London, by mak-

ing concessions to Italy in respect to economic or colonial matters.

5. If Italy refuses to sign the peace with Austria unless her un-just demands are granted, and there is placed before America the choice of signing an unjust peace or of making a separate peace with Austria, we should choose the latter alternative. With the treaty with Germany signed and the League of Nations assured, our position and our prestige would be stronger if, when it came to the Austrian treaty, we were to maintain a firm stand in favor of justice and morality in international dealings. We cannot afford, by our actions, to set the seal of approval upon the policy by which Italy has sought to extort immoral gains for herself, or to repudiate our rôle as the defender of the liberties of small peoples, or to begin our leadership in the League of Nations by guaranteeing, as a member of the League, a solution which we believe to be morally indefensible. The very fact that we were unable to sign a peace, not because it was unfair to us personally, or to our interests, but because it was in flagrant conflict with the new spirit of interna-tional morality, of which the League of Nations is one of the visible signs, would give enormous weight to American opinion in world affairs in the future. More than ever would our country be trusted and respected; more than ever would other nations seek to bring their policies into harmony with our views in order to secure our valued support. Instead of being weakened, our influence would be enormously strengthened.

If we maintain a firm stand on the policy outlined above, I am confident that the Italian government will in the end accept the American solution. It is characteristic of Italian methods to press with passionate insistence for every advantage they can hope to secure, and to yield quickly only at the last possible moment. Such has repeatedly been the history of various Italian claims before the Territorial Commissions of the Conference and elsewhere. Borsa[2] and other Italians of importance have admitted to me that it is ab-solutely impossible for any Italian government to accept a solution of the Adriatic problem which does not carry America's signature. They say, and I think with good reason, that if America refused to sign, the world as a whole would inevitably brand the Italian claims as unjust; Italy's moral isolation would be complete, with disas-trous consequences to her financial, economic, and political posi-tion; the Jugo Slavs and the Tyrolese patriots would be enormously stiffened in their opposition to Italian occupation of their lands; and in the conflict which must then ensue, the Jugo Slavs at least would have the support of world opinion, while the Italians could hope for little sympathy.

In other words, America has much to gain by declining to sign an unjust peace, whereas Italy must lose much which is vital to her if she refuses to sign unless her demands are met. Under these circumstances it would seem that America can well afford to throw her full weight on the side of justice, and to maintain that position to the end. Indeed, America could herself decline to sign the Austrian Peace until the Adriatic question, arising from the dissolution of Austria, was satisfactorily settled; for Italy needs America's signature guaranteeing her frontiers in the Tyrol as well as in support of the large areas of Slavic lands which even the American line transfers to her sovereignty.

T MS (SDR, RG 256, 186.3411/646, DNA).
    [1] About which, see Mantoux's minutes of the Council of Four, June 7, 1919, n. 13, Vol. 60.
    [2] Dr. Mario Borsa, correspondent for the Milan *Secolo*. Baker (Diary, May 27, 1919, Vol. 59) called him "a real Italian liberal."

From the Diary of Vance Criswell McCormick

June 26 (Thursday) [1919]

At 3.00 went to President's house to talk with him, along with Baruch, Davis and Lamont to see whether it would be wise for us to go home with him Saturday. He said he recognized that the principal questions of policy had been decided but wanted someone here with good judgment who, if anything new developed, would know enough to act intelligently or refer to higher powers at home. He asked us each what we had done to close up our work and who we proposed to have represent us. We all agreed that on reparation and financial clauses Foster Dulles was the best man and with his complete knowledge of the subject, he was perfectly reliable and safe in every respect and we asked the President to write him a letter requesting him to stay, which he said he would do. He was in a good humor and told us one of Lincoln's stories which he is so fond of doing. He quoted him several times and you can see continually signs of his being a close student of Lincoln's war time experiences.

At 5.00 o'clock Lloyd George and others came in so we got out, delighted with his final consent to our all sailing with him on the George Washington Saturday. He was convinced the Germans would send their delegates Friday and we could have the ceremonies on Saturday afternoon.

From the Diary of Ray Stannard Baker

Thursday the 26th [June 1919]

When I reached the President's house in the Place des Etats-Unis this afternoon I found Admiral Grayson—who has two young sons[1] at home—in the process of winding up a wonderful mechanical tiger which he had just brought home. This extraordinary French beast crouches back, turns his head menacingly, growls, and then suddenly leaps forward in a way to send delicious chills down the spine of any little boy. Brooks,[2] the President's colored valet, was there, enjoying it hugely, & Close. The Admiral also had a gray elephant which waggled its ears & walked in ponderous elephantic style about the floor.

Upon sudden inspiration we took these marvelous creatures down-stairs, and into the President's study, & when the President & Mrs. Wilson came in we had them ready wound up & the precious tiger quite prepared to growl & leap at the President—which he did to perfection. The President laughed heartily—and yet, as one could feel, not without restraint. He unbends with the greatest difficulty! And he is tired.

He told me that L.G. & Clemenceau were worried about the escape from Holland of the Crown Prince—thought it an added insult (after the sinking of the German ships at Scapa Flow, & the burning of the French flags)

"They were savage enough to start war again," he said.

[1] That is, James Gordon Grayson and Cary Travers Grayson, Jr.
[2] That is, Col. Arthur Brooks.

To Joseph Patrick Tumulty

Paris, 26 June 1919.

Please thank Mr. Gompers as President of the Federation for his message[1] about the endorsement of the League of Nations. It is most cheering.   Woodrow Wilson.

T telegram (WP, DLC).
[1] S. Gompers to WW, June 24, 1919.

David Hunter Miller to Gordon Auchincloss

Washington June 26 [1919].

114. For Auchincloss from Miller. Following is memorandum on Root letter:[1]

Root continues think adoption of Covenant of enormous importance as it contains "great deal of high value."

His first point is that arbitration has not been strengthened.

This subject sympathetically considered Paris and found it would involve prolonged discussion and perhaps with neutrals, and accordingly subject was left for future development by Council and powers.

Root's second point is the provision for development international law. But Assembly meets "at intervals" and doubtless will appoint committees of jurists to report upon improvements of international law.

Root admits that ratification of treaty need not await two additions he suggests, for he proposes subsequent negotiations regarding the word[ing?]. Root's four positive objections are now considered.

As to Article One, Root says that clause authorizing withdrawal on two years' notice leaves doubt whether a charge that we had not performed some obligation would not put it in power of Council to take jurisdiction of charge as disputed question and keep us in League indefinitely against our will and to remedy this doubt Root proposes that resolution of Senate contain following:

"The Senate consents to the ratification of the said treaty reserving Article One aforesaid with the understanding that whenever two years' notice of withdrawal from the League of Nations shall have been given, as provided in Article One, no claim, charge or finding that international obligations or obligations under the Covenant have not been fulfilled will be deemed to render the two years' notice ineffectual or to keep the power of giving the notice in the League after the expiration of the time specified in the notice."

I do not think language of Article One should be construed as permitting a power to be kept in League against its will despite notice of withdrawal. Neither do I think Mr. Root would so construe it. True construction is that a power is bound to fulfill obligations up to date that notice of withdrawal goes into force. That this is reasonable construction is supported by last paragraph Article Sixteen and Article Twenty-six.

It was generally recognized at meetings of Commission[2] that it would be useless to attempt to keep in the League a power which did not want to stay. However there can be no objection to having doubt removed.

I much prefer that doubt might be removed by amendment by statement of an "understanding" in resolution of consent by the Senate but such an expression with nothing whatever more could not be specially objectionable. It is not a "reservation" but statement of belief by power ratifying as to meaning of language used in treaty. In my opinion it is correct statement of that language and changed slightly in verbiage should be acceptable to other members.

Such statement of construction would be applicable in favor of all powers.

As to Monroe Doctrine Root says:

"The clause which has been inserted regarding the Monroe Doctrine is erroneous in its description of the doctrine and ambiguous in meaning. Other purely American questions, as for example, questions relating to immigration, are protected only by a clause apparently empowering the Council to determine whether such questions are solely within domestic jurisdiction of the United States. I do not think that in these respects the United States is sufficiently protected against most injurious results which are wholly unnecessary for the establishment and maintenance of this League of Nations."

First, as to Monroe Doctrine, Root says that this is "ambiguous in meaning" but points out no ambiguity.

Substance of the provision is that nothing in Covenant affects validity of Monroe Doctrine. Could any statement be more sweeping?

Furthermore, mention of Monroe Doctrine as a regional understanding is accurate. Doctrine is an American policy announced nearly a century ago and has been basis of position taken by the United States in international affairs. It may thus be properly described as understanding relating to Western Hemisphere. True, it has never been specifically limited or exclusively defined, but this makes very apt use of word "understanding" which is applicable to status indefinite rather than formal.

One great purpose of Monroe Doctrine has been to secure maintenance of peace.

Language of Covenant reserves in express terms Monroe Doctrine from its operation. A recognition by all nations including Latin-America that Monroe Doctrine exists and is not affected by entrance of the United States into League affords complete protection to American interests and is great diplomatic triumph for United States.

Vague phrase of Root regarding traditional attitude of United States toward purely American questions is almost meaningless in comparison with direct language of Article 21. Monroe Doctrine has never been purely American question, for it was originally announced as attitude of United States in reference to relations of Europe and America.

There is probably no one question as to which less possibility of doubt as to meaning of Covenant than that of immigration. Various Japanese proposals were made. Final Japanese proposal was simply to insert in preamble few words regarding principle of equality of nations. These words, words in themselves so harmless that members of the Commission generally in favor of them but because it was known that they would be thought to have some bearing on race question their insertion was refused upon the positive insistence, not of United States, but of Great Britain at meeting of peace conference at which Covenant was adopted. Makino alluded to failure of efforts of (?). There can thus be no possible doubt that this question is absolutely reserved. Going still further there is positive provision, the eighth paragraph of Article 15.

Root says that this question is:

"protected only by a clause apparently empowering the Council to determine whether such questions are solely within domestic jurisdiction of the United States."

The clause is not "empowering" clause at all but one which removes a dispute from jurisdiction of Council. Council cannot make even recommendations regarding such a question and is given no discretion.

Provision regarding disputes submitted to Council for investigation are by this clause much more limited than those which United States has previously adopted in *assigning* [arbitration] *treaties*.[3] By those treaties of which this [thirty] were negotiated and twenty ratified any disputes of every nature whatsoever is referred to international commission for investigation and report. Language used in treaties is of most sweeping character. For example, language of treaty with China:

"Any disputes arising between the Government of the United States of America and the Government of the Republic of China, of whatsoever nature they may be, shall be submitted for investigation."

We offered to negotiate a similar treaty with any country. Under Bryan peace treaties, which represent policy of United States of America, a dispute regarding immigration would be subject for investigation and report, but under Covenant it would not.

The "understanding" regarding the Monroe Doctrine and immigration which Root suggests for resolution of ratification is the following:

"The Senate consents to the ratification of the said treaty, excepting Article X aforesaid, with the understanding that nothing therein contained shall be construed to imply, first, relinquishment by the United States of America of its traditional attitude towards purely American questions, or to require the ? [submission] of its policy regarding questions which it deems to be purely American questions, to the decision or recommendation of other powers."

This language adds nothing to protection of Monroe Doctrine or immigration. Its use would be highly unfortunate for it would invite use of similar language by other powers, such as Japan with relation to Asia, and be highly unfortunate from point of view of our relations with Latin-America. For since it is intended to refer to Monroe Doctrine it would separate our attitude from that of Latin-America.

First portion of above quoted over again is copied from reservation of American Delegation upon signing convention for the pacific settlement of international disputes at first Hague Conference.[4] This reservation will be further considered in subsequent memorandum on Article X.   Polk, Acting.

T telegram (WP, DLC).
  [1] That is, Root's letter to Lodge of June 19, 1919, about which see JPT to WW, June 21, 1919, n. 3.
  [2] That is, the Commission on the League of Nations.
  [3] This correction and the following addition from the copy in the Diary of Gordon Auchincloss, T MS (G. Auchincloss Papers, CtY), entry for June 27, 1919.
  [4] Miller here referred to the declaration appended to the Convention for the Pacific Settlement of International Disputes, one of the Hague Treaties of 1899, by the American delegation to the Hague Conference of that year, which stated that nothing in the convention should be construed as requiring the United States to depart from its traditional policy of not becoming involved in the internal or external affairs of any foreign nation. See J. A. Metzger to JPT, July 29, 1919, and Calvin DeArmond Davis, *The United States and the First Hague Peace Conference* (Ithaca, N. Y., 1962), pp. 176-80.

From the Diary of Dr. Grayson

Friday, June 27, 1919.

The President arose early and he and the Council approved the final details of the ceremony to be gone through with on Saturday afternoon at Versailles. It was decided that there would be no effort to make the scenes incident to the signing ceremonious. Instead of court dress it was agreed that all of the delegates would wear the ordinary black afternoon costume.

The President proceeded to the Crillon, where at 2:15 o'clock he met the assembled newspaper correspondents. Probably never before had the President shown to such advantage as he did at this conference. Gathered there were more than fifty representatives of the American newspapers and of the various magazines. Many of these men were avowedly hostile to the President. Some of them were hostile because of political reasons; others were hostile because of socialistic tendencies. However, at no time did a single man succeed in putting a question to the President that in any way embarrassed him. The President at the outset explained very carefully to the men that he would be very glad to be perfectly frank with them, but that they must understand that what he said to them was said to them entirely for their guidance and must not be attributed either to him or to that mythical "high authority" which many of them had utilized as a medium for the dissemination of erroneous information.

The President was asked how he felt regarding the accomplishment of the task which he came to Europe to assume. He replied: "I am very well satisfied; I think a good job has been done." Asked whether he considered the treaty followed his original fourteen points, the President said that he thought it did so in every way. In fact, he said that he was surprised that he had been able to keep the treaty as closely to the lines laid down in advance as he had done. The President paid a generous tribute to the work of the men with whom he had been associated. There was not a single note of criticism in his reference to the other members of the Council of Five. He openly praised both Clemenceau and Lloyd George for the manner in which they had cooperated, and he pointed out that in an exchange of views such as had taken place in this connection, it was natural that men would want to know all sides of all questions before they finally reached a decision.

When the President was asked to sum up what he believed had been accomplished in connection with the treaty, he said: "The Treaty is severe on Germany, but why should it not be? Germany caused the war. Germany ran amuck and tried to rule the world. Germany must accept the consequences of her own acts. We make individuals responsible for their own acts. In capital cases we make individuals responsible for their own acts even to the extent of giving up their lives because of such acts. We have not attempted to exact Germany's life. We have only compelled her to make such reparation as she is capable of making. But it is not alone Germany in this case. We have done something that no one would have believed possible only a year ago. We have liberated peoples who never hoped for liberation. We have recreated ancient Poland—a dream that was only a dream even to the Poles themselves. We have liberated the peoples who were oppressed parts of the Austria-Hungary Empire. They are given back their original sovereignty.

We have made possible the restoration of liberty to the world itself."

The President was asked whether he cared to say anything about the settlement in connection with the Shantung Peninsula. He replied that he would be very glad to tell the correspondents all of the actual facts. He made it plain, however, once more that this information was entirely for their guidance and must not be attributed to him. The President then said that when the question of Shantung came before the Council, the Japanese delegates produced the secret treaties which were entered into during the war between Japan on the one side and Great Britain and France on the other side, whereby these two nations assured Japan that she would be given as her reward for her participation in the war all of the rights enjoyed by the Germans under their original understandings with China. He said that after this had been agreed upon the Japanese sent to Peking a representative who took up the matter with the Chinese Government. This Japanese representative told the Chinese that while they had abandoned, upon the protest of the United States, what was known as the "21 points," yet Japan intended to carry through a good portion of these demands in connection with her understanding with England and France. The President said that when he learned this he found that it was necessary to exert the utmost influence to secure for China the rights which she deserved, and also to protect China from the imposition under a new guise of these so-called points, which had been the medium of a sharp protest by America to Japan. As a result of this, the Shantung agreement was reached, whereby Japan agreed to restore to China all her territorial rights in the Shantung Peninsula, with the exception of the ownership of the railroad itself and with the establishment of certain commercial stations. Japan agreed that these commercial stations should not at any place infringe upon the Kiao Chau fortifications. He said that as a result of the agreement China had received far more than she possibly could have received in other circumstances, and, in addition, was in a position later on to appeal to the League of Nations to restore to her the railroad rights which Japan was to retain under the present arrangement. The President was asked why it was when this arrangement was approved he took such a positive stand in connection with the Dalmatian question. The President said that there was absolutely no comparison between the two problems. The so-called Treaty of London, he said, was an unholy alliance. France and Great Britain both recognized this fact. However, Italy had insisted that it would stand squarely upon the London Pact, and the United States was therefore compelled to declare that it could not participate in any settlement under it.

The President was asked why it was that there had been no decision reached in connection with the Hungarian problem. He said that was due to the fact that Hungary at the present time was like a basin of quick-silver—there was no government that could be pinned down for a single moment. Béla Kun was in power only in Budapest. The rest of Hungary was in a state of chaos, and until a stable government should evolve itself there was nothing that the Allies could do to settle the questions there.

The President was asked what had been done in connection with the suggestion that America be given mandatories in Turkey. He said that that was a matter which Congress itself must decide. So far as he personally was concerned he did not favor accepting any mandatory except possibly one for Armenia and another for Constantinople. In the case of Armenia there were sentimental reasons that would affect a decision. In the case of Constantinople he said the United States was the only nation which could administer it unselfishly. Any European nation must naturally have a selfish interest, while the United States would have none, and he likened the proposition of America carrying this mandatory to its position in connection with the Panama Canal, as it would keep open the Dardanelles at all times and leave a free sea route to the Black Sea.

The session with the correspondents was most illuminating, and the President made it very clear to them that so far as the United States was concerned, it had not sacrificed a single principle during the weary months of negotiation.

Lloyd George and Clemenceau are very anxious that the President come back to Europe later on. The President said: "This is practically out of the question. Lincoln one time told the story of a little girl who had some blocks with letters on them. She was learning her A B C's with the use of these blocks, and one night before going to bed she was playing with them. When she got into bed she started to say her prayers, but she was so sleepy all she could say was: 'Oh, Lord, I am too sleepy to say my prayers; here are the blocks and the letters—you spell it out.' " The President continued: "I have worked over here and laid down all the principles, the rules and regulations that I could think of. Someone else now will have to take the blocks and spell it out."

Today I lunched with Lord Derby.[1] Lloyd George, Balfour, Sir Ian Malcolm[2] were also present at the luncheon. I had asked Lord Derby whether I could call and say goodbye to him. He replied by saying that he wanted me to lunch with him; that he would ask

[1] That is, Edward George Villiers Stanley, 17th Earl of Derby, British Ambassador to France.
[2] That is, Sir Ian (Zachary) Malcolm, Balfour's private secretary at the peace conference.

Lloyd George and Mr. Balfour, who were good friends of mine, to come if they could find the time; if they were not engaged, he felt sure they would come. Lord Derby referred to Lloyd George in his conversation as "L.G.," and to Balfour as "Arthur." He refers to me as "Admiral Grayson" but always addresses me as "Grayson." The question of having Lord Derby accept the vacant Ambassadorship at Washington came up at the luncheon table. Lloyd George and Balfour joined with me in urging him to accept the vacant post. They told Lord Derby that he was my selection, and that they not only endorsed it but that they agreed with me, and that they were anxious to see that I had my way in this matter. Lord Derby said that he regretted very much that his business interests were such that he could not afford to be absent, or to be as far away from them as would be necessary were he to go to Washington. Lloyd George slyly suggested to me that possibly it might not be so much a matter of business interest as it was his deep interest in racing and his love for his thoroughbred stables. I then told Lord Derby that if this was the only obstacle we could very easily remedy it. I told him about the wonderful racing in the United States, of our good tracks there, of the attractions such as the Latonia Derby, the Kentucky Derby, the Preakness and other big fixed stakes; that if this was not sufficient we would construct a race-track especially for his benefit. When I concluded my persuasive speech, Lord Derby turned and said to the others: "I see now why it is that President Wilson considers Grayson such a good doctor." To my proposal he then said: "It cannot be done, but I will tell you what I will do. I will agree to offer you every inducement to come to England as my guest and spend the month of July with me." This would bring me to England for the two famous meetings—the meeting at Epson and that at Ascot.

This afternoon I called on the King of Montenegro[3] at the Ritz Hotel. The call was made at the King's request. He said to me that he was very glad to meet me; that he had been in poor health; that he had heard I was a famous doctor, and when he had heard that I had taken such good care of the President he wanted to offer the highest honor at his command. He said that the people of Montenegro looked upon the President as the big man of the world and that they wanted to show their appreciation to me for the good health that I had given him. They were, therefore, presenting me with a decoration. He expressed regret that he had not been able to "show" me this honor earlier.

The President dined quietly at home with the family tonight and retired early, realizing that he had a very serious ordeal before him tomorrow.

[3] That is, Nicholas I.

Notes of a Press Conference by Walter Edward Weyl[1]

PRESIDENT WILSON'S REMARKS TO AMERICAN
CORRESPONDENTS, JUNE 27, 1919:

Regarding the proposition that the United States accept a mandate for Armenia, the President said he considered that he had no right to make a personal decision without consulting the American people. He regarded Anatolia as an integral part of Turkey, not to be linked with Armenia. He was personally inclined to favor accepting a mandate for Armenia and stated that the question of Constantinople was like that of Armenia. He said the moment you separate Constantinople from the Turkish Empire, it is of small consequence. The real job about Constantinople was like the Panama Canal job—one of keeping the Black Sea passage open.

Asked if he was going to put this question before the people or Congress, he answered: "Both." He said he intended touring the country to "explain what we have been trying to do over here—to report to the folks." Would he go as far as the Pacific? "I'd go the limit."

If an effort were made by any power to amend the Treaty before ratification, that would mean that the war would not be over for that power until the negotiations had been worked through with over 20 other powers.

The President said that any attempt by any congress or parliament to amend the Peace Treaty, to ratify partially or with reservations would mean: "an interminable process indefinitely delaying the resumption of normal relations." He said that reservations would be the equivalent of amendment and would require a reconvocation of the Peace Conference. Asked about the proposal to reserve Article 10 of the Covenant, which guarantees territorial integrity, he said: "Article 10 is the backbone of the whole thing."

Regarding Senator Fall's proposition that Congress delcare the War at an end,[2] he said, heatedly: "It would be a national disgrace. It would mean allying ourselves with Germany. My God! It would put us in such contempt as no nation has ever suffered. I cannot imagine such a thing. It would be stepping over to Germany's side." Asked if he would amplify that statement, he said: "It would make me too mad! Not a handful of people in the United States would stand for that."

The President said he was grateful that the contact had been long enough to bring about a general understanding between

---

[1] Cofounder, with Herbert Croly and Walter Lippmann, of the *New Republic* in 1914 and one of its editors from 1914 to 1916 and again since 1917.

[2] About the Fall Resolution, see JPT to WW, June 25, 1919 (sixth telegram of that date).

France and America. He thought this not merely a personal, but a national mutual understanding. He was proud to notice that the views of the American technical experts had almost always prevailed. This, he thought, was because we had no material interests.

Had he felt the influence of concessionaires and financial interests? He was surprised how little of such interests there were. They had very rarely been present. He had seen little of that sort of thing.

(LINCOLN STEFFENS) "They're as invisible as with us?" The President smiled but said that wherever those interests put their heads up they got "swatted." He instanced a case of oil interests in Mesopotamia which, when called to the attention of Lloyd George, were cancelled.[3]

"Did you feel the pressure of international banking interests?"

(The President) "No. I must in honesty say 'no.' In the question of reparations, you saw them, in not a sinister way but to safeguard things. We had much help from American financial interests."

(Frederick Moore)[4] "Don't you consider the consortium to be one of the saving graces out there in China?"[5]

(Woodrow Wilson) "That depends on how graceful it is. We've got to watch it but if they play square—Yes."

"We (Great Britain and the United States) think the League of Nations offers abundant protection to France. If there is a danger from Germany, it is not within a twelve-month or two years, or ten years. The peculiarity of the military occupation is that it is for the years without danger. In that fifteen years, the League of Nations will prove itself, for good or for bad. We think France is well safeguarded. The French didn't think so. They are in a tense state of mind. Their worst fears of the past have been realized, and that convinces them that the danger still exists.

"Lloyd George and I therefore promised to lay before our legislatures the proposition that, subject to the approval of the Council of the League of Nations, we pledge ourselves not to wait for the advice of the Council (as provided for in the Covenant) before taking military action against a future German aggression. That leaves us free to judge ourselves whether it is a case of crying 'Wolf! Wolf!' or really an unprovoked movement of aggression. This undertaking is not yet formal and is only in the form of a letter to the French promising to lay this before the Senate. The final undertaking must be in the form of a treaty ratified by the Senate.

[3] About this matter, see the minutes of the Council of Four, May 22, 1919, 11 a.m., printed in PPC, V, 807-12.
[4] Correspondent for the New York Tribune at the peace conference.
[5] About the organization of a new international financial consortium for China, see n. 3 to the extract from the Diary of Edward T. Williams printed at April 22, 1919, Vol. 57, and RL to WW, May 26, 1919 (second letter of that date), Vol. 59.

"As to the Shantung affair, before we entered the war, Great Britain and France had agreed with Japan that in case of victory, Japan should have whatever Germany had in Shantung. Later, Japan agreed with China to restore Chinese sovereignty over Kiaouchaow. That promise was based upon an 'if' going back to the time of Japan's twenty-one demands upon China, against which we had protested at the time. Our protest was influential at the time in restraining Japan from more extravagant demands. The 'if' was a sort of repetition of the 21 demands. In our conferences here, Japan distinctly undertook—not only in writing but orally— to cede back to China everything in the nature of sovereign rights, with the reservation of a residential district in the city of Kiaouchaow Bay. As to the railroads and mining concessions, Japan would merely succeed to the German rights and concessions with the addition that a special police force was to be maintained on the railroad with Chinese police but trained by the Japanese. Japan would withdraw her troops from the railroad at the earliest possible time, leaving things to the Chinese civil administration. The forts were not to be included in the residential area. In our conversations, I made it explicit that nothing we said could be construed as in any way recognising the validity of the twenty-one demands.

"That seemed the best that could be got out of a complicated situation in which two of the other great powers were bound. There was distinctly a danger that if we did not concede at least that much Japan would not adhere to the Treaty and would not become a member of the League of Nations. I said to our Chinese friends that I thought that would be a grave danger because the League of Nations is our only instrument of bettering conditions. I hoped all the nations would ultimately give up their extraterritoriality and semisovereignty in China. There was a difference from the Dalmatian case because this undertaking, with Great Britain and France, was clearly binding as far as they were concerned. I never regarded the Treaty of London as binding. The situation is absolutely different. I think England and France feel so too, although they feel it would be dishonorable for them to say so. (?)

"There has been no suggestion of giving Poland an undertaking similar to that given France.

"We took particular pains not to interfere with revolutions. That's why Article 10 speaks of external aggressions."

(Question) "What about outside assistance to revolutions?"

(W.W.) "That depends on the circumstances."

(Steffens) "What about Russia, Hungary, and Mexico?"

(W.W.) "I will publish a volume on that some day."

(Hill)[6] "And Ireland?"

(W.W.) "The Irish question takes new shape every day. I am a good deal at sea about it."

(Alsberg)[7] "What about Ruthenia?"

(W.W.) "Something is being done about Ruthenia, but I am ashamed to say I don't remember what."

(Swope)[8] "Was there any play of international finance in the Russian lobbies?"

(W.W.) "No. The play of the Russian lobbies was not apparent at all."

Apropos of Roumania and the alleged moderations of our [limitations of her] sovereignty,[9] the President said:

"I had to point out[10] that 'there wouldn't be no Roumania' but for the great powers, and that these things had to be guaranteed by the great powers. The great powers had to be the responsible powers and to dominate the extensive [executive] councils of the League whether that were an ideal arrangement or not. That's not creating an aristocracy among powers. It's a physical fact."

"I had the necessity of keeping the great powers together constantly in mind, but not more so than the others."

In answer to a question by Oulahan,[11] the President said:

"Clemenceau often urged his view but said that he would not urge it so far as to break up the unity. It was the reason for a great many concessions on all sides. I did not find as many divergencies of opinion as might have been expected."

(Swope) "Are you more satisfied with the Treaty than dissatisfied?"

(W.W.) "Oh, I should say so!"

(Swope) "Well—what do you really think of it?"

(W.W.) "All things considered, it is a wonderful success! It's rough on Germany but never forget that Germany did an unpardonable wrong; did it deliberately, and of course the reparation of that wrong is rough on her. In law, we carry the responsibility of reparation to the extent of lives of individuals, but you can't do that with nations. It is just that Germany should repair the wrong to the very utmost of her ability. We have liberated peoples that have

[6] That is, Laurence Hills of the New York *Sun*.
[7] Henry Garfield Alsberg of the *New York Call*, the Socialist daily.
[8] That is, Herbert Bayard Swope of the New York *World*.
[9] About this matter—the stipulations for the protection of minorities in Rumania—see Hankey's minutes of the Council of Four printed at May 28, 1919, 11:45 a.m., Vol. 59, and the minutes of the Plenary Session of May 31, 1919, printed in *PPC*, III, 394-410.
[10] In his address to a Plenary Session printed at May 31, 1919, Vol. 59.
[11] That is, Richard Victor Oulahan of the *New York Times*.

never had a chance and had hardly dreamed of it. We have bound the people of the world together to see that what was done remained done. We have cleared the air of international law and given a charter to Labor. We have provided for a convention to remove unreasonable restrictions on intercourse and provide for joint human enterprises. It's a colossal Peace such as the world never dreamed of before. It's all on paper now but it's up to us to see that it's realized."

(Question) "What about lending part of our Army or Navy to a permanent international police force?"

(W.W.) "The question was never raised."

(Question) "What is the greatest difficulty now?"

(W.W.) "I don't see any special difficulty. It's a new job that we may bungle at."

(Apropos of the blockade) "We have told Germany that the Blockade will be raised so soon as Germany ratifies the Treaty. The Blockade continues legally so long as the Armistice continues. The Treaty is in force as soon as three of the great powers sign. We told Germany we only waited for that.

"There really is no blockade against Russia. That's an incidental part of the German Blockade. Theoretically, Russia is free to trade now, but there is nobody to trade with. The real difficulty is the uncertainty of credit.

"I'd raise the war-time prohibition if I could and I wish Congress would."

In answer to a question, the President said:

"My own principles of recognition are two: First—it's absolutely none of my business what kind of government another country has. Second—I am entitled to wait until they have time to find one that suits them and until it has held power for a time.

"We haven't found a Russian government yet. We are looking for it. The one we bet on is being chased eastward just now."

(Swope) "You have analysed the Treaty. Now characterize it. What do you think of it?"

(W.W.) "It's a long job that I'm hoping to see finished."

(Swope) "A good job?"

(W.W.) "On the whole, a good job."

(Swope) "A liberal job?"

(W.W.) "Undoubtedly a liberal job. The temper of all the men I have dealt with has been genuinely liberal."

(Swope) "Are you proud of it?"

(W.W.) "Yes. I am proud of it."

(Question) "Does it adhere to the Fourteen Points? You know you are quoted as saying so."

(W.W.) "Yes, I know; but I didn't say it adheres to the Fourteen Points. But really, I think it adheres more closely to them than I had a right to expect."

(Question) "What about Hungary?"

(W.W.) "Search me! Apparently, the government of Hungary— so-called—resides only in Budapest and doesn't extend its authority throughout Hungary. We are genuinely seeking for light."

(Question) "Will the United States sign the treaties with Turkey and Bulgaria against whom we have not declared war?"

(W.W.) "Yes. You see those treaties include the Covenant of the League of Nations and that brings us in, necessarily."

(Question) "When will Germany be admitted into the League?"

(W.W.) "I can't make a guess."

(Question) "Do you think France will enter into the League as heartily as she would if there were no separate undertaking?"

(W.W.) (Warmly) "Oh yes."

(Q) "What about Mexico, Costa Rica, and other countries omitted from the League?"

(W.W.) "That's their own lookout. They've got to find themselves to qualify as respectable nations.

"The American people have been misled, not to say lied to, about the Treaty. I count upon them to support it with a considerable degree of confidence."

(Q.) "What parts have been misrepresented?"

(W.W.) "Time fails to enumerate them. Pretty nearly every part—especially about the League of Nations. It is really [blank]

(Q.) "Do you think frontiers can be readjusted easily after the signing of the Treaty?"

(W.W.) (Confidently) "Oh yes. The principle is recognized that any unsatisfactory frontier can be changed. It will be a perfectly normal process. If it is shown that a boundary is not drawn as well as it could be on ethnic lines, and that a ferment is setting up there which might upset the peace of the world, it would be perfectly normal."

T MS (received from Nathaniel Weyl).

A Report of a Press Conference by Charles Thaddeus Thompson[1]

[June 27, 1919]

The President talked quite freely this afternoon, summing up the work of the Peace Conference. He was evidently well pleased with the favorable turn of affairs and looked well and smiling, with little trace of fatigue from the strain he has been under of late. He talked for a full hour, a remarkably straight and open talk on all the phases of the Conference. First he answered a question as to an American mandate in Turkey.

"I have made no promise as to an American mandate in Turkey," he said, "as I have no right to promise anything of that kind. The most that could be done has been to say that the question of an American mandate will be presented to our people at home and it will be for them to decide.

"As to a mandate for Armenia," continued the President, "I am inclined to think that our people would consider it favorably, for they have always shown much interest in Armenia. But after all, that is only my personal opinion, and it will be for the people to decide what will be done."

"And how about Constantinople?" the President was asked.

"It is the same with Constantinople as with Armenia. The people at home will decide. I have felt there would be a certain advantage in our being at Constantinople, in that it would keep it out of European politics. With any other power there, questions of self-interest would be raised. But everyone recognizes that we are completely disinterested as to Turkey, so that if we took the mandate for Constantinople it would be completely removed from the field of European politics. And it would be a job worth the doing," pursued the President with a glow of enthusiasm, "it would be something on a large scale, for the benefit of the whole world, like the building of the Panama Canal—and besides administering Constantinople, the task would be to keep open the Strait as an international highway, with a free route to and from the Black Sea for the commerce of the world."

"It is understood, Mr. President, that you will make a tour of America on your return, and address the people?"

"Yes, I have thought it would be well to make a tour and try to explain what has been accomplished here at the Peace Conference. What is needed most of all is a thorough understanding of what has been done, and it needs explanation rather than argu-

[1] Correspondent for the Associated Press at the peace conference.

ment. There has been too much misunderstanding, to use a very
mild world, and the effect of it has been that our people at home
have not been able to see clearly what has happened here in its
true light, and they have seen some things in a distorted light."

"How far will you go—as far as the Pacific Coast?"

"I will go to the limit," answered the President.

"Are there reasons, Mr. President, why the Senate should ratify
the Peace Treaty without amendments?"

"There are very important reasons why that should be done. In
the first place, if any power seeks to make amendments, then the
war is not over until every one of the twenty-one Allied nations
learns the result of the changes and decides whether they will be
accepted. The only way I know of to do this is by negotiation back
and forth between these twenty-one powers. It would be a hopeless
process of delay. It would keep us out of the Treaty and out of the
League of Nations."

"If the Senate ratified with reservations, as has been proposed,
would the reservations be the same as amendments?"

"That would depend on the terms of the reservations. But in
general reservations are much the same as amendments. And certainly the proposed Root reservation to Article X of the Covenant of
the League of Nations would be an amendment, for it destroys the
entire meaning of the Article."

"And what do you think of Senator Fall's amendment, declaring
the war between the United States and Germany at an end, and
for a separate treaty of peace with Germany?"

The President's face took on a very stern look. He did not answer
at once, and seemed to be choosing his words of criticism. Finally
he said:

"My God, that Fall resolution would be a disgrace. It would put
on us a contempt that no nation has ever suffered. It would make
us the ally of Germany. No, this Fall resolution, I do not believe a
handful of people in America would support such a disgraceful
measure."

"It is difficult for me to avoid profanity in referring to that resolution," the President went on after a pause. "It makes me feel like
the man with the sand wagon. You remember the story. He was
going up hill with a load of sand, when some mischievous boys
took out the tail board of the cart so that all the sand ran out.
Reaching the top of the hill, and turning to find that his load of
sand had run out, he said: 'Well, there ain't no words to express
my feelings on that job.' And that is the way I feel as to the Fall
resolution—there simply ain't no words to express my feelings on
that job."

The conversation turned to the length of the Peace Conference.

"With everyone in the Conference having pretty positive views," said the President, "it naturally took time to mould all these strong contentions into something like a co-ordinate and harmonious whole. The result of a long discussion is usually much better than a short one in bringing about an understanding, particularly when the interests involved are very great and the differences in view sharply defined as they were in this Conference. But after all, the length of this Conference has not been great—six months—as compared with the Vienna Congress, and when one considers the vastness of the world problems brought here for settlement, for we have been engaged practically in making over the whole world.

"I have been very proud during this work that the views of our American experts usually prevailed. It was probably because America had no selfish interests to serve, and our experts approached every subject without the prejudice of self-interest and with the sole desire to reach a just decision. They brought to every discussion something more than full and well ordered information. Of course they had that, but others had that also. But the one thing which was preeminently theirs in all this play of divergent interests was the complete disinterestedness of America. That gave them a voice of sincerity and authority, and it was the reason, I believe, why the voice of our American experts usually prevailed in the adjustment of the many difficult issues."

The President was asked if the influence of any "interests" had been made manifest during the Conference. This led him to relate an incident which occurred when Mesopotamia was under consideration in the Council of Four. It was disclosed during the discussions that one of the big oil concerns was much interested in a certain provision. Lloyd George thereupon suggested that if the oil interest was involved, the provision had better go out.

"And out it went," said the President, indicating that the mere mention of a selfish interest had been sufficient to prejudice a proposition.

"Has the influence of the banking interests—high finance—been felt to any extent?" the President was asked.

"Not to any appreciable extent, and I am bound to say that very little of that influence has had a sinister aspect. The governments have in fact received a great deal of help from some of these banking interests, particularly the American."

At this point, the undertaking of the United States and Great Britain to come to the help of France with military force, came up and was explained in detail by the President. It was considerately referred to as an "undertaking" as the President did not like the word "alliance." And yet, at first, he was in doubt as to what was meant by the inquiry on the "undertaking."

"Oh, yes, the French agreement," he said at last. "Ah, yes, that is the undertaking, and I suppose we are the undertakers."

The President smiled grimly at this identification of the undertaking, and then he said:

"The point is this. The British view and the American view was that the League of Nations gave France abundant protection against Germany. For if there was any real danger from Germany it would probably not be within the next few years, while Germany is prostrate and disarmed, but after a certain lapse of time, by which time the League would have proved itself an effective instrumentality for preserving the peace of the world. But France did not see it that way. France has been under the spell of the German menace so many years that it is simply beyond the French comprehension that anything can ever check this menace in the slightest degree. While we did not share that view, yet we had to recognize it was a natural view for France, placed as she has been. And so we yielded in a certain measure, to meet this French viewpoint. Yet all we pledged to France in this undertaking is that we will not wait in coming to their assistance. All beyond that was already provided in the Covenant of the League of Nations. In that, you will remember, the Council of the League puts in motion the measures for coming to the relief of a power threatened or attacked by a covenant-breaking power. But that would take time, and the threatened nation would have to wait. So we agreed to go a step further— to come to the assistance of France without waiting.

"This is the form it will take in a treaty, to be submitted to the Senate. If the Treaty is ready, I will sign it before leaving; if not, I will authorize Secretary Lansing to sign it."

The Kiau Chau question and the knotty Japanese problem was next brought to the President's attention, and he said:

"I will tell you some of the inside facts which show how that question was very difficult to handle. At the outset it developed that Japan and Great Britain had made an agreement that Japan was to have what Germany previously possessed in Shantung. Then Japan made an agreement with China, conditioned on China's recognizing the twenty-one demands made by Japan.

"When the subject came before the Council, Japan was ready to cede back to China all the rights in Kiau Chau except in the foreign residential district. Japan agreed to withdraw also from all administration in Shantung. It is to be noted, also, that we have not recognized the twenty-one points contained in Japan's demands on China, which are the conditions on which Kiau Chau is to be returned by Japan to China."

The President referred with satisfaction to what was being done to protect the rights of minorities, and the establishment of an international tribunal, which would have jurisdiction over all questions affecting minorities and their racial, educational and religious rights. He spoke in passing, also, of Ireland, saying: "It presents new phases every day and I am much confused by it."

Taking up the objections made to the League Covenant on the ground that England with her colonies had six votes to America's one vote, the President disposed of them in this way:

"The real guide as to the voting strength is in the Council of the League, and not the Assembly. The Assembly meets only occasionally, but the Council is the executive body always ready to act and with suitable powers of action. Now while the British colonies have a voice in the Assembly—the consultative body which occasionally meets—yet they are not represented on the Council, except through the one vote of the home government. In the Council of nine members, the United States has the same voice as Great Britain, and each of the other Great Powers, and of four Smaller Powers. There can be no question, therefore, of having six British votes arrayed against us in the most vital organ of the League—the organ which is the directive force of the whole structure—as there is complete equality of vote in that body."

The President had thus far spoken of the detailed work of the Conference, but now, turning to the general results, he summed them up thus:

"I am more than satisfied with the net results, and all things considered, I think a wonderful success has been achieved. It is a pretty tough peace for Germany, to be sure. But Germany did great wrong and it is quite natural and just that she should make full reparation for that great wrong. But aside from Germany, consider what we have accomplished here: we have liberated peoples that never had a chance of liberty before—Poles, Jugoslavs, Czechoslavs. Then we have banded together the peoples of the world to see that what is done shall stay done. We have given a charter to labor. We have established a new colonial system in which the development of the native population is the dominant purpose instead of colonial exploitation. We have removed the petty restrictions and barriers on international commerce, making the great waterways and highways neutral and open to all without restriction or discrimination. These are only a few of the really great results we have been able to accomplish. There are many others."

And then with impressive earnestness the President added:

"It is a colossal business, such as the world has never dreamed of before."

Returning to some of the specific questions which had arisen, the President said the blockade on Germany would be raised as soon as Germany ratified the Treaty. But until Germany showed her good faith by ratifying, the blockade would remain in force, and this would be made known to Germany in a letter delivered to the German plenipotentiaries at the time they signed the Treaty.

"I think Germany will carry out the Treaty substantially," said the President in reply to a question which implied that Germany would first sign the Treaty and then systematically avoid it.

Referring to the conclusion of the work, the President said:

"It's a long job that I'm glad to see finished. And it's a good job."

The Fourteen Points were here brought up for the first time, and the President said:

"I think the Treaty adheres to the Fourteen Points more closely than I had a right to expect, in view of the difficulties which arose and the great number of divergent views which had to be reconciled. The Fourteen Points were the guiding principle throughout and their spirit entered into pretty much everything that was done."

When the President was asked why Mexico and Costa Rica were not in the League of Nations, he said:

"That is their own affair; those governments have got to find themselves."

He dismissed the matter with that, and then turning to the opposition to the Peace Treaty in the American Senate, he said:

"I have absolute confidence in the judgment of the American people, and when they fully understand the facts, I rely confidently on their support. There has been so much misrepresentation that their judgment has been clouded. But once the people understand the facts, their judgment will be, in my opinion, swift and conclusive, and I feel absolutely confident it will approve the work we have done here."

With this the talk closed and the President withdrew. But a little later he again referred to the Treaty and its ratification, and said:

"Aside from the unwisdom of the Senate's changing the Treaty, there is the further question of the Senate's right to change the Treaty, or to make any amendments or reservations equivalent to a change. The Constitution gives the treaty making power specifically to the executive. The Senate is to advise and consent as to treaties, but that does not mean it is to participate in the actual making of the Treaty, which is distinctly an executive function.

Their right to consent to the Treaty as it stands, or withhold consent, is absolute. But if they go beyond that, and undertake to change the Treaty, then the executive can reject such action as exceeding the Senate's prerogative, and entering upon that of the executive.

"It would be well for the Senate to keep to its own proper functions, and leave the executive to his functions," added the President, smiling, as it recalled to him this incident:

"There was a place in Virginia where they had a lot of hens, and two big roosters in the midst of the hens. The roosters had fought each other until one of them had no tail feathers left, and the other had just one solitary tail feather remaining. But with all their fighting, neither of the roosters had been able to establish dominion over the place, and so they decided on a truce. There was a brick walk running through the middle of the yard, dividing it into two sides. By common consent one of the roosters took the other side of the walk. Each was supreme on his side of the walk. But if either of them ventured on the dividing line or across the line, then there was war."

Printed in Charles T. Thompson, *The Peace Conference Day by Day: A Presidential Pilgrimage Leading to the Discovery of Europe* (New York, 1920), pp. 406-16.

From the Diary of Ray Stannard Baker

Friday June 27 [1919]

Another whirling day, getting ready for the signing of the treaty. Badgered nearly to death with tickets. At 2:15 the President came down & talked for over an hour with the correspondents in Secretary Lansing's room. He should do this oftener because he always makes an extremely favorable impression.

I went up as usual in the evening & he told me of the doings of the day: the appointment by the Four of a new Mandatory Commission consisting of Lord Milner, Colonel House, M. Simon, Signor Crespi & Chinda, the Japanese.

I asked the President who wrote the remarkable reply to the Turkish letter[1] & he told me that Balfour did it and said that he would have felt proud if he could have done it.

His talk to-day to the correspondents was most interesting & helpful, especially in guiding them as to his own views. I wish he would do it oftener: but he dreads it, & is keenly sensitive to those who are hostile in their questioning, & is likely to assume a defensive tone. He never appeared to better advantage than on this occasion—better by far than in one or two conferences with correspondents which I have attended at Washington. He met the fire of questions with humor and simplicity & with a plain desire to give the men exactly what he had in his mind. He told one or two excellent stories to illustrate his points—and answered questions in all for more than an hour.

As to mandatories he said he felt inclined to recommend to the American people that they take a mandate for Armenia: he would not "take anything out of which we could make anything." As to Constantinople he said that if we took it it would be only to keep it out of European politics. He could only "report to the folks" in regard to mandates, explain the questions involved and take the decision of Congress.

Asked about the Senate resolution (introduced by Senator Fall) providing for peace with Germany without conditions, he said it would be a "national disgrace" if it were to pass. The proposal to ratify the treaty with reservations would also be disastrous, because it could not then be made effective until we got replies from 21 nations. As to Article 10 of the Covenant he regarded it, he said, "as the backbone of the whole thing."

He was questioned closely regarding the much-mooted guarantee to France. "We think," he said, "that the League of Nations affords abundant protection to France, but the French are in a tense state of mind. They saw this fearful thing coming. Other people said it would not come. It did. They are still fearful & require our assurances for their safety. As a matter of fact any new threat to France could not come for a dozen years: & in that period the L. of N. will prove itself one way or another."

He was asked about the protection of minorities: Irish and Jews especially. "It must not be thought of as a new question," he said, "majorities have always been troubled by minorities & always will be."

He summed up the whole matter: "All things considered the treaty adhered more nearly to the 14 points than I had a right to expect. Considering the incalculable difficulties we had to face it comes remarkably near. Never forget that Germany did an irreparable wrong, & must suffer for it. It is just that Germany be required to repair the wrong done. Think of the positive achievements of the peace—the newly liberated peoples, who had not before dared to dream of freedom—the Poles, the Czechoslovaks, the Slavs, the peoples of Turkey. The peace has given a new charter to labor, has provided for economic equality among the nations, has gone far toward the protection of racial & religious minorities, and finally & greatest of all, it has banded the peoples of the world in a new League of Nations. It is a colossal business. It is all on paper so far of course but it is up to us to see that it is made effective. There are great difficulties ahead of us and heavy burdens will fall upon us—but I never believed more firmly than I do now in our own people."

He said he would admit Germany to the League when she had proved her new democratic government to be permanent. Mexico & Costa Rica must "qualify as respectable nations before being admitted."

[1] About which, see n. 3 to the minutes of the Council of Four printed at June 21, 1919, 4 p.m.

Hankey's Notes of a Meeting of the Council of Four[1]

C.F.94.

President Wilson's House,
Paris, June 27, 1919, 11 a.m.

The Council had under consideration the Report of those members of the Reparation Commission, who had been deputed to negotiate with Poland, Czecho-Slovakia, Serbia and Roumania with regard to the payment of contributions towards the cost of the war.[2]

I. COLONEL PEEL[3] explained that they had initiated negotiations on the basis of the instructions given at the last meeting of the Council on this subject. Taking the value of the Kroner at 25 per cent of its par value they had finally suggested a total sum in respect of the four states amounting to 2 milliards Francs Swiss gold. Generally speaking these states were reluctant to undertake this liability though Czecho-Slovakia had undertaken to do so if the other three would consent. Serbia and Roumania had not absolutely declined but he doubted whether they were seriously willing to pay. We did not know what decision had been taken by the Polish representatives as they had not been present at the last discussion on the subject. He pointed out therefore that this liability must either be imposed on these States, or the sum might be discussed and proposals for its revision considered or the matter dropped altogether.

PRESIDENT WILSON asked what method it was proposed to adopt to impose this obligation on the States in question.

MR. DULLES suggested that they should be told that in the event of a refusal they would again come under the terms of the Austrian Treaty and be liable to pay reparation.

MR. LLOYD GEORGE agreed that this was the best method of dealing with them, and reminded the Council that, as he had pointed out before, with regard to Serbia and Roumania, a kind of bookkeeping transaction could be conducted i.e. the amount of their contributions could be deducted from their claims to reparation.

M. LOUCHEUR said that in his opinion to impose on these small Powers the sum of 1, 1½ or 2 milliards was to incur a great deal of odium for very little profit. His attitude might be different if substantial sums were in question. He reminded the Council of the burden of war expenses which would have to be borne by Serbia and Roumania. If, however, it was decided to impose this obligation on these States, he agreed that Mr. Dulles' suggestion was the right one. He added that he had understood from a Roumanian Delegate on the previous day that these States were prepared to offer 1½ milliards.

M. CLEMENCEAU said that he adhered to M. Loucheur's opinion.

MR. LLOYD GEORGE asked whether in effect M. Loucheur intended that Serbia and Roumania should present in full their reparation claims against Germany, while acquiring between them something like half the former Austrian Empire.

M. CLEMENCEAU explained that he had not looked at the matter in this light. Serbia and Roumania would certainly have to diminish their claims against the reparation fund.

M. LOUCHEUR thought that Mr. Lloyd George's position was right but in view of what had been embodied in the German Treaty with regard to the principle of "solidarity" he did not think that his attitude could now be maintained.

MR. LLOYD GEORGE said that he was not calling in question the principle of solidarity. His point was that the Reparation Commission must strike a balance in the case of Serbia and Roumania and deduct the amount of their contributions from their reparation claims.

M. LOUCHEUR said that the negotiations which, as had been reported, had proved unacceptable to these smaller States, had been conducted on this basis. In any case the balance would be enormously in favour of Serbia and Roumania and he adhered to his opinion that the amount in question was not worth the trouble involved. The reparation claimed by these States would very likely amount to 20 milliards and contributions as suggested to 2 milliards only.

MR. LLOYD GEORGE said that if this position was taken up with regard to Serbia and Roumania, the Czecho-Slovaks would, he supposed, agree to make a payment. He added that it was well known that in Czecho-Slovakia there were a very large number of rich Germans. He could not consent to a proposal which would relieve them of the burdens to be borne by men in similar positions in the Allied countries.

M. LOUCHEUR suggested therefore that the total amount of contributions to be demanded should be 2 milliards of francs.

MR. LLOYD GEORGE said that he would not express an opinion as to a figure and thought that it should be left to the Reparation Commission, when this came into being, to assess it.

MR. DAVIS said that they had attempted, without success, to persuade these States to agree to this proceeding.

COLONEL PEEL suggested that the experts there present and previously delegated for these negotiations should have authority to settle a figure at once.

IT WAS AGREED

That Poland, Czecho-Slovakia, Serbia and Roumania should be called upon to accept liability for the payment of contributions in respect of the expenses of the liberation of formerly Austrian territory to be acquired by them.

That the amount of the contributions should be fixed by the experts of the Reparation Commission who would already be deputed to negotiate with them.

That if these States refused this settlement they should be liable for the payment of reparation under the Clauses of the Treaty with Austria.

II. The Council approved the following provision for insertion in the Financial Clauses of the Polish Treaty:

Poland shall undertake responsibility for a part of the Russian Public Debt and of all other financial obligations of the Russian State as these shall be determined by a special Convention between the principal Allied and Associated Powers of the one part and Poland of the other. This Convention shall be drawn up by a Commission appointed by the said Powers. In case the Commission should not arrive at an agreement, the questions in dispute shall immediately be submitted to the League of Nations.

A copy of the above provision, initialled by Council of Five was handed to M. Cheysson[4] for immediate communication to the Drafting Committee.

BARON MAKINO said that he initialled the document on the assumption that provision would be made for the representation of Japan when the matter in question was under consideration.

III. Voting in Austrian Section of the Reparation Commission.

The following addition to paragraph 3 of Section 3 of Annex II of the Reparation Clauses was initialled for insertion in the Treaty of Peace with Austria, to follow immediately after this clause, "the composition of this section * * * claims."

When voting takes place the representatives of the United States of America, Great Britain, France and Italy shall each have two votes.

T MS (SDR, RG 256, 180.03401/94, DNA).
   [1] The complete text of these minutes is printed in PPC, VI, 716-19.

[2] About this matter, see the minutes of the Council of Four printed at June 4, 1919, 11 a.m.; the extract from the Diary of V. C. McCormick printed at June 4, 1919; and the minutes of the Council of Four printed at June 16, 1919, 5:15 p.m., all in Vol. 60. For a detailed record of the protracted negotiations about the question of the reparation liability of the Austro-Hungarian successor states, see also the abstracts of the documents printed in Philip M. Burnett, *Reparation at the Paris Peace Conference From the Standpoint of the American Delegation* (2 vols., New York, 1940), I, 275ff.

[3] That is, Lt. Col. Sidney Cornwallis Peel, M.P., a financial adviser in the British delegation.

[4] Pierre Cheysson, Inspector of Finance and expert on financial questions in the French delegation.

Hankey's Notes of a Meeting of the Council of Four[1]

President Wilson's House,

C.F.95.   Paris, June 27, 1919, 12 noon.

NOTE: The following decisions were taken immediately after and during the dispersal of the meeting in regard to the Reparation and Financial Clauses in the Austrian Treaty, which is recorded as a separate Meeting.

1. The Council approved the attached additional Clause for inclusion in the Treaty with Poland (Appendix I).

The Clause was initialled by the representatives of the Five Principal Allied and Associated Powers, and was taken by M. Cheysson for immediate communication to the Drafting Committee, since the Treaty with Poland is to be signed on Saturday, June 28th.

2. With reference to C.F.92,[2] Minute 8, the Council took note that since the last meeting the attached resolution in regard to their decision on the subject of the raising of the Blockade of Germany[3] had been approved and initialled by the representatives of the Five Principal Allied and Associated Powers, and, after being initialled, had been forwarded by Sir Maurice Hankey to the Secretary-General for the information of the Superior Blockade Council.

It was agreed that the above decision in regard to the raising of the Blockade should be communicated to the German Delegates in writing by M. Clemenceau on behalf of the Allied and Associated Powers immediately after the signature of the Treaty of Peace.

M. CLEMENCEAU read the draft of the letter he proposed to send to the German Delegation.[4]

3. With reference to C.F.93, Minute 6, Conclusion (1) and C.F.93.A.,[5] Minute 2, the Council took note of the immediate telegram to the Dutch Government, which had been drafted by Mr. Balfour, and which had been approved for despatch on behalf of the Council on the previous day by M. Clemenceau, President Wilson and Mr. Lloyd George, but had immediately been communicated to M. Sonnino and Baron Makino.

BARON MAKINO asked that, in the sentence "He is also the potentate," the word "was" might be substituted for "is."

(This was approved, and Sir Maurice Hankey was instructed to use the utmost expedition to endeavour to secure the change before the telegram was despatched.

It was further agreed that this telegram should be published in the morning papers of Sunday, June 29th).

A copy of this telegram, as finally approved, is attached (Appendix II).

4. With reference to C.F.93, Minute 6, Conclusion (2) BARON MAKINO said he would agree to Mr. Lansing's draft telegram to the Dutch Government.

(This telegram was accordingly taken note of for use when the time came to give effect to Article 227 of the Treaty of Peace with Germany.)

5. (It was agreed that, as soon as the Reparation and Financial Clauses have been approved, the outstanding portions of the Treaty of Peace with Austria should be communicated to the Austrian Delegation by the Secretary-General.)

(It was agreed to hold a Meeting of the Council at Versailles on the conclusion of the signature of the Treaty of Peace with Germany.)

APPENDIX I TO C.F.95.
TREATY WITH POLAND.

Poland agrees to assume responsibility for such proportion of the Russian public debt and other Russian public liabilities of any kind as may be assigned to her under a special convention between the principal Allied and Associated Powers on the one hand and Poland on the other, to be prepared by a commission appointed by the above States. In the event of the Commission not arriving at an agreement the point at issue shall be referred for immediate arbitration to the League of Nations.

26 June, 1919.

APPENDIX II TO C.F.95.
TELEGRAM TO THE DUTCH GOVERNMENT.

The Allied and Associated Powers desire in the interests of Peace to call the attention of the Dutch Government to the position of the German ex-Kaiser and the German ex-Crown Prince who, early in last November sought safety in Dutch territory.

The Allied and Associated Governments have heard with great surprise that the titular Crown Prince, who is a German combatant officer of high rank, has been permitted in violation of the laws of war to escape from the neutral country in which he was interned. They trust that no similar breach of international obligation will be permitted in the far more important case of the ex-Kaiser. He is not only a German officer who has fled to neutral territory, he was also the potentate whom all the world outside Germany deems guilty of bringing on the great war, and of pursuing it by methods of deliberate barbarism. According to the Treaty of Peace which is about to be signed with Germany his conduct will be judicially arraigned. But he still represents the military party whose influence has ruined his country and brought infinite suffering on the human race. His escape would raise their credit and revive their waning hopes. It would threaten the peace so hardly achieved and even now not finally secured. To permit it would be an international crime, which could not be forgiven those who have contributed to it by their carelessness or their connivance.

The Allied and Associated Powers are confident that these considerations will commend themselves to the Dutch Government. But they desire to add that should that Government feel that in existing circumstances the safe custody of the ex-Kaiser involves responsibilities heavier than any which it is prepared to bear, the Allied and Associated Governments are willing to undertake the duty and so relieve a neutral State of a thankless task which it never sought but which it is under grave obligation to carry out. *26th June, 1919.*

T MS (SDR, RG 256, 180.03401/95, DNA).
    [1] The complete text of these minutes is printed in *PPC*, VI, 720-22.
    [2] That is, the minutes of the Council of Four printed at June 25, 1919, 4 p.m.
    [3] This resolution does not accompany Hankey's minutes. However, it reads as follows:
"The Superior Blockade Council is instructed to base its arrangements for rescinding restrictions upon trade with Germany on the assumption that the Allied and Associated Powers will not wait to raise the Blockade until the completion of the ratification, as provided for at the end of the Treaty of Peace with Germany, but that it is to be raised immediately on the receipt of information that the Treaty of Peace has been ratified by Germany." "RESOLUTION IN REGARD TO THE RAISING OF THE BLOCKADE," June 26, 1919, T MS (WP, DLC).
    [4] This draft, too, is missing in Hankey's minutes. However, it was G. Clemenceau to "Mr. President," June 27, 1919, a TCL of which is in *ibid.*
    [5] That is, the minutes of the Council of Four printed at June 26, 1919, 11 a.m., and at June 26, 1919, 4 p.m.

To Edward Mandell House, with Enclosures

My dear House: Paris, 27 June, 1919.

The British have put Lord Milner to work on drafting mandates, and here is the result. Will you not be kind enough to compare this with Cecil's[1] and Beers' drafts and let me know your opinion at the earliest possible hour? Mr. Lloyd George wants to discuss them this afternoon, but of course I can put that off if necessary.

Affectionately yours,   Woodrow Wilson

TLS (E. M. House Papers, CtY).
¹ See R. Cecil to EMH, May 24, 1919, Vol. 59, and Enclosure II printed below.

E N C L O S U R E   I

SECRET.   MEMORANDUM ON MANDATES.
W.C.P. 1074.   *By Lord Milner.*

Several months ago when it was in contemplation that a Commission should be appointed by the Peace Conference to deal with the question of Mandates, I was requested to draw up some typical forms of Mandate for the consideration of that Commission, on which I understood I was to be one of the British representatives. I accordingly did so to the best of my ability with the assistance of our British legal experts, and submitted the result with a covering Memorandum to the British Empire Delegation, which considered the forms and made several suggestions for their amendment. The Commission, however, was never appointed, and after waiting some time in Paris with a view to taking part in its labours, I returned to England and took no further steps in the matter, except that I from time to time during subsequent visits to Paris submitted my proposals privately to various members of the Peace Conference to have the benefit of their opinion, and have also somewhat modified them to bring them into closer accord with Article 22 of the Covenant of the League of Nations, as contained in the Draft Treaty of Peace. The forms of mandate thus amended, which do not differ materially from those which I originally drafted, I once more submit for consideration.

Article 22 of the Covenant of the League of Nations contemplates three different classes of mandated territories. It will be convenient to set them out here in the language of that Article. For the purpose of reference I will describe them as I described them in my original proposals as Class A. B. and C.

A. Certain communities formerly belonging to the Turkish Empire have reached a stage of development where their existence as independent nations can be provisionally recognised subject to the rendering of administrative advice and assistance by a Mandatory until such time as they are able to stand alone. The wishes of those communities must be a principal consideration in the selection of the Mandatory.

B. Other peoples, especially those of Central Africa, are at such a stage that the Mandatory must be responsible for the administration of the territory under conditions which will guarantee freedom of conscience and religion, subject only to the maintenance of public order and morals, the prohibition of abuses such as the slave trade, the arms traffic and the liquor traffic, and the prevention of the establishment of fortifications or military or naval bases and of military training of the natives for other than police purposes and the defence of territory, and will also secure equal opportunities for the trade and commerce of other Members of the League.

C. There are territories, such as South-West Africa and certain of the South Pacific Islands, which, owing to the sparseness of their population, or their small size, or their remoteness from the centres of civilisation, or their geographical contiguity to the territory of the Mandatory, and other circumstances, can be best administered under the laws of the Mandatory as integral portions of its territory, subject to the safeguards above mentioned in the interests of the indigenous population.

The forms of Mandate which I now submit deal only with Class B. and C. For reasons which I explained at length at the time when I was first requested to deal with the matter I found it impossible to suggest any typical form of Mandate for Mandated territories of the "A" Class. It is unnecessary to state those reasons, which have lost none of their force in the interval, at any length here. But briefly stated the position is this; that the number and nature of these territories is still so uncertain, and their condition so various, that it is difficult to conceive any single form of Mandate which would be applicable to them all. With regard to Mandated territories of the "B" and "C" class on the other hand, the case is quite different. We know all about them. We know exactly what they are, and as a matter of fact the Conference has already decided to what Powers the Mandate for each of them is to be entrusted. Moreover, their social and ethnological conditions are comparatively simple, and in either class pretty homogeneous. There is no reason that I can see why a single typical Mandate should not be applied, merely altering the name of the country and the Mandatory Power, to every one of the Pacific Islands and to S. W. Africa (Class C); and another single typical Mandate to the other ex-German Colonies in Africa (Class B).

The suggested Mandates for those two Classes of Mandated territories are as follows:

MANDATE. CLASS B.
(Applicable to any ex-German Colony in Africa, except South-West Africa)

1. Germany having renounced all rights over X (here insert the description of the mandated territory) the Allied and Associated Powers hereby confer upon Y (here insert the name of the Mandatory Power) a mandate to govern this territory. Y hereinafter referred to as the Mandatory Power shall have full rights of administration and legislation.

2. The Mandatory Power hereby accepts the mandate thus conferred upon it, and undertakes to execute the same in accordance with the following provisions. The Mandatory Power shall be responsible for the peace, order and good government of X hereinafter referred to as the territory, and undertakes to do everything possible to promote the moral and material welfare and progress of the inhabitants.

3. The Mandatory Power undertakes to eliminate all forms of the slave trade and to prohibit forced labour. The traffic in arms and ammunition within the territory shall be controlled in accordance with the General Convention entered into by the Allied and Associated Powers on this subject. The supply of spirituous liquors to natives shall be prohibited, and the trade in such liquors throughout the territory shall be kept under effective control.

4. No native armed forces shall be organised except such as are necessary for the preservation of order and then only upon a voluntary basis. No military or naval works or bases shall be erected or maintained except for the defence of the territory.

5. Subjects or citizens of all States, members of the League of Nations, shall be entitled on an equal footing to enter into, travel or reside in the territory, and to carry on their trade, establish factories, carry on industries, or exercise their professions or occupations, and to buy or sell goods or hold or transmit property of every description, subject only to the requirements of public order and compliance with the local law. The rights conferred by this Article extend equally to companies and associations organised in accordance with the law of any of the States, members of the League of Nations.

6. The Mandatory Power undertakes to maintain throughout the territory, subject only to any necessary limitation in the interest of public order or morals, complete freedom of conscience and religious toleration together with the free and open exercise of all forms of worship. Missionaries shall have full right to enter into, travel and reside in the territory with a view to prosecuting their calling, and shall be entitled on behalf of the missionary or educa-

tional institutions with which they are connected to buy and hold property of every description and to erect buildings for missionary or educational purposes, and to maintain schools and institutions in connection with their work without distinction of creed, but the Mandatory Power will retain full right to exercise such control as may be necessary in the interests of peace, order and good government.

7. The commerce and navigation of all States members of the League of Nations while engaged in lawful enterprises shall enjoy equal treatment in the territory. No attempt shall be made by the Mandatory Power to obtain for the commerce or navigation of its own nationals treatment more favourable than that which is accorded to the commerce and navigation of other States members of the League. Customs duties shall be levied equally on the importation of goods the produce or manufacture of any state a member of the League and export duties shall also be levied equally on goods exported to any State a member of the League. Nothing in this Article however shall preclude the formation of a Customs Union between the territory and any contiguous territories administered by the Mandatory Power.

8. The Mandatory Power will adhere in respect of this territory to the Air Convention, and to the Conventions for the control of the Arms Traffic, for equality of Trade Conditions and for Freedom of Inland Transit.

9. The Mandatory Power undertakes to co-operate in the execution of any common policy adopted by the League of Nations for preventing and combatting disease, including diseases of plants and animals.

10. In the framing of any laws relating to the holding or transfer of land within the territory the laws and customary rights of the natives shall always be taken into consideration by the Mandatory Power and their interests shall be protected and preserved.

11. The Mandatory Power shall make to the Council of the League of Nations an Annual Report on the moral and material condition of the inhabitants of the territory and on the measures taken to give effect to the provisions of the Mandate. This Report shall include full information as to the local revenue and expenditure and as to the customs tariffs in force in the territory in the year under review. Copies of any legislation passed during the year directly affecting the welfare of the natives shall be communicated to the league, together with full particulars of all concessions for mining, ranching or other purposes involving grants of rights over land.

12. The expenses of the administration of the territory, if the

revenue obtained from local sources is insufficient, shall be defrayed by the Mandatory Power.

13. The native inhabitants of the territory shall be entitled to the diplomatic protection of the Mandatory Power when in foreign countries.

MANDATE. CLASS C.
(Applicable to any Ex-German Colony
in Africa except S. W. Africa.)

1. Germany having renounced all rights over X* the Allied and Associated Powers hereby confer upon Y** the Mandate to govern X in accordance with the following provisions.

2. Y shall have full rights of administration and legislation over X as an integral portion of Y and may apply the laws of Y to X subject to such local modifications as circumstances may require.

3. Y, hereinafter referred to as the Mandatory power, accepts the Mandate to govern X, hereinafter referred to as the territory, as a trustee for the wellbeing and development of its inhabitants. The Mandatory power undertakes that the slave trade and forced labour shall be prohibited, and the traffic in arms and ammunition shall be controlled in accordance with the General Convention entered into by the Allied and Associated Powers on this subject. The sale of liquor to the natives of the territory shall be prohibited, and no military training shall be imposed upon the natives otherwise than for the defence of the territory. Furthermore no Powers shall be allowed to establish military or naval bases or erect fortifications in the territory.

4. The expense of the administration of the territory, if the revenue obtained from local sources is insufficient, shall be defrayed by the Mandatory Power.

5. The Mandatory Power shall make an annual report to the Council of the League of Nations, containing full information with regard to the territory and indicating the measures taken to carry out the obligations assumed under Article 3, and the extent to which the wellbeing and development of the inhabitants is progressing.   MILNER.

* X.—the Mandated territory.
** Y.—the Mandated Power.

T MS (WP, DLC).

ENCLOSURE   II

MANDATES—(Beer's suggestions)[1]

MEMORANDUM FOR COLONEL HOUSE   10 June, 1919.

Attached is a copy of Mr. Beer's suggestions with regard to the betterment of the mandate for "Class B" colonies or territories.

The mandate as originally submitted by Lord Robert has not been changed in the sense that anything has been struck out, but certain additions have been made which Mr. Beer has scored on the side in blue pencil.[2] He is now at work on the "Class C" mandate.

I have been told in confidence that Lord Robert is ur[g]ing that these draft mandates be published in order that they may be subjected to the same sort of criticism that was brought to bear on the Covenant of the League. Inasmuch as Mr. Beer has thought it advisable to make so many various additions as he has made, it is likely that careful examination by a number of the officials attached to these delegations might considerably improve these mandates before they were made public. At all events, I think it would be very unfortunate to subject them to criticism until we are sure that they are absolutely the best thing that can be produced in Paris.

CENTRAL AFRICA ("CLASS B") MANDATES
PROPOSED MODEL CLAUSES

1. Germany having renounced all rights over _____, the High Contracting Parties confer upon _____, a mandate to govern this territory. _____ hereinafter referred to as the Mandatory Power shall have full power of administration and legislation.

2. _____ hereby accepts the mandate thus conferred upon it, and will execute the same in accordance with the provisions of this Treaty, and shall be responsible for the peace, order and good government of this territory, and for doing everything in its power to promote the moral and material welfare and progress of the inhabitants.

_____ recognizes the obligation accepted by it under this Convention to be matters of international concern of which the League of Nations has jurisdiction.

3. The Mandatory Power undertakes to eliminate all forms of the slave trade and to prohibit forced labor. The traffic in arms and ammunition shall be controlled in accordance with the General Convention entered into by the High Contracting Parties on this

[1] WWhw.
[2] Beer indicated his additions both by this method and also by underlining in blue pencil. We have put all of his additions in italics.

subject. The supply of spiritous liquors to natives shall be prohibited, and the trade in such liquors throughout the territory shall be kept under effective control.

(Proposed new articles, instead of Number 3.)

(3. The Mandatory Power undertakes: 1, to provide for the emancipation of all slaves and for as speedy an elimination of domestic and other slavery as social conditions will allow; 2, to suppress all forms of the slave trade; 3, to prohibit all forms of forced or compulsory labor, except on essential public works yielding no income and then only in return for adequate wages; 4, to protect the natives from fraud and force by the careful supervision of labor contracts and the recruiting of labor.)

(3a. The traffic in arms and ammunition shall be effectively controlled in accordance with the Brussels Act of 1890 and any subsequent General Convention entered into by the High Contracting Parties on this subject.)

(3b. The trade in spirituous liquors shall be effectively controlled in accordance with the Brussels Acts of 1890, and 1899 and 1906 and the zones of prohibition provided for in the act of 1890 shall be clearly delimited. Any subsequent General Convention entered into by the High Contracting Parties on this subject shall be put into effect.)

4. No native armed forces shall be organized except such as are necessary for the preservation of order. Such forces as are organized shall be raised by a voluntary basis. No military or naval works or bases shall be erected or maintained except for the defence of the territory (east Africa only "or of the great lakes").

5. Subjects or citizens of all Members of the League of Nations shall be entitled on an equal footing to enter into, travel or reside in this territory, and to carry on their trade, establish factories, carry on industries, or exercise their professions or occupations, and to buy or sell goods or hold or transmit property of every description, subject only to the requirements of public order and compliance with the local law. The rights conferred by this Article extend equally to companies and associations organized in accordance with the law of any of the Members of the League of Nations.

6. The Mandatory Power undertakes to maintain through this territory, subject only to any necessary limitation in the interest of public order or morals, complete freedom of conscience and religious toleration together with the free and outward exercise of all forms of worship. No political or civil disability shall be imposed on the ground of religious belief or in consequence of a change of

faith. Missionaries shall have full right to enter into, travel and reside in the territory with a view to prosecuting their calling, and shall be entitled on behalf of the missionary or educational institutions with which they are connected to buy and hold property of every description and to erect buildings for missionary or educational purposes, and to maintain schools and institutions in connection with their work without distinction of creed. No difficulty shall be placed in the way of any community (*missionary institution*) carrying on its schools in its own language.

The Mandatory Power will retain full right to exercise such control as may be necessary in the interests of peace, order and good government, provided that such control be applied equally to subjects of all Members of the League of Nations.

7. The commerce and navigation of all Members of the League of Nations while engaged in lawful enterprises shall enjoy equal treatment in this territory. No attempt shall be made by the Mandatory Power to obtain for the commerce or navigation of its nationals treatment more favorable than that which is accorded to the commerce and navigation of other Members of the League. (*This equality of treatment shall apply likewise to the navigation from the open sea and vice versa, to the navigation of all rivers, and also to the coastwise trade.*) Customs duties shall be levied equally on the importation of goods the produce or manufacture of any Member of the League (*or imported from them*) and export duties shall also be levied equally on goods (*shipped*) to any Member of the League. No preference in these respects shall be accorded to goods imported or exported under any flag over those imported or exported under the flag of any Member of the League. (*Further, there shall be no inequality or discrimination as regards subjects or citizens of Members of the League of Nations in port-dues, fees, or any taxes whatsoever, nor in the tariffs for transportation by railway, by river or by other means of transit. No administrative orders shall be issued regarding weights and measures, gauging, etc., which might discriminate against the merchandise of any subjects or citizens of Members of the League of Nations.*)

(*7a. All concessions for railways, ports, telegraphs, wireless stations, and all other public works, shall be granted without regard to the nationality of the applicant provided he is a subject or citizen of a Member of the League of Nations, but the right is reserved to the Mandatory Power both to construct such works for the account of the local government and also to provide that the concessions are granted only on such conditions as will maintain intact the local government's authority over these undertakings of public interest. Likewise, there shall be no discrimination in the granting of concessions for the development of the country's natural resources.)*

(7b. Contracts for the execution of public works and for supplies of sufficient magnitude to warrant such procedure (or in excess of a specified amount) shall be awarded on the basis of public tender, but it is left to the judgment of the local government to determine in the light of the various factors involved the relative advantage of the different tenders.)

(7c. Provided all other States, whether Members of the League of Nations or not, refrain [from] similar measures in regard to ___ ____, the Mandatory Power shall not admit merchandise from ___ ____ at lower rates of duties than the same commodities of other origin, and shall not encourage such imports from _____ by direct or indirect bounties, and, further, shall not grant direct or indirect shipping subsidies for the specific purpose of fostering commerce between _____ and itself.)

8. The Mandatory Power will adhere in respect of this territory to the Air Convention, and to the conventions for the equality of Trade Conditions and for freedom of Inland Transit and for the suppression of the Opium Traffic.

9. The Mandatory Power undertakes to co-operate in the execution of any common policy adopted by the League of nations for preventing and combating disease, including diseases of plants and animals.

10. In the framing of any laws relating to the holding or transfer of land within the territory the laws and customary rights of the natives shall always be taken into consideration by the Mandatory Power and their interests shall be protected and preserved. *(No transfers of land shall be valid, except with the specific approval of the public authorities appointed for the purpose.)*

11. The Mandatory Power will make to the Mandatory Commission of the League of Nations an Annual Report on the moral and material condition of the inhabitants of this territory, and on the measures taken to given effect to the provisions of the present convention. This Report shall include full information as to the local revenue and expenditure and as to the customs tariffs in force in the territory in the year under review, and shall be divided into the following principal headings and sub-headings:

(1) Political: organization and results.
   (a) Administration
   (b) Finance
   (c) Judicature
   (d) Legislature.

(2) Education and religion so far as not included under heading (1).

(3) Economic.

(a) Public works *(and supplies)* including detailed schedule of concessions and concessionaries *(and of tenders and contracts)*.

(b) Development of natural resources including detailed list of concessions and concessionaries.

((b 1) *Labour conditions and contracts)*

((b 2) *Land tenures, holdings, grants, and transfers.)*

(c) Commerce, Customs tariff, and statistics of imports and exports.

(4) Military and Police: numbers, organization, sources of recruitment, Measures taken for public security including police regulations.

(5) Medical and Sanitary organization and results.

(6) Action taken to fulfil adherence to provisions of Art. 8.

The Mandatory Power further undertakes to supply, so far as possible, any information which the Mandatory Commission may at any time require of it.

12. The expenses of the administration of this territory, if the revenues obtained from local sources are insufficient, will be defrayed by the Mandatory Power. *(All local revenues must be devoted solely to local purposes)*

13. The native inhabitants of this territory shall be entitled to the diplomatic protection of the Mandatory Power when in foreign countries.

14. The consent of the Council of the League of Nations is required for any modification of the terms of this Convention, and it shall be the duty of the Council to advise their reconsideration at any time, should they, in its opinion, have become inapplicable to existing conditions.

15. If any dispute whatever should arise between the Members of the League of Nations relating to the interpretation or the application of the present Convention which cannot be settled by friendly negotiations, this dispute shall be submitted to the Permanent Court of International Justice to be established by the League of Nations.

T MS (WP, DLC).

A Memorandum by George Louis Beer

Paris, June 27th, 1919.

Memorandum on drafts of mandates.

The drafts submitted by Lord Milner are essentially the same as those drawn by Lord Robert Cecil with this exception, that Lord Milner has submitted no form of mandate for the first class, namely, for the territories that formerly were a part of the Turkish Empire. Neither Lord Milner's nor Lord Robert Cecil's drafts are altogether satisfactory, especially in that they do not give adequate protection to the native populations; nor do they provide fully for the open door. If these mandates were accepted in their present shape there is no question that they would call forth considerable hostile criticism from people who have interested themselves earnestly in the welfare of the native peoples of Africa and elsewhere. For instance, the class C mandate contains no provision for the protection of missionary activities. Yet, American missionaries have extensive interests in the Caroline and Marshall islands that are to go to Japan under a mandate.

Even if these mandates in their present shape were satisfactory to the American delegation it is exceedingly doubtful if they would be accepted immediately and without careful scrutiny by the French, hence the only practical procedure seems to be to appoint a Commission composed of delegates from the five Allied and Associated Powers to draw up satisfactory mandates as was proposed in the letter of Colonel House to the President a few days ago. The issues at stake are of great moment and the question should be carefully studied in all its aspects. The mandates drawn up by this Commission would then go for approval either before the Council of the League of Nations or before the five Allied and Associated Powers in whose favor Germany has relinquished her rights over the territories in question.

T MS (WP, DLC).

Hankey's Notes of a Meeting of the Council of Four[1]

President Wilson's House,

C.F.96.   Paris, June 27, 1919, 4 p.m.

1. (M. Paderewski and Mr. Hurst were present during this discussion.)

M. PADEREWSKI said he had come to ask the Council to make certain modifications in the Convention to be signed between Poland and the Principal Allied and Associated Powers under Article 93 of the Treaty of Peace. The various points to which he alluded were dealt with fully in a letter, dated 26th June, 1919, he had sent to M. Clemenceau,[2] and to which he made frequent reference.

2. The first point raised by M. PADEREWSKI is contained in the following extract from his letter to M. Clemenceau:

"I have the honour to declare, in the name of the Polish Delegation to the Peace Conference, that we are ready to sign the proposed Convention in execution of Article 93 of the Treaty of Peace with Germany, while asking you, M. le Président, in the name of justice, to stipulate that the numerous Polish population destined to remain under German domination shall enjoy the same rights and privileges so far as concerns language and culture as those accorded to Germans who become, by reason of the Treaty, citizens of the Polish Republic."

There was considerable discussion on this point, which is only briefly summarised below.

PRESIDENT WILSON pointed out that the claim was a just one, but it was impossible now to put it in the Treaty with Germany. There were no means by which the Peace Conference could compel the Germans to observe any stipulation of this kind. The Poles, however, might enter into negotiation with the Germans with a view to some arrangement between them.

M. SONNINO said that the obligation by Poland to Germans resident in Poland contained in the Convention might be subordinated to reciprocity by Germany.

MR. LLOYD GEORGE suggested that the best plan would be for Poland to make an appeal to the League of Nations on the subject. He felt sure that the Council of the League would sustain them. He thought this would be a much better plan than by making any stipulation on the subject. If there were a bargain by which the Germans were compelled to treat the Poles in their territory in the same manner as the Poles were bound to treat Germans in their

---

[1] The complete text of these minutes is printed in *PPC*, VI, 723-34.
[2] Paderewski's letter does not accompany Hankey's minutes. However, its full text, in French, is printed in Halina Janowska *et al.*, eds., *Archiwum Polityczne Ignacego Paderewskiego* (4 vols., Wroclaw, 1973-74), II, 220-23.

territory, there would continually be disputes as to whether Germany had extended these privileges, and it would be an encouragement to extremists to refuse just treatment on the ground that the other party had not done the same. It was, however, to the interests of Poland to treat Germans in their territory as well as possible and to make them contented. Troublesome times might come and it would then be a great advantage that the German population should have no cause for discontent. Further, the Poles' appeal to the League of Nations would be much stronger if they had treated the Germans well.

M. PADEREWSKI shared Mr. Lloyd George's point of view in principle, but pointed out that the question arose as to when the authority of the League of Nations would extend over Germany.

PRESIDENT WILSON pointed out that this depended upon when Germany was admitted to the League of Nations and the conditions for this had been laid down in the reply to the German counter-propositions.[3] He considered that Mr. Lloyd George's plan was the best one. He pointed out that Germany was eager to qualify for admission to the League of Nations, since she was handicapped as against other nations until she had qualified. He suggested that the League might be asked to insist on corresponding treatment to the Poles in German territory as a condition for Germany's entering into the League of Nations. He regretted that provision for just treatment of Poles in Germany had not been made in the German Treaty and that it would be necessary to postpone the matter for the present, but, in the circumstances, he thought this was the best plan.

M. CLEMENCEAU agreed that the best plan was for Poland to apply to the League of Nations. In reply to an observation by M. Paderewski that the League of Nations might not always consist of persons actuated by the same motives as the Council of the Principal Allied and Associated Powers, he pointed out that, in effect, the Council of the League of Nations could consist of the same persons as the present Council.

3. A second alteration in the Treaty, proposed by M. PADEREWSKI, is contained in the following extract from his letter of June 26th to M. Clemenceau:

"At the same time, we beg you, M. le Président, to be so good as to modify the text of Article 9 by editing the second paragraph as follows:

'In the towns and districts where a considerable proportion of Polish subjects of Jewish faith reside, there shall be assured to

---

[3] For which, see Appendix IV to the minutes of the Council of Four printed at June 12, 1919, 11 a.m., Vol. 60.

this minority an equitable part in the division of the sums which shall be raised from public funds, municipal or otherwise, for the object of education, religion or charity. These sums shall be employed for the establishment, under the control of the Polish State, of primary schools, in which the needs of the Jewish faith shall be duly respected and in which the popular Jewish language (Yiddish) should be considered as an auxiliary language.' "

This modification, M. Paderewski explained, had been asked for by the Polish Jews.

MR. LLOYD GEORGE pointed out that this proposal went far beyond what was contemplated under the present draft of the Treaty.

PRESIDENT WILSON agreed and pointed out that the intention of the present Treaty was that Yiddish should only be used as a medium of instruction and was not to be taught as a separate language.

M. PADEREWSKI said that, as this had been put forward by an influential Jewish body, he had felt it his duty to present it to the Council.

4. M. PADEREWSKI further raised objection to the provision in the Convention with Poland for the Internationalisation of the River Vistula and its tributaries. He feared that this would enable the Germans to obtain advantages. Germany already had advantages in the control of many of the markets affecting Poland. He was ready to conclude any arrangement with the Allied and Associated Powers, but Poland had to remember that Germany did not consider herself bound by treaties. It was being openly declared in German newspapers that Germany would not be morally bound by the Treaty of Peace. The internationalisation of the Vistula was not provided for in the Treaty with Germany. It had been proposed in Commissions and Sub-Commissions, but the proposal had been withdrawn, and thus the Vistula had been recognised as a national Polish river. This was why the Polish Delegation proposed the suppression of Article 6. In reply to questions as to how far the Vistula ran through territory other than Polish, he said that the river itself ran entirely through Polish territory. Its tributary, the Bug, ran part of its course through Ruthenian territory.

PRESIDENT WILSON pointed out that by this article Poland was merely bound to accept for her rivers, the same international regime as Germany had accepted for German rivers. Poland was only asked to come into the same international scheme as was contemplated in other parts of Europe.

M. PADEREWSKI said he felt that this clause gave privileges to the Germans.

5. In the course of the above discussions, the question was raised as to the equipment of the Polish military forces.

MR. LLOYD GEORGE said that in a short conversation he had had with M. Paderewski on entering, he had asked him about the condition of the Polish army. He was disturbed to find that this bore out the accounts that he had lately received from General Sir Henry Wilson, namely that part of the Polish forces were quite inadequately armed. The Allied and Associated Powers had plenty of material, and he could not imagine how Poland had been allowed to be short.

PRESIDENT WILSON thought it was due to the difficulty in getting supplies through.

M. PADEREWSKI regretted that this was not really the reason. He had been told to appeal to the Supreme Council. When he had appealed some time ago not one had been willing to help except the Italian Government who had sent several trains of ammunition through Austria. Except for General Haller's army, however, he had received nothing from the United States of America, France or Great Britain.

MR. LLOYD GEORGE said that Great Britain had been asked to supply Admiral Koltchak, General Denikin and the Archangel Government, and they had done so. He asked if they had refused any specific appeal from Poland.

M. PADEREWSKI said that the appeal had not been made individually to Great Britain but was made to the Council without any result.

PRESIDENT WILSON said that his own recollection was that nothing had been sent, because it was impossible to get any material through.

MR. LLOYD GEORGE said there should be no difficulty about getting it through now. The whole of General Haller's army had been transported and Dantzig was also available.

M. PADEREWSKI said that the passage of food through Dantzig was being stopped. Many of the soldiers in Poland had not even cartridge belts. He had applied to the United States Army and to Mr. Lansing personally and in writing but could not get any belts, though the surplus of these was actually being burnt in some places. The equipment of General Haller's army was absolutely first-class, but Poland had some 700,000 men who needed everything. They had no factories themselves, and had an entire lack of raw material.

(It was agreed that the Military Representatives at Versailles should be informed that the Council of the Principal Allied and Associated Powers were anxious to complete the equipment of the Polish Army. The Military Representatives should be directed to make immediate enquiry as to the deficiencies of the Polish Army in equipment and supplies, and to advise as to how and from what sources these could best be made good. The Military Representatives should be authorised to consult the Polish Military Authorities on the subject.)

6. Importance of ratification by Poland of the Treaty with the Allied and Associated Powers.

M. MANTOUX read the following note from M. Fromageot.

(translation.)

The Treaty with Germany must be ratified by Poland in order that it may benefit from it. On the other hand the application of this Treaty so far as concerns Poland is not subordinated to the ratification by Poland of this special Treaty with the Powers for the guarantee of minorities.

It might happen from this that Poland, while refusing to ratify this special Treaty, might become the beneficiary of the Treaty with Germany, a Treaty of which Article 93 however, provides for the protection of minorities in Poland in the form of an engagement with this country.

M. FROMAGEOT has notified the Minister of Foreign Affairs of this question, and Mr. Hurst has equally notified Mr. Balfour.

M. PADEREWSKI said there was no doubt that the Polish Diet would ratify the Treaty.

(It was agreed that no action was called for on this note.)

(M. Paderewski and Mr. Hurst withdrew.)

7. The Council had before them forms of Mandates which had been prepared by Lord Milner and circulated by Mr. Lloyd George.

PRESIDENT WILSON said that there was some criticism to make against Lord Milner's proposals. In his view they hardly provided adequate protection for the native population; they did not provide sufficiently for the open door; and the Class "C" Mandates did not make provision for missionary activities. He thought that if the Council devoted themselves to this question now, they would find themselves in the position of drafting the Mandates themselves, and he did not feel they were suitably constituted for that purpose. He thought the best plan would be to appoint a special Committee for the purpose.

MR. LLOYD GEORGE did not agree that Lord Milner's draft did not go sufficiently far as regards the open door. He thought that in some respects his Forms went beyond what was originally contemplated. He agreed, however, in remitting the matter to a special Committee. He thought that perhaps the Committee might transfer its activities to London as this would be more convenient for

Lord Milner. Colonel House was about to proceed to London, and as he was informed by Baron Makino, Viscount Chinda, the Japanese Ambassador in London would be the Japanese member of the Committee.

PRESIDENT WILSON suggested that the best plan would be to set up the Commission at once and ask them to hold a special preliminary meeting to arrange their own procedure. He thought it would be a good plan to draw up the Mandates and publish them in order to invite criticism before adopting them. He was prepared, however, to leave this also to the Commission.

MR. LLOYD GEORGE said that a closely connected question was that of the Belgian claims to a part of German East Africa. Lord Milner had agreed upon a scheme with the representatives of the Belgian Government which the British Government was ready to accept. He felt bound to mention, however, that the Council of the Aborigines Society[4] had lately come to Paris and had raised objections to the allocation of this territory to Belgium. He understood the difficulty was that Belgium desired these territories mainly for the purpose of raising labour rather than for what they contained.

PRESIDENT WILSON said that he believed Belgium had reformed her Colonial administration but the difficulty was that the world did not feel sure that this was the case. He thought the best plan would be to ask the special Committee to hear the Aborigines Society.

SIR MAURICE HANKEY, alluding to a proposal that M. Clemenceau had made that the question should be discussed on the afternoon of the following day at Versailles after the signature of the Treaty of Peace, said that not only the Belgian representatives would have to be heard, but in addition, the Portuguese representatives who had asked to be heard when questions relating to German East Africa were under consideration.

PRESIDENT WILSON suggested that the Special Committee might hear the Portuguese representatives in addition.

SIR MAURICE HANKEY pointed out that this would considerably extend the reference to the special Commission.

PRESIDENT WILSON said that the Aborigines ought to be heard in connection with the Mandates.

MR. LLOYD GEORGE said he supposed the question of German East Africa would have to be put off until the Aborigines Society had been heard.

---

4 The Aborigines Protection Society, founded in London in 1837 as a result of an inquiry by a Royal Commission into the treatment of indigenous populations in the British colonies. It had merged, in 1909, with the British and Foreign Anti-Slavery Society to form the Anti-Slavery and Aborigines Protection Society.

It was agreed that a special Commission should be immediately set up composed as follows:

Colonel House for the United States of America.

Lord Milner for the British Empire.

M. Simon for France.

M. Crespi for Italy.

Viscount Chinda for Japan.

for the following purpose:

1. To consider the drafting of Mandates.
2. To hear the views of the Aborigines Society in regard to the Belgian claims in German East Africa.

   To hear the Portuguese claims in regard to German East Africa.

   (Mr. Philip Kerr was summoned into the room and given instructions to invite Lord Milner immediately to summon a preliminary meeting of the Commission.)

8. With reference to C.F.93,[5] Minute 11, MR LLOYD GEORGE suggested that a telegram ought to be sent to Admiral Koltchak asking him whether he was willing to agree in the scheme for the co-operation of the Czecho-Slovak forces in Siberia with the right wing of his army.

(It was agreed that a telegram in this sense ought to be sent, and Mr Lloyd George undertook to submit a draft to the Council at the Meeting on the following morning.)

9. PRESIDENT WILSON suggested that after he himself and Mr Lloyd George had left, the main work of the Conference should revert to the Council of Ten at the Quai d'Orsay. He said that Mr Lansing's presence was required for a time in the United States, and that Mr Polk would temporarily take his place.

MR LLOYD GEORGE agreed in the new procedure.

(It was agreed that on the departure of President Wilson and Mr Lloyd George, the Council of Ten should be re-established at the Quai d'Orsay as the Supreme Council of the Allied and Associated Powers in the Peace Conference.)

10. MR LLOYD GEORGE said he understood that the upshot of recent conversations was that the Turkish question must be postponed until it was known whether the United States of America could accept a mandate.

(It was agreed:

1. That the further consideration of the Treaty of Peace with Turkey should be suspended until such time as the Government of the United States of America could state whether

---

[5] Hankey's minutes of the Council of Four printed at June 26, 1919, 11 a.m.

they were able to accept a mandate for a portion of the territory of the former Turkish Empire.

2. That the Turkish Delegation should be thanked for the statements they have made to the Peace Conference,[6] and that a suggestion should be conveyed to them that they might now return to their own country.

The view was generally expressed that Mr Balfour should be invited to draft the letter to the Turks.)

11. (M. Tardieu was introduced.)

The Council had before them the attached report on the proposals of the French Government in regard to the allocation of certain former German passenger ships to relieve the difficulties of France in regard to passenger tonnage, especially so far as her Colonial lines are concerned (Appendix I).[7]

MR LLOYD GEORGE commented that if France and Italy were in a difficult position as regards tonnage, so was Great Britain. He said he could not accept the report because no representative of the Ministry of Shipping had been available to take part in it. He could neither give an assent or a dissent on a shipping question unless the proper expert was available. He had telegraphed on the previous day to the Minister of Shipping, and he hoped that an expert would be available immediately.

(It was agreed that the report should be considered as soon as a representative of the British Ministry of Shipping was available.)

(M. Tardieu withdrew.)

12. (M. Dutasta entered.)

With reference to C.F.91,[8] Minute 1, M. DUTASTA handed a letter from the German Delegation on the subject of the signing of the special Convention in regard to the Rhine to M. Mantoux, who translated it into English (Appendix II).[9] In this letter the German Delegation protested against having to sign the Rhine Convention simultaneously with the Treaty of Peace, on the ground that Article

[6] About these statements, see the extract from the Grayson Diary printed at June 17, 1919, and n. 1 thereto, Vol. 60, and n. 14 to the minutes of the Council of Four printed at June 25, 1919, 4 p.m.

[7] Printed in PPC, VI, 732. This brief untitled report, dated June 26, 1919, had been submitted by a committee composed of Capt. Charles Talbot Hardy, Assistant Director of the Trade Division of the British Admiralty, John R. Gordon, a representative of the United States Shipping Board, Étienne Clémentel, André Tardieu, and Silvio Benigno Crespi. The committee stated that it had no authority to propose a distribution of enemy ships. However, it recommended that, in view of the critical position of France with regard to passenger tonnage, the Reparation Commission should report to the Council of Four on the possibility of placing at the disposal of France the passenger ships used for the transportation of American troops as soon as those vessels became available. In a postscript, Crespi observed that, while he agreed with the report, Italy's position, which was even more serious than that of France, would also have to be considered.

[8] The minutes of the Council of Four printed at June 25, 1919, 11 a.m.

[9] It is printed in PPC, VI, 733-34.

232 provided only for a subsequent convention. They intimated, however, that they would not press their objection if conversations could take place later on the subject.

(On M. Clemenceau's suggestion, it was agreed to reply in the sense that the Rhine Convention must be signed on the same day as the Treaty of Peace with Germany, but that the Allied and Associated Powers would not object to subsequent meetings to discuss details.

Captain Portier drafted a reply, which was read and approved.[10] M. Clemenceau undertook to dispatch it immediately.)

13. M. DUTASTA also handed a Note from the German Delegation to M. Mantoux, which he translated into English, containing the German consent to the addition of a special Protocol to the Treaty of Peace with Germany, as proposed some days before. (Appendix III.)[11]

(M. Dutasta withdrew.)

14. The Council had under consideration the question of the size of the Army of Occupation of the Provinces west of the Rhine. In this connection they had before them the report of the special Commission appointed to consider that question as well as to draw up a Convention regarding the military occupation of the territories of the Rhine.[12]

(It was agreed to refer the question to the Military Representatives of the Supreme War Council at Versailles.)

15. (With reference to C.F.79,[13] Minute 4, it was agreed that the Secretary-General should be authorised to communicate the decision concerning the frontier between Roumania and Jugo-Slavia in the Banat to the representatives in Paris of the countries concerned.)

16. With reference to C.F.92,[14] Minute 20, the following telegram was approved and initialled by the representatives of the Five Principal Allied and Associated Powers:

"The Supreme Council of the Allied and Associated Powers has decided to authorise the Polish Government to utilise any of its military forces, including General Haller's army, in Eastern Galicia."

N.B. It was explained that this decision was consequential to the decision that the Polish Government be authorised to occupy with its military forces Eastern Galicia up to the River Zbruck, and had

[10] It does not accompany Hankey's minutes.
[11] It is printed in *PPC*, VI, 734.
[12] For this report, see Enclosure I printed with J. W. Davis to WW, June 10, 1919, Vol. 60.
[13] The minutes of the Council of Four printed at June 21, 1919, 3:45 p.m.
[14] The minutes of the Council of Four printed at June 25, 1919, 4 p.m.

been recommended by the Council of Foreign Ministers on June 25th.

(Captain Portier undertook to communicate the initialled telegram to the Secretary-General for despatch.)

17. (M. Claveille and General Mance[15] were introduced.)

GENERAL MANCE explained that the Südbahn was the railway from Vienna to Trieste with a branch to Fiume and a branch to Innsbruck, which went through to Trent. By the Treaty of Peace, it was divided into five parts. The bondholders were largely French. The Governments of Austria, Jugo-Slavia, Italy and Hungary each had the right under the Treaty of Peace with Austria to expropriate the portion running through its territory. Various proposals had been made for meeting the difficult situation created. The simplest was that of the Czecho-Slovak Government, which, moreover, was disinterested. Their proposal was that there should be an agreement between the four Governments in regard to the status of the railway, including the rights of expropriation and the financial arrangements. Failing agreement between the four Governments, arbitration should be arranged by the Council of the League of Nations.

(At M. Sonnino's request, the subject was postponed until the following day, when Italian, as well as British and French experts, might be present.)

T MS (SDR, RG 256, 180.03401/96, DNA).

[15] That is, Albert Claveille, French Minister of Public Works and Transportation and an adviser on communications questions in the French delegation; and Brig. Gen. Harry Osborne Mance, Director of Railways, Light Railways, and Roads in the British War Office and an adviser on railroad questions in the British delegation.

Hankey's Notes of a Meeting of the Council of Four[1]

President Wilson's House,
C.F.96.A.   Paris, June 27, 1919, 4:30 p.m.

1. MR. LLOYD GEORGE said that Mr. Hurst had prepared a text of a Convention to give effect to the agreement in regard to the guarantee to be given by Great Britain to France. The draft was based on an American draft, but one important alteration had been made. The American draft made the agreement subject to approval by the League of Nations in accordance with the Covenant of the League of Nations. It had been pointed out, however, that in this case one member of the Council could interfere with the validity of the agreement. Consequently, in the British draft, it was made subject to the agreement of the majority of the Council of the League of Nations.

PRESIDENT WILSON accepted the new draft and asked Mr. Hurst to arrange with Mr. Brown-Scott[2] to make a corresponding alteration in the American draft.

MR. LLOYD GEORGE said that M. Clemenceau must realise that he was not in a position to bind the self-governing Dominions, which had their own Parliaments, and this was provided for in the Draft Convention.

M. CLEMENCEAU said that he quite understood this.

(Mr. Hurst was instructed to prepare a final draft.)

(The final draft is contained in Appendix I.)

APPENDIX I TO C.F.96A.

ASSISTANCE TO FRANCE IN THE EVENT
OF UNPROVOKED AGGRESSION BY GERMANY

Amended copy read to and approved by President Wilson,
M. Clemenceau, and Mr. Lloyd George, 27.6.19.

WHEREAS there is a danger that the stipulations relating to the Left Bank of the Rhine contained in the Treaty of Peace signed at Versailles on June 28, 1919, may not at first provide adequate security and protection to the French Republic, and

WHEREAS His Britannic Majesty is willing subject to the consent of His Parliament and, provided that a similar obligation is entered into by the United States of America, to undertake to support the French Government in the case of an unprovoked movement of aggression being made against France by Germany: and,

WHEREAS His Britannic Majesty and the President of the French Republic have determined to conclude a Treaty to that effect and have named as their Plenipotentiaries for the purpose, that is to say:

His Britannic Majesty

. . . .

The President of the French Republic

. . . .

In case the following stipulations relating to the left bank of the Rhine contained in the Treaty of Peace with Germany signed at Versailles the 28th. day of June, 1919, by the British Empire, the French Republic and the United States of America among other Powers:

"42. Germany is forbidden to maintain or construct any fortifications either on the left bank of the Rhine or on the right bank to the west of a line drawn 50 kilometres to the East of the Rhine.

"43. In the area defined above the maintenance and assembly of armed forces either permanently or temporarily, and military

manoeuvres of any kind as well as the upkeep of all permanent
works for mobilisation are in the same way forbidden.

"44. In case Germany violates in any manner whatever the provisions of Articles 42 and 43, she shall be regarded as committing
a hostile act against the Powers signatory to the present treaty and
as calculated to disturb the peace of the world."

may not at first provide adequate security and protection to France,
Great Britain agrees to come immediately to her assistance in the
event of any unprovoked movement of aggression against her
being made by Germany.

II.

The present treaty, in similar terms with the Treaty of even date
for the purpose concluded between the United States of America
and the French Republic, a copy of which Treaty is appended
hereto, will only come into force when the latter is ratified.

III.

The present Treaty must be submitted to the Council of the
League of Nations and must be recognised by the Council, acting
if need be by a majority, as an engagement which is consistent
with the Covenant of the League; it will continue in force until on
the application of one of the parties to it the Council acting if need
be by a majority agrees that the League itself affords sufficient protection.

IV.

The present Treaty shall before ratification by His Majesty be
submitted to Parliament for approval.

V.

The present Treaty shall impose no obligations upon any of the
Dominions of the British Empire unless and until it is approved by
the Parliament of the Dominion concerned.

The present Treaty shall be ratified and shall, subject to Articles
2 and 4, come into force at the same time as the Treaty of Peace
with Germany of even date comes into force for the British Empire
and the French Republic.

In faith whereof the . . . .

Done in duplicate at the City of Versailles,
on the ..... day of ...... 1919.

T MS (SDR, RG 256, 180.03401/96¼, DNA).
  [1] The complete text of these minutes is printed in *PPC*, VI, 735-37.
  [2] That is, James Brown Scott.

From the Diary of Colonel House

June 27, 1919.

This has been a trying day because so many people have come in to say good-bye since I am leaving on Sunday. A great number are also leaving with the President Saturday night.

The President came to the Crillon today and had a talk with the newspaper men, and later with the Commissioners. Just before lunch he sent a letter to me which is a part of the record. I immediately set to work, and when he arrived at 2.15 I had the answer ready for him. It had to do with the very important questions of mandates. Lloyd George, he said, was pressing him for an immediate decision and he wanted my advice. He also wished to know the difference between the memorandum made by Lord Milner and that made by Lord Robert Cecil. I advised in the memorandum, which Louis Beer had prepared at my suggestion, that we had best do nothing at the moment, and pointing out that we disagreed sharply with the British upon some essentials. I told the President in person that in my opinion he should not let Lloyd George crowd him into immediate action.

The reason for this discussion was that in the afternoon meeting of the Council of Three, a commission was appointed to pass upon this question of mandates. Besides myself, the other members are Lord Milner for England, Viscount Chinda for Japan, M. Simon for France and Signor Crespi for Italy. Milner undertook to call a meeting for tomorrow morning, and I undertook not to go, which made things even. I sent Beer to tell them we would take the matter up later when we reached London.

To John Foster Dulles

My dear Mr. Dulles: Paris, 27 June, 1919.

I hope that you will not feel that I am imposing a too onerous or too unwelcome duty upon you if I beg very earnestly that you make arrangements to remain in Europe for the present to handle the very important and difficult matters with which you have become so familiar and which you have so materially assisted in handling. My request is justified by the confidence we have all learned to feel in your judgment and ability, and I am acting upon the opinion of the men with whom you have been collaborating, as well as upon my own, in making this earnest request.

Cordially and sincerely yours,   Woodrow Wilson

TLS (J. F. Dulles Papers, NjP).

To Douglas Wilson Johnson

My dear Major Johnson: Paris, 27 June, 1919.

I have your letter of yesterday with the accompanying memorandum, and find myself in substantial agreement with all that you urge. I have recently sent a brief memorandum to my colleagues of the American Peace Delegation which is substantially along the same lines, though perhaps even a little more drastic and uncompromising.[1] I am going to send your memorandum to Mr. Lansing as a commentary and am sure it will be most useful. Thank you very much.

Cordially and sincerely yours,   [Woodrow Wilson]

CCL (WP, DLC).
[1] That is, the Enclosure printed with WW to RL, June 25, 1919 (first letter of that date).

To Robert Lansing

My dear Lansing: Paris, 27 June, 1919.

Here is a memorandum from Douglas Johnson which I think you will read with the same acquiescence with which I have read it. I have told him that I was going to send it to you as a sort of commentary on the Italian memorandum I sent you the other day.

Cordially and faithfully yours,   Woodrow Wilson

TLS (RG 256, 186.3411/646, DNA).

From Herbert Clark Hoover, with Enclosure

My dear Mr. President: Paris 27 June 1919.

You will please find enclosed herewith a memorandum which I propose to introduce to the Supreme Economic Council in reply to the memorandum of the various other Governments demanding the erection of some continuing economic body.[1] I trust this is in accord with the understanding which we reached a few days ago.[2]

I am deeply impressed with the necessity for coordinated action within the United States in connection with the granting of private and public credits and in the supplying of raw material and food to various countries in Europe. That is, it would seem to me to be a disaster if we allowed our merchants and bankers to expend either American private or public credits to Governments in Europe who did not maintain stability, who did not cease hostilities and who do not busy themselves with sound economic reconstruction and return to production. I would like to lay before you for consideration whether it would not be desirable to set up some sort of an economic committee in the United States representing the different departments of the Government and such other persons as you might select, and who would in a general way pass upon the policies to be pursued by the American Government and people in these matters. Such a council could quite well have relations with similar Councils set up in other countries and could no doubt affect a great deal of constructive order towards rehabilitation in Europe without submerging American policies in these matters in those of foreign Governments. I have discussed this matter with Mr. Davis[3] who will no doubt take it up with you on the steamer enroute home.   Faithfully yours,   Herbert Hoover

TLS (WP, DLC).
   [1] Memoranda by the British delegation, June 20, 1919; the French delegation, June 20, 1919, and the Italian delegation, June 16, 1919; and E. de Cartier to HCH, June 20, 1919, all printed in *PPC*, X, 414-27. The memoranda and De Cartier's letter all strongly urged the continuance of the Supreme Economic Council, or some similar body, after the signing of the peace treaty. Such a supranational agency, they argued, was essential for the rational and constructive solution of all the postwar economic problems—continued relief and reconstruction, control of food supplies and raw materials, satisfaction of the financial needs of the new states, the solution of the problem of inter-Allied indebtedness, possible assistance to Russia, etc. Of these proposals, that of the French delegation was the most elaborate and explicit, and it spelled out in detail the role, composition, and powers of the new agency.
   [2] See the extract from the Diary of Vance C. McCormick printed at June 23, 1919.
   [3] That is, Norman H. Davis.

E N C L O S U R E

Paris 27 June 1919.

MEMORANDUM:

   The American Delegates on the Supreme Economic Council, being as they are, officials for the period of war only, have felt that the establishment of some form of international conference on economic matters must rest for decision, so far as the United States is concerned, with the permanent departments of the Government. In conference with the President on this matter, he has taken the same view and feels that on his own authority alone he could not establish such an American representation in a body of this character as would make it an effective organ from the American point of view. The matter therefore requires to be laid before the leading officials in the Government at Washington and their views obtained. It is my understanding that this will be undertaken. I also understand that the present Council in any event continues until the end of July pending the signature of peace with the Governments with whom the Entente have been at war. It seems to the

American Delegates undesirable that the present Council should continue after such a date lest it should give the impression to the world of an economic block of the Governments who have been aligned in war.

T MS (WP, DLC).

From Edward Mandell House

Dear Governor: Paris, June 27, 1919.

It seems to me that, as soon as the treaty is signed, it will be highly advisable for us to resume relations of some kind with the German Government, principally in order to lend stability to a Government which will have need of all its vitality to resist the efforts of reaction which are sure to be set up against it and, incidentally, so that our exporters may not be placed at a disadvantage with regard to other nationals who will undoubtedly attempt to establish themselves in Germany on the eve of the signing of peace.

While I understand that relations cannot be officially resumed until the ratification of the treaty by the Senate, I believe it will be possible to appoint a Special Agent, who might be designated as Chargé d'Affaires after the ratification of the treaty. I am satisfied that Mr. Ellis Loring Dresel is well qualified to fill such a post but I suggest that you discuss the matter with Lansing. Mr. Dresel spent two years at our Embassy in Berlin with Ambassador Gerard and has a fluent knowledge of the German language in addition to his wide diplomatic experience; for a time he was in charge of the organization of American prisoners relief in Swi[t]zerland in connection with the Legation at Berne and the American Red Cross. Later on he became the American representative of the War Trade Board in Switzerland.   Affectionately yours,   E. M. House

TLS (WP, DLC).

From Philip Henry Kerr, with Enclosure

Dear Mr. President,   Paris. 27th June 1919.

The Prime Minister asked me to send over to you immediately the enclosed draft telegram to Admiral Koltchak prepared in the Military Section for your consideration.
                                        Yours sincerely,   P. H. Kerr

TLS (WP, DLC).

ENCLOSURE

Following for Admiral Koltchak.   *27th June 1919.*

I. The principal Allied and Associated Governments have under consideration the following scheme for repatriating and utilising Czecho-Slovak troops in Siberia:

(a) Allied and Associated Governments to find shipping to move all Czecho-Slovak troops who can reach Archangel before the closing of the port by ice and to do their best to find shipping at Vladivostok.

(b) 30,000 men to take part in an operation on right wing of Koltchak's army with a view to establishing a junction with Archangel forces at Kotlas, whence they would be repatriated before end of current year.

(c) Remainder of Czecho-Slovak troops to be moved gradually to Vladivostok, and thence embarked to Europe as shipping becomes available.

(d) Sector of railway now guarded by Czecho-Slovaks to be taken over by Americans or by Japanese, or by both conjointly.

II. Apart from the very substantial advantages which it is hoped to obtain by enabling you to effect a junction with the Archangel forces, above scheme offers prospect of relieving dangerous situation now developing in Central Siberia through the discontent which has arisen among the Czecho-Slovak troops.

III. It is recognised that the morale of these troops is at present low, and success of scheme is obviously dependent on sufficient men being willing to fight the Bolsheviks with a guarantee of earning repatriation as a reward for success.

IV. It is also recognised that transportation of Czecho-Slovaks by rail to Perm will interfere with your normal despatch of supplies and munitions unless running of increased number of trains can be arranged for the purpose.

V. It is obviously impossible to guarantee success of proposed operation, and even assuming success, there is a risk of the Czecho-Slovaks reaching Archangel too late for repatriation before the port is ice-bound. It has, however, been calculated that there is a reasonable possibility of Czechs reaching Kotlas before middle of October provided the military operations involved are successful in which case, repatriation this year would be possible.

VI. The Governments of the principal Allied and Associated Powers wish you to consider this project carefully in all its aspects, and to telegraph your views on the various points raised above with the least possible delay, since, if the project is to be carried out, every day is of importance. The project, is of course, dependent on the consent and co-operation of the Czecho-Slovaks Government, which the Powers will endeavour to obtain if you consider this scheme both practicable and desirable. To avoid subsequent mis-understanding, it is pointed out that there can be no question of retaining any of the Czecho-Slovak troops once their junction with Archangel forces has been effected.

T MS (WP, DLC).

Frank Lyon Polk to Robert Lansing and Vance Criswell McCormick

Washington, June 27, 1919

URGENT. For the Secretary of State and McCormick: I under-stand your 2794, June 25, 6 P.M.¹ to mean that we can deal openly with representatives of Kolchak who are now here and desire to purchase supplies. However, I fear that even this will lead nowhere unless we can work on credit basis with ten percent initial cash payment. Can I assure Secretary of War and any others concerned that this is what the Mission understands to be the President's pur-pose. Please let me know as soon as you possibly can do so.

Polk

TS telegram (SDR, RG 59, 861.01/71, DNA).
¹ RL and V. C. McCormick to FLP, June 25, 1919.

From Vi Kyuin Wellington Koo, with Enclosure

My dear Mr. President: [Paris] June 27, 1919.

Aggreably to the conversation I had had with you in the evening of the 25th instant, I consulted Mr. Lansing yesterday and later saw Mr. Pichon who asked for the meaning of the Chinese reser-vation. After my explanation, he wrote down the following notes, which he would show to Mr. Clemenceau:

"The Chinese plenipotentiaries will sign the treaty, but will first send a letter to the President of the Conference declaring that the Chinese plenipotentiaries will sign the treaty under the reservation of May 6, 1919, which was intended to enable the Chinese Govern-ment after the signing of the treaty, to ask at a suitable moment for a reconsideration of the Shantung question."

At 5:30 this afternoon I was informed verbally by Mr. Pichon that Mr. Clemenceau could not admit any reservation sent in be-fore the signing of the treaty but would accept a declaration after the signing. I said that I feared it would be very difficult for the Chinese Delegates to sign without being able in advance of the signature to send in some form of declaration. To this he pleaded the decision of the President of the Conference.

The acceptance of a declaration merely reserving the right of re-opening the question of Shantung, while it means a great deal to the Chinese Delegation, does not appear, in the absence of any ex-planation from Mr. Pichon, an insurmountable difficulty with the Supreme Council, and therefore I appeal to you to exercise your friendly influence with a view to enabling the Chinese Delegates to sign the treaty without sacrificing their sense of national honor and pride. China can have no desire to withdraw from the Council of the Allied and Associated Powers by refraining from signing the treaty until and unless every honorable compromise is denied her.

Pardon me for taking the liberty of writing you so informally and I beg to assure you that if you have any word to convey to me, I am entirely at your disposal.

I am, Mr. President,

Yours respectfully,   V. K. Wellington Koo

TLS (WP, DLC).

E N C L O S U R E

In proceeding to sign the treaty of peace with Germany today, the undersigned, plenipotentiaries of the Republic of China, con-sidering as unjust articles 156, 157 and 158 therein which purport to transfer the German rights in the Chinese Province of Shantung to Japan instead of restoring them to China, the rightful sovereign over the territory and a loyal co-partner in the war on the side of the Allied and Associated Powers, hereby declare, in the name and on behalf of their Government, that their signing of the treaty is not to be understood as precluding China from demanding at a suitable moment the reconsideration of the Shantung question, to the end that the injustice to China may be rectified in the interest of permanent peace in the Far East.

Y. R. Loutsengtsiang

Chengting Thomas Wang[1]

TS MS (WP, DLC).

[1] That is, Lu Cheng-hsiang and Wang Cheng-t'ing.

From Robert Lansing

My dear Mr. President: Paris June 27th, 1919

With reference to your letter dated June 25th regarding the appointment of Mr. Whitlock as Ambassador to Rome,[1] I hasten to inform you that the formal nomination which I transmitted to you for signature with my letter dated June 12th has already been forwarded to the Department of State by mail and will be at your disposal upon your arrival in Washington.

Faithfully yours,   Robert Lansing.

TLS (WP, DLC).
    [1] WW to RL, June 25, 1919, CCL (WP, DLC), saying that it would probably be wise to have the formal nomination of Whitlock ready for him to take home with him.

To Thomas William Lamont

My dear Mr. Lamont: Paris, 27 June, 1919.

I have just been greatly shocked by receiving the following message from Mr. Tumulty:[1]

"Present indications are that Republicans will make an effort to put through joint resolution which proposes to have Congress declare a state of peace between Germany and the United States unconditionally. It also instructs the Executive to withdraw troops from Europe. Committee considered resolution today without action but may report the same Monday."

"Today" means Wednesday, the 25th. Personally I am filled with dismay at the possibility of an action which would absolutely forfeit for us the confidence of the whole world. I am sending this to you with the thought that possibly you may think of some channel through which influence can be exerted to prevent this disgrace. I do not mean the passage of the resolution—I take it for granted that is impossible—but the serious proposal of it.

In haste,

Cordially and sincerely yours,   Woodrow Wilson

TLS (T. W. Lamont Papers, MH-BA).
    [1] JPT to WW, June 25, 1919 (sixth telegram of that date).

Three Telegrams to Joseph Patrick Tumulty

Paris, June 27, 1919.

Surely no responsible Republican is mad enough openly to support a resolution for unconditional peace with Germany. Such an action, and I am afraid even the proposal of such an action, on the part of Congress would instantly win and earn for us the hatred and contempt of every other free nation, undo all we have done in the war and brand us as the friend of the nation that has done the greatest wrong in history. It would be nothing less than an act of treachery at the very moment when there is the most need of honor and co-operation. I am firmly convinced that our people will be profoundly shocked by the suggestion and will firmly repudiate it. Is it in fact seriously proposed and supported?[1] (Paragraph.)

Please see John R. Mott and discuss with him the possibility of my speaking at the Great Joint Meeting of the Northern and Southern Methodist Churches in Ohio.[2] I am afraid the meeting ends too soon for me to attend it. (Paragraph)

I entirely agree with the general tenor of your cable of the 25th, number 211, about the Irish question and I firmly believe that when the League of Nations is once organized it will afford a forum not now available for bringing the opinion of the world and of the United States in particular to bear on just such problems. The Republicans will commit another great blunder if they make use of the Irish agitation and will endanger the lining up of the whole country along religious lines. That would be a calamity which would not be compensated for by the defeat of the Republicans. (Paragraph.)

Sorry to say that I am convinced I have no legal power in the matter of the ban on liquor.[3] It does not specify in the law that it shall end with the signing of peace, but with the demobilization of the troops, and we cannot say that that has been accomplished for it is far from being accomplished. (Paragraph.)

I agree with McAdoo as quoted in your number 210[4] that it would be a mistake to seek to pass through New York unnoticed and of course I am willing to receive any sort of informal welcome that may be planned, provided the danger you speak of can be avoided. (Paragraph)

Please say to the Attorney-General[5] that I am quite willing that seventy thousand dollars should be allotted to the Department of Justice from the National Security and Defense Appropriation for 1918 to complete the payment of all liabilities arising on account of railway transportation of alien enemies and other miscellaneous matters for the period ending June 30, 1918, if there is a balance in the fund sufficient to cover the amount and available for the purpose.   Woodrow Wilson.

T telegram (WP, DLC).
  [1] There is a WWsh draft of this paragraph in WP, DLC.
  [2] Wilson was replying to J. R. Mott to RL, n.d., T telegram, enclosed in RL to WW, June 25, 1919, TLS (WP, DLC).
  [3] Wilson was replying to JPT to WW, June 25, 1919 (third telegram of that date).

⁴ JPT to WW, June 25, 1919 (first telegram of that date).
⁵ Wilson was replying to FLP to Ammission, June 24, 1919, T telegram, enclosed in
J. C. Grew to GFC, June 26, 1919, TLS (WP, DLC).

Paris, June 27, 1919.

Please release following to the Press when you receive word that the treaty has been signed:

"My fellow-countrymen: the treaty of peace has been signed. If it is ratified and acted upon in full and sincere execution of its terms it will furnish the charter for a new order of affairs in the world. It is a severe treaty in the duties and penalties it imposes upon Germany but it is severe only because great wrongs done by Germany are to be righted and repaired; it imposes nothing that Germany cannot do; and she can regain her rightful standing in the world by the prompt and honorable fulfillment of its terms. And it is much more than a treaty of peace with Germany. It liberates great peoples who have never before been able to find the way to liberty. It ends, once for all, an old and intolerable order under which small groups of selfish men could use the peoples of great empires to serve their own ambition for power and dominion. It associates the free governments of the world in a permanent league in which they are pledged to use their united power to maintain peace by maintaining right and justice. It makes international law a reality supported by imperative sanctions. It does away with the right of conquest and rejects the policy of annexation and substitutes a new order under which backward nations— populations which have not yet come to political consciousness and peoples who are ready for independence but not yet quite prepared to dispense with protection and guidance—shall no more be subjected to the domination and exploitation of a stronger nation but shall be put under the friendly direction and afforded the helpful assistance of governments which undertake to be responsible to the opinion of mankind in the execution of their task by accepting the direction of the League of Nations. It recognizes the inalienable rights of nationality; the rights of minorities and the sanctity of religious belief and practice. It lays the basis for conventions which shall free the commercial intercourse of the world from unjust and vexatious restrictions and for every sort of international cooperation that will serve to cleanse the life of the world and facilitate its common action in beneficent service of every kind. It furnishes guarantees such as were never given or even contemplated before for the fair treatment of all who labour at the daily tasks of the world. It is for this reason that I have spoken of it as a great charter for a new order of affairs. There is ground here for deep satisfaction, universal reassurance, and confident hope."

Woodrow Wilson.[1]

T telegram (J. P. Tumulty Papers, DLC).
[1] There is a WWT draft of this telegram in the C. L. Swem Coll., NjP.

Paris, 27 June, 1919.

Please ask Secretary Baker to be thinking over this suggestion which I will discuss with him when I get back:

That upon Pershing's return to America he be made Chief of Staff and General March be sent to this side of the water to take charge of military matters remaining to be directed here.

Woodrow Wilson.

T telegram (WP, DLC).

Two Telegrams from Joseph Patrick Tumulty

Washington June 27 1919.

Number 217 Springfield Republican leading editorial commenting on Irish situation says quote Is it true that British statesmanship is utterly comma hopelessly comma bankrupt in dealing with Ireland period The average American of plain comma homely speech comma who desires that the United States and Great Britain shall hereafter get on well together comma is asking quote why in thunder doesn't England do something to end the everlasting row over Ireland unquote paragraph quote Do Englishmen know that here in America comma and in this Commonwealth of Massachusetts comma for example comma the Irish question comma like questions of religion comma is getting dangerous to discuss freely comma except in small groups of peoples whose views are known in advance unquote quote If the reactions of the Irish question on Anglo-American relations is deadly comma deadlier comma sadliest comma there ought not to be a moments delay in taking whatever remedial action remains in the reach of practical statesmanship unquote quote If there is no longer a cooperative solution of the question attainable for whatever reason dash Ulster's opposition or Sinn Fein's desperation dash then the internal troubles of the English speaking world are not entirely of the past unquote Thought you would be interested in this view.   Tumulty

[The White House] June 27, 1919.

No. 218 There are only four days left before nation-wide prohibition becomes effective and the country will get on a whiskey basis, unless you act to suspend it. Everything that has happened in
the last few weeks confirms the views I expressed to you in May,[1]
except that added force has been given to every argument made,
especially by the action of the American Federation of Labor whose
membership almost unanimously voted at its convention for lifting
the ban. The action of Canada in lifting the ban is regarded by the
country as significant. Working men and common people all over
the country cannot understand why light wines and beer cannot
be permitted until the constitutional amendment becomes effective. Only this week the Pennsylvania Legislature voted to legalize
two and three-quarters per cent beer and light wines. Similar action will follow in other states. The consensus of opinion in the
Press is that if prohibition is to be effective, it might better be by
action of three-quarters of the states than by presidential proclamation, for which you alone and our party would bear the responsibility. The prohibitionists in Congress are fearful that the enforcement of war-time prohibition will cause a harmful reaction on
real prohibition, and I believe that they are secretly in favor of your
lifting the ban for this reason. Demobilization figures officially announced by the War Department show that the number of troops
now remaining in service is practically only the number in the
Regular Army. Samuel Gompers, Mary Roberts Rinehart,[2] Mrs.
Douglas Robinson,[3] sister of the late Theodore Roosevelt, Miss
Gertrude Atherton,[4] Frank J. Goodwin,[5] president of Johns Hop-
kins University, and Cardinal Gibbons out in strong statement favoring retention of beer and light wines. If you do not intend to lift
the ban on July first, you can announce your intention to suspend
it as soon as the War Department notifies you demobilization is
accomplished which, the best opinion says, will be August first.
The feeling all over the country is one of harmful uncertainty and
I strongly believe that a definite announcement of some nature
which will clear the atmosphere should be made. Since your last
announcement, all your friends on the Hill, even Senators from
Southern states, agree with the attitude you took in your message
on this question.[6] I cannot tell you how deeply it has embarrassed
the Republicans.   Tumulty.

T telegrams (WP, DLC).
  [1] See JPT to WW, May 9, 1919 (second telegram of that date), Vol. 58.
  [2] Prolific author and playwright.
  [3] Corinne Roosevelt Robinson.
  [4] Gertrude Franklin (Mrs. George H. Bowen) Atherton, prolific author.
  [5] Actually, Frank Johnson Goodnow.
  [6] That is, in Wilson's special message to Congress printed at May 20, 1919, Vol. 59.

David Hunter Miller to Gordon Auchincloss[1]

Washington June 27, [1919]

115. For Auchincloss from Miller. Following summary second memorandum on letter of Root. Major criticism is against article ten. In first sentence this article are two distinct covenants first of

[1] It seems very likely that Wilson read this telegram, as well as others from Miller, since he, Wilson, made all of Miller's points, for example, on his western tour in September.

Wilson saw only the badly garbled version printed below. It is impossible to reconstruct it by corrections in square brackets. Hence, we print the text from the carbon copy in the D. H. Miller Papers:

"Following summary second memorandum on letter of Root: Root's major criticism is against Article ten. In first sentence this Article are two distinct covenants, first of which is agreement to respect, etc. Nowhere any objection to this feature which Root does not mention. But this provision of greatest importance. If this part Article ten stands, one of greatest incentives to war eliminated. This engagement Austria Hungary refused to give to Russia regarding Serbia in July, 1914. For breach of this Member may be expelled. If League includes all nations observance of this would mean that guarantees would never require enforcement. Effect of striking this out morally would be in favor of aggression and technically that covenant would in case of dispute upon which opinions in Council differed authorized war of aggression.

"With such agreement in Covenant, Members are to see it lived up to in spirit. No League of Nations could otherwise endure. Thus remaining covenant of Article criticised by Root is natural and necessary result of League based upon mutual forebearance and is vital.

"From another viewpoint such agreement is necessary consequence of war and of Treaty.

"Allies and United States have united in peace which restores Belgium, returns Alsace Lorraine to France, creates Poland, etc. etc.

"Only one answer to such question, which Root gave on March 29th when he supported Article ten. Root admits this now when he favors French Alliance.

"But he adds, QUOTE. But let us not wrap up such a purpose in a vague universal obligation under the impression that it really does not mean anything likely to happen. UN-QUOTE.

"But this obligation does not mean QUOTE anything likely to happen. UNQUOTE. By Article ten moral force of United States would alone prevent aggression. Root would protect France but if new Russia comes in as helpless member may she again be treated as at Brest-Litovsk?

"Root would reject Article ten because we should keep out of quarrels of Europe and in same breath says he favors not keeping out of quarrels of France.

"Argument based upon possible QUOTE dissension and hatred among our own inhabitants of foreign origin UNQUOTE too long to quote but to favor French alliance and in next paragraph to ask QUOTE How can we prevent bitterness and disloyalty toward our own Government on the part of those against whose friends in their old homes we have intervened for no cause of our own UNQUOTE leaves doubt whether Root wrote all of letter.

"World policy described in Article ten not without precedent in engagements of United States.

"Familiar instances are New Granada, 1846. Panama, 1903.

"Similar policy expressed in language to which the language of Article ten bears close resemblance was announced by Root in exchange of notes with Japan, November 30th, 1908.

"Memorandum here compares language of Article ten with language of Root Takahira notes which see.

"Taking into account purposes of League and Article eleven moral force of Council would of itself prevent any aggression.

"Root recognizes this when he speaks of provisions which QUOTE ought not to be lost UNQUOTE as including QUOTE the arrangement to make conferences of the powers automatic when there is danger of war; provisions for joint action as of course, by representatives of the nations concerned in matters affecting common interest; the agreement for delay in case of serious disputes, with opportunity to bring the public opinion of the world to bear on the disputants, and to induce cool and deliberate judgment. UNQUOTE.

which is agreement to respect, et cetera. Nowhere any objection to this feature which Root does not mention. But this provision of greatest importance. If this part Article X stands one of greatest incentives to war eliminated. This engagement Austria-Hungary refused to give to Russia regarding Servia in July 1914. For breach

"Memorandum next discusses meaning of QUOTE external UNQUOTE and of article generally, and shows that Article is intended to accomplish a certain result, but that means to be adopted are discretionary and that advice of Council must be unanimous.

"As practical matter obvious that war would never be necessary unless aggression were that of Great Power or of great combination. Idea that dispute in Balkans would require troops of United States is fantastic. NO Balkan States could challenge moral force of or economic pressure of Great Powers. Vital result accomplished by Covenant and never before is unity of Powers against aggression which in advance defeats all aggression.

"Root says Article ten is independent alliance but not so for it is bound up with Covenant, and Council advise how obligation fulfilled. Root says agreement might involve parties in war against Power which had not broken any other provisions of Covenant, but this statement is strong argument for Article X for no one could desire Covenant which contemplated that integrity and independence of Member could be destroyed by another Member or non-Member.

"Doubtless Root refers to case of dispute either between Members or between Member and non-Member of the League, which is submitted to Council and as to which unanimity in Council does not prevail. In such case Members by Article fifteen reserve liberty of action and striking out Article ten would in effect add to that reserve QUOTE and may commence a war of subjugation and annexation. UNQUOTE.

"Mr Root's proposed QUOTE reservation UNQUOTE as to Article ten is as follows: QUOTE. In advising and consenting to the ratification of the said treaty, the Senate reserves and excludes from its consent the tenth article of the covenant for the league of nations, as to which the Senate refuses its consent. UNQUOTE.

"Memorandum here argues that so called reservation is really amendment differing from alleged precedents of certain Hague conventions.

"How can United States by Article one ask Latin American countries not belligerents to accede to Article ten if United States does not, and at same time say if they do not accede to the whole Covenant including Article ten without reservation, they must stay out of League.

"Council has certain duties and representative of United States is always member of Council. How can Council perform duty under Article ten unanimously if United States is not party to Article ten? Beyond doubt Covenant with Article ten in force as to some Powers and not as to others is impossibility.

"Inevitable conclusion is that Article ten is essential part of Covenant. Under clause permitting withdrawal, any Power may end its obligations, but while League of Nations exists, Article ten must remain.

"Language used by Root in paragraph three of his proposed resolution of ratification is QUOTE. Inasmuch as in agreeing to become a member of the league of nations, the United States of America is moved by no interest or wish to intrude upon or interfere with the political policy or international administration of any foreign State, and by any existing or anticipated dangers in the affairs of the American Continents, but accedes to the wish of the European States that it shall join its powers to theirs for the preservation of general peace, the Senate consents to the ratification of the said treaty, excepting article ten aforesaid, with the understanding that nothing therein contained shall be construed to imply a relinquishment by the United States of America of its traditional attitude toward purely American questions, or to require the submission of its policy regarding questions which it deems to be purely American questions, to the decision or recommendation of other Powers. UNQUOTE.

"Incorporated in this language is much of declaration made at First Hague Conference by United States and adopted as a reservation the ratification of both Conventions of 1899 and 1907 for pacific settlement International Disputes which see.

"Striking differences between proposal of Root and earlier reservations.

"First. By earlier reservations United States was not required to depart from policy of not interfering with political questions of foreign state; by Root's proposal, United States says merely that in joining League it is moved by no wish or interest to so interfere.

of this member may be expelled. If League includes all nations observance of this would mean that guarantees would never require enforcement. Effect of striking this out morally would be in favor of aggression and technically that covenant would in case of dispute upon which opinions in council differed authorize war of aggression.

With such agreement in covenant members are to see it lived up to in spirit. No League of Nations could otherwise endure. Thus remaining covenant of article criticised by Root is natural and necessary result of League based upon mutual forbearance is vital.

From another view point such agreement is necessary consequence of war and of treaty.

Allies and U. S. have united in Peace which restores Belgium, returns Alsace-Lorraine to France, creates Poland, et cetera.

Only one answer to such question which Root gave on March 29th when he supported Article X.[2] Root admits this now when he favors French Alliances.[3]

Recognition by Root that earlier language is inappropriate, is significant. While arguing against keeping out of QUOTE quarrels of Europe UNQUOTE Root recognizes that League in which United States declared it could not be concerned with political questions of Europe, would be absurdity.

"Second. Root proposes that United States say it QUOTE accedes to wish of EUROPEAN States that it shall join its powers to theirs for preservation of general peace. UNQUOTE.

"Reference only to QUOTE wish of European Powers UNQUOTE would be slight to Far East and Latin America, but such a declaration goes much farther than Article ten.

"Latter is carefully limited to prevention of external aggression means to accomplish object are not only discretionary but subject of consultation by Council, but proposed declaration is revolutionary by comparison and if added by us might be urged against our own ideas of Monroe doctrine.

"Third. Final language proposed by Root commencing QUOTE understanding UNQUOTE is only partly taken from earlier reservations but is not only unnecessary but objectionable. Speaks of QUOTE purely American questions UNQUOTE and admits by inference that contrary would be true as to our policy in questions which may be American but not purely American. Why make such admission? Questions of domestic jurisdiction are outside covenant by express language and Monroe doctrine excluded by name. No reason for creating argument as to whether any of these are purely American.

"Language used in 1899 and 1907 doubtless harmless, in view of nature of Conventions but not apt in connection with Covenant which in specific words leaves Monroe doctrine outside provisions and excludes even from inquiry matters within domestic jurisdiction.

"Proposed changes in that language and additions thereto would extend obligations of United States under Covenant, without changing those of any other Power."

The Editors have not found a copy of Miller's memorandum, of which it is a summary, in the files of the State Department. They have also not found a copy of Miller's memorandum in any collection.

[2] Miller here refers to the following paragraph in Root's letter to Will Hays of March 29, 1919:

"The fourth point upon which I think there should be an amendment is article 10, which contains the undertaking 'To respect and preserve as against external aggression the territorial integrity and existing political independence of all members of the league.'

"Looking at this article as a part of a perpetual league for the preservation of peace, my first impression was that the whole article ought to be stricken out. If perpetual it would be an attempt to preserve for all time unchanged the distribution of power and territory made in accordance with the views and exigencies of the Allies in this present juncture of affairs. It would necessarily be futile. It would be what was attempted by the peace of Westphalia at the close of the Thirty Years' War, at the Congress of Vienna

But he adds,

"But let us not wrap us such purpose in a vague universal obligation under the impression that it really does not mean anything to the Siberian Government to happen."

But this obligation does not mean "anything likely to happen," by Article X moral force of United States would alone prevent aggression. Root would protect France but if new Russia comes in as helpless member may she again be treated as at Brest Litovsk?

Root would reject Article X because we should keep out of quarrels of Europe and in same breath says he favors not keeping out of quarrels of France.

Argument based upon possible "dissension and hatred among our own inhabitants of foreign origin" too and henceforth to "but to favor French alliances and in next paragraph to ask "how can we prevent bitterness and disloyalty toward own own Government on the part of those against whose friends in their old homes we have intervened for no cause of our own" leaves doubt whether Root wrote all of letter.

World policy described in Article Ten of the precedent in engagements of United States.

---

at the close of the Napoleonic wars, by the Congress of Berlin in 1878. It would not only be futile; it would be mischievous. Change and growth are the law of life, and no generation can impose its will in regard to the growth of nations and the distribution of power upon succeeding generations.

"I think, however, that this article must be considered not merely with reference to the future but with reference to the present situation in Europe. Indeed, this whole agreement ought to be considered in that double aspect. The belligerent power of Germany, Austria, Bulgaria, and Turkey has been destroyed; but that will not lead to future peace without a reconstruction of eastern Europe and western Asia. The vast territories of the Hohenzollerns, the Hapsburgs, and the Romanoffs have lost the rulers who formerly kept the population in order, and are filled with turbulent masses without stable government, unaccustomed to self-control, and fighting among themselves like children of the dragon's teeth. There can be no settled peace until these masses are reduced to order. Since the Bolsheviki have been allowed to consolidate the control which they established with German aid in Russia, the situation is that Great Britain, France, Italy and Belgium, with a population of less than 130,000,000, are confronted with the disorganized but vigorous and warlike population of Germany, German Austria, Hungary, Bulgaria, Turkey, and Russia, amounting approximately to 280,000,000, fast returning to barbarism, and the lawless violence of barbarous races. Order must be restored. The allied nations in their council must determine the lines of reconstruction. Their determinations must be enforced. They may make mistakes. Doubtless they will; but there must be decision, and decision must be enforced. Under these conditions, the United States can not quit. It must go on to the performance of its duty, and the immediate aspect of article 10 is an argument to do that. I think, therefore, that article 10 should be amended, so that it shall hold a limited time, and thereafter any member may withdraw from it. I annex an amendment to that effect."

Root's proposed amendment to Article X reads as follows:

"After the expiration of five years from the signing of this convention any party may terminate its obligation under this article by giving one year's notice in writing to the secretary general of the league." *Cong. Record*, 66th Cong., 1st sess., pp. 1548, 1549.

[3] That is, in his letter to Lodge of June 19, 1919, as follows:

"If it is necessary for the security of Western Europe that we should agree to go to the support of, say, France, if attacked, let us agree to that particular thing plainly, so that every man and woman in the country will understand the honorable obligation we are assuming. I am in favor of that."

Familiar instances are *violation of neutrality* 1846 Panama 1903.[4]

Similar policy expressed in language to which the language of Article Ten bears close resemblance was announced by Root in exchange of notes with Japan November 30th, 1908.[5]

Memorandum here compares language of Article Ten with language of Root-Takahira notes which paragraph taking into account purposes of League and Article Eleven moral force of Council would of itself prevent any aggression.

Root recognizes this when he speaks of provisions which "ought not to be lost" as including "the arrangement to make conferences of the powers automatic when there is danger of war, provisions for Japanese subjects as of course by representatives of the nations concerned in matters affecting common interest, the agreement for delay in case of serious disputes, with opportunity to bring the opinion of the world to bear on the disputants and to induce cool and deliberate judgment."

Galway next discussing meaning of "external" and of Article generally and shows that article is intended to accomplish a certain result, but much means to be adopted are discretionary *and that* advice of council must be unanimous.

As practical matter obvious that war would never be necessary unless aggression were that of great power or of great combination. Idea that dispute in Balkans would require troops of United States is fantastic. No Balkan States could challenge moral force of or economic pressure of great powers. Vital result accomplished by covenant and never before is unity of powers against aggression which in advance defeats all aggression.

Root says Article Ten is independent alliance but not so for it is bound up with covenant and Council advise how obligation fulfilled. Root says agreement might involve parties in war against power which had not broken any other provisions of covenant but this statement is strong argument for Article for no one could desire covenant which contemplated that integrity and independence of member could be destroyed by another member or non member.

Doubtless Root refers to case of dispute either between members, or between member and non member of the League, which is submitted to council and as to which unanimity in council does

[4] Miller here of course referred to Theodore Roosevelt's actions during the so-called Panamanian revolution of November 1903, when he ordered United States warships to Panama to protect the free transit across the isthmus guaranteed by the treaty with New Granada of 1846.

[5] The so-called Root-Takahira agreement of 1908, about which, see E. T. Williams to W. J. Bryan, Jan. 27, 1915, Vol. 32. The Root-Takahira correspondence is printed in *FR 1908*, pp. 510-12.

not prevail. In such case members by Article Fifteen reserve liberty of action and striking out Article Ten would in effect add to that reserve "and may commence a war of subjugation and annexation."

Mr. Root's references "reservation" as to Article Ten is following "In advising and consenting to the ratification of the said treaty the Senate reserves and excludes from its consent the tenth article of the covenant for the League of Nations as to which the Senate refuses its consent."

Memorandum here argues that so-called reservation is really amendment differing from alleged precedents of certain Hague Conventions.[6]

How can United States by Article One ask Latin-American countries not belligerents to accede to Article Ten if United States does not at the same time say if they do not accede to the whole covenant including Article Ten without reservation, they must stay out of League.

Council has certain duties and representative of United States is always member of Council. How can Council perform any duty under Article Ten unanimously if United States is not party to Article Ten. Beyond doubt covenant with Article Ten in force as to some powers and not as to others is impossible.

Inevitable conclusion is that Article Ten is essential part of covenant. Under clause committee withdrawing any power may end its obligations, but while League of Nations exists Article Ten must remain.

Language used by Root in paragraph three of his proposed resolution of ratification is "Inasmuch as in agreeing to become a member of the League of Nations United States is moved by no interest or wish to intrude upon or interfere with the political policy or international administration of any foreign state, and by any existing or anticipated dangers in the affairs of the American continent, but accedes to the wish of the European states that it shall join its powers to theirs for the preservation of general peace. The Senate consents to the ratification of the said treaty except Article Ten aforesaid with the understanding that nothing therein contained shall be construed to imply a relinquishment by the United States of America of its traditional attitude toward purely American questions, or to require the submission of its policy regarding ques-

---

[6] About the reservations of the United States to certain provisions of the Hague Conventions of 1899, see D. H. Miller to G. Auchincloss, June 26, 1919, n. 4, and J. H. Metzger to JPT, July 29, 1919. The Senate had consented to the ratification of the Hague Conventions of 1907 concerning arbitration with reservations affirming the principles of isolationism and the Monroe Doctrine. See the Metzger letter, just cited, and Richard W. Leopold, *The Growth of American Foreign Policy* (New York, 1962), p. 292.

tions which it deems to be purely American questions to the decision or recommendation of other powers."

Incorporated in this language is much of declaration made at first Hague Conference by United States and adopted as a reservation the ratification of both conventions of 1899 and 1907 for pacific settlement international disputes which see striking differences between proposal of Root and earlier reservations.

First, by earlier reservations U. S. was not required to depart from policy of not interfering with political questions of foreign state. By Root's proposal U. S. says merely that in joining League it is moved by no wish or interest that interfer[e]. Recognition by Root that earlier language is inappropriate is significant. While arguing against keeping out of "quarrels of Europe" Root recognizes that League in which U. S. declared it could not be concerned with political questions of Europe would be absurdity.

Second, Root proposes that U. S. says it "accedes to wish of European States that it shall join its powers to theirs for preservation of general Peace."

Reference only to "wish of European powers would be to slight to far East and Latin-America but such declaration goes much farther than Article X.

Latter is carefully lent to prevention of external aggression. Means to accomplish object are not only discretionary but subject of Consultation by Council, but proposed declaration revolutionary by comparison and if added by us might be urged against our own ideas of Monroe Doctrine.

Third, final language proposed by Root commencing "understanding" is only partly taken from earlier reservations but is not only unnecessary but objectionable. Speaks of "purely American questions" and admits by inference that contrary would be true as to our policy in questions which may be American but not purely American. Why make such admission. Questions of domestic jurisdictions are outside covenant by express language and Monroe Doctrine excluded by name. No reason for creating argument as to whether any but they are purely American. Language used in 1899 and 1907 doubtless harmless in view of nature of conventions but not apt in connection covenant whether we in specific words leave Monroe Doctrine outside provisions and excludes even from inquiry matters within domestic jurisdiction.

Proposed changes in that language and additions thereto would extend of United States under covenant without changing those of any other power.   Phillips,   Acting.

T telegram (WP, DLC).

From the Diary of Dr. Grayson

Saturday, June 28, 1919.

Today crowned the President's trip to Europe. The Treaty was signed. The work of months had culminated in success. The President arose very early and after his breakfast proceeded to Lloyd George's house, where Clemenceau and Lloyd George were in waiting. Shortly afterwards Colonel Henry[1] and Secretary-General Dutasta put in an appearance, bearing the credentials of Dr. Hermann Müller and Herr Johannes Bell. Müller is the Foreign Minister under the new German government, and Bell is the Minister of Communications. They reached Versailles at 2:55 this morning and immediately turned their credentials over to Colonel Henry for transmission to the Council. The credentials were found to be perfect and were sent back with a notification that the ceremony of signing the Treaty would take place promptly at three o'clock in the afternoon at Versailles.

There were no guests at luncheon, and the President, Mrs. Wilson and myself left the house at two o'clock and proceeded to the Elysée Palace, where we paid our farewell visit to President and Madame Poincaré. We then proceeded along the troop-guarded road to the Palace at Versailles, where the signing of the Treaty took place.

The day had been overcast but before we reached the Palace grounds the sun had broken through the clouds. The entire city of Versailles was policed with troops; every entrance was guarded. The soldiers were in field uniform. The only dash of color was on the marble staircase that led up to the Hall of Mirrors, where the signing took place. There picked troopers of the Republican Guard lined the steps. They stood with drawn swords, silver and gold helmets, from which streamed black horse-hair manes; they wore red and black tunics, and white buckskin breeches, tucked into very high top patent-leather boots. The Hall of Mirrors itself had been arranged with a table directly in the center, where the signing was to take place. Directly in front of it was a horse-shoe table that extended almost around the middle chamber. In the center sat Clemenceau, with President Wilson on his right, and Lloyd George on his left. The remaining delegations were seated in the order that they had occupied at the various Plenary Sessions at the Quai d'Orsay. The right end of the room had been reserved for distinguished guests, and Mrs. Wilson and Miss Wilson were furnished with seats well to the front. The opposite end of the room had been set

[1] That is, Lt. Col. Marie Joseph Léon Augustin Henry.

aside for the newspaper correspondents from all over the world. On paper the arrangements were ideal. However, the French with their customary unfairness failed to live up to the promises that were made. They had furnished guest tickets in proportion to all of the powers and tickets for the newspaper correspondents in the same ratio. They then issued the same number of tickets to French people, which resulted in there being two persons present for every seat available. This resulted in indescribable confusion, and made it absolutely impossible for any one to actually see what went on.

The ceremony itself was absolutely devoid of any spectacular feature. After the Allied and Associated delegates had been seated the German delegates were ushered into the room, escorted by Colonel Henry and his staff. Colonel Henry is the French marshal who was assigned to take charge of them. Müller and Bell were accompanied by Herr Schmidt, Herr Kraus[2] and Count von Haniel, who occupied the position of expert advisers, and by the four secretaries who had arrived at Versailles with Brockdorff-Rantzau when the latter first came.

As soon as the German delegates were seated Clemenceau arose and addressing them told them that the hour for signatures had arrived and that they would be expected to sign the Treaty first. The decision to have the German delegates sign first was arrived at by the Council when attention was called by the President to the fact that it would be necessary to have them sign first because if they were allowed to wait until the last they might change their minds and this would result in making the whole procedure ridiculous. It was a very necessary decision. The Germans arose and escorted by Master of Ceremonies Martin and Secretary-General Dutasta proceeded to the table in the center of the room and affixed their signatures. As soon as they re-traced their steps, the signing for the Allied and Associated Powers was commenced, with the American delegation heading the line, the order being fixed in alphabetical procedure. President Wilson was the first to sign the treaty. Although special souvenir pens had been provided for the occasion, the President wrote his name with a little black pen that he purchased for Mrs. Wilson some three years ago when she told him she had none that would write very well, and which he has since used in signing his name to the majority of important state papers.

After the American delegation had signed the other nations proceeded in order, with Great Britain following. It was just 3:14 when the German signatures were completed, and at 3:50 the last

---

[2] Robert Schmidt, Minister of Food, and Prof. Herbert Kraus, a legal adviser in the Foreign Office.

of the Allied and Associated delegates had finished, and the Treaty
of Peace was an accomplished fact.

There were two incidents of a disturbing nature, however. The
Chinese delegation had asked to be allowed to sign the Treaty with
a reservation regarding the Shantung settlement. When they were
told that this would be utterly impossible, as it would invalidate the
whole document, they sent word that they could not participate in
the proceedings, and in consequence the Chinese seats were vacant.

Just before the British delegation signed, General Smuts, the former Boer Commander, issued a bitter statement assailing certain
portions of the Treaty.[3] Smuts said that he signed because it was
necessary to send the world back to work, but that he took objection to the provision that called for the punishment of the Kaiser
and other authors of the war. He maintained to the last the position
which he assumed regarding this question of personal guilt, although his associate, General Botha, made no public protest whatever.

After the signatures were completed Clemenceau, Lloyd George
and the President started out of the building, but Clemenceau lost
his way and they got into the wrong corridor. However, when they
finally got out in the square in front of the Palace the crowd started
cheering and shouting, "Vive Wilson," and crushed forward past
the guards in an effort to get a close view and, if possible, to shake

[3] Smuts' statement was hardly a "bitter statement assailing certain portions of the
treaty." Smuts said that he had signed the treaty, not because it was a satisfactory document, but because it was imperatively necessary to end the war. He did not believe
that the treaty achieved the real peace for which the peoples of the world were waiting,
and he felt that the real work of making peace would only begin after the treaty had
been signed. Muted contriteness and a spirit of forgiveness and mercy, generosity, and
humanity could alone heal the wounds that the war had inflicted upon Christendom.
To that end, many provisions in the treaty, such as certain territorial settlements, questions concerning guarantees, punishments, and indemnities, and numerous pin-pricks
would have to be revised.

However, Smuts continued, the treaty did record two achievements of far-reaching
importance for the world—the destruction of German militarism and the establishment
of the League of Nations. The League would yet lead Europe out of the path of ruin
brought about by the war, but only if the world, filled with a pacific spirit, converted it
into an instrument of progress. It was necessary for the enemy peoples to join the
League at the earliest possible moment, so that they could collaborate in the common
service for humanity.

Smuts then appealed to the peoples of the United States and the British Empire to do
their utmost to repair the wreckage of life and industry on the continent of Europe. He
warned the Germans that any effort by them to evade their responsibilities under the
treaty would be fatal to reconciliation, and he reminded the Allied peoples that God had
given them the victory only for the attainment of the great human ideals for which their
dead had given their lives.

Actually, about punishments, Smuts said only: "There are punishments foreshadowed, over most of which a calmer mood may yet prefer to pass the sponge of oblivion."
He did not mention the Kaiser or anyone else.

The statement is printed in W. K. Hancock and Jean van der Poel, eds., *Selections
from the Smuts Papers* (7 vols., Cambridge, 1966-73), IV, 256-59. A partial text is printed in
the *New York Times*, June 30, 1919.

the President's hand. Women cried out that they just wanted to touch him, and it was a personal ovation for him. The troops were unable to control the crowd, and for a time it was necessary for the President's own guard to crowd around him and to protect him from the exuberations of the multitude. Finally, the President with Lloyd George and Clemenceau started around the Palace and walked all the way around the old structure, with the people following, crowding in and cheering loudly. It was rather remarkable that the one person they wanted to see and applaud was President Wilson. Neither Clemenceau nor Lloyd George took very much of a part in this picture. Clemenceau was very nervous. For the first time his lips trembled and he seemed on the point of a nervous collapse.

The President, Lloyd George, Clemenceau, Baron Sonnino, and Baron Makino proceeded to the old Senate Chamber, where they held a brief meeting, and took up the questions that were to be decided after the President left. This included the Italian settlement.

Clemenceau had tea served for the party while they were there. He also had wine brought in and proposed a toast to the peace and good health of the party. After the toast had been drunk, he turned to me and said: "You had better have another one because you will not be able to get any more of this when you get back home." This was a reference to the fact that the United States was to go dry under the wartime prohibition enactment on July first.

After the meeting the President proceeded to his automobile, and the return trip to the temporary White House was begun. All along the line the roads were crowded with people, who waved flags and shouted, "Vive Wilson." The crowds were dense along the streets of Versailles and through St. Cloud, and then into Paris it was a continuous ovation to the President from the time he left the ancient Palace at Versailles until he alighted at the temporary White House.

Immediately after dinner, Lloyd George, who had been very much exhausted by his efforts of the afternoon, came over to say good-bye to the President. He stayed with him for half an hour and expressed the deepest regret over the fact that he was leaving for home. He said that owing to the fact that there would be a great crowd at the station he was going to ask the President to excuse him from going to the station to say his farewell, as he was very much fatigued and was still somewhat very weak from his recent illness. He referred to the fact that while there had been many occasions when they had differed very seriously in their deliberations, yet he had at all times appreciated the President's position and had grown to appreciate him very much. His parting words to the President were: "You have done more than any one man to bring about further cordial and friendly relations between England and the United States. You have brought the two countries closer together than any other individual in history."

We left the house for the Gare Invalides at 9:20. The trip to the station was made through the back streets, it being the shortest route. However, the people recognized the black cars and the President was cheered all along the line.

Outside of the station one of the biggest crowds that had ever gathered was in evidence. They were held in control by both troops and gendarmes, and as the President's car came up they cheered him wildly. All of the principal officials of the various governments were on the station platform to say good-bye to the President. Mr. Balfour had come down, among others, because he wanted to assure the President of his great personal admiration. He has been very, very fond of the President and has been very anxious to co-operate with him at all times. President Poincaré, Premier Clemenceau, and the members of the French Cabinet, were also on hand to say good-bye. General Pershing and the members of the American Commission were also on hand. Clemenceau was very fluent in his expressions of sorrow over the President's departure, and when I said good-bye to him, he said to me: "In saying good-bye to the President I feel that I am saying good-bye to my best friend." Parting greetings were exchanged until 9:45, when the whistle of the train sounded, and to the strains of the National Anthem, played by the Guard Republic Band, we steamed slowly out of Paris, the work of seven months finally accomplished.

To Robert Lansing, with Enclosure

My dear Lansing: Paris, 28 June, 1919.

Here is a supplementary memorandum about our future dealings with the Italian question. It is the substance of our conversation of yesterday and, I hope, will meet with your approval and the approval of our colleagues.

Always faithfully yours,   Woodrow Wilson

TLS (SDR, RG 256, 186.3411/651, DNA).

E N C L O S U R E

Paris, 27 June, 1919.

MEMORANDUM OF ADDITIONAL SUGGESTIONS CONCERNING
CONFERENCES WITH ITALIAN DELEGATION

In regard to Asia Minor, I think it ought to be made clearly evident to the Italians that we can in no case entertain their claim to the Dodecannesos, and that it is impossible to consider the wishes of Italy with regard to any other claims in Asia Minor until they have shown by action their wish and intention absolutely to cooperate upon equal terms with the United States and the Entente. The question, I suggest, should be put to them somewhat in this way. Either they do or they do not desire to act with the Entente. If they do desire to act with it, they must withdraw their armed forces from all parts of Asia Minor ⟨and also from Fiume⟩. If they retain their armed forces in these places, we will understand that they desire to be left to their own resources and to a forcible assertion of right wherever they choose to assert it, action which would clearly make it impossible for us to cooperate with or assist them in any way.

It ought to be made plain to them that the cooperation and assistance of the United States, including material and financial assistance of all kinds, is dependent upon her accepting as completely as the other powers have accepted the principles upon which the settlements of this peace have been made in respect of all other questions than those affecting Italy. We desire to be the friends of Italy and to render her every kind of assistance that it is in our power to render, but we cannot do so at the sacrifice of any of the principles upon which we have taken our unalterable stand in these negotiations.   Woodrow Wilson

TS MS (SDR, RG 256, 186.3411/651, DNA).

Hankey's Notes of a Meeting of the Council of Four[1]

Mr. Lloyd George's Residence,

C.F.96.B.   Paris, June 28, 1919, 10:30 a.m.

1. PRESIDENT WILSON read a draft of instructions to the United States Delegation which he had prepared.

M. CLEMENCEAU said he did not think that the Allies ought to insist on the evacuation of Fiume. They had no right to demand this. What they had a right to complain of was the assumption that the Italians were masters there and could issue orders in the name of the King of Italy.

MR. LLOYD GEORGE said that Italy had no more right to issue proclamations at Fiume in the name of the King of Italy than France had in the name of the President of the Republic, or Great Britain in the name of King George.

PRESIDENT WILSON said the difficulty was to make the Italians recognise this. All the evidence we had was that the Italians had issued orders and proclamations for the action of their troops in the name of the King of Italy.

MR. LLOYD GEORGE said he understood that it had been arranged informally on the previous day that President Wilson on the one part and Great Britain and France on the other part were to present M. Tittoni on his arrival with written memoranda explaining the attitude of their respective Governments. He thought this would make it easier for Mr. Lansing and Mr. Balfour who, though plenipotentiaries, were not Heads of States, in dealing with Italy.

PRESIDENT WILSON said he had thought the best plan would be to give written instructions to his colleagues who could then inform the Italian Delegation that they had instructions in this sense.

MR. LLOYD GEORGE thought their position would be stronger still if they were left a document which they were to hand to the Italian Delegation.

PRESIDENT WILSON thought it possible that M. Tittoni might use the document in the press to the disadvantage of the Allied and Associated Powers.

SIR MAURICE HANKEY, at Mr. Lloyd George's request, read aloud a draft statement to M. Tittoni on behalf of the British and French Governments, prepared by Mr. Balfour. The draft was not quite complete.

MR. LLOYD GEORGE thought the draft was admirable, but pointed out that the operative words were lacking. He would like to conclude the memorandum by stating that it was no use to have a discussion with the Italian Delegation while their troops remained in Asia Minor, and that before any discussion of Italian claims took place, we must insist on their moving out.

(Sir Maurice Hankey was instructed to ask Mr. Balfour to draft the last paragraph in the sense of Mr. Lloyd George's remarks, combined with the first paragraph of President Wilson's instructions to his colleagues.)[2]

T MS (SDR, RG 256, 180.03401/96½, DNA).
[1] The complete text of these minutes is printed in *PPC*, VI, 738-39.
[2] Balfour's draft, as adopted, is printed as Appendix I to the minutes of the Council of Four, June 28, 1919, 6 p.m.

Mantoux's Notes of a Meeting of the Council of Four

June 28, 1919, 10:30 a.m.

President Wilson reads the text of a note which will be presented in the name of the United States to M. Tittoni upon his arrival.

Wilson. Concerning Asia Minor, I favor saying clearly that in no case will we admit Italian claims to the Dodecanese, and that, for the rest, no solution will be possible so long as Italy has not given proof of her willingness to act in accord with the Entente, and not outside it. That is the essential point; Italy must be with us or outside us. If she is with us, she must evacuate the regions where she is despite our protests, that is Asia Minor and Fiume. If she does not do it, she must give up counting on our assistance, and I must say that, in particular, the financial assistance of the United States to her can be continued only if she gives up the conduct which we condemn.

I have an observation to make concerning Fiume. We cannot ask the Italians to evacuate it, in view of the fact that we also have troops there. What we have the right to ask is that Italy does not assert her sovereignty there. As for the evacuation, no Italian government could consent to it.

Lloyd George. In any case, the Italians do not have the right to promulgate decrees in Fiume in the name of the King of Italy, no more so than we have in the name of King George or President Poincaré.

Wilson. The Italians will claim they have done no such thing, and that the King's name is only found at the bottom of manifestos and other acts which do not have the character of acts of sovereignty.

Clemenceau. What is necessary is to indicate frankly the position of France and England.

Wilson. The text that I have just read you constitutes my instructions to Mr. Lansing.

Lloyd George. I believed that we would send a note in common.

Wilson. No: you yourself said that, because of the treaty that binds you to Italy, you would write a separate note.

Lloyd George. In Asia, I reckon that we must take the same position that you do.

Wilson. Mr. Lansing might say: "Here are my instructions." That commits you to nothing. What is obviously to be feared is that Italy will publish this document, directly or indirectly, to inflame opinion by saying that we want to exclude Italy.

Reading of text prepared by Mr. Balfour to be presented to M. Tittoni in the name of the French and English governments.

Lloyd George. The conclusion is missing. In my opinion, we

must say that we judge it pointless to talk so long as Italian troops
are in Asia Minor; they have stayed there only against our repeated
protests.

Clemenceau. I ask that this text be reread. I notice that it men-
tions the Sykes-Picot agreement;[1] it would be more correct to designate it under the name of "the agreement between M. Paul Cam-
bon and the Foreign Secretary of Great Britain."

Lloyd George. Why mention it?

Hankey. The text speaks of different agreements which, like
that of Saint Jean de Maurienne, must today be called into question.

Lloyd George. That seems pointless to me. I do not recognize the
validity of the convention of Saint Jean de Maurienne, concluded
subject to the consent of Russia.

Lloyd George. Lord Robert Cecil came to Paris to present to you
a recommendation of the Supreme Economic Council.[2] During the
period of transition between the state of war and the establishment
of the League of Nations, it is a matter of continuing, under a form
to be determined, the work of cooperation undertaken by the Economic Council, to avoid the serious consequences that an abrupt
halt of this cooperation could not fail to cause in the world's present situation.

Wilson. The difficulty for the government of the United States is
of a legal nature. The signing of the peace makes it impossible for
us to continue to collaborate with you on the same basis as before.
Once the peace is reestablished, we can study under what form
and to what extent that collaboration might be resumed.

Lloyd George. Lord Robert Cecil proposes to establish a provisional organization until the effective constitution of the League of
Nations.

Wilson. I will see what it is possible to do from the legal point of
view.

Lloyd George. Lord Robert Cecil is very concerned about this
question, and he came expressly to submit it to you.

Wilson. What I want is to manage not to give the impression that
we are creating an economic bloc, a sort of coalition which would
last after the war. That is the objection which the Germans would
not fail to make, and it would be justified. At the same time, I recognize the necessity of warding off the danger that the abrupt halt
of the system that functioned during the war could create.

At 11 a.m. takes place the signing of the two treaties intended to
assure to France the assistance of the United States and of Great
Britain in case of unprovoked aggression by Germany.

Mantoux, II, 553-55.
  [1] About which, see n. 7 to the minutes of the Council of Ten printed at Feb. 6, 1919, 3 p.m., Vol. 54.
  [2] About which, see HCH to WW, June 27, 1919, n. 1.

[APPENDIX]

AGREEMENT BETWEEN THE UNITED STATES AND FRANCE, SIGNED AT VERSAILLES JUNE 28, 1919.

Whereas the United States of America and the French Republic are equally animated by the desire to maintain the Peace of the World so happily restored by the Treaty of Peace signed at Versailles the 28th day of June, 1919, putting an end to the war begun by the aggression of the German Empire and ended by the defeat of that Power; and,

Whereas the United States of America and the French Republic are fully persuaded that an unprovoked movement of aggression by Germany against France would not only violate both the letter and the spirit of the Treaty of Versailles to which the United States of America and the French Republic are parties, thus exposing France anew to the intolerable burdens of an unprovoked war, but that such aggression on the part of Germany would be and is so regarded by the Treaty of Versailles as a hostile act against all the Powers signatory to that Treaty and as calculated to disturb the Peace of the world by involving inevitably and directly the States of Europe and indirectly, as experience has amply and unfortunately demonstrated, the world at large; and,

Whereas the United States of America and the French Republic fear that the stipulations relating to the left bank of the Rhine contained in said Treaty of Versailles may not at first provide adequate security and protection to France on the one hand and the United States of America as one of the signatories of the Treaty of Versailles on the other;

Therefore, the United States of America and the French Republic having decided to conclude a treaty to effect these necessary purposes, Woodrow Wilson, President of the United States of America, and Robert Lansing, Secretary of State of the United States, specially authorized thereto by the President of the United States, and George Clemenceau, President of the Council, Minister of War, and Stéphen Pichon, Minister of Foreign Affairs, specially authorized thereto by Raymond Poincaré, President of the French Republic, have agreed upon the following articles:

ARTICLE I.

In case the following stipulations relating to the Left Bank of the Rhine contained in the Treaty of Peace with Germany signed at Versailles the 28th day of June, 1919, by the United States of America, the French Republic and the British Empire among other Powers:

"ARTICLE 42. Germany is forbidden to maintain or construct any fortifications either on the left bank of the Rhine or on the right bank to the west of a line drawn 50 kilometres to the East of the Rhine.

"ARTICLE 43. In the area defined above the maintenance and assembly of armed forces, either permanently or temporarily, and military manoeuvres of any kind, as well as the upkeep of all permanent works for mobilization are in the same way forbidden.

"ARTICLE 44. In case Germany violates in any manner whatever the provisions of Articles 42 and 43, she shall be regarded as committing a hostile act against the Powers signatory of the present Treaty and as calculated to disturb the peace of the world.",

may not at first provide adequate security and protection to France, the United States of America shall be bound to come immediately to her assistance in the event of any unprovoked movement of aggression against her being made by Germany.

ARTICLE II.

The present Treaty, in similar terms with the Treaty of even date for the same purpose concluded between Great Britain and the French Republic, a copy of which Treaty is annexed hereto, will only come into force when the latter is ratified.

ARTICLE III.

The present Treaty must be submitted to the Council of the League of Nations, and must be recognized by the Council, acting if need be by a majority, as an engagement which is consistent with the Covenant of the League. It will continue in force until on the application of one of the Parties to it the Council, acting if need be by a majority, agrees that the League itself affords sufficient protection.

ARTICLE IV.

The Present Treaty will be submitted to the Senate of the United States at the same time as the Treaty of Versailles is submitted to the Senate for its advice and consent to ratification. It will be submitted before ratification to the French Chambers of Deputies for approval. The ratifications thereof will be exchanged on the deposit

of ratifications of the Treaty of Versailles at Paris or as soon thereafter as shall be possible.

In faith whereof the respective Plenipotentiaries, to wit: On the
part of the United States of America, Woodrow Wilson, President,
and Robert Lansing, Secretary of State, of the United States; and
on the part of the French Republic, Georges Clemenceau, President of the Council of Ministers, Minister of War, and Stéphen Pichon, Minister of Foreign Affairs, have signed the above articles
both in the English and French languages, and they have
hereunto affixed their seals.

Done in duplicate at the City of Versailles, on the twenty-eighth
day of June, in the year of our Lord one thousand nine hundred
and nineteen, and the one hundred and forty-third of the Independence of the United States of America.

                              [SEAL.]   WOODROW WILSON.
                              [SEAL.]   ROBERT LANSING.
                              [SEAL.]   G. CLEMENCEAU.
                              [SEAL.]   S. PICHON.

Printed in *Assistance to France in the Event of Unprovoked Aggression by Germany.
Message from the President of the United States*, 66th Cong., 1st sess., Sen. Doc. No.
63 (Washington, 1919).

Hankey's Notes of a Meeting of the Council of Four[1]

President Wilson's House,
C.F.97.   Paris, June 28, 1919, 11 a.m.

1. The following Treaties were signed to provide for assistance
to France in the event of unprovoked aggression by Germany.

(1) For assistance by the United States, signed by M. Clemenceau, M. Pichon, President Wilson and Mr. Lansing.

(2) For assistance by Great Britain, signed by M. Clemenceau,
M. Pichon, Mr. Lloyd George and Mr. Balfour.

2. The representatives of the five Principal Allied and Associated
Powers initialled the Reparation Clauses for the Austrian Treaty.

3. The representatives of the five Principal Allied and Associated
Powers initialled the Financial Clauses for the Austrian Treaty.

Sir Maurice Hankey was instructed to forward both the Reparation and Financial Clauses to the Secretary-General for communication to the Drafting Committee.

4. With reference to C.F.93.A.,[2] Minute 2, owing to the receipt
of information that the Crown Prince had not escaped, it was
agreed that the despatch to the Dutch Government in regard to the
security of the ex-German Kaiser[3] should be communicated to the
Dutch Government but not published.

5. The Council had before them a letter addressed by Mr. Hoover to President Wilson,[4] suggesting the appointment of a single temporary Resident Commissioner to Armenia, who should have the full authority of the United States of America, Great Britain, France and Italy, in all their relations to the de facto Armenian Government, as the joint representative of those Governments in Armenia. (Appendix 1.)

(This proposal was accepted.)

6. With reference to C.F.96,[5] Minute 10, the Council had before them a draft letter prepared by Mr. Balfour inviting the Turkish Delegation to return to Paris.

MR. LLOYD GEORGE suggested that the first paragraph of the letter should make it clearer that the Turkish Delegation had come here on their own initiative and had not been invited by the Powers.

(Sir Maurice Hankey was instructed to ask Mr. Balfour to modify the letter accordingly.)[6]

7. With reference to C.F.96, Minute 7,

SIR MAURICE HANKEY reported that he had not been quite clear as to the precise terms of reference to the Commission on Mandates, which it had been decided to set up on the previous day.

It was agreed that the terms of reference should be as follows:

(1) To consider the drafting of model mandates.

(2) To hear statements of the Belgian and Portuguese claims in regard to German East Africa.

(3) To hear statements by the Aboriginese Societies in regard to German East Africa.

(4) To make a report on the Belgian and Portuguese claims in German East Africa.

> NOTE. At this point there was a long discussion on the question of the Süd-Bahn railway, in which M. Claveille, General Mance, M. Crespi and Captain Young[7] took part. This is recorded as a separate meeting.

8. Mr. Hoover, Lord Robert Cecil, Mr. Wise,[8] M. Clémentel and M. Crespi were introduced.

LORD ROBERT CECIL said he had asked to see the Council because he was afraid of a hiatus occurring between the disappearance of the Supreme Economic Council and the setting up of new machinery for economic consultation under the League of Nations. As the Council were aware, the Supreme Economic Council provided all the necessary means of consultation at present. He felt it was hardly necessary to notify to the Council the very serious position that existed in regard to the economic state of Europe in matters of relief, transportation, supplies, etc. It was not too much to say that we were on the verge of disaster in the majority of the countries in Europe. At any moment there might be the greatest necessity for the Governments to consult on the subject. It would be most serious if there were a gap in the means of consultation. If only the ordinary diplomatic channels were available for consultation,—it would be impossible to get anything done. The decision required might be a question of days or almost of hours. He was anxious, therefore, to remove any possibility of such a gap. He hoped that it would be one of the first tasks of the Council of the League of Nations to provide for machinery for economic consultation. At one time the French representatives had put forward a scheme,[9] but this had happened at the very end of the proceedings of the Commission and it had not been thought possible to adopt it. President Wilson, he thought, would not be disposed to underrate the importance of the economic side of international relationships. These were the reasons for formulating the following proposal.

"That in some form international consultation in economic matters should be continued until the Council of the League of Nations has had an opportunity of considering the present acute position of the International economic situation, and that it should be remitted to the Supreme Economic Council to establish the necessary machinery for the purpose."

Lord Robert Cecil said he was prepared to substitute the word "propose" for "establish."

M. CLEMENCEAU, after reading the French text, accepted.

PRESIDENT WILSON said he understood that he was the only obstacle to the acceptance of this resolution. All agreed that the Economic Council would continue to function till Peace was ratified, which, he feared, might be some six weeks or two months hence. Consequently, there was ample time in which to consider other methods. What he wished to guard against was any appearance that the Powers who had been Allies and Associates in the war were banding themselves together in an economic union directed against the Central Powers. Any appearance of an exclusive economic bloc must be avoided. Any means of consultation set up must not be open to this suggestion. He agreed, however, that some means of consultation was desirable and even necessary. As regards his own powers, he had to point out that his authority to sanction such consultation ended with the ratification of peace. After that, he would have no authority, and he was not entitled to delegate authority. Hence, it would be necessary for him to consult with his advisers as to whether any machinery could be devised within the Statutes of the United States of America, and if this was impossible, he might have to get a new Statute. He had no objection to the Economic Council considering plans of consultation not having that appearance, but the wording must be very careful, and he must be very careful about his own attitude.

LORD ROBERT CECIL said that the Trades Union Congress at Southport had voted a demand for the Supreme Economic Council to continue as the only means of assisting Germany to tide over her economic difficulties. Credit, currency and many other matters must be dealt with as a whole for a year or two. Economic questions were very much interlaced. They could not be considered for one country alone, hence consultation was essential.

PRESIDENT WILSON said he was fully agreed in this. After some further discussion the following resolution was adopted:

"That in some form, international consultation in economic matters should be continued until the Council of the League of Nations has had an opportunity of considering the present acute position of the International economic situation and that the Supreme Economic Council should be requested to suggest for the consideration of the several Governments the methods of consultation which would be most serviceable for this purpose."

9. The Council had before them the attached draft telegram to Admiral Koltchak in connection with the proposal for the use of the Czecho-Slovak forces in Siberia to co-operate with the right wing of Admiral Koltchak's Army (Appendix II.)[10]

(It was agreed that subject to the approval of the Military Representatives of the Supreme War Council at Versailles, who, with the addition of representatives of Japan and Czecho-Slovakia, are considering this subject, the telegram should be dispatched on behalf of the Allied and Associated Powers by M. Clemenceau as President of the Peace Conference, to Admiral Koltchak.)

T MS (SDR, RG 256, 180.03401/97, DNA).
    [1] The complete text of these minutes is printed in *PPC*, VI, 740-45.
    [2] Hankey's minutes of the Council of Four printed at June 26, 1919, 4 p.m.
    [3] Printed as Appendix II to the minutes of the Council of Four printed at June 27, 1919, 12 noon.
    [4] HCH to WW, June 27, 1919, printed in *PPC*, VI, 743-44. The original of this letter is in WP, DLC.
    [5] Hankey's minutes of the Council of Four printed at June 27, 1919, 4 p.m.
    [6] A revised version of this note is printed as Appendix II to Hankey's minutes of the Council of Four, June 28, 1919, 5 p.m.
    [7] Actually, Capt. Guido Jung, a secretary for economic and financial questions in the Italian delegation.
    [8] Edward Frank Wise, Second Secretary in the British Ministry of Food and chairman of the Subcommittee on Germany of the Supreme Economic Council.
    [9] That is, the French memorandum cited in n. 1 to HCH to WW, June 27, 1919.
    [10] Printed as an Enclosure with P. H. Kerr to WW, June 27, 1919.

Hankey's Notes of a Meeting of the Council of Four[1]

President Wilson's House,
C.F.98.   Paris, June 28, 1919, 12 noon.

Railroads of the former Austro-Hungarian Monarchy.

PRESIDENT WILSON asked M. Crespi to be good enough to explain the situation.

M. CRESPI said that an agreement had almost been reached and all felt that it was very necessary to reach one. The only objection was that questions of private financial interests between Companies and States should not find a place in a Treaty of Peace. This principle had been asserted by the Supreme Council which had declared that no clause in the Treaty should mention any private interest. The Italian Delegation had a new proposal to make on this question, of which the following was the text:

"With the object of ensuring regular utilisation of the railroads of the former Austro-Hungarian Monarchy owned by private companies, which, as a result of the stipulations of the Treaty, will be situated in the territory of several States, the administrative and technical reorganisation of the said lines shall be regulated in each instance by an agreement between the owning Company and the States territorially concerned. Any differences on which agreement is not reached, including questions relating to the interpretation of contracts concerning the expropriation of lines, shall be submitted to an arbitrator designated by the Council of the League of Nations."

M. CRESPI thought that this proposal covered all the difficulties, as it referred technical questions as well as those regarding the interpretation of the contract between the various Companies to an arbitrator appointed by the League of Nations.

M. CLAVEILLE said that he had certain observations to make. He wished to have a hearing, because if the proposals just made were accepted, the result would be that only States territorially concerned would have a share in the ultimate agreement. It was only just that France should not be detrimentally affected. The capital invested in these Companies was largely French. More than three-quarters of the bond-holders were French, and they represented a capital of more than a milliard and a half. He made no mention of the shares which were mostly held by Austro-Hungarians. When this railroad system was partitioned it was inconceivable, seeing that the capital invested in it belonged to France, that France should have no share in the discussion. He thought a remedy to

---

[1] The complete text of these minutes is printed in PPC, VI, 746-50.

this could easily be found by a slight alteration in the proposal just made, namely, by substituting for the words "states territorially concerned" a list of the States, including France.

PRESIDENT WILSON said that the text used the word "contracts." He presumed that this meant contracts between the companies and the heirs of the Austro-Hungarian Monarchy.

GENERAL MANCE observed that each company would have to make new contracts with the new States.

PRESIDENT WILSON said that if the rights were not transferred automatically by the Treaty, the inclusion of new parties would from the legal aspect be wrong.

M. CRESPI said that he could not accept the addition proposed by M. Claveille. There were bond-holders in Italy also. Their interests were quite well represented by the directors of the Company, whose business it was to look after the interests of its creditors. It would be contrary to all commercial laws to allow shareholders to intervene in the administration of a Company.

M. CLAVEILLE said that the Board of Directors was Austro-Hungarian and a centre of Germanisation. It represented worthless paper, the only paper of any value being French. The bond-holders therefore in equity had a right to intervene, and it was intended to put them aside at the very moment when the railway system was to be partitioned. He thought this proposal inacceptable.

M. CLEMENCEAU said that France was simply being denied what she had a right to. A milliard and a half was being taken from her pocket.

MR. LLOYD GEORGE said that the British interest was relatively small as compared with the interest of France. He quite understood the reasons brought forward by the French representatives, but on the other hand he had been impressed by M. Crespi's argument. It was a serious matter to have France and Great Britain represented in matters regarding Austrian, Czecho-Slovak, Italian or Yugo-Slav railways, simply because these countries had invested capital in these concerns. It was alleged that the Board of Directors was Austro-Hungarian and more or less controlled by Germany, but this must surely have been the case at the time when French and British shareholders invested their capital. M. Crespi had shown the danger of introducing into this matter any State whose intervention could put a stop to everything. He said this after a prolonged conversation with his experts. He repeated that it was a very serious thing that France and Great Britain should intervene in matters regarding the administration of railroads in foreign countries merely because their subjects had invested money in them. He thought M. Crespi had gone a long way in accepting arbitration by the Council of the League of Nations for technical matters as well as for the expropriation of the lines.

M. CLAVEILLE said that it was not merely a question of purchase. The railroad was nearly 2,000 kilometres long, and France, by reason of the capital invested, owned three-quarters. The railroad was to be partitioned among four Powers, each of which would be in a position to make a separate contract. This might result in the destruction of the work accomplished by France. Could the country which had paid the bill be excluded from the debate? This appears to him inadmissible. France did not ask to settle the question alone, but only to take a share in the discussion.

M. CLEMENCEAU said that it amounted to taking money from French pockets. He regarded this as scandalous. This would be very deeply felt by public opinion in France, and such an action could not be represented as in the interests of justice.

M. CRESPI said that there was a misunderstanding. The arbitration of the League of Nations was accepted for the solution of the whole matter.

M. CLEMENCEAU said this was no doubt so, but it was also true that if the four contracting States agreed, there would be no arbitration, and the game would be lost to France. After the war waged by France, and the losses sustained by her in it, such a situation was quite unendurable, and he refused with the utmost energy to accept the proposal. He regretted having to take such a decision, but the uncompromising spirit shown forced him to do so.

PRESIDENT WILSON said that such a question could not remain an open one, as it was part of the Treaty with Austria, which could not indefinitely wait for settlement.

MR. LLOYD GEORGE said that General Mance had explained the French point of view to him, and he thoroughly understood it. He would observe that under the previous regime the Austro-Hungarian State had the right to expropriate the Company at any moment. He would ask therefore what change had been brought about by the new situation.

M. CLAVEILLE said that the proposal was unacceptable, both in form and in substance. It would amount to this—that the four States could come to an agreement, though they owned but a very small share of the invested capital. It was indeed extremely likely that they would reach an agreement. Arbitration would then not be resorted to, and French interests would be eliminated without even a hearing. The question of expropriation was not as simple as it seemed. The railroad stretched over four States, and afforded access for Czecho-Slovakia to the Adriatic. France had taken a considerable share of this. According to the Treaty, the four States were free to purchase or not to purchase the line. They would be in a position to share it and to partition the material constituting it. It could not be permitted that French savings, which had invested a milliard and a half, should have no voice in the final settlement. France had already lost 10 milliards in Russia. She had suffered more than any other country in the war, and now she was to be robbed of a milliard and a half. If this were done, there would be an overwhelming torrent of indignation in public opinion.

PRESIDENT WILSON asked whether it was not obvious that the four States would have every interest in developing the lines, as they were essential to their economic life.

M. CLAVEILLE said that he did not expect them to destroy the line, but he thought they would appropriate it at a low rate.

MR. LLOYD GEORGE said he could not see any difference between the new situation and that which existed before the war. If Austria-Hungary still existed, she would be able to expropriate, and France could not make any resistance. It seemed to him that expropriation was less likely at the present time since it required agreement of the four States.

M. CLAVEILLE said that there was yet a further point that had not been mentioned. The Company until 1875 had owned lines in Italy. At that period the Italian lines had been expropriated. Since then Italy had paid an annual indemnity of 29,000,000 francs. According to the Treaty, he gathered that this sum was to be paid in future by the Austrians. In regard to Austria, France took her place, with all the other Allies, among the creditors, and it was well-known how little would be received under this head. Hitherto, payment had been made by the Italian Government in Paris. This showed to what extent French interests were concerned in those lines.

M. CRESPI said that the Italian Government had always paid in Rome.

M. CLAVEILLE said he was ready to demonstrate the contrary.

M. CRESPI said that in the Convention it was stated that payment should be made in gold in Rome. If no gold were available, payment should be made on Paris or London, [preferably?] in Paris.

M. CLEMENCEAU said that France would be ready to accept payment in Rome, but not to be referred to Austria, which would pay nothing.

MR. LLOYD GEORGE said that this discussion might reopen the whole question. It appeared to him impossible to delay the Treaty of Peace with Austria merely because of shareholders. If this were to come about, it would be necessary to make it quite clear that it was for reasons of this sort that France had opposed the settlement of the question. This was his view.

M. CLEMENCEAU said that he held a different view. Moreover, he was quite ready, as far as he was concerned, to reveal all the details of the question to public opinion.

(The discussion was adjourned, and no solution was reached.)

T MS (SDR, RG 256, 180.03401/98, DNA).

A Memorandum by Robert Lansing

THE SIGNING OF THE TREATY OF PEACE WITH GERMANY
AT VERSAILLES ON JUNE 28TH, 1919

The Treaty of Peace with Germany was signed today in the Galerie des Glaces of the Palace of Versailles.

The hour set for the ceremony of signature was three o'clock and promptly on the hour the great assembly was opened by M. Clemenceau and before four o'clock the last delegate had affixed his name to this greatest of treaties.

For two or three days there has been much anxiety about who was to see the signing and who was not. The Secretariat of the Commission has had a very unhappy time with the applications for tickets, and I imagine that the Secretariat General of the Conference must have been nearly wild with the pressure brought to bear to obtain admission.

Friday night the matter was settled, the lists revised and the tickets issued. We obtained 60 tickets for the conference room, a lesser number for the gallery outside, and about 50 for the grounds of the Palace. There were some heart-burnings I know but that was unavoidable.

It seemed best in view of the possibility of confusion to go early to Versailles, so at one o'clock Mrs. Lansing and I accompanied by Foster and Allen Dulles[1] and Captain Garfield[2] started from the Hotel de Crillon in an automobile driven by Corporal Chavariat who had Private Seymour, my personal orderly, with him. Mr. Kirk,[3] my Secretary, came in our other car with his mother[4] and some of the staff. We ran out through the Bois de Bologne, up the winding road to the terraced gardens of St. Cloud and then on to

---

[1] That is, his nephews, John Foster Dulles and Allen Welsh Dulles.
[2] James S. Garfield, a secretary in the Secretariat of the A.C.N.P.
[3] That is, Alexander Comstock Kirk.
[4] Clara Comstock (Mrs. James Alexander) Kirk.

the Versailles road through the Forest. All along the route were French soldiers with red flags to direct the way. On the windshield was pasted a circular device like a target, blue in the center, then a white circle and outside of that a red one. This acted as a pass. On entering Versailles the curious crowds lined the way while soldiers and gens d'arm[e]s kept them back from the pavement.

We drove to the Palace by the broad approach at the front. On either side of the spacious roadway was a row of cavalry in horizon blue and trench helmets and carrying their long lances from which fluttered little red and white streamers. Behind these rows and about 20 feet from them were poilus shoulder to shoulder; and behind the poilus were dense masses of people. We drew up at the entrance to the basement, where our hats were checked, and we then mounted the staircase to the main floor of the Palace. On every third step stood two dragoons in their white trousers, black boots, dark blue coats with red facings, and glittering silver helmets with black horse tails over their shoulders. They stood like statues with sabres drawn looking neither to the right or left.

Passing through several ante-rooms we finally reached the Hall of Mirrors where a great table extended along the inner side of the gallery with short wing tables at either end. The seats of the delegates were on the outside in the usual order followed at the Preliminary Conference except that delegates sat on both sides of the wing tables. The place for the German delegates was on the left wing table next to the long table. In the center of the long table was the seat of the presiding officer, M. Clemenceau. Directly opposite his seat in the center of the room was a gold Louis XVth table on which lay the great treaty in a case of brown leather. On both sides of this table and filling all the available space between the tables of the delegates were the members of the Secretariat General and the Secretaries of the various Commissions. The space thus occupied took up about one third of the Hall, the rest of the space being filled with benches without backs, but beautifully upholstered in tapestry, for spectators and members of the press, the latter being to the right of M. Clemenceau.

When we arrived only a few people were in the room, but delegates and invited guests gathered rapidly. It was about two o'clock when M. Clemenceau arrived. He passed through the spectators section shaking hands right and left and causing perturbation to the ushers who were making way for him and who constantly got so far ahead that they had to turn back to find him. I was standing near the table where the aisle ended. When he saw me his face lit up with a smile and he exclaimed, "This is a great day for France." I replied, "A great day for the world, Mr. President." I had reached out my hand to shake hands, when he said, "No, give me both your hands, that is the way France and America should greet each other today." He then passed on toward his seat. A little later I followed him and he turned as I passed and showed me a wonderful gold pen and holder which lay in a leather case, a present from some organization. I discovered that he was sitting in President Wilson's seat and pointed out the fact to him. "Oh," he exclaimed, "I am glad you told me before the President came. He might have been embarrassed and I would have been very much annoyed."

It was soon after this, as the delegates began taking their seats in considerable numbers that there began a regular field day in writing autographs. Most of these were put upon the place-programs but every now and then an album appeared. During this occupation the President arrived and was at once deluged with requests for his signature, which he gave at first willingly but later with evident unwillingness.

Soon, however, there was a stir at the entrance behind the spectators. The President said, "Here they come." Preceded by ushers and French officers and followed by four or five secretaries the German Commissioners, Müller and Bell came down the aisle. Their appearance was not prepossessing. Their expressions were tense or possibly stolid. They were nervous and unquestionably felt deeply the humiliation which they, as representatives of a vanquished and hated country, had to bear. They came to the table and were directed to their seats by Dutasta, the Secretary General of the Conference. No one rose and no acknowledgment of their arrival was given. I think that I would have felt a deep compassion for these scapegoats of Germany, save for the fact that I could not think of the joy which would have filled their hearts if they were there representing a victorious Germany with the Emperor William seated in the place of "The Old Tiger" of France. It would have been an awful, not a glorious, day for the world and civilization.

As soon as they were seated M. Clemenceau stood up and briefly stated that the treaty was ready and that it was necessary for Germany to perform the conditions, which were irrevocable. After being interpreted into English, the remarks were rendered into German and, when the interpreter spoke of the necessity of performance and the unchangeable character of the conditions, Dr. Müller nodded his head and said in a low voice "Oui! Oui!" In some ways the scene was painful. It was as if men were called upon to sign their own death warrants, fully realizing that they were at the mercy of those whom they had wronged beyond the possibility of pardon. They seemed anxious to get through with it and be off.

After the translation of the words of M. Clemenceau, Dutasta and Martin, the fussy little head of "the protocol," walked over to the German delegates and conducted them to the table where lay the treaty, open at the place where they were to sign. Their seals like the seals of all other delegates had been previously affixed. With pallid faces and trembling hands they wrote their names quickly and were then conducted back to their places. Their names were at the end of the pages containing the signatures.

When the Germans had signed, the pages were turned back to the beginning. Then President Wilson rose and walked down to the right wing table and around the end and proceeded to the table with the treaty upon it. I followed, then Mr. White, Colonel House and General Bliss. In that order we signed opposite our individual seals, the old Lansing coat of arms being finely impressed. The President's seal was a small one with his name written stenographically. It had been made with a gold ring thus engraved. We then in turn signed the Polish treaty and the Rhine agreement which were on small side-tables.

I used, in signing, a plain steel pen in a silver penholder, the latter presented for the occasion by my office. The same penholder and pen I had used this morning at the President's house to sign the treaty with France by which the United States promises to come to her aid in the event of aggression by Germany. The Treaty was signed by Clemenceau, Pichon, the President and me, and is to be sent to the Senate at the same time as the Treaty of Peace is laid before that body.

When we had signed the Treaty of Peace and returned to our seats by way of the left wing table, the President whispered, "I did not know I was excited until I found my hand trembling when I wrote my name." I had noticed that his signature was unusually cramped. My own name I wrote without any feeling of nervousness. Possibly I was not as sensitive to the occasion as the President. It is hard to understand why I was not more responsive to the emotional impulses of such a momentous event. I cannot explain it myself.

After the American delegation had signed, the delegates of the British Empire followed, then those of France, Italy and Japan and so on down the list in the alphabetical order of the countries. From the time that the Germans affixed their signatures to the document to the end of the signing about forty-five minutes elapsed. It became a monotonous business after the first few had signed, and so the delegates and spectators visited with their neighbors, while the autograph-hunters continued their efforts, clustering about the

Wilson and Albert upon the arrival of the presidential party
at Adinkerke, June 18, 1919

At the ruins of Ypres

"This immortal spot" on the Yser River near Nieuport

With Brand Whitlock on the battlefield near Nieuport

With Elisabeth in the trenches at Nieuport

A royal picnic in the Forest of Houthulst

At Les Usines de la Providence near Charleroi

At the harbor of Zeebrugge

With Cardinal Mercier at Malines

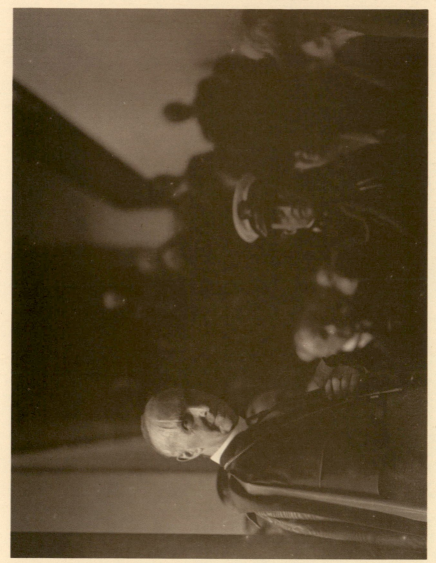

Cardinal Mercier and Dr. Grayson at Malines

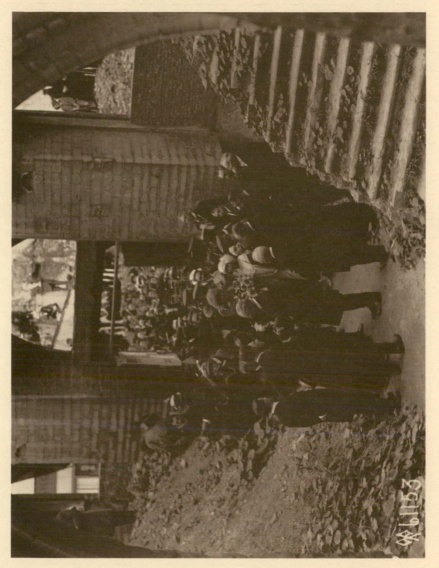

Amid the ruins of the library of the
University of Louvain

At the Royal Palace in Brussels

At the Versailles Palace before the signing of the treaty

The Big Four

central group of M. Clemenceau, President Wilson and Mr. Lloyd George. It certainly took from the dignity of the occasion.

There was one circumstance which caused a feeling of disquietude and, in a measure, of surprise, and that was the absence from the assembly of the Chinese delegates.

In the morning Baron Makino, the head of the Japanese delegation, came to see me at my request. For three quarters of an hour I labored with him endeavoring to persuade him to issue a formal public statement embodying the assurances of Japan to the Council of Four as to the surrender of Shantung to China and the liberal policy Japan intended to pursue. I gave him a draft of the statement[5] and urged him to see the Chinese and, if he was unwilling to issue the statement at once, to tell them that he would issue it after the signing of the treaty. I pointed out to him that such a course would gain general applause and cause satisfaction everywhere and that, if he failed to do it, I believed China would not sign the treaty since the Council of Four had refused to permit them to sign with reservations. I said that, if the Chinese failed to sign, the blame for their failure would fall chiefly upon Japan whatever the justice of the case might be, that it would cause the Shantung articles and Japan's designs to be the source of serious criticism, and might even endanger the ratification of the treaty in certain countries, while it would undoubtedly arouse bitter resentment in China and might result in forceful resistance to the Japanese throughout the country.

[5] It reads as follows:

"1. Japan claims no right of sovereignty in Shantung Province.

"2. Japan will restore the Lease of Kiaochow and will relinquish to China all rights, title and privileges acquired by Japan from Germany within the Leased Territory, except as regards railways, on condition that China compensate Japan for properties thus relinquished and that China agree to make the city of Tsingtao an international settlement and of the port an open port.

"3. Japan will endeavor to make this restoration complete within two years from the signing of the Peace Treaty.

"4. Japan relinquishes the benefit of any provision or provisions in the conventions and agreements between Germany and China which gave an exclusive preferential position in the Province of Shantung.

"5. In the administration of the existing railways which have been conceded to her, Japan will not discriminate against the trade of China or of other nations.

"6. The new railway lines, for the construction of which concessions have been accorded to Japan, shall be built by the Japanese for the Chinese Government.

"7. Japan will use special police only along the railways and only to ensure security for traffic. These police shall be Chinese, with such Japanese instructors as the Directors of the Railway may select, these instructors to be appointed by the Chinese Government.

"8. Japan will withdraw all military forces from Shantung as soon as practicable, it being the intention, if conditions permit, that the withdrawal shall be completed within a period of not more than two years." CC MS, filed with B. Long, "MEMORANDUM OF CONVERSATION WITH THE JAPANESE CHARGE D'AFFAIRES," Aug. 3, 1919, TS MS (SDR, RG 59, 793.94/946, DNA).

Baron Makino listened with great attention and expressed appreciation of my efforts but said that on account of Japanese public opinion he was afraid that the proposed action could not be taken and that he did not believe that the Chinese would refuse to sign the treaty. I repeated that I was sure that he under-estimated the intensity of China's sense of being unjustly treated and that I was firmly convinced that the Chinese delegates would not sign unless some public statement of policy in the nature of the one which I had given him was issued or at least promised. I asked him again to study the draft and to act for his government in a way to relieve the situation and insure China's participation. I felt, however, that, while Makino was very courteous and apparently impressed, I had not made a dent in his armor of oriental inscrutability. In a word, I know that I have completely failed in persuading him.

Subsequent events proved the correctness of my assertion so far as the signature of the treaty by China was concerned, and I believe that the consequences will be like those prophesied unless Japan changes the course taken by her delegates and gives out a statement. Even then it may be too late to remove the impression already made.

The President was greatly disturbed at the absence of the Chinese. When I pointed it out to him, he exclaimed, "That is most serious. It will cause grave complications." I told him of my interview with Makino and he said that he was sorry that they had not listened to me, as he believed trouble would result. He then added, "this is most unfortunate, but I don't know what we can do."

It was also a subject of remark that neither President Poincaré nor Marshal Foch was present. The impression seemed to be general that Poincaré was not there because Clemenceau did not want him, as the report is that there is little love lost between them. I believe, however, that the reason was that it would have caused embarrassment to find him a seat in conformity with his official dignity. Of course he could not preside and yet as head of the French Republic he could not have taken a position below the French premier. This seems to me the most plausible explanation of his absence, though the former may have had some influence.

I do not know what excuse will be offered for Foch's not being present. Probably the call of duty will be given, a convenient but inconclusive reason, though possibly the true one. My own belief is that he purposely absented himself to show that he did not approve the treaty. At the plenary session of the Conference, preceding the delivery of the treaty to the Germans on May 7th he made an address bitterly condemning the conditions of peace and declaring that the treaty ought not to be signed as it was not severe enough on Germany and failed to protect France from future aggression.[6] Having taken this radical position, to which little or no attention was paid by anybody, he would have been in rather a humiliating position if he had sanctioned by his presence the celebration of a treaty to which he had so unequivocally objected. His absence, however, caused general remark, astonishment and regret.

After the signature and after M. Clemenceau's announcement that the session was ended, the German delegates were formally conducted out of the Hall. When they had gone, the other delegates without ceremony left their seats, some going to the windows to look at the famous fountains and the crowds swarming on the terraces, others chatting with the spectators, examining the signed treaty or making their way to the exit. Even before the last delegate had signed the cannon had begun to boom out the news while the whirring of aeroplanes over the palace and gardens was clearly audible.

One of the striking features of the ceremony was the presence of twenty poilus and twenty doughboys in the embrasures of the windows facing the long table. The French soldiers were hideously disfigured by face wounds, some appearing to have grotesque masks of Greek comedy and tragedy. The American boys were from different units and selected under General Pershing's direction.

M. Clemenceau accompanied by President Wilson and Mr. Lloyd George proceeded to the Terrace, where immense throngs crowded about them cheering as they walked slowly between the playing fountains. Mrs. Wilson, Mrs. Lansing, Ambassador and Mrs. Wallace and I stood in one of the balconied windows of the Galerie des Glaces and watched the scene which was most inspiring, a wonderful demonstration of popular joy.

We then went down to the grand entrance and found our car after some little delay, and, foregoing tea with M. Clemenceau, we were soon on our way to Paris along roads black with people who waved flags and cheered as we passed. It was surprising how many American flags were in evidence.

Tonight Paris is a seething mass of rejoicing people. They are dancing, shouting, carrying flags of various nationalities and dragging about the streets captured German guns which have adorned the Place de la Concorde and Champs Elysées. Great army trucks,

[6] About this incident on May 6, 1919, see n. 1 to the extract from the Grayson Diary printed at May 6, 1919, and R. Borden to T. White, May 6, 1919, both in Vol. 58.

French, American and British, pass along simply hidden with men in uniform, and the cocottes are reaping a rich harvest of soldiers' caps as souvenirs. The scene is one hard to describe. Paris seems delirious.

We were dining this evening with the Paderewskis at the Hotel Ritz, but I had to leave at 9:15 to go to the Gare des Invalides to see the President and his party start for Brest. It was no easy matter to drive a motor car through the revellers who filled the roadway. Crowds were about the station and the President received a great ovation as he entered the decorated way to his train.

I saw M. Clemenceau at the station and said to him, "This is your day, Mr. President." "And yours, yes, yours too," he answered, his face beaming. "It is not the same," I said, "You are the great figure." He smiled even more broadly and shook my hand warmly as we parted.

The revelry is continuing as I write. It is after one o'clock now, and songs, cheers, and horns are making a joyous din, while the streets and the great square still are filled with men and women. Paris does not intend to sleep tonight. So ends this great day.

T MS (SDR, RG 59, 763.72119/5597½, DNA).

From the Peace Conference Diary of William Linn Westermann

June 28, 1919

The Signing of the Treaty of Versailles.

I found a card on my desk Saturday at eleven, admitting me to the Galerie des Glaces at Versailles. Went out in an automobile with Shotwell, Moran of the White House Detective Service, Shepherdson and one other man.[1] It was a beautiful drive through Saint Cloud. As we approached Versailles the crowds began to line the streets. French poilus were stationed at the crossroads with red flags with which they pointed out the route to follow, indicating it with a rather noble sweep of the flag.

As we got into Versailles we were often stopped and made to show our entry cards. There were companies of French infantry lined up along many of the streets. As we turned into the Avenue de Paris which leads up to the Palace at Versailles the sight was worth all the trip to Europe. There was a continuous line of French

---

[1] That is, James T. Shotwell, William H. Moran, and Whitney H. Shepardson.

lancers on horseback on either side of the street. Horizon-blue uniforms, lances topped with little red and white guidons which waved in the breeze, the dignified motions of head or body of these long lines of horses, the statuesque but easy seats of the lancers, and the long quarter mile lines of these stationary Centaurs—it made a wonderful picture, with just enough motion to make it living.

At the head of the court of the palace there were several companies of Guards of the Republic. Their uniforms were very bright in colors, but I cannot remember anything but the tall hats, black, with a visor, and flaring out at the top, surmounted by gay red pompoms. The stairways on the inside of the palace were lined by big cuirassiers, with gilded helmets, each with a red pompom at the side; black coats with the tails thereof pinned back showing the seats of the spotless while pantaloons, high black boots and spurs. These were picked men, all about six feet or more, each with a black or brown moustache and each with his sabre at carry arms. It was a thrilling sight.

Up these steps, in the time of Louis XVI, my Westermann ancestors must have gone, father's grandfather and grandmother, on state occasions. Father's grandmother, whom he knew and remembered was a lady-in-waiting to Marie Antoinette.

Arrived in the entrance hall to the Galerie des Glaces before two o'clock we waited outside for some time until some of the notables had gone in. Then I went in and took my seat. I saw many of these so-called "Great" of the world. General Castelnau[2] was a little bright faced old gentleman, with very great energy, about the size and with the alertness of Dean Birge.[3] I saw Generals Mangin, Monoury and possibly Maudit.[4] One of these men had a great hole in one side of his face, but which one it was I do not know. Among other notables who stand out in my memory are the Maharajah of Binkaneer;[5] King[6] the negro Secretary of State of Liberia; Mastry,[7] a very tall and heavy man, who is Premier of New Zealand. I saw also Jon Smuts, all the British delegation, the American delegation and many others. General Nuri Said[8] came in and stood across the

[2] Noël-Marie-Joseph-Édouard Castelnau, Vicomte de Curières.
[3] Edward Asahel Birge, Dean of the College of Letters and Science of the University of Wisconsin; President since December 1918.
[4] Charles-Marie-Emmanuel Mangin and Michel Joseph Maunoury; "Maudit" was actually Gen. Louis-Ernest de Maud'huy.
[5] Actually, the Maharajah of Bikaner.
[6] That is, Charles Dunbar Burgess King.
[7] Actually, William Ferguson Massey.
[8] Nuri as-Said, close associate of Emir Faisal in the Arab revolt against the Ottoman Empire; later Prime Minister of Iraq.

hall from me, unmoved and utterly unabashed by the presence of greatness.

The hall must have seated about 1,200 people. Opposite me sat the French members of the Chamber of Deputies a rather intelligent looking group of elderly men. Madame Paderewski sat near me, but I did not see Paderewski.

The Germans Müller and Bell, escorted by French, British and American officers came in about 3:10. There were five of them in all. Müller was tall with a high pompadour, long neck, large spectacles and a sagging walk, much like a camel. Bell was short, dark haired. My expectation that there would be something of the old haughty pride of the German aristocrat, was not in the least realized. Müller was deadly pale. Their entry was the one high moment of the whole conference. As they passed me—I had an end or aisle seat and could have touched them—I had a deep pang of pity for them, five Germans amid all this crowd, come to sign away the old glory of the Deutsches Reich after all the high expectations, the pride, and dreams of power.

They tell me that Müller and Bell were skilled laborers, both being Social-Demokraten. I can well believe it. They looked so. As they came to the center of the room where sat the allied diplomats and the groups from the lesser states which were to sign the treaty, Müller jerked curious, self conscious bows to right and left. Bell did better. He did not bow.

I have asked many people who were present what they felt when these two came in—all Americans, however. They have all confessed to this feeling of pity and compassion.

When they were seated, Clemenceau made a brief speech in which he gave his word that no change had been made in the document since it had been communicated to the German government, and said that it must be signed by the German plenipotentiaries with the full intention of living up to its provisions. In translating into English Paul Montaux used the phrase "German Republic," but was corrected by some one and changed the words to "German Reich." This, I later learned, was at the request of the Germans themselves. Montaux translated falteringly and badly, I thought.

The remainder of the seance seemed undignified to me. Many of the people in the room would rise to get a look over the room. The people would hiss "Assis, Assis" and a big curassier would instruct them to sit down. When there was too much noise the people would hiss for silence.

The signing occupied about forty-five minutes and was without incident. As soon as the signing of the treaty was over, and before the real close of the affair I went out and asked Col. Wallace[9] if I might ride back with him, as he was going. We rode around to the back of the palace and walked in to see the gardens, with the fountains playing and the thousands of people there. It was a wonderful sight, colorful, movement of white waters, green trees, crowds of moving humanity.

Going out Shepherdson said that the German envoys had been told that they would have to submit to a search of their persons before they went in. They protested, but said that they must submit. They insisted that they must see the treaty which they were to sign in order to be confident that nothing had been slipped into it since their government had agreed to its signature.

Before I left the Hall of Mirrors the Germans were taken out. They had recovered their color. Bell looked around, almost with curiosity.

This was the great day. It had singularly little of grandeur. Except for the one thrill of emotion when the five Germans first entered it left me cold.

I cannot believe that this treaty is a great document. It is certainly, possibly rightly, based upon the theory of punishment. Many of the territorial settlements made will soon be unmade, and it will cost some human blood to do it.

It seems to me to be a peace of the old type, in an age and for an age which must look upon life more generously than the past has done. The League of Nations unfortunately is a Siamese Twin with the Peace of Versailles. In the League of Nations lies a hope which must be cherished. It underwrites a very bad world situation. There is no naval disarmament, except as the German exploit in sinking the German fleet at Skapa Flow has reduced naval armament. I must stand for the League of Nations, as must every man until it has proven itself. The gain of the world has come through the war, in the overthrow of feudal land tenure in Hungary, in the overthrow of an effete despotism in Russia, in the overthrow of Kaiserism in Germany. The forced abandonment of militarism in Germany will be a great gain to the German people.

The little peoples of the world came to Paris with hopes of justice, the perverted view of his own justice that each one had. Despite the gradual withering of these hopes, despite the fact that their voices were but little heard, they were there. And they will not forget it. They have had tremendous publicity for their hopes; even Haidar Bammate of Daghestan has been heard. The Egyptian

9 Lt. Col. William B. Wallace, an officer in the General Staff Corps and an assistant to General Bliss in the A.C.N.P.

delegation is in Paris, though no one sees them except Lieut. No-ble.[10]

The British Empire comes out of the war the great victor—in the old sense.

The Peace Conference at Paris was wrong in its spirit and quite wrong in its methods. The secret and unorganized meetings of the "Great" Four were not the thing to gain the confidence of the modern world.

Perhaps it is altogether too close upon the action to permit of a judgment now. But I cannot believe that the world has much faith in the treaty evolved with Germany, nor great respect for the "Great" Four, or the Ten, who were chiefly instrumental in making it.

T MS (W. L. Westermann Papers, NNC).
    [10] George Bernard Noble, an assistant in the Division of Current Intelligence Summaries of the A.C.N.P. His book, *Policies and Opinions at Paris, 1919: Wilsonian Diplomacy, the Versailles Peace, and French Public Opinion* (New York, 1935), is still considered the standard work on the subject.

From the Diary of Colonel House

June 28, 1919.

This is the great day. I did very little in the morning. Beer went to the meeting of the Commission on Mandates and represented me. The next meeting will be in London ten days from now.

For the last ten days I have repeatedly suggested to Lansing, White and Bliss that they make a memorandum of questions they wished the President to pass upon before he leaves. At the meeting this morning they only had two of these questions ready, one regarding the Adriatic[1] and the other had to do with Turkey which Westerman[n], our expert on Turkey, had prepared on his own initiative.[2] When the President asked them if there was anything further, Lansing replied that they had not prepared anything yet, but they hoped he would come down again today. The President could not do so since every moment of today will be filled.

I was successful in getting practically all my Secretariat still in Paris, to Versailles to witness the ceremonies. Among them were Miss Denton, Gordon, Frazier, Colonel Moore and Shepardson;[3] Ensign Andrews and Capt. Montgomery[4] going on the terrace. The demand for tickets was unprecedented. Someone told me that one hundred thousand francs had been offered for a ticket, but this I doubt.

Nearly all the Delegates were seated before I arrived. Some of them started as early as one o'clock. I did not leave the Crillon until about 2.15 and reached my seat about ten minutes before the Germans arrived. The arrangements for getting into the hall were badly done. The approach to Versailles was an imposing sight, as indeed, was the entrance to the Palace. Thousands of people lined the roadway from Paris to Versailles, increasing in numbers as we drew near the Palace. There was a great display of cavalry with pennants flying, and upon the Grand Stairway, which witnessed the last stand of the Swiss Guard during the French Revolution, chasseurs in gorgeous uniforms lined both sides up to the very entrance of the Salle des Glaces, where the signing took place.

Balfour and I went in together, and presently were joined by Lloyd George and Sonnino. I lingered behind in order not to get into the crowd that was pressing through the only door at which entrance was possible. The ceremonies lasted nearly an hour and I shall not go into details since it had been and will be so fully described.

Most of my time was taken up signing souvenir programs for the different delegates. This is a pastime I did not indulge in. The signing of autograph albums, photographs and what not has become a great nuisance.

When the Germans had signed, and the great Allied Powers had done so, the cannons began to boom. I had a feeling of sympathy for the Germans who sat there quite stoically. It was not unlike what was done in older times when then [the] conquerer dragged the conquered at his chariot wheels. To my mind, it is out of keeping with the new era which we profess an ardent desire to promote. I wish it could have been more simple and that there might have been an element of chivalry, which was wholly lacking. The affair was elaborately staged and made as humiliating to the enemy as it well could be.

After the signing we went to the terrace to see the fountains, which were playing for the first time since the war began. Aeroplanes were in the air, guns were being fired and the thousands surrounding Versailles made a brilliant and momentous scene.

We went to the station to see the President and his party off. There was a large crowd of notables, including nearly every prominent man in Paris, other than the British Delegation, which was noticeably absent. I compared it to the last leave-taking very much to the credit of this one. There was more enthusiasm, there were more people, and the whole affair was more brilliant and successful.

[1] That is, the Enclosure printed with D. W. Johnson to WW, June 26, 1919.
[2] Printed as an Enclosure with GFC to RL, June 24, 1919.
[3] Frances B. Denton, Gordon Auchincloss, Arthur Hugh Frazier, Benjamin Moore, and Whitney H. Shepardson.
[4] Edward House Andrews and Stuart Montgomery.

From Robert Lansing

My dear Mr. President: Paris June 28th, 1919

It occurs to me that after your departure it will probably be necessary for me on different occasions to refer to conversations which have taken place at the meetings of the Council of Four and as no records of these meetings are at my disposal, I take the liberty of bringing the matter to your attention for such action as you may consider appropriate.

I believe that Sir Morris Hankey has the reports of these meetings and at your request will no doubt furnish me with a copy.

Faithfully yours,   Robert Lansing

TLS (WP, DLC).

Hankey's Notes of a Meeting of the Council of Four[1]

C.F.99. NOTES OF A MEETING HELD IN THE FOYER OF THE SENATE CHAMBER OF THE CHATEAU AT VERSAILLES shortly after the signature of the Treaty of Peace with Germany at 5:00 p.m. on the 28th June 1919.

1. M. MANTOUX at M. Clemenceau's request, read the English translation of a letter from Herr Bethmann Hollweg insisting that any responsibility on the part of the German Government for the events that precipitated the War in August 1914 was his and not the Kaiser's, since he had been Imperial Chancellor of the German Empire. From this he deduced that the Allied and Associated Powers ought to call him and not the Kaiser to account (Appendix 1).

M. CLEMENCEAU suggested that the reply should be that when the Tribunal was constituted his letter would be put before it.

MR. LLOYD GEORGE pointed out that the Tribunal had nothing to de except try the Kaiser and could not be made responsible for this matter.

M. CLEMENCEAU asked if Bethmann Hollweg was on the list of persons to be tried.

PRESIDENT WILSON said that there were two categories. The Kaiser was in one category alone to be tried, for a supreme offence against international morality and the sanctity of treaties. Those in the second category were to be tried for acts in violation of the laws and customs of war. Bethmann Hollweg did not fall into either category.

MR. LLOYD GEORGE suggested that the answer should be he could

[1] The complete text of these minutes is printed in *PPC*, VI, 751-58.

not be accepted as responsible for the Kaiser who, by the German Constitution, was alone responsible.

PRESIDENT WILSON said that Bethmann Hollweg was acting on the theory that the German Constitution was similar to that of Great Britain or France, [under] either [of] which the Minister was responsible. The Chancellor of the German Empire, however, was under the direct control of the Kaiser.

M. SONNINO said that the text of the letter would require careful study before a reply was sent.

PRESIDENT WILSON said that the reply should express the recognition of the Allied and Associated Powers of the spirit in which the offer was made, but should state that Bethmann Hollweg's interpretation of the German Constitution could not be accepted.

M. MAKINO expressed the view that by constitutional law the Minister would be the responsible party.

(It was agreed that the Commission on Responsibilities, of which Mr. Lansing was Chairman, should be asked to draft a reply to Bethmann Hollweg's letter, but that a general indication should be given to the Commission of the Council's view as to the nature of the reply formed without an opportunity for close examination of the facts, namely, that the Allied and Associated Powers recognised the spirit in which the offer was made but could not accept Bethmann Hollweg's interpretation of the German Constitution.)

2. PRESIDENT WILSON said that immediately before the Meeting of the Peace Conference for the signature of the Treaty of Peace with Germany, Mr. Hoover had sent him word that two of his relief agents for the distribution of food had been arrested by the Germans in Libau.

(It was agreed that Marshal Foch should be asked, through the Armistice Commission, to make an immediate demand for the release of these agents, laying special emphasis on the fact that this incident had occurred before an apology had been offered for the recent arrest by the Germans of British Naval Officers in the Baltic Provinces, if the Council are correct in assuming that no such apology has been made to the demand approved by them on June 4th (C.F.46, Min. 6. and Appendix IV.)[2]

3. SIR MAURICE HANKEY said he had been asked by various officials to supply copies of the Notes of the Meetings of the Council of the Principal Allied and Associated Powers and he asked for instructions.

[2] See the minutes of the Council of Four printed at June 4, 1919, 5 p.m., and n. 10 thereto, Vol. 60.

M. CLEMENCEAU said that in his view they ought not to be communicated to anyone and that there should be a general agreement to this effect.

M. SONNINO pointed out that the question would arise immediately in connection with the Italian Delegation as to whether these records should be handed by one Government to their successors in Office. In his view this was indispensable. He could not vouch for it that M. Orlando had not already given them to M. Tittoni. It would be very difficult for the new Government to conduct the business if it did not know what had been decided by its predecessors in the Council.

PRESIDENT WILSON expressed a strong view that these documents ought to be treated as purely private conversations. He recalled that it was on his initiative that the meetings of this small group had been held. He had invited his colleagues to meet him for the purpose of private conversations at his own house. For a long time no notes had been kept at all. Later, however, it had been realised that this was not a very convenient procedure and Secretaries had been admitted. If, however, he had thought that these Notes were to be passed on to Government Departments, he would have insisted on adhering to the system under which no secretaries were present. All the decisions had been communicated to the officials who had to carry them out, but he had the strongest objections to the communication of the accounts given in the Notes of the private conversations. All present had spoken their minds with great freedom. Contradictions could, no doubt, be found in the Notes to what had been said at different times and under different circumstances. It was even conceivable that political opponents who came into possession of these documents might misuse them. He did not think that properly speaking the Council could be described as an official body. The only official body was the Conference of Peace. The present group had rightly, as he thought, taken upon itself to formulate the decisions for the Peace Conference, but their conversations ought not to be regarded as official. He saw no objection to the communication of the notes to individuals in the personal confidence of members of the Council, for example, he had instructed Sir Maurice Hankey to communicate a complete set of the documents to Mr. Lansing, who was a minister appointed by himself and in his entire confidence.

M. CLEMENCEAU said that if he had to resign Office, he would find it a great embarrassment not to hand over these documents to his successor in Office. He did not think that they could be regarded as private property.

M. SONNINO said that perhaps these need not be regarded as official reports since they had not been carefully checked and corrected. Nevertheless, they contained important statements which, in some cases, were not recorded as conclusions. He quoted one case for example, where M. Orlando had made an important statement of which the Council had taken formal note, and this, he believed, was merely recorded in the procès-verbal. It might be very important for M. Orlando's successor in office to have a copy of this.

M. CLEMENCEAU recalled a similar case where he had insisted on the importance of interpreting certain provisions in the resolutions regarding mandates, so as to enable France to use African soldiers for the defence of her territory, and Mr. Lloyd George had suggested that it would be sufficient to mention it in the procès-verbal.[3]

PRESIDENT WILSON said that certainly such statements should be regarded as official, but nevertheless, he thought the actual conversations which led up to the conclusions reached should be regarded as private.

MR. LLOYD GEORGE suggested that the precedents ought to be looked up. For example, he would like to know whether the procès-verbaux of all conversations which took place in the Treaty of Berlin had been published.

PRESIDENT WILSON said that probably at the Congress of Berlin, there had been recorded formal Conferences and informal conversations which were not recorded.

MR. LLOYD GEORGE said that he had never had time to look at the notes at all.

M. CLEMENCEAU said that he also had never had time. He recalled, however, that Sir Maurice Hankey had several times been called upon to refer to what had occurred at the Council, for example, an important statement by Marshal Foch had been referred to at a recent meeting.

PRESIDENT WILSON said that when such references had been made, he had been much struck with the accuracy of the record. He thought that every action taken and every conclusion reached should be recorded as official and should be available in the appropriate offices, but not the conversations.

M. SONNINO said that they certainly should not be publishable or even presentable to Parliament, but he thought that the successors of the Government in office, if challenged, must be in a position to know what had happened.

[3] Clemenceau was referring to the meeting of the Council of Ten of Jan. 30, 1919, 3:30 p.m., the minutes of which are printed in Vol. 54.

PRESIDENT WILSON laid emphasis on the difference between handing on to a successor or to a set of Government officials, and to a confidential and trusted colleague.

M. SONNINO thought it would be very hard on a new Government not to have these documents.

PRESIDENT WILSON said he realised that the United States worked under a different Parliamentary system. There, no one had the right to claim documents of this kind. One adverse comment that might be made was that no Secretary had been present representing the United States of America. His reply would be that he had had complete confidence in the Secretaries who had been present, but the criticism might be made. The net result seemed to be that each Government must take the course traditional in its own country with the clear and distinct understanding that no one should, under any circumstances, make the procès-verbal public.

MR. LLOYD GEORGE said that if an attack were made on the political heads, he might feel bound, in particular cases, to refer to these notes. He gave fair warning that he might have to do this unless someone protested now.

M. CLEMENCEAU said it would not be possible to refuse extracts from the procès-verbal to prove particular facts.

4. With reference to C.F.97,[4] Minute 6, the attached re-draft by Mr. Balfour of a letter to the Turkish Delegation was approved. (Appendix II.)

The letter was handed to Capt. Portier to prepare a French copy for M. Clemenceau's signature.

5. With reference to C.F.92,[5] Minute 4, the Council had before them a memorandum by M. Larnaude on the suggestion that steps should be taken to make the execution of Clauses 214 to 224 (Repatriation of Prisoners) and Clauses 227 to 230 (Penalties) in the Treaty of Peace with Germany interdependent.

MR. LLOYD GEORGE suggested that each case ought to be considered on its merits. He would like to consider the particular case proposed by Sir Ernest Pollock, namely, supposing Germany, without adequate reason, fails to deliver up the culprits, was the return of German prisoners to be slowed down?

M. SONNINO said that the suggestion was all right in a general way, but the question was how far the principle should be applied in particular cases.

MR. LLOYD GEORGE said that M. Larnaude's proposal dealt with a substantial failure on the part of the Germans to carry out the

[4] The minutes of the Council of Four printed at June 28, 1919, 11 a.m.
[5] The minutes of the Council of Four printed at June 25, 1919, 4 p.m.

Treaty, which was tantamount to a refusal to accept it. When the names of the persons to be surrendered was communicated to Germany, the Allies ought to be in a position to say that they would not complete the surrender of prisoners until Germany handed them over.

M. SONNINO said he did not like linking one case with another in the manner proposed by M. Larnaude.

M. CLEMENCEAU said he was afraid that all the prisoners would have been handed over before the Germans were bound to fulfil their part of the Treaty.

PRESIDENT WILSON said that it was physically impossible to do this. He hoped that before all the German prisoners had been surrendered, some indication would be given as to whether the Germans were carrying out the Treaty.

6. M. CLEMENCEAU said that Herr von Haniel had asked M. Dutasta whether some Conferences should not now take place with the Germans in regard to the execution of the Treaty of Peace. He saw no objection to this, and if his colleagues would permit, he proposed to ask M. Dutasta to make some arrangement with the Germans.

MR. LLOYD GEORGE pointed out that it had been agreed to set up a Committee in regard to the execution of the Treaty and he thought that they might be the medium for these conversations.

(Both M. Clemenceau's and Mr. Lloyd George's proposals were agreed to.)

7. With reference to C.F.97, Minute 5, Sir Maurice Hankey said that he had encountered difficulty in giving effect to the decision taken at the meeting in the morning, to appoint a single temporary resident Commissioner to Armenia. It appeared to him that the matter required a good deal of administrative action.

(It was agreed that the Council of Ten should be asked to concert the necessary administrative steps to give effect to this decision.)

8. (It was agreed that the Joint Note by the Admirals of the Allied and Associated Powers, dated 27th [25th] June, 1919, on the subject of the disposal of German and Austro-Hungarian warships[6] should be referred to the Council of Ten.)

9. With reference to C.F.93,[7] Minute 9, the Council took note of the attached letter from General Bliss, reporting that he had no information to confirm the statement of Béla Kun to the alleged resumption of hostilities by the Roumanians. (Appendix III.)

[6] About which, see n. 3 to the minutes of the Council of Four printed at June 25, 1919, 11 a.m.
[7] The minutes of the Council of Four printed at June 26, 1919, 11 a.m.

APPENDIX I TO C.F.99.

W.C.P.*1088*.   Hohenfinow, 25th June, 1919.
(Translation)

Sir,

I have the honour to request that Your Excellency will be so good as to bring the annexed letter to the notice of the Governments of the Allied and Associated Powers.

I have the honour, etc.,   (Sgd)   Bethmann Hollweg.
His Excellency
    M. Clemenceau.

Enclosure in Above.

According to Article 227 of the Conditions of Peace, the Allied and Associated Powers publicly arraign His Majesty William II of Hohenzollern, ex-Emperor of Germany, for a supreme offence against international morality and the sanctity of Treaties. At the same time they declare that they will address to the Royal Government of the Netherlands a request to deliver the former Emperor into their hands in order that he may be put to trial.

With reference to these stipulations, I beg leave to request the Governments of the Allied and Associated Powers to direct against my person the procedure which they propose to initiate against His Majesty the Emperor. With this object I declare that I place myself at the disposal of the Allied and Associated Powers.

In accordance with the constitutional laws of Germany, it is I who, in my capacity of former Chancellor of the Empire, bear the exclusive responsibility for political acts of the Emperor during my tenure of office. I feel justified in considering that the Allied and Associated Powers who wish to submit these acts to their judgment should call me only to account therefor.

I feel convinced that the Governments of the Allied and Associated Powers will not refuse to admit that the rule established by the public law of a State deserves to be recognised in international relations, and I express the hope that they will be so good as to grant the urgent request which I submit to them.

(Sd)   Bethmann Hollweg.
Hohenfinow, 25th June 1919.

APPENDIX II TO C.F.99.

The Principal Allied and Associated Powers desire to thank the Turkish Delegation for the statements which they requested permission to lay before the Peace Conference.

These statements have received, and will continue to receive, the careful consideration which they deserve. But they touch on other interests besides those of Turkey and they raise international questions whose immediate decision is unfortunately impossible. Though, therefore, the Council are most anxious to proceed rapidly with the final settlement of Peace, and fully realise the inconvenience of prolonging the present period of uncertainty, an exhaustive survey of the situation has convinced them that some delay is inevitable.

They feel that in these circumstances nothing would be gained by the longer stay in Paris at the present time of the Turkish Delegation which the Turkish Government requested leave to send to France. Though, when the period arrives at which for her interchange of ideas seems likely to be profitable, they will not fail to communicate with the Turkish Government as to the best method by which this result may be conveniently and rapidly accomplished.

28th June, 1919.

APPENDIX III TO C.F.99.

AMERICAN COMMISSION TO NEGOTIATE PEACE.

Hôtel de Crillon, Paris, June 28th, 1919.

My dear Sir Maurice,

Referring to your letter of June 27th, 1919, enclosing copy of a despatch from Béla Kun (SSS de Budapest Nr 319 W 192 le 26/6/−4 h 20), in which you state that the Council wishes to be informed whether Béla Kun's statements in regard to the attitude of the Roumanians are correct, I beg to inform you that there is no information on file with the American Commission that would confirm the statements of Béla Kun. I have been informed by the Information Section of the British Delegation that that Section also has no information that would indicate a resumption of hostilities by the Roumanians.

Sincerely yours,   (Sd)   TASKER H. BLISS.

Colonel M. P. A. Hankey
   Villa Majestic,
      Paris.

T MS (SDR, RG 256, 180.03401/99, DNA).

Hankey's Notes of a Meeting of the Council of Four[1]

C.F.99A. NOTES OF A MEETING HELD IN THE FOYER OF THE SENATE HOUSE IN THE CHATEAU AT VERSAILLES,

on Saturday, June 28th, 1919, at 6:00 p.m.

1. With reference to C.F.96.B.,[2] Minute 1, PRESIDENT WILSON read aloud a re-draft of the proposed statement to the Italian Government, prepared by Mr. Balfour.[3]

NOTE: During the Meeting Baron Makino and Baron Sonnino arrived, but Mr. Lloyd George left the room to explain to them that the subject under consideration was Declarations by France and Great Britain on the one hand, and by the United States of America, on the other hand, to the new Italian Delegation, and they withdrew.

The above statement was approved, subject to some small amendments, the most important of which was the omission of a reference to the Dodecanese, which, it was considered, might be interpreted as a repudiation of the Treaty of London.

The draft as finally approved is attached in Appendix I. Sir Maurice Hankey was instructed to obtain the signature of Mr. Lloyd George before his departure, and subsequently that of M. Clemenceau, who undertook to communicate it to the Italians.

PRESIDENT WILSON said he was forwarding a separate statement, which he intended should contain a reference to the Dodecanese, as he was not bound by the Treaty of London.

---

[1] The complete text of these minutes is printed in *PPC*, VI, 759-62.

[2] The minutes of the Council of Four printed at June 28, 1919, 10:30 a.m.

[3] This document is printed as an Appendix. As the minutes of the Council of Four cited in n. 2 above reveal, Sir Maurice Hankey read a draft of a statement, prepared by Balfour, to be handed to Tittoni on behalf of the British and French governments. It was agreed that the draft was incomplete, and Lloyd George said that there was no point in having a discussion with the Italians while their troops remained in Asia Minor. Sir Maurice was instructed to ask Balfour to draft the last paragraph in the sense of Lloyd George's remarks, combined with the first paragraph of Wilson's instructions on the Dodecanese Islands and Asia Minor (printed as an Enclosure with WW to RL, June 28, 1919).

Balfour's redraft is missing in the Balfour Papers and other collections. The only copy that we possess is a carbon copy of one typed by Charles L. Swem, in the C. L. Swem Coll., NjP, on the face of which Wilson wrote "Allies to Italy." This is the copy that Wilson had before him at this, the last meeting of the Council of Four, and presumably Clemenceau and Lloyd George had copies of the same document. Wilson made a few changes on his copy and struck out a reference to the Dodecanese, but it seems altogether likely that he did this during the course of discussion about the document.

The style and wording of the document seem to be Balfour's, not Wilson's. The Editors do not know why Swem was asked to type up Balfour's redraft, but it is certainly possible that Wilson offered his services because Hankey was so busy on this day. We print the draft, with Wilson's changes on Swem's copy. The final draft, printed in *PPC*, VI, 760-62, conforms almost exactly if one reads the Swem copy en clair. Mantoux, II, 568, notes that the reference to the Dodecanese was omitted at Lloyd George's suggestion.

[Appendix]4

Allies to Italy

28th June 1919.

The change in the Italian Delegation has occurred at a moment in which the associates of Italy were feeling considerable anxiety with regard to the part she was playing in the common cause. While nothing could be more friendly than the personal relations which have united the representatives of the Five Powers through many months of anxious discussion, and while we gladly recognise the aid and co-operation which the Italian Delegation have rendered in the framing of the peace with Germany, we feel less happy about the general course of the negotiations affecting other aspects of the world settlement.

There is no doubt that the present uncomfortable condition of affairs is largely due to the complications which the development of political and military events has brought about since the Treaty of London was signed in 1915. Since then the aspect of the world has changed. The Treaty was contracted with Russia, France and Britain, but Russia is no longer in the war. It contemplated a victorious peace with the Austro-Hungarian Empire; but while victory of the completest kind has been achieved, the Austro-Hungarian Empire had ceased to exist. It assumed that if Turkey was completely defeated, fragments of the Turkish Empire might be assigned to the victors; but while Turkey has indeed *been* completely defeated, and the alien peoples which she misgoverned are to be separated from her Empire, they are not to be handed over in possession to the conquerors, while any spheres of influence which the latter may acquire will be held by them not independently, but as Trustees or mandatories of the League of Nations. In 1915 America was neutral; but in 1917 she entered the war unhampered by any Treaty, and at a period when the development of this order of political ideas to which she gave a most powerful impulse, were in process of rapid accomplishment.

It is not surprising that the situation thus created presents complexities which only the utmost good will and the most transparent loyalty can successfully deal with. The Treaty of London, with which the history may be said to open, was from the very beginning not strictly observed. Italy had undertaken to employ all her resources in prosecuting the war in common with her Allies against all their enemies. But she did not declare war on Germany for more than a year, *and she took no part in the war against Tur-*

---

4 Words in italics in this document WWhw; words in angle brackets deleted by him.

key. By the Treaty of London, the central portion of Albania was to be made into an autonomous State under Italian protection; while Northern and Southern Albania, were under certain circumstances to fall respectively to Serbia and Greece. But in 1917 Italy declared a Protectorate over the whole country—a Protectorate which she seems to have exercised ever since. By the Treaty of London Fiume was *with Italy's consent* assigned to Croatia. But since the Armistice, Italy has been accumulating troops in that neighborhood and local laws appear to have been promulgated in the name of the Italian King. Meanwhile America, which, unlike France and Britain, was not a party to the Treaty of London has, in conformity with the general principles of settlement on which all the Allied and Associated Powers, including Italy, are agreed declined to hand over reluctant Slav majorities in the Eastern Adriatic to Italian rule; and no arrangement on this vexed question has been arrived at.

Evidently the situation thus described is one of peculiar difficulty; but we feel bound to add that the difficulties have been greatly augmented by the policy pursued in Asia Minor by the Italian Government and Italian troops. This matter, as perhaps Your Excellency is aware, was the subject of warm debate in the Council of Four. President Wilson, Monsieur Clemenceau and Mr. Lloyd George complained in the strongest terms of the proceedings at Scala Nuova and elsewhere in South-Western Anatolia. They drew the sharpest contrast between the policy of the Greek Government, which moved no troops except with the cognizance, and usually at the request of the Allied and Associated Powers *including, of course, Italy herself*; while Italy, which was one of those Powers, and as such cognizant of all that was being done by her friends, landed troops and occupied important positions without *giving* the least inkling of her proceedings to those whose ⟨councils⟩ *counsels* she ⟨shares⟩ *shared*, whose general policy she professed to support, but whose remonstrances on this point she persistently ignored.

We find it difficult fully to understand this action on the part of a friendly Power. At first sight it might seem to be animated by the idea that territories occupied by troops of a given nationality would be assigned to that nationality by the final terms of Peace. But this has never been the view of the other Allied and Associated Powers, and we had the best reason for supposing that it was not the view of Italy. We venture to quote a paragraph on the subject to which the Italian Representative gave his adhesion:

"No State will be rewarded for prolonging the horrors of war by any increase of territory; nor will the Allied and Associated Powers be induced to alter decisions made in the interests of

Peace and justice by the unscrupulous use of military methods."[5]

It is needless to say that we have not made the recital of our common difficulties for any other purpose than to contribute to their removal. The Treaty of London, the Anglo-French Declaration of November 1918,[6] President Wilson's fourteen points all bear on the situation, all have in different ways to be considered when Italy is discussing with her Allies and Associates the aspects of the final settlements which most clearly concern her. But they cannot be treated as contracts susceptible only of a strict legal interpretation. Italy herself has not so treated them; and if her partners attempted the task an amicable settlement would seem beyond the wit of man. For, as has been pointed out, they were framed in different periods in a rapidly changing world and under the stress of widely different motives. They could not be and are not in all respects consistent. They are in part obsolete or obsolescent, and cannot in their entirety be carried out. What in these circumstances seems to be required is a re-survey of the whole situation. Let the four great Powers of the West, America, France, Britain and Italy, consider together with a fresh mind and perfect frankness, whether some solution cannot be found which is consistent both with the material interests of Italy, her enduring aspirations and the rights and susceptibilities of her neighbours. The difficulties in the way of such a solution may be great. But they should not be insuperable. We feel however compelled to add that it is wholly useless in our judgment to discuss Peace Terms in Paris as friends and associates, while one of our number is elsewhere pursuing an independent and even antagonistic course of action. ⟨If for example, Italy insists on retaining the Dodecanese she cannot be a fellow worker in the Settlement of Peace, for she is deliberately violating the principles, on which in our opinion, Peace should be established.⟩ If ⟨she⟩ *for example, Italy* insists, after our earnest protests, on maintaining troops in Anatolia, it can only be because she intends to obtain by force all she claims to be hers by right. This is quite inconsistent with genuine alliance; its inevitable end is complete isolation. It is for Italian Statesmen to say whether or not this is in Italy's interests. To us and the world the loss will be immense for the aid which Italy can render to mankind by helping in the establishment of a durable Peace through international co-operation is beyond price. To Italy it will mean the loss

[5] Printed in *PPC*, VI, 411.
[6] This declaration, quoted in n. 1 to R. Cecil to C. A. de R. Barclay, Oct. 31, 1918, Vol. 51, declared that Great Britain and France aimed only to achieve the complete and final liberation of the peoples of the Near East and "the establishment of governments and administrations deriving their authority from the initiative and the free choice of the native populations."

of all claim to further assistance or aid from those who were once proud to be her associates. To us such a consummation seems to be disasterous; but if Italian policy runs its course unchanged it seems also to be inevitable.

T MS (SDR, RG 256, 180.03401/99½, DNA); CC MS (C. L. Swem Coll., NjP).

A Memorandum on Future Relations with Italy

28 June, 1919.

It is very necessary, in the interest of friendly candour and the successful settlement of the difficult questions still remaining to be settled, that the position of the United States should be defined with the utmost clearness and frankness. It is right, therefore, that I should say that the Government of the United States can in no case entertain the Italian claim to the Dodecannesos Islands, and that it does not feel that it would be right for it to consider the wishes of Italy with regard to any other matters in Asia Minor until the Italian Government has demonstrated its intention to cooperate in all respects upon equal terms in these matters with the United States and the Entente. If the Government of Italy desires to act with the Entente and with the United States, it should at once withdraw its armed forces from all parts of Asia Minor. Those forces were sent there without consultation with the other Allied and Associated Powers, and are being retained there in spite of very explicit protest more than once made in the council of the Principal Allied and Associated Powers. If Italy is to retain its armed forces in Asia Minor, the other Powers will be forced to infer that it desires to be left to its own resources and to a forcible assertion of right wherever it chooses to assert it, action which would clearly make it impossible for the other Powers to cooperate with it or to assist it in any way.

The Government of the United States, in common with its associates, desires to render Italy every kind of assistance that it is in its power to render, but it cannot do so at the sacrifice of any of the principles upon which the present negotiations have been conducted and the decisions of the present peace settlements founded. It confidently hopes, therefore, that the representatives of Italy will be prepared to forego all claims which are not consistent with those principles, and to enter the common counsel of the Powers in a spirit of complete cooperation and with a frank acceptance of the fundamental standards which have determined all territorial questions and all questions with regard to the assignment of mandates wherever constituted.   Woodrow Wilson

TS MS (R. Lansing Papers, DLC).

To Robert Lansing

My dear Lansing: Paris, 28 June, 1919.

The simple peasants whose pictures are enclosed[1] walked some forty or fifty miles to a railway station in their mountain country, and came all the way to Paris to beg that their little mountain pocket might be attached to Poland, and as I am clearing up my papers I am deeply chagrined to find that I forgot to pay attention to their claims at the proper time. If it is not too late, as I sincerely hope it is not, will you not be kind enough to have someone look into the matter and rectify the frontier as they plead it may be rectified, so as to include them in Poland.

Cordially and sincerely yours,   [Woodrow Wilson]

CCL (WP, DLC).
    [1] About these peasants and their meeting with Wilson, see the extracts from the Baker Diary printed at March 31, 1919, Vol. 56, and from the Grayson Diary printed at April 11, 1919, Vol. 57.

To Eduard Beneš

My dear Doctor Benes: Paris, June 28, 1919.

It is with sentiments of particular gratification that I have received the diploma which constitutes the evidence of my having had conferred upon me by the University of Prague the title of Doctor of that university,[1] and I beg that you will convey to the authorities of the University an expression of my very deep and sincere appreciation. It will always be a matter of pride to me that I have received this evidence of the friendship and confidence of my colleagues—if I may call them so—of the University of Prague. It is delightful to be associated in this way with the affairs of a university which will henceforth ornament the scholarship of a great and independent people.

Cordially and sincerely yours,   [Woodrow Wilson]

CCL (WP, DLC).
    [1] See E. Beneš and K. Kramář to WW, June 24, 1919.

From Henry White

Dear Mr. President   [Paris] June 28 1919 8 P.M.

I am enclosing, for your perusal at sea, two clippings from yesterday's London Times which I think you will find interesting. Willert's on the League is encouraging[1] and the one from Rome[2] shows that Tittoni will probably be in a receptive mood. I shall hope to get hold of him before he commits himself and advise him "as an old friend" to steer his course in such a way as not to render the Italian situation an "impasse" from our point of view; giving him to understand what he may expect and will certainly encounter, if he does not take the hint.

I shall be grateful, dear Mr President, when you get home if you can see your way to appointing a new Minister to Siam. Apart from the fact that the post has been vacant for more than a year, I should like very much to get my son[3] out of that very enervating climate in which he has now spent—or will have done so before he can be relieved—two summers. He knows a great deal about—and takes a great interest in—far, & near, Eastern questions, and if he can get home by October, I think he might be useful at the State Department in connection with the League of Nations, Labor or other Conferences which are to take place in Washington—or hereafter in connection with the Treaty. But I am not suggesting any post for him, as he is in the regular Diplomatic Service—a 2d Secretary—and the Department of State knows his merits & will deal with him accordingly.

Admiral Grayson & Grasty both know him also. All that I am venturing to suggest to you is the appointment of a new Minister, or that another Secretary in the service be sent to take his place as Chargé d'Affaires within the not very distant future.

As I shall not have an opportunity for any private word with you at the station this evening, I avail myself of this opportunity to thank you for your kindness to me during the past six months and especially for having enabled me to take part in a great historical occasion, such as that of today must always be considered.

I shall hope to be of use in the settlement of the many questions still remaining and with every good wish for your success in getting the Treaty ratified by the Senate, I am dear Mr President

Most Sincerely Yours   Henry White

ALS (WP, DLC).

[1] This dispatch from Arthur Willert, Washington correspondent of the London *Times*, datelined Washington, June 26, reported that it had been a bad week for Republican opponents of the Covenant. The debate on the Knox Resolution had apparently been indefinitely postponed, and the Foreign Relations Committee had failed to report the Fall Resolution. Evidence was growing that the Republicans had not been attracting recruits lately for their fight against the League. Moreover, as the *New York Times* had reported, leading midwestern and western Republican newspapers had deprecated the tactics of the Republican senators. All this, Willert concluded, did not mean that Wilson would necessarily win the adoption of the Covenant as it then stood, but it made it much more than likely that he would obtain the Senate's consent to ratification with reservations not calculated to bar the United States from effective membership in the League. London *Times*, June 27, 1919.

[2] *Ibid.* This dispatch from Rome, datelined June 25, reported on Tittoni's speech to the Italian Senate of that same day, about which, see n. 2 to Hankey's minutes of the Council of Four printed at June 26, 1919, 11 a.m.

[3] John Campbell White, Chargé of the American legation in Bangkok.

From John Foster Dulles

My dear Mr. President: [Paris] June 28, 1919.

I am in receipt of your very kind letter of June 27, in which you ask me to remain in Europe for the present to continue to handle the matters with which I have become familiar.

It is not only a duty, but it becomes a pleasure, to continue in a task in which I have had the honor to have gained the confidence of yourself and the men with whom I have been collaborating. Accordingly, I shall be very happy to comply with your request.

I am, my dear Mr. President,
                    Faithfully yours,   John Foster Dulles

TLS (WP, DLC).

From Tasker Howard Bliss

My dear Mr. President: Paris, June 28th, 1919.

M[a]y I ask whether you have reached a decision in regard to the subject matter of my letter of June 26th, on the subject of allowing the two railway companies at Murmansk to remain not later than September 1st, *provided* they volunteer for this service? I talked with General Pershing yesterday about the matter and he expressed the opinion that, if they volunteer to do so, they should be permitted to remain.   Cordially yours,   Tasker H. Bliss.

TLS (WP, DLC).

To Tasker Howard Bliss

My dear General Bliss: Paris, 28 June, 1919.

The proposal contained in your letter of June 26th has my entire approval. I believe that the wishes of General Maynard, Commanding the British and Allied forces at Murmansk should be complied with. Our two companies of railway troops should be left at the service of the British and Allied forces until September first, provided those companies volunteer to stay and provided the British can assure us that they will be embarked by September first next.

I have consulted Mr. Lloyd George about this matter and am happy to find him in entire agreement and quite prepared to give this assurance.
                    Cordially and sincerely yours,   Woodrow Wilson
                         I concur   DLG

TLS (T. H. Bliss Papers, DLC).

A Statement Upon Leaving France

[Brest] June 28, 1919.

As I look back over the eventful months I have spent in France, my memory is not of conferences and hard work alone, but also of innumerable acts of generosity and friendship which have made me feel how genuine the sentiments of France are towards the people of America, and how fortunate I have been to be the representative of our people in the midst of a nation which knows how to show its kindness with so much charm and such open manifestation of what is in its heart. Deeply happy as I am at the prospect of joining my own countrymen again, I leave France with genuine regret, my deep sympathy for her people and belief in her future confirmed, my thought enlarged by the privilege of association with her public men, conscious of more than one affectionate friendship formed, and profoundly grateful for unstinted hospitality and for countless kindnesses which have made me feel welcome and at home. I take the liberty of bidding France God-speed as well as good-bye, and of expressing once more my abiding interest and entire confidence in her future.

                                        Woodrow Wilson

T MS (WP, DLC).

Three Telegrams from Joseph Patrick Tumulty

                                Washington June 28 1919

Two nineteen I would suggest this as a tentative program upon your return colon arrival at New York semicolon reception by committee comma as Mr McAdoo suggests semicolon informal address period Return to Washington semicolon address to Congress period Spend two or three weeks in Washington comma conferring with Senators and Congressmen and cleaning up your desk period Tour of the country comma extending to the Pacific Coast comma if possible arriving there when the new Pacific Fleet arrives at San Francisco period Paragraph I am just in receipt of two remarkable optimistic letters comma one from Homer Cummings who has spent the last six weeks covering all parts of the west comma from Michigan through to the Coast and back through Arizona comma through New Mexico comma North and South Dakota period The other from Senator Lewis[1] comma saying the tide is turning our way period Both were very pessimistic two months ago period Am keeping in touch daily with everything going on at the Capital period Things are moving smoothly period   Tumulty

---

[1] That is, James Hamilton Lewis, former Democratic senator from Illinois.

The White House, 28 June 1919

Number 220. Please do not issue any statement about beer ban until you receive my memorandum of the proposed statement to be issued by you.   Tumulty.

Washington June 28 1919

Number 221 Received your message saying you do not intend to lift the ban period The Republicans have been industriously spreading the story throughout the country that you in fact have power under the act of November 21 1918 to lift the ban period I think it is important wise and politic therefore for you to make a statement which we can issue from the White House along the following lines quote I am convinced that the Attorney General is right in advising me that I have no legal power at this time in the matter of the ban on liquor period Under the act of November 1918 my power to take action is restricted period The act provides that after June 30 1919 until the conclusion of the present war and thereafter until the termination of demobilization comma the date of which shall be determined and proclaimed by the President comma it shall be unlawful etc period This law does not specify that the ban shall be lifted with the signing of peace but with the termination of the demobilization of the troops comma and I cannot say that that has been accomplished period My information from the War Department is that there are still a million men in the service under the emergency call period It is clear therefore that the failure of Congress to act upon the suggestion contained in my message of the twentieth of May 1919[1] asking for a repeal of the act of November 21 1918 so far as it applies to wines and beers makes it impossible to act in this matter at this time period When demobilization is terminated comma my power to act without Congressional action will be exercised unquote

Tumulty

T telegrams (WP, DLC).
  [1] Printed at that date in Vol. 59.

Two Telegrams to Joseph Patrick Tumulty

Paris, 28 June, 1919.

Please say to the Attorney General and the Postmaster General that it is my earnest desire to grant complete amnesty and pardon to all American citizens in prison or under arrest on account of anything they have said in speech or in print concerning their personal opinions with regard to the activities of the Government during the period of the war. It seems to me that this would be not only a generous act but a just act to accompany the signing of the peace. I do not wish to include any who have been guilty of overt crimes of course but I think it would be a very serious mistake to continue to detain anyone merely for the expression of opinion. Will you not be kind enough to ask them to prepare the proper papers if action by me is necessary and make this announcement for me.   Woodrow Wilson.

                                              Paris, 28 June, 1919.

Please issue following statement: QUOTE.

I am convinced that the Attorney General is right in advising me that I have no legal power at this time in the matter of the ban on liquor. Under the act of November, 1918, my power to take action is restricted. The act provides that after June 30, 1919 until the conclusion of the present war and thereafter until the termination of demobilization, the date of which shall be determined and proclaimed by the President, it shall be unlawful etc. This law does not specify that the ban shall be lifted with the signing of peace but with the termination of the demobilization of the troops, and I cannot say that that has been accomplished. My information from the War Department is that there are still a million men in the service under the emergency call. It is clear therefore that the failure of Congress to act upon the suggestion contained in my message of the twentieth of May 1919 asking for a repeal of the act of November 21, 1918 so far as it applies to wines and beers makes it impossible to act in this matter at this time. When demobilization is terminated, my power to act without Congressional action will be exercised. UNQUOTE.   Woodrow Wilson.

T telegrams (WP, DLC).

From Joseph Patrick Tumulty

                                    The White House, 28 June 1919.

#224. The Attorney General thinks you ought to wait until you return before granting complete amnesty and pardon to all American citizens in prison or under arrest on account of anything they have said in speech or in print. He says there have been no convictions of people for mere expression of opinion. Every case has been a conviction for obstructing the war under statute.

                                                    Tumulty

T telegram (WP, DLC).

From William Howard Taft

[The White House] June 28-19

Number 223 Mr. Taft sends following:

"I would like to send a return message and that is that the President argue to the League and its necessity: the impossibility of secure peace without it, the dreadful unrest in Europe, the pressure of our allies to ratify and secure peace at once, the need of the League with the United States to stabilize and to resist Bolshevism, the necessity for renewal of negotiation if an important amendment like striking out article ten is made, the absurdity of a Congressional declaration of Peace on one side, the giving up of all objects of the war in such a peace if Germany were to make a similar declaration. I hope sincerely he will not attack the Republican senators. His appeal will be much more influential if he pleads his cause and does not attack the opposition."   Tumulty

T telegram (WP, DLC).

George Andrew Sanderson[1] to Joseph Patrick Tumulty

Sir: [Washington] June 28, 1919.

I hand you herewith a resolution of the Senate of June 27, 1919,[2] requesting the President immediately to inform the Senate, if not incompatible with the public interest, of the reasons for sending United States soldiers to Siberia, what duties are there to be performed by these soldiers, how long they are to remain, and generally to advise the Senate of the policy of the United States Government in respect to Siberia and the maintenance of United States soldiers therein.

Will you kindly acknowledge receipt of the resolution upon the enclosed form?   Respectfully,   George A. Sanderson
                                                          Secretary.

TLS (WP, DLC).
[1] Secretary of the United States Senate.
[2] Senator Hiram W. Johnson, on May 20, 1919, had introduced Senate Resolution No. 13, which stated "That the Secretary of State and the Secretary of War be, and they are hereby, requested immediately to inform the Senate of the reasons for sending 8,000 United States soldiers to Siberia, what duties are there to be performed by these soldiers, how long they are to remain, and generally to advise the Senate of the policy of the United States Government in respect to Siberia and the maintenance of United States soldiers therein." *Cong. Record*, 66th Cong., 1st sess., p. 63. This was a considerably revised version of the resolution about American troops in Russia that Johnson had introduced on December 12, 1918, for the text of which see NDB to WW, Jan. 1, 1919, n. 6, Vol. 53.
When the Senate Foreign Relations Committee reported back Senate Resolution No. 13 on June 26, 1919, it had amended the earlier part of the resolution to read: "That the President be, and he is hereby, requested immediately to inform the Senate, if not

incompatible with the public interest, of the reasons for sending United States soldiers to Siberia. . . ." *Cong. Record*, 66th Cong., 1st sess., pp. 1783-84. The Senate adopted the revised resolution on June 27, 1919. *Ibid.*, p. 1864.

From the Diary of Dr. Grayson

Sunday, June 29, 1919.

We had breakfast on the train and reached the harbor docks at Brest at 11:50. The Mayor of Brest[1] and all of the city's dignitaries, together with all of the American Army officers stationed there, and a large delegation of soldiers, were on hand to say good-bye to the President. A small tender, well decorated with flags and bunting, was in waiting, and after the usual salutes the President and Mrs. Wilson were escorted to the tender and taken out to the George Washington, which was anchored just outside of the breakwater. All of the ships in the harbor were gaily bedecked with flags and bunting, and as the tender passed out the forts inside fired a parting salute. The President said good-bye to the various French officials, and then proceeded on board the George Washington.

There was a delay of two hours while the balance of the party and the baggage were put on board, and at two o'clock the signal to start was given. The President and Mrs. Wilson went to the bridge and stood there as the George Washington, preceded by the Battleship OKLAHOMA, and flanked by American destroyers, passed on out of the harbor into the open sea. A French escort squadron steamed behind for two hours.

The President was in excellent condition, and after dinner went up into the dining salon and sat through a motion picture exhibition.

[1] Either Ernest Amélie Hervagault or [Jules Gustave] Hippolyte Masson.

From the Diary of Colonel House

June 29, 1919.

My last conversation with the President yesterday was not reassuring. I urged him to meet the Senate in a conciliatory spirit. I was certain if he treated them with the same consideration he had used with his foreign colleagues here, all would be well. In reply he said: "House, I have found one can never get anything in this life that is worth while without fighting for it." I combatted this, and reminded him that Anglo-Saxon Civilization was built up on compromise. I said that a fight was the last thing to be brought about, and then only when it could not be avoided. My own plan in negotiations had been to get all I could by friendly methods, but if driven to fight, then it was to do it so effectively that no one would wish to drive me to it again.

A Translation of a Letter from Albert, King of the Belgians

Mr. President, Bruxelles, le 29 juin 1919.

I am truly very happy to know from your gracious letter[1] that you and Mrs. Wilson carried back, from a time too short for us that you spent in Belgium, also good memories.

I take this occasion to say to you again how much we were charmed by your visit, which was the first that we have received since the Armistice. Your stay in Brussels will remain one of the most outstanding events to have happened in these first months in which the country has recovered her independence.

Belgium, so attached to her freedom, has appreciated above all the visit of the statesman who, by his creation of the League of Nations, is the symbol of the future security of small countries.

Your fine portrait, which accompanied your friendly letter, has given me extreme pleasure; it will remain for me a precious souvenir of your high friendship, and I thank you for it most sincerely.

I am certain that the wishes that you express for Belgium will bring to it happiness, and it is with all my heart that I express to you my wishes for the greatness of the noble American people and for the realization of the so elevated ideal of which you are the defender. I would ask you to transmit to Mrs. Wilson my respectful greetings, and I beg you to believe, yourself, Mr. President, in my faithful friendship, and I remain, Sincerely yours, Albert

T MS (WC, NjP).
[1] WW to Albert, June 20, 1919.

From the Diary of Dr. Grayson

Monday, June 30, 1919.

Early this morning I was awakened by an announcement that the Transport Great Northern was in sight. The reason for my being awakened was that I had been notified while in Paris that the Great Northern had on board a mail pouch from the White House, and I sent orders for her to transfer it to the George Washington enroute. In order to avoid hurting any one's feelings I transferred the orders through the various official channels so that they went to a number of people with the result that as soon as the Great Northern was located, Captain McCauley[1] saw that I was

personally notified with the result that my early morning beauty
sleep was seriously encroached upon. This early morning beauty
sleep was a habit that had been contracted only in France. When
I first arrived I was in the habit of getting up at my usual early
hour. After having done this two mornings in succession, and having had the French help at the temporary White House look at me
in a most reproachful manner, I decided that it was unfair to them
to interfere with the custom of the country of sleeping late, and I
remained in bed myself.

The mail bag was transferred and delivered to me. It was tied
with cords of rope and then re-tied, and I with a small pen knife
started a surgical operation to extricate the bag from its casing.
After I got the rope off I found underneath a canvas bag. I managed to cut it, although the stout canvas resisted my small knife to
a very material extent. Feeling, however, that my task was ended
after I had slit the bag across, I dumped it out only to find that
there was still another canvas-bag. I got that off after awhile, and
with a smiling countenance over duty well performed, started to
open the leather bag. However, I encountered three locks on the
pouch and no key with which to open them, so I was finally compelled to call in a locksmith to finish the job. In the pouch were a
number of letters, including one from Mrs. Grayson, which naturally I was more than delighted to receive. There were also two bills
that had been sent from the White House for the President's signature. They were the Indian Bill and the Urgent Deficiency Bill.
They were placed upon the President's desk, and at 11:15 this
morning he signed them. In signing these bills the President broke
another precedent, inasmuch as it was the first time in the history
of the United States that national legislation had been completed
upon the high seas.

The weather was fine and calm, and the President spent a great
part of the day resting. He worked for a while on an introduction
to his Message to Congress, which he intended to deliver soon
after his arrival in Washington.

In the evening after dinner the President and Mrs. Wilson attended a moving picture performance.

[1] That is, Capt. Edward McCauley, Jr.

To Raoul Gautier[1]

U.S.S. GEORGE WASHINGTON
My dear Mr. Rector: [c. June 30, 1919]

It was with feeling of the profoundest gratification that I received at the hands of your colleague, Dr. Rappard,[2] the diploma

creating me a Doctor of Laws, Honoris Causa, of the University of Geneva, and your gracious letter of the 26th of June[3] gives the honor a peculiar flavor of friendship and confidence which render it all the more acceptable and valuable.

All my life I have known of the great position held by the University of Geneva and it will always be a matter of deep pride with me that I am by this gracious act henceforth to be associated with that University as one of her adopted sons.

In common with all of my fellow-countrymen, I have always entertained a feeling of admiration akin to affection for the people of Switzerland, whose record of sturdy liberty and enlightened policy has given them a place of peculiar distinction.

Cordially and sincerely yours,   [Woodrow Wilson]

CCL (WP, DLC).
[1] Rector of the University of Geneva.
[2] William Emmanuel Rappard, Professor of Economics at the University of Geneva.
[3] R. Gautier to WW, June 26, 1919, HwLS (WP, DLC).

From Robert Lansing

[Paris, June 30, 1919]

CONFIDENTIAL. In my letter of June 24th,[1] I submitted my views regarding Austrian frontier problems and recommended certain changes in the boundaries proposed for Austria. You replied on June 25th that you desired to give this matter careful study. The Austrian counter-proposals on territorial questions are now being considered with a view to submitting Allied reply. In general do you care to attempt to effect alterations in the territorial clauses of the draft Austrian treaty, with a view to making the Austrian frontier conform more closely with the ethnographic frontier.

Lansing.

T radiogram (WP, DLC).
[1] About which, see WW to RL, June 25, 1919 (first letter of that date).

From Samuel Gompers

Sir: Washington, D. C. June 30, 1919.

Permit me to bring to your attention the following resolution adopted by the 39th convention of the American Federation of Labor, expressive of the sentiments of the organized labor movement of America in opposition to mob rule and lynching:[1]

"WHEREAS, President Woodrow Wilson issued from the capital city of our nation on July 26th 1918,[2] a personal statement addressed to his fellow-countrymen, defining mob-spirit action, called upon the nation to show the world that while it fights for Democracy on foreign fields, it is not destroying democracy at home; and

"WHEREAS, While the President referred not alone to mob action against those suspected of being enemy aliens or enemy sympathizers, he denounced most emphatically mob action of all sorts, especially lynchings, and

"WHEREAS, In all wars, where our country and its interests were at stake the colored race, with their white brothers, fought, shed their blood and died in defense of Old Glory and over there gave their all that others may live in peace and happiness ever after; and

"WHEREAS, Lynchings, cowardly and unjust is also a blow at the heart of ordered law and human justice; and

"WHEREAS, The colored people, their workers, their bread winners, throughout the nation look with hope and anxiety in their hearts to those in the struggle for better conditions, for better homes and for the good things of life, as well as protection from mob rule and for a surging popular opinion behind them that will not tolerate a laxity in upholding the laws of our land; and

"WHEREAS, The hope of civilization is in democracy; the hope of democracy is in justice; the only hope of justice is in the tribunals through which justice can be secured, and the only hope of the functioning of these tribunals is in the sentiment which demands that they within their departments, shall be supreme and that any effort to incite mob violence shall be regarded as an attack upon the very foundations of society itself; and

"WHEREAS, The American labor movement, A. F. of L., knows no race, color or creed in its stand for the toiling masses to get justice; and

"WHEREAS, Through its representatives in convention assembled, at Perth Amboy, N. J., week of August 19th, 1918, the New Jersey State Federation of Labor, with a membership of over 90,000 endorsed this resolution; and

"WHEREAS, The great American labor movement through its conventions, city, state and national, is the very medium through which popular and public sentiment can best be expressed against mob rule and for proper enforcement of the laws of our land; therefore, be it

"RESOLVED, That we, the representatives of the 39th Annual Convention of the American Federation of Labor, go on record as endorsing the above as our sentiments in opposition to mob rule and lynchings; and be it further

"RESOLVED, That copy of the same be sent to our Representatives of Congress and United States Senate and Speakers of both

Houses, and to the press and to the President of our nation, Honorable Woodrow Wilson."

I have the honor to remain,

Respectfully yours,   Saml. Gompers.

TLS (WP, DLC).

¹ Adopted on June 17 during the A. F. of L. annual convention at Atlantic City. There had been an outbreak of lynchings and race riots during the spring of 1919. At least twenty-six blacks had been lynched in the United States from March through June. Riots between blacks and whites resulting in fatalities had occurred in Berkeley, Georgia, on February 27; in Millen, Georgia, on April 14; and in Charleston, South Carolina, on May 10. Much more serious and well-publicized race riots were soon to take place in Washington, July 19-22, and in Chicago from July 27 to August 9. See William M. Tuttle, Jr., *Race Riot: Chicago in the Red Summer of 1919* (New York, 1970), especially pp. 20-25, and Arthur I. Waskow, *From Race Riot to Sit-In, 1919 and the 1960s: A Study in the Connections Between Conflict and Violence* (Garden City, N. Y., 1966), especially pp. 12-16, 304.

² Printed at that date in Vol. 49.

From Norman Hapgood

Dear Mr. President,   Copenhagen June 30, 1919.

I felt enormously heartened by your letter of June 20th.¹ I shall try not to write you too much, but to put into the briefest form such things as may seem essential.

I enclose a page torn out of a book called "Ten Days that Shook the World," by John Reed.² Reed is an extreme Bolshevist in sympathy, and the lines I have marked are interesting because: (1) they reflect the fact that the Bolsheviks consider the Cooperatives moderate and bourgeois; (2) that nevertheless the Bolsheviks have realized that only through the Cooperatives has Russia been able to maintain such life as she has maintained.

I have been desperately hoping since January, 1917, that we might find some way of working with the Cooperatives, and that feeling has taken particular possession of me during the whole of the present year.

Mr. Berkenheim,³ Vice President of the All Russia Union of Cooperatives, is, I believe, still in America.

Perhaps I ought to add that in the misleading propaganda of our press, one item mentioned some cooperative associations as endorsing Kolchak, as if it referred to the greater All Russia organizations. As a matter of fact, the only such endorsements that have come to my knowledge are by two small local unions.

I also enclose a copy of a letter from Dr. M. Davidson,⁴ because it makes pointedly the distinction between the revolutionary forces and the Bolshevik forces.

With all best wishes, and with gratitude,

Sincerely yours,   Norman Hapgood

P.S. I attach hereto a clipping from *The Manchester Guardian*[5] describing an interview with Beloroussouff,[6] chairman of the Committee for preparing the elections to the Constituent Assembly for Kolchak. According to this interview, it is decided in advance of any elections that the result must be, first, to exclude internationalist tendencies, and second, to prevent the preponderance of any one social group. If this interview is authentic, it illustrates the reasons for the fear I have already expressed to you that it would be very easy for Kolchak to engineer the Constituent to a desired result.

As *The Manchester Guardian* is much better informed on Russian affairs than any other paper, I enclose herewith a general article on Russia taken from the same issue.[7]

TLS (WP, DLC).

[1] See WW to N. Hapgood, June 20, 1919.

[2] John Reed, *Ten Days that Shook the World* (New York, 1919). Hapgood enclosed pp. xix-xx.

[3] Aleksandr Moiseevich Berkenheim.

[4] M. Davidson to N. Hapgood, June 26, 1919, TCL (WP, DLC). About Davidson, see the minutes of the Council of Ten printed at Jan. 21, 1919, 10:30 a.m., Vol. 54.

[5] Clipping, June 17, 1919, entitled "Koltchak's Constituent Assembly. Universal Suffrage."

[6] The Editors have been unable further to identify him.

[7] Clipping, June 17, 1919, entitled "The Russian Quagmire. Counter-Revolutionary Activities. Baltic Peoples' Fears."

From the Diary of Dr. Grayson

Tuesday, July 1, 1919.

The President slept very late and after breakfast went to his office to resume work on his Message to Congress. However, he found probably for the first time in his entire life that his work of the day before had not satisfied him, so he was forced to begin all over. In characterizing this the President said that he had made a false start; that he was compelled to give more attention to what was being done in this case than ever before, because he had very little respect for the audience to which he would deliver the address. He said that if he thought more of the Congress, he might be able to do a better job, but that he was forced to remember that it was impossible to reason out of a man something that had not been reasoned into him.

The President had as luncheon guests Mr. Ray Stannard Baker and Mr. John E. Nevin. The luncheon was a most delightful affair. The President was in splendid form, and it was very apparent that the voyage was doing him a world of good. Discussing the message that he planned to deliver to Congress, he said that he wanted to be sure that it would fill the bill; he did not want it when completed to resemble that famous Latin proverb, which, literally translated into English, reads: "The mighty mountain labored and brought forth a miserable mouse."[1]

After lunch the President talked about the difference between Old World and American tradition. He said that he had read an article in a magazine by the head of the American Expeditionary Forces College at Beaune.[2] This article declared that America had no tradition, and the President said there was enough truth to it to be disturbing. He said that as a matter of fact even Jefferson was only a book personage to the majority of the people in America. This, he said, was not the fact in England especially. There families have lived for generations in the same place; their family traditions are well-known, and they are proud of the individuality of their noted men of history. He referred to the fact that it was likely the war would change a great deal of this.

Speaking of scenery, the President said that he thought the English lake region was about the prettiest he had ever seen. He described the various valleys in which the lakes are situated, with the mountain in the center and the valleys radiating out like spokes from a wheel. He and Baker commented upon this, and the talk then turned to American university life. The President said that so far as our American universities were concerned they were conservative to the utmost degree. Baker wanted to know why this was so, calling attention to the fact that many revolutions in Europe have started from the universities, while our universities are everything that is the opposite of revolutionary in sentiment. The President expressed the belief that there was a very good ground for this. He said that in his opinion the universities were not a center of interest for the student—rather the fraternities and the clubs were the one thing that the student aspired to. In other words, he said, that it was a case of the side-shows overshadowing the big circus. He said that he had found a great deal of conservatism in Princeton, and referred to the fight which he had carried on while head of that institution. He said that it was astonishing how so many students failed even to know the officials of the universities which they attended, citing a case where he had rebuked a band of students at Princeton for stoning the windows of a house only to find out through the personal confession to him of one of the party a year later that they had not known who it was. He also told of an incident in Princeton when he went into a hardware store to purchase a screw-driver; he got it from a salesman to whom he had talked on many occasions. When he asked him whether he would not send it up to the house, the salesman said he would be glad to do so, and then asked him, "What is your name and where is your address?"

He also said that on one occasion a man had called on the long-distance telephone and asked for him only to be told by the girl in charge of the university switchboard that there was no such individual in Princeton as Woodrow Wilson, although he was at the time President of the University.

In contrast to this the President told of his visit to Edinburgh, Scotland,[3] at the time Princeton was arranging for the celebration of its 150th Anniversary. He went there to invite a noted professor[4] to attend. This professor, the President declared, was "dry as toast," and his favorite topics were those on psychology. He went to the place but lost his way in the maze of circuitous streets that are characteristic of the Scottish city. He stopped a postman who was in uniform but not on his route and asked him if he could tell him where No. 10 Queen Circle is. The postman said: "That would be Professor McCorkle's,[5] Sir. Yes, I know where it is. I will show you." The President said that it was a mile away but it simply illustrated that the Scottish people took pride in their noted men and knew where they lived regardless of the subjects upon which they wrote.

The President said that one of the troubles with American history was that most of it has been written by New Englanders, and they have treated the development of the United States merely as the expansion of New England. He related an incident where he had told a noted historian that he thought this was not so, only to be amazed by the historian insisting that this actually was the case. The President said that the real America was an expansion going out into the form of an ever-increasing wedge from Manhattan Island, following the settlement there of the Holland Dutch. He said that in his opinion New York, New Jersey and Pennsylvania were the original American states, rather than New England. It was the President's view that New England was settled by the Puritans, while Virginia and the South were developed by the Cavaliers; and that New York, Pennsylvania, and the States further West were the first actual melting-pot, where the races of the world were amalgamated into Americans. He said that the South for the most part was settled by Scotch and English, and Louisiana by the French, and that the South had never had to absorb the mass of races that had come into the other States.

After luncheon the President resumed work on his Message to Congress. His dinner guests this evening were Ambassador and Madame Jusserand. After dinner he attended the moving pictures.

---

[1] The classic Latin formulation of this saying appears in Horace, *Ars Poetica*, as follows: "Parturient montes, nascetur ridiculus mus." An earlier version is attributed to Aesop, and another is in Plutarch.

[2] Col. Ira Louis Reeves, U.S.A., President and Commanding Officer of the American Expeditionary Forces University. The Editors have been unable to find this article.

3 Wilson briefly describes this visit in WW to EAW, June 13, 1896, Vol. 9.
4 Wilson was actually thinking of Andrew Seth Pringle Pattison, Professor of Logic and Metaphysics at the University of Edinburgh, 1891-1919, who represented that institution at the sesquicentennial celebration at Princeton University in 1896. Though Pringle Pattison was primarily a specialist in theistic philosophy, his chair then included the field of psychology, and he did occasionally write on this subject.
5 There was no one named "McCorkle," or any name resembling it, on the faculty of the University of Edinburgh in 1896.

From the Diary of Ray Stannard Baker

At Sea "George Washington" July 1st. Tuesday [1919].

This noon I lunched with President and Mrs. Wilson in their private apartments and greatly enjoyed the talk, which he apparently kept as far away from the Peace Conference as possible. He told of his experiences at Princeton & spoke of American universities as the centers of conservatism, especially in the undergraduate bodies. He said he could not explain why it was that in Europe revolutionary movements so often started among students while in the United States there seemed no such spirit. He told also of his first contribution to a journal—when he was a senior in college.[1] He commented laughingly on the fact that Senator Lodge was one of the editors: a journal called the "International Review." We also talked of various American histories & historians, & commented on the difficulty of getting original material upon life in the South before the war. He is looking wonderfully well.

This evening Mrs. Lamont[2] had a birthday dinner party which I enjoyed very much. She is a sparkling woman.

The President is working on his message to Congress. He always writes these messages out in full—says he cannot trust himself to speak extemporaneously upon such occasions. He said he found it a difficult message to write.

1 "Cabinet Government in the United States," printed at Aug. 1, 1879, Vol. 1.
2 That is, Florence Haskell Corliss (Mrs. Thomas William) Lamont.

To Edward Mandell House

U.S.S. George Washington 1 July, 1919.

I neglected before leaving to speak to you about the committee to formulate model mandates, of which we asked Lord Milner to act as chairman, associated with him yourself, Simon, Chinda, and Crespi. Milner is inclined to go the full liberal length, I think, and will have to be supported as against his Chief[1] who thinks that the outlines he drew[2] go too far. I believe that by devoting your most watchful attention to this business you can probably get it into shape that we will all be willing to support. The British Chief is too much inclined to think that this is a business for the Great Powers and only in form for the League of Nations and is apt to verify the impression that the mandates are after all only a means of distributing the spoils.   Woodrow Wilson

CC telegram (WP, DLC).
¹ That is, Lloyd George.
² Milner's "outlines" of a mandate system are printed as Enclosure I with WW to EMH, June 27, 1919.

From Samuel Gompers

Sir: Washington, D.C., July 1, 1919.

During your stay in Paris I had the honor of addressing a communication to you regarding Post Master General Burleson.¹ In connection with the general subject of that letter, permit me to bring to your attention the following preambles and resolutions adopted by the recent convention of the American Federation of Labor:

"WHEREAS, President Wilson in his message to Congress made this declaration: 'The question which stands at the front of all others, in every country amidst the present great awakening is the question of labor. The object of all reform in this essential matter must be the genuine demoralization [democratization] of industry, based upon a full recognition of those who work, in whatever rank, to participate in some organic way in every decision which directly affects their welfare or the part they play in industry'²; and

WHEREAS, Postmaster General Burleson has pursued a labor policy in direct conflict with this enunciation of principles, and in answer to President Gompers, of the American Federation of Labor, has characterized as 'silly' the right of collective bargaining,

WHEREAS, Mr. Burleson has ruthlessly invaded the rights of the employes and has interfered in defiance of law with the proper functioning of their organizations; and has not only refused to recognize the accredited representatives, but has also sought to have repealed the employes' constitutional right of direct petition to Congress,

WHEREAS, This labor policy—a policy fastened upon every governmental agency under Burleson's supervision—is in utter defiance of the wishes of the people and in complete opposition to the expressed words of President Wilson; and

WHEREAS, Burleson's archaic and autocratic attitude has resulted in a demoralized service, discontented and resentful employes, confused and choked industrial processes, and a people wrathful and indignant at a long series of administrative blunders; therefore, be it

RESOLVED, That the American Federation of Labor in convention assembled, speaking directly for four millions organized wage-earners and firm in the belief that this reflects the sentiments of the vast majority of the American people, request President Wilson to remove Postmaster General Burleson from office."

The above subject matter is thus submitted to you for your consideration and, I trust, favorable action.

Respectfully yours, Saml. Gompers.

TLS (WP, DLC).
[1] See S. Gompers to WW, April 23, 1919, Vol. 58.
[2] The quotation is from Wilson's special message to Congress of May 20, 1919, printed at that date in Vol. 59.

From Stephen Samuel Wise

Dear Mr. President: Lake Placid, N.Y. July 1, 1919

My heart rejoices in the victory of justice which you have won for our country, the *Pax Americana* which is to bless the whole world. You have met every hope of those, who see, that, in urging the country to accept and to trust in your leadership, they builded better than they knew.

I ought to see you soon, just as soon as you can send for me. I must tell you about the trip thru the country for the League with Messrs. Taft and Lowell, and what I learned of doubts to be resolved. Again, it is very important that a statement be given out by a friend in order to show how generously and effectively you have furthered the interests of the Jewish people the world over, more especially in view of certain misunderstandings that obtain. May not that friend be I to and thru whom you have always spoken *re* questions Jewish. Finally, I ought to have an early opportunity to discuss the Polish situation with you, in order to remove the difficulty that has been created for Gibson.[1] I am,

Faithfully yours, Stephen Wise

Seeing that I am twenty hours from Washington, I presume that I will have a telegram regarding such appointment as you may be good enough to make.

ALS (WP, DLC).
[1] Louis Marshall, in a lengthy interview given to Charles Albert Selden of the *New York Times* in Paris on June 14, 1919, had attacked the reports of Hugh Simons Gibson, United States Minister to Poland, to the State Department from Warsaw to the effect that there had been no recent anti-Jewish pogroms in Poland. Gibson's reports are printed in *FR 1919*, II, 750-69. Marshall rehearsed many reports of anti-Jewish atroci-

ties in Poland and cited statements by Polish leaders such as President Pilsudski, Premier Paderewski, and General Haller condemning such atrocities as clear evidence that they had in fact occurred, despite Gibson's professed ignorance of them. *New York Times*, June 17, 1919. Colonel House noted in his Diary on June 25, 1919, that, in a meeting with Gibson in Paris on the previous day, Felix Frankfurter had "had the temerity to tell Gibson that the Jews had almost determined to keep him, Gibson, from being confirmed by the Senate because of what he termed, his anti-Jewish feeling." If there was in fact an organized movement to prevent Gibson's confirmation, it did not get very far. He was confirmed by the Senate as Minister to Poland on June 26, 1919. *Cong. Record*, 66th Cong., 1st sess., p. 1823.

From the Diary of Vance Criswell McCormick

July 1-2-3 (Tuesday, Wednesday and Thursday) [1919]

Bernie[1] and I lunched with the President Tuesday and nearly every day we meet him on the deck and have interesting chats. One day we discussed with him Dr. Taussig's[2] theory that all the railroads, public utilities and hard coal mines should be nationalized in the near future as Taussig thought we could not escape it. The President said he also felt that the necessities of life, like water, electricity and railroads, which are as much a part of our national life as air for our lungs, would ultimately bring about governmental ownership or control and he thought the time was soon ripe for a well worked out scheme. I suggested it might come and was really upon us because the Government now attempts to fix the price at which the railroads sell their commodity and also attempts to fix the price of labor which produces the commodity but with the reaction that was now on at home it would certainly be the wrong time to advocate it.

[1] That is, Baruch.
[2] That is, Frank William Taussig.

From Newton Diehl Baker

Dear Mr. President: Washington. July 1, 1919.

I hand you herewith a printed statement concerning the treatment of conscientious objectors in the Army,[1] in which is embodied all of the orders and data on that subject. You will find, also, a comparison of the British experience with our own, which I think I may say indicates a very much higher degree of success attending our policy, although, of course, we were aided at the outset by our knowledge of the British experience.

All told, the British had 6,135 men who resisted the military service acts, and of this number 5, 596 were imprisoned after trial by court martial. Our court martials amounted altogether to 504, although a study of the records of the Provost Marshal General's Office seems to show that about 4,000 men with certificates of religious objection from their draft boards were inducted into the service and there presented their certificates, while about 16,000 men so certified, on being brought into the service abandoned their claims for noncombatant service and entered the combatant branch. In other words, the policy of treating these men considerately when they were first brought into the military machine enabled the vast majority of them to acquire a broader point of view and so to fit themselves without resistance into the Army; while of the 4,000 who actually presented such claims, the great majority accepted noncombatant service, leaving only about 12 per cent. of them, or something over 500, to be dealt with by court martial.

Even of this number of 504, a substantial group came from camps where it would appear that they had not been considerately or sympathetically treated and, for one reason or another, not offered the opportunity of noncombatant service, so that a number of them were court-martialed who, upon later study, it appears clear would have been saved from that had a uniform course been consistently followed.

From the beginning I realized that your desire, with which I had the fullest sympathy, was to protect from avoidable hardship and from all cruel and brutal treatment these men who found themselves in conflict with the law requiring military service. I was particularly anxious, too, if it were possible, to come to an informed conclusion as to those who were sincerely opposed to war, whether upon formal religious grounds or for other reasons, and to separate those out who were merely opposed to this war or who had enemy sympathies which led them to obstruct our military preparation for the purpose of weakening the Nation in the contest. I, therefore, appointed Judge Julian Mack of Chicago, Dean Harlan F. Stone of Columbia University,[2] and Major Walter G. Kellogg[3] of the Office of the Judge Advocate General, a Commission to review the records of trials and personally examine each of the conscientious objectors in prison. Their recommendations to me from time to time have been followed. In the meantime, the Clemency Board in the Office of the Judge Advocate General by its operations has brought about the discharge of a number of these men, and there now remain in prison 191 so-called conscientious objectors who are classified into some sixteen groups as indicative of the origin of their resistance to the law, some of them being purely religious objectors of the Seventh-Day Adventist type, some political absolutists, and others technical deserters and agitators.

A careful examination of the remaining prisoners and their records divides them into three groups, as follows: First, those adjudged sincere by Judge Mack and Dean Stone, and whose con-

1)[4]

duct during confinement has been satisfactory. In this group there are 78 men.

2) In the second group are those who have been court-martialed for refusal to obey military orders, and whose conduct in confinement has been satisfactory, but who were not certified as sincere in their objection by the Mack-Stone-Board. In this group there are in all 36 men.

3) The third group, consisting of 84 men, are those whose conduct in confinement has been unsatisfactory, who have been through-out the whole controversy agitators and trouble-makers, and who have sought by propaganda and every form of breach of prison dis-cipline to stir up riots in the Disciplinary Barracks and proclaim their hostility to the Government and even their sympathy with its enemies.

I believe that the time has now come to quite definitely dispose of this whole subject,5 and my recommendation is that the first group be immediately discharged; that after one month shall have elapsed the entire second group be discharged; and that at the end of six months the third group be made eligible to parole so that some control can be exercised over their subsequent conduct.

I do not want to burden your mind with the details of this ques-tion, but I know of your interest in it and of your general desire to exercise as wide an amnesty as possible, and I therefore lay these facts before you, hoping that I can have at your convenience an indication of your general wish in regard to the matter.

Respectfully yours,   Newton D. Baker

TLS (WP, DLC).
¹ STATEMENT CONCERNING THE TREATMENT OF CONSCIENTIOUS OBJECTORS IN THE ARMY; *Prepared and published by direction of the Secretary of War, June 18, 1919* (Washington, 1919), printed pamphlet in WP, DLC.
² That is, Harlan Fiske Stone, at this time Dean of the Columbia University School of Law.
³ Walter Guest Kellogg. Kellogg, a prominent New York lawyer, was chairman of the Board of Inquiry that Baker appointed in August 1918 to investigate and report on con-scientious objectors. For his extended treatment of this subject, see Walter G. Kellogg, *The Conscientious Objector, Introduction by Newton D. Baker* (New York, 1919); re-printed, with a new introduction by John Whiteclay Chambers II, by Garland Publish-ing, Inc., New York, 1972.
⁴ Numbering WWhw.
⁵ Wilson marked a vertical line on the left-hand margin to the end of this sentence and wrote in shorthand: "recommendations." For whatever reason, the shorthand was very badly written.

From Alexander Mitchell Palmer

[The White House, July 1, 1919]

#227. The Atty Genl sends following quote

The impression seems to have gone out that the war time pro-hibition law will expire when the President proclaims demobilization has been accomplished. The war time prohibition law, under its terms, remains in force "until the conclusion of the present war and thereafter until the termination of demobilization, the date of which shall be determined and proclaimed by the President of the United States."

It should be borne in mind that by this language the Congress contemplated that the termination of demobilization could only come after the conclusion of the present war. The President therefore should not proclaim the termination of demobilization until after he has proclaimed the conclusion of the present war. unquote

Tumulty.

T telegram (WP, DLC).

From Florence Haskell Corliss Lamont

United States Ship George Washington

Dear Mr. President,   [c. July 1, 1919]

How lovely of you to write me such a charming letter![1] And to send me Mrs. Wilson's congratulations as well as your own. It made memorable and gay what, owing to my weight of years, would otherwise have been a very mournful occasion!

With warmest thanks to you both,   Florence Lamont

ALS (WP, DLC).
    [1] She celebrated her forty-sixth birthday on July 1, 1919.

From the Diary of Dr. Grayson

Wednesday, July 2, 1919.

The President slept until 11:00 o'clock, and after he arose worked for a short time on the re-draft of his Message. He had as luncheon guests Mr. Charles T. Thompson of the Associated Press, and Mr. Lowell Mellett of the United Press. The President was very much interested in Mr. Thompson, who had three sons in the service.[1] One of them is a graduate of Annapolis, and the other a graduate of West Point. Thompson had been four years acting as a war correspondent, having been on all fronts. He did splendid work with the Italian Army and also was one of the few men from the United States who was able to please the French with his newspaper stories. Thompson told the President a number of personal incidents and experiences and gave him the viewpoint which he (the President) had himself acquired. The President was much interested in what Mr. Thompson had to say but was more interested in the fact that three of his sons had participated actively in the war. The President utilized this to call attention to the fact that the war had itself been a great force for democracy, inasmuch as it had brought home to all of the people in the United States exactly what the war itself meant in its original effort on the part of Germany to overwhelm the world, and the alignment of the nations which prevented this. After Thompson and Mellett left the President they took occasion to declare that their viewpoint concerning him had been very much changed. They said it was hard to realize how democratic he really was, especially when a person had not come into contact with him and found the man as he really was.

The dinner guest was Captain McCauley of the George Washington. The President attended the movies after dinner.

Today after luncheon the President said to me: "I will have to spend a little while on my message this afternoon. I am wondering whether I should address this message to the Senate alone or to a Joint Session of the Senate and House of Representatives. What do you think would be advisable?" I said: "You have been in the habit of addressing both Houses and I would do so in this case." The President replied that he was inclined to the belief that in this instance he would be compelled to address the Senate alone. He finally decided inasmuch as it concerned the Treaty that he would ask Secretary Tumulty for an opinion on this subject before making a final decision.

[1] The only one of Thompson's three sons who can be named is Frederick A. Thompson. He was probably the Frederick Arthur Thompson listed as an ensign in the Naval Reserve Flying Corps in the *Register of the Commissioned and Warrant Officers of the United States Navy . . . January 1, 1918* (Washington, 1918), p. 366. However, this Thompson was not a graduate of the United States Naval Academy.

From the Diary of Edith Benham

July 2, 1919

The P. is busy writing his message to Congress, and getting some rest. Mrs. W. hauls him out every day to walk, which he despises but does meekly. He spoke today with real regret of leaving old Clemenceau, of whom he is very fond despite his shiftiness, which he feels is more due to his advisers, for he says the old man's ideas are all straight, and if left alone he would be honest.

Two of the newspaper correspondents came to luncheon today— Mellett of the United Press, and Thompson of the Associated Press. Mellett looks a mere lad, and one has to look at the gray hair on his temples to realize he is old enough to hold such a responsible position. Conversation turned on the violent attacks made on the P. by Americans living abroad during the war, and the fact that we didn't go into the war sooner. The P. said he didn't go into the war until he was sure he had the country behind him, that he felt he could not have gone one minute sooner, for the American people were not ready. I asked him later if he was like so many, ready ahead, and he said, "No, I was like the majority of my countrymen and followed with them." He said he used to ask the members of the Cabinet at the meetings every week what they heard, and they said the Americans would follow him, and he said, "I couldn't have them follow, they had to go into it with a whoop."

To Robert Lansing

U.S.S. George Washington, 2 July, 1919.

The greatest caution should be exercised in any attempt to readjust the boundaries of Austria along ethnographical lines.[1] There is a certain district in Bohemia,[2] for example, which is undoubtedly predominantly German in population but which lies within the undoubted historic boundaries of Bohemia and constitutes an integral part of her industrial life. In such circumstances ethnographical lines cannot be drawn without the greatest injustice and injury. So far as they can be re-drawn along ethnographical lines without such injury, I fully agree that they should be.

Woodrow Wilson

T telegram (WP, DLC).
  [1] Wilson was replying to RL to WW, June 30, 1919.
  [2] That is, the Sudetenland.

From Joseph Patrick Tumulty

The White House, 2 July 1919.

Number 228. Tentative programme arranged by Mr. McAdoo and Committee provides for battleship PENNSYLVANIA and part of Atlantic Fleet which is in New York Harbor at this time, to meet you with Committee and some members of the Cabinet aboard; programme further provides for your leaving GEORGE WASHINGTON at the Battery where an escort from Army and Navy will conduct you up Fifth Avenue to Carnegie Hall. At Carnegie Hall short speeches of welcome will be made by Governor and Mayor[1] and a brief speech by you in reply expressing your pleasure, etc.

Tumulty.

T telegram (WP, DLC).
  [1] That is, Gov. Alfred E. Smith and Mayor John F. Hylan.

Joseph Patrick Tumulty to Cary Travers Grayson[1]

The White House, 2 July 1919.

Following are names and addresses of senators opposing League unless reservations are adopted COLON

William E. Borah—Boise, Idaho;
Frank B. Brandegee—New London, Conn;
Albert B. Cummins—Des Moines, Iowa;
Charles Curtis—Topeka, Kansas;
Albert B. Fall—Three Rivers, New Mexico;
Joseph I. France—Port Deposit, Maryland;
Joseph S. Frelinghuysen—Raritan, N.J.;
Frederick Hale—Portland, Maine;
Warren G. Harding—Marion, Ohio;
Hiram W. Johnson—San Francisco, Calif;
Frank B. Kellogg—St. Paul, Minn;
Philander C. Knox—Pittsburgh, Penna;
Robert M. La Follette—Madison, Wis;
Medill McCormick—Chicago, Ills;
Henry Cabot Lodge—Nahant, Mass;
George H. Moses—Concord, New Hampshire;
Knute Nelson—Alexandria, Minn;
Henry S. New, Indianapolis, Ind;
Boies Penrose—Philadelphia, Pa;
Miles Poindexter—Spokane, Washn;
Senator [Lawrence Cowle] Phipps—Denver, Colo;
Lawrence Y. Sherman—Springfield, Ills;
Truman H. Newberry—Detroit, Mich;
James A. Reed—Kansas City, Mo;
Reed Smoot—Provo, Utah;
Selden P. Spencer—St. Louis, Mo;
Thomas Sterling—Vermillion, S.D.;
Senator [Arthur] Capper—Topeka, Kans;
Charles E. Townsend—Jackson, Mich;
James W. Wadsworth, jr.,—Groveland, N.Y.;
Francis E. Warren—Cheyenne, Wyoming;
James E. Watson—Rushville, Indiana.

Borah, Brandegee, Reed, Johnson, Knox, La Follette unreservedly opposed. Following are names of particularly virulent anti-news-papers COLON

Wm. R. Hearst, New York American;
Hearst's organs throughout country;
Ogden Reid, New York Tribune;
Frank Munsey, New York Sun;

Robert McCormick, Chicago Tribune;

Nelson Estate, Kansas City Star;

Indianapolis News practically in opposition;

George Harvey's Magazine;

Detroit Free Press;

New Republic, edited by Walter Lippmann;

Philadelphia North American, edited by [Edwin Augustus] Van Valkenburg;

The Nation, edited by Oswald Villard;

Ohio State Journal, edited by Wolff Bros.;

San Francisco Chronicle;

Detroit Journal;

New York Herald;

Providence Journal, edited by John Rathom.

Following are names of League opponents not in the Senate co-LON

George Wharton Pepper, Philadelphia, Pa;

James M. Beck;

Henry A. Wise Wood;

Ex-Senator [Albert J.] Beveridge;

Elihu Root;

George Harvey.   Tumulty.

T telegram (J. P. Tumulty Papers, DLC).

¹ This telegram was sent in response to C. T. Grayson to JPT, July 2, 1919, T telegram (J. P. Tumulty Papers, DLC): "President asks you to send by code names and home addresses of Senators opposing League of Nations; also name and owner of any particularly virulent anti-newspaper; also name and address of any particularly influential League of Nations opponents not in the Senate."

Charles William Eliot to Joseph Patrick Tumulty

Dear Mr. Tumulty: Asticou, Maine 2 July 1919

Can you bring to the President's attention immediately on his landing the following suggestions which I have heard mentioned among his supporters in this part of the country during the last month?

1. That he cancel his proposed tour of public speaking, and substitute another letter addressed to his fellow-countrymen.

2. That, if he maintains the proposed tour, he speak to the Senate before speaking to anybody else in a public way.

3. That he invariably describe the influence of the American delegates at the Peace Conference as the influence of America and its institutions.

4. That he announce within a few days of his arrival in this

country that he shall not under any circumstances be a candidate for re-election to the Presidency, on the ground that he has always been opposed to a third consecutive term in the Presidential office, and sees no present emergency which would justify a departure from that policy.

I dare say that President Wilson already has these four points firmly in mind; but not being sure of it, I venture to bring them to your attention.   Sincerely yours   Charles W. Eliot[1]

TLS (WP, DLC).
[1] "Dear Tumulty: There is a lot of sense in this letter. The President." TL (WP, DLC).

From the Diary of Dr. Grayson

Thursday, July 3, 1919.

The President rested late this morning. He and Mrs. Wilson took a morning walk on the deck, spending quite a little while in the sunshine.

The luncheon guests today were Mr. Bernard M. Baruch and Mr. Vance McCormick. Among the questions touched on at luncheon were the labor problems, the legal profession and the composition of the Supreme Court. Reference was also had to college life, particular stress being laid on athletics. McCormick was captain of the Yale foot-ball team at the time when Phil King of Washington[1] was a star player on the Princeton team. McCormick spoke of the suspicions which arise in the minds of college students. The President then related an incident of Phil King's suspicion about one of the Princeton players.[2] The player had stomach trouble and went to New York to consult Dr. Delafield (a Yale graduate),[3] who was a stomach specialist. The Doctor gave the Princeton player a prescription. It was just before an important match game between Princeton and Yale. When the Princeton player—I think Lee was his name—returned to Princeton with the prescription, Phil King thought it was his duty to visé the prescription, and the only thing he could read in it was "strychnine." Whereupon, he said, "Look here, Delafield is a Yale man, and he may be tampering with our player."

The conversation turned to individuals with whom the President and his associates had conferred with in Paris. It centered chiefly upon Premier Clemenceau, especially concerning his eccentricities and peculiarities. It was remarked how often the old man would sit in the meetings and pretend to be asleep. The President said, however, that he was wide awake whenever anything was suggested in the conference that was not in the interest of France.

He was not hard to wake up then. The President said: "Did you ever notice how he yawns at our meetings? Every now and then he would yawn as if he could not keep awake." I noticed the other night, at the dinner given by the President of the French Republic, that Clemenceau would frequently yawn. He did not show any signs of being sleepy, for I noticed that he was very attentive to the ladies who were seated on each side of him. The President said that it was most amusing to see how he would come into the meetings some mornings apparently really mad and all upset. He would blow up and go up to the ceiling. They finally decided to let him remain up at the ceiling until all his gas had escaped and he would then come down and join in the conversation as if nothing had occurred. The President said: "While he has many lovable qualities, at times he is brutally frank in his statements. For instance, Baron Sonnino, the day after the Orlando government failed, said to the Big Four: 'I will probably not be with you many more days, as I understand I will be succeeded by Tittoni.' Whereupon Clemenceau spoke out and said to Sonnino: 'You are a bad man but your successor is worse.' He spoke this in a tone and manner no one knew whether he was joking or whether he was serious." The President continued: "On another occasion Hymans, the Prime Minister of Belgium, said: 'I wish there was something I could do for Belgium.' Clemenceau said: 'The best thing you can do for Belgium is to die or resign.' "

Clemenceau at one time said that the only reason he had his assistants and experts around him was to show them that they had a hand in things; that they were not completely ignored. He said most of them were not worth a cent. The President remarked that Clemenceau's mind seemed to vary considerably. There were days when his mind appeared old, and then he would not make a mental move without calling for his experts. The next two or three weeks he would not have one of them around him, and he would simply say that they were no good. However, the ones he seemed to depend upon mostly were Loucheur and Tardieu.

The President had Mr. and Mrs. Thomas W. Lamont as dinner guests.

In connection with a newspaper report from New York received during the day that a certain newspaper misstated the proposition,[4] the following reply was made:

"There is no alliance. We make specific promises to France on condition that England makes the same promise, but there is no alliance between Great Britain and America in the arrangement.

"There is only a single engagement and that is that we will not wait for the concerted action of other countries under the

League of Nations, but will come immediately to France's assistance if Germany makes any unprovoked movement of military aggression against her."[5]

[1] Philip King, Princeton 1893.
[2] Langdon Lea, Princeton 1896.
[3] Francis Delafield, Yale 1860; M.D., Columbia 1863. Wilson had consulted Dr. Delafield in the autumn of 1895. See Edwin A. Weinstein, *Woodrow Wilson: A Medical and Psychological Biography* (Princeton, N. J., 1981), p. 126.
[4] A report of the Franco-American Treaty of Guarantee in the *Chicago Daily Tribune*, July 3, 1919, referred to that treaty as "the French-American alliance." A report by Herbert Bayard Swope in the New York *World*, July 3, 1919, said that Arthur Balfour had referred to the Anglo-French and Franco-American treaties as "a tripartite alliance."
The French Foreign Ministry had printed several hundred copies of the Franco-American treaty, for confidential distribution, to the members of the Chamber of Deputies and Senate among others, and brief summaries of the treaty began to appear in the Paris newspapers. To quiet speculation, the Foreign Ministry issued the text of the treaty to the press on July 3. It was published, e.g., by the *New York Times* and New York *World* on July 4, 1919.
[5] Perhaps this statement, which was almost certainly written by Wilson, was sent by wireless and not received. To the Editors' knowledge, it was not printed in any newspaper.

To Joseph Patrick Tumulty

[*U.S.S. George Washington*, July 3, 1919]

Cannot accept the New York programme suggested. Naval escort all right of course but I will proceed to the Hoboken dock on the George Washington. Hope Baker and Daniels will meet me there. Will cross on ferry to 23rd St. where I will expect the McAdoo Committee to meet me. Will proceed from ferry to Carnegie Hall and from there to Pennsylvania station. Are you sure there will be no embarrassment in the make-up of the New York Committee? Please see that automobiles are ready at Hoboken landing. Do not permit any modification or enlargement of this.

Woodrow Wilson[1]

WWhw telegram (C. L. Swem Coll., NjP).
[1] Wilson seems to have written the body of this message with his left hand. His signature, which is clearly right-handed, is a cramped scrawl—a striking contrast to the script of the text.

Two Telegrams from Joseph Patrick Tumulty

The White House, July 3, 1919.

#229. Please advise me as soon as possible by wireless if you will address Senate or Joint Session so that arrangements may be made at Capitol.

Dr. Anna Howard Shaw, suffragist leader, died yesterday. She had just undertaken strenuous speaking tour in behalf of League of Nations. It would be gracious thing if you could send word to Mrs. Catt asking her to convey expressions of sympathy to Dr. Shaw's family and members of National Woman's Suffrage Association.   Tumulty.

The White House, July 3, 1919.

#230. Following your direction will arrange program as follows:

Dock Hoboken about 2:40 p.m. Tuesday, motor slowly to 23rd Street Ferry passing through lines of school children and citizens of Hoboken. Met at 23rd Street by New York Committee, motor to Carnegie Hall, brief address, motor to Pennsylvania Station. Leave New York five p.m. Dine on train, arrive Washington 10 p.m. Transfer of train from pier at Hoboken to Pennsylvania Station will require two hours. Have therefore suggested 5 p.m. as leaving time. Please let me know if this meets your approval.

Tumulty.

T telegrams (WP, DLC).

From Samuel Gompers

Washington, D.C. July 3, 1919.

It is hoped you will find it possible to have a committee present to you in Washington a most constructive plan endorsed by the American Federation of Labor regarding the railroads[1] before you make any further official utterance upon that subject.

Samuel Gompers

T telegram (WP, DLC).
[1] That is, the Plumb plan, about which see n. 2 to the Enclosure printed with W. D. Hines to WW, Feb. 24, 1919, Vol. 55, and the index references to it in Vol. 62.

From the Diary of Dr. Grayson

Friday, July 4, 1919.

The President worked on his message after he rose today and completed his draft of the document. There were special Fourth of July games on the ship, and on the program was an address by the President after luncheon.

The luncheon guests were Norman Davis and Dr. Taussig of the Tariff Commission. The President told a number of stories, and they discussed at length socialism. The conversation was varied and pleasant.

It had originally been arranged that the President should make an address from the after part of B deck to the soldiers and members of the crew. The arrangement included the rigging up of a wireless telephone, which was to have taken in the escorting destroyers and the Battleship Oklahoma. However, when the alignment was made up the wires were carried through as far as the main switchboard, and it was stated that the President would be able to talk to Washington via New Brunswick. However, the President's intention was to talk to the soldiers and the sailors, and he felt very little concerned for the audience that had been embarrassed at Washington. The result was that he notified me at luncheon that he did not intend to make any address into any megaphone, but that he intended going out on the after hatch on C Deck and talk directly to the soldiers and members of the crew who would be assembled there. This program was carried out in full. His address was devoted to an explanation of what in his viewpoint the "new independence" which the war had forced upon the United States really meant.

After returning to his state-room the President rested for a short time, and I then called his attention to the fact that in his address he had referred exclusively to the Army. He made no comment on this fact but stated that he would accompany Ambassador Jusserand to the theatre on D Deck, where the French diplomat was to talk to members of the crew of the George Washington. When the President started down he said that he had no intention of making any speech, but after he got there the inspiration seized him and he paid a wonderful tribute to the work of the Navy in ferrying the American Army across to France and making it possible for them to be there in sufficient numbers to swing the tide of battle and really to "win the war."[1]

After dinner, at which there were no guests, the President and Mrs. Wilson attended the movies.

[1] There is no transcript of this speech.

An Address to His Fellow Passengers

On board George Washington, Fourth of July, 1919.

Fellow countrymen: It is very delightful to find myself here and in this company. I know a great many of you have been homesick on the other side of the water, but I do not believe a man among you has been as homesick as I have. It is with profound delight that I find myself bound westward again for the country we all love and are trying to serve. And when I was asked to make a speech and sat down and tried to think out what I should say, I found that the suggestions of this Fourth of July crowded into my mind in such a way that they could not be set in order, and I doubt if I can find expression to them. Because this Fourth of July has a significance that no preceding Fourth of July ever had in it, not even the first. I think that we can look back upon the history of the years that separate us from that first Fourth of July with very great satisfaction, because we have kept the vision in America, we have kept the promise to ourselves that we would maintain a regime of liberty and of constitutional government. We have made errors of judgment, we have committed errors of action, but we have always tried to correct the errors when we have made them. We have always tried to get straight in the road again for that goal for which we set out in those famous days when America was made as a government. So there has always been abundant justification for what was not self-glorification, but self-gratulation in our Fourth of July celebrations. We have successfully maintained the liberties of a great nation. The past is secure, and the past is glorious; and in the present the Fourth of July has taken on a new significance.

We told our fellow men throughout the world when we set up the free state of America that we wanted to serve liberty everywhere and be the friends of men in every part of the world who wanted to throw off the unjust shackles of arbitrary government. Now we have kept our pledge to humanity as well as our pledge to ourselves, for we have thrown everything that we possessed—all the gifts that nature had showered upon us and our own lives—into the scales to show that we meant to be the servants of humanity and of free men everywhere.

America did not at first see the full meaning of the war that has just ended. At first it looked like a natural raking out of the pent-up jealousies and rivalries of the complicated politics of Europe. Nobody who really knew anything about history supposed that Germany could build up a great military machine like she did and not refrain from using it. They were constantly talking about it as a guarantee of peace, but every man in his senses knew that it was a threat of war, and the threat was finally fulfilled and the war began. We, at the distance of America, looked on at first without a full comprehension of what the plot was getting into, and then at last we realized that there was here nothing less than a threat against the freedom of free men everywhere.

Then America went in, and if it had not been for America the war would not have been won. My heart swells with a pride that I cannot express when I think of the men who crossed the seas from America to fight on those battlefields. I was proud of them when I could not see them, and, now that I have mixed with them and seen them, I am prouder of them still. For they are men to the core, and I am glad to have had Europe see this specimen of our manhood. I am proud to know how the men who performed the least conspicuous services and the humblest services performed them just as well as the men who performed the conspicuous services and the most complicated and difficult. I will not say that the men were worthy of their officers. I will say that the officers were worthy of their men. They sprang out of the ranks, they were like the ranks, and all—rank and file—were specimens of America.

And you know what has happened. Having sampled America that way, Europe believes in and trusts America. Is not that your own personal experience and observation? In all the councils at Paris, whenever they wanted to send soldiers anywhere and not have the people jealous of their presence or fear the consequences of their presence, they suggested that we should send Americans there, because they knew that everywhere in Europe we were believed to be the friends of the countries where we sent garrisons and where we sent forces of supervision. We were welcome. Am I not, therefore, justified in saying that we have fulfilled our pledge to humanity? We have proved that we were the champions of liberty throughout the world, that we did not wish to keep it as a selfish and private possession of our own, but wanted to share it with men everywhere and of every kind.

When you look forward to the future, do you not see what a compulsion that puts upon us? You cannot earn a reputation like that and then not live up to it. You cannot reach a standard like that and then let it down by never so little. Every man of us has to live up to it. The welcome that was given to our arms and the cheers that received us are the compulsion that is now put upon us to continue to be worthy of that welcome and of those cheers. We must continue to put America at the service of mankind. Not for any profit we shall get out of it, not for any private benefit we shall reap from it, but because we believe in the right and mean to serve it wherever we have a chance to serve it.

I was thinking today that a new freedom has come to the peoples of the world out of this war. It has no date. It has no Fourth of July. There has nowhere been written a Declaration of Independence. The only date I can think of for it is the eleventh of last November, when the Central Powers admitted they were beaten and accepted an armistice. From that time they knew they had to submit to the terms of liberty, and perhaps some of these days we shall date the freedom of the peoples from the eleventh of November 1918. And yet if that be not the date of it, it interests my thought to think that,

as it had no date for beginning, we should see to it that it has no
date for ending; that as it began without term, it should end without term, and that in every council we enter into, in every force we
contribute to, we shall make it a condition that the liberty of men
throughout the world shall be served and that America shall continue to redeem her pledge to humanity and to mankind.

Why, America is made up of mankind. We do not come from any
common stock. We do not come from any single nation. The characteristic of America is that it is made up of the best contributed
out of all nations. Sometimes, when I am in the presence of an
American citizen who was an immigrant to America, I think that
he has a certain advantage over me. I did not choose to be an
American, but he did. I was born to it. I hope if I had not been, I
would have had sense enough to choose it. But the men who came
afterwards deliberately chose to be Americans. They came out of
other countries and said, "We cast in our lot with you, we believe
in you, and will live with you."

A country made up like that ought to understand other nations.
It ought to know how to fraternize with and assist them. It is already the friend of mankind, because it is made up out of all people, and it ought to redeem its lineage. It ought to show that it is
playing for no private hand. It ought to show that it is trying to
serve all the stocks of mankind from which it itself is bred. And
more than that, my fellow countrymen, we ought to continue to
prove that we know what freedom is.

Freedom is not a mere sentiment. We all feel the weakness of
mere sentiment. If a man professes to be fine, we always wait for
him to show it. We do not take his word for it. If he professes fine
motives, we expect him thereafter to show that he is acting upon
fine motives. And the kind of freedom that America has always represented is a freedom expressing itself in fact. It is not the profession of principles merely, but the redemption of those principles,
making good on those principles and knowing how to make good
on those principles.

When I have thought of liberty, I have sometimes thought how
we deceive ourselves in the way we talked about it. Some people
talk as if liberty meant the right to do anything you please. Well, in
some sense you have that right. You have the right to jump overboard, but if you do, this is what will happen: nature will say, "You
fool, didn't you know the consequences? Didn't you know that
water will drown you?" You can jump off the top of the mast, but
when you get down your liberty will be lost, and you will have lost
it because if it was not an accident you made a fool of yourself. The
sailor, when he is sailing a ship, talks about her running free in the

wind. Does he mean that she is resisting the wind? Throw her up into the wind and see the canvas shake, see her stand still, "caught in irons," as the sailor says. But let her fall off; she is free. Free, why? Because she is obeying the laws of nature, and she is a slave until she does. And no man is free who does not obey the laws of freedom. The laws of freedom are these: accommodate your interests to other people's interests, that you shall not insist on standing in the light of other people, but that you shall make a member of a team of yourself and nothing more or less, and that the interests of the team shall take precedence in everything that you do to your interest as an individual. That is freedom, and men who live under autocratic governments are not free because the autocrat arranges the government to suit himself. The minute he arranges it to suit his subjects, then his subjects are free.

But if I disobey the laws of freedom, if I infringe on the rights of others, then I presently find myself deprived of my freedom. I am clapped in jail, it may be, and if the jailor is a philosopher, he will say, "You brought it upon yourself, my dear fellow. You were free to do right, but you were not free to do wrong. Now what I blame you for is not so much for your malice as for your ignorance." One reason why America has been free, I take leave to say, is that America has been intelligent enough to be free. It takes a lot of intelligence to be free. Stupid people do not know how, and we all go to the school of intelligence that comes out of the discipline of our self-chosen institutions. That is what makes you free, and my confident ambition for the United States is that she will know in the future how to make each Fourth of July as it comes grow more distinguished and more glorious than its predecessor, by showing that she, at any rate, understands the laws of freedom by understanding the laws of service, and that mankind may always confidently look to her as a friend, as a cooperator, as one who will stand shoulder to shoulder with free men everywhere to assert the right. That is what I meant at the outset of these few remarks by saying that the suggestions of this Fourth of July crowd too thick and fast to be set in order. This is the most tremendous Fourth of July that men ever imagined, for we have opened its franchise to all the world.[1]

T MS (WP, DLC).
[1] There is a WWT outline, dated July 4, 1919, of this address in WP, DLC.

To Joseph Patrick Tumulty

U.S.S. GEORGE WASHINGTON, July 4, 1919.

My address in Washington will be in effect a report on the Conference, and it was my idea that it would be appropriate to make it to a joint session of two Houses, * * * (noon?) Thursday, in order to give time for printing after I reach Washington. I will address it to the Senate alone if you think best, notwithstanding my strong preference for a joint session.

Please let me have your advice in this matter before making final arrangements.   Woodrow Wilson.

T telegram (J. P. Tumulty Papers, DLC).

From the Diary of Ray Stannard Baker

At Sea July 4th [1919].

Wilson makes confidant of no one. No one gets his whole mind. Grayson is probably as near him as anyone, but Grayson gets the personal, physical side, certainly not [blank]

Wilson never does anything twice: does it right the first time.

Wilson lacks the essential trait of the executive, which is the courage to trust other people & to use other peoples' wits. He is the artistic type which wishes to perfect its own work.

From the Diary of Vance Criswell McCormick

July 4 (Friday) [1919]

This was a great day for sailors and passengers. The day was given up to deck sports and speeches. The racing, boom fight, boxing matches, etc., by the sailors and soldiers were a great success and the President's speech was most inspiring; standing on the deck in the midst of the sailors and soldiers, who covered every available space within sight, even up on the rigging and astride the booms. He made an excellent speech and later with Ambassador Jusserand spoke to the sailors in their hall on E deck.

The usual movies in the evening in the main dining hall. I can't see how the regular movie fan stands it every night. The President and Mrs. Wilson go every night as does the Captain. One interesting feature every evening at the movies is the singing by everyone of the popular airs, the words of which are thrown on the screen. The President and Mrs. Wilson enjoy this immensely.

John Foster Dulles to Bernard Mannes Baruch and Others

Paris July 4, 1919

2964 Will you please confidentially communicate the following from Dulles to Baruch, Davis, Lamont and McCormick who will arrive with the President.

"On the proposal of Clemenceau the Supreme Council has created an interim reparation commission to inaugurate in an informal manner the work of the permanent commission contemplated by the Treaty. The members of Interim Commission are Loucheur, Crespi, Peel, De Cartier and myself with Mori[1] designated by Japan to act when questions entitling Japan to representation are under consideration. The first meeting of the Interim Commission was held July third Loucheur being elected chairman. It was decided to look into the matter of securing permanent offices to be occupied by the Interim Commission when appointed. It was understood that the Interim Commission could assume no financial obligations, but Loucheur stated that if the Interim Commission approved of the selection of permanent offices and if it were necessary to act at once to secure them, the French Government would be prepared to do so entirely on its own risk. The Interim Commission also decided to establish at once a secretariat which might be taken over by the permanent commission.

The Supreme Council has authorized the carrying on of informal conversations with the Germans relative to reparations, which conversations have already been invited by the Germans. The interim reparation commission accordingly decided to confer with the Germans at Versailles, probably July 5th, to hear what the Germans might have to say and ascertain:

(A) The willingness of the Germans to supply labor to replace prisoners to be repatriated.

(B) The attitude of Germany toward the immediate restitution and reparation in kind required by the treaty and any suggestions of a practical nature the Germans might have to make relative to facilitating the performance of the treaty in this respect.

(C) The character of the proposals which the Germans intimate they are prepared to make relative to the restoration by Germany on a large scale of the devastated areas of France and Belgium.

(D) The requirements of the Germans themselves for minette ore.

You will appreciate from the foregoing that the reparation work is developing very rapidly and it becomes increasingly important that permanent United States representatives be here at the earliest possible moment. With the staff which is at present at Paris, and which is daily being depleted, it is impossible for me to deal adequately with the matters which are coming up for discussion and many of which are technical in character. Even were this not the case the present work should be handled by those who can be here permanently. Otherwise these latter will be at a great disadvantage and will find many of the most important questions of policy prejudged. We cannot well ask France and Belgium to defer consideration of these problems. Their interests are too great and their need is too pressing.

Very confidential. De Cartier has been offered the position of Belgian delegate on the permanent commission but tells me he hesitates to accept as he would like to be the first Belgian Ambassador to the United States."   American Mission

T telegram (SDR, RG 59, 763.72119/5521, DNA).
  ¹ Kengo Mori, Financial Agent of the Japanese embassies at London and Paris and adviser on economic and financial questions in the Japanese delegation.

From the Diary of Dr. Grayson

Saturday, July 5, 1919.

The President rested quite late and had no guests at luncheon. After luncheon he sent for me and told me that he wanted to confer with Messrs. Baruch, McCormick, Davis, Lamont and Dr. Taussig. I rounded them up and the President read his message to them and explained to them what his plans were. The President asked if there were any suggestions or criticisms to be made, but inasmuch as he had fully covered the ground none were forthcoming that were of a tangible nature.

After dinner the President attended the movies as usual.

From the Diary of Vance Criswell McCormick

July 5 (Saturday) [1919]

The President sent for Lamont, Davis, Baruch and me with Dr. Taussig to come to his room after lunch to read us his message to Congress to get our suggestions and criticisms. Mrs. Wilson, Miss Wilson and Grayson were also present in his stateroom.

We had few changes to suggest as it was an excellent general statement of the situation at Paris and the problems that confronted him. We raised the question as to the praise given his colleagues and developed from him a real feeling of friendship for his

colleagues whom he said privately were in accord with the principles we were fighting for but were hampered and restricted by
their own political conditions at home, due to the temper of their
people. He said he was surprised to find they had accepted the
Fourteen Points not for expediency only but because they believed
in them. He told us frankly of the Shantung settlement because it
was in his opinion most criticized and most difficult part of Treaty
to defend. He referred to the agreement made by France and England with Japan, binding them absolutely to the Shantung agreement. This he said Lloyd George criticized himself and said it had
been made by Asquith when Grey was sick, that the War Cabinet
was astounded when it was presented but had to accept it. He said
it only gave Japan an economic control, not political in any sense,
and by this settlement they kept Japan in the conference and made
her a party to the Allied policy toward China in all other respects
and by getting her in the League of Nations will maintain the open
door policy in China and make it possible to compel Japan to give
up an exclusive sphere of influence in that country, and you could
see he was far from satisfied but felt it was the best that could be
done under all the circumstances. He further stated Japan had
agreed with him verbally to pull out of Shantung but would not put
it in writing as it reflected on their good faith.

We all discussed the advisability of reading message to Congress
as a whole or to Senate alone. He said he had cabled to Tumulty to
get advice from friends in Senate on this point. He also told us he
was ready to make a tour of the country if necessary to speak for
the League of Nations and read us topics of his speeches.[1]

[1] This list does not seem to have survived.

From the Diary of Thomas William Lamont

July Saturday 5 1919

Pres. summoned us at 3 pm & read us his message to Congress
in presenting the Treaty. It was skilfully done—a report in the
large of his stewardship at Paris; of how the Treaty was worked
out. He started as a basis with the work of our Army & what it
stood for, paying it a fine tribute. "Our soldiers," he said, "were
terrible in battle—gentle out of it." All Europe looked to us, he said.
It became our business "to quiet the fears & realize the hopes etc."
Then he went on to show how the Treaty had to be built up in the
League of Nations etc.

We made various suggestions. FWT[1] made the best one that, in
showing the utilitarian and mechanical necessity of League of Nations he omitted any ideal reference to it as something to prevent

further wars. I pointed out that in speaking of the Covenant, he had described it as "a definite constitution." By this he gave a charge to the critics who had in mind the definite idea of a written, unchangeable constitution. W.W. made note & said he wd cover both these pts. NHD[2] said he thought some allusion shd be made to the Treaty not being a perfect one. We discussed that pt at considerable length. W.W. had covered it pretty well by pointing out the difficulties of getting together & the necessity of reconciling many divergent views. I said I would *not* apologize for Treaty, because such apology would give handle to his more dangerous opponents. The critics who called the Treaty unjust were not dangerous to ratification. The critics who tried to split the Covenant from the Treaty were the dangerous ones & we must not say to them that the Treaty was a poor, weak thing. This general view prevailed at the Conference.

We discussed at considerable length W.W.'s tributes to his colleagues—their "unfailing" sincerity & endeavor to do the right thing. W.W. said to be sure that was going pretty strong, but that he was actually convinced that on the whole the other three had made sincere efforts, in the face of many secret handicaps which they had. For instance, he said, when he first came over he had thought that they adopted the 14 Points, for sake of policy to end the war. But as he became acquainted w his colleagues he became convinced that they thoroughly believed themselves in the 14 Points.

They (L-G & Clemenceau) were to be sure badly handicapped by secret treaties etc. For instance take the Shantung settlement. 1st the Japs wd have kept out of the L of Nations unless there had been carried out for them the agreement that Eng. & France made with them early in the war that they should have what Germany had had in China. W.W. considered that the Shantung settlement was the severest compromise that we had been obliged to make & he made it only after saying again & again to the Japs that the settlement must not mean any exploitation of China by Japan or the closing of the open door. He was in hopes that all special spheres of influence in China could be abandoned after a while.

As to these secret handicaps, W.W. remarked that the other premiers were astonishingly frank in describing their difficulties. For instance as to the Treaty of London L-G said it wd never have been executed if Grey had been on his feet. But Asquith did it all by himself & then brought it in to the Cabinet as *un fait accompli*. When they read it the whole British cabinet threw up their hands in despair. But Asquith said that Italy had named her price & he had had to pay it. L-G was bitter against Asquith for giving way.

FWT asked the Pres't about Southern Tyrol wh. was not Italian

& wh. should not have gone to Italy. W.W. said frankly I made a mistake there. I wasn't familiar with the map. They told me it was one of the provisions of the Treaty of London that was O.K. I accepted & O.K.'d it without study & when I found out my mistake the Italian plot was already so thick that I felt I could not back track.

The President read us a series of titles for speeches on the Covenant that he intended to make if forced to fight for the Covenant. One title struck me particularly: "I don't want to wait & enter the League in company w. Germany: I want to enter now"

Hw bound diary (T. W. Lamont Papers, MH-BA).
  [1] That is, Frank W. Taussig.
  [2] That is, Norman H. Davis.

Two Telegrams from Joseph Patrick Tumulty

The White House, July 5, 1919

#232 Received your message with references to address to joint session Thursday. Senate so wedded to precedents would resent address to joint session. Clark[1] and Senate leaders agree that address to Senate alone would be wisest course. House leaders are arranging with Senate leaders to attend session in a body. May I arrange for session of Senate Thursday and announce it? For publicity purposes speech ought to be given out by Wednesday morning in order to reach all over country, especially country press.

Tumulty

  [1] That is, Champ (James Beauchamp) Clark, Democratic minority leader of the House of Representatives.

The White House, July 5, 1919.

#233 Dr. Mott[1] advises me that joint meeting of Northern and Southern Methodist Churches will remain in session until and including the thirteenth. He has just returned from Columbus and states that he is more than ever impressed with the desirability of your speaking before this great meeting; that not only the Methodist Church, North and South, is represented, but that the leaders of all other denominations have been invited so that it furnishes a wonderful opportunity to send a message to the whole religious element of the country. Dr. Mott thinks there might be some advantage if you could address the meeting on Saturday the twelfth which has been designated as Farmer's Day, although any day up to and including the thirteenth would be satisfactory. In my own mind the question arises whether it is wise to address a sectarian gathering on this subject at this time.   Tumulty.

T telegrams (WP, DLC).
  [1] That is, John R. Mott.

From Herbert Clark Hoover, with Enclosure

Dear Mr. President: [Paris] July 5th, 1919.

In a liesure [leisure] moment you may find the opportunity to read the enclosed memorandum in which I have tried to sum up my views on the economic situation on this side.

Faithfully yours,   Herbert Hoover

TLS (WP, DLC).

E N C L O S U R E

Economic Situation in Europe[1]

MEMORANDUM ON THE ECONOMIC SITUATION OF EUROPE.[2]

3 July 1919.

The economic difficulties of Europe as a whole at the signature of peace may be almost summarized in the phrase "demoralized productivity." The production of necessaries for this 450 million population (including Russia) has never been at so low an ebb as at this day.

A summary of the unemployment bureaus in Europe will show that 15 million families are receiving unemployment allowances in one form or another and are in the main being paid by constant inflation of currency. A rough estimate would indicate that the population of Europe is at least 100 million greater than can be supported without imports and must live by the production and distribution of exports, and their situation is aggravated not only by lack of raw materials imports but by low production of European raw materials. Due to the same low production, Europe is today importing vast quantities of certain commodities which she formerly produced for herself and can again produce. Generally, not only is production far below even the level of the time of the signing of the armistice, but far below the maintenance of life and health without unparalleled rate of import.

  [1] WWhw.
  [2] All sentences in the following document *sic*.

Even prior to the war these populations managed to produce from year to year but a trifling margin of commodities over necessary consumption or to exchange for deficient commodities from abroad. It is true that in prewar times Europe managed to maintain armies and navies, together with a comparatively small class of non-producers, and to gain slowly in physical improvements and investment abroad, but these luxuries and accumulations were only at the cost of a dangerously low standard of living to a very large number. The productivity of Europe in pre-war times had behind it the intensive stimulus of individualism and of a high state of economic discipline, and the density of population at all times responded closely to the resulting volume of production. During the war the intensive organization of economy in consumption, the patriotic stimulus to exertion and the addition of women to productive labor largely balanced the diversion of man power to war and munitions. These impulses have been lost.

II.

It is not necessary to review at length the causes of this decrease of productivity. They comprise in the main as follows:

The industrial and commercial demoralization arising originally out of the war but continued out of the struggle for political rearrangements during the armistice, the creation of new governments, the inexperience and friction between these governments in the readjustment of economic relations.

The proper and insistent demand of labor for higher standards of living and a voice in administration of their effort has unfortunately become impregnated with the theory that the limitation of effort below physical necessity will increase the total employment or improve their condition.

There is a great relaxation of effort as the reflex of physical exhaustion of large sections of the population from privation, mental and physical strain of the war.

To a minor degree considering the whole volume, there has been a destruction of equipment and tools and loss of organization and skill due to war diversions with a loss of man power. This latter is not at present pertinent in the face of present unemployment.

(The demoralization in production of coal in Europe today is an example in point of all these three forces mentioned above and promises a coal famine and with industrial disaster unless remedied. It is due to a small percentage from the destruction of man power of the physical limitation of coal mines or their equipment. It is due in the largest degree to the human factor of the limitation of effort.)

The continuation of the Blockade after the armistice has undoubtedly destroyed enterprise even in open countries, and of course prevented any recovery in enemy countries. The shortage in overseas transportation and the result of uncertainties of the armistice upon inter-national credits have checked the flow of raw materials and prevented recovery in the production of commodities especially needed for exchange for imports from overseas. The result of this delay has been unemployment, stagnation, absorption of capital in consumable commodities to some extent all over Europe.

From all these causes, accumulated to different intensity in different localities, there is the essential fact that unless productivity can be rapidly increased, there can be nothing but political, moral and economic chaos finally interpreting itself in loss of life on a scale hitherto undreamed of.

III.

Coincident with this demoralization in production, other disastrous economic phenomena have developed themselves, the principle one of which is that the very large wage paid special workers and the large sums accumulated by speculation and manufacture during the war have raised the standard of living in many individuals from the level of mere necessities to a high level of luxuries. Beyond this class there is a reflex in many other classes from the strenuous economies against waste and the consumption of non-essentials in all countries, and as a result there is today an outbreak of extravagance to a disheartening degree.

Another economic change of favorable nature from a human point of view, but intensifying the problems of the moment, has been the rise in the standard of living in large sections of the working classes through the larger and better wage distribution, separation allowances, etc., during the war. Parallel with these classes are those of fixed income, the unorganized workers, the unemployed to whom the rising cost of living is inflicting the greatest hardship.

IV.

During some short period, it may be possible for the Western Hemisphere, which has retained and even increased its productivity, to supply the deficiencies of Europe. Such deficiencies would have to be supplied in large degree upon credits; but aside from this the entire surplus productivity of the Western Hemisphere is totally incapable of meeting the present deficiency in European production if it is long continued. Nor, as a practical fact, could credits be mobilized for this purpose for more than a short period, because all credits must necessarily be simply an advance against the return of commodities in exchange, and credits will break down the instant that the return of commodities becomes improbable. Further, if such credits be obtained in more than temporary purposes, it would result in economic slavery of Europe to the Western Hemisphere and the ultimate end would be war again.

The solution, therefore, of the problem, except in purely temporary aspects, does not lie in a stream of commodities on credit from the Western Hemisphere, but lies in a vigorous realization of the actual situation in each country of Europe and a resolute statesmanship based on such a realization. The populations of Europe must be brought to a realization that productivity must be instantly increased.

V.

The outcome of social ferment and class consciousness is the most difficult of problems to solve. Growing out of the yearning for relief from the misery imposed by the war, and out of the sharp contrasts in degree of class suffering, especially in defeated countries, the demand for economic change in the status of labor has received a great stimulus leading to violence and revolution in large areas and a great impulse to radicalism in all others. In the main these movements have not infected the agricultural classes but are essentially a town phenomena.

In this ferment Socialism and Communism has embraced to itself the claim to speak for all the downtrodden, to alone bespeak human sympathy and to alone present remedies, to be the lone voice of liberalism. Every economic patent medicine has flocked under this banner, Europe is full of noisy denunciation of private property as necessarily being exploitation. Considerable reliance upon some degree of Communism has been embraced by industrial labor even in non-revolutionary countries. Its extremists are loud in assertion that production can be maintained by the impulse of altruism alone, instead of self-interest. To often they are embracing criminal support and criminal methods to enforce their ideals of human betterment. Every country is engaged in political experimentation with varying degrees of these hypothesis, and so far every trial has reduced production. The Western Hemisphere with its more equitable division of property, its wider equality of opportunity still believes that productivity rests on the stimulus from all the immutable human qualities of selfishness, self-interest, altruism, intelligence and education. It still believes that the remedy of economic wrong lies not in tampering with the delicate and highly developed organization of production and distribution, but in a better division of the profits arising from them. It still believes in the constitutional solution of these problems by the will of the majority while Europe is drifting toward the domination of extremist minorities. The Western Hemisphere's productivity is being maintained at a surplus over its own needs.

The first and cardinal effort of European statesmanship must be to secure the materials and tools to labor, and to secure its return to work. They must also secure a recognition of the fact that whatever the economic theory or political cry it must embrace the maximum individual effort for there is no margin of surplus productivity in Europe to risk revolutionary experimentation. *No economic policy will bring food to those stomachs or fuel to those hearths that does not secure the maximum production. There is no use of tears over rising prices; they are, to a great degree, a visualization of insufficient production.*

VI.

During the period of reconstruction, and recovery from reduced productivity, the conservation in the consumption of non-essential commodities is more critical than any time during the war. The relaxation of restriction on imports and on consumption of articles of this character since the armistice is disheartening in outlook. It finds its indication in the increased consumption of beverages and articles de luxe in many countries, even above a pre-war normal. Never has there been such a necessity for the curtailment of luxury as exists today.

VII.

The universal practice in all the countries at war of raising funds by inflation of currency is now bringing home its burden of trouble and in extreme cases the most resolute action must be taken, and at once. In other countries of even the lesser degree of inflation, such currency must be reduced and included in the funded debt or alternately the price of wages, living and international exchange must be expected to adjust itself to this depression. The outcry against the high cost of living, the constant increase of wages and the fall in exchange that is going on, is in a considerable degree due to this inevitable readjustment.

VIII.

The stimulation of production lies in the path of avoidance of all limitations of the reward to the actual producer. In other words, attempts to control prices (otherwise than in the sense of control of vicious speculation) is the negation of stimulation to production, and can only result in further curtailment of the total of commodities available for the total number of human beings to be fed, clothed and housed. There still exist in Europe great bureaucracies created from the necessity of control of price and distribution by the conditions of the war who are loath to recognize that with world markets open no such acute situation exists and that their continued existence is not essential except in the control of speculation. The argument so much advanced that world shortage may develop and justifies continued control of distribution and price is based upon the fallacious assumption that even if the world markets are freed of restraint that there is a shortage today in any commodity so profound as to endanger health and life. From any present evidence, thanks to the high production outside Europe, no shortage exists that will not find its quick remedy in diminished consumption or substitution of other commodities, through minor alteration and price. All attempts at international control of price, with view to benefitting the population in Europe at the cost of the producer elsewhere, will inevitably produce retrogression in production abroad, the impact of which will be felt in Europe more than elsewhere. A decrease of 20 percent of Western Hemisphere wheat would not starve the West, it would starve Europe. It must never be overlooked that control of price and distribution cannot stop with a few prime commodities, but once started its reprocussions drive into a succeeding chain of commodities and that on the downward road of price control, there can be no stoppage until all commodities have been placed under restriction, with inevitable stifling of the total production. It is also often overlooked by the advocates of price control that whereas the high level of production was maintained during the war even under a restraint of price, this high production was obtained by the most vivid appeal to patriotic impulse on both sides of the front. This stimulus to production and distribution no longer maintains and the world must go back to the prime impulse, and that is the reward to the individual producer and distributor.

That body of advocates who have deduced from war phenomena that production and distribution can be increased and maintained by appealing to altruism as the equivalent of patriotism or self-interest should observe the phenomena of Russia where the greatest food exporting country is today starving.

IX.

It must be evident that the production cannot increase if political incompetence continues in blockade, embargoes, censorship mobilization, large armies, navies and war.

X.

There are certain foundations of industry in Europe that no matter what the national or personal ownership or control may be they
yet partake of the nature of the public utilities in which other nations have a moral right. For instance, the discrimnatory control of
ships, railways, waterways, coal and iron in such a manner as to
prevent the resumption of production by other states will inevitably
debar economic recuperation and lead to local spats of economic
chaos with its ultimate infection abroad, to say nothing of the decrease in productivity. These mis-uses are already too evident.

XI.

The question of assistance from the Western Hemisphere during
a certain temporary period, and the devotion of its limited surplus
productivity to Europe, is a matter of importance and one that requires statesmanlike handling and vision. It is but a minor question compared to those stated above and it is in a great degree dependent upon the proper solution of the factors already touched
upon. It is a service that the Western Hemisphere must approach
in a high sense of human duty and sympathy. This sense will,
however, be best performed by the insistence that their aid would
not be forthcoming to any country that did not resolutely set in
order its internal financial and political situations, that did not devote itself to the increase of productivity, that did not curtail consumption of luxuries and the expenditure upon armament and did
not cease hostilities and did not treat their neighbors fairly. If these
conditions were complied with, it is the duty of the west to put
forth every possible effort to tide Europe over this period of temporary economic difficulties. Without the fulfillment of these conditions, the effort is hopeless. With Europe turned toward peace
with her skill and labor alligned to overcome the terrible accumulation of difficulty, the economic burden upon the West should not
last over a year and can be carried and will be repaid. To effect
these results the resources of the Western Hemisphere and here
must be mobilized.   Herbert Hoover.

T MS (WP, DLC).

From the Diary of Dr. Grayson

Sunday, July 6, 1919.

After the President had breakfast I read him the wireless despatches, which carried a statement that Holland had agreed to surrender the Kaiser to the British Government,[1] and that he was to

be conveyed to the Tower of London and there held a prisoner until the International Tribunal that was suggested under the Treaty could be assembled in order to try him for the "crimes" outlined in the Treaty. The President said that so far as he was concerned he thought it would be a great mistake to place the Kaiser on trial. He said that his position had been announced by him while he was in Paris, and that he had carefully explained to the Big Four that any action of this kind would be a great mistake inasmuch as it must naturally tend to the German people making a martyr of their former ruler. The President said that Lloyd George had promised during his campaign that the Kaiser would be placed upon trial and that as a result the English insisted that some arrangement must be made whereby this promise made to secure Lloyd George's reelection should be carried out. The President said that in his opinion the worst punishment that could be meted out to the Kaiser would be to leave him alone in his isolation, where he would have only the memory of his former greatness and the realization of what Germany's effort to conquer the world had resulted in.

The President was wondering whether Chief Justice White[2] of the United States Supreme Court would be in good enough health to make the trip and be the American representative on the board that would try the Kaiser. If the Chief Justice's health would permit, the President was thinking of asking him to assume the task.

The President discussed the problem which he had on his hands of selecting a new Ambassador to Germany and an Ambassador to Belgium, to replace Brand Whitlock, who is being transferred to Rome. The President said that the health of Mr. Frank Polk, Assistant Secretary of State, was giving him deep concern. He said that Mr. Polk was so valuable and he appreciated his services so much that he was loath to lose him. However, he realized that his health was so precarious that Mr. Polk could no longer be held down to the duties in the State Department, and he was wondering whether an appointment as Ambassador to either of these positions might not be welcome in order to allow him to recuperate and get back into normal health. If not, the President was thinking that it might be advisable to transfer Mr. Polk to Paris to substitute for Mr. Lansing in the Peace Commission.

The President went on deck late in the afternoon in an effort to get a little fresh air, the weather being extremely warm. He had not much more than appeared on the deck when Mr. Lamont and his associates gathered around and endeavored to start a discussion of matters affecting the Treaty and the Peace Conference. The President was not in a mood for business that was to be forced upon him and he quickly changed the situation by telling a number of stories that apparently satisfied the economic experts.

The President, Mrs. Wilson, Dr. Axson and myself had dinner with Captain McCauley in his quarters behind the bridge. Later the President came down and attended the moving pictures.

¹ The report that the government of the Netherlands had agreed to the extradition of William II to Great Britain seems to have originated with the London *Daily Mail*. The *New York Times*, July 5, 1919, reported on the matter as follows: "*London*, Saturday, July 5. The Allies, according to The Daily Mail, have received assurances that the Dutch government in the last resort will not refuse to surrender the former German Emperor for trial. The newspaper says that the necessary formal objections will doubtless be raised to maintain the rights of Dutch sovereignty, but as the demand for the ex-Kaiser's person can be made in the name of the League of Nations, national rights will not be infringed and there is no doubt that the Dutch Government will be quite ready to get rid of the unwelcome guest. It is not considered likely, The Mail continues, that the matter will come before the Dutch courts, despite certain statements at The Hague." The article continued with a detailed account of how the trial in London of the former Emperor would be conducted.

In fact, the Dutch government never officially made known its attitude toward the possible extradition of William II until January 1920 when, in response to a direct request for his surrender by the Supreme Council of the Paris Peace Conference, it finally stated publicly its refusal to do so. *New York Times*, Jan. 24, 1920.

² That is, Edward Douglass White.

To Joseph Patrick Tumulty

Ottercliffs, Maine, July 6, 1919.

Please make arrangements for me to address the Senate on Thursday and (announcement of) plan.

Since I cannot reach Washington with a copy of my address before Tuesday evening it seems quite impossible to have the address given out by Wednesday morning. All well.

Woodrow Wilson.

T telegram (J. P. Tumulty Papers, DLC).

From the Diary of Dr. Grayson

Monday, July 7, 1919.

The President rested late and at luncheon the conversation turned to various stories. The President expressed the opinion that the second best American story, following very close on the story of President McKinley and the Irish laborer,¹ was the story which had for its chief actors former President Van Horne and O'Shaughnessy,² the "railway builders" of the Dominion of Canada. Both men began in minor positions on the Canadian Pacific Railway. Van Horne held a minor official position on the railroad, while O'Shaughnessy was a section boss. A vacancy occurred in Van Horne's department and O'Shaughnessy determined that he would get that job if it were possible. So with his hat on his head and his pipe in his mouth, he stalked into Van Horne's office, passing through the door without knocking, and leaning across the desk, he said: "Boss, I want that job." Van Horne looked up and scowled and then turned around to O'Shaughnessy and said: "What do you mean by coming into this office without knocking, and what do you mean by asking for a job in that tone of voice. Take that pipe out of your mouth when you come in this office." O'Shaughnessy looked at him for a minute in bewilderment, and then turned on his heel and walked out. A minute later there was a knock on the door and Van Horne yelled "Come in." O'Shaughnessy walked through the door and as he did so he took off his hat and took his pipe out of his mouth. He then stood in a respectful attitude on the other side of the desk and addressing Mr. Van Horne said: "Mr. Van Horne, I understand there is a vacancy in your department and I would like to apply for the job." Van Horne said: "Yes, Mr. O'Shaughnessy, there is a vacancy. Do you think that you can do the work?" O'Shaughnessy said: "I can, and to show you, here are some letters of reference which are extremely good." Van Horne, after reading them, said: "I think you can have the job, Mr. O'Shaughnessy. Your qualifications seem satisfactory." O'Shaughnessy, resuming his hat and sticking his pipe in his mouth, turned to Van Horne and said: "You and your job can go to hell. I don't want it." Van Horne realizing that he had the man whom he needed for the job, jumped up and grasping him by the hand said: "Let's go out and have a drink and forget it." And thus another railroad king was made.

The President attended the moving pictures, and at the conclusion of the pictures the usual song of "God be with you till we meet again" was sung.

[1] The Editors have been unable to find any reference to this alleged McKinley story.
[2] Sir William Cornelius Van Horne, successively from 1881 to 1910 general manager, president, and president of the board of directors of the Canadian Pacific Railway; and Thomas George Shaughnessy, 1st Baron Shaughnessy, successively from 1885 to 1918 assistant general manager, vice-president, and president of the Canadian Pacific Railway.

From John Nevin Sayre

My dear Mr. President,   Brookwood Katonah, N. Y. July 7, 1919.

First of all I wish to congratulate you on your safe return to the United States. We are all glad to have you home with us again. When it is convenient for you to do so I hope that you will perhaps see me and two friends from the National Civil Liberties Bureau, Mr. Hollingsworth Wood and Mr. Albert de Silver.[1] We are anxious to talk with you about the question of granting amnesty to certain

classes of persons convicted or under trail [trial] for violations of
the Espionage Law and Selective Service Act. The last time that
you wrote me,[2] you said that your mind was still open on this question. I am hoping very much that this remains so, and that you will
give us the opportunity to talk with you. We will of course suit our
time to your pleasure.

   With warmest good wishes, I am

                    Very sincerely yours,   John Nevin Sayre

ALS (WP, DLC).
   [1] Levi Hollingsworth Wood and Albert De Silver, both lawyers of New York. De Silver
was director of the National Civil Liberties Bureau.
   [2] WW to J. N. Sayre, March 3, 1919, Vol. 55.

From Casper Salathiel Yost[1]

Dear Mr. President: St. Louis, July 7th, 1919.

I am a Republican. As a Republican editor I have opposed you in
your campaigns with all the strength I could command. No doubt
I would do so again in the same circumstances. But throughout
the war I have supported you loyally, vigorously opposing any partisan action against you in the great work you have had to do. I
have been from the beginning, and am now, an ardent advocate of
the League of Nations.

I state all of this merely as justification of the opinion I take the
liberty of expressing. The covenant is in my estimation the most
important measure that has ever come before the American people,
not even excepting the Constitution. It is of the utmost importance
that it be accepted. The majority of the people favor it. A large percentage of Republicans approve it and have no sympathy with the
fight that is being made against it. Permit me to say, Mr. President,
that whether that Republican support is retained depends very
much upon you. Some of the Republicans of the Senate have tried
to make the question a party issue. We have opposed that with all
our might. But any semblance of a partisan movement on your part
would quickly solidify the mass of the party in a position of opposition and make it difficult for the Republican Senators who are
disposed to approve the covenant to maintain that attitude.

I am confident that a majority of the Republican Senators are
now so disposed. And that brings me to another point. They are for
it, but in the face of the opposition within the party, and particularly within the Senate, they find it difficult to swallow it whole.
Some emollient in the shape of reservations is desirable if only for
this reason. If such reservations are merely interpretive, merely
put into the record the meaning that most of us who have studied

the document believe to be already there, and are not amendatory, what harm can they do? It is important, Mr. President, that this matter be put through as quickly and as amicably as possible. The nation without regard to parties should be behind it and the less animosity aroused the more general and more sincere will be the support the people will give to it.

Permit me to extend my congratulations on your great work and to subscribe myself   Sincerely yours,   Casper S. Yost

TLS (WP, DLC).
    [1] Editorial director of the *St. Louis Globe-Democrat*.

From the Diary of Dr. Grayson

Tuesday, July 8, 1919.

The President arose very early, and with Mrs. Wilson went on the bridge of the George Washington in order to see the approach of the escorting squadron sent out from the Atlantic Fleet. The escort was discerned on the horizon shortly after nine o'clock and was composed of four battleships, headed by the Battleship Pennsylvania, flying the flag of Secretary of the Navy Daniels and Admiral Wilson,[1] Commander of the Atlantic Fleet. When the Washington reached the squadron a Presidential salute was fired from the Pennsylvania, and then the Pennsylvania took a position ahead of the Oklahoma, and the start into the harbor was commenced.

Just before the Ambrose Channel light-ship was picked up, it was learned that one of the French brides, who were being brought home with their soldier husbands, had been robbed of some money, and a collection was taken up to replace the cash, which the girl needed badly.

Arriving in the Upper Bay the George Washington was met by two of the big Municipal Ferry boats and the New York Police Boat Patrol, carrying the Mayor's Reception Committee, who had put in an appearance to welcome the President. Originally, it had been intended by the committee that they would go on board the George Washington, but the President vetoed this plan, and so the boats escorted the Presidential ship as far as the Hoboken Army Dock.

There was a delay in warping into the pier, caused by the fact that the tide was low and it was necessary to have entirely slack water so that the George Washington could be pushed in by tugs without damage and without colliding with the great Leviathan, which was anchored on the south side of the pier.

It was nearly four o'clock before the start was made from the

George Washington. The President was accompanied by Governor Smith of New York and Mayor Hylan of New York City.

Mrs. Grayson met me at the gang-plank, and I was overjoyed to see her after our long separation.

The progress through the streets of New York was a triumphant procession. Admittedly the largest crowd that has ever greeted the President in this great metropolis thronged both sides of the street, and the President was compelled to stand in his auto and bow repeatedly all the way from the 23rd Street Ferry, as far as Carnegie Hall. The Carnegie Hall meeting was a splendid one, and the President was in excellent form in responding to the addresses.

Leaving Carnegie Hall the party proceeded directly to the Pennsylvania Station, where the special train was boarded and the trip to Washington made. Although it was midnight when Washington was reached, more than 100,000 people were gathered in and about Union Station to welcome the President back, and before he started for the White House he thanked the local committee very briefly for its efforts in arranging the demonstration.

The President, Mrs. Wilson and I went directly to the White House. On our way the President said: "The reception here tonight is one of the greatest surprises in my life. It is very touching." When we drove into the White House grounds I exclaimed: "I am one person who is very thankful to be back on this spot." Mrs. Wilson acquiesced with a smile, and the President said: "This house never looked so beautiful."

[1] Adm. Henry Braid Wilson.

An Address in Carnegie Hall

[[July 8, 1919]]

Fellow countrymen: I am not going to try this afternoon to make you a real speech. I am a bit alarmed to find out how many speeches I have in my system undelivered, but they are all speeches that come from the mind, and I want to say to you this afternoon only a few words from the heart.

You have made me deeply happy by the generous welcome you have extended to me. But I do not believe that the welcome you extend to me is half as great as that which I extend to you. Why, Jerseyman though I am, this is the first time I ever thought that Hoboken was beautiful. I have really, though I have tried on the other side of the water to conceal it, been the most homesick man in the American Expeditionary Force, and it is with feelings that it would be vain for me to try to express that I find myself in this beloved country again.

I do not say that because I lack in admiration of other countries. There have been many things that softened my homesickness. One of the chief things that softened it was the very generous welcome that they extended to me as your representative on the other side of the water. And it was still more softened by the pride that I had in discovering that America had at last convinced the world of her true character. I was welcome because they had seen with their own eyes what America had done for the world. They had deemed her selfish; they had deemed her devoted to material interests; and they had seen her boys come across the water with a vision even more beautiful than that which they conceived when they had entertained dreams of liberty and of peace. And then I had the added pride of finding out by personal observation the kind of men we had sent over. I had crossed the seas with the kind of men who had taken them over, without whom they could not have got to Europe; and then when I got there I saw that army of men, that army of clean men, that army of men devoted to the high interests of humanity, that army that one was glad to point out and say, "These are my fellow countrymen."

It softens the homesickness a good deal to have so much of home along with you, and these boys were constantly reminding me of home. They did not walk the streets like anybody else. I do not mean that they walked the streets self-assertively; they did not. They walked the streets as if they knew that they belonged wherever free men lived, that they were welcome in the great Republic of France and were comrades with the other armies that had helped to win the great battle and to show the great sacrifice.

Because it is a wonderful thing for this nation, hitherto isolated from the large affairs of the world, to win not only the universal confidence of the people of the world, but their universal affection. And that, and nothing less than that, is what has happened.

Wherever it was suggested that troops should be sent and it was desired that troops of occupation should excite no prejudice, no uneasiness on the part of those to whom they were sent, the men who represented the other nations came to me and asked me to send American soldiers. They not only implied, but they said, that the presence of American soldiers would be known not to mean anything except friendly protection and assistance. Do you wonder that it made our hearts swell with pride to realize these things?

But while these things in some degree softened my homesickness, they have made me all the more eager to get home where the rest of the folks live; to get home where the great dynamo of national energy was situated; to get home where the great purposes of national action were formed; and to be allowed to take part in the counsels and in the actions which were to be taken by this great nation, which from first to last has followed the vision of the men who set it up and created it.

We have had our eyes very close upon our tasks at times, but whenever we lifted them we were accustomed to lift them to a distant horizon. We were aware that all the peoples of the earth had turned their faces toward us as those who were the friends of freedom and of right, and, whenever we thought of national policy and of its reaction upon the affairs of the world, we knew we were under bonds to do the large thing and the right thing. It is a privilege, therefore, beyond all computation, for a man, whether in a great capacity or a small, to take part in the counsels and in the resolutions of a people like this.

I am afraid some people, some persons, do not understand that vision. They do not see it. They have looked too much upon the ground. They have thought too much of the interests that were near them, and they have not listened to the voices of their neighbors. I have never had a moment's doubt as to where the heart and purpose of this people lay. When anyone on the other side of the water has raised the question, "Will America come in and help?", I have said, "Of course America will come in and help." She cannot do anything else. She will not disappoint any high hope that has been formed of her. Least of all will she in this day of new-born liberty all over the world fail to extend her hand of support and assistance to those who have been made free.

I wonder if at this distance you can have got any conception of the tragic intensity of the feeling of those peoples in Europe who have just had yokes thrown off them. Have you reckoned up in your mind how many peoples, how many nations, were held unwillingly under the yoke of the Austro-Hungarian Empire, under the yoke of Turkey, under the yoke of Germany? These yokes have been thrown off. These peoples breathe the air and look around to see a new day dawn about them, and whenever they think of what is going to fill that day with action, they think first of us. They think first of the friends who through the long years have spoken for them, who were privileged to declare that they came into the war to release them, who said that they would not make peace upon any other terms than their liberty, and they have known that America's presence in the war and in the conference was the guarantee of the result.

The Governor has spoken of a great task ended. Yes, the formulation of the peace is ended, but it creates only a new task just

begun. I believe that if you will study the peace, you will see that
it is a just peace and a peace which, if it can be preserved, will save
the world from unnecessary bloodshed. And now the great task is
to preserve it. I have come back with my heart full of enthusiasm
for throwing everything that I can, by way of influence or action,
in with you to see that the peace is preserved—that when the long
reckoning comes men may look back upon this generation of
America and say: "They were true to the vision which they saw at
their birth."[1]

Printed in the New York *World*, July 9, 1919, with one correction from the text in the
New York Times, July 9, 1919.
   [1] There is a WWT outline of this speech, dated July 8, 1919, in WP, DLC.

From Robert Lansing and Henry White

VERY CONFIDENTIAL no distribution
Paris, 8th July 1919

3034 For immediate communication to the President
   In private conversation with Tittoni, Italian Foreign Minister and
new Chief of Delegation, soon after his arrival, he expressed an
earnest desire to place Italy on the most friendly relations with the
United States. Said that he counts on us for economic and financial support, without which impossible for Italy to exist, being
practically ruined by the war. He deeply regrets course pursued by
his predecessors and expressed apprehension lest they had for-
feited your sympathy and goodwill for Italy, which he considers to
be of the highest importance. It is his desire and intention, if feasible, to settle the Italian question soon as possible on best terms
obtainable. In view, however, of great excitement in Italy over
Fiume, he hoped it might be possible to obtain nominal Italian sovereignty there, circumscribed by every possible restraint with a
view to saving face of Italy. He was frankly told that Italian sovereignty over Fiume is absolutely out of the question and that the
object of the private conversation with him so soon after his arrival
was to prevent him from placing himself in a position, by demanding unobtainable terms, from which he could not with dignity re-
cede, as had been the case with his precedessors. He was furthermore told that other terms demanded by his predecessors would be
absolutely unobtainable, as set forth in your memorandum of June
25,[1] and that if any such were insisted upon, United States would
prefer separate peace with Austria rather than sign Treaty embodying them. He evidently appreciated friendly spirit in which these
facts were communicated and said he would see what could be

done in the way of meeting our views. Next day he told us in strictest confidence he had given up idea of Italian sovereignty and would accept proposed neutral state, but necessary for him in the statement of claims which he had been asked to make by Council of Five, to put in a demand for such sovereignty, it being, however, agreed with us that he would expect to have it rejected. Before being able to assent officially to any agreement relinquishing sovereignty over Fiume, it would be necessary for him to return home to obtain possible support of various Parliamentary chiefs in accepting terms; otherwise present Ministry would have to resign, which would be unfortunate, as he feared no one else able to form responsible Ministry. He has been negotiating with French and British governments with reference to compensation in Africa for claims relinquished by Italy in Adriatic; and seems to have effected satisfactory arrangements with British, but finds French very difficult to deal with. Matters seemed progressing favorably toward arrangement satisfactory to us when an unfortunate riot occurred Fiume two days ago between French and Italian sailors which, unless carefully handled, may have serious consequences. No account yet allowed to appear in papers here and private information received by us differs from Italian, but several apparently killed both sides. Clemenceau brought incident before Council of Five yesterday, when agreement reached to send Interallied Mission of five generals, none of whom connected previously with Adriatic affairs, to investigate facts on spot and advise as to punishment of those responsible. Tittoni tells us confidentially that if Italians in wrong, he will express regret and punish offenders. Owing to Fiume incident he left by special train for home this morning. Had two hours interview with us last night and suggested, in exchange for his relinquishing all claims respecting Dalmatia and accepting your proposed free state about Fiume, that Cattaro be assigned to Italy, with Montenegro and Albania free states under League of Nations. Cattaro, which has no commercial value, is landlocked harbor, surrounded by inaccessible mountains and unconnected with Montenegro, whose port is Antivari. 3034

Lansing Ammission[2]

T telegram (SDR, RG 256, 186.3411/682A, DNA).

[1] For which, see the Enclosure with WW to RL, June 25, 1919 (first letter of that date).

[2] The State Department sent a copy of this telegram to Wilson on July 9, 1919. Notation on RL to Sec State (for the President), No. 3034, July 8, 1919, T telegram (SDR, RG 59, 763.72119/5575, DNA).

From Frank Lyon Polk

My dear Mr. President: Washington July 8, 1919.

The members of the Abyssinian Mission[1] arrived in Washington on Monday morning, July 7th, and are now at the La Fayette Hotel. They arrived in New York on the MAURETANIA about noon on July 5th. I received them this morning at the Department of State.

As you probably know they visited Rome, Paris, and London. Our understanding is that they communicated with you from London and requested an audience, and that you replied that it would be impossible to arrange an audience in Paris, but that you would be glad to receive them at Washington.

It was not known whether it was your desire that they should be the guests of the Government, but being suddenly confronted with the situation upon their arrival on Saturday, and to avoid what might have been construed as discourtesy, they were met at the steamer but not till several hours after the passengers had landed, and after advices had been received by us that they expected some courtesy. They were taken to a hotel in New York, and have been brought to Washington and are continuing under the same arrangement.

It is our understanding that they have brought some presents to you from the Queen of Abyssinia.[2] They have requested that they be received by you, and I will be glad if you would let me know when it will be agreeable for you to receive them, and whether you think it will be necessary for you to have them to lunch with you—having in view the many other matters of great importance which are now demanding your attention.

Faithfully yours,   Frank L Polk

TLS (WP, DLC).
    [1] The Abyssinian, or Ethiopian, mission to the United States consisted of four persons headed by Dedjazmatch Nadao. They had arrived in New York on July 5, 1919. Their objective was to congratulate the United States on the victory of the Allied and Associated nations in the World War. For more details on the mission, see B. Long to JPT, July 12, 1919, and its Enclosures.
    This was the first Ethiopian diplomatic mission to the United States. Relations between the two countries had been desultory, to say the least. What might be called formal diplomatic relations were established in 1903, when Robert Peet Skinner, Consul at Marseilles, led a mission to Addis Ababa and negotiated a ten-year commercial treaty with Emperor Menelik II, who had defeated an Italian invasion force in 1896. The State Department stationed a low-level representative in Addis Ababa from 1906 to 1913, when the commercial treaty was renewed. American interests in Ethiopia were entrusted to the British legation in Addis Ababa and the American consulate in Aden from 1914 to 1928, when a formal United States presence in Addis Ababa was established. Frank J. Manheim, "The United States and Ethiopia: A Study in American Imperialism," *The Journal of Negro History*, XVII (April 1932), 141-55, and Russell Warren Howe, *Along the Afric Shore: An historic review of two centuries of U.S.-African relations* (New York, 1975), pp. 68-71.
    [2] The Empress of Abyssinia, or Ethiopia, was Zaouditou.

From William Phillips

Dear Mr. President,   Washington July 8th/19.

On this day of general thanksgiving for your safe return, may I add a personal word of hearty welcome and congratulation?

You have been so constantly in our thoughts that your absence has never seemed quite real.

Day by day we have followed you in the midst of the over-whelming problems and difficulties and have marvelled at your patience and steadfastness.

It is comparatively easy, as others have done, to demand the maximum of everything in the idea that that is loyalty to one's country, but to weave out of material of national selfishness a permanent structure for insuring unselfishness among nations, seems to me a superhuman accomplishment.

I am thrilled by the result of your labors and offer you my very very sincere congratulations.

Faithfully yours   William Phillips

ALS (WP, DLC).

From Elbert Henry Gary[1]

My dear Mr. President: New York July 8th, 1919.

As a plain citizen, a Republican in politics, I make bold to express my congratulations on and gratitude for the splendid work you have done for the United States and for the world during the last six months.

The number and perplexity of the problems presented at the Peace Conference are not, as yet, fully comprehended by those who did not participate in the deliberations.

However, the large majority of the people of this country believe the League of Nations will have a decided influence in preventing war, and therefore they approve it. In due time your efforts will receive universal commendation.

With high esteem, I am,   Sincerely yours,   E. H. Gary

TLS (WP, DLC).
[1] That is, the chairman of the board of directors and of the finance committee of the United States Steel Corporation.

From Edward Mandell House

London July 9th, 1919.

Urgent. 2496. Secret. For the President from Colonel House "Second meeting of the commission on Mandates was held yesterday afternoon at Sunderland House, the London office of the League of Nations. Besides myself there were present Lord Milner for Great Britain, M. Simon for France, Signor Marconi[1] for Italy. Viscount Chinda for Japan, Mr. Beer[2] and Lord Robert Cecil were also present as advisers. Principal matters discussed were: One, It was agreed that the discussion should proceed on the assumption that the Principal Allied and Associated Powers conferred the mandates upon trust to the mandatories and that the League of Nations will supervise the execution of mandates made. Two, a tenative draft of class C mandate. Chinda urged that the proper construction of the fifth and sixth paragraphs of article 21 of the Covenant of the League of Nations required a provision to be inserted in the class C mandates giving equal opportunities for the trade in commerce of the members of the League in the territories affected by the class C mandate. The British representatives opposed this construction and said that it was agreed in Paris before the Prime Ministers of the dominions left that there should be no change in the verbiage of the mandatory which would give the Japanese the privilege which they now demanded. After some discussion in which I called attention to the impossibility of the British changing this part of the mandatory at this time Chinda withdrew his active opposition and merely made a reservation in behalf of his Government. I offered a clause for the protection of missionaries which was agreed to in substance and the form will be drafted tomorrow. The full text of the proposed class C mandatory will be cabled to you as soon as it has been redrafted.

Two (Three)? Consideration of B mandate was met at the outset by the following proposal for article two[3] made by the French representatives "The mandatory power undertakes not to establish any military or naval base; not to erect any fortifications and not to organize any native military force, except for local police purposes and the defense of its territory whether colonial or metropolitan." The American proposal which was substantially the same as the British proposal reads as follows: "No native armed forces shall be organized except such as is necessary for the preservation of order. Such forces as are organized shall be raised on the voluntary basis. No military or naval works or bases shall be erected or maintained except for the defense of the territory."

French representative had positive instructions to insist upon the exact words of French proposal. Proces verbal of meeting of January thirtieth[4] at which you, Monsieur Clemenceau and Mr. Lloyd George were present was cited by French representative in support of his position. Proces verbal is not clear, but partially supports his position. As you can appreciate matter is of fundamental importance and I propose, if you approve, to stand firm on the general principles of our proposal. I have privately sounded the Japanese the Italians and the British representatives and they are sympathetic to our views as opposed to the views of the French. The next meeting of the Commission will be held in the morning of July 9th."   Davis

T telegram (WP, DLC).
    [1] That is, Guglielmo Marconi.
    [2] That is, George Louis Beer.
    [3] For the drafts which the commission was considering, see the Enclosures printed with WW to EMH, June 27, 1919.
    [4] See Hankey's minutes of two meetings of the Council of Ten printed at Jan. 30, 1919, Vol. 54.

From Prince Faisal

Damascus July 9, 1919.
Via Cairo 12th.
Recd. 13, 505 a.m.

538. Following from American Consul Damascus[1] July 9, 6 am. Prince Emir Faisal has requested me to transmit the following:

"To His Excellency, President Wilson. There is no doubt that after the arrival of your honorable commission[2] and the statements made to it expressing unreservedly the true desires and aspirations, the people and particularly myself have incurred as a matter of course the risk of a terrible strong current against us. I earnestly beg you not to leave me between the paws of the devourers. I beg to tender my highest respect. Faisal."   Gotlieb

T telegram (WP, DLC).
    [1] Bernard Gotlieb.
    [2] That is, the so-called King-Crane Commission, about which see the numerous references to it in Vols. 58 and 59.

From Adolf Kraus[1]

Chicago, Illinois, July 9, 1919.

We rejoice that you and Mrs. Wilson have returned home in safety.

You had the kindness on last Thanksgiving Day to say that

proper guarantees should be secured for the just treament of the Jewish peoples in countries where they have not been justly dealt with. Since then the Press brought news from Paris showing that that was your position. I would now like to publish in the Jewish Press your remarks as mailed to me by your secretary, unless otherwise instructed by you. I have the honor to be obediently yours,   Adolf Kraus.[2]

T telegram (WP, DLC).
    [1] Lawyer of Chicago, international president of B'nai B'rith.
    [2] "Please say, in reply to this letter, that the President feels that the matter of securing guarantees for the fair treatment of the Jewish people is in a very satisfactory position, but that it is a matter not yet clinched and put beyond danger. He therefore thinks that it would be wise, for the present at any rate, not to take further public part in the discussion of a matter in which he is much more interested in immediate results than in anything else." G. F. Close to White House Staff, T MS (WP, DLC).

The Postscript of a Letter from John Sharp Williams

[Washington] July 9, 1919.

P.S.—I want to congratulate you with all my heart on saving everything that you *could* save for the liberty and peace of the world at Paris. I, of course, realize—as you do more acutely than I—that in some things the Treaty of Peace doesn't square with what you wanted, and what America wanted, and what ought to have been; but, knowing European diplomats, and the bickering, and jealousy, and selfishness existing between European races and nations, I am astounded, as if it were by a miracle, at your having been so nearly successful in getting all that was desirable.

I shall find it right hard to swallow the Shantung clause, as doubtless you did; but, as my daughter Sally[1] said to a friend who had curly hair, while Sally had straight hair and wanted curly hair, when the other girl was complaining about something, "You can't have everything *and* curly hair"; and I think people are stupid who want to reject a great document, giving peace and promising enduring peace, merely because of one or two clauses which do not measure up to the standard.

Regardless of what the Senate may do—and I think things will come out all right ultimately, even there—the plaudits of posterity, at any rate, will await you. In addition to that, our time for ratifying this Treaty, including the Covenant of Peace among the nations of the world, is not limited. If it should be adopted by three nations, it goes into effect as to the balance of the world, at any rate, and we can wait until the American people have the opportunity to elect another Senate, which won't be quite as long practically as politicians think.

I realize the truth of what the New York World says in a recent editorial "that most of the objectionable clauses of the Treaty would never have been written into it had it not been for the bitter attacks upon you at home, which deprived you of the moral support of a united public opinion at a time when such support was imperative to a peace that represents the highest ideals of the American people."[2] I endorse the *World*'s further language which is to the effect that regardless of that opposition you succeeded in making the League of Nations the very foundation of the Treaty of Peace and that was the distinctive achievement of the Conference.

I know you will excuse me for just a suggestion; please show a little bit *more tact* in dealing with some of the obstructionists. Of course no amount of tact could have any effect upon Borah, or Poindexter, or Jim Reed, but it may have some upon a good many other Senators, hopefully even upon Knox himself, though of that I don't feel sure. Sometimes a fellow must grit his teeth and says "I am going to be pleasant to A, although I think A is deficient in intellect and public spirit." Maybe after awhile he finds that A was very easy to make all right, because he was sympathetically and elementally all right all the time.

I am, with every expression of regard,

Very truly yours,   John Sharp Williams

TLS (WP, DLC).
  [1] Sally Shelby Williams (Mrs. Joel William) Bunkley.
  [2] "PRESIDENT WILSON'S RETURN," New York *World*, July 8, 1919.

From William Cox Redfield

My dear Mr. President: [Washington] 9 July 1919

May I send a few lines to express my gladness that you have returned home safely, and I trust without too great fatigue, after accomplishing a great and noble work for our country and for the world.

It may interest you, but will hardly surprise you, to know that having long friendships with men in the Republican Party, who have been in the past the esteemed wise counselors and strong financial supporters of that Party, they do not hesitate to tell me that the present official representatives of that organization are in serious error and that the intelligence and conscience in the Party does not support them. I think you may rest securely in confidence that the judgment of the country is with you in the work that lies ahead.

With renewed welcome and kindest personal regards, I am,

Yours very sincerely,   William C. Redfield

TLS (WP, DLC).

From Walker Downer Hines

Dear Mr. President: Washington July 9, 1919.

I am enclosing memoranda dealing (1) with the financial, economic and social problem of the Railroad Administration involving
the question of an increase of rates, questions of new wage increases now being vigorously demanded, and the closely connected question of the high cost of living; and (2) with the permanent solution of the railroad problem.[1]

I believe these subjects are the most vital domestic problems
with which the United States has to deal and the necessity for
practically immediate decision with respect to the rate increases
and wage increases makes particularly urgent the adoption of an
aggressive policy with respect to the general evil of the constantly
increasing cost of living.

The rate and wage problems are:

Whether rates shall be increased to meet the deficits being
currently incurred on account of the increases in wages and
prices and if not what if any assurance should be given that the
railroads will not be turned back at the end of the year without
ability to support themselves.

Whether wages shall be still further increased to meet new
demands now being pressed by various classes of railroad employes on the ground that present wages do not meet increased
cost of living.

Both problems are of the most urgent character. As to wage increases, the shop crafts, numbering nearly 500,000 employes, are
in a pronounced state of ferment and there are prospects of serious
strikes at a very early date. As to rate increases, the demands for
prompt action are so general that a definite announcement of policy is highly desirable.

The decision of these questions will be influenced substantially
by a decision of the broad question of policy as to what can and
ought to be done to arrest the present continuing upward movement in the cost of living. I believe the increasing high cost of living is the greatest domestic problem confronting the Nation. The
habit of increasing prices on every pretext, and more than even the
pretext suggests, appears to have become the ruling passion of the
country and is creating a rapidly growing unrest on the part of Labor. These conditions are prompting Labor to demand additional

[1] These (all by W. D. Hines) were "A. INCREASE IN COST OF LIVING AND MEANS TO
COMBAT IT"; "B. SHALL THE GOVERNMENT NOW MAKE AN INCREASE IN RATES, OR OTHER-
WISE ASSURE THE TEMPORARY SELF-SUPPORT OF THE RAILROADS?"; "C. DEMANDS OF
RAILROAD EMPLOYES FOR FURTHER INCREASES IN WAGES"; and "D. PROPOSALS FOR RAIL-
ROAD LEGISLATION AND CONSIDERATIONS RELATING THERETO," all TS MS (WP, DLC).

wages. If these demands are granted they will immediately be followed by further increases in prices and again the increases in prices will be greater than the increase in the labor cost. Thus the cost of living will rise to still higher levels and discontent of Labor will become still greater, industrial turmoil will become even more pronounced and the evil will continue to grow by what it feeds on.

I respectfully urge that it is of the highest importance to the general public welfare, as well as to the successful and creditable handling of the Government's railroad responsibilities, to launch at once an aggressive campaign for the purpose of halting the increases in the cost of living, and to employ every available governmental agency capable of working to that end. I believe these results should be sought through executive action and through the development of an effective public sentiment rather than through processes of additional investigations or additional legislation because such processes will work far too slowly to get the quick relief which I believe the situation sorely needs. To protect the labor situation, what can be accomplished in the next thirty days will be worth a great deal more than what can be accomplished within six months or twelve months as the result of further investigation and further legislation.

I believe important results can be accomplished through immediate activity by the Department of Justice and by the Federal Trade Commission, and probably by the Department of Agriculture, through stimulating activity as to local matters in the District of Columbia, and encouraging similar municipal activity throughout the country, and through a general appeal which will arouse the public sentiment and will awaken a greater sense of responsibility upon the part of the influences which are controlling prices (including house rents) and which appear still to be increasing prices without regard to the consequences.

I do not submit specific recommendation as to increases in rates, as I would prefer first to have an opportunity to get the benefit of your views, but I am inclined to the belief that it is better not to increase rates at present, since the present conditions are transitional and an increase in rates would be a still further adverse influence upon the cost of living, and that instead it would be better to give assurance of a sympathetic attitude toward some plan of a temporary guaranty of an adequate railroad income for a few months after the corporations resume control of their properties. I do not make any recommendation at the moment as to increases in wages, because I think that situation will be largely influenced by a determination of what can and will be done in arresting further increases in the high cost of living.

I submit memoranda presenting my views more in detail upon these propositions as follows:

A. Increase in cost of living and means to combat it.
B. Shall the Government now make an increase in rates or otherwise assure the temporary self-support of the railroads.
C. Demands of railroad employes for further increases in wages.

I enclose a further memorandum, D, setting forth briefly the leading proposals for railroad legislation. The sum of this memorandum is that there is no prospect for absolute Government ownership and operation; that of the provisions which will be seriously urged we have at one extreme the Plumb Plan which promises to have unanimous and emphatic support of Labor and which contemplates Government ownership but operation by a corporation made up of the official and non-official railroad employes, profits to be divided between all such employes and the Government, and we have at the other extreme various plans which contemplate going back virtually to the old regime with various modifications which will not cure fundamental evils. The reactionary tendencies in Congress would make the return to the old regime almost certain but for the strong insistence of Labor on the Plumb Plan. The conflict between these radical demands of Labor and the reactionary tendencies in Congress may render possible some intermediate plan which will be really constructive and progressive.

I believe that any return to the former principles of so-called private management, through a vast number of corporations differing widely as to earning capacity, will prove a failure through its inability to attract the necessary additional capital and through its inability to satisfy Labor and the Public that they are not being exploited for private profit. I think that either now or a few years later we must come to a plan which will remove these fears of exploitation and which will attract the necessary new capital. Broadly, I think this can be accomplished through the compulsory consolidation of the railroads into a few large systems to be managed by Boards of Directors upon which the Government and Labor, in addition to the stockholders, will be adequately represented, with a statutory requirement insuring an adequate earning capacity but providing for a division of the excess profits with the Government or Labor or both.

Such plan as I have in mind will have the hearty support of Senator Cummins,[2] Chairman of the Senate Committee on Interstate Commerce, and he is hopeful that such a plan may be the outcome of the conflicting forces which are respectively pressing the Plumb

[2] That is, Albert Baird Cummins.

Plan and the reactionary plans. He believes, however, that success in this direction will be largely dependent upon the conclusions you may reach. Senator Cummins appoints today a sub-committee of five and hopes such committee will agree upon a bill along the lines he advocates, within the next thirty days, by which time he hopes the ratification of the Peace Treaty will have taken place and he thinks from that time on the railroad problem will occupy the attention of the Senate. Congressman Esch,[3] Chairman of the House Committee on Interstate and Foreign Commerce, does not so far appear to perceive the necessity for really fundamental changes.

The problem is so large and presents such opportunities for discussion that the prospect of a solution in the current calendar year is not bright unless great pressure shall be continuously applied to Congress to act. There is quite a disposition to assume that the railroads will not be turned back to their owners at the end of this calendar year unless Congress has acted. I believe that action by Congress could be stimulated if renewed emphasis were placed upon the proposition that the railroads undoubtedly will be turned back to the owners at that time in accordance with the statement you have already made in your message.[4]

There is a feeling that if the railroads were turned back on December 31st without additional legislation, the railroad companies would immediately find themselves insolvent. This matter can be met as above indicated either through an increase in rates to increase the earnings so as to take care of the expenses, fixed charges and dividends, or through some form of temporary guaranty.

As I have heretofore written you,[5] I hope you can conveniently discuss with me these difficult and closely inter-related problems at any early date.

The wage matter and with it the problem of the high cost of living are most acute.   Cordially yours,   Walker D Hines

TLS (WP, DLC).

[3] John Jacob Esch, Republican congressman from Wisconsin.

[4] That is, Wilson's special message to Congress of May 20, 1919, printed at that date in Vol. 59.

[5] W. D. Hines to WW, April 24, 1919, Vol. 58, and W. D. Hines to WW, July 7, 1919, TLS (WP, DLC).

From the Diary of Ray Stannard Baker

Wednesday the 9th [July 1919]

My son Roger[1] met me in New York and I arrived at home in Amherst about 6 o'clock & very glad, deeply glad to be here on our hillside.

Wilson never commends anyone, unless prompted to do so.

When I came to say good-bye to the President on our arrival in New York, although I had been seeing him daily—& intimately— for months—had occupied a confidential position—not one word did he say about it, either commendatory or otherwise, or intimate that he cared ever to see me again. He said good-bye to me just as he would have said it to a visitor of an hour. Mrs. Wilson said she would miss my daily calls. I am not saying this because I feel aggrieved about it, but merely as a bit of evidence regarding the President's nature. Mr. Roosevelt never let any man get away from him like that! The President sets high store upon a man's doing his duty. He does his, as he sees it—and goes ahead: expects every other man [to] do the same & make no fuss about it. But even the President is very sensitive to praise or blame & I know, from what I saw in the great celebrations in Europe, expands warmly to the welcome of crowds.

One of the secretaries of the President (Close), who has been closer to him for years than almost anyone else, told me on the ship that Wilson had never in his life spoken a word of commendation to him. Yet no man in the Presidential office ever stuck to his appointees, his official family, so faithfully as Wilson. He makes no changes: no matter what a man does Wilson sticks by him. Many men in his cabinet—Burleson!—ought long ago to have been turned out, but he keeps them. This is perhaps deliberate policy, not any special regard for the men themselves, not personal loyalty! A reputation for never being forced to dismiss a man under fire is a valuable asset to an administrator. It saves a great deal of trouble.

[1] Roger Denio Baker.

From the Diary of Dr. Grayson

Thursday, July 10, 1919.

The President completed his European labors at noon today when he laid down before the Senate the Treaty of Peace with its accompanying Protocols. Probably no state paper that the President has been responsible for was the subject of as much interest as was his address today. For hours before the Senate galleries were opened a crowd besieged the front doors of the Capitol Building and despite the fact that a torrential rain was falling, they remained there, although only persons holding tickets of admission were allowed to enter the building itself. The President came to the Capitol shortly after twelve o'clock and went directly to the President's room on the second floor, where he remained until the committee named by the Vice-President came and escorted him. The committee was composed of Senators Lodge, Borah, John Sharp Williams, Hitchcock and McCumber. The President, with the Treaty under his arm, started to march into the Senate Chamber. Senator Lodge, who was walking by the President's side, said: "Mr. President, can I carry the Treaty for you?" The President smiled and said to him: "Not on your life." Senator Williams said: "Don't trust him with it, Mr. President." All parties laughed.

The President's speech was listened to with the deepest attention. But the only applause that greeted him was at the start and at the finish. After he concluded his speech, he went back to his office room and there he met the majority of the Democratic Senators and discussed very briefly with them the procedure that is to be followed in the fight for the ratification of the Treaty.

A Report of a Press Conference[1]

July 10, 1919.

The President: I am very glad to see you, gentlemen. The job, the main part of it, is over, and the rest of it is outlined. Before I left Paris I think we were substantially agreed. We had agreed upon all the lines of the Austrian treaty and we had substantially agreed upon everything else that the United States had any part in—though that latter is hard to determine, what we had a part in and what we hadn't. For this reason: the Covenant of the League of Nations is to go into each treaty. If these treaties are ratified by the United States, that makes the United States a party to the execution then of the treaties with Turkey and Bulgaria, though we were not at war with Turkey and Bulgaria. For that reason, our men, the expert advisers, and so forth, who are over there are not only sitting in on the conferences on the Bulgarian and Turkish treaties, but are giving actual advice. In one sense they have no determining voice, but I am happy to say that the people over there have learned to seek their advice and have found it very valuable.

[1] Held in the East Room of the White House at 10:15 a.m. More than 100 correspondents were present.

Therefore they are taking part in the framing of them. I thought you would be interested to know where we came in on the rest of the job that remains to be done in Paris. But in working out the German treaty we tackled every tough subject that there was, and found the way around it, and established the main lines that would govern in all the treaties. So that I felt that I was free to come away, inasmuch as the main things were determined.

I am very much interested to learn by the papers this morning that the German Assembly has ratified the treaty.[2] That lifts the blockade, because we told them that we would not wait for the other ratifications to lift the blockade, since there were sure to be enough to put the treaty into effect, but would lift the blockade when they ratified.

I thought you would be interested to see the document. It is a nice little book. One of the things that makes it heavy is that it contains the maps in connection with the territorial settlements. It has elaborate maps and things of that sort in it, and in fact it is only half as big as it looks, because one page is French and the other is English. The two languages were put on an equal footing as an authoritative text of the treaty, so that it is printed in both languages, on the one side French and the other English. I had to bring an unsigned copy, because the only signed copy had to stay in one place and remains in Paris.

Q. If the blockade is lifted, does it follow that the Trading With the Enemy Act is suspended?

The President. No. I cannot answer that with as much confidence as I could if I had recently consulted the Act, but as I remember it, the Act remains in force if we choose to enforce it, until the proclamation of peace is made by the United States. That is my recollection of it.

Q. Is there any likelihood of its being retained?

The President. I really hadn't thought of that at all. I just assumed that we would not exercise any more restraint than special circumstances demanded.

Q. Is there anything you could say with regard to the resumption of trade relations with Germany?

The President. I have nothing special to say about that. Of course, the resumption of trade relations with Germany is a very important part of the carrying out of the treaty, because Germany cannot pay reparation unless her trade is resumed, and it becomes

[2] The German National Assembly at Weimar adopted a resolution ratifying the peace treaty on July 9 by a vote of 208 to 115, with ninety-nine abstentions. President Friedrich Ebert signed the resolution that same evening. *New York Times*, July 10 and 11, 1919.

important, therefore, to the whole group of nations, not to ourselves particularly, but to the whole group of nations, that her trade should be resumed. By the way, do not quote me on any of these things.

Q. Does lifting the blockade remove all obstacles from trade with Germany?

The President. No. It does not create ships enough and it does not release ships enough. Of course, until we bring all our men home, for example, our ships are tied up in the transport movement.

Q. Does it remove all legal obstacles?

The President. Yes.

Q. She is free to trade with Russia?

The President. Yes.

Q. There is no restraint on the part of the other Allied nations?

The President. They would exercise restraint if they could.

Q. Is the United States free to trade with Germany before the treaty is ratified here? Does the Trading with the Enemy Act remain in force?

The President. Yes. That is literally right, but of course it is left largely to the discretion of the government how far it exercises the restraint. Again I am speaking with a distant recollection of the Act.

Q. I understand it is in force unless the President proclaims the Act at an end?

The President. The board which exercises that control goes out of existence for lack of breath—otherwise known as lack of money. The instrumentalities for control are largely gone. I do not mean gone altogether, because the things that turned out to be useful in these boards are turned over to the regular departments.

Q. Can you say anything about your trip to the West?

The President. No. I have not been home long enough to more than see that terrible looking table in my study with documents piled on it.

Q. Have you anything to say about when demobilization will be completed.

The President. No. I have not. That depends—well, I should say the chief thing it depends on—is the rate at which the various governments ratify the treaty. And then there is another element in it which has been somewhat overlooked, apparently. I mean by general opinion. It has not been overlooked by the army. The treaty provides for a period of from one to four months for the execution of various parts of it that have direct bearing on the military status of Germany. For example, the yielding up of military materials of which they have still a great store. You see, the situation is this. Germany still has several million men, and she has munitions for several million men. Commissions acting under the treaty are going to superintend the delivery of all of that material, except that which she is allowed to retain. Now, while that process is going on, it will be wise to maintain sufficient forces of occupation to keep everybody from being nervous, and so that will be an element in the situation.

Q. Are the men under arms chiefly regulars?

The President. They are being more and more reduced to regulars. There are not many drafted men remaining to come home, as I understand it.

Q. Would you be willing to make a statement about Shantung?

The President. No. That is a long story and a very complicated one. I would not like, off-hand, to try to explain it.

Q. Can you say anything about Fiume?

The President. I understand that the street in Rome that they had called "Via Wilson" has been changed to "Via Fiume." That is the latest information I have, which is a practical joke on myself. The Fiume business is very singular. Because, as I dare say you all know, it was expressly provided in the Treaty of London that Fiume should go to the Croatians. Italy signed the document that it was not to go to her but to the Croatians. She was indeed to get a number of islands and a big slice of the Dalmatian coast, but Fiume she gave up, and now she seems indifferent to the other parts of the thing and she wants Fiume.

Q. These other things, she has obtained?

The President. No indeed. Things are at a complete standstill. You see, in the Austrian treaty this is an important thing to note. In the Austrian treaty, Austria renounces any political claims she may have had to any of those territories outside of the boundaries fixed by the treaty and assigns to the principal Allied and Associated Powers the right to make such disposition as they think proper of those territories. So that is the present status of Fiume and those islands. I mean, when the Austrian and Hungarian treaties are signed, they are in the hands of those five powers to determine their political future.

Q. Do you intend to discuss the French alliance?

The President. I am going to ask the Senate's permission to bring it up later, because it is too complicated. I will take it up separately.

Q. Can you say what part America will have in financing reconstruction?

The President. No, Sir. I wish I were wise enough to answer. I think we are all agreed that it should not be governmental assistance, but assistance, I was going to say, on the usual bases of credit. But that will not be possible, because it will have to be on a delayed basis of credit, but it will be on a sound basis.

Q. Would you be willing to discuss the criticism of Article X of the League Covenant?

The President. No, only to say that if you leave that out, it is only a debating society, and I would not be interested in a debating society. I have belonged to them and have found them far from vital.

Q. Won't this alliance be submitted to the Senate until after the treaty is disposed of?

The President. Yes, but not immediately. As soon as I can write a proper exposition of it. I have not had time to do that yet.

Q. Is the alliance of equal importance with the treaty itself?

The President. No, it is subsidiary to the treaty. But don't call it an alliance, for it is not an alliance with anybody. This is the point. You see, it hangs on the League of Nations, because in its terms it is made dependent upon the approval of the Council of the League. I am assuming, of course, that the League of Nations will be adopted. If it is, the process is this. There is no provision for military action except upon advice of the Council, advice given to the several governments. Of course it follows that the several governments will take the advice or not, as they please, and it will be a matter of honor with them whether they will or not. There is no legal obligation. So that what we assumed in discussing the Covenant was this. If fire broke out in the Balkans, for example, a Council of the League would advise that certain nations mobilize their armies and undertake the military pressure that was necessary, and the others play some other part, and that some natural arrangement for exercising a portion of the forces be devised. But of course it might take some time for the advice to materialize in action. One nation would be prompt, another would be slower, and so forth. Now, all that this treaty contemplates is this: that until a majority of the Council of the League of Nations shall declare that the permanent arrangements are sufficient, the United States agree, upon any unprovoked aggression by Germany against France, to immediately come to her assistance with military forces. That is to say, she promises not to wait for the advice of the Council. Now, inasmuch as that is an anticipation of the advice of the Council, we all agreed that it was necessary that the Council itself should assent to the treaty, so we put in the assent of the Council so as to tie it right in and make it consistent.

Q. In the event the Senate failed to accept the agreement, what would be the attitude of France toward the League of Nations?

The President: I don't think it would affect that. I think the French would be cut to the heart if we didn't do it.

Q. Who is to judge of provocation?

The President. I have to answer that the way I answered the question a year or two ago, when I said, if Germany committed an act of aggression, we would go to war with her. I did not know, but I was sure I would know it when I saw it. Now I feel that way about this. I think you can tell an act of aggression when you see it. In the region of the Rhine there will be a number of persons looking on, and it could not go unnoticed.

Q. Would the determination rest with the executive?

The President. I should assume that it would be the legislative. In other words, I suppose the process would be this: the executive would advise that such an act had occurred and ask for the necessary means of action, but the legislature could refuse it, of course.

Q. It does not rob Congress of its power to declare war?

The President. No. I explained that so often that I got tired, that I had no power to define the causes or to make war. That is really the reason the clause was put in about advice with regard to military action. Not only the United States, but Brazil and other countries are in the same case. We could not suspend the right of the legislature to make war.

Q. It has been suggested in the Senate that some of the objections raised would be removed by a reservation defining the right of Congress, making that clear just as you have expressed it here. Would that be regarded as an amendment, and would that prevent the ratification of the treaty itself?

The President: Well, I do not think that any explanation of the power of Congress is necessary. Reservations are a complicated problem. I take it for granted that no reservation would be of effect unless it passed by two-third majority, by the same majority that is necessary to ratify the treaty.[3] And if it had to be considered as an "if" in the adoption of the treaty, then we would have to go all over the process of the treaty again. All the countries concerned would

[3] For whatever reason, either ignorance of the Senate rules or memory loss, Wilson was mistaken on this point. Senate Standing Rule 37 stipulated that any action by the Senate on a treaty, except a motion to postpone indefinitely and, of course, a motion to consent to the ratification of a treaty, would be decided by majority vote. Senator Lodge was quick to point out Wilson's error, and Senator Hitchcock had to admit that Lodge was correct. See the *New York Times*, July 11, 1919. Also, someone in the Washington bureau of the New York *World* sent Wilson a copy of Standing Rule 37, probably on July 10, 1919. Undated T MS (WP, DLC). Wilson repeated his error in his conversations with senators at the Capitol immediately following his address to the Senate printed below. However, he stood corrected and never repeated this mistake.

have to be consulted. For you have to find out just what the reservation meant, and then they would have to decide whether they consented to it. In the meantime we would be at war with Germany for months together. That is the most serious side of it.

Q. The suggestion is made that a number of these reservations that are desired would be what they call innocuous. An innocuous reservation, I take it, is one that does not go to the vitals of the treaty.

The President: But who is to certify that it is innocuous? That is the difficulty of that class of reservations. The other countries would have to know just what they meant. If you had been at Paris with us, you would have found that things do not look the same to different nations, and what the United States would consider so and so, probably nobody else would. There were many curious points of view, and so I could not be sure that what we considered innocuous would be so considered by any other country.

Q. I think the Senate is going on the assumption that it can make reservations by majority vote.

The President. That is a very dangerous assumption.

Q. If war should break out in the Balkans, would the nations selected to put it down be governed by proximity?

The President. I am not going to run the League of Nations until it is adopted. I cannot answer questions of that sort. Nobody could.

Q. You said there would be a natural selection. What assurance is there that there would be?

The President. You have to take it for granted that they are going to have horse sense. They would not ask Japan to go into the Balkans when everything was on fire.

Q. We noticed that the order in which the representatives of the various countries signed the treaty was changed at the last moment. Was that because there was some fear that the Germans would back out?

The President. What was changed was the information of the press. It was all along intended that we get them salted down.

Q. In the cable dispatches on the Anglo-French and the American-French agreements, there is a difference of language. It looks as though we were bound to come to the immediate relief of France, but England only assents to come to her assistance.

The President. It means the same thing. There is no difference in the obligation.

Q. In the message of wartime prohibition, you said, when the army was demobilized, you would act. Mr. Palmer expressed the view that you were not empowered to act now.

The President. You see, I cannot declare demobilization completed until I declare peace. The peace declaration has to precede that.

Q. Do you expect to ask that the United States act as mandatory for Armenia?

The President: Let us not go too fast. Let's get the treaty first.

Q. Do you care to express your attitude toward the Kolchak government or the other governments of Russia?

The President. No sir. That is an athletic feat, to adjust one's mind to those things.

Q. Do you care to say anything about Mexico?

The President. I am not informed on Mexico as yet.

Q. Do you hold that if the Senate were to adopt reservations to the treaty of peace with Germany, the treaty could not be ratified?

The President: I do not think hypothetical questions are concerned. The Senate is going to ratify the treaty.[4]

T MS (WP, DLC).
[4] Of course, the Senate only consents to ratification of a treaty; the President himself exchanges articles of ratification. Wilson was obviously using language in common parlance then and now.
Close's shorthand notes of this press conference are in the G. F. Close Coll., NjP.

A News Report

[July 10, 1919]

OVATION TO THE PRESIDENT
But Most Republican Senators Fail to Join in Applause.

Washington, July 10.—President Wilson personally delivered the Peace Treaty with Germany to the Senate in open session this afternoon. It was the first time that a treaty had been submitted by a President in such a manner.

The President spoke before an audience such as is seldom seen in the Senate Chamber and received a most enthusiastic greeting except by the Republicans of the Senate. Both when he entered under escort of the committee, headed by Senator Lodge, and when he concluded his address, 37 minutes later, he was the recipient of stirring ovations from the galleries, the Democrats of the Senate, the Cabinet officers, seated in a semicircle in front of the Vice President, and members from the House who had crowded into the circular space behind the Senators. There were cheers mingled with the rebel yell.

But most of the Republicans took no part in the demonstration. When the President entered the Chamber the Republicans arose in unison with all on the floor and the galleries, but few joined in the applause. Senator Nelson applauded while the President was being escorted to the rostrum. Senator Warren also applauded a little when the President appeared. After the President's speech Senator McCumber was the only Republican seen to applaud.

The President's address was heard with the keenest interest by his splendid audience, but it was heard in silence. He was not at his best in the delivery of his speech, but this may have been due to a purpose on his part not to try for effect. Several times during the first half of his address he dropped a word in reading the type-written copy, on small cardboards, which he held in his hand, and then reread these sentences. His reading improved when he reached the portions dealing with the League of Nations, and it was there that he placed greater emphasis upon his sentences.

The President attempted only a general characterization of the scope and purpose of the treaty, discussed the role the American Peace Commissioners played at Paris, and declared that a League of Nations was "a practical necessity" for the maintenance of the new order of affairs, and was recognized as "the hope of the world." He added that the only question now was whether we could reject the confidence of the nations of the world.

It was when the President discussed the league that he appeared at his best. The league, he asserted, "was the practical statesman's hope of success in many of the most difficult things he was attempting." He traced the progress of the league idea, told how "the most practical, the most skeptical" men around the peace table had turned to the league more and more "as the authority through which international action was to be secured, the authority without which, as they had come to see it, it would be difficult to give assured effect either to this treaty or to any other international understanding upon which they were to depend for the maintenance of peace."

The impression developed as he proce[e]ded in his address that he was speaking not so much to the ninety-six Senators before him or even to the crowds in the galleries as to the people of the entire country. From the outset he seemed to sense the hostility on the Republican side of the Chamber and to feel the virtual futility of an appeal to them. The latter feeling may have been responsible for a sort of halting several times during his address.

The end of the President's address was splendidly dramatic. Up to this point he had read it to the Senate page by page. Then disregarding his manuscript, the President faced the Republican side of the Chamber and concluded:

"The stage is set, the destiny disclosed. It has come about by no plan of our conceiving, but by the hand of God, who led us into this way. We cannot turn back. We can only go forward, with lifted eyes and freshened spirit, to follow the vision. It was of this that we dreamed at our birth. America shall in truth show the way. The light streams upon the path ahead, and nowhere else."[1]

Printed in the *New York Times*, July 11, 1919.
    [1] This peroration, which this news report implies was extemporaneous, appears in the text of Wilson's speech printed below. It also appears in the text of the address printed, among other newspapers, in the *New York Times*, July 11, 1919, which was obviously an advance text given to the press on July 10. Hence, one can only conclude that Wilson had memorized the last paragraph and delivered it without reading from his text.

An Address to the Senate[1]

[July 10, 1919]

Gentlemen of the Senate: The treaty of peace with Germany was signed at Versailles on the twenty-eighth of June. I avail myself of the earliest opportunity to lay the treaty before you for ratification and to inform you with regard to the work of the Conference by which that treaty was formulated.

The treaty constitutes nothing less than a world settlement. It would not be possible for me either to summarize or to construe its manifold provisions in an address which must of necessity be something less than a treatise. My services and all the information I possess will be at your disposal and at the disposal of your Committee on Foreign Relations at any time, either informally or in session, as you may prefer; and I hope that you will not hesitate to make use of them. I shall at this time, prior to your own study of the document, attempt only a general characterization of its scope and purpose.

In one sense, no doubt, there is no need that I should report to you what was attempted and done at Paris. You have been daily cognizant of what was going on there,—of the problems with which the Peace Conference had to deal and of the difficulty of laying down straight lines of settlement anywhere on a field on which the old lines of international relationship, and the new alike, followed so intricate a pattern and were for the most part cut so deep by historical circumstances which dominated action even where it would have been best to ignore or reverse them. The cross currents of politics and of interest must have been evident to you. It would be presuming in me to attempt to explain the questions

    [1] According to the *New York Times*, July 10, 1919, Wilson did not finish writing this address until late in the afternoon of July 9. His British spelling of words such as "vigour" and "honourable" indicates that Wilson did read from a WWT draft, which Wilson later sent to the Public Printer. The WWT draft does not seem to have survived. There is an early and incomplete WWsh draft in WP, DLC.

which arose or the many diverse elements that entered into them. I shall attempt something less ambitious than that and more clearly suggested by my duty to report to the Congress the part it seemed necessary for my colleagues and me to play as the representatives of the Government of the United States.

That part was dictated by the role America had played in the war and by the expectations that had been created in the minds of the peoples with whom we had associated ourselves in that great struggle.

The United States entered the war upon a different footing from every other nation except our associates on this side of the sea. We entered it, not because our material interests were directly threatened or because any special treaty obligations to which we were parties had been violated, but only because we saw the supremacy, and even the validity, of right everywhere put in jeopardy and free government likely to be everywhere imperiled by the intolerable aggression of a power which respected neither right nor obligation and whose very system of government flouted the rights of the citizens as against the autocratic authority of his governors. And in the settlements of the peace we have sought no special reparation for ourselves, but only the restoration of right and the assurance of liberty everywhere that the effects of the settlement were to be felt. We entered the war as the disinterested champions of right and we interested ourselves in the terms of the peace in no other capacity.

The hopes of the nations allied against the central powers were at a very low ebb when our soldiers began to pour across the sea. There was everywhere amongst them, except in their stoutest spirits, a sombre foreboding of disaster. The war ended in November, eight months ago, but you have only to recall what was feared in midsummer last, four short months before the armistice, to realize what it was that our timely aid accomplished alike for their morale and their physical safety. That first, never-to-be-forgotten action at Château-Thierry had already taken place. Our redoubtable soldiers and marines had already closed the gap the enemy had succeeded in opening for their advance upon Paris,—had already turned the tide of battle back towards the frontiers of France and begun the rout that was to save Europe and the world. Thereafter the Germans were to be always forced back, back, were never to thrust successfully forward again. And yet there was no confident hope. Anxious men and women, leading spirits of France, attended the celebration of the fourth of July last year in Paris out of generous courtesy,—with no heart for festivity, little zest for hope. But they came away with something new at their hearts: they have themselves told us so. The mere sight of our men,—of their vigour, of the confidence that showed itself in every movement of their stalwart figures and every turn of their swinging march, in their steady comprehending eyes and easy discipline, in the indomitable air that added spirit to everything they did,—made everyone who saw them that memorable day realize that something had happened that was much more than a mere incident in the fighting, something very different from the mere arrival of fresh troops. A great moral force had flung itself into the struggle. The fine physical force of those spirited men spoke of something more than bodily vigour. They carried the great ideals of a free people at their hearts and with that vision were unconquerable. Their very presence brought reassurance; their fighting made victory certain.

They were recognized as crusaders, and as their thousands swelled to millions their strength was seen to mean salvation. And they were fit men to carry such a hope and make good the assurance it forecast. Finer men never went into battle; and their officers were worthy of them. This is not the occasion upon which to utter a eulogy of the armies America sent to France, but perhaps, since I am speaking of their mission, I may speak also of the pride I shared with every American who saw or dealt with them there. They were the sort of men America would wish to be represented by, the sort of men every American would wish to claim as fellow countrymen and comrades in a great cause. They were terrible in battle, and gentle and helpful out of it, remembering the mothers and the sisters, the wives and the little children at home. They were free men under arms, not forgetting their ideals of duty in the midst of tasks of violence. I am proud to have had the privilege of being associated with them and of calling myself their leader.

But I speak now of what they meant to the men by whose sides they fought and to the people with whom they mingled with such utter simplicity, as friends who asked only to be of service. They were for all the visible embodiment of America. What they did made America and all that she stood for a living reality in the thoughts not only of the people of France but also of tens of millions of men and women throughout all the toiling nations of a world standing everywhere in peril of its freedom and of the loss of everything it held dear, in deadly fear that its bonds were never to be loosed, its hopes forever to be mocked and disappointed.

And the compulsion of what they stood for was upon us who represented America at the peace table. It was our duty to see to it that every decision we took part in contributed, so far as we were able to influence it, to quiet the fears and realize the hopes of the peoples who had been living in that shadow, the nations that had come by our assistance to their freedom. It was our duty to do everything that it was within our power to do to make the triumph of freedom and of right a lasting triumph in the assurance of which men might everywhere live without fear.

Old entanglements of every kind stood in the way,—promises which Governments had made to one another in the days when might and right were confused and the power of the victor was without restraint. Engagements which contemplated any dispositions of territory, any extensions of sovereignty that might seem to be to the interest of those who had the power to insist upon them, had been entered into without thought of what the peoples concerned might wish or profit by; and these could not always be honourably brushed aside. It was not easy to graft the new order of ideas on the old, and some of the fruits of the grafting may, I fear, for a time be bitter. But, with very few exceptions, the men who sat with us at the peace table desired as sincerely as we did to get away from the bad influences, the illegitimate purposes, the demoralizing ambitions, the international counsels and expedients out of which the sinister designs of Germany had sprung as a natural growth.

It had been our privilege to formulate the principles which were accepted as the basis of the peace, but they had been accepted, not because we had come in to hasten and assure the victory and insisted upon them, but because they were readily acceded to as the principles to which honourable and enlightened minds everywhere had been bred. They spoke the conscience of the world as well as the conscience of America, and I am happy to pay my tribute of respect and gratitude to the able, forward-looking men with whom it was my privilege to cooperate for their unfailing spirit of cooperation, their constant effort to accommodate the interests they represented to the principles we were all agreed upon. The difficulties, which were many, lay in the circumstances, not often in the men. Almost without exception the men who led had caught the true and full vision of the problem of peace as an indivisible whole, a problem, not of mere adjustments of interest, but of justice and right action.

The atmosphere in which the Conference worked seemed created, not by the ambitions of strong governments, but by the hopes and aspirations of small nations and of peoples hitherto under bondage to the power that victory had shattered and destroyed. Two great empires had been forced into political bankruptcy, and we were the receivers. Our task was not only to make peace with the central empires and remedy the wrongs their armies had done. The central empires had lived in open violation of many of the very rights for which the war had been fought, dominating alien peoples over whom they had no natural right to rule, enforcing, not obedience, but veritable bondage, exploiting those who were weak for the benefit of those who were masters and overlords only by force of arms. There could be no peace until the whole order of central Europe was set right.

That meant that new nations were to be created,—Poland, Czecho-Slovakia, Hungary itself. No part of ancient Poland had ever in any true sense become a part of Germany, or of Austria, or of Russia. Bohemia was alien in every thought and hope to the monarchy of which she had so long been an artificial part; and the uneasy partnership between Austria and Hungary had been one rather of interest than of kinship or sympathy. The Slavs whom Austria had chosen to force into her empire on the south were kept to their obedience by nothing but fear. Their hearts were with their kinsmen in the Balkans. These were all arrangements of power, not arrangements of natural union or association. It was the imperative task of those who would make peace and make it intelligently to establish a new order which would rest upon the free choice of peoples rather than upon the arbitrary authority of Hapsburgs or Hohenzollerns.

More than that, great populations bound by sympathy and actual kin to Rumania were also linked against their will to the conglomerate Austro-Hungarian monarchy or to other alien sovereignties, and it was part of the task of peace to make a new Rumania as well as a new Slavic state clustering about Serbia.

And no natural frontiers could be found to these new fields of adjustment and redemption. It was necessary to look constantly forward to other related tasks. The German colonies were to be disposed of. They had not been governed; they had been exploited merely, without thought of the interest or even the ordinary human rights of their inhabitants.

The Turkish Empire, moreover, had fallen apart, as the Austro-Hungarian had. It had never had any real unity. It had been held together only by pitiless, inhuman force. Its people cried aloud for release, for succour from unspeakable distress, for all that the new day of hope seemed at last to bring within its dawn. Peoples hitherto in utter darkness were to be led out into the same light and given at last a helping hand. Undeveloped peoples and peoples ready for recognition but not yet ready to assume the full responsibilities of statehood were to be given adequate guarantees of friendly protection, guidance, and assistance.

And out of the execution of these great enterprises of liberty sprang opportunities to attempt what statesmen had never found the way before to do; an opportunity to throw safeguards about the rights of racial, national, and religious minorities by solemn international covenant; an opportunity to limit and regulate military establishments where they were most likely to be mischievous; an opportunity to effect a complete and systematic internationalization of waterways and railways which were necessary to the free economic life of more than one nation and to clear many of the normal channels of commerce of unfair obstructions of law or of privilege; and the very welcome opportunity to secure for labour the concerted protection of definite international pledges of principle and practice.

These were not tasks which the Conference looked about it to find and went out of its way to perform. They were thrust upon it by circumstances which could not be overlooked. The war had created them. In all quarters of the world old established relationships had been disturbed or broken and affairs were at loose ends, needing to be mended or united again, but could not be made what they were before. They had to be set right by applying some uniform principle of justice or enlightened expediency. And they could not be adjusted by merely prescribing in a treaty what should be done. New states were to be set up which could not hope to live through their first period of weakness without assured support by the great nations that had consented to their creation and won for them their independence. Ill governed colonies could not be put in the hands of governments which were to act as trustees for their people and not as their masters if there was to be no common authority among the nations to which they were to be responsible in the execution of their trust. Future international conventions with regard to the control of waterways, with regard to illicit traffic of many kinds, in arms or in deadly drugs, or with regard to the adjustment of many varying international administrative arrangements could not be assured if the treaty were to provide no permanent common international agency, if its execution in such matters was to be left to the slow and uncertain processes of cooperation by ordinary methods of negotiation. If the Peace Conference itself was to be the end of cooperative authority and common counsel among the governments to which the world was looking to enforce justice and give pledges of an enduring settlement, regions like the Saar basin could not be put under a temporary administrative regime which did not involve a transfer of political sovereignty and which contemplated a final determination of its political connections by popular vote to be taken at a distant date; no free city like Dantzig could be created which was, under elaborate international guarantees, to accept exceptional obligations with regard to the use of its port and exceptional relations with a State of which it was not to form a part; properly safeguarded plebiscites could not be provided for where populations were at some future date to make choice what sovereignty they would live under; no certain and uniform method of arbitration could be secured for the settlement of anticipated difficulties of final decision with regard to many matters dealt with in the treaty itself; the long-continued supervision of the task of reparation which Germany was to undertake to complete within the next generation might entirely break down; the reconsideration and revision of administrative arrangements and restrictions which the treaty prescribed but which it was recognized might not prove of lasting advantage or entirely fair if too long enforced would be impracticable. The promises governments were making to one another about the way in which labour was to be dealt with, by law not only but in fact as well, would remain a mere humane thesis if there was to be no common tribunal of opinion and judgment to which liberal statesmen could resort for the influences which alone might secure their redemption. A league of free nations had become a practical necessity. Examine the treaty of peace and you will find that everywhere throughout its manifold provisions its framers have felt obliged to turn to the League of Nations as an indispensable instrumentality for the maintenance of the new order it has been their purpose to set up in the world,— the world of civilized men.

That there should be a league of nations to steady the counsels and maintain the peaceful understandings of the world, to make, not treaties alone, but the accepted principles of international law as well, the actual rule of conduct among the governments of the world, had been one of the agreements accepted from the first as the basis of peace with the central powers. The statesmen of all the belligerent countries were agreed that such a league must be created to sustain the settlements that were to be effected. But at first I think there was a feeling among some of them that, while it must be attempted, the formulation of such a league was perhaps a counsel of perfection which practical men, long experienced in the world of affairs, must agree to very cautiously and with many misgivings. It was only as the difficult work of arranging an all but universal adjustment of the world's affairs advanced from day to day from one stage of conference to another that it became evident to them that what they were seeking would be little more than something written upon paper, to be interpreted and applied by such methods as the chances of politics might make available if they did not provide a means of common counsel which all were obliged to accept, a common authority whose decisions would be recognized as decisions which all must respect.

And so the most practical, the most skeptical among them turned more and more to the League as the authority through which international action was to be secured, the authority without which, as they had come to see it, it would be difficult to give assured effect either to this treaty or to any other international understanding upon which they were to depend for the maintenance of peace. The fact that the Covenant of the League was the first substantive part of the treaty to be worked out and agreed upon, while all else was in solution, helped to make the formulation of the rest easier. The Conference was, after all, not to be ephemeral. The concert of nations was to continue, under a definite Covenant which had been agreed upon and which all were convinced was workable. They could go forward with confidence to make arrangements intended to be permanent. The most practical of the conferees were at last the most ready to refer to the League of Nations the superintendence of all interests which did not admit of immediate determination, of all administrative problems which were to require a continuing oversight. What had seemed a counsel of perfection had come to seem a plain counsel of necessity. The League of Nations was the practical statesman's hope of success in many of the most difficult things he was attempting.

And it had validated itself in the thought of every member of the Conference as something much bigger, much greater every way, than a mere instrument for carrying out the provisions of a particular treaty. It was universally recognized that all the peoples of the world demanded of the Conference that it should create such a continuing concert of free nations as would make wars of aggression and spoliation such as this that has just ended forever impossible. A cry had gone out from every home in every stricken land from which sons and brothers and fathers had gone forth to the great sacrifice that such a sacrifice should never again be exacted. It was manifest why it had been exacted. It had been exacted because one nation desired dominion and other nations had known no means of defence except armaments and alliances. War had lain at the heart of every arrangement of the Europe,—of every arrangement of the world,—that preceded the war. Restive peoples had been told that fleets and armies, which they toiled to sustain, meant peace; and they now knew that they had been lied to: that fleets and armies had been maintained to promote national ambitions and meant war. They knew that no old policy meant anything else but force, force,—always force. And they knew that it was intolerable. Every true heart in the world, and every enlightened judgment demanded that, at whatever cost of independent action, every government that took thought for its people or for justice or for ordered freedom should lend itself to a new purpose and utterly destroy the old order of international politics. Statesmen might see difficulties, but the people could see none and could brook no denial. A war in which they had been bled white to beat the terror that lay concealed in every Balance of Power must not end in a mere victory of arms and a new balance. The monster that had resorted to arms must be put in chains that could not be broken. The united power of free nations must put a stop to aggression, and the world must be given peace. If there was not the will or the intelligence to accomplish that now, there must be another and a final war and the world must be swept clean of every power that could renew the terror. The League of Nations was not merely an instrument to adjust and remedy old wrongs under a new treaty of peace; it was the only hope for mankind. Again and again had the demon of war been cast out of the house of the peoples and the house swept clean by a treaty of peace; only to prepare a time when he would enter in again with spirits worse than himself. The house must now be given a tenant who could hold it against all such. Convenient, indeed indispensable, as statesmen found the newly planned League of Nations to be for the execution of present plans of peace and reparation, they saw it in a new aspect before their work was finished. They saw it as the main object of the peace, as the only thing that could complete it or make it worth while. They saw it as the hope of the world, and that hope they did not dare to disappoint. Shall we or any other free people hesitate to accept this great duty? Dare we reject it and break the heart of the world?

And so the result of the Conference of Peace, so far as Germany is concerned, stands complete. The difficulties encountered were very many. Sometimes they seemed insuperable. It was impossible to accommodate the interests of so great a body of nations,—interests which directly or indirectly affected almost every nation in the world,—without many minor compromises. The treaty, as a result, is not exactly what we would have written. It is probably not what any one of the national delegations would have written. But results were worked out which on the whole bear test. I think that it will be found that the compromises which were accepted as inevitable nowhere cut to the heart of any principle. The work of the Conference squares, as a whole, with the principles agreed upon as the basis of the peace as well as with the practical possibilities of the international situations which had to be faced and dealt with as facts.

I shall presently have occasion to lay before you a special treaty with France, whose object is the temporary protection of France from unprovoked aggression by the Power with whom this treaty of peace has been negotiated. Its terms link it with this treaty. I take the liberty, however, of reserving it for special explication on another occasion.

The rôle which America was to play in the Conference seemed determined, as I have said, before my colleagues and I got to Paris,—determined by the universal expectations of the nations whose representatives, drawn from all quarters of the globe, we were to deal with. It was universally recognized that America had entered the war to promote no private or peculiar interest of her own but only as the champion of rights which she was glad to share with free men and lovers of justice everywhere. We had formulated the principles upon which the settlement was to be made,—the principles upon which the armistice had been agreed to and the parleys of peace undertaken,—and no one doubted that our desire was to see the treaty of peace formulated along the actual lines of those principles,—and desired nothing else. We were welcomed as disinterested friends. We were resorted to as arbiters in many a difficult matter. It was recognized that our material aid would be indispensable in the days to come, when industry and credit would have to be brought back to their normal operation again and communities beaten to the ground assisted to their feet once more, and it was taken for granted, I am proud to say, that we would play the helpful friend in these things as in all others without prejudice or favour. We were generously accepted as the unaffected champions of what was right. It was a very responsible rôle to play; but I am happy to report that the fine group of Americans who helped with their expert advice in each part of the varied settlements sought in every translation to justify the high confidence reposed in them.

And that confidence, it seems to me, is the measure of our opportunity and of our duty in the days to come, in which the new hope of the peoples of the world is to be fulfilled or disappointed. The fact that America is the friend of the nations, whether they be rivals or associates, is no new fact: it is only the discovery of it by the rest of the world that is new.

America may be said to have just reached her majority as a world power. It was almost exactly twenty-one years ago that the results of the war with Spain put us unexpectedly in possession of rich islands on the other side of the world and brought us into association with other governments in the control of the West Indies. It was regarded as a sinister and ominous thing by the statesmen of more than one European chancellery that we should have extended our power beyond the confines of our continental dominions. They were accustomed to think of new neighbours as a new menace, of rivals as watchful enemies. There were persons amongst us at home who looked with deep disapproval and avowed anxiety on such extensions of our national authority over distant islands and over peoples whom they feared we might exploit, not serve and assist. But we have not exploited them. And our dominion has been a menace to no other nation. We redeemed our honour to the utmost in our dealings with Cuba. She is weak but absolutely free; and it is her trust in us that makes her free. Weak peoples everywhere stand ready to give us any authority among them that will assure them a like friendly oversight and direction. They know that there is no ground for fear in receiving us as their mentors and guides. Our isolation was ended twenty years ago; and now fear of us is ended also, our counsel and association sought after and desired. There can be no question of our ceasing to be a world power. The only question is whether we can refuse the moral leadership that is offered us, whether we shall accept or reject the confidence of the world.

The war and the Conference of Peace now sitting in Paris seem to me to have answered that question. Our participation in the war established our position among the nations and nothing but our own mistaken action can alter it. It was not an accident or a matter of sudden choice that we are no longer isolated and devoted to a policy which has only our own interest and advantage for its object. It was our duty to go in, if we were indeed the champions of liberty and of right. We answered to the call of duty in a way so spirited, so utterly without thought of what we spent of blood or treasure, so effective, so worthy of the admiration of true men everywhere, so wrought out of the stuff of all that was heroic, that the whole world saw at last, in the flesh, in noble action, a great ideal asserted and vindicated, by a nation they had deemed material and now found to be compact of the spiritual forces that must free men of every nation from every unworthy bondage. It is thus that a new role and a new responsibility have come to this great nation that we honour and which we would all wish to lift to yet higher levels of service and achievement.

The stage is set, the destiny disclosed. It has come about by no plan of our conceiving, but by the hand of God who led us into this way. We cannot turn back. We can only go forward, with lifted eyes and freshened spirit, to follow the vision. It was of this that we dreamed at our birth. America shall in truth show the way. The light streams upon the path ahead, and nowhere else.

Printed in *Address of the President of the United States to the Senate . . . July 10, 1919* (Washington, 1919).

Two News Reports

[July 10, 1919]

WILSON GREETS CALLERS
Holds Reception in Capitol Room to Discuss Peace Problems.
RESERVATIONS A THEME
President Holds Monroe Doctrine is Doubly Guarded by
Being Recognized.

Washington, July 10.—Following his address in the Senate Chamber, President Wilson went to his reception room adjoining, where for three quarters of an hour he discussed with callers the Shantung settlement, the Monroe Doctrine reservation, the Irish question, and other matters bound up in the Peace Treaty of [and] the League covenant.

About thirty visitors called upon him, including most of the Democratic Senators. Senator Kenyon was the only Republican Senator to pay his respects. The President seemed in the best of spirits, and laughed and chatted with his callers. He expressed himself with the same frankness that characterized his conference with newspaper correspondents earlier in the day, answering all questions freely.

At one time he held what amounted to an informal conference around the marble topped table in the centre of the room, Senators King of Utah, Gerry of Rhode Island, Pomerene of Ohio, Pittman of Nevada, Swanson of Virginia, Phelan of California, and Walsh of Montana, and Attorney General Palmer participated.

The first topic taken up was the question of the vote on reservations, and the President reiterated his statement of the forenoon to the newspaper men, that a two-thirds' vote of the Senate would be necessary. He told the Senators that he was opposed to any reservations, particularly as these would cause delay in the final ratification of the treaty.

There was considerable diversity of opinion on the parliamentary situation. Senators Pittman and Phelan took the ground that the majority could not force the Senate to vote for an amended treaty without an alternative.

After the conference, Senator Phelan said:

"I should think the Senate should be allowed to vote on the treaty with or without amendments. By no rule could the Senate be denied the right to vote for the League in its purity; in other words, the majority could not force the Senate to vote for an amended treaty and nothing else."

Touching on the Monroe Doctrine the President said that he brought the matter up in Paris, and as a result there was an acknowledgment of the doctrine which had never before had any standing in international law, being only a declaration of the President of the United States. He held that the action in Paris was a guarantee of recognition of the doctrine, and that furthermore the League would, by its terms, prevent aggression by European powers against any Central or South American powers. The President appeared perfectly certain on this point, and the Senators present understood him to believe that recognition by the League of the doctrine constituted a sort of second line of defense.

It came out during the conversation that the President expected the Japanese to fix a definite time when they would retire from the Shantung Peninsula granted them in succession to the German rights. It is understood here that the President used strong efforts, while in Paris, to induce the Japanese to fix definitely the time of their retirement from Shantung.

The Irish question was brought up by Senator Phelan. Mr. Wilson said that this problem was one of the most difficult ones he had to consider while abroad, involving many discussions of the subject. But he held that as the Irish question related to the territory of Great Britain, recognized by international law, and as the questions before the conference related wholly to territory taken from the enemy and not possessed by the Allies, no headway could have been made with the Irish situation. Mr. Wilson said that he wished the American people to understand the delicacy of his position in the matter.

Mr. Wilson stated that Lloyd George had arranged a hearing and also for passports for the American delegates sent to Ireland with a view to enabling them to get information at first hand.[1]

Senator Phelan asked the President if the Ishii-Lansing "agreement"[2] did not recognize Japan as having rights over China. The President said the Ishii-Lansing "agreement" was not an agreement at all, but an "understanding" and related only to superior rights of Japanese in Manchuria.

[1] See EMH to WW, May 9, 1919, and its Enclosure, and EMH to D. Lloyd George, May 9, 1919, all in Vol. 58.
[2] About this "agreement," see the index references to Japan and the United States in Vol. 44.

Did Not Like Shantung Settlement.

Washington, July 10. (Associated Press.)—In his talk with League supporters at the Capitol the President is quoted as saying that he was not satisfied with the treaty provision giving Shantung to Japan, but as declaring that there was an informal understanding among the peace delegates that eventually Japan must make an acceptable agreement with China in the matter. He was represented as expressing confidence that Japan would deal rightly in the final settlement.

Discussing the failure of the Peace Conference to receive the representatives of Irish-American organizations on behalf of Irish freedom, Mr. Wilson is said to have told Senators that the representatives had so identified themselves with the revolutionary element in Ireland that it became impossible to receive them. He is quoted as saying that both he and David Lloyd George, the British Premier, had been anxious to arrange for a hearing.

The decision not to bind Germany to a definite indemnity, the President was reported to have said, was reached over his protest. He is quoted as saying that he consented to the indeterminate plan to help Premier Lloyd George over domestic obstacles.

The President is said to have taken a firm hand against any reservations in the Senate's ratification of the treaty. It is asserted that he would not be disposed kindly even toward interpretive reservations to make the Senate's position clear, pointing out that there always might be doubt as to whether any particular reservation was innocuous or would vitiate some league principle.

Regarding the proposed reservation under which the Senate would declare that the nation could not enter war under Article X. without a war declaration by Congress, Mr. Wilson is reported to have declared such a stipulation unnecessary. He is quoted as saying that the constitutional inability of the United States to make war without a Congressional declaration was one of the reasons why the League Council was authorized only to "advise" as to the steps to be taken.

Printed in the *New York Times*, July 11, 1919.

From Edward Nash Hurley

My dear Mr. President: Washington July 10, 1919.

Although I have been anxious to return to private life, ever since the war ended, I have withheld my resignation, first because I did not want to trouble you while you were in the midst of the international settlement, and second because in view of proposed and announced investigations of the various departments of the government by Congress I wanted to remain long enough to give the legislative committees ample time to make their inquiries.

With the extra session already assembled, I feel that the Congressional Committees will have sufficient opportunity between the present date and August 1 to inquire into any matters affecting contracts about which they may have doubt. I have already informed the Chairmen of the Senate and House Committees that I am at their disposal. I am hopeful, therefore, that you will find it possible to relieve me on August 1.

You will recall that when I retired as Chairman of the Federal Trade Commission it was with no thought of returning, at a later date, to public life. I want to spend more time with my own family. The war, however, forced all of us to put aside our own personal inclinations. When you asked me to serve on the War Council of the Red Cross, and later on the War Trade Board, and finally appointed me Chairman of the Shipping Board, I felt proud of the opportunity to give you and the government the best that was in me.

We were put to the necessity of creating an entirely new and enormous industry. We had no time to waste, but the whole nation rallied to the call, and the situation was met. Now that we have a very large portion of the fleet we set out to build, the next large problem is one of operation. I have submitted a plan to Congress, which should form the basis for the discussion which will lead to a permanent ship-operating and shipbuilding policy.

I feel that my own work has been done. The Shipping Board and its Emergency Fleet Corporation both are well organized and all that remains is for Congress to work out the legislation that will serve as a compass for the future.

In handing you my resignation, please let me express my heartfelt appreciation of your constant aid, counsel and sympathetic cooperation. Your leadership has been an inspiration to all who have served under you. My whole experience as part of your administrative course has increased my faith in human nature.

The remembrance of your generosity and kindness, and the satisfaction of having served under your leadership, in so critical a period, will remain with me always.

With sincere appreciation, I am,

Faithfully yours, Edward N. Hurley

TLS (WP, DLC).

To Edward Nash Hurley

My dear Hurley: [The White House] 10 July, 1919.

As Chairman of the Shipping Board, you have done work of a very exceptional character both at home and abroad, and it is with genuine and very deep regret that I accept your resignation, only because you desire me to do so. It would not be just to insist upon your continuing. Yielding to your wishes, I accept it to take effect the first of August, 1919.

In more than one capacity you have served the country with distinction in these difficult times, and I am sure that you can carry away from your tasks the sense of duty well performed. No one ever served his country's interests more devotedly than did you, and personally I am deeply grateful to you. I am sure that my gratitude and appreciation are shared by all those who know the importance of the work you have done.

Cordially and sincerely yours,   Woodrow Wilson

TLS (Letterpress Books, WP, DLC).

From Carter Glass

Dear Mr. President: Washington July 10, 1919.

Shortly after the receipt of your wireless message of February 19, 1919,[1] I arranged with your approval for the establishment of a credit in favor of Italy of $25,000,000, to be availed of for such purchases in neutral countries as I should from time to time approve. There has been advanced to the Italian Government $7,000,000 chargeable to said credit and about $5,500,000 thereof must be reserved to meet an excess, of which the Italians advise me, over their previous estimate of their existing commitments in the United States thus leaving a balance of about $10,500,000.

The Treasury has been informally asked by the representatives of the Italian Government if it would object to the use of all or part of the balance of said credit to cover new purchases by Italy in the United States instead of in neutral countries. In my judgment it is to the advantage of the United States to advance money to Italy for expenditure here rather than for expenditure elsewhere.

Since Mr. Davis[2] communicated from Paris your wishes on the subject the Treasury has not approved any applications for new purchases by Italy either in the United States or in neutral countries.

In view of the repeated requests that have been made by the representatives of the Italian Government for my approval of new purchases, I am constrained to ask you whether it is your wish that the Treasury should continue to refuse to approve additional Italian purchases, under credits already established, either in the United States or in neutral countries. As a financial matter only and without regard to political considerations, I should permit Italian applications for new purchases to be approved in proper cases within the limits of the remaining balance of credits heretofore assured Italy by the Treasury.

Cordially yours,   Carter Glass.

TLS (WP, DLC).
¹ WW to C. Glass, Feb. 19, 1919, Vol. 55.
² That is, Norman Hezekiah Davis. See N. H. Davis to WW, April 18, 1919, and WW to N. H. Davis, April 19, 1919, both in Vol. 57; N. H. Davis to WW, April 23, 1919, Vol. 58; and Enclosure II printed with N. H. Davis to WW, May 13, 1919, Vol. 59.

From Charles Richard Crane, with Enclosure

Dear Mr. President: Beirut, Syria. July 10, 1919.

We are sending you various papers bearing upon our experiences in Syria,¹ including a copy of the partial report cabled to you in code.

We feel that our mission has been very worth while and that there is raw material here for a much more promising state than we had in the Philippines. The every-day people are sober, industrious and intelligent. There is a great deal of national feeling which has been revealed from time to time when the country has come under great strain or menace. The present situation is such a situation. There are three special elements of nationality here extending over a wide area. They are: (1) the rich and beautiful Arabic language; (2) both Christian and Moslem faiths; (3) the ancient and interesting culture.

The people have been touching in the confidence they have shown in us and we feel that it would have been difficult for a general commission to have been given so much self-revelation, even in a very long time.

I hope that if Howard Bliss is still in the U.S.A. you will ask him to look over these papers and see if our conclusions and observations based on so brief an experience tally with his own.

Cordial messages to you and Mrs. Wilson and your official family, from us all.   Sincerely yours,   Charles R. Crane

TLS (WP, DLC).
¹ "STATEMENT OF THE EMIR FAISAL TO THE AMERICAN COMMISSION," n.d.; "Statement of Syrian Conference, Damascus, July 3, 1919"; and A. H. Lybyer, "The Apparent Situation in Syria, July 1, 1919," T MSS (WP, DLC). All three documents came to essentially the same conclusions as those of the Enclosure printed below, except that Faisal did not propose himself as the head of the Syrian state and did not mention Palestine or the Zionists.

ENCLOSURE

Report of the American Section of the International Commission on Mandates in Turkey, cabled in code to President Wilson, from Beirut, Syria, July 10, 1919.

Commission has now covered strategic points from Beersheba to Baalbek and from the Mediterranean to Amman. Every facility has been given the Commission by the various Military Governors though inevitably some steering. Heartily welcomed everywhere. No doubt of great interest of people, some Bedouin delegates riding thirty hours to meet Commission. Gratitude to you and America constantly and warmly expressed. Popular program developing in range and definiteness, showing considerable political insight. Much to indicate our inquiry greatly worth while and freer expression of opinion to American Section than could have been made to mixed commission.

Certain points are unmistakable. Intense desire for unity of all Syria and Palestine and for as early independence as possible. Unexpectedly strong expressions of national feeling. Singularly determined repulsion to becoming a mere colony of any power, and against any kind of French mandate. Only marked exceptions to these statements are found in a strong party of Lebanese who demand complete separation of Lebanon with French collaboration.[1] In our judgment proclamation of French Mandate for all Syria would precipitate warfare between Arabs and French, and force Great Britain to dangerous alternative.

America genuinely first choice of most for mandatary because believed has no territorial ambitions. General demand that essentially same conditions should hold for Irak as for Syria. Both British and French officers share conviction that unity of whole of Syria and Palestine is most desirable. They feel that constant friction and dangers to peace are otherwise inevitable, between British, French and Arabs. But there is little clear evidence that either British or French are willing entirely to withdraw.

Subsequent experience only confirms earlier despatch concerning Zionism.[2]

Syrian National Congress, composed of sixty-nine regularly elected representatives, Moslems and Christians, from Syria, including Palestine and Lebanon, met at Damascus July 2nd. Formulated program acceptable to all Moslems and many Christians, except that Christians prefer strong mandatary power for their protection. Congress asks immediate complete political independence for united Syria. Government a civil, constitutional, federal monarchy, safe-guarding rights of minorities, under Emir Faisal as king. Affirm Article twenty-two[3] of Covenant does not apply to Syria. Mandate interpreted to mean economic and technical assistance limited in time. Asks this earnestly from America. Should America refuse, then England. Denies all right and refuses all assistance of France. Vigorously opposes Zionistic plan and Jewish immigration. Asks complete independence of Mesopotamia. Protests against Sykes-Picot agreement and Balfour Declaration. Concludes requesting that political rights be not less than under the Turks.

Whole situation here involves elements of world-wide importance. Solution proposed in Paris putting Syria under France would not strengthen friendly relations of France with England but the contrary. Arabs would certainly resist by every means. England would be obliged to choose between Arabs and French with Egypt and India in the background. Moslem world undoubtedly unhappy at seeing its last independent state disappear. Reduction of Turkey accepted as necessary political measure but if followed by resistance to formation of Arab state, interpretation will be hostility to Moslem world, an attitude neither Britain nor France can afford. But important move can be made greatly strengthening position of both. Emir Faisal, despite limitations of education, had become unique outstanding figure capable of rendering greatest service for world peace. He is the heart of the Moslem world, with enormous prestige and popularity, confirmed believer in Anglo-Saxon race, really great lover of Christianity. Could do more than any other to reconcile Christianity and Islam, and longs to do so. Even talks seriously of American College for Women at Mecca. Most important Faisal be encouraged, supported and given opportunity to work out his plans. Given proper sympathy and surroundings, no danger of his getting adrift or taking big step without Anglo-Saxon approval. Every doctrine and policy concerning Syrian state should take this into consideration.

We are sending by courier important documents showing general convictions of people.   (Signed: Crane, King)

T MS (WP, DLC).
    [1] The Maronite Christian community in the region of Lebanon centered around Beirut had long favored greater political autonomy for Lebanon under French protection for both religious and economic reasons. See Philip S. Khoury, *Syria and the French Mandate: The Politics of Arab Nationalism, 1920-1945* (Princeton, N. J., 1987), pp. 27-32.
    [2] See C. R. Crane and H. C. King to WW, June 20, 1919.
    [3] That is, the article concerning mandates.

From John Sharp Williams

My Dear Mr. President: [Washington] July 10, 1919.

I was just asked for an interview of what I thought of your Address to the Senate, and I gave this out—what is more I meant it:

"You ask me what I think of the President's Address to the Senate: I think that in breadth of vision, in height of humanitarianism, in fundamental world statesmanship, and in the delicacy of dovetailed-English, it is the greatest thing that he himself has ever ut-

tered, and when I say that that means the greatest thing ever uttered by any President of the United States since Lincoln died. His
words are a fitting close to his magnificent and unselfish and upon
the whole effective work at Paris as a member of the Peace Conference."

I am, Mr. President, with every expression of regard,

Very truly yours,   John Sharp Williams

TLS (WP, DLC).

From the Diary of Henry Fountain Ashurst

July 11, 1919.

When Abraham Lincoln delivered his oration at Gettysburg in
1863, (which oration nobody discovered to be "immortal" until Lincoln had been dead some years) he turned to his friend, Mr. Ward
H. Lamon, and said: "Lamon, that speech won't scour." Scour was
then a folklore word analogous to our slang "make good." President
Wilson's speech to the Senate yesterday may in the long future be
highly regarded, but it did not "scour" today. Everyone in the Senate was on tiptoe of expectation. The President's opponents as well
as his supporters expected a masterpiece. Here was the President
just home from Europe where he had met and had matched wits
with cunning men. Here were the League supporters hungry for
arguments in support of the League, whilst supporter and opponent alike, expected explanations of obscure portions of the Covenant; for example: Why was Shantung Peninsula awarded to Japan when it is the Chinese Holy Land? What about the
safeguarding of the Monroe Doctrine? What does Article Ten
mean? Why are Poland and Czecho-Slovakia set up as independent states and Ireland's 700 years of struggle for independence
unrecognized? How may the U. S. withdraw from the League?
What mandatories do we assume? These and many other vital
questions were ignored.

I was petrified with surprise. The League opponents were in
state of felicity; they winked, thrust tongue against cheek, and
whispered that Wilson had failed to "make good." Wilson's speech
was as if the head of a great Corporation, after committing his company to enormous undertakings, when called upon to render a
statement as to the meanings and extent of the obligations he had
incurred, should arise before the Board of Directors and tonefully
read Longfellow's Psalm of Life. Wilson was called upon to render
an accounting of the most momentous cause ever entrusted to an
individual. His audience wanted raw meat, he fed them cold tur-

nips. Completing his speech, the President laid the bulky Versailles Treaty upon the Vice-President's rostrum and walked from the Senate Chamber oblivious to the failure of his address.

There was a contraction of the back of his neck and a transparency of his ears; infallible indicia of a man whose vitality is gone.[1]

The moral elevation of his address may not be doubted and he may have had a wise purpose in refusing to furnish a popular speech.

The portion of the Press, supporting the League Covenant, aver that he acted wisely in leaving details to be explained to the Senate Committee on Foreign Relations. A copy of the "Treaty of Peace with Germany" ordered printed yesterday was today as "Document No. 49" placed upon each Senator's desk.

T MS (AzU).
[1] The contraction in the back of the neck was clearly a sign of tension and might well have been an indication that Wilson was in some pain from a headache, which would help to account for the uncharacteristic awkwardness, noted earlier, with which Wilson delivered the address. The transparency of the ears was an indication of a lack of proper blood supply to the head.

From Thomas William Lamont, with Enclosures

Personal.

Dear Mr. President: New York. July 11th, 1919.

This afternoon the League of Free Nations Association,[1] which, as you know, embodies membership throughout the country, brought down to me (inasmuch as I have been a director of the association since its inception), the attached copy of resolutions, recently adopted; such copy having been submitted to you, I understand, and also to Senator Lodge.

The interesting part is that Senator Lodge made immediate reply, in a letter of which I attach a copy to you for your personal and private perusal. To this letter of Senator Lodge I have suggested that the Association reply in accordance with the attached draft. Whether they will send such reply I am not certain, but I am inclined to think they will do so.

The object of the resolutions, as suggested, is not, in any way, to serve as a reservation, but simply to indicate a programme of proposals, for the future to be brought up to the League and discussed there in due course. The hope of the Association as indicated to me, was that such resolutions as these, if adopted in the way that I indicate, would not harm the situation in any way, and might serve as a constructive suggestion to certain senators. In haste

Sincerely yours,   T. W. Lamont

TLS (WP, DLC).
¹ About this organization and its activities, see Wolfgang J. Helbich, "American Liberals in the League of Nations Controversy," *Public Opinion Quarterly*, XXXI (Winter 1967-1968), 568-96. After April 1921, the organization was known as the Foreign Policy Association.

ENCLOSURE I

RESOLVED:

That the League of Free Nations Association in accordance with a referendum of its full membership, calls upon all forward-looking citizens to urge the United States Senate:

1. To ratify without reservations the Treaty with Germany, including the League of Nations Covenant.

Such ratification would establish immediate peace, the world's most urgent need in the interest of order and progress; would abolish many international injustices which have proved prolific causes of war, and would create an agency for the rectification of remaining injustice and for the establishment of mutually advantageous and just relations between nations.

2. To accompany its ratification with a resolution, declaring it to be the purpose of the United States, as made possible by the League of Nations Covenant, to:

(a) Press for the immediate restoration of Kiao-Chau and the German concessions in Shantung to the Chinese Republic.

(b) Hold that nothing in the Treaty or Covenant shall be construed as authorizing interference by the League in internal revolutions; or as preventing genuine redress and readjustment of boundaries, through orderly processes provided by the League, at any time in the future that these may be demanded by the welfare and manifest interest of the people concerned.

(c) Call for the inclusion of Germany in the Council of the League as soon as the new republic shall have entered in good faith upon carrying out the Treaty provisions; for the inclusion of Russia as soon as the Russian people establish stable government; and for the full participation of both Germany and Russia on equal footing in all economic intercourse as the best insurance against any reversion to the old scheme of balance of power, economic privilege and war.

(d) Press for the progressive reduction of armaments by all nations.

(e) Throw its whole weight in behalf of such changes in the Constitution and such developments in the practice of the League as will make it more democratic in its scheme of representation, its procedure more legislative and less exclusively diplomatic; an in-

strument of growth invigorated and molded by the active democratic forces of the progressive nations.

CC MS (WP, DLC).

E N C L O S U R E   I I

Henry Cabot Lodge to James Grover McDonald[1]

Personal.

My dear Sir: [Washington] July 10, 1919.

I have received your letter of July 9 with the resolutions which
you enclosed and which I shall be very happy to present to the
Senate if you desire or if you have not made arrangements to have
somebody else present them. The difficulty with the resolution
which you desire the Senate to pass and which includes some
points which ought to be, in my opinion, covered by reservations is
that the chances of amending the League of Nations after its ratification seem to me slight in the extreme. I think the only safety
for those who desire to make the League promote the peace of the
world and not dissensions between the nations and to guard the
rights and interests of the United States the abandonment of
which can do no good to the cause of peace, would be to make the
reservations now.   Very truly yours,   H. C. Lodge.

TCL (WP, DLC).
  [1] Chairman of the board of directors of the League of Free Nations Association, who
was just beginning his long career as a publicist and journalist in support of numerous
initiatives for international cooperation. First United States Ambassador to Israel, 1949-
1952.

E N C L O S U R E   I I I

A Draft of a Letter by Thomas William Lamont

Memorandum—Suggested reply to Mr. Lodge:

My dear Mr. Lodge: July 11, 1919.

We were glad to receive your letter of July 10th, and to note that
the resolutions that our Associations propose are of interest to you.
The matter is, as you indicate, of such importance to the interests
of our country and of the whole situation, that we should be glad
of the opportunity to confer with you at your early convenience in
Washington, with the idea of asking you to introduce the resolutions as you suggest.

Our Associations represent, as you undoubtedly are aware, a very large membership of intelligent and thinking people throughout the country, all devoted to the cause of permanent peace and to the idea that America shall continue to take in the future, as she has in the past, a leading part in the establishment and development of a League of Nations.

We are frank to say that, in our own view, the resolutions that we have forwarded to you, should be adopted as representing a constructive programme for the future, but not in the form of reservations to the ratification of the present proposed Treaty. We are convinced, from the information that we have received from abroad, that delay in the ratification of the Treaty will mean continued unsettlement of worldwide conditions, an encouragement of the Bolshevist movement, and a playing into the hands of the Germans. Further, it is difficult for us to see a danger point for America in the situation, and we venture to believe, with profound respect for your own judgment, that it will not only be not a difficult matter to amend the League from time to time, but that it will be an ordinary and accepted course of procedure; that the League of Nations is, in its present form, a tentative instrument, a basis of a great compact, but subject to constant amendment and improvement, in which America must take a leading part. We haven't any doubt as to the ability of America to guard her rights and interests, as you properly put it, either now or in the long future. Her position is too strong to make the case otherwise.

This view that we present to you for your consideration is one that we believe is shared, not only by the members of our Associations throughout the country, but, if we catch public sentiment correctly, by the public at large, quite regardless of party lines.

However, our minds are open in the matter and we shall welcome a brief conference with you, if you so determine, preferring that our resolution should be offered by as [a] statesman of your standing, who, in years past, has pronounced so emphatically in favor of an effective League of Nations.

With great respect,   Very truly yours,

T MS (WP, DLC).

Frank Lyon Polk to the American Mission in Paris

July 11, 1919, 4 p.m.

2546. Your [Our] 2499, July third eight p.m.[1]

Department announced to-day that all restrictions in regard to trade with Germany would be immediately removed and blanket license given permitting such trade, an exception however being made in regard to dyes, potash and chemicals. The President is surprised at the suggestion that the British and French intend to maintain any control in the nature of restrictions. He was very positive that all the Allied Governments and the United States were committed to remove all restrictions as soon as Germany ratified and the continuation of restrictions would lay the Governments making the restrictions open to the charge of bad faith and would involve the honor of the United States, as this Government is a party to the treaty which assured free, unrestricted trade.

The President wished me to convey his views to you so his position could be made clear in case there was any attempt to continue restrictions.   Polk.   Acting.

T telegram (SDR, RG 59, 763.72112/12382, DNA).
    [1] W. Phillips to Ammission, No. 2499, July 3, 1919, T and Hw telegram (SDR, RG 59, 763.72119/5509, DNA), which reads as follows:
"There is tremenduous pressure on the Department for definite information as to when and by what means trade relations with Germany may be reestablished. It is the unanimous opinion here that if the Allied countries are allowed to facilitate trade with Germany by sending consular officers or other commercial representatives into Germany in advance of the United States even if only for a few weeks, advantages would be gained by them which it would be very difficult to overcome. In view of this as definite answers as possible to the following questions are requested: (1) If the ratification of the peace treaty is delayed by Senate action when will it go into effect as to other signatories. (2) If Germany and three of the principal Allied Powers ratify the Peace Treaty will those Allied Powers be able to open trade with Germany and to send consuls and official or private trade representatives. (3) If so, is there no means by which American traders may have access to Germany pending ratification by the United States. (4) Is it to be understood from your telegram that the Department may exercise discretion in respect to the appointment of consular representatives, even unofficial, to Germany pending ratification by the United States. The Department has no thought of allowing Germans, except interns, to return to Germany, but is greatly interested in having definite advice upon the foregoing points to be used in answering numerous inquiries from all quarters. In view of the feeling here, as I interpret it, I fear that if the United States is unable to open trade with Germany pending ratification of the treaty by the Senate, the administration will be charged with postponing commercial intercourse with Germany in order to influence ratification of the treaty, since the ratifying powers will have begun trade with Germany and Germany will as a practical matter be at peace with the United States.
    "In this relation please see telegram 289 from Edwards, The Hague, to McCormick, which I am repeating to you and which indicates that the British and French are not even awaiting ratification before resuming trade relations with Germany. If the practice described in that telegram should become generally known here, I cannot but think that the effect would not only be unfortunate for the Department but might well create an embarrassing irritation toward Great Britain and France unless the U.S. shall insist upon like privileges for its own citizens. Phillips"

From Edward Mandell House

London. July 11, 1919.

Urgent. 2511. (Special Green) Secret. For the President from Colonel House. After a session of three days, the Commission on mandatories have finished mandates for class B and C, and I herewith submit them for your consideration and approval. The report was unanimous with the exception that the French reserved the right to discuss further article two in mandatory B. They accepted all of the clause but wished to add at the end of words: "whether colonial or metropolitan." This, of course, would give them the power to raise troops for national defense and would vitiate the entire mandatory theory. The Japanese desire to substitute paragraph one of article five of form B for article four in form C. They will not insist upon it, but merely make the reservation in conformity with the position they took in Paris. I hope that you will approve as early as possible so that I can communicate your decision to the other members of the Commission. In the event an agreement is reached it is the purpose of the Commission to make the text of these mandates public. The A type of mandate will not be formulated until some time in August. The reason why we defer this class of mandate is because of the uncertainty regarding the mandates which will be issued for the Turkish Empire.

(Green) "B" type of mandate.

(Type of mandate for such territories as may be governed in accordance with paragraph five of article twenty-two of the Covenant of the League of Nations.)

Preamble. Germany, having by article blank of the peace treaty signed at Versailles on the twenty-eighth June 1919 renounced all rights to blank, the Principal Allied and Associated Powers confer upon blank a mandate to govern this territory. Blank accepts the mandate thus conferred upon it and will execute the same on behalf of the League of Nations and in accordance with the following provisions:

Article one. The mandatory power shall be responsible for the peace, order and good government of the territory and undertakes by all means in its power to promote the material and moral well being and the social progress of its inhabitants. The mandatory power shall have full powers of legislation and administration.

Article two. The mandatory power undertakes not to establish any military or naval base, not to erect any fortifications and not to organize any native military force except for local police purposes and the defense of its territory.

Article three. The mandatory power undertakes: one, to provide for the eventual emancipation of all slaves, and for as speedy an elimination of domestic and other slavery as social conditions will allow; two, to suppress all forms of slave-trade; three, to prohibit all forms of forced or compulsory labor except for essential public works and services and then only in return for adequate remuneration; four, to protect the natives from fraud and force by the careful supervision of labor contracts and the recruiting of labor; five, to exercise a strict control over the traffic in arms and munitions and the sale of spirituous liquors.

Article four. One, the mandatory power undertakes that in the framing of laws relating to the holding or transference of the land it will take into consideration native laws and customs and will respect the rights and safeguard the interests of the native population; two, no native land may be transferred, except between natives, without the previous consent of the public authorities and no real rights over native land in favor of non-natives may be created except with the same consent; three, the mandatory power undertakes to promulgate strict regulations against usury.

Article five. One, the mandatory power undertakes to secure to all citizens and subjects of members of the League of Nations the same rights as are there enjoyed by its own nationals in respect to proceeding into any residence in the territory, the protection afforded to their person and property, the acquisition of property movable and immovable, and the exercise of their profession or trade, subject only to the requirements of public order and compliance with the local laws. Two, further the mandatory power undertakes to ensure to all citizens and subjects of the members of the League of Nations on the same footing as to its own nationals complete economic, commercial and industrial equality, and freedom of transit and navigation, provided, that the mandatory power shall be free to organize essential public works and services on such terms and conditions as it thinks just. Three, concessions for the development of the natural resources of the territory shall be granted by the mandatory power without distinction on grounds of nationality between the subjects or citizens of all members of the League of Nations but on such conditions as will maintain intact the authority of the local government. Four, the rights conferred by this article extend equally to companies and associations organized in accordance with the laws of any of the members of the League of Nations subject only to requirements of public order and compliance with the local law.

Article six.

The mandatory power undertakes to ensure to all complete freedom of conscience and the free exercise of all forms of worship, without distinction which are consonant with public order and morality.

Missionaries of all such religions shall be free to enter the territory and to travel and reside therein, and to acquire and possess property to erect religious buildings and to open schools throughout the territory, but the mandatory power shall have the right to exercise such control as may be necessary for the maintenance of public order and good government and to take all measures required for such control.

Article Seven. One, in accordance with these provisions the mandatory power undertakes to apply to the territory the benefits of any general international conventions already existing or that may be concluded hereafter respecting the slave-trade, the traffic in arms and ammunition, the liquor traffic and the traffic in drugs, as well as the conventions relating to commercial equality, freedom transit and navigation, the laws of aerial navigation and of postal, telegraphic and wireless communication. Two, the mandatory power undertakes to cooperate in the execution of any common policy adopted by the League of Nations for preventing and combating disease, including diseases of plants and animals.

Article eight. The mandatory power shall be authorized to constitute the territory into a customs, fiscal and administrative union or federation, with the adjacent territories under its own sovereignty, provided that the measures adopted to that end do not infringe the provisions of this mandate.

Article nine. The mandatory power shall extend its diplomatic protection to the natives of the territory when in foreign lands, under the same conditions as to its own nationals.

Article ten. The mandatory power shall make to the Council of the League of Nations an annual report, to the satisfaction of the Council, containing full information concerning the measures taken, to apply the provisions of the present mandate a copy of all laws and regulations made in the course of the year and affecting property, commerce, navigation or the moral and material well-being of the natives, shall be communicated therewith.

Article eleven. The consent of the Council of the League of Nations is required for any modification of the terms of this mandate.

Article twelve. One, if any dispute whatever should arise between the members of the League of Nations relating to the interpretation or application of this mandate, which cannot be settled by negotiations, this dispute shall be submitted to the Permanent Court of International Justice to be established by the League of Nations. Two, states members of the League of Nations may likewise bring any claims on behalf of their subjects or citizens for infractions of their rights under this mandate before the said court for decision.

Mandate class C. (type of mandate for such territories as may be governed in accordance with paragraph six of article 22 of the covenant of the League of Nations.) Revised draft agreed to July 10, 1919.

Preamble. Germany having by article blank of the Peace Treaty signed at Versailles on the twenty-eighth of June nineteen nineteen renounced all her rights to X. the Principal Allied and Associated Powers confer upon Y. a mandate to govern X. Y accepts the mandate thus conferred upon it and will execute the same on behalf of the League of Nations and in accordance with the following provisions.

Article one. Y shall have full power of administration and legislation over X as an integral portion of Y and may apply the laws and regulations Y to X subject to such local modifications as circumstances may require. Y undertakes by all means in its power to promote the material and moral well-being and the social progress of the inhabitants of X.

Article two. Y hereinafter referred to as the mandatory power undertakes that the slave trade shall be prohibited and that no forced labor shall be permitted, except for essential public works and services and then only for adequate remuneration. It further undertakes that the traffic in arms and ammunitions shall be controlled in accordance with the principles contained in the Brussels Act 1890 or any convention amending the same. The supply of intoxicating spirits and beverages to the natives of the territory shall be prohibited. X equals the mandated territory, Y equals the mandatory power.

Article three. The military training of the natives otherwise than for purposes of internal police and the local defense of the territory shall be prohibited. Furthermore, no military or naval bases shall be established or fortifications erected in the territory.

Article four. Subject to the provisions of any local law for the maintenance of public order and morals the mandatory power guarantees in the territory freedom of conscience and the free exercise of all forms of worship and undertakes to allow all missionaries, the subjects or citizens of any member of the League of Nations to enter into, travel and reside in the territory for the purpose of prosecuting their calling.

Article five. The mandatory power shall make to the Council of the League of Nations an annual report to the satisfaction of the Council containing full information with regard to the territory and indicating the measures taken to carry out the obligations assumed under articles one, two, three and four.

Article six. The consent of the Council of the League of Nations is required for any modification of the terms of this mandate. If any dispute whatever should arise between the members of the League of Nations relating to the interpretation of the application of these provisions which cannot be settled by negotiations this dispute shall be submitted to the Permanent Court of International Justice to be established by the League of Nations.

T telegram (WP, DLC).

From Frank Lyon Polk

My dear Mr. President: Washington July 11, 1919.

We have $1,000,000 accruing from the sale of foodstuffs from the $5,000,000 revolving fund for rationing North Russia, which we can still use for the same purpose. Telegrams from Archangel and Paris show:

1. That Mr. Hoover has no supplies for Archangel and Murmansk.
2. That the present stocks of flour there will be exhausted by August first.
3. That we have a moral obligation to continue the assistance which we have been rendering for the past year.
4. That the rationing of North Russia will, necessarily, have a bearing upon the support which has been promised to Kolchak.
5. That from a political point of view it is obviously unwise to let North Russia revert to Bolshevism through starvation, especially in view of Mr. Hoover's undertaking to supply Petrograd upon the overthrow of the Bolsheviki.[1]

I arranged a contract with the Grain Corporation which will enable us to ship at once about 5000 tons of flour to Archangel, but have not authorized the expenditure until I could get your views.

I believe the shipment should be made and hope that you will let me know that you approve.

I am, my dear Mr. President,
                    Faithfully yours,   Frank L Polk

Approved
    Woodrow Wilson[2]
12 July, 1919.

TLS (SDR, RG 59, 861.48/905, DNA).
    [1] Hoover had ordered increased shipments of food to Vyborg, then held by Finland, and other points in the vicinity of Petrograd in anticipation of the possible capture of the latter city by anti-Bolshevik forces. Hoover later recalled that he had taken this step at the request of the State Department. Herbert C. Hoover, *The Memoirs of Herbert Hoover* (3 vols., New York, 1951-52), I, 418-19. However, one scholar has concluded

that Hoover had in fact acted entirely on his own initiative. John M. Thompson, *Russia, Bolshevism, and the Versailles Peace* (Princeton, N. J., 1966), pp. 331-32.
    [2] WWhw.

From Carter Glass

Dear Mr. President: Washington July 11, 1919.
    By letter bearing date April 21 last the Treasury assured Italy of the establishment of credits in its favor

A. To meet commitments in the United States (including May interest on Italian obligations held by the United States Government) for which provision could not be made by the bank balances of the Italian Government in the United States or from the proceeds of sale of certain food products then being negotiated

$69,000,000

B. To meet claims of the United States War Department

22,000,000

C. For new purchases in the United States approved by the Treasury

5,000,000

D. To meet British claims for purchases made in the U.S. for Italy to the extent approved by the Treasury and to make payment for cereals under the allocation plan previously agreed upon

67,000,000

TOTAL $163,000,000

This letter was delivered before Mr. Davis communicated to me from Paris your wishes regarding future advances and credits to Italy.[1] It now transpires that the $5,000,000 of the said credits allocated to meet new purchases must be used wholly to meet commitments made by Italy and approved by the Treasury prior to the receipt of the aforementioned advices from Mr. Davis. Subsequently on advices from Mr. Davis further credits were assured Italy to provide for its share of purchases to be made in the United States for Austrian relief in the amount of $5,000,000 and the Treasury promised to establish a further credit in favor of Italy of $1,000,000 for the same purpose.

The aggregate of these credits is within the amounts of credits for Italy which you had previously approved.

Of the above mentioned credits $70,000,000 have been formally established and the balance, $99,000,000, remains to be formally established. If it meets with your approval, I propose to meet the Treasury's commitments in this respect and formally establish at an early date the balance of these credits. In view of the fact that these credits must, under the terms of the Liberty Loan Acts, be established before the termination of the war as proclaimed by you,

I deem it wise from the Treasury point of view not to longer delay the formal establishment of the credits mentioned.

If the early establishment of these credits meets with your approval may I ask you to so indicate at the foot of this letter.

Cordially yours,   Carter Glass.

The White House.
Approved: July   1919.

TLS (WP, DLC).
    [1] Again, see, e.g., N. H. Davis to WW, April 18, 1919, and WW to N. H. Davis, April 19, 1919, both in Vol. 57.

From Norman Hezekiah Davis

Dear Mr. President: Washington, D. C., July 11, 1919.

I have had a thorough discussion with Secretary Glass, Mr. Leffingwell, and Mr. Rathbone[1] on the financial situation of Europe, and the various measures which may be taken in connection therewith, and am leaving today to join my family in Stockbridge, Mass., for a short vacation. I expect to return to Washington in about two weeks, but in the meantime if any questions should arise in connection with the Peace negotiations or anything else, in which you think I can in any way be useful, I shall be only too glad to hold myself available and return at any time.

It has been a great source of satisfaction to me to have co-operated in the important and far-reaching work of the Peace Conference, and especially to have been privileged to work under your inspiring leadership, and it was therefore a great pleasure yesterday to witness your deserved reception at the Senate when you brought back this treaty.

Believe me, my dear Mr. President,

Most cordially and faithfully yours,   [Norman H. Davis]

CCL (N. H. Davis Papers, DLC).
    [1] That is, Russell Cornell Leffingwell and Albert Rathbone, both Assistant Secretaries of the Treasury.

From Newton Diehl Baker

Personal and Confidential.

My dear Mr. President: [Washington] July 11, 1919.

I attach this personal and confidential note to the record in the case of the United States against _____ and _____.

In this case the death penalty by hanging was imposed upon these two men for the crime of murder. They were privates who deserted from the Army and secreted themselves in a woods where they were for a long time sustained with food furnished by relatives and friends. The young men were heavily armed, and had proclaimed their intention to shoot any officers who attempted to apprehend them.

On the night of the crime they approached the house of the father of one of them, near which two Texas Rangers had stationed themselves for the purpose of capturing them. On their approaching the house firing started, with the result that one of the Rangers was killed, and the other severely wounded. Neither of the accused was injured. They were subsequently surrounded by a larger body of Rangers and surrendered.

The doubtful questions of fact presented by the conflicts of testimony may be assumed to have been correctly judged by the court as the trial was carefully conducted throughout, and the rights of the accused fully protected. The Acting Judge Advocate General finds no error in the record, and I have been able to find none in my examination of it.

It does appear, however, from the record, that these two young men, each twenty-four years of age, had had no education beyond the second grade in the public schools, which, I assume, since the[ir] entire experience was limited to three months in a remote country school, did little more than teach them their letters and the spelling of one syllable words. The whole record discloses the remoteness of their lives from the general civilization prevailing throughout the country. They were rough, illiterate, ignorant men. Their environment was rude and violent. Undoubtedly the idea of "crossing the water" terrified their imaginations, and the whole idea of being taken to France presented a picture to their minds of which it is impossible for us to conceive. Their desertion from the Army, their going about armed, and their ultimate attack upon the Rangers was a crime of violence, and yet it was not a premeditated murder, based upon any calculation of gain to themselves or hatred or ill will toward the individual victims.

I have read the record and tried to put myself in their place. I may have overdrawn the nameless terrors which their untutored imaginations conjured up and against which they resorted to violence to protect themselves, and yet I confess that under all the circumstances my strong feeling is that the society which left them illiterate might well exact less than the extreme penalty which it would rightfully exact from men who have had wider opportunities of contact and better equipment for appreciation of all the circumstances with which they were confronted.

If this aspect of the case appeals to your judgment I shall be very glad to have an order drawn commuting the death penalty to life imprisonment, and as the men are both young an opportunity would be had to see whether the educational processes of the prison will ultimately so reform these men as some day to justify further executive clemency.

Respectfully yours, [Newton D. Baker]

CCL (N. D. Baker Papers, DLC).

From William Gibbs McAdoo, with Enclosure

Dear Governor: New York July 11, 1919.

Your address to the Congress was a noble message and will appeal to the people, but I fear it is like casting pearls before swine, so far as the Senatorial cabal is concerned.

A good many of your best friends are very eager to have you make argumentative speeches, in your irresistible style, to the people when you go to the country on the League of Nations. I believe that such speeches from you would rout the opposition. From my observation and experience, I am sure that the average man, while sympathetic to the League, wants to be convinced by an argument that will make clear to him how the League will function and how it will prevent war.

I am sending you a copy of the Outlook of last week containing a speech I made on the League of Nations[1]—not as a suggestion to you, but merely as a sample of the kind of a speech which has evoked many letters from people I do not know who express themselves with some enthusiasm about it as giving the first clear comprehension of the League of Nations and its effects that they have yet had.

Nell joins me in dearest love for Edith and yourself. We are very happy that you are safely at home again.

Affectionately yours, W G McAdoo

P.S. I enclose a letter from Judge Wheeler of the Supreme Court of Connecticut. He is an ardent supporter and admirer of yours, a strong Democrat and did magnificent war work in Connecticut. WGM

[1] William G. McAdoo, "The League of Nations," *The Outlook*, CXXII (July 2, 1919), 367-72.

George Wakeman Wheeler to William Gibbs McAdoo

My dear Sir: Bridgeport, Conn. July 8th, 1919.

I want to thank you for your article in the Outlook. It is the most useful article I have seen. It really gets down to argument and that is what the thoughtful American is looking for.

I was in charge of the War Activities in Bridgeport and have charge of the Americanization work here. These connections have thrown me among all classes of people. I know what they are talking of and thinking of on this subject. They are afraid the League imperils American interests, and ties up our National existence to European dominance. A great many fear this is the substitution of Internationalism for Nationalism. They are sincere and conscientious. Some of the Senators I place in this class.

It wont do to meet these men with talk upon fundamentals, or on the philosophy of the League. Mr. Wilson has put these concepts as no other man could have done.

We have now reached another stage of this debate. The specific objections must be taken up in good humor, dispassionately discussed and overwhelmingly buried. And while this is being done the most intense Americanism must be preached, and American Nationality run up so that everybody can know the speaker means just that. I wish if you agree with me that you could present this view to Mr. Wilson.

I think the case of the League of Nations depends on how well and fairly Mr. Wilson argues the case. If he defends on generalities, or makes the same sort of speeches he has made, the League may lose in America. And I say this fully appreciating that the addresses he has made in Europe are to live always and are filled with passages no other living man could have uttered. And one thing more. If only Mr. Wilson could say a generous word for the Republicans for what they'd done in the war, for their stand for the country it would be invaluable to our great cause. And following this, if ignoring their patent hatred of him, he'd assume their opposition to the League was due to conscientious motives and that it was his purpose to try to make clear the doubts, there'd be a universal feeling that that was fair play. The exigencies of the fight may break down this neutral attitude but the advantage of the start will be with Mr. Wilson.

Please excuse my writing you at such length. This cause is near my heart and so is Mr. Wilson.

Very sincerely yours,   George W. Wheeler

TLS (WP, DLC).

To Frank Lyon Polk, with Enclosure

My dear Polk: The White House 12 July, 1919.

Will you not be kind enough to ask the Commission in Paris to present the following message to the gentlemen who so generously signed the enclosed message which I am returning herewith?

"It moves me very deeply that you should so fully realize the heartfelt sympathy I feel for the cause of Justice, and particularly for the nations which, because they are less strong than the strongest, have hitherto struggled with little hope for the realization of the highest and most legitimate ambitions. It gives me new courage and new pleasure in the work I am trying to do, that you should hearten me with such a greeting."

Cordially and faithfully yours,   Woodrow Wilson

TLS (SDR, RG 59, 763.72119/5872, DNA).

ENCLOSURE

Paris July 7 1919.

3019. The following message addressed to the President has been received by the Commission with the request that it be transmitted to him.

"Permit us on the eve of your return to America and in the name of the small nations to express to you the profound impression we have received of your sincerity, disinterestedness and good will, as shown in your utterances and in your unremitting labors for a peace which shall be enduring because founded on justice.

The services which you have rendered to this generation and posterity cannot be adequately measured until time has brought them into their true perspective, but none can attest so truly as we, the sympathy and solicitude you have manifested to struggling nations, lifting us from despondency to hope and dispelling the apprehensions and misgivings which have afflicted us in the past.

That our peoples look to the future with confidence is to a large extent a tribute to your leadership and work and we beg that you will carry home to the great American republic, whose disinterestedness, efficiency and altruism you so well applied to stricken Europe, our grateful acknowledgements. E. K. Venizelos, Nik P. Pashitch, ? Edward Benes, Boghos Nubar Pasha, Nahum Sokolow."[1]   American Mission

T telegram (SDR, RG 59, 763.72119/5545, DNA).
[1] Nahum Sokolow, Polish-born author and journalist who wrote in the Hebrew language; general secretary of the World Zionist Organization.

To William Phillips

My dear Phillips: [The White House] 12 July, 1919.

Your letter of July eighth has made me very glad. I value your friendship and approval very highly, and it takes away a lot of the fatigue and of the self-dissatisfaction with which I have come out of the work on the other side of the water to have such cordial approval from you. I thank you with all my heart, and your commendation is made all the more delightful by your generous way of expressing it.

Cordially and faithfully yours,   Woodrow Wilson

TLS (Letterpress Books, WP, DLC).

To William Cox Redfield

My dear Redfield: The White House 12 July, 1919.

Thank you warmly for your generous note of July tenth.[1] I have been anxious to see you and grasp hands with you since my return, and in the meantime am heartily obliged to you for your commendation of my address to the Senate.

Hoping that you are all well,

Cordially and sincerely yours,   Woodrow Wilson

TLS (W. C. Redfield Papers, DLC).
[1] It is missing.

To Newton Diehl Baker

My dear Baker: The White House 12 July, 1919.

No commendation of my address on Thursday can gratify me more than yours does,[1] and I thank you for it from a full heart.

In haste,

Cordially and faithfully yours,   Woodrow Wilson

TLS (N. D. Baker Papers, DLC).
[1] Baker's note, undoubtedly an ALS, is missing in WP, DLC.

To John Sharp Williams

My dear Senator: The White House 12 July, 1919.

Nothing could have gratified me more than what you have said about my address to the Senate. Your approval makes me very happy and gives me new spirit for the work ahead of us. It was generous of you to let me know what you had said. You must have known how it would cheer and help me.

Cordially and faithfully yours,   Woodrow Wilson

TLS (J. S. Williams Papers, DLC).

To John Spargo

My dear Mr. Spargo: The White House 12 July, 1919

Accept my cordial thanks for your generous letter of the eighth of July,[1] which has given me a great deal of pleasure and satisfaction. I deeply appreciate your kind approbation.

Cordially and sincerely yours,   Woodrow Wilson

TLS (J. Spargo Coll., VtU).
[1] It is missing in WP, DLC, and the J. Spargo Coll., VtU.

To Frank Irving Cobb

My dear Cobb: The White House 12 July, 1919.

Your letter of July ninth[1] gave me the kind of pleasure that goes deep and makes the day's work easier, and I thank you for it with all my heart. I was mightily disappointed when I got to the other side to find that you had returned to this side, because I was looking forward with such pleasure to working with you over there. It would have been a joy and a benefit to have had your advice, and now that I am back home I am sure I shall get many a tip that will be of profit, from your own thoughtful head, about the fight that is ahead of us. I have a "hunch" that it is not going to be quite as hard and long as it looks.

With warmest regards,

Cordially and faithfully yours,   Woodrow Wilson

TLS (IEN).
[1] It is missing in WP, DLC.

To the Right Reverend James Henry Darlington[1]

My dear Bishop Darlington: [The White House] 12 July, 1919.

I have related with great amusement your vigor in sticking the badge *into me*,[2] but unluckily in the rush that was made for me the badge was almost torn out of my hand and it[3] was a good deal injured. I appreciated very much the impulse which made you try to attach it to me.

Thank you for telling me about the Russian Metropolitan's[4] presence in this country. I shall certainly seek an early half hour of leisure to see him. I cannot name it just now, but shall not forget to see so important a person.[5]

In haste,

Cordially and sincerely yours,   [Woodrow Wilson]

TLS (Letterpress Books, WP, DLC).
    [1] Protestant Episcopal Bishop of Harrisburg, Pennsylvania.
    [2] The letter to which this was a reply is missing in WP, DLC.
    [3] The badge, not Wilson's hand.
    [4] Platon, Metropolitan of Odessa and Kherson.
    [5] Darlington brought Platon to the White House for a brief meeting with Wilson at 2 p.m. on July 23, 1919. The *New York Times*, July 25, 1919, reports on their conversation on that occasion.

To Henry Paul Merritt[1]

[The White House] 12 July, 1919.

I hope that you will not think that I am taking an unwarranted liberty in saying that I earnestly hope, as do all friends of the great liberal movement which it represents, that the Legislature of Alabama will ratify the Suffrage Amendment to the Constitution of the United States. It would give added hope and courage to the friends of justice and enlightened policy everywhere and would constitute the best possible augury for the future of liberal policy of every sort.

Woodrow Wilson

T telegram (Letterpress Books, WP, DLC).
    [1] Speaker of the House of Representatives of Alabama.

To Thomas Erby Kilby[1]

[The White House] 12 July, 1919.

I hope you will pardon me if I express my very earnest hope that the Suffrage Amendment to the Constitution of the United States may be ratified by the great State of Alabama. It would constitute a very happy augury for the future and add greatly to the strength of a movement which in my judgment is based upon the highest considerations both of justice and expediency.

Woodrow Wilson

T telegram (Letterpress Books, WP, DLC).
    [1] Governor of Alabama.

From William Cox Redfield

My dear Mr. President: Washington July 12, 1919.

The situation as regards passenger carrying vessels from our ports to South America is giving me a good deal of concern. The number of American vessels is so few that our citizens who wish to visit South America on business are obliged to wait for British ships and, even with these, there are not enough.

The War Department has a number of large passenger carrying vessels which, before many months, will be released from their service. It would be unfortunate if all or even most of these were to be held and turned over for civilian use together. There are not facilities for repairing all of these ships at one time. A far better arrangement would be to have them turned over one at a time so that they may be refitted and put into use with the least possible delay.

Respecting this and the general subject as to how these passenger vessels are to be handled in our commerce, may I say that after a talk with Mr. Hurley before whom I brought the matter, we concur in thinking that it is desirable that a conference should take place between the Secretary of War, the Secretary of the Navy, Mr. Hurley and myself. We should be glad if you would suggest to the first two named the desirability of such a conference, with the thought in mind of reaching a result which we might later lay before you.

Awaiting the favor of your response, I am

Yours very truly,   William C. Redfield

TLS (WP, DLC).

From Frank Lyon Polk

My dear Mr. President: Washington July 12, 1919.

Mr. McCormick tells me that after conferring with you he understands that you approve of selling to Kolchak's Government, on a credit basis, any available surplus materials which may now be in the hands of the War Department, provided that no formal or diplomatic recognition of the Omsk Government results.

I am quite confident that the Secretary of War can deal with the representatives of Admiral Kolchak in this country and contract with them for the purchase of materials without conferring on the Kolchak Government any form of recognition on the part of the United States. I have written Mr. Baker that I shall be glad to discuss how this result can be achieved as soon as he reaches a decision with you as to whether or not the materials are to be sold.

Personally, I feel very strongly that we should translate into action the desire and purpose of the Government to assist Russia which you have so clearly and convincingly formulated from time to time. Consequently, I hope very much that after conferring with the Secretary of War that you can see your way clear to putting the very much needed supplies which the War Department has, at the disposal of Kolchak and his associates.

The most recent telegram we have from the Counsul General at Omsk[1] expresses the hope that we may be able to adopt the same liberal attitude, which has already been adopted by the French and British. Mr. Harris tells us that England has already furnished about 300,000 uniforms to Denekine[2] and 200,000 to Kolchak, and about 500,000,000 rounds of cartridges and 2000 machine guns and some tanks, on the understanding that they will be paid for by some future all-Russian Government; while France has supplied 400 heavy guns and is shipping 135 aeroplanes on the same principle.

I hope our assistance may not be limited to such a purely military character. The Russians look to us for disinterested assistance quite as much as do any of the other nations who are now struggling to reestablish normal conditions.

Faithfully yours,   Frank L. Polk

TLS (WP, DLC).
  [1] That is, Ernest Lloyd Harris.
  [2] That is, Gen. Anton Ivanovich Denikin.

Georges Clemenceau to Robert Lansing

Paris July 12, 1919.

3105. Following reply received from Clemenceau with regard to Senate resolution concerning the cause of Ireland.[1]

"Paris. June 25, 1919. Mr. Clemenceau to Mr. Lansing. Your Excellency. I have the honor to acknowledge to your Excellency receipt of the communication which you have been good enough to make to me, in the name of the American Commission to Negotiate Peace, of a resolution adopted by the Senate of the United States concerning 'the Exposition of the cause of Ireland before the peace Conference.'

Your Excellency is good enough to call my attention to the request of the Senate, as a result of which the American Commission to Negotiate Peace desires the hearing of Edouard de Valera, of Arthur Griffith, and of Count George Noble Plunkett by the Peace Conference.

After due reflection, it appears to me absolutely impossible to grant the request of which you are the interpreter, without deliberately exposing myself to exceed the limits of our task. The Peace Conference, instituted by the Allied and Associated Governments, has endeavored in so far as possible, to institute better conditions of peace in parts of the territories which joined in the war against us. No one knows better than you how far from easy this task is, but it forced itself upon our deliberations and we have resolutely accepted it. Intervention in the affairs of Allied states seems to me a question which the present Peace Conference can in no way consider under any circumstance whatsoever. If such a thing were attempted, I cannot doubt that it would bring about very animated retorts, and the object of our work might be brought to nothing by endless dissensions.

Your Excellency will thus be good enough to excuse me if I am obliged to bring to your attention the fact that I would fail in my first duty as President of the Peace Conference by carrying out the suggestion which you have done me the honor to communicate to me.

I beg Your Excellency to receive the assurance of my high consideration G. Clemenceau."   American Mission

T telegram (WP, DLC).
    [1] See the Enclosure printed with RL to WW, June 7, 1919 (second letter of that date), Vol. 60.

From Prince Faisal

Paris, July 12, 1919

3115. Following for President Wilson from Emir Feisul dated Egypt July 9: "At this great historic moment I beg to tender to your highly esteemed person and the American nation my sincerest and most heartfelt congratulations and wishes on signing the peace through your personal efforts and the valuable support of your noble nation. Justice has secured a brilliant victory and your efforts have been crowned with success. I pray the Almighty to make it a complete and everlasting peace for the world."

American Mission.

T telegram (SDR, RG 59, 763.72119/5800, DNA).

A News Report

[July 12, 1919]
LEAVES LEAGUE FIGHT
Hitchcock Takes Rest as Wilson Shows "Lack of Warmth."
SENATOR SWANSON IN CHARGE

A change of plan in the program of defense of the President's league of nations covenant in the Senate, involving the absence of Senator Hitchcock, minority leader, from the helm, became known yesterday when it was announced that the opening salvo of oratory and the leadership in the fight would be assumed by Senator Swanson. Senator Hitchcock, who has been the mainstay of the defense and defended the league against opposition onslaughts on every occasion, has gone to Swampscott, Mass., to get the benefit of the refreshing airs of the North coast and an opportunity for some good golf. He has decided to spare himself active work on behalf of the covenant fight for the immediate present.

The departure of Senator Hitchcock at this crucial time is understood to be associated with some lack of warmth between the President and the Nebraska senator, which has apparently developed within the past forty-eight hours. Friends of the senator admitted frankly that Mr. Hitchcock was not altogether pleased with the signs of recognition of his leadership which came from the President.

Anyway, Senator Hitchcock did not participate in the conferences which the President held with administration leaders at the Capitol on Thursday afternoon and he does not intend to figure prominently in the role of leader when the big fight starts on Monday. It is hoped that matters will be smoothed over, but in the meantime the senator is going to enjoy a well-earned rest.

In explaining what is described as the "lack of warmth" in the greetings between the President and Senator Hitchcock, it is said that when the special committee of five senators, all members of the committee on foreign relations and headed by Senator Lodge, went to the White House on Wednesday morning to notify the President that the Senate would give ear to his explanation of the purposes of the league of nations, the President did not make the welcome to Mr. Hitchcock much more cordial than the one he extended to Senator Borah.

On Thursday when the same committee went forth to welcome the head of the nation and lead him through the Senate portal there developed the same lack of warmth. When the President retired to his ante-room at the conclusion of the presentation of his case Democratic Senators gathered about him for counsel but Senator Hitchcock was not in the group. The President consulted principally with Senators Swanson, Williams, Phelan and Pittman. Following this Mr. Hitchcock made arrangements for his visit to the Swampscott golf links.

No explanation is offered as to the President's indicated change of administration leader in the Senate. It is well known in senatorial circles, however, that Senator Hitchcock has worked for the league because he sincerely believed in it and not because he wished to climb aboard the administration bandwagon.

During the whole period of the war and even before the entry of the United States into the struggle Senator Hitchcock has often been at odds with the President. Long before the war first signs of this disagreement developed. They were first disclosed when Senator Hitchcock was a member of the Senate banking and currency committee and the Federal reserve currency act was in the making. Then Senator Hitchcock stood with Senators Weeks and Reed against some suggestions for the formulation of the system which William Jennings Bryan wanted incorporated.[1]

In the early days of the war in Europe the attitude of Senator Hitchcock was adverse to the President's course in dealing with the imperial German government. More than eighteen months ago he joined with Senator Chamberlain[2] in a campaign of investigation concerning alleged shortcomings in the management of the War Department. It is suggested that the President may not have forgotten this part of Senator Hitchcock's activities and that the President personally prefers Senator Swanson to lead the league fight.

Printed in the *Washington Post*, July 12, 1919.
[1] About this matter, see Arthur S. Link, *Wilson: The New Freedom* (Princeton, N. J., 1956), pp. 228-31, 233-34, 237. Senators Weeks and Reed were John Wingate Weeks, Republican of Massachusetts, and James Alexander Reed, Democrat of Missouri.
[2] That is, George Earle Chamberlain, Democrat of Oregon.

A Press Release

12 July 1919.

Statement by the Secretary to the President:

The stories appearing in the morning papers of a disagreement between the President and Senator Hitchcock are without the slightest foundation. There has been no conference between the President and the Democratic senators, either at the White House or at the Capitol, since his return. What the newspapers referred to as a conference was merely an informal meeting at the President's room in the Capitol which took place immediately after the President addressed the Senate, when many Democratic senators, including Senator Hitchcock, came to greet the President and to congratulate him upon his address. I was present when the President met Senator Hitchcock. The meeting was most cordial in every way. The President deeply appreciates Senator Hitchcock's fine support as the ranking member of the Committee on Foreign Relations and will at the earliest moment seek an opportunity to confer with him on all phases of the Peace Treaty.

T MS (J. P. Tumulty Papers, DLC).

Breckinridge Long to Joseph Patrick Tumulty, with Enclosures

My dear Mr. Tumulty: Washington July 12, 1919.

I am attaching hereto the following papers in relation to the visit of the Abyssinian Mission which the President will receive at noon on Monday next:

1. Translation of autographed letter from the Empress of Abyssinia;
2. Translation of autographed letter from the Heir-Apparent to the throne of Abyssinia;
3. Translation of remarks which His Excellency Dedjazmatch Nadao, the Chief of the Mission, will read, and,
4. Draft of proposed response of the President.

The name of the Empress of Abyssinia is Zaouditou and is pronounced as though spelled "Zowdeetoo." The Heir-Apparent is Prince Ras Taffari,[1] which is pronounced as though spelled "Ras Taffar*ee*" (the "a" is pronounced as in "car" and the accent is on the "ee").

I will escort the Mission and will be accompanied by Mr. G. Cornell Tarler,[2] of the Department of State who is attached to them, and by Captain P. R. Morrissey,[3] of the United States Army who has been in attendance upon them since their arrival in New York.

It would be very much appreciated if the President would indicate to the Mission that he will cause to be delivered to them, before their departure from this country, autographed letters addressed to the Empress of Abyssinia and to the Heir-Apparent in response to those sent to him.

Proposed drafts of such responses will be sent over later unless the President disapproves.

They are bearing various gifts to the President from the Empress of Abyssinia. In England the King received the gifts and stated to them that he would send gifts to the Empress and the Heir-Apparent of Abyssinia. They understand, however, that it is not the custom for the United States to send gifts but it would be most appropriate if the President would send, in place of the gifts, an autographed picture to the Empress and the Heir-Apparent. If he approves of this he may want to state that to them upon the occasion of their reception by him.

It is customary, I believe, that the gifts should be carried to the White House before the arrival of the Mission and that they be displayed upon a table in the room in which the President will receive them. After receiving the Mission, and after the formalities, he may want to proceed with them to the table and examine the gifts and make some expressions of pleasure at receiving them. Proceeding upon this theory, I will see that the gifts are delivered to the White House on Monday morning, unless the arrangement is disagreeable to the President, in which case if you will notify me I will, of course, see that his every desire is executed.

Yours very sincerely,   Breckinridge Long

TLS (WP, DLC).
  [1] Later Emperor Haile Selassie I.
  [2] George Cornell Tarler, a career diplomat at this time on duty at the State Department.
  [3] Actually, Capt. Patrick J. Morrissey.

E N C L O S U R E   I

WOODROW WILSON
PRESIDENT OF THE UNITED STATES OF AMERICA,

To Her Majesty
  Zaouditou,
    Empress of Ethiopia.
Great and Good Friend:
  I have received at the hands of the Ethiopian envoys the letter expressing Your Imperial Majesty's pleasure and the joy of the Ethiopian Empire, that the part taken by the United States in the war for the liberty of the world has helped to bring about the victory of the nations fighting for equality and independence.

Your Majesty's good wishes afford me deep satisfaction and I share the hope that the friendly relations established between our peoples in the time of His Majesty Menelik II, will lead to the development of commercial ties by which both nations will be greatly benefited.

I trust that your reign will continue to redound to Your Majesty's glory and to the prosperity and happiness of your people, in whose affections may Your Majesty long live.

And I pray God to have Your Imperial Majesty in His safe and holy Keeping.

>Your Good Friend,   (Signed) Woodrow Wilson
Washington, July 23, 1919.

TC of engrossed letter (WP, DLC).

E N C L O S U R E   I I

TRANSLATION OF THE AUTOGRAPHED LETTER
FROM HER MAJESTY THE EMPRESS OF ABYSSINIA.

>(Seal)

The Lion of the Tribe of Juda has conquered.

Zaouditou, Empress of Ethiopia, to His Excellency, Mr. Wilson, President of the United States of America.

We extend to you our honorable compliments.

The Ethiopian Empire was glad to hear that America had entered the European war of 1914 for the liberty of the world and was victorious; our Government was therefore happy and has sent this mission to express our pleasure.

Our principal thoughts and desires are those of His Majesty, Menelik II, whose friendly relations with the United States we are desirous of continuing and strengthening; it is our further desire to strengthen and develop commercial ties between both Governments.

We feel in our hearts that America has arisen with firmness to proclaim the equality and independence of all the nations of the world.

May God grant to your country blessings and prosperity, and to your people peace and rest.

Written at Addis Abeba, 15 Meizia 1911.

>(English calendar 22 April 1919)

E N C L O S U R E   I I I

TRANSLATION OF THE AUTOGRAPHED LETTER
FROM THE HEIR APPARENT OF ABYSSINIA.

>(Seal)

RAS TAFFARI, Heir-Apparent to the throne of Ethiopia, to his Excellency, Mr. Wilson, President of the United States of America:

We are very glad that America, entering into the war of 1906

(1914), has been victorious. It was our greatest desire to be of assistance to the Allies, but as our country was then unsettled, we regret very much our inability to realize our wishes; however we are very delighted that the final victory was for the Allies.

When your consul at Aden, Mr. Addison E. Southard, came to Addis Abeba and told us of the purpose of America to give independence to the entire world, my heart was comforted with hope.

I beg to inform your Excellency that my most earnest hope now is that the bonds of friendship between the Ethiopian Government and the United States of America may be strengthened and that closer commercial ties may be formed.

May God give to your Government peace and happiness.

Written in Addis Abeba 15 1911. (22 April 1919)

Signature (Seal)

ENCLOSURE IV

TRANSLATION OF THE REMARKS OF
HIS EXCELLENCY DEDJAZMATCH NADAO, JULY 14, 1919.

YOUR EXCELLENCY,

We have the honor to be the first mission to America to present the congratulations of our country on your work with the Allies for the successful termination of the war with Germany.

More than five thousand years have elapsed since the establishment of the Ethiopian Government. In the time of David and Solomon this Government was well known. The queen of Ethiopia, Macada, ruled over all Sheba at that time. She heard of King Solomon and came to listen to his wisdom and see the country, and as she returned to her own dominion she proclaimed the religion of the living God. From that time until Constantine the Great Ethiopia has believed in God according to the laws of the Old Testament. In the time of Constantine Ethiopia became Christian according to the gospel of Jesus Christ, and since that time has fought for her Christianity and independence against the surrounging [surrounding] Mohammedans and heathens.

Undoubtedly Your Excellency knows more about the history of our race and religion than I am able to tell.

All the people of Ethiopia, knowing that the United States of America, after securely establishing her own independence, has taken upon herself the wonderful duty of assisting the Allies in gaining equal liberty and independence, rejoiced and praised the American people.

We hope that the friendship with the United States that began during the reign of Emperor Menelik II will continue and develop, and that commerce will be renewed and increase as a result of that friendship.

This is the anxious desire of Her Majesty, our Empress, of the Heir-apparent to the throne, and of all our people.

We owe many thanks to all your kind officers who received and treated us always with the greatest courtesy and hospitality since our arrival in New York.

You are the blessed peace-maker; may God grant you a long and happy life.   July ———, 1911 (July ——— 1919)

T MSS (WP, DLC).

A News Report

[*July 13, 1919*]
WILSON TO CONSULT CONGRESS MEMBERS

Washington, July 13.—President Wilson has appointments for tomorrow with a number of members of both branches of Congress. While the statement is made in circles close to the White House that this marks no new Presidential policy, the feeling is growing in Washington that the President has returned to Washington with a more generous attitude in the matter of his personal relations with the legislative branch of the Government. This is held to have been evidenced in the opening paragraphs of his speech of last week to the Senate, in which he declared his willingness to go before the Senate Foreign Relations Committee whenever requested to furnish any information its members might desire regarding the Peace Treaty and the League of Nations covenant.

The President has not been given to keeping open house for Congressmen in the matter of White House conferences, and for long periods during his administration members of both Senate and House, even men in his own party, found it rather difficult to see the President on matters in which they were deeply interested. Beginning tomorrow, the President will see a number of members from both houses. The appointments have been made at the request of the members who are to call at the White House and who want to talk over a number of matters with the President. Ever since his return the President has been importuned to grant conferences of this nature.

The impression has been created that the President intends to be a little more liberal in the future than in the past in the matter of granting appointments to members of the legislative branch. If so, the new policy is expected to win the President considerable popularity at the Capitol, especially among members of his own party, who frequently have found themselves embarrassed because they were not able to go freely to the White House to talk over matters in which they were interested.

In one quarter close to the White House it was asserted tonight that while the President had quite a list of appointments for tomorrow, the list was not considered unusual and that it was the result of a great number of requests from members who wished to see the President. However, the fact that the President, who has returned to find many matters facing him for consideration, has granted these requests for conference is considered to be not without significance, and it is altogether probable that, having granted these requests, the President will be importuned by numerous other members for appointments, especially in connection with letters members have received urging them to use their influence with the President to visit certain cities during his proposed tour of the country.

Printed in the *New York Times*, July 14, 1919.

From Henry van Dyke, with Enclosure

Dear President Wilson: [Ithaca, N.Y.] July 13. 1919.

Will you let me congratulate you on your return, safe and sound, bringing with you the fruits of your arduous and successful labors at the Peace Council? It is a wonderful achievement of skill, courage, patience, and singleness of purpose; and the address with which you presented the Treaty to the Senate was a masterpiece of sincere and convincing eloquence,—*suaviter in modo, fortiter in re.* The Treaty with the Covenant ought to be, and I hope will be, ratified without change or delay. The opposition is factional and factitious for the most part. The only part of it which has to be seriously considered is that which relies for its support upon the popular jealousy for the American Constitution.

In travelling through all parts of the country this year, working for the League, I have found the great majority of the people in favor of it; but even among this majority there are some who have an honest though not very intelligent misgiving lest in some way or other the Constitution should be impaired by our acceptance of all the covenants of the League. If in your judgment any concession should be necessary to remove this misgiving and thus secure a prompter and larger vote in favor of the Treaty including the Covenant, might this not be done by the addition of a simple proviso to the resolution of ratification? Such a "proviso" would not be an "amendment," nor even a "reservation" strictly speaking. It would simply be an interpretation of the Covenant in a sense entirely consonant with what seems to me its real meaning. It might do much to banish the bogey of a Super-state.

I venture to send you a suggestion in this line for your consideration if you deem it wise. The last sentence is not necessary.

With all good wishes, Faithfully yours   Henry van Dyke

ALS (WP, DLC).

E N C L O S U R E

The Senate hereby advises, and consents to, the ratification of the Treaty of Peace, including the Covenant of the League of Nations as an integral part thereof, with the following proviso, which is essential to the ratification:

Nothing in Article X, Article XVI, or any other Article of the said Covenant which refers directly to a recommendation of the Council that military or naval forces be used to protect the undertakings or covenants of the League, shall be deemed to abrogate or alter the provisions of the Constitution of the United States of America by which the power of declaring war and of making appropriations for the raising and equipment of military and naval forces on the part of this country is entrusted to the Congress of the United States of America. (In making this proviso it is understood that all the self-governing states which are, or may become, members of the League have, and shall retain, the right to observe the methods of procedure prescribed by their several constitutions.)

Hw MS (WP, DLC).

From Norman Kemp Smith[1]

My dear President Wilson,   Edinburgh. July 13. 1919.

I have been elected to the Logic Chair of Edinburgh University, & wish to thank you very heartily for your kindly and generous testimony in my support.[2] The good will that inspired it has given me keen personal pleasure, quite apart from the immediate needs of the candidature has. Mrs. Kemp Smith[3] & I leave Princeton & America with the deepest regret; & I shall ever be grateful to you for the opportunities you opened to me, in my appointment to a

Professorship in Princeton, of knowing and loving America in this intimate fashion.

With our united homage for the great work you have been achieving for the higher civilisation,

Yours ever sincerely,   Norman Kemp Smith.

ALS (WP, DLC).
[1] Stuart Professor of Psychology at Princeton University, 1906-1913; McCosh Professor of Philosophy since 1913.
[2] WW to the Authorities of Edinburgh University, June 3, 1919, CCL (WP, DLC). Wilson had written this testimonial in response to N. K. Smith to WW, May 29, 1919, ALS (WP, DLC).
[3] Amy Kemp Smith.

From Edward Mandell House

Dear Governor:	London, July 14, 1919.

When the Commission on Mandatories met in London I was agreeably surprised to find that outside of the French effort to make the natives subject to military service in defence of the mandatory power, there was general unanimity of purpose to protect the natives in every way possible. I had no difficulty with Milner. Lord Robert Cecil was invited to sit with us at my suggestion. I did this because his views were so nearly in accord with ours.

It has not yet been determined when we shall sit again to prepare mandatories for Class A. Cecil thinks we should get at it immediately and I have expressed a willingness to do so.

I am touching the League of Nations gently. I seldom go to Sunderland House but Drummond, Fosdick, Shepardson[1] and others keep me in intimate touch, and I am advising through them.

I hope you will not think that I shirked the work in Paris by leaving when you did. I thought the thing out carefully and came to the conclusion that it would be nearly impossible to continue there after you had gone and keep in cordial relations with the other Commissioners. You may or may not know that there was considerable resentment that you did not consult them sufficiently and I came in for my share of this feeling. With you away and Lansing in charge, and with Lansing gone and White in charge, my position would have been untenable. It seemed, therefore, on the whole, better to leave them to work things out alone.

The members of the other delegations would almost surely have brought their difficulties to me and I would have been under the necessity of having to decline to take them up or to have created friction with my colleagues. I suppose you understood that it was really this that brought me over here.

Affectionately yours,   E. M. House

TLS (WP, DLC).
    [1] That is, Sir (James) Eric Drummond, Raymond Blaine Fosdick, and Whitney Hart Shepardson, all active at this time in organizing the League of Nations at the temporary headquarters of its secretariat at Sunderland House in London.

From Frank Lyon Polk

My dear Mr. President: Washington July 14, 1919.

I hesitate to burden you with the attached copy of the NATION, although it features on the cover an article appearing on page 34, regarding a proposal to the Bolsheviki from Bullitt which I think you would like to note.[1]   Faithfully yours,   Frank L. Polk

TLS (WP, DLC).
    [1] "The Latest Allied-American Dealing with Lenin," New York *Nation*, CIX (July 12, 1919), 34. This article consisted of a fairly detailed and on the whole accurate account of the Bullitt mission to Russia in February and March of 1919, about which see the index references under "Bullitt, William Christian," in Vols. 55-57 of this series. The article was based upon a wireless statement issued by the People's Russian Information Bureau in Budapest after its receipt, in early June, by wireless from Moscow, over the signature of the Soviet government.

From Newton Diehl Baker

Personal and Confidential:

Dear Mr. President: Washington. July 14, 1919.

I had a talk with Governor-General Harrison of the Philippine Islands this morning and told him quite frankly that I had presented his case to you with my own belief that his divorce and marriage[1] made it inexpedient for him to remain Governor-General of a solidly Catholic country, and that you were disposed to accept that judgment; but that we both felt it would be better for him to return to the Islands now and submit his resignation later in the year. He accepted the decision graciously and said that he did not feel qualified to dissent from such a judgment, and that he would return at once to the Islands and tender his resignation in the Fall.

He asked me to endeavor to arrange an opportunity for him to see you, not in connection with this question but because he feels that the prestige of the Governor-General of the Islands would be affected prejudicially if he were not received by you during his visit. If you can arrange a time within the next few days when you can see him very briefly, I will explain to him the necessity of the interview being brief and wholly at your convenience.

Respectfully yours,   Newton D. Baker

TLS (WP, DLC).
    [1] About the scandal occasioned by the recent divorce and remarriage of Francis Burton Harrison, see the index references to Harrison in Vols. 59 and 60 of this series.

From John Crawford Anderson[1]

Sir: Montgomery July 14, 1919.

In behalf of all Alabamians friendly to progress, justice and righteousness, I wish to thank you for your timely messages to the Governor and the Legislature. You will note from enclosed clipping that the outlook for ratification is not very bright, and if this fight is won the victory will be yours.

Judicial propriety usually restrains me from participating in ordinary contests, but a realization not only of the justness of this cause but the far-reaching effect the rejection or adoption of this measure may have upon the future of our party has impelled me to throw what little weight and moral influence I may have into the fight.

Extending to you a hearty welcome upon your homecoming, and wishing for you health and happiness, I am,

Cordially yours,   Jno. C. Anderson.

TLS (WP, DLC).
[1] Chief Justice of Alabama.

To the American Mission in Paris

[The White House] 15 July, 1919.

With regard to the decision stated in your 2886, June 30,[1] to suspend further consideration of the treaty with Turkey until our Government can state whether it will be able to accept a mandate for a portion of the Turkish territory, I fear that this will involve a very considerable delay, and would be glad to know what it is proposed that the attitude of the powers should be towards Turkey in the meantime.   Woodrow Wilson

T telegram (WP, DLC).
[1] ACNP to FLP, June 30, 1919, T telegram (WP, DLC). This telegram quoted the decisions recorded in Minute 10 of the minutes of the Council of Four printed at June 27, 1919, 4 p.m.

To Newton Diehl Baker

My dear Mr. Secretary: The White House 15 July, 1919.

I would be very much obliged if you could make it convenient to have a conference with Mr. Hurley of the Shipping Board and the Secretary of Commerce with regard to the situation in respect of passenger service from our ports to South America.[1] It is a matter the importance of which I need not dwell upon, and I am in hopes that a conference such as I suggest can work out something practical.

I am writing a similar letter to the Secretary of the Navy.[2]

Cordially and faithfully yours,   Woodrow Wilson

TLS (N. D. Baker Papers, DLC).
 [1] About which, see WCR to WW, July 12, 1919.
 [2] WW to JD, July 15, 1919, TLS (J. Daniels Papers, DLC).

To William Gibbs McAdoo

My dear Mac: The White House 15 July, 1919.

Thank you very warmly for your letter of the eleventh. I am pondering very carefully the method of action best calculated to bring about the right results in these difficult days. Your own work in support of the League has been worthy of all praise and, I have no doubt, will be more and more useful as the days go on.

It is very, very delightful to be at home again, and even the work itself does not seem as hard as it otherwise would, because of the delight of being again among people I understand.

With warmest love to you both,

Affectionately yours,   Woodrow Wilson

TLS (W. G. McAdoo Papers, DLC).

To John Nevin Sayre

My dear Nevin: The White House 15 July, 1919.

I am sorry to say in the present rush it is not possible for me to make an appointment to see you and Mr. Wood and Mr. de Silver,[1] because I am in the midst of a pressure from which there is no let up. But I would greatly value a definite suggestion from you, if you would be willing to make it.

In haste,   Faithfully yours,   Woodrow Wilson

TLS (PSC-P).
 [1] Wilson was replying to J. N. Sayre to WW, July 7, 1919.

To Hugh Manson Dorsey[1]

[The White House] 15 July, 1919.

I am profoundly interested in the passage of the Suffrage Amendment to the Constitution, and would very much value your advice as to the present status of the matter in the Georgia Legislature. I would like very much to be of help, for I believe that it is absolutely essential to the political future of the country that this Amendment should be passed, and absolutely essential to the fortunes of the Democratic Party that it should play a leading part in the support of this great reform.   Woodrow Wilson

T telegram (Letterpress Books, WP, DLC).
¹ Governor of Georgia.

To Elbert Henry Gary

My dear Judge Gary: [The White House] 15 July, 1919.

Your generous letter of July eighth has given me a great deal of pleasure. It is particularly gratifying to know of your strong feeling for the League of Nations. Our prompt and cordial participation in this great enterprise of peace seems to me necessary as a vindication of the character and purpose of the country, which has now won a position in the world which it would be folly to impair.

With warmest thanks and appreciation,
          Sincerely yours,   Woodrow Wilson

TLS (Letterpress Books, WP, DLC).

To Casper Salathiel Yost

PERSONAL

My dear Mr. Yost: [The White House] 15 July, 1919.

I have just now been able to turn from public duties to the reading of your interesting letter of July seventh with its enclosure, "America and Article X."

I need hardly say I admire and warmly appreciate your patriotic attitude with regard to the great matters we have now in hand, and I have no doubt that your influence will be very great in enabling us to arrive at the proper conclusions and actions.

You may be sure that I am not in the least inclined to do anything that is not altogether helpful in these matters, which ought not to be touched in the least degree with partisan feeling or purpose, and I greatly value your generosity in advising me.
          Cordially and sincerely yours,   Woodrow Wilson

TLS (Letterpress Books, WP, DLC).

To John Sharp Williams

My dear Senator Williams: The White House 15 July, 1919.

Tumulty has laid before me your letter of July ninth[1] about Mr. Peyton. Unhappily, as you seem to surmise, the appointment of Graham was decided upon and authorized by me before I got back. It is distressing to me to have to turn away from your friend.

There was no reason to apologize for your advice about using gentleness and tact in our present task. It is good advice and I know that it is. I always value any "tip" from you, and I can subscribe to your estimate of the treaty.

Cordially and sincerely yours,   Woodrow Wilson

TLS (J. S. Williams Papers, DLC).
  [1] We print only the postscript of this letter. In the letter itself, Williams had urged Wilson to appoint Harry Peyton, a native of Mississippi who had practiced law in Washington for many years, to the United States Court of Claims. Wilson had already decided to appoint Samuel Jordan Graham.

To William H. Bolling[1]

My dear Mr. Bolling: [The White House] 15 July, 1919.

On my return home I find your letter of June 27th.[2] You may be sure that I am interested in anything that affects you, but I think you will realize upon reflection that it is not possible for me to appoint anyone related to myself to public office in any exceptional way. Relatives of the President are unfortunately under a special disability. If they are in the public service at all, they have to depend upon the regular routine of promotion.

I congratulate you on having had an opportunity to serve the country in these interesting times, and hope that you will continue to find ways of service.

With warm regards from us all,

Sincerely yours,   Woodrow Wilson

TLS (Letterpress Books, WP, DLC).
  [1] A nephew of Edith Bolling Wilson, formerly a Deputy Collector of Internal Revenue in the 5th District of Kentucky, at this time serving in the United States Navy at Guantánamo Bay, Cuba.
  [2] W. H. Bolling to WW, June 27, 1919, ALS (WP, DLC). Bolling asked Wilson to appoint him to any governmental position for which he was qualified.

From Henry White

Paris July 15, 1919.

Very urgent. 3152. For the President. The question of the attitude of the Allies toward trade with Bolshevist Russia has been reopened through a formal request by Sweden to be advised as to whether any restrictions will be attempted to be imposed by the Allies upon exports from Sweden to Bolshevist Russia. A particular instance in question involves shipment of munitions of war.

The British and French now propose that the Allies notify neutrals that traffic into and out of ports in the Gulf of Finland can only be conducted under permit from the local naval command.

You will perhaps recall that the question of commercial relations with Bolshevist Russia was considered by the Supreme Council, which decided in substance that there would be no legal basis for a continuation of restrictions after the termination of the blockade of Germany.[1] Hankey under date of June 17th, advised McCormick that the Supreme Council has "Decided that after the acceptance of the conditions of peace by Germany measures are not still to be taken to prevent commodities from reaching Bolshevist Russia or Hungary." At the meeting of Supreme Council held today Mr. Balfour urged a modification of this decision to the extent of giving notification above referred to on the following grounds:

First. The decision of June 17 was taken in expectation of an early fall of Petrograd, which would automatically have prevented Bolshevist Russia from receiving aid through the Gulf of Finland. This expectation has not been fulfilled.

Two. Military and naval operations are active in and about the Gulf of Finland and the Allies are making naval dispositions to prevent the Bolshevists taking the anti-Bolshevists in the rear through naval operations. The Allies cannot permit neutral shipping to proceed to Bolshevist territory as this would be the means whereby naval dispositions of the Allies would become known.

Three. The decision of the Supreme Council of June 17 related to both Bolshevist Russia and Hungary. The Supreme Council itself modified the decision in respect to Hungary prior to your departure, which it was urged indicated that the decision as a whole should not be regarded as final.

Mr. Clemenceau actively supported Mr. Balfour and urged particularly the moral obligations which the Allies were under by virtue of their promises of aid and assistance to Koltchak. Mr. Tittoni is prepared to concur with the British and French. I secured postponement today at Council of Five of decision for at least 48 hours in the hope that by that time I would be able to ascertain your wishes.

While fully appreciating the force of the arguments raised by Mr. Balfour and the practical advantages of taking the course suggested, I am impressed and so expressed myself, with the danger of admitting the right of one group of nations to control the high seas unless by virtue of recognized belligerent rights. This distinguishes the case of Hungary from that of Bolshevist Russia, with which latter we are not belligerent. I am also inclined to feel that the British and French overestimated the aid Bolshevists will receive in the absence of the proposed notification. Navigation is exceedingly hazardous by present naval operations in progress and above all by reason of the presence of great numbers of mines. Furthermore, the Bolshevist ports will normally be closed for the winter by the latter part of November.

I recognize, however, that it is desirable that we should go as far as possible with our associates in assisting Koltchak and preventing aid from reaching the Bolshevists and accordingly I shall take no action here until advised of your wishes.

It is also proposed that Koltchak shall declare a formal blockade of about 90 miles of the Black Sea littoral and that if this blockade is effective it be recognized by the Allied and Associated Powers. I shall accept this proposal unless you indicate otherwise. Please answer as soon as possible. White.   American Mission.

T telegram (SDR, RG 59, 661.119/433, DNA).
[1] See Minute No. 5 of the minutes of the Council of Four printed at June 17, 1919, 4 p.m., Vol. 60.

From Henry Cabot Lodge

To the President: [Washington] July 15, 1919

I have the honor to submit herewith a resolution[1] adopted today by the Committee on Foreign Relations and to ask for it your kind consideration.

I have the honor to be,

Very respectfully yours,   H. C. Lodge

TLS (WP, DLC).
[1] The enclosure is missing. However, Tumulty, at a later date, paraphrased it as follows:
"July 15, 1919—Resolution of a Committee on Foreign Relations—Senate—All drafts or forms presented to or considered by the peace commissioners relating to a league of nations, and particularly the draft or form prepared or presented by the commissioners of the United States; and All proceedings, arguments and debates, including the transcript of the stenographic reports of the peace commission relating to or concerning a league of nations, or the league of nations finally adopted; and all data bearing upon or used in connection with the treaty of peace with Germany now pending." CC MS (WP, DLC).

From Newton Diehl Baker, with Enclosure

Confidential.

My dear Mr. President: Washington. July 15, 1919.

The attached cablegram has just come. I assume that General Bliss expects this application for additional troops to be made to you, or to be brought to your attention by the State Department. In any case, you may desire to confer with Mr. Polk prior to his departure about your attitude in the matter.

Respectfully yours,   Newton D. Baker

TLS (WP, DLC).

                    E N C L O S U R E

Versailles [July 14, 1919].

Number 341. Confidential. For the Secretary of War and Chief of Staff. I understand that it is possible that the Council of Five[1] may ask Washington whether United States will send troops to Siberia to replace fifty or sixty thousand Czecho-Slovaks in case latter are repatriated. I have not favored this proposition because I believe our aid can better be given in some other form than that of troops. I believe that it would have a steadying effect on European affairs if government took advantage of first good opportunity to plainly declare that Europe can expect no troops from America unless Germany should renew the war.   Bliss

T telegram (WP, DLC).
[1] That is, the heads of the delegations of the Principal Allied and Associated Powers in Paris.

From Newton Diehl Baker, with Enclosure

My dear Mr. President: Washington. July 15, 1919.

I return herewith the dispatch you handed me this afternoon. I have directed that Colonel William N. Haskell[1] be not recalled without the matter being presented to you and receiving your approval.

Colonel Haskell is a Captain in the Regular Army, but holds emergency rank as Colonel. All of this emergency rank will, of course, expire with the emergency as that phrase is defined in the Act of Congress authorizing the creation of the present Army. That, however, will not be for some months.

I refer to this fact only because if Colonel Haskell is to be abroad a considerable length of time this automatic reduction in rank may take place under embarrassing circumstances. Incidentally, there are a fairly large number of officers abroad who have no Regular Army status but are emergency officers. It will be necessary for us to get them home in time to discharge them here by the end of the emergency. The number of Regular Army officers is perhaps not great enough to permit all the places of these emergency officers to be filled by Regulars so that we ought to keep in mind the possibility of our being obliged to employ civilians for some of the tasks which are at present being done by Army officers in various parts of Europe.

The portion of this dispatch dealing with a mission to be sent to Armenia, headed by General Harbord,[2] I have not undertaken to execute, because I feel somewhat doubtful about the wisdom of such a mission until the Senate shall have acted upon the treaty. It may be that my feeling on the subject is not justified, but every advantage is taken by those opposed to the treaty of the presence of our troops in various parts of the world, and it occurred to me that the Senate might feel that we were anticipating its action if it discovered that General Harbord and a group of American officers were in Armenia.

If you wish me to take any action about this will you be good enough to indicate it?

Respectfully yours,   Newton D. Baker

TLS (WP, DLC).
  [1] William Nafew Haskell.
  [2] That is, Maj. Gen. James Guthrie Harbord.

E N C L O S U R E

Paris. July 5, 1919.

2982. American Mission's 2961, July third.

Following telegram sent to President is repeated for your information and for communication to Charles E. Hughes Committee[1] if you see fit.

"July 5, 10 p.m. After receiving General Harbord's views, and discussion with the Peace Mission, we have concluded that the temporary measures necessary to strengthen relief and administration in Armenia should be separated from the problems involved in repatriation and expulsion of present trespassers, and permanent pacification of the territory. We have therefore recommended the appointment of Colonel William N. Haskell, at present in charge of relief measures in Roumania to be a temporary commissioner as proposed by us to you and accepted in principle by the heads of state, and we trust he will not be recalled by the War Department. The broader question of repatriation etc., requires an examination as to the measures and force necessary successfully to cope with the problem and will require congressional action to grant sufficient funds and forces. We therefore recommend that a mission should immediately be sent to Armenia headed by General Harbord who should choose his own assistants to investigate this question together with the general political and economic problems involved in setting up the new state of Armenia. Such investigation as a basis of determination of policy is, in our minds, necessary before even the repatriation of refugees can be begun. We believe General Harbord could be persuaded to undertake such a mission. Hoover. Morgenthau. We endorse the recommendations made in the above telegram. American Mission."

American Mission.

T telegram (WP, DLC).
¹ Charles Evans Hughes was a member of the executive board of the American Committee for the Independence of Armenia.

From Newton Diehl Baker

Confidential.

My dear Mr. President: Washington. July 15, 1919.

Some weeks ago while you were in Paris, the forces of the bandit Villa approached the city of Juarez and it became fairly clear that an attack was intended upon that city, which, as you know, is immediately across the Rio Grande from El Paso. There was a good deal of anxiety among the people of El Paso as to their safety. I instructed General Cabell,¹ commanding general of the Southern Department, not to permit firing across the border by anybody, and that in the event of firing which imperiled life or property in El Paso he should proceed across the border with force enough to drive the combatants away, and immediately return to the American side.

A few days later the Villistas did attack Juarez and a good many shots were fired across the border. Several persons were wounded in the streets of El Paso. General Erwin,² who was immediately in command at El Paso, thereupon crossed the border, notifying the Mexican commander of his coming. The regular Mexican troops were withdrawn to a nearby fort. General Erwin drove the Villistas out of the neighborhood, and we crossed the border the next day into the United States.

For a day or two there was some anxiety lest the Villistas should undertake to execute revenge upon Americans elsewhere in Northern Mexico. This apprehension, however, did not materialize, and the bandit forces have since that time kept away from the border. Meantime, I think the action of our forces now has the very general approval of all the Americans along the border, and the Mexican Government made no serious protest against our action. With the details of this transaction you have probably been made familiar by Mr. Polk, with whom, of course, I was in constant consultation throughout the incident.

I now have a letter from General Cabell dealing with the capture of Mr. T. J. Robertson, a cattle man of El Paso, by bandits who raided across the border, captured Mr. Robertson and required a ransom of five thousand dollars for his return. This incident took place in May, and General Cabell says of it:

"As this is the third capture of Americans in the sector south of Columbus in which they were held for ransom, I recommend that authority be given for an attempt to capture the bandits making captures in future. A small expedition of a troop of cavalry, guided in the night by the man sent for the reward, might succeed in capturing the bandits. It would no doubt endanger the lives of the captives, but a well organized expedition might succeed. Doing nothing encourages the bandits to continue the practice."

My inclination is to authorize General Cabell, within the limits of his previous instructions, to follow where possible the hot trail of bandits thus making raids across our border, cautioning him that he should in each case have due regard to the chances of success and the possibility of fatal consequences to the person or persons captured, but leaving it largely to his discretion whether to undertake such a pursuit, with the strict understanding that he is in no case to make any permanent or long-continued occupation of Mexican soil, but is merely to cross and recross the border rapidly, and not to penetrate many miles in any case. I do not, however, want to give instructions of this kind without first submitting them to you.

Shall I take the course indicated?

Respectfully yours,   Newton D. Baker

TLS (WP, DLC).
[1] Maj. Gen. De Rosey Carroll Cabell.
[2] Brig. Gen. James Brailsford Erwin.

From Brand Whitlock

Dear Mr. President: Brussels, July 15th, 1919

During the ever memorable two days that you spent with us in Belgium, I spoke to you of Whistler's "The Gentle Art of Making Enemies."[1] I have succeeded in procuring a copy from London, and I send it to you herewith, in the hope that it may distract you for a moment now and then in the midst of your heavy cares. Its wit is often terrible in its irony, but it affords sometimes, even to us of a milder manner, a certain vicarious consolation. It is not a book to be read through at a sitting; but rather to be taken in small pinches—like salt, though not necessarily cum grano salis. I have marked a few typical passages to give you the taste of it. And yet, read through, one sees that it was not without a plan, and that, as a whole, it is a rather liberal education in the matter of art, not always appreciated by the British and American public whom he was trying to instruct.

I have the honour to be, dear Mr. President,
          Your devoted and obedient servant,   Brand Whitlock

TLS (WP, DLC).
  [1] James Abbott McNeill Whistler, *The Gentle Art of Making Enemies, As Pleasingly Exemplified, in Many Instances, Wherein the Serious Ones of this Earth, Carefully Exasperated, Have Been Prettily Spurred on to Unseemliness and Indiscretion, While Overcome by an Undue Sense of Right* (London and New York, 1890). There is a copy of this book in the Wilson Library, DLC.

Henry Winslow Williams[1] to Joseph Patrick Tumulty, with Enclosure

My dear Mr. Tumulty: Baltimore, Md. July 15th, 1919.

I was sorry to miss you yesterday, but I had a very pleasant chat with the assistant secretary.[2] He told me that he did not think that the President would be able to visit Baltimore this time, as his itinerary had not yet been arranged, and also that there was strong pressure to have him make his first address in St. Louis or some other Western city. However, I certainly hope that he will be able to speak here at some time, and then of course the Maryland Branch of the League to Enforce Peace will cooperate with the Press Club and with the State and City officials to give him a proper welcome. Needless to say the meeting is sure to be a success.

As I wrote you the Maryland Branch of the League is having its luncheon and conference tomorrow, and I only wish that the President or some one representing him could be present. However, I understand this is impossible. The luncheon is at 12:30 at the Belvedere Hotel, and even a telegram of regret would be appreciated.

I left with the assistant secretary a draft of a proposed resolution of ratification by the Senate, and as I told him I saw Senator France with regard to the matter later in the day. I talked with the Senator for an hour, and I found, as I had been told by his friends who had requested me to call upon him, that he was very much interested in the humanity features of the covenant for the League of Nations, his principal objection being that various great nations, particularly China, Russia and Germany were not members of the League at this time, and if their membership was unduly delayed, which he thought probable, they might form an opposition coalition. We discussed this matter at length, and I think he is willing to be convinced that China and Germany will become members of the League in a very short time, and thus his main objection will be removed. I see by the paper, in fact, that China will probably sign the Austrian treaty, which will of itself make it a member of the League, as I understand it, and the Senator should be assured if possible that Germany's membership is expected within a short time.

I gave him a copy of the resolution which I handed the assistant secretary yesterday, and he commended it very highly. He said he agreed with me that the reservations as proposed by Mr. Root would amount to amendments of the Treaty, and in such case the Treaty would have to be re-ratified by the other parties thereto, and I should judge from the way he spoke that he considers this result unfortunate. He said he thought probably resolutions in the form suggested would be satisfactory, and then the Government, if it saw fit, could give notice of withdrawal from the League if the outcome was not satisfactory. He asked me if we could not have the resolution in the form suggested introduced by some advocate of the League, meaning, of course, a Democrat. I answered that I was not speaking officially for the League to Enforce Peace, or for any other organization, and therefore I could not say anything as to that, but that I hoped he would give the entire matter consideration, and suggest it to his colleagues, and that I would take the liberty of seeing him again shortly about the entire matter. He said he would give the matter careful consideration, and be very glad to see me at any time.

In addition to the three "understandings" in the resolution submitted, which cover the interpretations of Mr. Root, I find that Senator France, as well as others, are much concerned with regard to the domestic questions, and also the Shantung situation, and therefore the resolution as submitted might be made more effective as a basis of adjustment if there was added to it a statement that the Senate understood that the League of Nations had no jurisdiction over domestic questions, such as the tariff, or immigration, and also understood that the occupation of the Peninsula of Shantung by the Empire of Japan was only temporary. I enclose an additional form of the resolution with these additions.

I write at this length because it seems to me that this is an important matter, and I would be very glad if you could submit it to the President, so that I could receive his view upon it. Of course I would be delighted to come to Washington to see the President or yourself any time you might suggest.

The suggestion of Senator France that a resolution in this form should be introduced by some Democratic Senator, and then referred to the Committee on Foreign Relations may be worthy of consideration. It seems to me that an adjustment might possibly be worked along these lines, though of course I do not want to take any action that is disapproved by the President.

Permit me to extend my congratulations to the President upon the result of his labors in Europe.

Yours very sincerely,   Henry W. Williams

TLS (WP, DLC).
  ¹ Lawyer of Baltimore, chairman of the executive committee of the Maryland branch of the League to Enforce Peace.
  ² That is, Warren Forman Johnson, Tumulty's secretary.

E N C L O S U R E

RESOLVED that the Senate of the United States advises and consents to the ratification of the said Treaty.

BE IT FURTHER RESOLVED that the Senate understands that under the Covenant for the League of Nations, the United States cannot be committed to war otherwise than through the exercise by the Congress of the United States of its constitutional power; that whenever two years' notice of withdrawal from the League of Nations shall have been given as provided in Article I of the Covenant, no finding that an international obligation or an obligation under the Covenant has not been fulfilled shall conclude [preclude] the member giving such notice unless such obligation shall have been established by an award of arbitration, a decision of the Court of International Justice, a unanimous report of the Council or an equivalent report by the Assembly before the filing of such notice; that nothing contained in the Covenant shall imply a relinquishment by the United States of its traditional attitude towards purely

American questions; that the League of Nations has no jurisdiction over domestic questions such as the tariff or immigration; that the occupation of the Peninsula of Shantung by the Empire of Japan is intended to be but temporary.

T MS (WP, DLC).

From the Diary of Henry Fountain Ashurst

July 15, 1919.

The President and Mrs. Wilson attended a reception at the French Embassy, last night, given by the French Ambassador and Mme. Jusserand, in honor of Bastille Day (the French Fourth of July). This is the second time that W.W. and his lady have thus honored Ambassador and Mme. Jusserand; the other occasion being last November to celebrate the entrance of French troops into Alsace-Lorraine. The guests assembled in the Reception Rooms of the Embassy and were welcomed by the exquisite Jusserand and his wife. Daniels, Burleson, Lane and Redfield of the Cabinet were there; Burleson wore white clothes in contrast to the dress-suits and flashing military and naval uniforms. In the dining room, a buffet dinner was served. Soon W.W. came in escorting Mme. Jusserand and the Ambassador escorting Mrs. Wilson.

Mr. Jusserand, in speaking, recalled how gloomy the outlook was one year ago and how changed now. W.W. responded but observed the proprieties by not making a better speech than did his host. Representatives of the foreign powers which declared war upon Germany were present. Senator Lodge left before W.W. came in. The other Senators were Overman, Pomerene and Lady, Warren and Lady, Newberry and Lady, Ashurst and Lady. Speaker Gillett and Representatives Flood, Nicholas Longworth and Jno. J. Rogers[1] were present.[2]

[1] John Jacob Rogers, Republican of Massachusetts.
[2] Jusserand, in his weekly report to the Foreign Ministry, No. 102, July 15, 1919, CC MS (J. J. Jusserand Papers, FFM-Ar) reports on this reception in some detail. The Wilsons, Jusserand wrote, came unannounced at 10 p.m., which Jusserand considered a mark of great honor and good will. Among the numerous flowers sent to the French embassy, one group came from Mrs. Wilson. Jusserand does not mention Wilson's little speech. For another account of this affair, see the *Washington Post*, July 15, 1919.

To Charles Linza McNary[1]

My dear Senator: [The White House] 16 July, 1919.

Matters of so grave a consequence are now under consideration that I would very much appreciate an opportunity to have a talk with you about the Treaty and all that it involves. I wonder if it would be possible for you to see me at the White House at 3 o'clock Friday afternoon, July 18th.

Cordially and sincerely yours,   Woodrow Wilson[2]

TLS (Letterpress Books, WP, DLC).
[1] Republican senator from Oregon.
[2] Wilson wrote the same letter, *mutatis mutandis*, to A. Capper, W. S. Kenyon, F. B. Kellogg, K. Nelson, L. B. Colt, W. L. Jones, and P. J. McCumber, all dated July 16, 1919, and all TLS (Letterpress Books, WP, DLC).

To Thomas Staples Martin

My dear Senator: [The White House] 16 July, 1919.

I am deeply distressed, on reaching home again, to find that you are not well, and write to express not only my very warm sympathy but my hope that you are rapidly mending. We miss you sadly in the fight that is going on here. Your counsel and assistance would be of the greatest service to us, and I am sure your thoughts are with us. But do not let the situation distress you in any way. Only get well. We will take care of matters in your absence.

Cordially and sincerely yours,   Woodrow Wilson

TLS (Letterpress Books, WP, DLC).

From Frank Lyon Polk

My dear Mr. President: Washington July 16, 1919.

I saw Senator Lodge in regard to your appointing a representative on the Reparation Commission.[1] I pointed out why you hesitated to act, and also pointed out the tremendous importance of having this country represented on this commission from the beginning. He seemed to be impressed with the necessity of action, and suggested that if you would write the Committee a letter stating that you desired to appoint some one, and pointing out the importance, that there would probably be no criticism or complaint on the part of the Committee.

It seems to me he felt that a letter to the Committee would save its face, as it would be in the nature of a formal consultation with the Senate on your part.   Yours faithfully,   Frank L Polk

TLS (WP, DLC).
[1] Wilson had probably asked Polk to talk to Lodge about this matter in response to J. F. Dulles to B. M. Baruch *et al.*, July 4, 1919.

From Frank Lyon Polk, with Enclosure

My dear Mr. President: Washington July 16, 1919.

I enclose a copy of a telegram from the American Consul General at Omsk[1] which I have repeated to Ambassador Morris for his information. Mr. Morris is now in Siberia on his way to Omsk.

All the reports we have show that Allied troops will probably be required to replace the Czechs when they are withdrawn. You will recall that the Czechs are now understood to be guarding the line from Irkutsk through Krasnoyarsk and apparently as far West as Novo Nikolaievsk. Possibly Japanese troops may be used effectively for railway guards in this section.

As regards Japanese troops proceeding to the Volga front, my personal opinion is that their presence would stiffen the Bolshevik resistance to a greater degree than they would help Kolchak.

                    Faithfully yours,   Frank L Polk

TLS (WP, DLC).
    [1] That is, Ernest L. Harris.

E N C L O S U R E

Telegram from the American Consul General at Omsk
dated July 10, 1919, noon, SECRET, *No. 317—*
sent via Peking.

From reliable source have learned that on June 14th Japanese proposed to Omsk Government plan of sending Japanese troops to front. Omsk Government apparently favorable to plan. Negotiations being carried on at present which provides that a Japanese division of 40,000 men shall be sent in Siberia under guise of protecting railway when Czechs evacuate. Japanese troops however are to be sent immediately to Ural front to participate in fighting.

T telegram (WP, DLC).

From the American Mission in Paris

                              Paris July 16th 1919.

3170. For the President. Technical advisor has inquired whether the United States is to be a party to and bound by the treaties of peace with Turkey and Bulgaria. Replying the Commissioners referred to your statement to the press representatives before your departure to the effect that the United States would sign these treaties and that consequently the United States would be bound by these treaties.[1]

Commission's technical experts state that if the United States were not to guarantee these treaties the position which they would adopt in drawing up the terms of the treaties might perhaps be different.

Do you approve of the Commissioners' action in the matter?

American Mission

T telegram (SDR, RG 59, 763.72119/5658, DNA).
¹ See the reports of Wilson's press conference printed at June 27, 1919.

George Andrew Sanderson to Joseph Patrick Tumulty

Sir: [Washington] July 16, 1919.

I have the honor to hand you herewith a resolution of the Senate of the United States of July 15, 1919, requesting the President, if not incompatible with the public interest, to furnish the Senate with information relative to treaties or negotiations purported to have taken place between Japan and Germany during the war.

Will you kindly acknowledge receipt of this resolution upon the enclosed form?   Respectfully,   George A. Sanderson

TLS (WP, DLC).

From Robert Latham Owen

My dear Mr. President: Washington, D. C. July 16, 1919.

Europe needs supplies from the United States to restore the productive powers of Europe to pre-war conditions, to enable Europe to pay its debts to America, to stop the growing discontent of unemployed men, and to check the growth of Bolshevism.

America has the supplies abundantly available.

Europe requires credit to buy these things.

The Secretary of the Treasury does not approve the extension of further credits by the United States Government to cover European purchases. I believe that the American people would approve the extension of these credits properly safeguarded if it were explained to them—that the credits would open a way to market their goods at satisfactory prices.

I understand that Holland, for instance, is now extending governmental credits to France for such peace purposes, that Sweden is also doing the same thing, and that some of the South American Republics have the same matter under advisement. The urgency is great, and this policy would be of benefit to both buyer and seller.

We have an investing public in America, however, well suited to extend these credits to Europe by buying European securities. There is needed a mechanism qualified to pass upon the validity of European securities offered for sale to the investing public. These securities consist of "promises to pay" of private merchants, of syndicates, of underwriting banks, and of bonds of European municipalities and Nations, and of combinations of such securities.

Against these securities, properly selected, debentures could be issued by American corporations and sold to the American investing public on a six per cent basis, provided the Government of the United States would lend its good offices in granting a suitable charter or charters to such institutions, with governmental supervision, the charter rights to be exercised under governmental patronage and favor.

Unless immediate steps are taken to accomplish these results I fear a serious business reaction will take place in the United States by cutting off a large part of our foreign market for our surplus products, throwing these products back on the United States and causing a very serious recession of prices due to over production. I agree that prices should come down, but the reduction should be by the elimination of excess profits artificially placed upon goods, and they should not come down by cutting down the wages paid to labor. There is a natural increase in prices in the United States due to the expansion of our currency by excess gold imports and by the development of Federal Reserve notes against commodities which have taken the place of gold as a basis of note issue.

With a view to providing a mechanism for accomplishing these purposes, I introduced on February 20, 1918, a Bill (S.3928) to establish a Federal Reserve Foreign Bank—copy inclosed.[1]

You referred this Bill to the Comptroller of the Currency for a report, and he made you a favorable report, but you took no action upon it as far as I know, and I was unable to get the support of the Treasury Department for the Bill, and it died with the 65th Congress, to my great regret.[2]

I drew up a Bill some months ago providing for the organization of a large corporation with a billion dollars of capital to handle these European securities, issue debenture bonds, and provide the means of marketing European securities in America with the investing public—a copy of which I inclose.[3]

The virtue of this Bill consisted in the Government of the United States having a very substantial interest in it and therefore being in a position from the standpoint of the public to protect the interests of the public as well as the interest of the stockholders who might otherwise deal too largely from a selfish standpoint.

The New York banks dealing in foreign exchange have been

hostile to both of the above Bills, since they regard such measures as having a tendency to deprive them of the monopoly of foreign exchange and to deprive them of the opportunity of speculating in foreign exchange. I am opposed to their speculation to the injury of our industries and commerce, and I allege that they have made millions out of speculation in foreign exchange to the disadvantage of American commerce and to the disadvantage of the American producers and the American consumers alike. I allege their interest is a private interest, and that they are not concerned to deal with the matter from the public standpoint. I do not intend this comment as any reproach to them in their natural attitude to deal with the subject matter from the standpoint of their private interest. I merely call your attention to it and to what I assume should be our attitude as public servants to protect the public against private monopolies in international exchange.

Senator Edge introduced, on July 15, 1919, Senate Bill 2472, authorizing the organization of corporations to deal in foreign banking, a copy of which is inclosed,[4] and which I understand meets the views of the Federal Reserve Board and of the Secretary of the Treasury. I believe the banks dealing in international exchange would make no objection to this latter Bill for the reason that it simply gives a Federal charter to corporations to engage in international banking. While I should greatly prefer a Federal Reserve Foreign Bank that would be a medium through which all American banks could function with assurance of equitable treatment, it will probably be better to pass Senate Bill 2472 rather than take no action at all, for at least it would expand the facilities in the international banking field, and the Federal Reserve Foreign Bank might be developed later. Indeed, I think, under your authority the Federal Reserve Board could establish a division handling international exchange in the public interest rather than for private interests to do so, and which would function as a Federal Reserve Foreign Bank without the name, and this might be acceptable to the Federal Reserve Board.

The Federal Reserve Act authorizes the Federal Reserve Banks to transact international banking business and authorizes the Federal Reserve Board to require them to do this, so that you have the power now to direct the Federal Reserve Banks to immediately open up foreign branches and transact foreign business for the protection of the public. If you do not support a Federal Reserve Foreign Bank, I then appeal to you to compel the Federal Reserve Banks to open up foreign branches and transact the business which the Federal Reserve Act contemplates, and in respect to which they have not discharged their full functions.

I venture to remind you that under the Act of June 15, 1917, known as the Espionage Act, you directed the Secretary of the Treasury to administer the regulations relative to the export of coin, bullion and currency, by Executive Order of September 7, 1917, and under the Act known as the "Trading with the Enemy Act," by Executive Order of October 12, 1917, you further vested in the Secretary of the Treasury the authority to supervise the foreign exchange operations, etc.

You have recently, by proper orders, vacated this machinery, but you have not cancelled the original Executive Orders. I respectfully suggest that these Executive Orders should be cancelled so as to leave the field open for the supervision and action of the Federal Reserve Board to the extent of their existing powers under the Federal Reserve Act in relation to foreign exchange business free from a possible technical complication.

Mr. President, the suggestions of this letter would be valueless if I had no concrete proposal to make.

I make a concrete proposal.

I request that you submit this entire subject matter to the Secretary of the Treasury, to the Federal Reserve Board and to the Secretary of Commerce, and require of each of them an immediate written report upon these several Bills, and direct them to submit recommendations as to what shall be done to protect the foreign commerce of the United States and stabilize international exchange, with a view to submitting such reports and recommendations to Congress.   Very respectfully,   Robt L. Owen

TLS (WP, DLC).
[1] It is missing, but it was entitled, "A bill (S. 3928) to amend the act approved December 23, 1913, known as the Federal reserve act, as amended by the acts of August 4, 1914, August 15, 1914, March 3, 1915, September 7, 1916, and June 21, 1917." *Cong. Record*, 65th Cong., 2d sess., p. 2370. Owen discussed this bill in some detail and introduced various documents in its support in the Senate on February 25, 1918. *Ibid.*, pp. 2604-16. A copy of the printed bill is enclosed in R. L. Owen to JPT, March 23, 1918, TLS (WP, DLC).
[2] Wilson had referred Owen's bill to William G. McAdoo on February 7, 1918, with a request for McAdoo's opinion of it. WW to WGM, Feb. 7, 1918, CCL (WP, DLC). WGM to WW, Feb. 13, 1918, TLS (WP, DLC), characterized the bill as "a very bad measure." McAdoo promised to send a full report on it as soon as it could be prepared. "Meanwhile," he concluded, "I hope you will not commit yourself in any way to this measure." This full report, if it ever was prepared, is missing.
On July 10, 1918, Owen urged Wilson to submit the bill to a banking expert, such as John Skelton Williams. Wilson did so on July 11. Williams replied on July 16 with a report that favored Owen's bill with some modifications. In his reply of July 23, Wilson expressed the hope that "under the influence of the Treasury Department this idea may be developed and brought to a stage where we can urge action by Congress." R. L. Owen to WW, July 10, 1918, TLS; WW to J. S. Williams, July 11, 1918, CCL; J. S. Williams to WW, July 16, 1918, TLS; and WW to J. S. Williams, July 23, 1918, CCL, all in WP, DLC.
McAdoo remained opposed to Owen's bill as late as September 1918. He professed to be in favor of Owen's "purposes and objects" in supporting a federal foreign exchange bank but argued that it would be a "grave mistake" to create such an institution at that time: "Any division of responsibility and any unneeded multiplication of agencies . . . would be most unfortunate and hurtful." WGM to WW, Sept. 26, 1918, TLS (WP, DLC).

³ It is missing, but it was S.2590, introduced by Owen on July 22, 1919, a bill "to incorporate a foreign finance corporation to provide means of acquiring and selling public and private foreign securities, extending credits against the same and assisting in the development of the foreign trade of the United States." It was referred to the Committee on Banking and Currency, whence it never emerged. *Cong. Record*, 66th Cong., 1st sess., p. 2982.
⁴ Following a lengthy passage through both houses of Congress and a conference committee, the Edge bill was approved by Wilson on December 24, 1919. 41 *Statutes at Large* 378.

From Julius Howland Barnes

My dear Mr. President: New York July 16, 1919

There are two important policies on which I greatly desire your views.

First: Shall we at this time announce a policy of resale of wheat at lower than the guarantee price which the Grain Corporation must pay?

Second: To what extent, if at all, shall we use the authority in the Act of March 4th to sell wheat and wheat products for credit?

May I comment on certain phases of each question. The Grain Corporation at present owns no wheat, unsold. Its total stocks of wheat on hand are less than 4,000,000 bushels, all of it due under contract to the Allied agencies. There is no authority in law by which it is assured purchases of wheat, except as the export embargo control may create a natural pressure of the crop to the Government buying-basis at the guarantee price. This will undoubtedly happen shortly, although for three months wheat prices in the United States have ruled at substantially above the guarantee price basis. In fact, since February, last, the Grain Corporation has resold in America from its holdings accumulated last fall a total of about 90,000,000 bushels, which it had expected to market overseas.

Our analysis of the crop movement, obtained through the thousands of dealers' and millers' reports, indicates that the estimate for the crop of 1918, 918,000,000 bushels, was probably 50,000,000 bushels above the quantity actually secured.

The crop estimate of July 1 this year of 1,161,000,000 bushels, based on current threshing and crop-condition reports, is, I believe, materially larger than will be actually demonstrated.

I estimate that the world overseas requirements for this coming crop-year, as far as one may forecast them at this time, indicate a requirement upon the United States of 410,000,000 to 460,000,000 bushels. (Mr. Hoover places these figures even larger.) A separate statement showing analysis on which I base my estimate is hereto attached.[1] Should our crop yield shrink to 1,000,000,000 bushels, as now seems possible, it would be, in my judgment, impossible to provide for export more than 400,000,000 bushels.

For several years, under the stress of war helpfulness, we have reduced our carryover between crops in the United States to a dangerously low level. On July 1, this year, our total stock of wheat, in all positions, remaining from the second largest wheat crop ever grown, did not exceed the equivalent of one month's consumption. With our numerous congested industrial centers and large sections of foreign-born population this is not a sound situation to allow to develop when avoidable.

I am also somewhat apprehensive as to the wheat-acreage to be sown this coming fall. The guarantee price basis of $2.26, with no assurance on other grain, was a great stimulation to the winter-sown acreage of last fall—49,261,000, against 42,301,000 the year before. The spring wheat acreage showed no expansion—22,593,000 against 22,489,000 acres. The effect of this increased winter wheat acreage is probably reflected into the corn acreage of this spring's sowing—102,977,000 against 107,492,000 acres. The old relation of, roughly, corn at one-half the price of wheat has been definitely broken. To-day, against the Government guarantee for No. 1 Wheat of $2.26, Chicago, standard corn is selling at $2.00 per bushel. Such a situation, if continued to the fall sowing season, with no guarantee on either grain, will undoubtedly deflect much wheat acreage into corn, and possibly, with a year of poor prospective yields, we might find uncontrolled wheat prices sharply higher than the guarantee fair-price basis. The present comparison, per pound, Chicago basis, is: Wheat, 3.77; Corn, 3.57. An artificial reduction in wheat prices would put wheat actually at a lower price per pound than corn, against the old ratio of wheat double the value of corn and would be almost sure to demoralize the wheat acreage and to exhaust the reserves which might soundly be constructed to prevent possible wheat scarcity the coming season.

The practical difficulties of making effective to the grower the guarantee price basis of $2.26, Chicago, and establishing a lower resale basis have, I believe, been overcome as far as is humanly possible. Our problem was to make, in case of need, such adjustments by payment from the National Treasury but so framed as to reduce to a minimum the opportunity for fraud and abuse and to make sure that the reduced prices so made effective should actually reach the consumer. We have done this by trade contracts

---

[1] "FORECAST OF PROBABLE WORLD WHEAT SITUATION FOR CEREAL YEAR 1919-20," T MS (WP, DLC).

executed with individual mills providing for the sale of their products on such a readjusted basis and that, during such directed reduction, their gross operating margin of profit is definitely set and controlled. Nevertheless, with all these safeguards, a reduced price basis is difficult to police, and for this reason alone, to be avoided until the last moment.

I believe a sounder policy is that the wheat which comes to the Government in protection of the guarantee price, shall be sold on a fair reflection of that price basis, plus charges, and no more; that the necessities of the world which might easily force a much higher basis than the Government guarantee shall not be used for national profiteering; that control over exports shall be used to protect, as far as can be humanly estimated, our domestic requirements and then apportion fairly to those entitled to claim upon our food supply, and I am inclined to believe that this can be and will be as practical a one as the hitherto popular conception of a world price basis forcing a reduction in our own guarantee price.

I feel quite confident that if the law of supply and demand could be reinstated to operate freely it would be as likely to produce a basis for wheat higher than the guaranteed price as one lower. The guarantee was made as an extension of the Fair Price Decision of your special Price Commission and is probably as fair a reflection of a proper basis between buyer and seller as can be determined, with the free action of supply and demand influences suspended as they are at present. I believe it a possible outcome that the wheat price may be held steady by the pressure of our undoubted large crop at the guarantee level, at least until the latter end of the crop year when new-crop influences become decisive. I believe our surplus can be fairly distributed, helpfully, and without perhaps any loss on the National Treasury, whatever. I therefore strongly recommend that, until circumstances materially alter, we shall assume the Government guarantee price is a fair basis for our own people and for our foreign buyers to pay, and that we shall operate on that basis without any present attempt to produce a readjusted lower basis.

In regard to the second policy, that of credit extension. Those Neutrals that profited by war stimulation and without war destruction, Spain, Holland, Denmark, Norway, Sweden, should be expected to pay cash and in full for such purchases as they may desire to make, and such as we may allot to them when our stock is better ascertained. Allied countries—Great Britain, France, Italy, and probably Belgium—should probably be helped to resume the normal course of business by the extension of part credit accommodation under the authority of this Act. Would it meet your approval to state a present policy of extending to them one-half credit and one-half actual payment, in the expectation that they will thus be stimulated to make an effort to resume the normal and orderly course of payment? The character of such obligations as we may conclude to take I would desire to discuss with the Treasury Officials, unless you have a specific suggestion.

As to Germany, should there be any accommodation? There will be, probably, intense popular resentment against any credit extension to Germany.

As to the newly-liberated countries—Finland, Poland—and as to Jugo-Slavia, Czecho-Slovakia and Roumania, in case they should need cereal help, what attitude shall we assume? As to Portugal and Greece, what position would you recommend?

There is under contemplation, as you know, some method of extending financial accommodation for raw materials to be furnished European countries. Is it your desire that I should cooperate with them, perhaps using whatever agencies for credit they may establish?

Trade Contracts. I wish to add just a word of explanation of these, because they are a new departure, and a hopeful one. I have conceived that our people desire as little as possible of license regulation and administrative control. In the trade contracts which will be executed with the trades, dealers and millers bind themselves to pay a fair reflection of the Government guarantee price, and in the contracts of the trade facilities that reach the producer, provision is made that the producer feeling himself aggrieved as to grade or dockage or price, may appeal to the Grain Corporation officer, and then to the Wheat Director, and these decisions shall be conclusive. In this manner we have offered the producer a ready and impartial settlement of the age-long dispute between grain-seller and grain-buyer, and I am hopeful of the result.

In order that the trade facilities may function and that they may handle as much of the crop in the ordinary processes as possible, the Grain Corporation has contracted to take at any time their unsold wheat and flour at the guaranteed price, and its reflection.

In order that their credit may be secure, this guarantee is operative at any time, and particularly as to May 31, next. But in order that the trade may adjust itself with as little radical price disturbance as possible and that the flow of flour may continue without interruption, we are contracting that the trades may exercise an option to keep their wheat and continue to distribute and market their flour for forty-five days longer than that. By July 15 the outcome of the new winter wheat crop is ascertained and the progress of the new spring wheat crop demonstrated, and at that time the trades are given the opportunity of turning in their unsold balances of wheat or flour to the Grain Corporation or retaining them for their own account.

These contracts extend also to flour jobbers and to bakers, binding them in case of a readjusted flour price and the payment by the Grain Corporation for such readjustment, that it will be immediately reflected in their resale prices. I attach a set of these trade contracts for your reference should need arise.

These trade contracts were perfected after numerous conferences with advisory bodies of the trades affected and a final large conference, in New York, June 10-11th, at which time some four hundred delegates from all sections of the United States and of all trades affected, discussed these contracts and the various phases of their trade controls, and without, broadly speaking, a single discordant note against that control. I believe them to be fair; I believe them to offer the readiest and most effective means of making the guarantee price reach the producer and of constructing the engine for reduced wheat prices should that be demonstrated necessary, and I hope by means of them to provide the solution for what was a most discouraging problem. I ask your approval of that method of trade control by voluntary agreement, while we have all these trades under license for license regulation, should that later prove necessary.   Sincerely,   Julius H. Barnes.

TLS (WP, DLC).

From Albert Sidney Burleson

My dear Mr. President: Washington, D. C. July 16, 1919.

With reference to the attached telegram from Mr. Rolph,[1] Mayor of San Francisco, California, the facts are as follows:

The International Brotherhood of Electrical Workers several months ago voted a general strike, and the strike was called for June 16th. On June 14th a committee appointed by the American Federation of Labor, then in session at Atlantic City, called on the Postmaster General, and after a conference it was fully agreed that there was no need for a strike, and the committee stated that if certain orders were issued by the Postmaster General (and these orders substantially had been theretofore issued by the Postmaster General) and the companies were specifically directed to comply with these orders that the strike would be called off. These orders were issued, and the companies were notified by telegram of their issuance and to comply strictly with the same.

Therefore, a committee representing the employees waited on

the officials of the Pacific Telephone Company, and the company stated that it was prepared to take up immediately negotiations for all matters in controversy. The committee stated that it was not prepared to do so until June 19th. In the meantime, however, on June 16th, without any further negotiations they went out on strike, and the national officers of the Brotherhood of Electrical Workers have stated that they were not able to control these persons. Negotiations have continued between the company and representatives of the employees, and so far as the Postmaster General knows there has been no actual violation of the order issued on June 14th, and it is understood that the employees and the representatives of the company have reached an agreement in all matters in controversy except that of retroactive pay, which the Postmaster General asked be referred to the Wire Control Board, which would act on it within three days after the presentation of the case to that board. Advices received this morning indicate that a settlement will no doubt be reached within the next twenty-four hours in this matter.

The statement by Mayor Rolph that the Wire Control Board is composed of representatives of corporations owning telephone and telegraph lines is an error, as this board is composed of the Postmaster General, the First Assistant Postmaster General, and the Solicitor for the Post Office Department,[2] who own no stock and have no interest in any telephone or telegraph company. The only desire they have in the matter is to see that the owners of the properties and the employees are both treated in a just and equitable manner.

I am attaching hereto a tentative draft of a telegram which I suggest be sent to the Mayor of San Francisco and to the Mayor of Berkeley, California.[3]   Faithfully yours,   A. S. Burleson

TLS (WP, DLC).

[1] James Rolph, Jr., to WW, July 9, 1919, T telegram (WP, DLC). Rolph stated that the telephone strike in California had continued for three weeks, "causing great inconvenience to all classes and intolerable conditions in business and social life." The employees, he said, were willing to submit all matters in controversy to "a fair and impartial board of arbitrators composed of members having no connection whatever with wire companies or Postmaster General's Department." "Repeated efforts," he continued, "to induce the Postmaster General to order the company under his control to arbitrate have been unavailing. Relief from him seems impossible." Burleson had suggested only that the questions in dispute be submitted to the Wire Control Board. This was unacceptable to the employees, who believed that the board was composed of representatives of corporations owning telephone and telegraph lines and was dominated by Burleson. Rolph appealed to Wilson, as Burleson's superior, to order the submission of all questions in dispute to arbitrators acceptable to all parties concerned.

[2] That is, John Cornelius Koons and William Harmong Lamar.

[3] "Tentative Draft of a Telegram," T MS (WP, DLC). This draft telegram repeated the substance of the second, third, and fourth paragraphs of the above letter. The Mayor of Berkeley was Louis Bartlett.

A Communication

[c. July 17, 1919]

It is pleasant to learn from a statement sent us by the American Red Cross that their 1918 War Fund was increased by $49,333.57 resulting from the sales of the wool clipped from the White House sheep,[1] a price that would indicate wild profiteering if the transaction had been commercial, but justified by the objects of the sales which were publicly understood as a device to augment the funds of Red Cross and thereby enable it both to contribute to the comfort of our soldiers and sailors in their stern task of defending the liberties of the world and to render mercy to the harassed peoples of the nations associated with us in the war against the common enemy. We congratulate you upon the contribution which you have made to a fund devoted to these patriotic and humane purposes.

Woodrow Wilson
Edith Bolling Wilson

TS MS (WP, DLC).
[1] About which, see K. Neville to WW, May 28, 1918, n. 3, Vol. 48.

To Josephus Daniels, with Enclosure

My dear Daniels: The White House 17 July, 1919.

I send the enclosed to you because I do not know whether any of our ships are available for this purpose. If they are, it might be well to comply with the request herein contained, though perhaps it would be best to do it through Admiral Knapp, who is in touch with our colleagues on the other side of the water as we are not.

Faithfully yours,   Woodrow Wilson

TLS (J. Daniels Papers, DLC).

ENCLOSURE

From Frank Lyon Polk

My dear Mr. President: Washington July 14, 1919.

I enclose a copy of a telegram from the American Embassy at Archangel[1] making an urgent plea that one American warship be allowed to remain at Archangel in order to make the withdrawal of our land forces from North Russia appear less pointed and abrupt. Personally, I believe this would be an excellent move to make if you can see your way clear to issuing the necessary instructions to the Secretary of the Navy.

Faithfully yours,   Frank L Polk

TLS (WP, DLC).
  [1] About which, see JD to WW, July 23, 1919, n. 1.

From Edward Mandell House

Dear Governor: London, July 17, 1919.

I am enclosing for your files copies of Mandates B and C as drafted by the Commission on Mandates, as there may have been some error in the transmission by cable.[1]

I have not heard from you yet as to your approval, but hope to do so in a day or two.

I want to congratulate you upon your presentation of the Treaty to Congress last Thursday. No one but you could have done it so well. I was particularly glad to read the tribute you paid to the American soldiers and sailors in the war. They deserve all that can be said.   Affectionately yours,   E. M. House

TLS (WP, DLC).
  [1] The text of EMH to WW, July 11, 1919, conforms to the text of House's enclosure, with variations only in paragraphing, numbering, and capitalization. Hence, the enclosure in EMH to WW, July 17, 1919, is not printed.

To Thomas William Lamont

My dear Lamont: The White House 17 July, 1919.

Thank you very much for your letter of July 11th with its interesting enclosures. I am very much interested in what you have suggested to the League of Free Nations Association, and believe that such things will bear very valuable fruit.

In haste,   Faithfully yours,   Woodrow Wilson

TLS (T. W. Lamont Papers, MH-BA).

To William Allen White

My dear Mr. White: The White House 17 July, 1919.

Mr. Tumulty has called my attention to your recent editorial "The President and the Peace."[1] I want you to know how thoroughly I appreciate your attitude and the patriotic support you are giving to the programme which it seems to me is absolutely necessary to redeem the reputation and establish the influence of the country we love.

Cordially and sincerely yours,   Woodrow Wilson

TLS (W. A. White Papers, DLC).
¹ "THE PRESIDENT AND THE PEACE," *Emporia*, Kan., *Daily Gazette*, July 11, 1919. "President Wilson's appeal," White wrote in comment on Wilson's address to the Senate on July 10, "to the country through the Senate was fair and temperate and should be convincing, but it was not definite."

White continued: "It was vague where it should have been specific. Mr. Wilson should have gone down the treaty, line upon line, precept upon precept. But he didn't. He cannot. It's not his nature to be concrete in his discussions. President Wilson has his obvious faults, he should not be elected to a third term, and the Democratic party should not get and will not get any credit for his endeavors in Europe. Moreover, his endeavors in Europe, while they were honest and certainly uninfluenced by considerations of personal ambition, were no more important in results than any other American charged with his mission might have achieved. It was the character of his mission that gives him importance. For he really did strive sincerely and well for genuinely wise things. And for his ideals and for the way those ideals have been impressed upon the minds and hearts of Europe, even if not in the treaty, he deserves great credit, because sooner or later those ideals will bear fruit in the amended Covenant and the revised treaty, and the world will be better for it. The President was the sower who went forth to sow. The Covenant and the treaty in the present form are by no means the full and final harvest.

"But on the other hand, the Covenant and the treaty are the best compromise obtainable from the constituted authorities of the Peace Conference. Possibly the Senate can improve these documents. They are not God-given. It is not necessary to regard them as having been handed down from Sinai; the Covenant is about where the constitution of the United States was when it was adopted and before the amendments began making it a workable document. Doubtless, the states considering the American federal constitution saw many flaws, but the very fact that they saw where it could be improved and made a living instrument of justice, was the reason for their adopting the American constitution with its bald imperfections. The treaty also has its faults as well as the Covenant of the League. But if the League is secured, the League will furnish a court of appeal to which the faults and injustices of the treaty may be taken for readjustment.

"The real danger in the situation is a political danger. We may as well face the fact. The Republicans are hungry for an issue. They can't get together on the issue of the social, industrial and economic reconstruction of this country. For they don't think in the same language—Penrose and Johnson, Watson and Borah, McCormick and Sherman, but they can get together on anything to beat the Democrats. So they are intent on discrediting the President. They want an issue and they are jeopardizing the peace of the world to make it. It is small business. And what is more, it will wipe the Republican party off the map. For one more smashing defeat, and that defeat upon a fake issue, will start the daisies sprouting out of the toes of what was once a grand old party. And the good Lord knows the Democratic party is too rotten, to[o] imcompetent and too generally untrustworthy to deserve the pudding of a victory, which the Republicans will put in the Democrats' hands, by forcing this issue as the Republicans are trying to force it now.

"These are hard times for the world."

To Joseph Patrick Tumulty, with Enclosure

Dear Tumulty: [The White House] 7/17/19.

I greatly appreciate the attitude of the Red Cross in this matter, but feel that I ought to pay for the wreath nevertheless, and would be obliged if you would tell them that I would be pleased to do so, if they will tell me how and when.   The President.

TL (WP, DLC).

ENCLOSURE

Stockton Axson to Joseph Patrick Tumulty

My dear Mr. Tumulty: Washington, D. C. July 11, 1919.

You may recall a correspondence of some months ago concerning a monument to the American soldiers and sailors who lost their lives in the wreck of the transport "Otranto" and were buried at Islay in Scotland,[1] and that the American Red Cross engaged to erect a monument as a memorial to these. At that time it was stated that the President would place a bronze wreath on this monument. A letter from the Red Cross Commissioner in London states that the design and estimate for the wreath has been prepared, but that the wreath is not to be manufactured until the President has been consulted as to the inscription which shall be placed upon it. The design, which accompanies this letter, is merely the suggestion and recommendation which has come from London.

The cost of the wreath will be £65. Personally, I am very much inclined to recommend that this expense be borne by the Red Cross and I am glad to find that my view is shared by some of my associates. I do not know how this question of a "President's wreath" originated, but I fear it may have been rather forced upon the President and it is certainly not fair to impose upon him so heavy a cost. At the same time, knowing the President as I do, I fear he may feel that he should pay for anything that appears in public as "A Contribution from Woodrow Wilson," as the present inscription reads.

I am rather embarrassed by the whole episode and simply submit this to you for your consideration and shall await your reply.

Very sincerely yours,   Stockton Axson

P.S. Let me make it quite clear that the Red Cross can and will assume this expense (upwards of $325) if the President will permit us to do so.

TLS (WP, DLC).
[1] The British troop transport *Otranto* was rammed by a British commercial steamship, *Kashmir*, in thick fog in the North Channel between Ireland and Scotland near the island of Islay on October 6, 1918. A British destroyer from the convoy of which *Otranto* was a part rescued some of the soldiers and sailors on board. However, the helpless vessel quickly drifted on the rocks of Islay and was soon dashed to pieces by the stormy seas. It was officially reported on October 15, 1918, that the total loss of life from the disaster was 527, including 357 American troops, 164 members of the ship's crew, and six men from a French fishing vessel. London *Times*, Oct. 12, 1918, and *New York Times*, Oct. 12, 13, and 16, 1918. The *New York Times*, October 12, 1918, mistakenly identified *Otranto* as an American vessel.

To Joseph Patrick Tumulty

Dear Tumulty: The White House, 17 July, 1919.

This is an amazing article.[1] I know of no such "Allied terms" as are here quoted, and do not for a moment believe that it is true that "The Nation itself is in a position through information received direct from Paris, to state * * * that Messrs. Bullitt and Steffens did take a memorandum into Russia and that the memorandum was in the handwriting of Philip Kerr, Private Secretary to Mr. Lloyd George."[2] I would very much like your advice as to whether you think it would be wise to do anything about this. I have an utter contempt for the Nation and its editor,[3] and do not want to get into a controversy with it, though my inclination is to have its statement challenged in some way and a demand made for the evidence which the editor alleges to be in his hands.   The President

TL (WP, DLC).
  [1] See FLP to WW, July 14, 1919, n. 1.
  [2] As W. C. Bullitt to WW, March 16, 1919, n. 1, Vol. 55, reveals, Kerr had sent to Bullitt, just before his departure for Russia, an unofficial memorandum outlining eight terms for a settlement between the Allies and the Soviet government. There is no evidence on the question of whether or not Bullitt took Kerr's original handwritten memorandum with him to Russia, but the similarity of the terms of the Soviet proposal that he brought back to those of Kerr's memorandum indicates clearly that he took that document in some form on the mission. There is also no written evidence to contradict Wilson's statements that he knew nothing of the "Allied terms," and that he did not believe in the truth of the *Nation*'s statement about Kerr's memorandum.
  [3] Oswald Garrison Villard.

From Joseph Patrick Tumulty

Dear Governor: The White House, 17 July 1919.

Unless the Nation's story is carried more extensively, I would not do anything in this matter.

Bullitt is discredited and no one pays any attention to the Nation. If we notice this article, we will be advertising Bullitt as well as the Nation. I think we ought to wait, at least, until later. Perhaps, this slander will finally reach Senators Lodge or Borah, who will use it. Then we can in a dignified way call for proof.

                                        Sincerely yours,   Tumulty
    Okeh W.W.

TLS (WP, DLC).

George Andrew Sanderson to Joseph Patrick Tumulty

Sir: [Washington] July 17, 1919.

I have the honor to hand you herewith a resolution of the United States Senate of July 17, 1919, requesting the President, if not incompatible with the public interest, to send to the Senate a copy of any letter or written protest by any member or members of the American Peace Commission or of any officials attached thereto against the disposition or adjustment which was made with reference to Shantung, and so forth.

Your acknowledgment of the receipt of this resolution is requested on the enclosed form.

                          Respectfully,   George A. Sanderson

TLS (WP, DLC).

From Frank Lyon Polk

Dear Mr. President: Washington July 17, 1919.

I enclose a carbon copy of a despatch received from the American Consul at Tampico, Mexico, reporting the murder of John W. Correll, an American citizen, and the outrage committed on his widow.[1] This is the case referred to in the telegram from the Governor of Oklahoma,[2] and it will probably be brought to your attention by Representative McKeown[3] of Oklahoma.

                          Faithfully yours,   Frank L Polk

TLS (WP, DLC).
[1] Claude Ivan Dawson to FLP, June 20, 1919, T telegram, (WP, DLC).
[2] James Brooks Ayers Robertson to WW, July 12, 1919, T telegram (WP, DLC).
[3] Thomas Deitz McKeown, Democrat.

From Robert Latham Owen

                                              [Washington]
My dear Mr. President: July seventeenth, Nineteen Nineteen.

I inclose a demand from the Governor of Oklahoma[1] for a full reparation from Mexico for the murder of John W. Correll and the rape of his wife, near Tampico on June sixteenth.

American citizenship in Mexico not only does not seem to protect but on the contrary seems to aggravate the Mexicans to assault and murder.

I do not believe this condition should be tolerated, and if no other means can be provided for the protection of American life in Mexico I believe that the armed force of the United States should be used for that purpose.

Yours very respectfully,   Robt L. Owen

TLS (WP, DLC).
  [1] J. B. A. Robertson to R. L. Owen, July 12, 1919, T telegram (WP, DLC). See also WW to J. B. A. Robertson, July 18, 1919.

From Josephus Daniels

My dear Mr. President: Washington. July 17, 1919.

I have received a letter from Rev. Dr. G. B. Winton,[1] Editorial Secretary of the Protestant Missionary work in Latin America, who, after expressing his regret that you could not come to Columbus at the Methodist Centenary Celebration,[2] says:

"Two phases of the situation there would have interested him. The first was that the audiences which gathered from day to day, each a new one, were overwhelmingly in favor of the League of Nations. To a Southern Democrat this was impressive, as they must have been predominantly Republican.

"In the second place the President would have found all our Latin American contingent, missionaries and natives alike, and not from Mexico alone but those from South America as well, a unit against intervention in Mexico. It was felt by all that such a step would deal a deadly blow to mission work. Every Latin nation would resent it and would promptly take sides with Mexico. The present era of good will, the like of which we have never before known, would come to an abrupt end.

"Since all my information from Mexico indicates that conditions there are better than at any previous moment since 1913 and that no important movement against the Government is left in the field, I have been surprised on coming to New York to find the feeling prevalent here that we are on the verge of armed intervention. If the Republican majority in Congress is proposing to yield to pressure from the capitalists and investors and force President Wilson to abandon an attitude which has won us the friendship of all our neighbors to the south, the public should be exactly appraised of what is taking place. We are especially concerned because of the direct effect a change of policy will have on Protestant missionary situation. It is better to-day than ever before."

I am sending you this quotation from his letter about the Mexican situation, because he is quite familiar with it from the standpoint of Protestant missionary work. I knew this would interest you.   Sincerely yours,   Josephus Daniels

TLS (WP, DLC).
   [1] George Beverly Winton.
   [2] About which, see JPT to WW, July 5, 1919 (second telegram of that date).

From Thomas James Walsh

My dear Mr. President: Washington July 17, 1919.

Reflecting after leaving you yesterday on the subject of our conversation, two ideas occurred to me, which I thought ought to be conveyed to you.

1. If you could find some occasion to say publicly here what you said to Lloyd George concerning Carson,[1] it would be helpful in a high degree. Perhaps his recent outbreak,[2] apparently universally condemned in England,[3] may afford you an excuse.

2. It would be invaluable if, in elucidating the manner in which the cause of Ireland could be brought before the League, as discussed by us, you could declare your purpose to present the matter, Congress concurring, at the first opportunity.

I have it in mind in connection with the discussion of the subject when I again address the Senate to submit a resolution declaring it to be the sense of the Senate that the Government of the United States should, in case the treaty is ratified, ask the League, under Article XI, to take into consideration the existing state of affairs in Ireland. I believe that under the influence of action along the line suggested the formidable opposition which has been aroused would fade away. The present status of affairs is illustrative of what may happen at any time when a controversy of any character arises between this country and Great Britain. If the sentiment is anywhere nearly evenly divided otherwise, the resentment of those of Irish blood in this country against England would mass them almost solidly against a peaceful solution. I was told last night that Mr. Hurley had said that even such conservative and broad-gaged men as John D. Ryan and James A. Farrell[4] are intensely wrought up over the fact that the Peace Conference has brought freedom to practically every submerged people in Europe except the Irish. It might be wise for you to call in Mr. Hurley and ascertain what he knows.   Sincerely yours,   T. J. Walsh

TLS (WP, DLC).
   [1] Wilson probably had reiterated to Walsh his belief that England's Irish problem could have been largely solved if the English government had hanged Sir Edward Henry Carson for treason when he tried to force a division between northern and southern Ireland in 1913-1914. For Wilson's first reported statement of this belief, see the extract from the Diary of Dr. Grayson printed at March 12, 1919, Vol. 55.
   [2] Carson had delivered a speech at an Orange party celebration of the anniversary of the Battle of the Boyne (1690), held at Holywood, about six miles northeast of Belfast, on July 12, 1919. He presented a resolution for the repeal by Parliament of the Irish Home Rule Act of 1914 and for a parliamentary union between Ireland and England.

He asserted that the Home Rule Act was only a step toward an independent Irish republic. He threatened to call out his Ulster Volunteers if any attempt was made to deny the citizens of Ulster their rights as British citizens. He warned his listeners of the great anti-British propaganda campaign being carried on in the United States by Irishmen and Irish-American sympathizers, backed, he asserted, by the Roman Catholic Church. He declared that the United States should attend to its own affairs, while England and Ulster did the same. He also attacked the Irish-American mission headed by Frank P. Walsh for its meddling in Irish affairs. The fullest account of Carson's speech is in the London *Times*, July 14, 1919.

[3] The *New York Times*, July 17, 1919, reported that British newspapers of all persuasions were condemning Carson's speech.

[4] That is, John Dennis Ryan and James Augustine Farrell, president of the United States Steel Corp.

From Vance Criswell McCormick

Personal

Dear Mr. President: Harrisburg, Penn. July 17th, 1919

I have been in Washington several times since my return and made no effort to see you because I felt that your time could be more profitably spent in interviewing others.

I have arranged for the liquidation of the War Trade Board with Mr. Polk and will complete the job when Secretary Lansing returns, with whom I will immediately confer. Its affairs are in good shape and the Congressional appropriation will enable us to carry our work to its ultimate conclusion.

It is needless for me to say that, while I have returned to my normal life here and am taking up the loose ends of my private business, if I can ever be of service to you, I am always at your call.

I am deeply grateful to you for the opportunity you gave me to attend the Peace Conference in Paris. It has been one of the most wonderful experiences of my life and I am proud even if in a small way to have been a party to the consummation of what to my mind is one of the world's greatest achievements—the completion of a Peace Treaty under almost insurmountable difficulties, due to your leadership; and I want to confess now that you were right and I was wrong when I advised against your going to Paris, as I do not believe as satisfactory settlement, if any at all, could have been made, if you had remained in this country.

I have been getting next to the people. They are behind you in the League of Nations and in my opinion the Senate will have to ratify it.

With many thanks for giving us this opportunity of enjoying the delightful and restful return voyage on the George Washington and with very kind regards, I am

Sincerely yours,   Vance C. McCormick

TLS (WP, DLC).

From Frank William Taussig

My dear Mr. President: Washington July 17, 1919.

You will recall that you have in your hands my resignation, which was to take effect on July 1st, or at such later date as in your judgment might be desirable.[1] Since returning I have taken up Tariff Commission business and have acted with my fellow commissioners in disposing of it. I take the liberty of suggesting now that my resignation be accepted by you as of August 1st.

I have already brought to your attention some suggestions concerning the type of men who might be chosen in my place,[2] and I hope to bring to your attention before long a possible appointee or appointees.

I need hardly add that I shall be at your disposal and at that of Mr. Baruch, so far as I may be helpful, in clearing up matters connected with the Peace Treaty.

Not least, you will let me express again my appreciation of your constant consideration and kindness, and my faith in the high purposes and high achievements of the Administration.

Very sincerely yours,   F. W. Taussig

TLS (WP, DLC).
  [1] F. W. Taussig to WW, May 31, 1919, TLS (WP, DLC).
  [2] F. W. Taussig to WW, May 31, 1919, TLS (WP, DLC).

Breckinridge Long to Joseph Patrick Tumulty

Dear Mr. Tumulty: Washington July 17, 1919.

At five o'clock Friday afternoon, July 18th, the President will review the Czecho-Slovak contingent which is en route from Siberia to Europe.

The President was so interested in the movements of the Czech troops in Siberia and in the heoric [heroic] conduct of their army of 80,000, that it has occurred to the officers of the department that it would be a very fitting occasion for him to address a few remarks to them.

These men have been in a territory which has been infected with Bolshevism; they are going from here to another territory which is infected with Bolshevism and the thought has occurred that every way in which they could be bolstered up would re-act to the good of all concerned. Aside from that, any remarks which the President might see fit to address to them would be heard around the world and be read with particular interest in Siberia where encouragement is badly needed and in Czecho-Slovakia where the new nation is just beginning to get on its feet.

It could be very easily arranged that the column halt in its procession past the reviewing stand and that the officers proceed to the reviewing stand and stand before the President during his remarks.

Realizing how very busy he is, an attempt has been made to draft some remarks[1] which, however, inadequate they may be, may save him some trouble.

Since the review is at five o'clock Friday afternoon, I will ask you to let me know as soon as you conveniently can, what the pleasure of the President will be and I will see that his desires are complied with.   Yours very sincerely,   Breckinridge Long

TLS (WP, DLC).
    [1] "The Czecho-Slovaks in Washington," T MS (WP, DLC).

A News Report

[July 18, 1919]

THREE HEAR WILSON
McCumber, Colt and Nelson Are Enlightened on the League.
By ALBERT W. FOX.

President Wilson yesterday began his personal conferences at the White House with Republican senators and the effect of this move is awaited with intense interest on all sides. Contrary to the expectations of the opposition, the President did not begin by inviting any of the 40-odd Republicans known to be against the present league covenant, but issued invitations to those Republican senators understood to be inclined toward the league.

At first this plan caused some mystification, but as the day progressed administration spokesmen began to see in the move another specimen of the President's well-recognized political strategy. He has first sought out and found the weak point in the opposition's armor, they said, and has taken timely and full advantage of opportunity.

The Republicans expressed confidence last night even while admitting the shrewdness of the President's move. It cannot, however, be said that the conferences between the President and the Republicans who are weakest in their opposition to the covenant are taking place without causing some uneasiness in the ranks of the opposition.

The main purpose which the President hopes to achieve has apparently become clearer, according to senators on both sides, and it is believed that this is to insure a majority on his side in the Senate prior to leaving the battleground for his tour to the west coast. From this viewpoint, it is far more practical and promising for the President to confer with senators like McCumber, Colt, Jones, Nelson, Kenyon, Kellogg, McNary and Capper than with other Republican senators.

The senators here named all received invitations yesterday excepting Senator Jones, who is out of the city.

The letters sent from the White House were, in substance, as follows:

My dear senator: Matters of so great a consequence are now under consideration that I would very much appreciate an opportunity to have a talk with you about the treaty and all that it includes.

Senators McCumber, Colt and Nelson responded to the invitation yesterday. Senators Kenyon, Kellogg, McNary and Capper will go today.

The President spent an hour or more with each of the three senators yesterday. Senator McCumber, who has all along been a staunch supporter of the league, made the following statement after his long and cordial talk with the President:

"The President gave me much confidential information that I am not at liberty to discuss, or to use in a speech. His conversation tended to show how conclusions were reached in the peace conference regarding various matters in the treaty. It did not change my views in any regard, and I am still of opinion that some reservations are necessary in connection with our ratification. The President made no effort to change my attitude."

Senator Colt, who has had leanings toward the league covenant though he favors reservations in a few particulars, talked with the President at great length over the Shantung decision which has so stirred the country. The President went over the details of Japan's diplomatic battle for Shantung, and without defending Japan's course explained that the necessity of a compromise caused the peace conference to arrive at its final decision in this case. The President, according to Senator Colt, made the fullest sort of an expose of facts leading up to the Shantung affair.

The President did not seek to influence Senator Colt's view of the covenant excepting by explaining his own side of the case and it is understood that the senator discussed the possibility if not probability of some reservations. Senator Colt feels that if unimportant reservations threaten the covenant it would not be wise or worth while to press the reservations. But it is believed that the senator is still very uncertain as to whether Article X, "the teeth of the covenant," as it is called, should be modified. The President's view is that reservations, even of an unimportant character, would reopen the whole question of reservations to the other powers and jeopardize the treaty as a whole, according to Senator Colt.

Senator Nelson, following his conference, said that the President talked with him for about an hour. It was a very friendly and pleasant discussion, he said, in which the President went into many of the difficult features of reaching agreement on different phases of the treaty. He did not attempt to present any new reasons why its ratification was necessary. The conversation took a wide range, dealing with Shantung, Russia, the Balkans and other topics.

Senator Nelson suggested the desirability of bringing into existence a federated republic of the Balkans and found the President kindly disposed toward the plan. Mr. Nelson has indicated heretofore that he favors certain reservations in the ratification and he said yesterday that nothing in his discussion at the White House had changed his position. His impression seemed to be that the President in his present talks with senators is laying the foundation for further talks with them later, as new controversial points develop.

Printed in the *Washington Post*, July 18, 1919.

To the Senate and House of Representatives

The White House, *18 July, 1919.*

To the Senate and House of Representatives:

I take the liberty of calling your attention to a matter which I am sure is at the heart of the whole country, and which I have had very much in mind throughout all these months when we were trying to arrange a peace that would be worthy of the spirit and achievements of the men who won the victory in the field and on the sea. After mature reflection, I earnestly recommend that you give the permanent rank of general to John J. Pershing and Peyton C. March, expressing the law in such a way as to give precedence to Gen. Pershing; and that you give the permanent rank of admiral to William S. Benson and William S. Sims. I take it for granted that I am only anticipating your own thoughts in proposing these honors for the men upon whom the principal responsibilities devolved for achieving the great results which our incomparable Navy and Army accomplished.[1] Woodrow Wilson.

Printed in 66th Cong., 1st sess., House Doc. No. 153 (Washington, 1919).
[1] Congress passed on August 28 and September 2 and Wilson signed on September 3, 1919, an act reviving for Pershing the title of General of the Armies, a rank previously held only by George Washington. 41 *Statutes at Large* 283; *Cong. Record,* 66th Cong.,

1st sess., 4468-69, 4619, 5208; Frank E. Vandiver, *Black Jack: The Life and Times of John J. Pershing* (2 vols., College Station, Texas, and London, 1977), II, 1038-39.
    However, Congress took no action in the cases of March, Benson, and Sims, and they reverted to their permanent ranks of major general and rear admiral.

Remarks to Czechoslovak Soldiers[1]

July 18, 1919.

Major Vladimir Jirsa, Officers, and men of the detachment of the Czechoslovak Army:

It gives me great pleasure to have this opportunity to review this detachment of your valiant army and to extend to you, its officers, and the brave men associated with you a most cordial welcome. Though we have been far away, we have watched your actions and have been moved by admiration of the services you have rendered under the most adverse circumstances. Having been subjected to an alien control, you were fired by a love of your former independence and for the institutions of your native land, and gallantly aligned yourselves with those who fought in opposition to all despotism and military autocracy. At the moment when adversity came to the armies with which you were fighting, and when darkness and discouragement cast a shadow upon your cause, you declined to be daunted by circumstances and retained your gallant hope. Your steadfastness in purpose, your unshaken belief in high ideals, your valor of mind, of body, and of heart have evoked the admiration of the world. In the midst of a disorganized people and subject to influences which worked for ruin, you consistently maintained order within your ranks, and by your example helped those with whom you came in contact to reestablish their lives. I cannot say too much in praise of the demeanor of your brave army in these trying circumstances. Future generations will happily record the influence for good which you were privileged to exercise upon a large part of the population of the world, and will accord you the place which you have so courageously won. There is perhaps nowhere recorded a more brilliant record than the withdrawal of your forces in opposition to the armies of Germany and Austria, through a population at first hostile, or the march of your armies for thousands of miles across the great stretches of Siberia, all the while keeping in mind the necessity for order and organization.

You are returning now to your native land which is today, we all rejoice to say, again a free and independent country. May you contribute to her life that stamina which you so conspicuously manifested through all your trying experiences in Russia and Siberia, and may you keep in mind after your return, as you have kept in mind hitherto, that the laws of God, the laws of man, and the laws of nature require systematic order and cool counsel for their proper application and development, and for the welfare and happiness of the human race.

T MS (WP, DLC).
¹ Led by the United States Marine Band, 1,000 troops of the Czech Army, en route from Siberia to Czechoslovakia, had marched down Pennsylvania Avenue into the White House grounds and past the front portico of the White House, where they were reviewed by Wilson. Mrs. Wilson, Gen. March, Adm. Benson, Newton D. Baker, Josephus Daniels, and military and naval representatives of the Allied governments in Washington were among those present. The marching veterans were followed by twelve U. S. Army ambulances filled with wounded Czech soldiers. After the review, the Czechs reassembled before the portico to hear Wilson's remarks, which were translated for them by Charles (Karel) Pergler of the Czechoslovak legation in Washington. Following the President's speech, the soldiers gave him three cheers. *New York Times* and *Washington Post*, July 19, 1919.
In his speech, Wilson followed the text prepared by Long with only a few literary changes.

To Henry Cabot Lodge

My dear Senator: [The White House] 18 July, 1919.

There are some things in connection with the execution of the Treaty of Peace which can hardly await the action of the several governments which must act with regard to the ratification of the Treaty, and the chief of these is the functioning of the Reparation Commission. It is of so much importance to the business interests of the United States, as well as to the nations with which we are associated, that the United States should be represented on that commission, and represented now while the work of the commission is taking shape, that I am taking the liberty of writing to ask if you will not be kind enough to consult the Committee on Foreign Relations with regard to this particular appointment, and say to them that I would very much appreciate their approval of my appointing provisionally a representative of the United States to act upon the Reparation Commission.

Very sincerely yours,   Woodrow Wilson

TLS (Letterpress Books, WP, DLC).

To Edward Mandell House

The White House, 18 July, 1919.

I find the model mandates B and C quite satisfactory. Would it not be worth while to work out a mandate for Constantinople and the Straits, which will have to be of a special character? I do not quite understand why it is not possible to work out a model mandate A. Should not the mandates of that class be the same, no matter who becomes the mandatory?   Woodrow Wilson

T telegram (WP, DLC).

To William Phillips, with Enclosure

My dear Phillips: The White House 18 July, 1919.

The enclosed cable was read to the Cabinet the other day and discussed at some length. It was the unanimous judgment, so far as I could gather, that the plan proposed by the Supreme Economic Council on July 10th was perhaps better than the substitute proposed by Hoover and Dulles, inasmuch as one seems to involve us as much as the other, and in the present state of nerves of European politicians and business men it is perhaps best to relieve their anxiety as much as possible by frankly entering into a consultative scheme such as that suggested.

The only doubt suggested was whether we have the legal right to take part in commissions not sanctioned or recognized by our own legislation. My own judgment is that inasmuch as the body set up is merely consultative, that obstacle does not exist.

Cordially and faithfully yours,   Woodrow Wilson

TLS (SDR, RG 59, 763.72119/6063, DNA).

E N C L O S U R E

Paris July 12, 1919.

3111, July 12th, 11 P.M.

For the President. Hash 690. Supreme Economic Council July 10th passed the following resolutions proposed organization for carrying into effect international consultation in economic matters pending the formation of the League of Nations. The Council of the principal Allied and Associated Powers at their meeting on the 28th June decided as follows:

"That in some form international consultation in economic matters should be continued until the council of the League of Nations has had an opportunity of considering the present acute position of the economic situation and that the Supreme Economic Council should be requested to suggest for the consideration of the several Governments the methods of consultation which would be most serviceable for this purpose. The subcommittee of the Supreme Economic Council appointed to report upon the means of carrying into effect the above decision makes the following recommendations.

One. An International Economic Council shall be formed to consult together on economic matters and to advise the various Governments concerned pending the organization of the League of Nations.

On the termination of the Supreme Economic Council, the Interallied organizations then existing which have been previously responsible to the Supreme Economic Council shall report to the International Economic Council.

Two. The membership of the International Economic Council shall comprise two delegates of ministerial or High Commissioners rank from each of the nations represented on the Supreme Economic Council, viz. United States, British Empire, France, Italy, Belgium with the addition after the first session one delegate each of the same rank from four other Governments to be invited by the International Economic Council.

Three. The council may in its discretion, invite a representative of any other country to sit as a member at any meeting of the Council during the consideration of matters specially affecting the interests of that country.

Four. The Council shall normally meet once a month in London, Paris, Washington, Brussels or Rome according as the Council may decide.

Five. The Council shall have full authority to create the necessary organization and machinery to carry on its work.

Six: The first session of the Council shall be held at Washington not later than the 15th of September."

In respect to the above, we would like to lay before you our views:

First. That it is desirable that the American Government should show no disinclination to join in any real world necessity of an economic character.

Second. In order that coordinate, efficient and disinterested action can be taken by the United States, it is desirable that some kind of Committee be created within the United States comprised of the head of the Departments bearing on creditors and foreign relations, such a committee to determine the broad policies to be pursued in economic assistance to Europe.

Third. We have the feeling that if these matters are left solely to an organization of bankers, it will create distrust both at home and in Europe and may be charged with economic exploitation no matter how wise its intentions.

Fourth. Such a Governmental committee could coordinate our economic support so as to maintain political stability in Europe without stifling individual initiative.

Fifth. If this plan were adopted such a committee could extend an invitation to similar departmental heads in Europe to a conference such as outlined in the above resolutions of Supreme Economic Council. If this suggestion should meet with your views it would seem desirable to reply somewhat as follows to each of the representatives of the above Governments at Washington.

"With respect to the recommendations of the Supreme Economic Council the American Government is giving consideration to the creation of a committee comprising the necessary Cabinet Ministers and other officials who will direct the American Policy in economic relationship to Europe so far as this may prove necessary or possible and this committee will extend an invitation to the Governments mentioned by the Supreme Economic Council and such other countries as may be determined by these governments to a general conference on world economic matters and it would seem to the American Government that questions of permanent organization should be left to determination by this conference." Hoover Dulles.   American Mission

T telegram (WP, DLC).

From Frank Lyon Polk

My dear Mr. President: Washington July 18, 1919.

You remember the question came up the other day in regard to your power to appoint a representative on the International Economic Council. I enclose a telegram referring to this subject,[1] and also a memorandum from the Solicitor's office, in regard to your right to make the appointment.[2]

With this information before you, you may feel that you would be justified in either appointing a representative to sit on the proposed conference, or to appoint delegates to meet delegates from the other countries for the purpose of creating the proper kind of board.   Yours faithfully,   Frank L Polk

TLS (WP, DLC).
¹ Just printed.
² L. H. Woolsey to FLP, July 17, 1919, TLI (WP, DLC). Woolsey discussed the various legal aspects of the case and concluded that Wilson did have the right to appoint representatives to international commissions without authorization from Congress under his prerogative as Chief Executive. Normally, Congress would have to authorize salaries or compensation for such appointees, but at present there were funds available for such expenses in either the "President's Fund" or the "President's Emergency Fund."

To William Phillips, with Enclosure

My dear Phillips: The White House 18 July, 1919.

I can quite understand the embarrassments caused to our representative in the matter referred to in the enclosed cable. May I suggest that you get from Vance McCormick a leader as to the best reply to make?   Faithfully yours,   Woodrow Wilson

TLS (SDR, RG 59, 763.72112/12381, DNA).

ENCLOSURE

Paris, July 15, 1919.

3166. Department's 2546, July eleventh four p.m.¹ We have carefully noted this cable and particularly the President's positive view that all the Allied Governments and the United States were committed to remove all trade restrictions as soon as Germany ratified the treaty, and that the continuation of restrictions would lay the government making the restrictions open to the charge of bad faith. We shall make every effort to ensure the adoption and application of this position and indeed have already had occasion to express ourselves to this effect at meetings of the Supreme Economic Council and of its sections. It would however be very much appreciated if the Department would advise us in considerable detail as to the character of the control which the Department cables indicates is to be retained with respect to dyes, potash and chemicals. These commodities of course represent Germany's principal available exports and we have already been embarrassed by inquiries from the British and French as to the basis for the restrictions which they understand we are to maintain against the export from Germany to the United States of this important group of commodities. We are not here aware of any protective legislation by Congress upon which these restrictions can be based and can only assume that they depend upon war legislation enacted to render effective the blockade of Germany. If so it is difficult for us to differentiate these restrictions from those the abandonment of which we have been urging upon our associates in order to give effect to our understanding as to the obligation assumed toward Germany and which understanding seems to be confirmed by the President's statement in your cable.

You will therefore appreciate how greatly our position would be strengthened were we in a position to discuss our control of dyes, potash and chemicals with a full knowledge of the facts which would enable us to differentiate such control from that which the British and French desire to maintain and which superficially at least appears to be very similar in character. DULLES.

American Mission.

T telegram (SDR, RG 59, 763.72112/12382, DNA).
  [1] See FLP to Ammission, July 11, 1919.

Two Letters to William Phillips

My dear Phillips: The White House 18 July, 1919.

I am clear that our answer to the enclosed[1] should be in the affirmative, because these treaties are to include the Covenant of the League of Nations, and by that means we are to guarantee the results.[2]   Cordially and faithfully yours,   Woodrow Wilson

TLS (SDR, RG 59, 763.72119/5760, DNA).
  [1] See Ammission to WW, July 16, 1919.
  [2] Wilson's answer was sent as W. Phillips to Ammission, Paris, July 21, 1919, T telegram (SDR, RG 59, 763.72119/5658, DNA).

My dear Phillips: The White House 18 July, 1919.

I would be very much obliged if you would ask the Commissioners in Paris to express to Emir Faisul my warm appreciation of his cordial message[1] and my assurances of a friendship which we shall always try to exercise in his behalf.[2]
                 Cordially and faithfully yours,   Woodrow Wilson

TLS (SDR, RG 59, 763.72119/5800, DNA).
  [1] Faisal to WW, July 12, 1919.
  [2] Wilson's message was sent as W. Phillips to Ammission, Paris, July 19, 1919, T telegram (SDR, RG 59, 763.72119/5800, DNA).

To Newton Diehl Baker

CONFIDENTIAL

My dear Mr. Secretary: The White House 18 July, 1919.

Referring to your letter of July fifteenth with regard to the action of our troops on the Mexican border, let me say that your letter expresses my own judgment and that I am quite willing that you give General Cabell the authority you suggest, if you have entire confidence in his discretion.

Confidentially and faithfully yours,   Woodrow Wilson

TLS (N. D. Baker Papers, DLC).

To James Brooks Ayers Robertson

[The White House] 18 July, 1919.

Your telegram of July twelfth[1] has received my most serious consideration, and I beg to assure you that through the State Department I am seeking to do everything that is possible with regard to the tragical and terrible case of the treatment of Mr. Correll.

Woodrow Wilson

T telegram (Letterpress Books, WP, DLC).
[1] J. B. A. Robertson to WW, July 12, 1919, T telegram (WP, DLC).

From Frank Lyon Polk, with Enclosure

My dear Mr. President: Washington July 18, 1919.

Referring further to my letter of July 14, I enclose herewith a copy of a telegram from Mr. Poole,[1] the Chargé d'Affaires at Archangel, who is now in Paris on leave of absence.

I endorse Mr. Poole's views thoroughly and hope you will be able to arrange with the Secretary of the Navy to retain an American naval vessel at Archangel, at least for a time. I think we owe it to the people of North Russia to afford them this tangible evidence of our good will, especially as it can be done without active participation in military movements.

Faithfully yours,   Frank L Polk

TLS (WP, DLC).
[1] That is, DeWitt Clinton Poole, Jr.

ENCLOSURE

Paris. July 16, 1919.

3180. The Commission accepts no responsibility for the following personal message for Mr. Polk from Poole.

I beg to bring especially to your attention Cole's telegram 1315, July eleventh five p.m. from Archangel respecting the possibility of leaving one American naval vessel there for a time longer as an indication that we are not totally abandoning the Anti-Bolshevik movement in Northern Russia or seeking positively to discredit it.

The revolt of the inhabitants of the Northern region against the Bolsheviki was instigated by the Allies and was an indispensible part of the American program of protecting stores in the Archangel region. It created an obligation from which we cannot escape at will. The departure of our military forces has caused misgiving and disquiet, though the necessity for it was somewhat understood. The complete withdrawal of our recently arrived naval representation, following closely thereon, will seem and in fact will be hardly less than a betrayal.

The successful development since spring of the Anti-Bolshevik movement in the North has been one of the most hopeful aspects of the Russian situation. About twenty thousand Russian Anti-Bolshevik troops are under arms. Relative political contentment exists back of the front and the orderly processes of government are being revived along satisfactorily democratic lines. It would be in keeping with our general policy to encourage this development in every practical way.

The North Russian region is not strategically a unit and without a junction with Siberia can hardly be expected to withstand by itself—in the absence at least of our moral support—an aggressive central Russian government.

I appreciate the considerations motivating the early departure of American forces from Europe. The presence for a time longer of one American vessel at Archangel not participating in operations does not seem to me inconsistent with this policy.

I feel sure that the considerations suggested above will have weight with you and I sincerely hope that you will consider it possible to bring them to the personal attention of the President. This is one of these situations in which there can be no doubt of the President's decision if the issue is squarely before him.

American Mission.

T telegram (WP, DLC).

Frank Lyon Polk to Henry White

Washington, July 18, 1919.

2594 For White. Your 3152, July 15. President directs me to say that he approves of the stand taken by you in connection with the proposals made by Mr. Balfour. A blockade before a state of war exists is out of the question. It could not be recognized by this Government. Personally, I agree with you that the Allies exaggerate danger of trade with the Bolsheviks in Russia.

Polk   Acting

T telegram (SDR, RG 59, 661.119/433, DNA).

From Frank Lyon Polk, with Enclosure

My dear Mr. President: Washington July 18, 1919.

As you probably have seen from the telegrams, another American has been killed by bandits in Mexico in the same general neighborhood as Correll was recently murdered. It seems to me that it would be desirable to send the Mexican Government rather a stiff message and see if they cannot be brought to their senses.

As far as I know, they have never captured any of the various bandits responsible for these crimes, and, as I told Bonillas[1] the last time I saw him, it seems to me General Carranza should either see that these bandits are captured, or remove the officers responsible for order.

If this telegram is too strong, would you be good enough to change it and return it to Mr. Phillips, as something a little stronger than the usual representation seems to be called for.

Yours faithfully,   Frank L Polk

TLS (WP, DLC).

[1] That is, Ignacio Bonillas, Mexican Ambassador to the United States.

E N C L O S U R E[1]

July 18, 1919.

AMEMBASSY MEXICO CITY (MEXICO)

Consul at Tampico telegraphs Department under date of July 15th that he has already informed Embassy that American citizen, Peter Catron, was shot to death by bandits near Valles, San Luis Potosi, on or about July 7th. Supplementing such representations as you may have already made under standing instructions, you will formally urge upon the Mexican Government the capture and punishment of those responsible for this murder, and the adoption of adequate measures to prevent a recurrence of the murders of American citizens. You will further state that should the lives of American citizens continue to remain unsafe, and these murders continue by reason of the unwillingness or inability of the Mexican Government to afford adequate protection, this Government ⟨will⟩

may be forced to adopt a radical change in its policy with regard to Mexico.[2]

CC MS (WP, DLC).
  [1] Word in angle brackets deleted by Wilson; the one in italics, Wilson's.
  [2] This was sent as W. Phillips to George Thomas Summerlin, Chargé in Mexico City, July 21, 1919, printed in *FR 1919*, II, 572.

From Frank Lyon Polk

My dear Mr. President: Washington July 18, 1919.

Allow me to attach a copy of a letter I have just written to the Secretary of War.[1] One of the most pressing needs in Siberia today is a supply of drugs, medicines, et cetera. The information we have shows that the situation is very bad indeed both among the civilian population and also the military forces of Admiral Kolchak.

I hope very much that you will feel inclined to confer with the Secretary of War and see what can be done under the legislation I am given to understand has recently been passed by Congress.

                    Faithfully yours,   Frank L Polk

TLS (WP, DLC).
  [1] FLP to NDB, July 12, 1919, CCL (WP, DLC).

From Thomas William Lamont

Personal   *Reparations Commission.*

Dear Mr. President: New York. July 18, 1919.

Frank Polk undoubtedly showed you the message from Dulles last week,[1] explaining that an Interim Reparations Commission had been appointed to avoid the very difficulty that you yourself pointed out to us, namely, that of having a break between all the arrangements which were worked out at Paris and the coming into office of the new Commission. As Dulles pointed out, however, this Interim Commission is obviously a patchwork affair, and it is of the highest importance to appoint the permanent Commission as soon as possible.

You have undoubtedly for weeks past been considering the matter of the American appointee. But the matter is of such moment, both for our own country and the world at large, that I am venturing by this letter to suggest to you again some of the considerations bearing upon the situation:

We are all agreed that the power of the Reparations Commission will be extraordinary, for good or for ill; not only for carrying out a most important clause in the whole treaty, but in composing the situation in a way to contribute to the ultimate peace, rather than unsettlement of the world. The power which the Commission will have over the exchanges of Europe and over its security markets will be great, and all this will have a certain reflex upon American industry and commerce.

Furthermore, as was constantly pointed out at Paris, the American representative upon the Commission will occupy a unique position, inasmuch as he will have no special interest to plead, and will probably, in effect, act as an umpire or arbiter in the vastly important decisions awaiting the Commission.

For all these reasons, the ideal man for the position must possess a large and generous mind, excellent organizing ability, a judicial temperament, calmness and courage. In my judgment, it is not necessary that he should be a judge, a financial man, or have had any one particular kind of training. It *is* essential that he should be a man of such large capacity as to be able to handle and get the best out of other men; for the organization, if the work is to be carried on effectively, must be large and complete, and must be designed to relieve the Commissioners themselves from all detail.

Norman Davis, Baruch, Vance McCormick and I discussed, among ourselves, a good many names but failed to agree upon any one name as a joint recommendation. There is no man to be found that could meet the ideal standard that we have set for ourselves, but any one of the following would, I believe, represent America adequately:

Benjamin Strong, Governor, Federal Reserve Bank,

Grayson M.-P. Murphy,[2] Vice-President, Guaranty Trust Company, formerly head commissioner of the Red Cross and a graduate of West Point.

Russell Leffingwell, Assistant Secretary of the Treasury,

Albert Strauss, Vice-Governor of the Federal Reserve Board,

John W. Davis, Ambassador to England,

John D. Ryan, Copper producer and former head of the Aircraft Production Board.

Ambassador Davis, of course, has, as I understand it, had no particular financial experience, but he is a man of such unusual capacity that he can always be relied upon to carry a matter through successfully.

Norman Davis and I were going to join in writing this letter to you, but he is up at Stockbridge and will undoubtedly write you direct. I think you will find that his ideas and mine are in substantial accord. Baruch seems to think that, on the whole, Eugene Meyer would be the best man that could be suggested. I do not agree with him in this estimate. Judge Parker,[3] of the present Liq-

uidation Commission, has been mentioned. Much as I admire
many of his qualities, I don't consider him to be a big enough man.

Very likely you already have arrived at a conclusion on the whole
matter, or have in mind other names, equally as suitable as, if not
better than, the ones mentioned above. But I feel that I should be
failing in a certain sense of duty if I did not record for you my
opinion on this all important matter, having to do with the completion of the work at Paris.

Let me take this occasion once again to express my gratefulness
for the opportunity of joining you in the work at Paris and for the
large measure of confidence that you were good enough to bestow
upon me.

With great respect and profound regard, dear Mr. President, I
am,   Most sincerely yours,   Thomas W. Lamont

P.S. Of course, I think that Norman Davis would be able to handle the job very effectively but, owing to his large family, eight
small children, it would hardly be fair to ask him to make the sacrifice.

TLS (WP, DLC).
    [1] Again, J. F. Dulles to B. M. Baruch *et al.*, July 4, 1919.
    [2] Grayson Mallett-Prevost Murphy.
    [3] That is, Edwin Brewington Parker.

From Newton Diehl Baker, with Enclosure

Information no answer

My dear Mr. President: Washington. July 18, 1919.

The statements contained in the attached sheets were made to
me in a conversation by Doctor Salmon[1] who, as a Colonel was
chief psychiatrist with our Army in France. He is a man of very
eminent scientific and professional reputation, and the statements
are so striking and interesting that I feel sure you will be glad to
glance them over at some leisure moment. They give me limitless
satisfaction, and they are, of course, the outcome of the work done
by Fosdick[2] and the great group which he gathered around him
and directed.   Respectfully yours,   Newton D. Baker

TLS (WP, DLC).
    [1] Thomas William Salmon, M.D., who served both before and after the war as medical
director of the National Committee for Mental Hygiene. He was a pioneer in the treatment and prevention of mental disorders.
    [2] As chairman of the Commission on Training Camp Activities.

ENCLOSURE

The Army organized and trained in the United States and sent overseas was the *sanest, most sober*, and *least criminalistic* body engaged in the great war, under any flag, or that could be found in any group the same size in civil life. This is not a rose-colored generalization, based upon a few facts hastily collected and advanced in support of a theory, but is the conclusion, arrived at after actual observation and careful study of statistics, by the experienced, scientifically sceptical, and unemotional officers who dealt with the problems of insanity, inebriety and crime in the American Expeditionary Forces.

First, as to *sanity*: Every ten thousand men in the regular establishment contributed, during the period 1912-1919, thirty discharges each year for mental diseases. The same number of men contributed each year five suicides. The rate for insanity in the American Expeditionary Forces, in spite of the terrific stress to which the one million three hundred thousand combat troops were exposed, was less than twenty per ten thousand. In the American Expeditionary Forces there were one hundred and twenty suicides. Had the rate been the same as in the Regular Army from 1912 to 1916, not less than one thousand men would have taken their own lives.

Second, as to *sobriety*: At a time when the hospitals of the American Expeditionary Forces had approximately two hundred and twenty thousand patients, a census was taken to determine the number of men with certain specified diseases. This census disclosed the fact that there was not a single American soldier with delirium tremens in a military hospital in France. In New York City there are approximately the same number of men as there were in the American Expeditionary Forces (with much less likelihood of all alcoholic cases receiving hospital care) ten thousand patients with delirium tremens passed through the "alcoholic" wards of one group of general hospitals in a single year. Out of the two million men who served in France less than one hundred have been returned to the United States for discharge for disability for chronic alcoholism or for any form of alcoholic insanity.

Last, as to the *absence of crime*: At the time of the armistice, there were in military prisons at Gievres one thousand men, sixty five per cent of whom were serving sentences of three months or less, and only twenty per cent of whom had been convicted of crime other than those of a military character. This prison had more than half of all the general prisoners undergoing confinement in France. Up to that time very few general prisoners had been returned to the United States, so this group of about two thousand men represented the accumulation of military criminals during fifteen months of the existence of the American Expeditionary Forces. It must be remembered that these men who were living far from home could, if they so desired, find opportunities for committing most of the crimes of civil life, and, in addition, were exposed to temptation to commit purely military offenses. The same number of men in New York City contribute two hundred and ten thousand arrests every year, not including summonses for violations of the traffic and sanitary laws. There are at all times in the correctional institutions of New York State not less than eight thousand men of New York City serving sentences. In the Regular Army in 1915, twelve per cent of the enlisted strength left the service through criminal procedure. That is to say, one man in eight of all who had made enlistment contracts had them terminated by desertion or by a court-martial sentence that included dishonorable discharge from the military service. Had the same rate prevailed in the whole army during the war, more than four hundred and twenty-thousand men would have had their service terminated in that manner. In the American Expeditionary Forces, there would have been two hundred and forty thousand—a number exceeding all the casualties.

The five greatest evils of mankind have been said to be disease, poverty, insanity, crime and inebriety. Three of these evils—not to mention here the triumphs over disease in the war—became, in the American Expeditionary Forces, problems of relatively slight importance in a body of men of the age-period which in civil life contributes *practically all the* crime, as large a share of insanity as any other group, and more than half the alcoholism.

Three causes for this extraordinary situation stand out above all others. They are:

1. The rejection of seventy-two thousand insane, mentally defective and mentally unstable men by the careful psychiatric examination in the camps at home.

No other army attempted this task and, in consequence, every other army found itself burdened to an enormous extent by the mentally unfit. One in five of all the soldiers discharged for disability from the British Army was discharged for mental or functional nervous diseases. The end of the war found special hospitals for the military insane in many parts of England and Canada. In France the same situation existed.

2. The control of the use of intoxicating drinks.

Probably no cause, not even the first one mentioned, influences so greatly the prevalence of crime in the American Army as the control of the use of alcohol and this factor was of course responsible for inebriety becoming a negligible problem. In the American Expeditionary Forces, where the regulations in force in the United States did not apply and alc[o]holic drinks, even the stronger ones, were readily obtainable, the influence of the period of abstinence in the camps at home, and the effect of self-respecting, sober months spent in training were sufficient to carry most of the men along the same path.

3. The extraordinary morale of officers and men.

Many causes contributed to the high morale of the officers and men in the American Expeditionary Forces. Beneath them all was the concept of individual duty and responsibility for winning the war. The fruits of the careful work done in the camps at home for improving morale were also seen. The absence of the high proportion of mentally defective and psychopathic individuals found in the old army, but rejected by the special examinations in 1917 and 1918, however, have aided in development of good standards of personal conduct, just as the existence of high morale aided in diminishing crime, inebriety and even insanity in the American Expeditionary Forces.

T MS (WP, DLC).

From Joseph Patrick Tumulty, with Enclosure

Dear Governor: The White House, 18 July 1919.

Is not Dr. van Dyke liable to show this letter? and would not any publicity about reservations be hurtful at this time?

The Secretary

TL (J. P. Tumulty Papers, DLC).

E N C L O S U R E

My dear Dr. van Dyke: The White House 17 July 1919.

I know what earnest work you have been doing in behalf of the League of Nations, and therefore know how to value your kind letter of the thirteenth of July. Thank you for the suggestion about a possible reservation. I am hoping that it will be possible to get the Treaty accepted without reservations, but if not, such action as you suggest is undoubtedly thoroughly worth considering.

With the warmest appreciation, in unavoidable haste,

Cordially and sincerely yours,[1]

TL (J. P. Tumulty Papers, DLC).
  [1] Wilson did not reply to Van Dyke's letter until September 2, 1919.

From Joseph Patrick Tumulty

Dear Governor: The White House 18 July, 1919.

It is clear to me that the Republicans will soon attempt to extricate themselves from the unenviable position in which Lodge's leadership has placed them, by voting for the Treaty with certain reservations. The only inroads the opposition has made have been those caused by the impression they have sought to give that the Treaty was indefinite about the following things:

1st. The Monroe Doctrine;
2d. Our control over domestic problems;
3d. The Shantung affair;
4th. Section X.;
5th. Interference with the right of Congress to declare war.

I think if you could anticipate the suggested reservations, you could destroy any need for them, so far as public opinion is concerned, by either making a public statement covering these matters or within a few days, making a speech. In other words, a speech or statement interpreting the Treaty would do a great deal to win the fight which is now being made for reservations. In this speech or statement, without taking a stand against reservations, you could show the embarrassment the reservations would cause; the difficulty of calling the conferees together and the possible breaking down of the whole League of Nations idea.

                              Sincerely,   Tumulty

TLS (WP, DLC).

From Alexander Mitchell Palmer

                    Washington, D. C. July 18, 1919.

MEMORANDUM TO THE PRESIDENT.

One of the most difficult problems which I inherited when I became Attorney General was that growing out of the oil situation on the public lands.[1]

Congress has been trying for some years to pass a general leasing bill. In the last Congress, the bill reached the stage of conference, but was caught in the jam caused by the Republican filibuster and did not come up for final passage. It contained a so-called relief measure intended to bring about an adjustment of the claims of persons who have been operating upon public lands under circumstances which make them, under the present state of the law and the decisions, trespassers against the Government.

When the legislation failed at the end of the last Congress, I directed that suits be brought in Wyoming to support the Government's contention with respect to these lands. As I was about to file the bill, the oil people asked for sixty days' time in which to take up with me the matter of adjustment of the cases. I granted this extension and numerous conferences have resulted. They have been participated in by representatives of the Navy and Interior Departments and we are about ready to make certain suggested changes in the relief measures contained in the Conference report,[2] the same measures being incorporated in several bills now pending in Congress.

I find that Lane and Daniels approach this whole question from entirely different points of view and I have received conflicting reports as to what your attitude is. I am informed Scott Ferris says that you approved of the terms of the bill as agreed to in Conference. If that is true, it will make our path easier because undoubtedly it would be more practicable to put through Congress now a measure which came so near passing the last Congress than it would be to put through a radically different measure. Personally, I think that some slight changes might be made in the relief sections of the leasing bill and Lane has agreed to this, but Daniels seems unwilling to commit himself to anything in the way of relief for the claimants.

Congressional committees are urging Lane to give his opinion on various bills introduced and they will probably expect my opinion, at least with reference to the relief sections. It would, of course, expedite the legislation considerably if Daniels, Lane and I could all agree on the exact terms, but evidently this cannot be done without an expression of your opinion. I think we would make the most rapid progress with this difficult matter if you could give the time to see Daniels, Lane and myself together some time soon. If you do not care to do that, I would be glad if you would tell me just how far I can go in trying to compose the differences between Lane and Daniels and between the Government and the oil claimants and still conform entirely to your views.

A Mitchell Palmer

TS MS (WP, DLC).
[1] Palmer referred to the longstanding controversy between Franklin K. Lane, on the one hand, and Josephus Daniels and former Attorney General Thomas W. Gregory, on the other hand, concerning the rights of private individuals and organizations to pros-

pect and drill for oil on the public lands of the United States in the areas reserved for the petroleum needs of the navy, particularly Naval Reserve No. 2 in Buena Vista, California. This dispute, which involved both the several bills for the leasing of mineral rights on the public lands considered by Congress during the Wilson administration and charges of fraudulent claims made by private interests for such rights both before and during the Wilson administration, dated back at least to 1916. For the development of the controversy and its ramifications to this point, see the index references under "general leasing bill" and "naval oil reserves" in Vols. 39, 52, and 54 of this series; Enclosure I printed with JD to WW, July 30, 1919; and J. Leonard Bates, *The Origins of Teapot Dome: Progressives, Parties, and Petroleum, 1909-1921* (Urbana, Ill., 1963).
  [2] *Oil and Gas Lands Bill. Conference Report on the Bill (S. 2812) to Encourage and Promote the Mining of Coal, Phosphate, Oil, Gas, and Sodium on the Public Domain,* 65th Cong., 3d sess., Sen. Doc. No. 392.

From Walker Downer Hines

Dear Mr. President: Washington July 18, 1919

I am so keenly alive to the great problems now pressing upon your time that I am extremely reluctant to try to engage your attention, but I feel I ought to advise you of the following developments affecting railroad labor which have taken place since I wrote you on the 7th inst. and on the 9th inst.[1]

Day before yesterday the members of the Railroad Administration's Board of Wages & Working Conditions submitted to me divided reports respecting the demands for increased wages by the shop men. The three labor members favored a 25% increase which they estimate will cost $165,000,000 per year. Two of these labor members claim that the action they think necessary as to the shop men will also necessitate corresponding increases to other railroad labor. All this would mean $500,000,000 or more increase in the existing deficit which must now be running at the rate of at least $350,000,000 per year.

The Board of Wages & Working Conditions has arranged to give a hearing next Monday to the Brotherhood of Railroad Trainmen which is urging substantial further increases in the wages of its members. The Brotherhood of Locomotive Firemen has just adopted resolutions contemplating similar action.

The shop men are in a state of decided unrest. In the Southeast, a convention held a few days ago has adopted resolutions in favor of a strike on August 1st unless their demands are granted. Similar action to some extent has already been taken in other parts of the country.

I am to hold a conference here with the representatives of the shop men on Monday, 28th inst., to discuss working conditions as well as the wage matter. I cannot, without serious injury to the situation, avoid indicating at that conference a policy on the wage question.

If, before I am forced to take a position on this far-reaching matter, I can have a conference with you on that and the related subject of the high cost of living, I believe the danger of my adopting a mistaken policy will be greatly reduced.

Cordially yours,   Walker D Hines

TLS (WP, DLC).
¹ W. D. Hines to WW, July 7, 1919, TLS (WP, DLC), and W. D. Hines to WW, July 9, 1919.

From Matthew Hale

"PERSONAL"

Dear Mr. President: Washington, D. C. July 18th, 1919

It was a great pleasure to hear that you are in close touch with the Alabama and the Georgia situation as far as the ratification of the Suffrage amendment is concerned.¹ My whole purpose in asking to see you was to have you know just what the facts were and also to have you know how vital to all of us Liberals a prompt ratification is. Looking at it from a purely political point of view, I can conceive nothing more damaging to the Democratic party in 1920 than to have a Democratic state refuse to ratify, after such a reactionary Republican state as Pennsylvania has ratified under the leadership of a man like Penrose. Surely it must be possible to make the Southern legislatures realize that we are no longer discussing whether we are going to have our women vote or not, since that question has already been decided by the country. They must realize now that it is a question of whether the Republican party is going to be the one which will have given them the vote or whether it will be the Democratic party.

Would it not be possible for you to send someone down to these two states for the next few days? In Alabama as you undoubtedly know, ratification was lost by three votes in the Senate yesterday. I understand that the matter is going to be reconsidered in the next day or two and that there is a chance of having the vote reversed. I feel sure that this could be done if a personal representative of yours was on the ground. The Prohibitionists are being very active down there and have sent several representatives. I sincerely hope you can see your way to having a representative of the National Democracy cooperating to accomplish the result desired.

In Georgia, with the active cooperation of Governor Dorsey who favors the amendment, I feel that ratification could be secured.

I understand that the Secretary of the Treasury, although opposed to Suffrage, sees the political inadvisability of resisting it and has very nearly come to the point of making a public declaration in regard to Virginia, urging the Virginian legislature to ratify the amendment. Of course, if he could be pursuaded [persuaded] to do this it would have a tremendous weight with all the Southern states.

In regard to Maryland, I understand that the majority of the legislators are now in favor of ratification but that the Governor[2] is unwilling to call the legislature in session. Could not he be pursuaded as to the advisability of calling this at once?

Please excuse my venturing to give you suggestions in regard to these four states. I do so because I feel so strongly not only that justice requires that we should give women the vote at the earliest possible moment but also that political expediency demands that we should not allow our reactionary opponents to claim the entire credit.

Your help in securing Senator Harris' announcement in Paris[3] showed so clearly the way you felt and was of such value to the Democratic party, that I am sure you will appreciate the similar opportunity now presented to you in regard to the four southern states.

With best personal wishes, believe me,

Very sincerely yours,   Matthew Hale

TLS (WP, DLC).
[1] See WW to H. P. Merritt, July 12, 1919; WW to T. E. Kilby, July 12, 1919; and WW to H. M. Dorsey, July 15, 1919.
[2] Emerson Columbus Harrington.
[3] See JPT to WW, May 2, 1919, (third telegram of that date), n. 1, and the extract from the Diary of Dr. Grayson printed at May 8, 1919, both in Vol. 58, and WW to JPT, May 13, 1919, n. 1, Vol. 59.

From Francis Joseph Heney

My dear Mr. President: Los Angeles July 18, 1919

The Hearst newspapers are cunningly and viciously fighting your League of Nations plan, out here, but it may give you some satisfaction to know that up to the present time, very little adverse impression has been made upon the minds of the public in this state, notwithstanding the fact that Senator Hiram W. Johnson has an enormous following here, and is throwing all of his influence against your plan, and is fighting it just as unfairly as, but more ignorantly than, the Hearst newspapers.

It is too bad that there is not some way by which Mr. Walter Weyl's "After the War"[1] cannot be put in the hands of every thinking person in the United States for perusal and consideration. It is not comprehensible to me how any progressive thinker in the

United States can fail to be an ardent and enthusiastic supporter ·
of your League of Nations policy. Of course, it is not a panacea for
all the woes of mankind, and is not certain to stop all wars in the
future, but it is certainly the greatest practical step in the direction
of the continued maintenance of a world's peace through gradual
disarmament and the arbitration of disputed questions, that has
ever been taken or even suggested. History will give you the full
measure of credit to which you are entitled for securing this great
initial triumph for the principles of a world's democracy. It seems
to me that the inevitable, irresistible tendency of your League of
Nations policy will be toward the further democratization of the
world and the bettering of the condition of the masses of mankind.

I am leaving on a camping trip to-morrow for a good long rest,
and simply felt that I was neglecting an important duty if I went
without first assuring you that I am ready and willing to help in
any and every way in my power to secure the ratification by our
country of your League of Nations policy without any reservations
whatsoever. I say this, notwithstanding the fact that I am the author of the anti-Japanese legislation which is now on the statute
books of California, and am strongly opposed to Japanese immigration (because I believe it means the injection of another race problem such as that which almost destroyed our Union, and has seriously retarded the development of the southern states), and am
mindful of the danger to democratic institutions of the dominence
[dominance] of the Japanese power on the Pacific Ocean.

With high esteem and hearty congratulations.

Sincerely yours,   Francis J. Heney

TLS (WP, DLC).
    [1] Walter E. Weyl, *The End of the War* (New York, 1918).

From Albert Sidney Burleson

My dear Mr. President: Washington July 18, 1919

I know you will be pleased to know that the telephone strike on
the Pacific Slope has been called off, and that orders by the national labor organizations have been given to all employees to return to work. The controverted points have been referred to the
Wire Control Board for decision. This is the agency created by the
Postmaster General to settle such controversies and I have insisted
that to set the Wire Control Board aside and enlist outside agencies
as arbiters would be an admission that the agency established by
the Government could not be relied upon to do justice between the
parties. Such an admission, as I see it, would be indefensible.

There are remaining only the strikes in the South, where the operators entered upon the strike without just grounds and where in a great measure they refused to respect the strike order. The service in the South is practically normal as only 200 operators in all the cities involved out of an aggregate of 16,000 employees are now out.

I hope in a few days to effect a settlement of the strike at Cleveland, where only 15 percent of the employees are out, and at East Saint Louis, where only 10 percent of the employees are still refusing to return to work. In both these cities the service is practically normal.   Faithfully yours,   A. S. Burleson

TLS (WP, DLC).

From Franklin Knight Lane, with Enclosure

My dear Mr. President: Washington July 18, 1919.

Here is a suggestion as to a possible testimonial to the dollar-a-year men. Might it not be worth while to be rather generous with these testimonials, we had so many men and women doing service for which they asked no recompense? I am thinking, for instance, not only of the specialists of many kinds here but of the members of the State Councils of Defense, the local councils, the Food Administration, and the Fuel Administration people, etc. etc.
                    Cordially and faithfully yours,   Franklin K. Lane

TLS (WP, DLC).

E N C L O S U R E

The President of the United States
to
[blank]

When the United States entered into the war with Germany it called upon men of special talent and experience to aid the government in the conduct of this unprecedented task. To this call you responded and at a known sacrifice to yourself, served so long as the need for your service lasted. Therefore I have thought it becoming as an evidence of the appreciation in which your spirit and effort are held, that you should be presented with this testimonial.

                    President.

T MS (WP, DLC).

From William Seaver Woods[1]

Dear Sir: New York July 18, 1919.

We have made a fine portrait of Mr. Samuel Gompers for use as a cover design on an early issue of *The Literary Digest*, in recognition of his splendid services to the country and to the preservation of sane and orderly policies in the ranks of labor in this country and Europe.

We are preparing an article to accompany this portrait in which we shall sketch briefly his career, achievements and personality, in quotation from various magazine and newspaper articles. It would add splendidly to this well deserved tribute to Mr. Gompers if you would be kind enough to send us a few words of appreciation of his services at this critical time.[2]

Hoping that you can find time among your many duties and demands to cooperate in this tribute to Mr. Gompers, I remain,

Very truly,   William Seaver Woods.

TLS (WP, DLC).
  [1] Editor of *The Literary Digest*.
  [2] "I would be very much obliged if you would make the usual explanations to this gentleman. I have the most sincere admiration for Mr. Gompers and the great services he has rendered, but if I contribute to tributes to one man, I shall have to contribute to those to others until presently some name will be suggested which I cannot admire, and then there will be heartburnings." WW to JPT, July 25, 1919, TL (WP, DLC).

Sir William Wiseman to Arthur James Balfour

British Embassy, Washington.   July 18, 1919.

Following for Mr. Balfour from Sir William Wiseman:

I have just had a conversation with the President regarding the situation here. He is confident that the Treaty will be ratified, but is dealing with the Senate opposition seriously and patiently in contrast to the attitude of some leading Democrats who regard the Republican attack as a complete failure and are more intent on scoring off their opponents than in securing the unanimous approval of the Treaty. He has abandoned, for the time being at any rate, his defiant, rather contemptuous attitude and every day interviews separately half a dozen Senators and endeavours to explain the Treaty.

The following is a summary of the President's observations:

It is impossible at the moment to say how long it will be before the Senate vote on ratification. In a few days more he will be able to judge. He has won over several of the opposing Senators who had not previously committed themselves in public. The trouble is that the Senate Foreign Relations Committee has been packed by his more irreconcilable opponents and a number of the Senators pledged themselves to defeat the League before they read the Covenant, although some of them now regret that course. They have burnt their boats and are anxiously searching for a bridge.

He complained rather bitterly that Mr. Taft is weakening in his support and now thinks there ought to be reservations to the League.[1] He is setting his face against any amendments or reservations, his main argument being that such a course would set a precedent which would be followed extravagantly by the newly created states who are not entirely satisfied with the terms and unless all the great Powers including the United States unite to support the Treaty and the League there is a grave danger that Bolshevism may over-run Europe. Objectors are found to most all the Clauses from Labour to German colonies, but the President thinks the only one which might gain support in the country centers round the right of withdrawal from the League. Senators contend that the United States may not be able to withdraw owing to a difference of opinion as to whether or not she has fulfilled her international obligations under the covenant.

He does not believe the Republicans can get a majority for any one amendment but they might secure the necessary majority by combining their chief objections into one reservation.

Confidentially he admits that he may be obliged, in order to secure a really satisfactory majority, to agree to some reservation defining or interpreting the language of one or more Clauses of the Covenant. Probably Clauses No. one relative to withdrawal[,] ten and twenty one.

The President is entirely satisfied that he has the support of the people and is most eager to tour the country in support of the Treaty. He will not do so unless he concludes that he cannot persuade sufficient Republican Senators by his present daily conferences.

The President points out that the Senate has one eye on the parliaments of the Allies and will be influenced by the progress of ratification by other powers.

Senator Lodge has told his supporters that he has received letters from a member of the Government in London to the effect that the proposed Republican Amendments would be welcomed at Westminster. The President does not believe this story but thinks you ought to know that such devices are being used.

The Irish Extremists are deliberately trying to wreck the Treaty on what he described as the devilish theory that without the League we may some day be able to pick a quarrel with England and go to war and liberate Ireland.

The agitation against the Shantung settlement he regards more as an expression of mistrust of Japan than serious objection to the terms themselves.

The President looks tired and Mrs. Wilson doubts if he can stand the heavy strain of a speaking tour through the country during the very hot weather. The President told me to send his warm regards to the Prime Minister and yourself and to say that he missed you both.

T MS (W. Wiseman Papers, CtY).
[1] See JPT to WW, with Enclosure, July 23, 1919, and the memorandum by W. H. Taft, printed following Tumulty's letter and Enclosure, and the notes for these documents.

From May Randolph Petty and Calvin H. Petty

My Dear Mr Wilson: Princeton N. J.   July 18, 1919

Enclose[d] you will please find my personal check for One hundred and thirty-five ($135.) dollars. My husband joins me in trying to express our deepest and most sincere appreciation of your kindness—both in this loan[1] and desiring no interest. We would both of us welcome the day, if it's ever possible, when we could express in actions or deeds, more fully—our thanks to you.

Will you please see to returning the note before you leave Washington.

With best wishes for your *safety* and health. I am with warmest regards   Most Sincerely   May Randolph Petty
                                        Calvin H Petty

P.S. If you are ever in this vicinity, we would be so glad to have you stop and see us, and look over the Generals[2] farm and have lunch with us. If such a pleasure should ever be ours please send a card that we might be home. Wouldn't miss seeing you for the world.   May

ALS (WP, DLC).
[1] About the Pettys and this loan, see WW to Helen W. Bones, Feb. 26, 1918, n. 1, Vol. 46.
[2] That is, Hugh Lenox Scott. Again, see the footnote cited in n. 1 above.

To Thomas William Lamont

My dear Lamont: The White House 19 July, 1919.

Thank you for your letter about the interim Reparations Commission and the necessity of getting it on a permanent basis.[1] I have the matter under very anxious consideration and am waiting to hear from the Senate Committee, whom I have consulted as to the propriety of making a permanent designation. I value very much indeed your advice in the matter and the list of names you suggest. It makes me feel pretty confident that I shall be able to find a competent man, if not the ideal one.

In unavoidable haste,

Cordially and sincerely yours,   Woodrow Wilson[2]

TLS (T. W. Lamont Papers, MH-BA).
   [1] T. W. Lamont to WW, June 18, 1919.
   [2] While signing his letters on July 19, Wilson's handwriting became increasingly deformed. Among the originals of letters printed herein, the signature on the letter to Daniels was particularly cramped and almost grotesque.

A News Report

[July 19, 1919]

WILSON TOLD LEAGUE CANNOT PASS INTACT
Friendly Republicans Firm in Views at White House

By ALBERT W. FOX.

An unexpected failure developed in connection with President Wilson's further conference with Republican senators favorable to the league yesterday. The President was told in the most friendly but firm manner that he must accept the inevitable and abandon his plan for obtaining ratification of the covenant in the present form. Coming from Senators who are anxious to be helpful and who are ready to assist toward any goal which they believe can be reached, these declarations are understood to have made a profound impression on the President.

In reply to the first positive statement that facts must be faced as they are and that fulfilment of the President's hope is, under the circumstances, impossible, the President is said to have expressed not only keen disappointment, but positive apprehension for the world's future.

So disturbed are world conditions and so great are the threatening dangers to international stability that the President dreads to look over his paper each morning, according to his senatorial visitors.

Mr. Wilson is described as feeling that the world at large has little idea of the perils still in the path of peace. The Balkan situation, the internal affairs of more than one European government, the increasingly delicate Far Eastern situation, all combine to make the outlook uncertain. It was believed that China would sign the peace treaty yesterday, but for some reason not explained action has been withheld.

Closely linked with this delicate European and Asiatic situation is the prospective attitude which America will assume toward the league of nations covenant, the President is represented as believing. The warning of the friendly Republicans came therefore as a shock, it is stated, but the President is represented as facing the issue in a practical way and determined to make the best of it.

After he had talked with Senators Kenyon, Kellogg, Capper and McNary, the President went to the Capitol, where he had a long conference with Senator Hitchcock, of Nebraska. The President's conference with Senator Hitchcock took place in the President's room in the Senate wing. The matters discussed were not divulged.

Senator Kenyon and the President discussed the league covenant very frankly and fully. The President is making a point of not attempting to influence his senatorial visitors excepting through explanation of the covenant clauses as he interprets them, and the senators are not attempting to picture the covenant's prospects in more rosy colors than the facts, in their opinion, justify. The senators are giving the President their best judgment regardless of whether it will be pleasant to listen to, and in this sense the interviews yesterday were perhaps unusually helpful.

Senator Kenyon did not disclose what he and the President talked about, but he did say that he had asked about the President's interpretation of one of the covenant clauses regarding the right of the United States to withdraw after two years, provided the United States regarded its own obligations under the league as having been fulfilled. Senator Swanson, in his recent speech, made this point and took the stand that the United States and not the league powers would be the judge of whether these obligations had been fulfilled. According to the text of the covenant the view was held by many senators that the league and not the United States would be the judge as to whether America's obligations had been fulfilled. The President is represented as indorsing this view.

Senator Capper, of Kansas, is understood to have been one of the senators who called a spade a spade in his talk at the White House. He apparently does not believe there is a chance for the covenant to pass without reservations. He is said to have told the President that sentiment in Kansas, which was first overwhelmingly for the league, has undergone a decided change.

Senator McNary, of Oregon, said, after leaving the White House, that he had not altered his views on the covenant. In many respects he and the President are in accord. But on the matter of reservations Senator McNary has already indicated his desire to see some features of the covenant changed.

After his talk with the senators the report became current that the President would shortly issue a statement to the country regarding the Shantung provision of the peace treaty. Indications are that the President has made a very decided impression on senators whenever he has gone into details regarding the need of meeting Japan's demands regarding Shantung. The belief prevails that the President will make a public explanation of the reasons why the American peace delegates, much against their inclinations, accepted Japan's demands.

As a result of the frank statements of friendly Republicans there is already talk of a new move on the President's part which may meet the situation. It is now reported that he will agree to "interpretative reservations," but will still oppose such reservations as would alter the sense of the treaty and make it necessary for other powers to concur in the changes.

On this score the President will be in a position to contend that if America makes reservations, other powers will want reservations made too, with the result that "the doors will be opened" and the basic structure of the covenant doubtless materially changed. "Interpretative reservations" would merely be expressions made by the Senate independent of the treaty and would not necessitate indorsement by foreign powers. But for this very reason the opposition is apparently determined to make the reservations very real and vital and to insist that foreign powers agree to them before the treaty is declared binding on the United States.

It may be that the President's first fight in the Senate will be to separate reservations from the covenant itself and make them merely expressions of interpretation, meanwhile ratifying the treaty and the covenant as they now stand. In other words, the interpretative reservations would merely by [be] for the guidance of America and not call for any international approval or disapproval.

So far as the foreign powers are concerned, America's position in the league would not be affected one way or the other, for the American Senate could never be denied the privilege of describing the league's clauses in any way it saw fit. In case of future international complications, however, the interpretation of the league and not that of the United States Senate would of course prevail, so that the "interpretative reservations" would not be of especial interest to other powers.

But reservations in the sense intended by the opposition are admittedly a very different matter. They would mean that the covenant is accepted by the United States, provided that the other powers recognize in advance that America is not obligated in specific matters mentioned, or that the league, so far as America is concerned, is not given jurisdiction over specific matters. Definite recognition of these changes—perhaps of vital importance—would have to come from the other powers as a condition for America joining the league. Therefore reservations in this sense necessarily imply all the complications mentioned by the President.

Should the President get a majority for "interpretative reservations" he might still hold the whip hand, but if the opposition holds the balance of power and real reservations begin the President's fight will be in perilous jeopardy.

Printed in the *Washington Post*, July 19, 1919.

To Newton Diehl Baker, with Enclosure

My dear Baker: The White House 19 July, 1919.

Thank you for sending me the enclosed. It is quite in keeping with the understanding which arose out of conferences I had with Bliss and Pershing, the substance of which I believe I communicated to you in one of our talks.

Cordially and faithfully yours,   Woodrow Wilson

ENCLOSURE

From Newton Diehl Baker

My dear Mr. President: Washington. July 15, 1919.

The following cablegram has been received from General Pershing:

"For Secretary of War and Chief of Staff. By direction of the President, I have discussed with Marshall Foch question of force to be left on the Rhine. Following agreed upon: The 4th and 5th Divisions will be sent to base ports immediately, the 2nd Division will commence moving to base ports on July 15th, and the 3rd Division on August 15th. Date of relief of 1st Division will be decided later. Agreement contemplates that after compliance by Germany with Military conditions to be completed within first three months after German ratification of treaty, American forces will be reduced to one regiment of Infantry and certain auxiliaries. Request President be informed of Agreement. This has not been given to Press here and I request it not be given out there because of political effect in Germany. Pershing."

Very sincerely,   Newton D. Baker

TLS (N. D. Baker Papers, DLC).

To Josephus Daniels

My dear Daniels: The White House 19 July, 1919.

Thank you cordially for your letter of July 17th containing the quotation from Dr. Winton's letter. It is instructive and cheering.

Cordially and faithfully yours,   Woodrow Wilson

TLS (J. Daniels Papers, DLC).

To Henry Cabot Lodge

My dear Senator: [The White House] 19 July, 1919.

I have just approved an estimate for an appropriation, prepared by the Department of State, for authorizing and providing for raising the rank of our Legation in Belgium to that of an Embassy. You will no doubt have noticed that France and Italy have recently taken this action, and it is authoritatively announced that Spain and Brazil will follow their example. It would be, it seems to me, a very proper thing at this time to show our deep interest, at the conclusion of the war, in the little nation in which so many of the causes of the war seemed to center and whose cause indeed will always seem one of the most striking evidences of the unscrupulous action of Germany. When I was in Brussels, I stated to the Belgian Parliament that it would be my purpose to propose this action on our part and earnestly urge its acceptance by the Congress. I take the greatest pleasure in doing this, and hope that it will commend itself to your judgment and to the judgment of the Nation.   Cordially and sincerely yours,   Woodrow Wilson[1]

TLS (Letterpress Books, WP, DLC).

[1] Wilson sent the same letter, on the same date, *mutatis mutandis*, to Senator Hitchcock, Representative Flood, and Representative Stephen Geyer Porter, Republican of Pennsylvania, Chairman of the House Committee on Foreign Affairs, all TLS (Letterpress Books, WP, DLC). Wilson's letters were prompted by FLP to WW, July 17, 1919, TLS (WP, DLC), enclosing FLP to C. Glass, n.d., CCL (WP, DLC).

To George William Norris

My dear Senator: [The White House] 19 July, 1919.

Matters of so grave a consequence are now under consideration that I would very much appreciate an opportunity to have a talk with you about the Treaty and all that it involves. I wonder if it would be possible for you to see me at the White House at 11 o'clock Monday morning, July 21st.

Cordially and sincerely yours,   Woodrow Wilson[1]

TLS (Letterpress Books, WP, DLC).

¹ Wilson wrote the same letter, *mutatis mutandis*, to the following Republican senators: Truman H. Newberry, Albert B. Cummins, Walter E. Edge, Carroll Smalley Page of Vermont, William Musgrave Calder of New York, George Payne McLean of Connecticut, and Thomas Sterling of South Dakota, all dated July 19, 1919, TLS (Letterpress Books, WP, DLC).

To Carter Glass

My dear Glass: [The White House] 19 July, 1919.

No doubt you have more than once considered the enclosed in substance at the earnest request of Senator Owen,¹ but I am so far from an expert in such matters that I would very much like your guidance as to the reply I should make to the enclosed letter of the Senator's.

Cordially and faithfully yours,   Woodrow Wilson

TLS (Letterpress Books, WP, DLC).
¹ R. L. Owen to WW, July 16, 1919.

To Julius Howland Barnes

My dear Mr. Barnes: [The White House] 19 July, 1919.

I know that you feel the same spirit of resentment that I do when you see articles like the enclosed,¹ but perhaps we are not at liberty to let them pass uncontradicted and unrebuked, and I am writing to ask whether you think it would be wise or feasible to offset them in a statement which would really put things in the right light.

Cordially and sincerely yours,   Woodrow Wilson

TLS (Letterpress Books, WP, DLC).
¹ It is missing in WP, DLC. However, it was "Wilson Order Will Keep Up Bread Prices," *New York Herald*, July 17, 1919. It began as follows:
"In the face of an admission by Julius H. Barnes, head of the United States Grain Corporation, that the latter had made a profit of $23,000,000 in handling the wheat crop of the country, President Wilson issued a proclamation tonight placing control of the wheat situation more definitely in the hands of Mr. Barnes than ever before. In view of Mr. Barnes' policy, this action insures continuation of the high price of bread."
The article then went on to describe what were, in fact, three proclamations issued by Wilson on July 16, 1919, which authorized Barnes to regulate, by a license system, the export and import of wheat and wheat flour, domestic and foreign distribution, and the baking of bread and other products. The article was especially critical of the elimination of competition among wheat producers resulting from the prohibition of wheat imports from Canada and other countries which had large surpluses that sold below the price of $2.26 per bushel guaranteed by the government to American producers. The announcement of the profits made by the Grain Corporation and Wilson's proclamations had revived the controversy over the government's method of meeting the wheat guarantee by artificially keeping up the price of bread and putting an "excessive tax" on the staple food of the poor. This policy, the article continued, had already come under sharp criticism from some members of Congress, and it concluded by quoting from a letter to Barnes by Representative Roscoe Conkling McCulloch, Republican of Ohio, as follows:
"In view of the strained conditions throughout the country which, so far as the cost of living goes, have reached almost the breaking point, I ask you for information, if you can furnish it, which will justify a government agency taking out of the pockets of the consumers of bread a net surplus of $23,763,320.93. This profit must come out of the

pockets of the consumers and the producers do not get it. In what way do you justify exacting this enormous profit at the expense of the consuming public?"

Wilson's letter had been prompted by JPT to WW, July 18, 1919, TLS (WP, DLC). Tumulty pointed out that stories of this kind had done "a great deal of damage," and he suggested that Wilson call on Barnes to make a statement "repudiating the intimations made in this article." For Barnes' explanation, see J. H. Barnes to WW, July 24, 1919, and n. 2 thereto.

To Frank William Taussig, with Enclosure

My dear Taussig: [The White House] 19 July, 1919.

I am yielding to your request and our agreement in sending you the enclosed. I hope you know how warmly I mean the expression of admiration and regret, and let me here add how highly I valued the admirable work you did in Paris.

I have been attempting to hold so many things in my memory recently that it is getting weak, and therefore I am going to take the liberty of requesting that you send me a brief memorandum of the advice you gave me concerning the type of man who might be chosen in your place or for membership on the Commission. You will readily understand why my memory leaks.

With warmest regard,

Cordially and sincerely yours,   Woodrow Wilson

E N C L O S U R E

To Frank William Taussig

My dear Dr. Taussig: [The White House] 19 July, 1919.

I cannot tell you with what regret I accept, at your urgent request, your resignation as a Member of the United States Tariff Commission, to take effect as of August first. Your services have been so helpful that I had hoped that you would feel at liberty to continue them, but since you give reasons which I am not at liberty to contest, for withdrawing, I can only express my admiration, my appreciation, and my deep regret.

Cordially and faithfully yours,   Woodrow Wilson

TLS (Letterpress Books, WP, DLC).

To Thomas James Walsh

My dear Senator: [The White House] 19 July, 1919.

I value your letter of July 17th. I am not sure that it would be wise at the present time to act upon its suggestions, but you may be confident that I shall do anything that seems possible for me to do in the great matter we are both so deeply interested in.

Cordially and faithfully yours,   Woodrow Wilson

TLS (Letterpress Books, WP, DLC).

To Lucy Marshall Smith

My dear Cousin Lucy: [The White House] 19 July, 1919.

It was a delight to get your letter of July 12th,[1] and we devoured it the minute we recognized your hand-writing. We hope that this time you and Cousin Mary will not go home again before turning your faces this way and giving us a glimpse of you. We are very anxious to learn what your plans are and in what direction they are likely to carry you. I am taking it for granted that now the war is over the calls homeward are less imperative and insistent than they were.

We are very well, I was about to say, considering what we have been through, but I do not think that qualification is necessary, for we are quite fit and beyond measure delighted to get back to this blessed country and to the dear friends on this side of the water. I have no doubt that if you have read the newspapers, you know more things about us than we know about ourselves, but it would be a delight to have a chance to tell you the inside of some of our experiences. Edith and Margaret join in love to you both and in the hope that you are perfectly well and that you think of us as often as we do of you.   Affectionately yours,   Woodrow Wilson

TLS (Letterpress Books, WP, DLC).
  [1] Lucy M. Smith to WW, July 12, 1919, ALS (WP, DLC).

From Henry White

Paris 19th July, 1919.

3238. Very confidential, for immediate transmission to the President No distribution

Referring to telegram No. 3034, July 8th.[1] Upon Tittoni's return from Italy, he sought interview with me and said he had called together the chiefs of Parliamentary parties, had discussed the situation in the light of conversations with our Delegation before his departure, and had obtained their promise to support him in any reasonable settlement of Adriatic question which he might be able to bring about. After some discussion I said that we should be glad to receive his proposal, based on the conversations reported in our telegram No. 3034 to which he replied that he would have a map prepared setting forth what he would be able to do. He asked me to prepare you for this proposal with a statement that he had returned from Rome in a most conciliatory frame of mind and was extremely anxious to comply with your wishes and effect a settlement which would be satisfactory to you. His proposal was, however, only presented to us on the 17th. Even at first sight pretty obvious it would not meet our views. Detailed examination since by [Douglas Wilson] Johnson clearly demonstrates that, though modifications in form of original Italian proposal, it had become, as a result of Tittoni's consultations with his experts, if possible less satisfactory in substance. I have therefore just had confidential interview with him and handed his proposal back to him, saying that I must decline to submit it to you, and was thereby saving him the humiliation of having it turned down, as it would assuredly be, adding that you had decided, before your departure,[2] that no further discussion in respect to the conditions thrashed out again and again by the Council of Four would be worth while, nor even possible for this Delegation, and I must therefore decline to enter upon any such.

Briefly, his proposal involved:

1. Cession to Italy of Assling Triangle, on the ground that Trieste railroad runs through it and would, even if freedom of transit guaranteed, be subject to constant Jugo-Slav interference, and therefore cause constant friction frequently with that government.

2. Removal of American line in Istria considerably east of Arsa River;

3. Assignment of Idria mines and band of territory stretching south therefrom to Fianona and eastward to railroad.

4. Not only town, but district of Zara, with islands in front, to be free state, but "under a formula to be worked out which would involve definite attachment to Italy."

5. The port of Cattaro to be Italian, with surrounding portions of Dalmatia and Montenegro, including Mount Lovcen, besides a very considerable expansion of Valona area to take in most of southern Albania; also Italian mandate over the rest of Albania.

There are other details which are immaterial, as the whole proposal is entirely turned down, and it was agreed between us that it should not be considered as having been made.

Tittoni expressed himself as deeply disappointed at what I had said, but appreciative of my frankness. He made a strong appeal for the Assling Triangle, solely on the ground previously stated; no mention being made of strategic reasons. I repeated that I could not discuss that question, as it is entirely settled so far as we are concerned. He then said "What can I do? Of course, you know, if

I am driven into a corner, I have got to sign the treaty and I have got to accede to what the President insists upon; Italy being absolutely dependent upon America for financial and economic assistance; but, I am afraid, if compelled to accept such conditions, that we shall have to go home as the Germans did and send second or third rate men to sign the Treaty as a protest." I replied that I thought this would be an unfortunate proceeding on his part, and would in no way help the situation; that, unfortunately, he and his countrymen are all acting on the theory that they are giving up something belonging to them by acceding to our terms in respect to Dalmatia; whereas, our point of view is that they have no right to be there at all and that in giving up claims to any part of that country they are making no concessions, and the stand we are taking is based upon the future peace of the world, not in the least upon a desire to diminish the importance of Italy. He also said that it would be necessary for him, if he conceded what I asked, to approach the French and the English and claim the rights of Italy under the Treaty of London, insofar as Dalmatia is concerned. I told him I agreed with him in feeling that, inasmuch as the Treaty of London, which we decline to recognize, had been made, he is entitled to claim compensations from British and French elsewhere than in Dalmatia and insofar as the coal mines of Heraclea or Italian aspirations in Africa or others elsewhere which might seem to us reasonable, we would certainly endeavor to support the Italians. He said "What about our claims in Asia Minor," to which I replied that I do not know, first of all, what those claims are; and, secondly, what your views would be in respect to any Italian claims whatever in Asia Minor; but that if he accepts our terms completely in regard to Dalmatia, I should be very glad to submit to you for an expression of your views any suggestions he might have to make in regard to the Italian claims in Asia Minor. By claims, I said "I suppose you mean a mandate for a certain portion of Asia Minor," to which he replied in the affirmative. I furthermore said that he knew, as was stated in the Council of Four yesterday, that the whole question of Asia Minor is being held up by the Council until the intention of the United States is known in respect to that region, and therefore I did not suppose you would be in a position to express any decided view, even if you were made aware of any Italian claims there. I finally left him to consider the matter for a day or two and told him that, if he sees his way to accept the situation as I had explained it as regards Dalmatia, I should be willing to submit the following proposals to you, namely:

1. The Italian occupation of the port of Cattaro alone, without any surrounding territory, particularly Mount Lovcen;
2. The inclusion of certain islands in front of Zara in the pro-

posed free state of Zara without any formula of attachment to Italy as proposed by him;

3. An Italian mandate over Albania, Montenegro being a free state;

4. Any opinion he wishes to express as to Italian aspirations to a mandate in Asia Minor;

5. No implication by submission of these four proposals to you of obligation or of promise on my part that you would take any of them into favorable consideration.

I have not discussed with any other members of the Council of Five my confidential conversations with Tittoni. I asked him today whether he had done so. He replied "Not with Balfour but in a general way, particularly Italian occupation of Cattaro, with Tardieu, who replied that he thought it might serve as a basis for discussion."

Unless asked by colleagues as to intent and purport of my talks with Tittoni, I do not propose mentioning the matter to them until I hear from you.

As at present arranged, Tittoni is to consider during the next day or two what steps he shall take and what proposal to make. He understands that no proposal assigning sovereignty of Italy over any part of Dalmatia east of the American line will be considered for a moment. Meantime I promised him that the matter should be considered as absolutely confidential. I shall inform you immediately of further developments.   White   Ammission.

T telegram (SDR, RG 256, 186.3411/717A, DNA).
  [1] That is, RL and H. White to WW, July 8, 1919.
  [2] See the Enclosure printed with WW to RL, June 25, 1919 (first letter of that date).

From William Phillips, with Enclosures

Dear Mr. President: Washington July 19, 1919.

Mr. Polk had a conversation with you yesterday afternoon about a telegram which Doctor Reinsch had sent us[1] and which states that the Japanese Minister at Peking had indicated to the Minister of Foreign Affairs of China that Japan would open negotiations for the restitution of the German properties in Shantung on the basis of the Treaties of 1915 and 1918 between China and Japan.[2] Acting under your direction, Mr. Polk had a conversation with the Japanese Chargé d'Affaires[3] before his departure from Washington. He asked the Japanese Chargé d'Affaires to talk to Mr. Long more in detail. Mr. Polk dictated a memorandum of his conversation with Mr. Debuchi but left before he could correct it. I enclose it.

Mr. Debuchi called upon Mr. Long this morning and took up the subject and I enclose herewith a memorandum of that conversation.

In these conversations Debuchi has raised a matter which it seems to me will have to be treated very carefully. He asks for definite information as to the interpretation of the Treaty of Versailles as regards Shantung and also our position regarding the 1915 and 1918 Treaties between Japan and China.

As I understand the situation, the question to be decided is whether we construe the treaty signed at Versailles to apply exclusively or whether it is to be modified or enlarged by the treaties between China and Japan of 1915 and 1918. While we have not recognized those treaties it would seem that we could not take the position that they are invalid except as regards any rights of the United States in China which might be affected thereby. It might be inferred that the treaty of Versailles superseded the treaties of 1915 and 1918, as far as the province of Shantung is concerned, but, those former treaties dealt with various other provinces of China, such as Manchuria, Mongolia and Fukian, and I am satisfied that the Japanese would not consent to a nullification of all the rights which they have established with China by virtue of these two agreements. Further than that, and except for the treaty of 1918, the rights conferred upon Japan under the treaty signed at Versailles are probably greater than the rights which Japan would inherit under the treaty of 1915—because she has definitely stated as part of the treaty of 1918 that she would return Kiauchau to China whereas that statement does not apply to the rights which Japan holds by virtue of the treaty of Versailles.

The matter is complicated and involves such a number of treaties and their interpretations, that I hesitate to commit the Government to any course until I have a definite knowledge of your views and wishes.

In this connection I beg to enclose a copy of a telegram received from the American Embassy at Tokyo yesterday, which shows that the Japanese Government have already begun to take steps to negotiate unofficially with China regarding the retrocession of Japan's rights in Shantung to China according to the treaties of 1915 and 1918.[4]   Faithfully yours,   William Phillips

TLS (WP, DLC).
[1] P. S. Reinsch to SecState, July 12, 1919, T telegram (SDR, RG 59, 763.72119/5626, DNA), which also included dire warnings of Japanese intentions in China.
[2] About which, see the index references to China, Japan, Shantung Province, and Paris Peace Conference in Vols. 52, 57, and 58.
[3] Katsuji Debuchi, Counselor of the Japanese embassy in Washington.
[4] Ray Atherton to SecState, July 18, 1919, T telegram (WP, DLC).

ENCLOSURE I

Frank Lyon Polk to Breckinridge Long

Dear Mr. Long: [Washington] July 18, 1919.

In accordance with the President's instructions, I told Mr. De-buchi, when he called to say good-bye, that the President was surprised to note the report from Peking to the effect that the Japanese Minister in Peking had told the Chinese Minister of Foreign Affairs, when asked as to when they would withdraw from Kiauchau, that he was withdrawing subject to the terms of the 1915-1918 agreement; that it was our understanding that the agreement reached in Paris superceded the 1915-1918 agreements in so far as Shantung was concerned, namely that the Japanese took the German concessions. Debuchi said he knew the President had formally notified the Conference that the United States did not recognize the 21 points, but he wanted to know whether we claimed that the 1915-1918 treaties had been annulled, as they affected a number of places besides Shantung.

I told him I was not going to discuss any question besides Shantung; my understanding was that the 1915 agreement gave them more than had been conceded by the Powers at Paris, and they therefore took it subject to the '19 treaty at Paris terms and not 1915-1918. He seemed surprised and said it was a very serious matter; that he would take it up with his Government. I said we would be very glad to have his views, as he must realize the Shantung question was making a great deal of trouble in this country and that the people understood that Japan not only got the benefit of the Treaty of Paris, but held on to the other concessions, and public opinion would be even more inflamed than it was at present.

He rather intimated that the Treaty of 1915 was between Japan and China and it was a little out of our province. I told him that we were party to the Treaty of Paris and had great interest in the settlement. F.L.P.

TL (WP, DLC).

ENCLOSURE II

A Memorandum by Breckinridge Long

**MEMORANDUM OF CONVERSATION WITH THE
JAPANESE CHARGE D'AFFAIRES.**

July 19, 1919.

Mr. Debuchi called this morning and resumed the subject of conversation he had had up with Mr. Polk last night, that is the Shantung question,—whether the Japanese rights in Shantung were fixed by the Treaty at Paris, or were to be considered also effected by the Treaties of 1915 and 1918. He gave me a summary of Mr. Polk's conversation with him. I told him that Mr. Polk had staid [stayed] at the Department until very late last night, and had subsequently left for New York and Paris; that his stenographers had worked very late, and had been unable to transcribe as yet the memorandum which Mr. Polk had left for me; that they had read it to me from their notes, but that I had only a general idea. He said in that case he preferred to postpone the conversation until I could get more definite information.

However, he proceeded to discuss and take up various phases of the Shantung situation, more or less as follows:

1st, He argued that the application of the Treaties of 1915 and 1918 was necessary; that even if we had not recognized the twenty-one demands of 1915 that China had recognized them; that only part of them applied to Shantung. To which I replied that we had not recognized the 1915 Treaty, and had taken exception to it, as evidenced in our indentic notes to Japan and China during 1915;[1] that we did not recognize the subsequent agreement of 1918, which pertained to the further administration of the railroad and rights in that province; and that the Treaty of Paris, which gave to them the rights which Germany had, superseded the Treaties of 1915 and 1918. He said that the prior Treaties could not possibly be considered as annulled, because they dealt with matters beside Shantung. He said that he was fully familiar with the position that the President had taken in the Counsel [Council] of Four at the time the matter was discussed, but that he felt sure that the Japanese delegates had not considered that those Treaties would be annulled.

2nd, He argued that China was not a signatory to the Treaty of Paris, and that its provisions were not binding upon China. I told him that we were a party to the Treaty; that his Government was a party to the Treaty, and that Germany was a party to the Treaty, and the rights in Shantung which were disposed of were German rights, over which China had alienated control and the exercise of sovereignty for a definite time, and that it was not necessary that China be a party to the Treaty in order to have its provisions apply to the German possessions in Shantung. He said that as a matter of international law, and with particular reference to the Chinese-German Treaty of 1898, under which the rights in Shantung had been granted to Germany, and in which there was a provision that Germany would not alienate her ownership to a third party without the consent of China, that it became necessary for China to consent to a transfer to Japan, and consequently to be a signatory to the Treaty of Paris, or to have expressed to the transferee a willingness that she could succeed to the German rights. To this I answered that the Great Powers of the world had decided that Germany was possessed of those rights, and that by a settlement to which all the Powers were parties those rights had been transferred, and that the consent of China would not seem to have been necessary. In response to this he suggested we might appear like using force upon China.

3rd, He indicated a very indirect line of thought by alluding to the Lansing-Ishii Agreement,[2] and joining it with the Twenty-one Demands, and stating that at the time the Lansing-Ishii Agreement was made we had made no reservation about the Twenty-one Demands, but had recognized Japan's special interest in China. I very positively stated that we had indicated some years prior to that agreement our position on the Twenty-one Demands, and that there was no relation between the two, and further that we had not recognized Japan's special interest in China, except in a limited and qualified way, and with particular reference to those territories to which she was contiguous, and that pertained to Manchuria, and further that in the Lansing-Ishii Agreement we had mutually agreed to respect the territorial integrity and political sovereignty in China, which we did not consider to have been done in the Twenty-one Demands, so that the two were necessarily quite contradictory and distinct. He rejoined that there could hardly be that close understanding between Japan and the United States if we did not recognize Japan's special position, and by virtue of it their right to make treaties with China, and recognize the Twenty-one Demands. I told him that it was necessary to our close understanding and proper cooperation in China that arrangements made like those in the so-called Twenty-one Demands should not be attempted.

He said that he would like to know the exact position of this Government as regards Shantung and the Paris Treaty, and the Treaties of 1915 and 1918 between Japan and China. He characterized the situation as rather a delicate one, and said that he would not telegraph his Government until he had some definite word, provided that he could have it by Monday. He did not see the necessity of sending a cable which was not explicit, and which might cause anxiety to his Government. He asked me if I could give him a written memorandum on Monday. I told him that I would be glad to see him, and would give the matter some thought before then.   Breckinridge Long

TS MS (WP, DLC).
    [1] WJB to G. W. Guthrie and to P. S. Reinsch, May 11, 1915, *FR 1915*, p. 146. A draft of these notes is printed as Enclosure II with WW to WJB, May 10, 1915, Vol. 33.
    [2] About which, see the index references under Japan and the United States in Vols. 43, 44, and 52.

From William Phillips

Dear Mr. President: Washington July 19, 1919.

I am sending you enclosed a preliminary sketch of the German rights in Shantung and various Treaty agreements thereto,[1] which has been prepared in the Far Eastern Division and which I understood from Mr. Polk you expressed a desire to have before you. A more comprehensive statement is being prepared and will be submitted to you upon completion.

                         Faithfully yours,   William Phillips

TLS (WP, DLC).
    [1] "I. GERMAN RIGHTS IN SHANTUNG . . . ," T MS (WP, DLC).

From Thomas Nelson Page

My dear Mr. President: Washington, D. C., July 19, 1919.

I wrote you some months ago that there were reasons of a personal nature which made me very desirous to return home as soon as the Peace should be concluded, to the attainment of which you had so largely contributed; and, the reasons having become more urgent, I felt obliged later to renew to you my request to be relieved when, in your judgment, it could be done with due regard to all considerations involved.

In tendering you now my resignation of the post of American Ambassador at Rome, to take effect immediately, or as soon as you can make appropriate arrangements as to my successor, I desire to express to you anew my high appreciation of the opportunity afforded me to serve under and with you during these crucial years marked by the unprecedented events which have involved the world. The inspiration derived from the spirit in which you were striving for so great ends, has caused me to regard labors, sometimes sufficiently arduous, as a very high privilege.

It has been my endeavor, in sympathetic understanding of your views and purposes, to interpret to Italy, so far as I might, the spirit of the American people, and, assisted by the zealous and loyal staff of our Embassy in Rome, and by the earnest efforts of our great relief organizations, I am happy to believe that the endeavor has not been wholly in vain. I believe that the Italian people today feel closer to the American people then ever before; and, having seen what the Italian people underwent and performed during the war, I feel profoundly that their friendship is an asset of the highest consequence. All that is necessary is to bring about and to foster a truer and fuller understanding of each other. To this end I hope I may still be permitted to contribute somewhat in a private station, and, should my knowledge of Italy appear at any time to be of value, you will, I hope, feel that I shall be entirely at your service.

Believe me, my dear Mr. President, with the highest appreciation of your personal kindness, as well as of your official consideration towards me,

Always most sincerely yours,   Thos. Nelson Page

TLS (WP, DLC).

From Newton Diehl Baker

Information only, no answer.

Dear Mr. President: Washington. July 19, 1919.

General Gorgas, who retired from the Army, having reached the age limit, in September last, has just returned from a visit of several months in various South American countries, where he has been acting for the Rockefeller Foundation in an effort finally to stamp out yellow fever by eliminating the sources of infection still to be found there. He was in Ecuador, San Salvador, and one or two other countries. He was also in those countries in 1913. He told me this morning that in 1913 it was necessary for him to have a military guard wherever he went, to protect him against anti-American sentiment based upon suspicion of our motives and general distrust of the American Government.

This year he finds a complete reversal of opinion, great enthusiasm for America and full confidence in the unselfishness of our national purposes. These countries were pro-German during the war, but since the conclusion of the armistice public opinion has changed, and General Gorgas told me that on every hand he heard most confident expressions of good will and trust in America and in your own leadership. Many of these comments were based upon our Mexican forebearance, and many of them were based generally upon your expressions of American policy from time to time with regard to the great war.

Respectfully yours,   Newton D. Baker

TLS (WP, DLC).

Sir William Wiseman to Edward Mandell House

[New York] 19 July 1919.

Following for Col. House from Wiseman:

Have just returned from Washington. Friday I lunched at White House. The President is dealing with the Senate opposition seriously and patiently. He is interviewing Senators daily and has won over several opponents who had not previously committed themselves in public. He cannot give any estimate of the situation for a few days.

He complained bitterly that Mr. Taft has weakened and now supports reservations to the Covenant. The President does not believe the Republicans can get a majority for any one amendment but they might secure the necessary majority by combining their chief objections into one reservation. At present he is refusing to discuss any amendments or reservations. His main argument being that such a course would set a precedent which would be followed extravagantly by the newly created states and powers not satisfied with the terms, and unless all the great powers, including the United States, stand solidly behind the Treaty and the League, there is a grave danger that Bolshevism may overrun Europe.

Objections are being raised to most of the clauses from Labour to German colonies, but the President thinks the only one which might gain support in the country centers round the right of withdrawal from the League. Senators contend that the U. S. may not be able to withdraw owing to a difference of opinion as to whether or not she has fulfilled her international obligations under the Covenant.

He foresees that he may be obliged, in order to secure a really satisfactory majority, to agree to some reservation defining or interpreting the language of one or more clauses of the Covenant.

Probably clauses No. one relative to withdrawal, ten and twenty-one.

The President is entirely satisfied that he has the support of the people and is most eager to tour the country for the League. He will not do so, however, until he is satisfied that he has done everything possible to persuade the Senate by his present method of personal conferences. The President points out that the Senate will be somewhat influenced by the progress of ratification by other Powers.

Lodge has told his supporters that he has received letters from a member of the Government in London to the effect that the proposed Republican amendments will be welcomed at Westminster.

The agitation against the Shantung settlement President regards more as an expression of mistrust of Japan than serious objection to the terms.

The above is a summary of the President's observations. From other sources I learn that the Republicans agree their attack is a failure. That big business interests have warned Senators not to delay the Treaty. That Republican leaders do not expect to carry more than interpreting resolutions paraphrasing the language of the President's speeches. Another suggestion is that the Senate might ratify without any reservation and pass a separate resolution condemning anything they disliked in the Treaty.

Personally I regard the situation as very satisfactory, particularly as the President has adopted a wise and patient attitude towards the Senate which cannot fail to bring him further public support.

The President and Mrs. Wilson told me to send you their affectionate regards.

I have sent the Foreign Office a cable summary of my interview with the President.

T telegram (W. Wiseman Papers, CtY).

Two News Reports

[July 20, 1919]

WILSONS ON CRUISE DESPITE THE STORM
Depart on Mayflower for Two Days—President Took No Papers

Despite the threat of stormy and dismal weather for two days, the President and Mrs. Wilson left Washington last night aboard the Mayflower for their first week-end cruise down the Potomac River and Chesapeake Bay in months. They expect to return early tomorrow morning.

The President motored from the White House to the Navy Yard in a shower, and as the Presidential yacht "shoved off" from the quay shortly after 6 o'clock, the heaviest storm of the day broke. Reports from lower river points last night stated that the thunderstorms, which were sweeping the lower Potomac during the day, continued unabated. Whether the President will go all the way to Hampton Roads, or not, is not known at the White House.

As the President had no appointments yesterday he spent the entire day in his study at work. He is understood not to have taken any papers with him on the trip.

Secretary Tumulty also left Washington yesterday for a weekend visit at Asbury Park, N. J.

Printed in the *Washington Post*, July 20, 1919.

[July 20, 1919]

35 TO BLOCK LEAGUE
List of Senators Who Oppose It Offered to the President.
MOST SIGNED ROUND ROBIN

To back their assertion that the league of nations in its present form is doomed, opposition leaders, it was learned yesterday, have offered to furnish President Wilson with a list of 35 senators who have solemnly pledged themselves to vote for the rejection of the whole treaty unless radical amendments or reservations are adopted.

Ratification of a treaty requires a two-thirds vote. Thirty-five senators would be two more than enough to reject the treaty. The senators whose names appear on the list are in most instances those who signed the Lodge "round robin"[1] last March and forced the revision of the covenant by the Paris peace conference. Each of these 35 senators, it was stated, has given his pledge in such form as to show his determination to vote against the treaty in its present form, at any risk or cost to his political future.

Republican senators who conferred with President Wilson Friday,[2] it is said, offered to give him the list to support the statements they made to the effect that the covenant could not be ratified without reservations.

The President, nevertheless, it was stated, takes an optimistic view of the prospect. His spokesmen yesterday denied reports to the effect that the President had cabled to other powers asking if they would be willing to accept "interpretations" by the Senate, and insisted the President had no thought of compromise.

Concessions by the administration were a long way off, it was

stated. Nothing of the kind would be forthcoming unless an absolute deadlock should develop over the treaty, and administration
leaders said they were confident no such contingency would arise.

Despite the fact that the canvass showed the President had
made no inroads on the opposition, Secretary Tumulty said the
President had authorized him to say he was very much pleased
with his conferences with Republican senators during the past two
days.

No conferences were held yesterday, but it was stated at the
White House the President had no thought of abandoning them
and would extend other invitations this week.

Reviewing the developments of the first week of the treaty in the
Senate, opposition leaders yesterday declared that the fight was
taking on a new aspect. Sentiment for the rejection of the whole
treaty is growing, they declared.

Careful study of the text of the document is revealing so many
obnoxious features, they declared, as to create doubt whether
American interests can be amply protected by mere reservations or
amendments.

One of the opposition leaders, who did not want his name used,
summed up the situation in this manner:

"The contest as to whether there shall be reservations is past.
The fight now enters upon a new phase—whether the United
States shall enter any league. I am convinced the President will
agree to accept reservations, seeking to make them as mild as possible. The final stage of the contest will be whether or not the
treaty shall be rejected. There is a strong growing sentiment in this
direction in the Senate."

Senator Moses, of New Hampshire, a Republican member of the
foreign relations committee, made this statement:

"There is a growing feeling in the Senate that the whole treaty
should be thrown out of the window. Senators are beginning to
believe that the wisest way to deal with the problem is to discard it
entirely and adopt a plain resolution declaring the status of war at
an end."

The two reasons held to be most responsible for the drift toward
flat rejection were:

First—That the close scrutiny to which the treaty has been subjected in the Senate during the past week has brought home to
senators a realization of the tremendous burdens assumed by the
United States as one of the "big five," apart from the obligations
under the league of nations.

Second—The reflex of public sentiment, as revealed in the correspondence of senators, following upon the revelation of the facts regarding the Shantung settlement.

Senator Knox, of Pennsylvania, came out yesterday for the rejection of the treaty unless the league of nations covenant is eliminated and reserved for future discussion.

"I cannot vote for the treaty unless the league covenant is separated from it and unless material modifications are made to the body of the document," said Senator Knox.

The senator reiterated his determination to push his proposal to separate the league covenant and the treaty. He feels confident this proposal is much stronger now than when it was first put forward.

Some of the President's advisers are urging him, it was learned yesterday, to abandon his country-wide campaign for the league. They pointed out that while the President undoubtedly would be received everywhere by large crowds, his receptions would have little or no effect on the Senate. He could work more effectively in Washington by attempting to conciliate the Senate, they thought.

A bill to create the machinery for the league of nations has been prepared by administration officials and has been given to Senator Hitchcock for introduction. This bill provides that the American officials in the league should be appointed by the President "by and with the advice and consent of the Senate."

Opponents of the league assert that the purpose of presenting this bill is to attempt to shut off some of the opposition, by showing that the Senate is to have a voice in the selection of the American representatives in the league organization.

The Shantung case is very much alive in the Senate and is likely to be the subject of more speeches. Senator Moses, discussing it yesterday, said:

"Does any one think that private conversations with Baron Makino at Paris are going to hold against the written word in the treaty? Is there anything in the treaty which says that Japan must return Shantung in six months? Not a bit of it. The treaty language is that 'Germany renounces all her rights in favor of Japan,' and it is well known that Germany was there to stay. Therefore, so far as the treaty is concerned, Japan may stay as long as she likes and nobody believes that she will not."

Printed in the *Washington Post*, July 20, 1919.
    [1] About which, see n. 1 to the extract from the Grayson Diary printed at March 3, 1919, Vol. 55.
    [2] Kenyon, Kellogg, Capper, and McNary.

From Henry White

Paris. July 20, 1919.

3240. For the President. Before Mr. Lansing's departure our representatives on the Bulgarian (Extension?) Commissions[1] Messrs. Coolidge, Johnson and Buckler, submitted to the three commissioners[2] their unanimous opinion that the Bulgarian territory bordering the Aegean Sea[3] should not be (*) [taken] from Bulgaria and annexed to Greece as was proposed by the Greek territorial commission. This territory, formerly a part of Turkey and still containing large Turk majority, was voluntarily ceded to Bulgaria by Austria Hungary and her allies in 1913 despite fact that Greek minority was slightly larger than Bulgarian minority in this area. At that time the territory was occupied by Greek troops and the Bulgarians came into occupation only upon voluntary withdrawal of Greek troops. Hence Bulgaria had clear title to this territory at the beginning of present war and since her occupation Bulgarian population has increased and Greek population practically disappeared, partly through natural exchange of population and partly (according to Greek allegations) by forcible expulsion of Greeks. Bulgarians deny latter accusation. Of the Mohammedan majority more speak Bulgarian than Greek and probably would prefer Bulgarian to Greek rule. Evidence to contrary presented by Greeks not convincing.

Absence of direct territorial access to Mediterranean Sea will affect unfavorably Bulgaria's economic development. Promises of free transit and port facilities in Greek territory do not appear to be equivalent of direct territorial access even in time of peace and have no value in time of war. This principle fully recognized by powers when they insisted on territorial access to sea for Poland. Route by Black Sea and Dardanelles not an equivalent because it is round about and hence more costly in time and money.

Unquestionably Bulgarians will profoundly resent apparent injustice of taking from them territory voluntarily given them in 1913 thus depriving them of direct and separate access to Mediterranean. This resentment will threaten future peace. Establishment of narrow band of Greek territory entirely adjoining Balkan Peninsula from mouth of Adriatic to Black Sea creates geographical anomaly, ? s in handling of single power, military and naval control of approaches to international state controls sea route to Russia and land route to India. All our information tends to show that the Bulgarians who are still in undisturbed possession of the territory have no idea it will be taken from them. An attempt to do so is likely to lead to armed resistance or revolution or both.

Commissioners unanimously approved conclusions of American experts and authorized them to take a stand in Central Territorial Committee against annexation of Bulgarian Thrace to Greece.

Italian delegation stands with Americans while British and French oppose strongly. Japan less strongly. Am informed by *Bile* [Balfour] that British particularly incensed by American attitude. Threatened to withdraw from committee and it has been reported to him they may oppose participation of Bulgarian treaty of any power not associated in war with Bulgaria. British geographical and military experts secretly approve American stand and (*) their satisfaction that the dangerous recommendation of the Greek territorial commission may be rectified.

In this connection, as I entered council room at the Foreign Office yesterday afternoon Clemenceau took me aside and said Venizelos had just been to see him in reference to the position by the American Commission on Bulgarian and German Claims regarding western Thrace. The reason which Venizelos had told him is the desire of our Government to have Thrace included in mandate for Constantinople, which he alleges we are eager to obtain. Clemenceau added that in his opinion the stand our experts have taken and which he understood is sustained by our delegation is exceedingly unfortunate and if adopted by the Council will undoubtedly lead to further (*) in the Balkans. I replied that Venizelos is entirely mistaken in attributing the position taken by our commission to any motive other than the maintenance of peace in the Balkans; that our Government is not seeking mandates anywhere and that the question therefore of Thrace or any other territory being incorporated [in] the Constantinople mandate is not under discussion by us. I added, we feel that the peace will be materially endangered by depriving Bulgaria of territory constituting her sole access to Aegean Sea, which has been assigned to her by the Conference of London in 1913 and of which she was consequently in possession more than a year before the war began. To this Clemenceau replied that it must not be forgotten that Bulgaria is an enemy and Greece a friendly nation and that in view of the punitive measures which have been adopted in the treaty with Germany, public would not sustain the absence of similar measures in the treaty with Bulgaria and that [he] thought the conference had already gone too far in the matter not to assign western Thrace to Greece. He hoped, therefore, that we would withdraw from our position to which I replied that we would be unable to do so save under instructions from you. If you have any suggestion to give us based upon your own or upon the view which public opinion at home is likely to take in the matter, we shall be grateful to receive it as soon as possible as the question is likely to come up in the Council of Five within the next few days. White.   American Mission

T telegram (SDR, RG 59, 763.72119/5719, DNA).
    ¹ The Commission on Greek and Albanian Affairs, of which Jules Cambon was president. This commission was a subcommission of the Central Territorial Committee, of which Tardieu was president and Archibald Cary Coolidge, Douglas Wilson Johnson, and William Hepburn Buckler were members. Buckler, special agent at the American embassy in London, had recently been attached to the A.C.N.P.
    ² The other three chief subcommissioners were Sir Robert Borden, Cambon, and Giacomo de Martino.
    ³ The area in dispute was West Thrace, which corresponds roughly to the present Greek administrative region of Thrace. It had been awarded to Bulgaria by the Treaty of Bucharest of August 10, 1913, which had ended the Second Balkan War.

From Henry Seidel Canby[1]

My dear President Wilson: Yale University July 20, 1919

Your work and ideas have had so large a share in my book "Education by Violence,"[2] that the copy I am sending you should be accompanied by acknowledgements.[3] I shall be pleased if it finds a place in your library.

I am   very sincerely   Henry S Canby

ALS (WW Library, DLC).
    ¹ Assistant Professor of English at Yale University.
    ² *Education by Violence: Essays on the War and the Future* (New York, 1919). This book is in the Wilson Library, DLC.
    ³ He inscribed it: "To President Wilson with acknowledgments of deep indebtedness."

From Alfred J. Colburn

Dear Mr. President: So. Boston, Mass. July 20, 1919.

As a disabled soldier who is taking up vocational training I wish to thank you for vetoing the bill that would cut down the appropriation for rehabilitation of disabled soldiers.[1]

The only thing that kept Hope alive within me while I was in the hospital was the knowledge that our government was going to teach me a vocation that would prevent me from becoming a pauper and were this chance for gaining a livelihood taken away now I do not know just what I would do, sir.

The thanks and gratitude of a common soldier may not mean a great deal to you, Mr. President, but I wanted you to know that I am very grateful for your efforts to see that we get a square deal.

I thank you, sir.   Gratefully yours   A. J. Colburn.

ALS (WP, DLC).
    ¹ Wilson had vetoed the Sundry Civil bill on July 11 because in his opinion it appropriated insufficient funds for the rehabilitation of disabled war veterans. The bill appropriated $6,000,000 for this purpose. Wilson pointed out in his veto message that even

$8,000,000 would barely provide subsistence for the estimated 8,000 veterans already enrolled or about to be entered in the rehabilitation program established by an Act of 1918 and would provide no funds at all for their tuition or travel or for job placement after they had completed the course. *New York Times*, July 13, 1919. Wilson's veto message is printed in *ibid.* and in *Cong. Record*, 66th Cong., 1st sess., p. 2493.

The House of Representatives voted on July 17 to increase the item for rehabilitation in the Sundry Civil bill to $14,000,000. The Senate concurred on July 18, and Wilson signed the revised bill on July 19. *New York Times*, July 18, 19, and 20, 1919.

A News Report

PRESIDENT WILSON RETURNS ILL, IS ORDERED TO BED; ALL CONFERENCES OFF; NORRIS DECLINES INVITATION

[*July 21, 1919*]

Washington, July 21.—President Wilson was ill when he returned to Washington this morning on the Mayflower from his weekend cruise down the Potomac River, and Rear Admiral Cary T. Grayson, his physician, ordered him to bed immediately.

Dr. Grayson stated then that the President was suffering from dysentery, but added that his condition, while it might require him to remain in bed several days, was not serious. Dr. Grayson said tonight that, although the President was resting easier, he had passed an uncomfortable day, and it would not be wise for him to undertake any work tomorrow.

The President seemed a picture of health when he reviewed the Czechoslovak troops in front of the White House Friday afternoon, but it was learned today he was not in the best of shape when he sailed Saturday night on the Mayflower. At that time it was thought that he was suffering from indigestion. The President was ill throughout the trip down and back.

His condition is attributed to the intense heat of the capital that faced him on his return from abroad, the bad weather of the past four days, and the strain he has been under from the attention he has been giving to the treaty situation.

The President had sent invitations to Senators Edge, Norris, Cummins, and Calder to confer with him today.[1] Senator Edge was preparing to go to the White House when word came, asking him to postpone the visit.

Senator Norris wrote to the President declining the invitation to call on him. He gave as his reason, it is understood, that he could not consistently make the visit in view of his uncompromising opposition to some provisions of the treaty. He told colleagues at the Capitol today that his mind was made up on the necessity of reservations and that nothing the President could say would change it.

Mr. Wilson's conferences on the treaty, when resumed, will be with Senators Edge, Calder, McLean, and Cummins. For Wednesday Senators Page of Vermont and Sterling of South Dakota had been invited. These conferences will be postponed if the President is not well enough tomorrow and Wednesday.

Printed in the *New York Times*, July 22, 1919.
　¹ The senators mentioned here and below, all Republicans, were Walter Evans Edge of New Jersey, George William Norris of Nebraska, Albert Baird Cummins of Iowa, William Musgrave Calder of New York, George Payne McLean of Connecticut, Carroll Smalley Page of Vermont, and Thomas Sterling of South Dakota.

From George William Norris

Dear Mr. President: 　　　　　Washington, D. C. July 21, 1919.

I acknowledge receipt of your letter requesting me to come to the White House to discuss with you the provisions of the Peace Treaty with Germany.

An unwritten law, universally respected, prohibits Members of Congress from giving publicity to information obtained, and conversations taking place, at conferences such as you propose. Our conversation at such a conference would undoubtedly cover many phases of the subject with which I am already somewhat familiar, and therefore, in any future public discussion of the subject, either in the Senate or elsewhere, I might find myself embarrassed in the use of information I already possess, or that by independent investigation I may be able to obtain.

Moreover, it is not fair to you that your valuable time should be taken up in going over with each individual Senator a lengthy argument in favor of the ratification of the Treaty without amendment. I hope therefore, you will pardon me when I most respectfully suggest that you follow the method prescribed in the Constitution in communicating to the Senate any information that in your wisdom is deemed advisable. Such a course would not only conserve your time and energy, but would give to all our countrymen as well as to the Senate, the benefit of your valuable argument and advise [advice].

I have the honor to remain,
　　　　　　　　　　　Very truly yours, 　G. W. Norris.

TLS (WP, DLC).

From William Phillips, with Enclosure

My dear Mr. President: [Washington] July 21, 1919.

I have the honor to enclose herewith copy of an interesting telegram from Ambassador Morris, despatched from Irkutsk and dated July 17, discussing conditions in Siberia.

I have shown the telegram to the Secretary of War and propose, with your approval, to repeat it to our Embassies at London and Paris to be read to the British and French Ministers for Foreign Affairs for their confidential information, in order that they may be fully informed of the situation as presented by Mr. Morris. The American Mission is also being informed.

Faithfully yours,   William Phillips

CCL (SDR, RG 59, 861.77/945, DNA).

E N C L O S U R E

Irkutsk.   July 17, 1919.

Confidential. I submit the following observations of the conditions under which the Chinese Eastern and Trans-Siberian Railways are being operated as far as Irkutsk.

The Allied inspectors in charge of operations are struggling with serious difficulties. On the division between Vladivostok and Pogranichnaya, Stevens and the Allied Technical Board are hampered by the interference of the Cossack military authorities who profess to represent Kolchak in Eastern Siberia and refuse to recognize the authority of the Technical Board. I am convinced that the Cossacks get sympathy and support from the Japanese military authorities. While Stevens and his men have won the confidence of the employees and of the railway management the continued military interference and the falling value of the ruble have created discontent and restlessness among the men and have resulted in the recent strikes. There is little, if any, Bolshevism among the railway employees, but there is a deep seated antagonism to the rule of the Cossacks and suspicion of the Kolchak Government which is apparently too weak to challenge the Cossack authority.

On that part of the Chinese Eastern Railway which passes through northern Manchuria, including Harbin and Manchuria Station, there is no Cossack problem, and the situation is somewhat better. The Japanese military authorities no longer interfere as they did when they took possession a year ago. To this extent they are loyal to the railway agreement. But they still maintain

troops at all the stations in Manchuria, they are holding all the barracks previously occupied, they have completed the erection of
their private telephone and telegraph wires, and are maintaining
their own force of despatchers, inspectors, and terminal experts,
who, while not attempting for the present to interfere in operation,
are quite obviously preparing for the future.

From Manchuria Station to Verkhneudinsk the railway is dominated by Semenoff[1] with the open support of the Japanese military
authorities. His relations with the Kolchak Government merely
nominal. His strength is wholly Japanese. He has constantly interfered with the Allied inspectors who have again and again sought
and have been refused the support of the Japanese military command supposedly guarding the railway in this section. I arrived at
Chita just after Semenoff's bandits in one of their armored cars
had seized the office car and equipment of Major Graves,[2] an
American engineer, and the Allied Divisional Inspector. I am using
this incident to bring the general question to definite issue. At
Chita I saw General Oba,[3] the Japanese Divisional Commander,
and discussed the entire situation for several hours. Later under
Japanese pressure Semenoff promised to return the car, but has
not yet done so. During our interview, General Oba frankly expressed to me his profound admiration for Semenoff, his confidence in Semenoff's purposes and motives and the close association which existed between them.

Between Verkhneudinsk and Mysovaya the presence of two
thousand American troops and the determined stand taken by
Colonel Morrow[4] under General Graves's instructions have destroyed Semenoff's influence in that sector, while from Mysovaya
to the Irkutsk, including the important Baikal tunnel district, the
Czechs are still in control.

On this situation I offer the following comment:

From Vladivostok to Irkutsk, excepting only two sectors guarded
by American troops, the military control of the railways is in the
hands of the Japanese who are using the Cossack organization
subsidized and supported by them to discredit Allied operation.
Kolchak is powerless to withstand this influence which has gone
so far as to force the appointment of the bandit Kalmikoff[5] as the
representative of Dutoff,[6] the Kolchak Commander of all military
operations in the east.

To my mind the Japanese plan is perfectly clear. Baffled by the
railway agreement in their organized attempt to take possession of
the Chinese Eastern and Trans-Siberian railways as far as Chita
and thus dominate Eastern Siberia and northern Manchuria the
Japanese Government is countenancing a less obvious, but a more

insidious scheme of operating through the Cossack organization which is the only substantial support Kolchak has east of Chita. It will not be difficult for Japan to dispose of the Eastern Cossacks when they have served the purpose.

I will discuss in a subsequent telegram the Czech situation, which I am now investigating, and the opportunity it might offer to defeat this Japanese military plan.   Morris.

T telegram (SDR, RG 59, 861.77/945, DNA).
  [1] That is, Gen. Grigorii Mikhailovich Semenov, Cossack leader and a notorious cut-throat and bandit in the pay of the Japanese government.
  [2] Ernest Graves.
  [3] Lt. Gen. Jirō Oba, commander of the third division of the Japanese army.
  [4] That is, Col. Charles H. Morrow, commander of American troops in the region of Lake Baikal.
  [5] That is, Ivan Pavlovich Kalmykov, hetman of the Ussuri Cossacks.
  [6] Aleksandr Il'ich Dutov, hetman of the Orenburg Cossacks, former chairman of the All-Russian Congress of Cossacks, and leader of the All-Russian League of Cossack Hosts. Although Dutov was a strong supporter of Kolchak, Morris is mistaken in identifying him as Kolchak's commander of all military operations in the East. That post was actually held by General Sergei Nikolaevich Rozanov, who had recently replaced General Horvath.

From William Phillips, with Enclosure

Dear Mr. President: Washington July 21, 1919.

Upon receipt of your note of the 18th,[1] I communicated with Vance McCormick,[2] as you requested, and beg to enclose a draft reply which has McCormick's approval. Unless you see any objection, I will forward the message as drafted.

                    Faithfully yours,   William Phillips

Approved
Woodrow Wilson

TLS (SDR, RG 59, 763.72112/12382, DNA).
  [1] WW to W. Phillips, July 18, 1919 (second letter of that date).
  [2] W. Phillips to V. C. McCormick, July 19, 1919, CCL (SDR, RG 59, 763.72112/12381a, DNA).

E N C L O S U R E

                    Washington, July 21, 1919

Your 3166, July 15, 1 p.m.[1] It was not intended in Department's 2546 July 11, 4 p.m.[2] to mean that the United States was committed to remove all restrictions whatsoever upon trade between this country and Germany. The restrictions to whose removal we feel committed are those which may be properly termed "Blockade Restrictions" which are directed against Germany's general freedom of trade with all countries, but we do not understand that any assurance has been given which could be construed as a relinquishment of the right of any one of the Associated Governments to impose its own municipal limitations either upon the importation or exportation into or from this country of commodities, whose export or import it is desirable to control for purely domestic considerations. We are not restricting Germany's general freedom to trade in dyes, potash and chemicals, but merely controlling their import into the United States for purely domestic reasons. Therefore, we feel clearly that we are according to Germany economic freedom as to exports in the full sense of the Supreme Economic Council's interpretation of the assurance given to Germany by Mr. Clemenceau as stated in your 3037, July 9, 1 p.m.[3] So long as we are fulfilling this assurance, it does not seem to us pertinent whether our municipal limitations exist by virtue of so-called "war legislation" or by what you term "protective legislation by Congress." There is now pending before Congress legislation similar to that already enacted by the British, which, for the purpose of protecting our dye industry, proposes to subject all importations of dyestuffs to a licensing system. In view of this legislation, the Department, under the authority of Section 11 of the Trading with the Enemy Act, will, for a short period, control the importation of German dyestuffs and permit the import of only those dyes which are urgently needed in this country.

The differentiation between our present control of dyes and the control measures desired to be maintained by the British and French is that the former constitutes merely an internal domestic regulation of the United States and does not affect Germany's general freedom of trade with other countries of the world, whereas the latter restrictions are understood by us to be directed against Germany's general freedom of trade with other countries and not to be purely municipal limitations of the countries imposing them. McCormick approves the foregoing.

Prepared for WTB
By Lawrence Bennett[4]

T MS (SDR, RG 59, 763.72112/12382, DNA).
[1] Printed as an Enclosure with WW to W. Phillips, July 18, 1919 (second letter of that date).
[2] See FLP to Ammission, July 11, 1919.
[3] Ammission to SecState, No. 3037, July 9, 1919, T telegram (SDR, RG 59, 662.1115/15, DNA).
[4] Secretary of the War Trade Board. This was sent as RL to Ammission, No. 2632, July 25, 1919, T telegram (SDR, RG 256, 700.62112/129, DNA).

From Henry White

Paris 21 July 1919

To Secstate, Washington, Confidential for the President

3245 The Giornale d'Italia, Sonnino's organ, in its issue of July 4th, carries a long editorial defending and explaining the Italian policy at Paris in respect to the Adriatic question. In as much as this is in some measure an official justification of Sonnino's Adriatic policy, and makes admissions which should perhaps affect our attitude in the matter, it seems wise to bring it to the President's attention.

After saying that "it is now necessary to lay all the cards on the table," the article proceeds to show that the fundamental object of Sonnino's policy was to establish on the eastern coast of the Adriatic three military, political and economic bridgeheads in view of Italy's future expansion in the Danubian and Balkan regions. These three bridgeheads were to be: Julian Venetia and Istria, together with Fiume, in the north; the Zara-Sebenico region with its islands in the center; and, Albania in the south. The article charges that others feared Italy's plan for expansion in the Balkans and that this was the reason of their opposition to Italy's Adriatic claims.

Italian policy in regard to the Free State of Fiume, which was to form part of the northern base of expansion, is given as follows: "To give to the small Free State of Fiume such a statute that during the first fifteen years it would be in effect governed by Italy through the long arm of a local government faithful to Italy, while ultimately it would have been annexed to Italy." The policy in regard to the Zara-Sebenico region is stated as follows: "To save in Dalmatia the harmonious system Zara-Sebenico-adjacent islands, thus creating a sufficiently large political, economic and military bridgehead to give a valid guarantee of the Italianita of Dalmatia and afford some protection for all future eventualities." As regards Albania the policy was to secure through possession of Valona and its hinterland and the mandate for an independent Albania, Italy's influence, strategical security, and future expansion in that region. Sonnino and Orlando are defended for having permitted no substantial concessions to be wrested from them which would compromise the fundamental objects of their policy. They are praised for having acted immediately after the victory in such a way as to solve the problem of Fiume, in the Italian sense, by immediate military occupation of the area, and for having insisted on arrangements which would have "created at Fiume an effective Italian situation susceptible of being transformed in due time into annexation to Italy."

It is interesting to note that the burden of the article is the necessity of establishing bridgeheads for Italy's future expansion in the Balkans and that the defense of Italy's eastern coast which was the alleged reason for Italy's need of naval bases on the Jugo-Slav coast is scarcely mentioned. 3245   White Ammission.

T telegram (SDR, RG 256, 186.3411/718A, DNA)

From John R. Shillady[1]

New York, July 21, 1919.

In the name of twelve million negroes of the United States, the National Association for the Advancement of Colored People respectfully calls your attention to the shame put upon the country by the mobs, including United States soldiers, sailors and marines, which have assaulted innocent and unoffending negroes in the national capital.[2] Men in uniform have attacked negroes on the streets and pulled [them] from street cars to beat them. Crowds are reported by New York TIMES to have directed attacks against any passing negro by cries of "there he goes." The effect of such riots in national capital upon race antagonism will be to increase bitterness and danger of outbreaks elsewhere. National Association for the Advancement of Colored People calls upon you as President and Commander-in-Chief of the armed forces of the nation to make statement condemning mob violence and to enforce such military law as situation demands.   John R. Shillady

T telegram (WP, DLC).
    [1] Secretary of the National Association for the Advancement of Colored People.
    [2] An estimated 100 soldiers, sailors, and marines on liberty in Washington, "said to have been aroused by repeated attacks on white women by colored men during the last few days," had entered a black residential district on the evening of Saturday, July 19. One black man was severely beaten before police and provost guards got to the scene. *New York Times*, July 20, 1919. A later report revealed that a policeman had been shot and seriously wounded in the rioting that continued into early Sunday morning. Further rioting involving both military men and civilians took place on Sunday evening and early Monday morning in various parts of the city; one incident occurred within "a stone's throw" of the White House. Again, the provost guard and police reserves had to be called out. *Ibid.*, July 21, 1919.
    The rioting became much more serious and spread to new areas of Washington on the night of July 21-22, as blacks began to organize to defend themselves and even to retaliate for white attacks. One policeman, one white civilian, and two blacks were killed; at least seventy persons of both races were injured, some very seriously; and "hundreds" of persons were arrested. Secretary Baker announced that he would use whatever military force was necessary to end the rioting. *Ibid.*, July 22, 1919.
    On Tuesday, July 22, an undisclosed but sizable number of soldiers, sailors, and marines from military facilities in and around Washington were put on duty under the command of Maj. Gen. William George Haan, then director of the War Plans Division of the Army General Staff, with orders to quell the rioting. Baker conferred with Wilson about the situation at the White House. About their meeting, see the second news report printed at July 23, 1919. Many congressmen called for martial law. Martial law was not put into effect, but the police and military forces, assisted by heavy rain showers, did prevent the assembling of crowds. One white member of the Home Guard (a police reserve created during the war) was shot to death

in an isolated incident, but there was no further widespread violence. *Ibid.*, July 23, 1919. The city remained calm on the night of July 23-24 and for the next several days, and the military forces returned to their bases on July 27. *Ibid.*, July 28, 1919. See also the second news report printed at July 23, 1919; NDB to WW, July 23, 1919 (first letter of that date); Constance McLaughlin Green, *The Secret City: A History of Race Relations in the Nation's Capital* (Princeton, N. J., 1967), pp. 191-94; and Waskow, *From Race Riot to Sit-In*, pp. 21-37.

From Upton Beall Sinclair

Pasadena Calif [July 21, 1919]

I earnestly implore immediate action regarding petitions for political amnesty. Surely all emergency which would justify holding prisoners for expression of anti war opinion is now past. Conditions under which Debs is held are menace to life of an old man and are causing deplorable embitterment of his supporters. You have opportunity for act of statesmanship in this matter.

Upton Sinclair.

T telegram (Records of the Office of the Pardon Attorney, RG 204, DNA).

Charles William Eliot to Joseph Patrick Tumulty

Dear Mr. Tumulty: Asticou, Maine 21 July 1919

I was glad to get your note of July 17th; although it has appeared from the President's doings since he got home that he already had in mind two out of the four suggestions I made in my letter of July 2nd.

If he decides on a letter to the American people, instead of a tour of speaking, I think he would do well to begin it "Fellow-countrymen," not "My fellow-countrymen." He gives a convenient handle to his opponents when he puts a considerable number of Is and mys into his speeches or writings.

If he has already decided not to be a candidate for a third consecutive term in presidential office, I think it would be expedient—would it not?—to make this decision known confidentially to the Senators and to the leaders of the House before he says anything about it to the public. That announcement would affect the minds of such men as Senators Lodge and Johnson a good deal in respect to desirable planks for the Republican platform, and make them hedge in urging objections to the Treaty and the Covenant. Lodge is hedging already. Massachusetts is not standing behind him, and he knows it.

After the Treaty has been ratified by the Senate, a candid statement by President Wilson to the effect, that the establishment of

Ireland as an independent republic and no part of the British Commonwealth is out of the question, would do a deal of good both in this country and in Great Britain. Obviously, Ireland must remain an integral part of the British Commonwealth; but she ought to be an independent State in precisely the same sense that Virginia or California is an independent State within the American Union. Many of our Irish Americans need to be told that squarely by President Wilson himself, after his experiences at Paris, and before the next presidential election comes on. The Sinn Feiners weaken the Democratic Party materially in all the States where they are much in evidence.   Sincerely yours   Charles W. Eliot

TLS (WP, DLC).

A News Report

[July 22, 1919]

WILSON STAYS IN BED
Weakened, But Not Seriously Ill, Dr. Grayson Reports.

President Wilson was in a weakened but no wise serious condition last night after having spent the day in bed with acute dysentery. Rear Admiral Cary T. Grayson, his personal physician, said the President had been in considerable pain during the day and had been very "uncomfortable." Admiral Grayson said he would insist that Mr. Wilson remain in bed until he had completely recovered.

The President's appointments for today with Republican senators had not been postponed last night, but at the White House it was considered extremely doubtful whether Mr. Wilson would be able to keep them.

While none of those close to the President would say whether his illness would result in postponement of his trip through the West, there seemed to be an opinion that should the illness be prolonged it could have no other effect. Rear Admiral Grayson was uncertain when the President might be able to resume his dutues [duties].

The President first complained of feeling ill Friday when he went to the Capitol to confer with Senator Hitchcock, of Nebraska, ranking Democratic member of the foreign relations committee.

He told Secretary Tumulty then he was slightly indisposed and expressed his intention of going down the Potomac over the weekend in the belief that a change of air might be beneficial.

During the trip, however, the weather was stormy and damp and Mr. Wilson appears to have contracted a slight cold. When he returned from the trip yesterday morning he was feeling worse and immediately upon arriving at the White House Rear Admiral Grayson diagnosed his ailment as acute dysentery and ordered him to bed. All appointments for yesterday were cancelled and those who were to have called were asked to postpone their visits until today.

Printed in the *Washington Post*, July 22, 1919.

To the President of the Senate[1]

Sir: [The White House] 22, July 1919.

For the information of the Senate, and in response to the Resolution[2] adopted June twenty-third, 1919, requesting the President to inform the Senate, if not incompatible with the public interest, of the reasons for sending United States soldiers to Siberia, the duties that are to be performed by these soldiers, how long they are to remain, and generally to advise the Senate of the policy of the United States Government in respect to Siberia and the maintenance of United States soldiers there, I have the honor to say that the decision to send American troops to Siberia was announced to the press on August fifth, 1918, in a statement from the Acting Secretary of State, of which a copy is enclosed.[3]

This measure was taken in conjunction with Japan and in concert of purpose with the other Allied powers, first of all to save the Czecho-Slovak armies which were threatened with destruction by hostile armies apparently organized by, and often largely composed of enemy prisoners of war. The second purpose in view was to steady any efforts of the Russians at self-defense, or the establishment of law and order in which they might be willing to accept assistance.

Two regiments of Infantry, with auxiliary troops—about eight thousand effectives—comprising a total of approximately ten thousand men, were sent under the command of Major General William S. Graves. The troops began to arrive at Vladivostok in September, 1918. Considerably larger forces were dispatched by Japan at about the same time, and much smaller forces by others of the Allied powers. The net result was the successful reunion of the separated Czecho-Slovak armies, and the substantial elimination in Eastern Siberia of the active efforts of enemy prisoners of war. A period of relative quiet then ensued.

In February, 1919, as a conclusion of negotiations begun early in the Summer of 1918, the United States accepted a plan proposed by Japan for the supervision of the Siberian railways by an international committee,[4] under which committee Mr. John F. Stevens would assume the operation of the Russian Railway Service Corps. In this connection, it is to be recalled that Mr. John F. Stevens, in response to a request of the provisional government of Russia, went to Russia in the Spring of 1917. A few months later he was made official adviser to the Minister of Ways of Communication at Petrograd under the provisional government. At the request of the provisional government, and with the support of Mr. John F. Stevens, there was organized the so-called Russian Railway Service Corps, composed of American engineers. As originally organized, the personnel of this Corps constituted fourteen skeleton division units as known in this country, the idea being that these skeleton units would serve as practical advisers and assistants on fourteen different sections of the Siberian railway, and assist the Russians by their knowledge of long-haul problems as known in this country, and which are the rule and not the exception in Siberia.

Owing to the Bolshevik uprising, and the general chaotic conditions, neither Mr. Stevens nor the Russian Railway Service Corps was able to begin work in Siberia until March, 1918. They have been able to operate effectively only since the railway plan was adopted in February, 1919.

The most recent report from Mr. Stevens shows that on parts of the Chinese Eastern and Trans-Baikal Railway he is now running six trains a day each way, while only a little while ago they were only able to run that many trains per week.

In accepting the railway plan, it was provided that some protection should be given by the Allied forces. Mr. Stevens stated frankly that he would not undertake the arduous task before him unless he could rely upon support from American troops in an emergency. Accordingly, as provided in the railway plan, and with the approval of the Inter-Allied Committee, the military commanders in Siberia have established troops where it is necessary to maintain order at different parts of the line. The American forces under General Graves are understood to be protecting parts of the line near Vladivostok, and also on the section around Verchna Udinsk [Verkhneudinsk]. There is also understood to be a small body of American troops at Harbin. The exact location from time to time of American troops is, however, subject to change by the direction of General Graves.

The instruction[s] to General Graves direct him not to interfere in Russian affairs, but to support Mr. Stevens wherever necessary. The Siberian railway is not only the main artery for transportation in Siberia, but is the only open access to European Russia today. The population of Siberia, whose resources have been almost exhausted by the long years of war and the chaotic conditions which have existed there, can be protected from a further period of chaos and anarchy only by the restoration and maintenance of traffic on the Siberian railway.

Partisan bands under leaders having no settled connection with any organized government, and bands under leaders whose allegiance to any settled authority is apparently temporary and transitory, are constantly menacing the operation of the railway, and the safety of its permanent structures.

The situation of the people of Siberia, meantime, is that they have no shoes or warm clothing; they are pleading for agricultural machinery, and for many of the simpler articles of commerce upon which their own domestic economy depends, and which are necessary to fruitful and productive industry among them. Having contributed their quota to the Russian armies which fought the Central Empires for three and one-half years, they now look to the Allies and the United States for economic assistance.

The population of Western Siberia and the forces of Admiral Kolchak are entirely dependent upon these railways.

The Russian authorities in this country have succeeded in shipping large quantities of Russian supplies to Siberia, and the Secretary of War is now contracting with the great cooperative societies which operate throughout European and Asiatic Russia to ship further supplies to meet the needs of the civilian population. The Kolchak Government is also endeavoring to arrange for the purchase of medical and other Red Cross supplies from the War Department, and the American Red Cross is itself attempting the forms of relief for which it is organized. All elements of the population in Siberia look to the United States for assistance. This assistance can not be given to the population of Siberia, and ultimately to Russia, if the purpose entertained for two years to restore railway traffic is abandoned. The presence of American troops is a vital element in this effort. The services of Mr. Stevens depend upon it, and, a point of serious moment, the plan proposed by Japan expressly provides that Mr. Stevens and all foreign railway experts shall be withdrawn when the troops are withdrawn.

From these observations it will be seen that the purpose of the continuance of American troops in Siberia is that we, with the concurrence of the great Allied powers, may keep open a necessary artery of trade, and extend to the vast population of Siberia the economic aid essential to it in peace-time, but indispensable under the conditions which have followed the prolonged and exhausting participation by Russia in the war against the Central powers. This participation was obviously of incalculable value to the Allied cause, and in a very particular way commends the exhausted people who suffered from it to such assistance as we can render to bring about their industrial and economic rehabilitation.

Very respectfully yours,   Woodrow Wilson

TLS (Letterpress Books, WP, DLC).
    [1] The following document was drafted by Frank L. Polk (the draft, dated July 2, 1919, is a T MS, WP, DLC) and was reviewed and redrafted by Newton D. Baker (NDB to JPT, July 22, 1919, ALS, WP, DLC, enclosing a CC MS dated July 22, 1919). Wilson had Baker's draft copied verbatim, and it was published as AMERICAN TROOPS IN SIBERIA . . . , 66th Cong., 1st sess., Sen. Doc. No. 60 (Washington, 1919).
    [2] That is, the Johnson Resolution, about which see G. A. Sanderson to JPT, June 28, 1919, n. 2.
    [3] The press statement, printed in AMERICAN TROOPS IN SIBERIA, is also printed at Aug. 3, 1918, Vol. 49.
    [4] About which, see FLP to RL, Dec. 30, 1918, n. 4, Vol. 53.

Three Letters from Henry Cabot Lodge

My dear Mr. President: [Washington] July 22, 1919.

In accordance with my note to you of Sunday last,[1] I laid your letter of July 18th before the Committee on Foreign Relations yesterday morning. In that letter you suggested that you would be glad to receive the approval of the Committee for the provisional appointment of a member of the Reparation Commission which is to be established when the treaty with Germany goes into effect.

The Committee instructs me to say that it is the judgment of the Committee that until the proposed treaty is ratified in accordance with its terms no power exists to execute any of its provisions, either provisionally or otherwise.

I have the honor to be Respectfully yours,   H. C. Lodge

    [1] It is missing in WP, DLC.

My dear Mr. President: [Washington] July 22, 1919

I have just received your letter of July 19th and laid it at once before the Committee on Foreign Relations, which was at that moment in session. The Committee are unanimously in favor of your plan for raising our legation at Brussels to an embassy and instruct me to say to you that they will do everything in their power to cooperate with you in securing the legislation which you suggest.

I have the honor to be Respectfully yours,   H. C. Lodge

To the President: [Washington] July 22, 1919.

I am instructed by the Committee on Foreign Relations to ask you if you will have the kindness to send to the Committee, if not incompatible with the public interest, the agreement referred to in Article 237 of the treaty with Germany,[1] in the event that such agreement has been determined upon by the Allied and Associated Governments.

I have the honor to be Respectfully yours, H. C. Lodge

TLS (WP, DLC).
  [1] Article 237 related to the distribution of German reparation payments. The significant sentence reads as follows: "The successive instalments, including the above sum [20,000,000,000 gold marks, stipulated as a preliminary payment in Article 235], paid over by Germany in satisfaction of the above claims will be divided by the Allied and Associated Governments in proportions which have been determined upon by them in advance on a basis of general equity and of the rights of each." PPC, XIII, 440.

From William Phillips

My dear Mr. President: Washington July 22, 1919.

In view of the prominence which has been given to the discussion of the Shantung Settlement, the Department took advantage of the presence in the United States on leave of Mr. John V. A. MacMurray, who recently returned from Tokyo, and asked him to make a memorandum of the whole question beginning with the circumstances which lead up to the acquisition of the German rights in 1898. It has been done with great care, and by a man who has made a particular study of treaties relating to the Far East, and he knows the subject very well.[1]

The memorandum is of considerable length,[2] but this seems to be necessary for a proper examination of the several treaties concerned and the rather intricate questions presented.

The most important features of it have been blue penciled and it may be that you will want to read those parts if not the whole memorandum.

Attached to it is a map of China and a list of citations used in making the memorandum.

Also attached is a statement compiled after a very careful analysis of the Treaty of Versailles, showing the benefits which would accrue to China under that Treaty.[3] It has been drawn with the fact in mind that China has not signed the Treaty.

Because of the importance of the subject and its complex nature I feel that you may want to have this, and without any desire, of course, to burden you, I take this means of placing it at your disposal.   Yours very sincerely, William Phillips

TLS (WP, DLC).
  [1] J. V. A. MacMurray "MEMORANDUM ON THE SHANTUNG QUESTION," July 21, 1919, TI MS (WP, DLC). Following a review of the historical background of the Chinese government's concessions to Germany in Shantung Province in 1898, the memorandum con-

centrated on a careful, detailed analysis of the exact nature of those concessions and of the process by which they were transferred to Japan through her military occupation of Shantung as well as through her diplomatic negotiations with China and with the other great powers. The provisions of the Treaty of Versailles relating to Shantung Province, MacMurray concluded, simply granted to Japan exactly the same *de jure* rights in Shantung Province which Germany had held prior to the war and which Japan had entered into *de facto* by virtue of military occupation of the province.

MacMurray's memorandum was in many respects similar to the two lengthy documents submitted by the Chinese delegation to the Paris Peace Conference in April 1919, about which see V. K. W. Koo to WW, April 17, 1919, n. 1, Vol. 57, and J. C. Grew to GFC, April 25, 1919, n. 1, Vol. 58. However, MacMurray's memorandum lacked the fervent arguments for the immediate restoration of full Chinese sovereignty over Shantung Province found in the two earlier documents.

² It consists of forty-seven pages and a map of northern China and Manchuria.

³ "CHINESE RIGHTS UNDER THE PEACE TREATY (Other than Shantung Provisions)," T MS (WP, DLC). This statement concluded that, under the peace treaty, China would enjoy all the rights, privileges, and protection provided for and guaranteed by the Covenant of the League of Nations and would secure the renunciation by Germany of all privileges and concessions which China had formerly made to that nation. However, as the phrase in the parentheses indicates, the statement said nothing at all about the privileges and concessions in Shantung Province which Japan had taken over from Germany.

From William Phillips, with Enclosure

Dear Mr. President: Washington July 22, 1919.

I beg to call to your special attention two important telegrams received from the Mission:

1. Text of a note sent by the French and British Governments to the Italian Government,[1] and the reply thereto of the Italian Government.[2]

2. Relating to the participation of the United States in the work of setting up Commissions provided for in the Treaty of Peace.   Sincerely yours,   William Phillips

TLS (WP, DLC).

¹ The text of this note is printed as the Appendix to the minutes of the Council of Four printed at June 28, 1919, 6 p.m. The telegram to which Phillips referred is Ammission to SecState, No. 3171, July 17, 1919, T telegram (SDR, RG 259, 763.72119/5669, DNA).

² Tittoni's reply of July 7, 1919, is included in the telegram just cited and is printed in French in Amedeo Giannini, ed., *L'Italia alla Conferenza della Pace* (Rome, 1921), pp. 117-23. René Albrecht-Carrié, *Italy at the Paris Peace Conference* (New York, 1938), pp. 238-42, summarizes Tittoni's note in great detail.

In his point-by-point reply to the Anglo-French note, Tittoni rehashed arguments in defense of Italy's past actions and present claims made many times by Orlando and Sonnino in the Council of Four.

ENCLOSURE

Paris, July 20, 1919.

3235. It was our understanding that the President, at about the time of his departure, expressed the view that there should be no participation by the United States in the work of setting up commissions provided for by the Treaty until ratification of the Treaty by the Senate. There are certain obvious difficulties in a literal application of this policy, which, it seems to us, we are warranted in bringing to your attention, so that we may be assured of knowing the precise views of the President with reference to the actual situation which confronts us and in which we are subjected to very considerable pressure by our colleagues.

The Treaty provides that nearly all of the commissions begin their duties within fifteen (*) after the coming into force of the Treaty. On account of the unsettled conditions in large parts of Europe it is necessary that the Boundary Commissions, Plebiscite Governing Commissions, etc., should be prepared to undertake their duties within the time specified, especially as areas will be evacuated by German passport and administrative officials, leaving no adequate provisions for local government. Delay in arrival of the commissions may involve serious local unrest which in turn may require the despatch of Allied forces. The smaller states are entitled to protection in these matters and probably will not be satisfied with commissions without the American members prescribed by the Treaty. On the other hand Germany can and probably will insist that the commissions shall not start upon their work without these American members. In the matter of arbitration, particularly concerning rivercraft and railway matters, commerce in Europe will be greatly impeded through lack of decision in cases where the United States is, by the Treaty, to name the umpires.

In order that these commissions and arbitral bodies may be able to enter upon their duties within the time specified by the treaty, not only must personnel be selected, but opportunity afforded for acquainting such personnel with the character of their duties and the history of the treaty clauses which they will be called upon to enforce. In discussion with our associates we have hitherto taken the position that while no definite appointments would be made by the United States except after ratification by the Senate, we would take informal preparatory steps necessary to enable us punctually to carry out our obligations in the event of ratification. If we are not to do so, we feel we should frankly so state.

It may also be pointed out that the treaty becomes effective when ratified by three principal powers, which may take place be-

fore America ratifies. Whether we ratify or not the small states and
Germany will doubtless demand American representation on the
Treaty commissions, and it is suggested that we might meet such
demands, as it is not unusual for the United States to designate
arbitrators, et cetera, to act under treaties to which the United
States is not a party.

The rapid withdrawal of American army officers from Europe,
many of whom are adapted for positions which, under the treaty,
the United States is required to suspend, will make it extremely
difficult for us to perform the obligations above referred to, unless
action is now taken to hold in Europe suitable officers. Authority
requested, therefore, to make immediately, temporary selections
here for all of these positions except for League of Nations Commission and the more important positions in other commissions, as
the Reparation Commission and the Rhineland Commission. Such
selections would, of course, be subject to any necessary approval
or change upon the Senate having acted on the Treaty. The persons selected would be able to participate, if desirable, in deliberations with their colleagues without binding the United States but
merely assisting in preliminary discussion and preparation in order
to become fully informed and ready to take part if and when they
are formally appointed.

This authority will further involve the granting of additional
funds to the Peace Commission.

A related and equally important matter is that of Hoover's economic commissions in control of the railways of central and eastern Europe, the Danube, Elbe and Vistula; his commissions in
control of coal distribution of practically all central European coal
fields; and his telegraphic communications syndicates upon which
we greatly rely for communication with Eastern Europe. All of
these are necessarily about to demobilize because of the exhaustion of his funds and expiration of his office. He is endeavoring to
hold on until the Austrian Treaty is signed, although he has no
adequate resources for payment of salaries and expenses. The various commissions created by the Treaty of Peace will, to a great
extent, replace Hoover's economic administration which is very
important for economic cooperation of central Europe, and, if authority is given to make selection for Treaty positions as above requested, we can, in large measure, bring about an orderly transfer
of the relief work to Treaty bodies. If, however, his commissions
are withdrawn before the various permanent commissions under
the Treaty are set up, [it] might jeopardize the good effects of the
work already accomplished and increase the danger of economic

chaos. Hoover states that if we can quickly install the new regime it will cover this situation.

General Bliss says that Marchal Foch has informed him that the general scheme for organization of the Commissions of Control, charged with supervising the disarmament of Germany, calls for an American General as president, a subcommittee on the disarmament of fortifications, and that he has requested the immediate designation of this officer. General Bliss informed the Marshal that he has no power to consider this question and that the officer must be appointed at the proper time by the Government in Washington. To this, the Marshal replied that it is absolutely necessary to make the appointment now in order that the commission may organize and block out its work. General Bliss suggests that in case an American officer cannot be designated prior to ratification of the Treaty by the Senate, he be directed to inform the Marshal that an officer of some other nationality must be selected as president of the sub-Commission on Fortifications. The American Mission understands that the permanent designations of all American representatives on commissions created by the Treaty of Peace will be made in Washington and that they shall so inform their colleagues here. White. Bliss.   American Mission.

T telegram (SDR, RG 59, 763.72119/5712, DNA).

From William Phillips

My dear Mr. President: Washington July 22nd, 1919.

I beg to acknowledge the receipt of your letter of July 18th, 1919,[1] with reference to the telegram from the American Mission at Paris regarding the proposal of the Supreme Economic Council for carrying into effect international consultation in economic matters pending the formation of the League of Nations, and regarding the alternative plan suggested by Messrs. Hoover and Dulles.

I note your statement that the matter was considered by the Cabinet and that doubt was suggested as to whether you had legal right to take part in commissions not sanctioned by legislation.

In this connection, I venture to suggest that while the Act approved March 4, 1913, making appropriations to supply deficiencies in appropriations for the fiscal year 1913 and for prior years and for other purposes, contains a provision that "hereafter the Executive shall not extend or accept any invitation to participate in any international conference, congress or like event without first having specific authority of law to do so," yet it is believed that, by virtue of your power under the Constitution to conduct the foreign relations of the United States, you have ample authority to appoint representatives on an international council such as it is proposed to establish, notwithstanding the provisions of the Act mentioned. If this view be sound, there would seem to be no legal obstacle in the way of participating in the proposed plan.

Practical difficulties, however, exist as to the source of the funds for the expenses of representation on such a council. In this connection you may desire to use the emergency fund to temporarily meet the expenses of participation in the proposed plan. I would call your attention, however, to the fact that the expenses of the American Mission to Negotiate Peace are chargeable to this fund and I would therefore suggest that any payments made from this fund should be of a temporary nature.

                              Sincerely yours,   William Phillips

TLS (WP, DLC).
[1] WW to W. Phillips, July 18, 1919 (first letter of that date).

From Henry White

Greece-Thrace
To be constituted a part of the international state of Constantinople[1]

                                        Paris July 22, 1919

3256. For the President. Referring to 3240 dated July nineteenth.[2]

At today's meeting of Council of Five[3] the necessity and importance were discussed of having the clauses of the Peace Treaty with Bulgaria completed before the arrival of the representatives of that country on the twenty fifth. Balfour urging that the delay which had occurred (*) connection with the Austrian Treaty, and which he described as little short of a disgrace to the Conference, should not be repeated; other three colleagues[4] being practically of the same opinion. Balfour insisted that the reparation clauses cannot be settled until the question of the amount of territory to be taken from Bulgaria is agreed upon, which he thought impossible until the frontiers of Bulgaria are finally settled. Informal discussion then took place during which Tardieu read extracts from re-

[1] WWhw and transcript of WWsh.
[2] Actually, H. White to WW, July 20, 1919.
[3] Actually, this meeting of the Supreme Council took place on July 21, 1919. The minutes of this meeting are printed in PPC, VII, 233-53. White's telegram was sent from Paris at 11:38 a.m., July 22.
[4] Clemenceau, Tittoni, and Makino.

port of the Commission on Bulgarian Coasts[5] from which it tran-
spired that the French, British and Japanese delegates on the
Commission strongly favor the assignment of western Thrace to
Greece while the American and Italian oppose it. It was thereupon
proposed to discuss the matter immediately with a view to arriving
at a decision to which I objected on the ground that, in the absence
of final instructions from you, I was not in a position to make one.
Discussion was thereupon adjourned until the meeting of the
Council on Thursday. The following is a quotation from the report
of the Commission on Bulgarian coasts giving the reasons of the
respective members thereof regarding the disposition of western
Thrace.

"American and Italian point of view: The American delegation
expresses the following opinion:

A. Bulgaria did not acquire western Thrace by right of conquest,
but by virtue of a cession made voluntarily by Greece and her Allies
who were enemies of Bulgaria and who, although they were the
conquerers, recognized the wisdom in their giving to defeated Bulgaria this natural outlet to the sea. The country was occupied by
Greek and not Bulgarian troops; and certainly only came into possession upon the voluntary retreat of the Greek forces. Bulgarian
title to the possession of western Thrace was not contested at the
commencement of the present war. The only point still under discussion at Bucharest was that of knowing whether Bulgaria should
not obtain rather more than less territory on the Aegean. The
American delegation thinks that it would be ill advised to inflict on
a nation the loss of a territory to which it possesses just title from
a legal, ethnic and economic point of view.

B. The report of the Commission on Greek affairs[6] contains a
fundamental error when it declares, as a first argument in support
of its conclusions, that 'the non-Mussulman population of Bulgarian Thrace is regarded as (*) Greek than Bulgarian' and that 'the
ethnic rights of Greece are therefore superior to those of Bulgaria.'
The statistics on which these assertions are based are of prior date
to the cession of western Thrace to Bulgaria; the verb can only
therefore be used in relation to the past. The non-Mussulman population was Greek rather than Bulgarian to a very small degree before the territory passed to Bulgaria. A well known fact however
and something which is not contested, is that the extent to which
the Greek troops withdrew from western Thrace after the cession
to Bulgaria, a part of the Greek population evacuated the region

[5] Actually, the "Report on the Boundaries of Bulgaria Presented to the Supreme
Council by the Central Territorial Committee," printed in PPC, VII, 242-48.
[6] That is, the Sub-Commission on Greek and Albanian Affairs.

and this exodus has continued since that time while the (?) of Bulgarians have arrived to take the place of the Greeks. The proofs of alleged deportations of Greeks, outside of this argument, are contradictory. In any event the relatively slight Greek majority has been inevitably replaced by a relative Bulgarian majority secured by natural causes subsequent to the cession of this territory to Bulgaria.

The proofs are contradictory regarding the question as to whether the Mohammedan majority prefers to be under Bulgarian or Greek authority. Should it be impossible to have a Turkish administration, the testimony of eight Mussulman deputies is not entirely convincing. It should be noted that the most probable tongue of a great proportion of these Mohammedans is Bulgarian while but a few of them speak Greek; it is therefore difficult to believe that these populations, speaking Bulgarian, should prefer to be under Greek rather than Bulgarian authority. The two principal arguments on which the Greek Commission has relied in support of its conclusions thus lose much of their force.

C. The lack of any direct access to the Mediterranean would seriously compromise the economic development of Bulgaria. The promises made by Greece not to interfere with the transit and to accord facilities in the ports of Greek territory do not represent the equivalent of direct access to the sea even in times of peace. In time of War this would have no value. This principle has been fully recognized by the powers when they insisted on assuring this access to the sea in the case of Poland. The route by the Black Sea and the Dardanelles does not take the place of direct access as it is a round about route which is longer and more expensive.

D. Even if the economic inconveniences could be overcome it would be impossible to convince the Bulgarian people that its future development is not affected by the loss of what all nations value most highly. The Bulgarians would cherish a profound resentment against the injustice which would be committed in imposing on them these frontiers and this sentiment would be an inestimable menace to the future peace of the world.

E. The cession by Turkey to Bulgaria in 1915 of the territory neighboring Adrianople has repaired a serious injustice which was imposed on Bulgaria in 1913 when Turkey closed the natural outlet of the valley of the Maritza [River] and cut the only railroad leading to the Bulgarian port on the Aegean. It is essential to maintain this rectification as it would be useless to give to Bulgaria a port on the sea if the natural route of access to the latter should remain blocked.

The ethnographic, economic and political arguments, as well as the actual fact of possession, which is based upon valid titles, all are in favor of maintaining the Bulgarian frontiers as they are at the present hour.

The American Delegation therefore make the following proposition: The southern frontier of Bulgaria shall be that which existed after the cession by Turkey in 1913 of the territory neighboring to Adrianople, the right of the principal Allied and Associated Powers being reserved to attach to the international state any part of the said territory which they may think desirable."

The Italian delegation adheres to the observations and conclusion of the American delegation.

Two. English, French and Japanese point of view:

A. Neither from a historical nor moral point of view has Bulgaria any title whatsoever to Western Thrace. This territory was given to her after the second Balkan war by Greece and Servia as a proof of their desire to live on terms of friendship and trust with an ally who had just betrayed them. Bulgaria flagrantly abused this generosity; she entered this war solely for the purpose of rapine; she conducted this war in the most barbarous fashion and for the second time has been completely defeated.

Under the circumstances the three delegations believe that Bulgaria has not justified the confidence which was originally accorded her. Neither do they think that it would be politic to recompense her for entering the European war by granting her additional territory as is proposed in the American program.

B. Bulgaria, from an ethnic point of view, is not justified in claiming Western Thrace, the Territory in which the Bulgarian element only ranked third, according to the latest Turkish statistics (1910). The three delegations believe that the value of these statistics has not been changed at all by the fact that deportations or emigrations *en* masse of the Greek population have taken place since the Bulgarian occupation. To accept such a criterion would be to accord a premium on the persecution of the native population and to establish a precedent which in other cases, such as Armenia, for example, would lead to the most unjust conclusions. As regards the aspirations of the Mussulman population of Western Thrace, we have the testimony of eight out of twelve Mussulman deputies to the Bulgarian Parliament who, in a recent petition addressed to General Franchet D'Esperey, expressed themselves as follows: "It would be unjust to leave us under the most cruel and most merciless yoke, the yoke of Bulgarian domination."

For these reasons the three delegations maintain that the conclusions of the Committee on Greek Affairs were fully justified.

C. As regards Bulgarian access to the sea, the three delegations consider that the economic situation of Bulgaria will be benefited by the Treaty of Peace which they propose to impose upon her.

On the one hand her outlet on the Black Sea will be rendered better and more secure through the internationalization of the Straits and of the Danube.

On the other hand, the natural outlet of Bulgaria in the Mediterranean is not situated in western Thrace but in Greek territory, either at Kavala or at Saloniki. The Greek Government has moreover offered to give to Bulgaria special privileges and facilities in one of these two ports and the Commission on Ports and Waterways has elaborated special provisions to make this offer effective.

The case of Poland cannot be compared to the case of Bulgaria, since, no matter what the solution may be, Bulgaria will always have access to the sea by her northern and eastern frontiers.

D. The three delegations frankly admit that in case of war between Greece and Bulgaria the rights obtained by the latter at Kavala or at Salonica will be valueless but they do not believe that a purely military or strategic argument can outweigh other conditions.

They also admit that taking western Thrace from Bulgaria would cause in Bulgaria too bitter resentment. They maintain however that this solution is just in itself and that the resentment caused in Greece and Servia by giving this territory to Bulgaria, territory to which she has not right, would be at least equivalent to the resentment which would be caused in Bulgaria by the (*) of this territory.

E. The three delegations likewise admit that the frontier rectifications obtained by Bulgaria from Turkey in 1915 are of great economic value to Bulgaria. They observe however that the territory in question is almost entirely inhabited by Greek and Turkish populations, moreover these delegations are loath to violate the ethnic principle in order to give Bulgaria economic advantages which are in fact the price paid to Bulgaria for entering the war against the Allied Powers. They are convinced that the militaristic spirit in Bulgaria could only be encouraged by this mode of action and that Bulgarian opinion would be led to believe that, no matter how unjustified, inhuman, or unfortunate a war might be, it is in the end an advantageous means of satisfying her appetite.

The three delegations, confining themselves to the precise question put by the Supreme Council and reserving the problem of the annexation of eastern Thrace, recommend in the most formal manner that this province, together with that portion which was added in 1915, should be ceded by Bulgaria to the Principal Allied and Associated Powers."

Please let me know if possible before Thursday whether I am to sustain position taken by our experts in the commission to the extent of preventing any other settlement even if left a minority of one. White.   American Mission

T telegram (WP, DLC).

A News Report

[*July 22, 1919*]

WILSON SAYS HE DECIDED SHANTUNG
Britain and France Had Him Umpire Claim,
He Tells Visiting Senators.

Washington, July 22.—During the renewal of his conferences with Republican Senators today at the White House, President Wilson, in explaining the reasons lying back of provisions in the treaty of peace with Germany to which opposition had been raised in the Senate, revealed that the foreign delegates at the Peace Conference put up to Mr. Wilson the delicate handling in Paris of the Shantung matter, over which such a storm of criticism has developed in debate in the upper branch of Congress.

President Wilson is said to have informed his callers that Great Britain and France, because of their private understandings with Japan, by which to obtain the entrance of the Mikado's Government into the war, they had agreed to support Japan's claim to the German rights on the Shantung Peninsula, had felt unable to deal with the situation when it arose in the Peace Conference. Great Britain and France felt bound by their agreement, the President said, and could take no other position than to support Japan's claim.

The two Governments, backed by others at the conference, Mr. Wilson said, had agreed to leave it to the President to work out such a solution of the problem as he might be able to make. Mr. Wilson, in the face of the agreements entered into between France and Great Britain with Japan, felt impelled to support the Japanese claim to the Chinese peninsula.

That the question of the inclusion of the Shantung agreement in the treaty of peace had been left to the President to determine was not known at the Capitol until after today's conferences. The President gave the impression to his callers, it was said, that he had come to the determination that the Shantung provision ought to be embraced in the treaty only after he was convinced that Japan would bolt the conference and decline to sign the treaty if Shantung were omitted.

The President's callers were Senators Calder of New York, Cummins of Iowa, and Edge of New Jersey, and with all of them, although not yet entirely recovered from his recent illness, he talked about Shantung along with other provisions of the treaty. All three of the Senators advocate reservations as to Shantung and provisions of the League covenant, embracing Article X, guaranteeing territorial integrity and political independence to nations in the League, the Monroe Doctrine, purely American policies, such as tariff, immigration, and race questions, and the right of America to determine if her obligations have been fulfilled when desiring to withdraw from the League.

After their conferences with the President, which, as in the case of the talks of other Senators with Mr. Wilson last week, were conducted individually, the Senators said their attitude on Shantung and the other provisions was unchanged. All of them were as unalterably in favor of reservations as ever. Senator Calder went so far as to say that unless the reservations he advocated were adopted he would vote against the treaty. The others did not commit themselves that far.

President Wilson talked earnestly with his callers on the treaty, expressing the view that, unless it were ratified without change a difficult situation would arise in requiring the Peace Conference to reopen the entire treaty negotiations. Mr. Wilson urged that the League of Nations covenant be accepted without amendment. He did not, so far as is known, indicate that he might approve even a resolution of interpretation of understanding to express the Senate views as to the application of any of the treaty provisions to which objection has been voiced. He intimated that he was opposed to any kind of reservation.

Japan, the President told his callers, did not intend to keep Shantung for an indefinite time. He appeared to have some assurance from the Japanese representatives at Paris that the Mikado's Government would give up its rights on the peninsula within a reasonable period. The only right retained by Japan, he explained, would be that her nationals remain on the peninsula and be not obliged to relinquish any commercial activities in which they might have engaged. No political right was exacted by Japan in her possession of the peninsula.

Mr. Wilson had felt, he said, that, in view of all the circumstances, the agreement between Great Britain and France and Japan must be respected. He spoke of it as the only solution of the problem as it confronted the Peace Conference.

Senator Calder told the President, he said, that he was not satisfied with the obligation imposed under Article X. He felt that it would compel the United States to plunge into small disputes of nations over territorial matters.

"I asked the President," said Senator Calder, "what he would think of a reservation to Article X. to provide that it should be operative up to 1921 and be renewed, after that, for another period of time. I suggested that that would give the United States opportunity to decide, after 1921, if it wanted to be bound further by Article X.

"The President looked at me sharply and shook his head.

" 'That article is one of the most vital ones in the covenant,' the President said. 'The nations of the world are looking to us to help maintain a status of peace.' "

Printed in the *New York Times*, July 23, 1919.

From James Henry Taylor[1]

My dear Mr President: [Washington] 22 July 1919

Owing to the fact that I shall be absent from the city during the month of August, the Session has advanced the communion service to next Sunday, July 27.

During my absence in August Dr. J. G. McAllister,[2] whom you know, will preach for us August 3rd, 10th & 17th. Rev. Thomas W. Hooper of our Presbytery,[3] who was released from his church work for the period of the war and served at the front as Captain of Company K. 319th Infantry, will preach for us August 24th and 31st.

I regret exceedingly to know that you are indisposed and trust that you are rapidly improving and that you will harbor your strength for the continuation of the great task from which, for so long a time, you have had no respite.

With regards to Mrs. Wilson and yourself,

I remain, Very sincerely   James H. Taylor

ALS (WP, DLC).
    [1] Pastor of the Central Presbyterian Church of Washington, where Wilson usually worshiped.
    [2] That is, James Gray McAllister.
    [3] Thomas Williamson Hooper, Jr., pastor of the Culpeper & Mitchells Presbyterian Church of Culpeper, Va., since 1907.

Four News Reports

[July 23, 1919]

DENY WILSON POWER
May Not Appoint Reparation Commissioner, Senators Vote.

By ALBERT W. FOX.

President Wilson and the foreign relations committee of the United States Senate are apparently not going to work in accord so far as consideration of the peace treaty is concerned. The President's efforts at conciliation appear doomed to failure so far as restoring harmony between himself and this important committee is involved, and yesterday's session of the committee showed many signs of increasing opposition to the President's whole peace plan.

When the committee met it had a letter from the President requesting acquiescence in the appointment of an American member of the reparation commission. This commission is not connected directly with the league covenant and will exercise a tremendous power in holding Germany to fulfillment of terms, collecting indemnities and otherwise liquidating consequences of the war.

As its existence is essential and as America admittedly should be represented on it, the administration believe[d] that the foreign relations committee would hasten to grant the President's request. But the temper of the committee was a matter which had not been reckoned with. The majority of the committee members were somewhat incensed over the failure of the President to forward to the Senate any reply to the various requests of the committee for information about certain phases of the treaty.[1]

Consequently the committee was not in a receptive mood when the President's letter came up for consideration. Whether this made any difference in the committee's action can only be surmised, but, anyway, the committee voted to refuse the President's request, and the plan for an American member of the reparation commission went aglimmering.

When the committee met there were pending a series of resolutions outlining the reply that Senator Lodge should make to the President's letter. Senator Williams had introduced a resolution agreeing that the President had power to make the appointment and Senator Harding, of Ohio, had proposed to instruct the chairman to reply that "neither the committee nor the Senate has any

---

[1] See, e.g., G. A. Sanderson to JPT, July 16 and 17, 1919. The committee had also not yet received Wilson's reply to the Johnson Resolution about American policy in Russia printed at July 22, 1919.

authority to take action in respect to any treaty provision until said treaty becomes effective through ratification."

Senator Hitchcock proposed to amend this by declaring that the President, while the treaty is in the stage of negotiation, has the power to make such appointments if they are necessary. But Senator Knox insisted that until the treaty is ratified "no power exists either in the President or in Congress to execute any provision of the proposed treaty, either provisionally or otherwise."

With the battle thus staged, the voting began. Mr. Hitchcock's proposal which had the full support of the administration was voted down 9 to 6. Mr. Knox's provision was sustained by a vote of 8 to 7. As anticipated the Republicans, excepting Senator McCumber, stood together and therefore the reply which Senator Lodge sent to the President stated that "till the treaty has been ratified in accordance with its terms no power exists to execute any of its provisions, either provisionally or otherwise."

The action of the committee came as a great surprise to some of the administration supporters who have been confident that whenever the test really came the President's stand would prevail. They firmly believed that the committee would not refuse point blank to accede to a request from the President having such a direct and vital bearing on the execution of the peace treaty.

The committee took little time in considering the reply to the President. There was much more interest attached to the discussion of why the committee had received no reply to its requests for documents relating to the treaty. It was pointed out that it is now more than three weeks since Senator Johnson asked concerning American purposes in Russia.

Senator Lodge pointed out that during his senatorial experience, covering all the administrations, beginning with that of Cleveland, there has never been a time when the Senate's requests for information were treated in such a "cavalier fashion" as they are now.

There are signs, too, that the Republican senators are beginning to deeply resent the President's sending for individual senators to hold private conversations with them while withholding from the Senate itself the documentary facts which the President uses in his private talks.

Senator Lodge insists that the Senate is now entitled to everything bearing on the treaty, because the treaty has passed out of the purview of the executive branch and into the Senate branch of the treaty-making power. Meanwhile the committee is continuing with its task of carefully reading the treaty, and Senator Lodge has been assuring the committee that he hoped to have the document reported in another week.

President Wilson yesterday resumed his conferences with Republican senators, interviewing Senators Cummins, Edge and Calder. Following their visits to the White House, the senators spoke of having had pleasant talks with the President, but stated that their views had undergone no change.

Senator Cummins said the President discussed among other things Article X, which is described as "the teeth of the league" because it pledges the league members to go to war in defense of [the] territorial integrity of any member threatened from outside aggression, &c. The Iowa senator is only in favor of this provision if it cannot involve the United States, and as the President takes a diametrically opposite view so far as the necessity of making Article X binding is concerned, the differences between Senator Cummins and the President on that score are for the present irreconcilable.

The President continued his discussion of the Shantung provision with his callers, but brought out no new points, Senator[s] say.

During his talk with Senator Calder there was much discussion about the importance of ratifying the treaty, including the league covenant, on account of the delicate state of the public mind in Europe. Senator Calder suggested important reservations concerning Article X, but it is understood that the President is still adverse to change.

After spending an hour with the President, Senator Edge said:

"I have nothing to say further than that I was very glad to hear the President's viewpoint. He was very interesting and gave me information I was glad to have. I still feel, however, that in any way the Senate can, from an American standpoint, clarify or strengthen the covenant or peace treaty, such action is not only our sworn duty, but in the final analysis will be in the interest of all parties concerned.

"Perhaps the Senate, through not having participated in the peace conference, is in a better position to make what we believe necessary reservations than was the President, who, of course, to an extent had to give and take. I believe such fair reservations would be promptly accepted by the other nations. I don't want to see the United States evade any responsibility, but looking to the future, America should never be a minority stockholder in an international corporation."

Printed in the *Washington Post*, July 23, 1919.

[July 23, 1919]

WILSON DISCUSSES RIOTS WITH BAKER
Feeling Better, President Resumes
His Treaty Talks With Senators.

President Wilson, who was confined to his bed Monday, was well on his way to recovery last night, even though he spent a busy day holding conferences with Republican senators and other officials. Admiral Cary T. Grayson, the President's personal physician, expressed the belief last night that, although Mr. Wilson would have to exercise care for several days owing to his weakened condition, no concern need be felt.

The President upon rising yesterday morning expressed a desire to resume his conferences with the Republican senators and by noon he was able to go to his study. In addition to discussing treaty subjects with Senators Calder, of New York; Edge, of New Jersey, and Cummins, of Iowa, he received reports on Monday night's race riots in Washington and later sent for Secretary Baker. With Mr. Baker he discussed for half an hour measures that might be taken by the Federal authorities to aid the District government in quelling the disturbances.

At the White House it was impossible to ascertain whether the President's illness might interfere with his proposed tour of the country. As it is understood that the President does not contemplate starting on his trip before August 1, it was not considered that his plans would be materially affected.

Printed in the *Washington Post*, July 23, 1919.

[July 23, 1919]

WILSON CONTINUES FIRM
Tells Senators Smaller Nations
Would Oppose Treaty Modifications.

Washington, July 23.—An unyielding attitude against reservations to the treaty of peace was taken by President Wilson in talks today with four Republican Senators at the White House. The President's firm position, in the minds of his callers, disposed of reports spread about the Capitol during the last few days that the Executive might accept mild reservations that would embrace the features under attack in the Senate debate.

The callers were Senators Page of Vermont, Sterling of South Dakota, McLean of Connecticut and Newberry of Michigan.[1] All of

[1] That is, Truman Handy Newberry, Republican.

these advocate reservations, chiefly bearing upon Article X, relating to guarantee of territorial integrity; the Monroe Doctrine, American matters like immigration, and unconditional withdrawal of the United States from the League of Nations upon two years' notice to the League Council.

Senators Page and McLean urged the President to undertake a compromise between the Republicans who want reservations and the Administration Senators supporting the treaty in its entirety. This the President indicated he would not attempt. Mr. Wilson, the Senators said, expressed the view that, while reservations might be accepted by Great Britain, France, Italy, and Japan, the smaller nations in the League had to be considered. Some of the minor nations, he is quoted as saying, undoubtedly would oppose any reservations that would vitally affect the obligation of the United States to remain solidly in the League in support of provisions that touched their welfare.

The treaty had been designed as much to protect the smaller nations as the greater ones, Mr. Wilson is said to have declared, and he would feel obliged to resist any reservations that he felt would be objected to by them.

President Wilson was reported by the Senators to have explicitly stated that he would accept no compromise with the opposition forces; he wants the treaty ratified as it is, League of Nations covenant, the Shantung award to Japan and all. The President did not urge his four callers to change their attitude, they said, the executive refraining from asking any of them how they expected to vote.

Mr. Wilson, as upon the occasion of the visits of the other Republican Senators, went into detail in explaining the reasons for the inclusion of features assailed in the Senate. One new point touched upon was the Anglo-American alliance to protect France against German invasion. This, the President said, in discussing it, could not go into effect until the League of Nations covenant had been adopted, along with the ratification of the treaty.

While the President was holding his conferences, which stretched throughout the whole day, there was talk in the Senate lobby that Senator Kellogg of Minnesota, who called upon the President last week, and who favors reservations to the treaty, had undertaken the task of intermediary between the opposing forces. The Minnesotan, it was stated, had approached Administration leaders in an endeavor to come upon some compromise that would embrace the points raised by the opponents of the treaty.

How far Mr. Kellogg had proceeded with his reported effort did not develop. While the Republicans have insisted that they have the votes to put reservations through, the Administration Senators have challenged the statement. They were not inclined, it is stated, after the President's attitude had been so clearly expressed to his visitors, to consent to any compromise.

All of the four Senators who went to the White House declared upon their return to the Capitol that they had not changed their minds as to the urgency of the need of reservations to the treaty. Senator Page frankly told the President, while suggesting that Mr. Wilson undertake the task of reaching an agreement with the opposition, that, for himself, he was unequivocally for reservations and that he would follow whatever policy the Republican leaders mapped out.

"I am a party man," Mr. Page told the President, "and as a party man I am essentially an American. As an American, I believe in reservations to this treaty that will explicitly safeguard the interests of America."

When Mr. Page urged that the President undertake an effort at compromise with the Republican forces, the President, it is said, plainly told him that he would not attempt it. Mr. Wilson went into a discussion of the treaty provisions under attack, the Senator said, explaining them from his point of view. He urged, as he had in his previous conferences with Senators, that the League of Nations was a vital part of the treaty and that to change it would entail indefinite delay by throwing the treaty back to the conference.

In his talk with Senator Sterling the President emphasized the danger of reservations, which, he is reported to have said, while perhaps acceptable to the greater nations in the Peace Conference, would arouse the smaller nations. The President was understood by Senator Sterling to be as unequivocally opposed to reservations as when he began his White House conferences.

Senator McLean said the President did not urge him to change his views and that he did not succeed. One point brought out by the President in his talk with Mr. McLean was that any action by the Senate in making changes in the treaty might be interpreted by nations abroad as meaning that the United States was only half-hearted in its engagement in the peace compact. Europe believed in the League of Nations, the President is reported as saying, and thinks the people of the United States want it.

Mr. McLean suggested to the President that he might take up the matter of reservations with the Foreign Relations Committee. The President replied, it was stated, that he did not want to put himself in the attitude of arguing with the committee, but wanted it to use its own judgment in considering the treaty.

Senator Newberry described his conference with the President as "informative and instructive." The President, he said, dwelt upon the extreme difficulties faced in reaching an agreement upon the treaty provisions. This exposition, Mr. Newberry said, threw light upon the problems that confronted the President at Paris.

"While I do not doubt that the President faced great difficulties at Paris," said Mr. Newberry, "still he did not say anything that inclined me to change my mind as to the necessity of reservations."[2]

Senator Norris of Nebraska, an ardent advocate of reservations to the League of Nations covenant, made public today his letter to President Wilson declining the invitation to a White House conference early in the week. In his letter Senator Norris wrote that he felt that to attend such a conference would impose an obligation that might affect his free discussion of the treaty afterward, either in the Senate or outside of it. He suggested that the President, instead of conducting the conferences, submit to the Senate any information he desired to impart on the treaty. The letter follows: . . .

In giving out the letter, Senator Norris explained that he had obtained the consent of the President's Secretary to make it public.

Senator Capper of Kansas, in a letter sent today to his newspaper in Topeka,[3] dealt with his talk with the President concerning the Shantung award at the White House last week.

"The President went into the Shantung piracy by Japan in detail, and I gathered that he is more disturbed over this surrender of principle which undoubtedly he regarded as inescapable if he was to secure the League of Nations, with Japan as a participant, than over any other feature of the treaty. My own view is that this indorsement of a most loathsome product of secret diplomacy is wholly indefensible and that the Senate must, by means of some declaration or reservation, show that the American people do not consent to Japan's false title to a dominion over this great Chinese province, with its population equal to that of the Japanese Empire itself."

---

[2] About this meeting, Newberry wrote shortly afterward: "I had a very agreeable interview of an hour with the President, during which he made no effort to argue for the adoption of the Treaty and League. He spent a great deal of time explaining the difficulties attending his negotiations in Paris, particularly as to the Shantung settlement. He has seen about 15 Republican Senators and has asked seven more to see him to-day or tomorrow. I believe all of them have told him the same thing: that the Treaty could not be ratified without definite reservations and I personally believe that he realizes now that the Treaty in its present form has no chance of ratification.

"You will notice he keeps deferring his proposed speaking tour. This would indicate that he is preparing to accept such changes in the Treaty as our party leaders have already suggested." T. H. Newberry to Charles Elroy Townsend, July 30, 1919, CCL (T. H. Newberry Papers, Burton Historical Coll., MiD).

[3] *Topeka Daily Capital.*

[July 23, 1919]

WILSON DENIES RESPONSIBILITY FOR THE SHANTUNG SETTLEMENT

Washington, July 23.—President Wilson today denied published reports that he had told Senators he was responsible for the Shantung settlement in the treaty with Germany. A statement, issued at the White House, read:

The President authorizes the announcement that the statement carried in several of the papers this morning that he originated or formulated the provisions with regard to Shantung in the treaty of peace with Germany is altogether false. He exerted all the influence he was at liberty to exercise in the circumstances to obtain a modification of them, and believes that the ultimate action of Japan with regard to Shantung will put the whole matter in its true light.

Printed in the *New York Times*, July 24, 1919.

To Empress Zaouditou

WOODROW WILSON
PRESIDENT OF THE UNITED STATES OF AMERICA.

To Her Majesty
   Zaouditou
      Empress of Ethiopia.

Great and Good Friend:

I have received at the hands of the Ethiopian envoys the letter[1] expressing Your Imperial Majesty's pleasure and the joy of the Ethiopian Empire, that the part taken by the United States in the war for the liberty of the world has helped to bring about the victory of the nations fighting for equality and independence.

Your Majesty's good wishes afford me deep satisfaction and I share the hope that the friendly relations established between our peoples in the time of His Majesty Menelik II, will lead to the development of commercial ties by which both nations will be greatly benefited.

I trust that your reign will continue to redound to Your Majesty's glory and to the prosperity and happiness of your people, in whose affections may Your Majesty long live.

And I pray God to have Your Imperial Majesty in His safe and holy   Keeping.

Your Good Friend,   (Signed)   WOODROW WILSON

Washington, July 23, 1919.

TCL (Letterpress Books, WP, DLC).
   [1] Empress Zaouditou to WW, April 22, 1919, printed as an Enclosure with B. Long to JPT, July 12, 1919.

To Ras Taffari

WOODROW WILSON
PRESIDENT OF THE UNITED STATES OF AMERICA.

To His Royal Highness,
    Ras Taffari,
        Heir Apparent to the Throne of Ethiopia.

Greeting:

The letter of Your Royal Highness[1] congratulating the United States on the victorious issue of the recent war has been delivered to me by the Ethiopian Special Mission, and I appreciate very highly the friendly sentiments expressed therein. I also realize and regret the difficulties which prevented your country from giving its valued aid to the Allies.

In the era of peace which is now at hand, it will be the grateful task of the Ethiopian and American Governments to strengthen the friendly bonds which unite our peoples, and to bring about a closer intercourse between them, which will lead to the development of commerce and redound to their mutual advantage.

The beneficent interest of Your Royal Highness will greatly promote the attainment of these ends.

I pray God to have Your Royal Highness in His safe and holy Keeping.   (Signed)   WOODROW WILSON.

Washington, July 23, 1919.

TCL (Letterpress Books, DLC).
    [1] Ras Taffari to WW, April 22, 1919, printed as an Enclosure with B. Long to JPT, July 12, 1919.

From Josephus Daniels

My dear Mr. President: Washington. July 23, 1919.

Referring to your letter of July 17th with reference to the availability of ships for Archangel, and in view of the telegram from Mr. Cole,[1] returned herewith, directions have been given that the DES MOINES remain there for the present.
                    Faithfully yours,   Josephus Daniels

TLS (WP, DLC).
    [1] F. Cole to FLP, July 11, 1919, T telegram (WP, DLC). Cole urged that at least one American cruiser, either *Des Moines* or some smaller one, be left at Archangel for "some time" after the departure of the American railway engineers. The rapid removal of American troops and naval vessels was playing into the hands of Bolshevik propagandists and depressing adherents of the anti-Bolshevik provisional government of North Russia, who felt that the Americans were letting them down. The continued presence of an American cruiser, Cole believed, would be an important symbol of continued American support.

From Joseph Patrick Tumulty

For the President: The White House, 23 July 1919.

Mrs. Catts [Catt], of the woman suffrage organization, wishes to know for her private information if the League of Nations is to meet in Washington in October.   The Secretary

Yes—unless rebuffed by the Senate   W.W.

TL (WP, DLC).

From Joseph Patrick Tumulty, with Enclosure

Dear Governor: The White House, 23 July, 1919.

You will be interested in the enclosed points made by Mr. Taft, in his letter to Will Hayes [Hays], which he suggests as reservations.[1]   Sincerely,   Tumulty

TLS (WP, DLC).

[1] Taft had written to Will H. Hays on July 20, 1919, about the best possible strategy to win enough votes from those Republican senators who had some reservations about the Covenant to make it possible to obtain the consent of two thirds of the senators to the ratification of the Treaty of Versailles. In this long and confidential letter, Taft analyzed the political situation in the Senate and pointed out that at least nineteen Republican votes would have to be added to the probable forty-five Democratic votes in favor of the treaty in order to assure the success of the treaty. The only possible way to obtain the favorable vote of the nineteen Republicans, Taft said, was to relieve "their consciences through reassuring interpretations of the League, of such a character that they are likely to be accepted, without further negotiations and conference and delay, by the other nations who dictated the peace."

Taft added that, as far as he was concerned, the Senate might well ratify the Treaty without any reservations or interpretations, and that he was confident that the actual operation of the Treaty after ratification "would bring about exactly the same result" as that which would be obtained by the acceptance of a list of reservations and interpretations, which he had sent to Hays a short time earlier. (The Enclosure in Tumulty's letter is a paraphrase of these reservations. Their nearly final text is printed in the following document.) However, Taft went on, Wilson was himself in large measure responsible for the present political situation, in which a basically good treaty might be defeated, because Wilson had alienated so many Republican leaders and a majority of Americans by his extreme partisanship in the conduct of the war, before the congressional elections of 1918, and in his conduct of the peace negotiations. Taft then went on to explain and justify his "interpretations," which he said would not weaken the effectiveness of the League in any substantial way and which, he added, he hoped would remove "the qualms and anxious concern of friends of the League whose votes are necessary to ratify it." W. H. Taft to W. H. Hays, July 20, 1919, CCL (W. H. Taft Papers, DLC).

In a second letter to Hays on July 20, 1919, TCL (W. H. Taft Papers, DLC), Taft wrote that he thought that it would be unwise for Hays to bring his suggestions to the attention of Elihu Root, Senator Lodge, or to Republicans unalterably opposed to ratification. However, Taft did send his first letter of July 20 to a number of friends, and it, along with Taft's second letter of that date, and a paraphrase of the "reservations" or "interpretations," were leaked to the Associated Press and published in the newspapers of July 24. All that a crestfallen Taft could do was to write to the A.P. on July 26: "These letters were personal and confidential and were so plainly marked, and were published without the knowledge or consent of Mr. Hays or myself." New York Times, July 27, 1919.

Obviously, Tumulty had also come into possession of a copy of Taft's first letter to Hays of July 20, as the Enclosure with his letter plainly shows.

There are numerous letters relating to Taft's initiative between about July 13 and July 21, 1919, in Series 3 of the Taft Papers.

ENCLOSURE

Point one made by Mr. Taft in his letter to Will Hays:

1. Provision is made for retirement from the League on two years notice without reservation that retirement shall be upon conditions that the United States has fulfilled all its obligations as a member of the league, this question of fulfillment to be determined by the council. The nation withdraws as a member and the question of damages arising out of any failure to fulfil its international obligations, while a member of the league, will be determined by the machinery set up for that purpose.

2. Self-governed colonies cannot ever be represented on the council, if the home government is represented or be included in any of those clauses where the parties to the dispute are excluded from its settlement.

3. Functioning of the council under Article X shall be advisory only and not binding on the members, each of whom shall be free to determine his own obligation which in the case of the United States, would be determined by Congress.

4. Differences between the nations regarding immigration or the tariff are domestic questions and are not to be submitted to the league.

5. The Monroe Doctrine is defined as a convention under international law applicable to this hemisphere, and the right of the United States shall not be challenged in objecting to or preventing any attempt by a non-American nation contravening the principle of the Monroe Doctrine.

6. Without a waiver of any rights on the part of the United States to withdraw from the league at an earlier date, the United States gives notice of withdrawal in ten years.

CC MS (WP, DLC).

A Memorandum by William Howard Taft[1]

(Taft) "Reservations."[2]

THE SENATE OF THE UNITED STATES ADVISES AND CONSENTS TO
THE RATIFICATION OF SAID TREATY WITH THE FOLLOWING
RESERVATIONS AND INTERPRETATIONS TO BE MADE A
PART OF THE INSTRUMENT OF RATIFICATION

FIRST:

That the obligations of the United States under Article X. shall
not continue longer than five[10+] years* from the exchange of ratification of the Treaty unless the President and the Senate of the
United States by vote of two thirds of the members present shall
consent to an extension of the same.

SECOND:

That the obligations of the United States under Article X. are to
be fulfilled only by action of the Congress of the United States in
which body is vested the final power of determining in good faith
for the United States, the extent of such obligations, the happening of the conditions on which they become immediate and the
method of their fulfillment.

THIRD:

That differences between nations in respect to immigration or
duties on imports into the country of one or the other when not
limited or effected [affected?] by treaties between them, involving
solely domestic questions of the one or the other, and are not to be
submitted for consideration, decision, recommendation, or other
action by the Council, the Assembly or any other agency or tribunal of the League.

FOURTH:

That Article XXI. of the Covenant providing that nothing therein
shall effect regional understandings like the Monroe Doctrine,
classifies the Doctrine as having required [acquired] the character
of a customary convention and recognizes it as a principle of International Law in the interest of Peace with the meaning and effect
that the United States may without violation of any olbigation [ob-
ligation] or restraining covenant of the League object to and prevent any attempt by non-American nations whether by war, purchase, voluntary transfer or intrigue, to make new or additional
territorial acquisitions, or to acquire new or additional strategical
foot-holds in the Western Hemisphere, or to establish or further
the establishment of Monarchial or non-democratic government in
such hemisphere, or to secure new or additional political control
therein.

* "after talk with French Representative make it 10 years instead of 5."

FIFTH:

That whenever two years notice of withdrawal from the League of Nations shall have been given as provided in Article I. the nation giving it, shall cease to be a member of the League or subject to its obligations at the time fixed in the notice, but this shall not relieve it from such liability for damanages [damages] or recoupment as it may have incurred for its violation of its International obligations or the Covenant of the League while a member of the league to be prosecuted under any proceedure [procedure] of the league that may be applicable to and binding upon member.

SIXTH:

That the intendment of Article IV. and Article XV. is that no self governing Dominion or Colony member of the league whose home government has always a representative on the Council shall be selected by the Assembly to send a representative to the Council and that the "Representatives of one or more of the parties to the dispute," who, by Article XV. are not to join in the report of the Council or the Assembly, include all the representatives of a home government and of all its Dominions or colony thereof, as a party to the dispute to the evident intent that the action of such Council or Assembly shall in accord with the preamble of the Covenant of the League, be impartial and be solely influenced by considerations of International justice, law and equity as applied to the fairly ascertainable facts of dispute.

T MS (WP, DLC).

¹ This is a discrete undated document in WP, DLC. It is the text of the "reservations" or "interpretations," a slightly later version of which Taft had sent to Hays on July 19 and a paraphrase of which was printed in the newspapers on July 24. Letters in the Taft Papers indicate that Taft had begun to draft this document as early as July 12, and that he made the changes indicated in the text on July 17. W. H. Taft to W. H. Hays, July 13 and 17, CCL (W. H. Taft Papers, DLC).

When and how Taft's memorandum came into Wilson's hands, the Editors cannot say with confidence. Taft's intimate friend, Gustav J. Karger, Washington correspondent for the *Cincinnati Times-Star*, told Taft that Senator Kellogg told him that he, Kellogg, had shown Taft's memorandum to Wilson on July 18, and it is possible that Kellogg left this copy with Wilson at that time. Kellogg also told Karger that Wilson had talked with Hitchcock about the memorandum. Karger added the following report: "Thus far I have no definite information to the effect that the President has indicated willingness to accept interpretations. His attitude has been courteous and even gracious, however, and I believe he has done some good. I think I see some signs of yielding and as I said before there should be no real difficulty in working out a compromise. Of course Wilson will decline to compromise if the conferences he is now holding convince him that he can get the treaty through without yielding anything." G. J. Karger to W. H. Taft, July 19, 1919, TLS (W. H. Taft Papers, DLC).

² WWhw.

³ Paul-Henri-Benjamin Balluat d'Estournelles de Constant, a member of the French Senate, identified as the "French represenative" in W. H. Taft to W. H. Hays, July 17, 1919, CCL (W. H. Taft Papers, DLC).

From Brand Whitlock

Brussels July 23, 1919

Important 294. For the President. The King has just told me that he wishes to visit America and I have suggested September and October as His Majesty must return to Belgium by 15th November when elections occur. He will be accompanied by the Queen. He asked me to arrange during my leave of absence in America the details of his visit saying that he would leave it all in my hands and that he wished me to accompany him. He suggested that no more than three days be devoted to official functions so that he may be free to study our institutions and to visit the Pacific coast. He is highly enthusiastic over going and it occurs to me that his visit might have great influence in favor of the peace treaty and of the League of Nations.   Whitlock

T telegram (SDR, RG 59, 033.5511/12, DNA).

From William Cox Redfield

My dear Mr. President: Washington 23 July 1919

I do not know whether the following suggestion will be helpful but it is offered in the hope that it may be so. In view of what I understand is the Senate's refusal to permit an American to be appointed on the Reparation Commission, is it possible that one of our own men could informally act in that capacity? We have a thoroughly experienced and capable man in Paris, Mr. Chauncey D. Snow, and as you may recall, Mr. Burwell S. Cutler is on the way and can be sent to Paris if you think best.[1] Should neither suffice, we can under our general law appoint a Special Trade Commissioner, whom you may select, to do anything which would "foster, promote or develop" the commerce of the United States.

If in this matter we can be helpful, it would be a pleasure.

Sincerely yours,
William C. Redfield

TLS (WP, DLC).
[1] Chauncey Depew Snow, lawyer who had held various positions in the Department of Commerce since 1910, at this time Commercial Attaché at the American embassy in Paris; Burwell Smith Cutler, Director of the Bureau of Foreign and Domestic Commerce in the Department of Commerce.

Three Letters from Newton Diehl Baker

Personal and Confidential.

My dear Mr. President: Washington. July 23, 1919.

I have gone very carefully over the police situation with General Haan last night. Apart from the one murder, the City was much quieter than it had been anticipated and no serious disturbances took place. Such small crowds as there were on the streets were largely boys from fourteen to twenty years of age, and there was a very general observance by both white and colored people of the request of the quthorities [authorities] that persons stay at home and avoid crowds on the streets. The attitude of the colored people, particular of their leaders, is reported to have been helpful generally. I have instructed General Haan to retain the troops which were brought to the District yesterday and he is making some modifications in his disposition of them, so that their presence on the streets will be somewhat less apparent to-night, but they will be stationed at available points to meet any emergency that may arise. So far as I have been able to discover, General Haan's judgment that he has the situation well in hand is justified.

The single murder which did take place grew out of no controversy or excitement, but seems to have been an unprovoked and impulsive act, perhaps the act of a man of unstable mind, deranged by excitement growing out of the general situation.

Respectfully yours,   Newton D. Baker

Confidential.

My dear Mr. President: Washington. July 23, 1919.

Some days ago the Committee on Rules of the House of Representatives called General Churchill,[1] head of the Department of Military Intelligence to give testimony with regard to Mexican conditions. I instructed him to decline to answer any question having to do with the internal political conditions of Mexico, or the international relations of the United States and Mexico, and to say that all such matters were within the province of the State Department and not the War Department, and that any information the War Department had on that subject came to it incidentally and was transmitted to the State Department.

General Churchill was not called as the matter was abandoned by the Rules Committee and turned over to the House Committee on Foreign Relations, but I am told that Mr. Fletcher,[2] our Ambassador to Mexico, had been called as a witness before the House Committee and had testified.

I venture to call this to your attention, because it seems to me that an American Ambassador to a foreign country ought not to be permitted to testify before a Committee of Congress with regard to the affairs of the country to which he is accredited; but that any information on such a subject which the Committee desires ought to be given through the State Department. Any testimony such an Ambassador gives will, of course, be printed in the country to which he is accredited, and would inevitably tend to embarrass his position, if not indeed to destroy his usefulness as an Ambassador.

I would make this suggestion to Mr. Lansing if he were here, but I have not been able to catch him today and so I venture to transmit this to you.

Respectfully yours,   Newton D. Baker

[1] That is, Marlborough Churchill.
[2] That is, Henry Prather Fletcher.

My dear Mr. President: Washington. July 23, 1919.

We are called upon in all manner of official documents and communications to give a name to the war. We have always named our wars, as "The American Revolution," "The Mexican War," "The Civil War," and "The Spanish-American War." Present usage with regard to this war is unsettled, and various names have been suggested, as, for instance, "The Great War," "The World War," "The War of 1917," and "The War Against Teutonic Aggression."

I am told that the Navy has more or less adopted the name "The War Against Teutonic Aggression."

The commanders of the Allied Armies in devising the Victory Medal put upon its reverse side, "The Great War for Civilization."

Some of these titles seem too long to be descriptive. Great Britain is reported to have officially named the war, so far as she is concerned, "The War of 1914-1918." My own preference is for the phrase "The World War." "The Great War" would be equally descriptive, as this was the greatest war in history.

As Commander-in-Chief of the Army and Navy, would you be willing to give us your judgment so that we can all adopt it and establish the name by official sanction?

Respectfully yours,   Newton D. Baker

TLS (WP, DLC).

From Francis Edward Clark[1]

Dear President Wilson: Boston, July 23, 1919.

I have refrained from sending you my congratulations and good wishes on your return to America, knowing the flood of correspondence that must await you, and not wishing to burden you with another letter.

But I hope I may now be allowed to tell you how thoroughly we in this office appreciate the tremendous difficulties of the task you undertook in Paris, and that we thank God you were able to secure the adoption of the League of Nations, which I pray may not be wrecked by the attitude of reactionaries at home. I have done what I could by word and pen to give to the Christian Endeavorers throughout the country my views on the supreme importance of the League of Nations.

In a letter to Secretary Tumulty[2] I forwarded the earnest invitation of our Convention Committee and ventured to express the hope that you might be able and willing to speak on the League of Nations at our great biennial, international Christian Endeavor Convention to be held in Buffalo from the 5th to the 10th of August. I trust that the request may have received your favorable consideration, for your message would reach, directly and indirectly, millions of young men and women in all parts of the country.

Praying that your health may speedily be restored, I am, with sincere respect, I am [sic]

Faithfully yours,   Francis E. Clark

TLS (WP, DLC).
[1] The Rev. Dr. F. E. Clark, president of the United Society of Christian Endeavor.
[2] It is missing in WP, DLC.

From Julius Howland Barnes

My dear Mr. President: New York July 24, 1919

Your note of July nineteenth with the enclosure of the clipping from the "New York Herald" of July seventeenth[1] only reached me to-day.

I can not find that there has been any repetition of the statements made in the "Herald" dispatch mentioned, and in fact since that time Representative McCulloch, on whose statement the whole erroneous point of view was emphasized, has quoted a letter of explanation of mine in the public press and apparently has abandoned his position of criticism.

His statement, and the whole article, was based on a misconception that the Grain Corporation profit report as of July 1, included an operation under the Guarantee Act of March 4th; whereas, as you are aware, no transactions had taken place under the Act to make the Wheat Guarantee effective, and my explanation to that effect which I did make on July eighteenth through the public press apparently has stopped that line of criticism.

I was very glad to have a challenge of the profit return of the Grain Corporation so that there was occasion to make a public explanation of the source of the $23,000,000. referred to.

Excess profits forced as a refund from the mills, amounting to $4,500,000., was so distinctly the result of a determined and successful effort to protect our domestic consumers that I was glad to have this part of the earnings emphasized by that criticism, and its answer.

Interest on national capital employed for the time that that capital was withdrawn from the national treasury, at a time when the national treasury was borrowing money through national loans and paying therefor a substantial rate of interest, was so just and proper an earning of the Grain Corporation that there can be no criticism of that item, amounting to $10,000,000.

The dispute allowed us to lay emphasis on the fact that the Grain Corporation had handled, largely in overseas traffic, the enormous total of almost $2,000,000,000. worth of foodstuffs and had on that enormous business so closely calculated its profit return as to show a final earning of only one-half of one per cent on that turnover. This last item of profit on turnover, of $9,000,000., also included profits which we were justified in taking on neutral business at a time when neutrals were assessing us very high ocean rates for urgently needed steamers, so that the analysis, I think, has strengthened our whole position.

I enclose you the statement I gave out in answer to the very "Herald" dispatch which attracted your attention, and I trust this statement will meet your approval.[2]

There is a broader question, and that is the possible retirement of the Grain Corporation and the Wheat Director from appearing to be the sole reason for the wheat price in America. Recent crop developments, here and abroad, including the terrific shrinkage in our own crop prospects, and in Canada, are developing a situation which in a very short time, I believe, will enable us to seriously consider opening export gates, retiring from foodstuffs handling except as standing ready to pay the guarantee price in case reinstated supply and demand do not absorb wheat at better prices, and then there can be no justification for any claim that the Government guarantee is maintaining a wheat price level which would otherwise collapse, with its related statements that the sustained wheat price is sustaining other food levels, also;—a claim which is easily demonstrated even now to be unsupported theory, and, in my judgment, largely erroneous.

But from your own expression to me last week, I feel confident that your desire runs parallel with Mr. Hoover's and my own to take out of the private currents of business these Government Agencies such as the Grain Corporation as fast as can be done without jeopardizing the national policies, and I hope to submit to you this week in a special statement for your earnest consideration some phases of that which may shortly offer us such a solution that the National Administration can no longer be even erroneously charged with any responsibility for food levels.

Yours truly,   Julius H. Barnes.

TLS, (WP, DLC).
    [1] About which, see WW to J. H. Barnes, July 19, 1919, n. 1.
    [2] "BARNES EXPLAINS PROFITS ON GRAIN," *New York Journal of Commerce and Commercial Bulletin*, July 18, 1919, clipping (WP, DLC). Barnes summarizes the explanation in his statement of the $23,000,000 "profit" on wheat in paragraphs four to six of this letter. The balance of his statement asserted that the poor prospects for the coming wheat crop, both domestic and foreign, made it likely that whatever wheat was available would sell at well above the price at which the Grain Corporation was willing to buy. Thus, the corporation could not be held responsible for the continuing high price of wheat and, hence, of bread.

Two Letters from Newton Diehl Baker

My dear Mr. President: Washington. July 24, 1919

Mr Tafts performance in the morning paper is the ne plus ultra! His statement with regard to your wishing "to monopolise the credit" takes his measure, not yours; as it means that he cannot understand anybody having a higher motive and therefore that would have been his motive had he gone.

But the way he treats Senators Lodge, Knox and company is even worse. He openly says that the covenant and the treaty ought to be ratified but that these senators are so full of partisan rage and personal jealously of you that they will on no account do their official and public duty—therefore he proposes a few reservations which will do no good and will not improve the treaty but will please the vanity of these Senators enough to induce them to do their sworn duty by their country! Surely nobody ever said so derogating a thing before about the statesmen of his own party and he says it with his hands flat on the table and his head turned, so that he obviously does not know he has said it.

And to think, I had about given him the next Republican nomination!

But it will help—they will all now be afraid Taft means them
Heartily & respectfully yours   Newton D. Baker

ALS (WP, DLC).

My dear Mr. President: Washington. July 24, 1919.

I hand you herewith a copy of the letter with regard to Conscientious Objectors to which I referred the other day.[1] As I look at it
now I realize that it is much too long. The meat of the matter begins at the middle of page three.

In view of our conversation, I shall assume your sympathy with
my suggestions so that it will not be necessary for you to write me
with regard to the matter.

Respectfully yours,   Newton D. Baker

TLS, (WP, DLC).
[1] Baker had already sent the enclosure to Wilson: NDB to WW, July 1, 1919. Wilson
must have misplaced it and asked Baker for another copy.

From Charles Henry Grasty

Dear Mr President: Washington July 24 1919.

I venture to lay before you the substance and implications of several suggestions appearing in a dispatch from me in *The Times*
today:[1]

1—Any interpretative resolution by the Senate changing the
treaty and requiring its resubmission to the contracting parties is
unthinkable in the present state of the world. Every nation wants
a great deal more than it got and many think that they got relatively less than some of their Allies. Agreement was secured while
matters were still fresh and under the influence of our effective
military and economic help. The wounds of the war are very deep
and unless healed by "first intention" may not be healed at all. To
fling the treaty back into the mumbo-jumbo of European controversy would be to take risks that would be unjustifiable, after securing a treaty that is satisfactory and which has already faced the
world away from war toward peace.

2—There should be no "reservations" (a word that would instantly alarm Europe) or any changes in the meaning of the terms
agreed to. The case is entirely different as regards interpretations
which shall have the effect of more clearly expressing the sense in
which the minds of the conferees met & of removing all ambiguity.
These would be advisable and welcome. Resolutions in an interpretative sense would be controlling if subsequently there ap-

peared any ambiguity. unless there were prompt dissent by other nations.

3—I pointed out Mr Clemenceau's success in meeting his very insecure situation in the Chamber by a full and frank exposition before that body.[2] I believe that similar statements by the President from time to time would profoundly affect this country, would bring to bear on the Senate the reflex of an informed opinion and result in an early and righteous settlement. The sincere efforts made to familiarize Senators with European conditions and the circumstances in which agreement was reached in the Conference have already influenced the American public. I believe that the same methods which prevailed over opposition in Paris will prevail here, and the more easily because the people can be appealed to.

I have the honor to remain

Most Sincerely Yours   Charles H Grasty.

ALS (WP, DLC).
    [1] Charles H. Grasty, "FINDS SENTIMENT FOR RATIFICATION. Observer Thinks Popular Feeling is Making Itself Felt in Washington," *New York Times*, July 14, 1919.
    [2] Grasty's argument in *ibid.* with regard to Clemenceau's success in the Chamber of Deputies ran as follows:
    "There is a certain parallel between Clemenceau's position in respect to the French Chamber and President Wilson's in respect to Congress.
    "Clemenceau's Government does not control a majority, but his opponents are unable to rally their vote against him. His audacity and his fitness to make war, especially in the last quarter of an hour, gave him the respect of public opinion, and his opponents have not yet been able to down him, although often, on a cloakroom count of noses, they could reckon a majority against him. Since the armistice Clemenceau has been vulnerable, owing to his acknowledged lack of capacity for reconstructive work. He is a critic and not a builder by instinct, and he is 78 years old, with a bullet in his lung. . . .
    "The difference in the two system[s] of France and America prevents the parallel between Wilson and Clemenceau from being extended too far. Clemenceau goes down like a shot when his lack of a majority in the Chamber discloses itself in a vote. No matter what Mr. Wilson's backing or lack of it in Congress, he will be President till March 4, 1921.
    "On the other hand, whenever he is threatened, Clemenceau faces the music and mounts the tribune. That is what he is required by practice and tradition to do. It gives him a wonderful, dramatic, sporting opportunity, which he enjoys and employs to the utmost.
    "The opposition may have him when he appears in the tribune. He melts away enough of it to save himself. If President Wilson, who is no less a fighter, had a similar advantage, who doubts that much of the secret, partisan, personal, and vindictive opposition would disappear?
    "He can go to the Capitol, but a visit implies his seeking an opportunity to intervene, whereas the Tiger has his back against the wall in the Chamber. It is a fight for blood and all France listens tensely.
    "It would be most useful now if just such a method could be adopted in thrashing out the differences between the President and the Senate. The great public would sit by, hearing and weighing every word, and an informed public opinion would be the deciding factor. It will eventually be the deciding factor anyway, but the interest and information will be in less degree."
    Obviously, Grasty's argument applied to the whole of Clemenceau's ministry. But he probably had specifically in mind the vote of confidence which the ministry had received in the Chamber of Deputies on July 22. The debate preceding the vote had been primarily upon domestic rather than foreign policy. At the climax, Clemenceau had in fact mounted the dais and addressed his opponents in defiant, though very general, terms. The vote was 272 in favor of Clemenceau's government to 181 against. *Ibid.*, July 23, 1919.

From Simon Wolf

My dear Mr President.   South Poland, Me. July 24/19

Personally, and officially as the Representative of the Independent Order of Bnai-Bri'th and as chairman of the Board of Delegates of the Union of American Hebrew Congregations, I take great pleasure in thanking and congratulating you for the outcome, as reported, in securing equal rights for the peoples of such countries, as have heretofore been denied. During your entire administration you have promptly answered every appeal to use your good offices at the Peace Conference. Your repeated assurances made to me as evidenced in the published correspondences have been redeemed, and the dawn of a better day, has at last been ushered in for my long suffering correligionists.

This is doubly gratifying, to have an American and a Christian work for the accomplishment so essential to the happiness of all peoples.

For what elevates the Jew elevates the Christian, and the converse is equally true.   Sincerely   Simon Wolf

ALS (WP, DLC).

From Frank William Taussig

My dear Wilson: Cotuit, Massachusetts, July 24, 1919.

I am going to drop formalities and address you as of old, to say how great is my regret on all personal grounds on severing my connection with your Administration. You know, but I am glad to say again, that I feel unbounded admiration for your purposes and achievements, and am sure of the place which your Administration will have in history. So far as domestic problems are concerned, you have not been able to accomplish all I suspect to have been in your hopes; for the war has brought unexpected complications and has interrupted the course of political and social reform. But what you have done during the war has justified the highest hopes of your friends and, most of all, they have been able to maintain unshaken their faith in the nobility of your character.

So far as concerns the Tariff Commission, I am enclosing a memorandum[1] which may go on [in] your files for consultation at any convenient time. I lay most stress of all on the desirability of putting in Page[2] at once as Chairman.

One final word about myself. I plan to resume work at the University in the autumn, and I have literary jobs cut out which will suffice to keep me busy for the rest of my life. I assume that no imperative calls for a return to public life will come to me. But one call there is, not to be considered imperative, which might tempt me. I have great intellectual interest in what is now going on in Germany, not only because the peace of the whole world is involved in her internal development, but because she is likely to try social and economic experiments of a radical and yet not necessarily impracticable sort. If I should by any chance be asked to serve as Minister to that country I should be tempted. Under existing circumstances a man of modest means and academic antecedents might be not acceptable. You have your own ideas on this matter, as on every other, and will quietly record this possibility without favor or prejudice.

I trust you have recovered from your indisposition and are able to take up the gallant fight with vigor. That I wish you success and have full confidence in the outcome needs not again be said.

Believe me,   Always sincerely yours,   F. W. Taussig

TLS (WP, DLC).
  [1] "MEMORANDUM FOR THE PRESIDENT ON THE TARIFF COMMISSION," TS MS dated July 24, 1919 (WP, DLC). It urged Page's appointment as Chairman of the Tariff Commission. It also urged the appointment of a Republican in good standing to take Taussig's place, in order to insure bipartisan support for the commission. "I will endeavor to find the right man," the memorandum concluded, "and at all events hope that the place will not be filled until he can be found."
  [2] Thomas Walker Page, who became Chairman of the Tariff Commission in January 1920.

Ronald Charles Lindsay[1] to the Duke of Devonshire[2]

Washington, Recd. by Post 24th July 1919.
Following sent to Foreign Office No. 1184 July 21st.

CONFIDENTIAL.

All last week in Senate the discussion on treaty proceeded, Shantung settlement being the main theme. Especially in view of reported Japanese atrocities in Corea[3] sentiment is strongly hostile, but it is recognised that America's attitude on Japanese demands of 1915 makes it difficult for her to dissent from this section of the treaty, and that the Powers have been compelled by events to acquiesce reluctantly in a distasteful arrangement.

Foreign Relations Committee is now reading treaty and will take a long time, it is really waiting on events. When final vote on ratification will take place it is difficult to foresee, but an utterance by Chairman of Committee indicates that he expects whole treaty to be finally disposed of about the end of September.

Am informed by Lodge that treaty cannot be passed without a reservation making it clear that in no case shall United States Government be under any obligation whether moral or expressed, to take any action merely at behest of League. Lodge claims that thirty three Senators are pledged definitely to make this a sine qua non of ratification, enough in fact to make a deadlock if their view is not accepted.

Everybody is making lists of Senators pledged to this or that view, but even the best are very conjectural. It is stated that President is engaged in constant conferences with individual Senators with good effect. Since his return his attitude has been very conciliatory, and this is so new that it has given rise to reports that he is prepared to make concessions on question of substance, but such reports are really quite unfounded.

Repeated to Canada by Post.   (Sd.)   Lindsay.

T telegram (R. L. Borden Papers, CaOOA).
  [1] First Secretary of the British embassy in Washington.
  [2] Victor Christian William Cavendish, 9th Duke of Devonshire, Governor-General of Canada.
  [3] About which, see FLP to the American Commissioners, March 22, 1919, n. 2, Vol. 56.

Two News Reports

[*July 25, 1919*]

URGING JAPAN TO SETTLE
Wilson Tells Spencer of Hope of Agreement in a Few Days.

Washington, July 25.—Negotiations with Japan over the Shantung provisions of the Peace Treaty, it became known today, have progressed to a point where President Wilson expects to announce a satisfactory settlement within a few days. This became known after a conference at the White House between the President and Senator Spencer, Republican, of Missouri. Senator Spencer presented the draft of a resolution of ratification previously submitted to the Foreign Relations Committee, and now discussed with the President, according to one account, at the suggestion of Chairman Lodge, one of those reservations related to Shantung, and this led to the intimations by President Wilson of the impending developments.

Senator Spencer said that he believed the acceptance of the reservations would insure the early ratification of the treaty by the Senate. Mr. Wilson promised to take them under consideration.

President Wilson intimated to Senator Spencer that the expected arrangement on Shantung would remove much, if not all, of the opposition to that part of the treaty. The State Department, Senator Spencer said, was at work on the matter. He declined to go into

detail, but it was believed that he referred to the visit of Mr. Debuchi, Japanese Chargé, to the State Department yesterday, followed by a call today by President Wilson on Secretary Lansing.[2]

The result of activities here is expected to be a statement by the
Japanese Government concerning the return of Shantung to
China, and another from China accepting the Japanese terms.

This was hinted at a week ago by Senator Hitchcock after a talk
with President Wilson, and was again touched upon today by Senator Spencer, who said that he thought that if Japan would make
an offer which China accepted, it would remove most, though not
all, of the objections. The suspicion would remain, he said, that
China, as usual, had been forced to take the settlement.

The reservations proposed by Senator Spencer read:

"Resolved (two-thirds of the Senators present concurring
therein)—That the Senate advise and consent to the ratification
of the treaty of peace between the allied and associated powers
and Germany, signed on the 28th day of June, 1919, and presented to the Senate by the President on the 10th day of July,
1919.

Resolved further, That the advice and consent of the Senate to
such ratification is given with the full understanding, which is
made a part of the instrument of ratification and is the basis of
the consent of the United States to the treaty, and is the condition of the identification of the United States with the League of
Nations, that nothing in the said treaty or in any part thereof
shall ever be construed as in any degree either interfering with
or restricting the following three essential principles which are a
part of the established policy of the United States.

First, that the Monroe Doctrine is an essential national policy
of the United States, and that the necessity and extent of its application and enforcement are matters to be determined by the
United States alone as the occasion for interpretation may from
time to time arise and without interference, direct or indirect, on
the part of any other nation.

Second, that internal questions entirely domestic in character,
such as immigration and tariff, notwithstanding certain international results that may from time to time naturally be connected therewith, are matters to be determined solely by the
country in which they arise, and are under no circumstances to
be regarded as within the jurisdiction or under the control of the
League of Nations.

Third, that inasmuch as the United States is governed by a
written Constitution, the provisions of which are supreme and
controlling in this Republic, over every act, legislative, executive

or judicial, and by such Constitution it is expressly provided that the power to declare war is vested exclusively in the Congress of the United States, it is apparent that the United States cannot bind itself in advance either to make war in the future or to send its army or navy into other lands for purpose of control, which is an act of war, without the express authorization of Congress at the time, and, therefore, whether the United States, as the necessity for such action in the future may arise, shall by any military or naval force co-operate in maintaining any of the provisions of the League of Nations, is a matter which the Congress, under the provisions of the Constitution of the United States is, and must be entirely free to determine by what in its judgment is at the time consistent with the honor and interest and duty of the American people, and

With the further understanding that the right of the United States to withdraw from the League of Nations, after giving notice of its intent so to withdraw and after the expiration of the time prescribed by the covenant, includes the right to determine for itself whether all its international obligations and all its obligations under the covenant have been fulfilled at the time of its withdrawal.

In thus ratifying the treaty of peace with the reservations hereinabove set out, the Senate cannot refrain from expressing its deep regret at the provisions of the treaty (Sections 156, 157, 158,) which transfer to Japan such broad rights and powers and physical possession over the territory and people in the Shantung Peninsula of China, as being alike disregardful of the true rights and deep seated desires of more than thirty-six millions of Chinese inhabiting the peninsula, unjust to the Republic of China, and threatening to the future peace of the world.

It is the sincere hope of the United States that this manifest injustice may be speedily reconsidered and remedied.

"I found Mr. Wilson afraid of action that would reopen negotiations," said Senator Spencer. "But I do not believe he would seriously oppose reservations, not inherently bad, if their adoption were necessary to insure acceptance of the treaty by the world.

"He is simply afraid that if the Senate does qualify the treaty in any way, complications will ensue through counter-reservations by other nations, which would threaten the destruction of all the work done."

Mr. Spencer also told the President, he said, that sentiment in the Senate and throughout the country was veering rapidly in the direction of a rejection of the treaty unless some provision was made definitely protecting American rights.

"The President, however, seemed to think," said Senator Spencer, "that so many diverse criticisms and objections will be raised, each starting a little current of opposition, that they will gradually neutralise each other."

Senator Warren, Republican, of Wyoming, also conferred with the President, but refused to discuss the conference. . . .

[1] Wilson talked to Lansing about Japan and Siberia in the morning of July 25. About their meeting, see the extract from the Lansing Desk Diary printed below. About this time, Wilson began to meet with Lansing on a daily basis. This is the time when Wilson seems to have had greatest confidence in his Secretary of State, as Breckinridge Long notes in a memoir dated 1924, T MS (B. Long Papers, DLC).

[*July 25, 1919*]

Wilson to Withhold French Treaty Till Tour Ends; Lodge Not to Press Request for Its Submission

Washington, July 25.—President Wilson intends to withhold the French treaty from the Senate until he has returned from his speechmaking tour. This was stated at the White House today.

When Senator Lodge was informed of the President's intention he at once indicated that it would be useless to try to pass the resolution requesting the immediate submission of the treaty, in accordance with the published text of Article IV. of the convention, which expressly provides that it be laid before the Senate at the same time as the Peace Treaty. He will not press his resolution.

Mr. Lodge and other members of the Foreign Relations Committee hold the view that every day President Wilson keeps back the French Treaty adds to his responsibility. They expect this responsibility to become embarrassing to him in the near future.

They asserted today in conversation that Mr. Wilson was not "breaking faith" with the Senate, but with Premier Clemenceau, who signed the treaty with him. It was indicated that the President's position was to be made the target for more attacks when the Senate resumed its sessions next week.

Republican Senators today sought from their Democratic colleagues some explanation of Mr. Wilson's delay on the French Treaty. None was forthcoming, except that he was the best judge of his obligation in the matter, and could be depended on not to be swayed from whatever course he deemed proper by Senate attacks.

Printed in the *New York Times*, July 26, 1919.

To Henry Cabot Lodge

My dear Senator: [The White House] 25 July, 1919.

In response to your letter of July 22nd[1] requesting me, on behalf of the Committee on Foreign Relations, to send to the Committee the agreement referred to in Article 237 of the Treaty with Germany, in the event that such an agreement has been determined upon by the Allied and Associated Governments, I would say that so far as I know such an agreement has not yet been reached. As I recollect the business, an attempt was being made to reach such an agreement, but I have not yet learned of an agreement having been arrived at.

May I not add, with regard to other requests which I have received from the Committee for papers and information of various sorts, that I was not able to bring from Paris a complete file of papers. I brought with me only those which happened to be in my hands when I left France. These alone constitute a considerable mass of papers, and I have been going over them as rapidly as time and my engagements permitted, and must beg the Committee's indulgence for the delay in informing them which I can supply them with.   Very sincerely yours,   Woodrow Wilson

TLS (Foreign Relations Committee Papers, RG 46, DNA).
[1] H. C. Lodge to WW, July 22, 1919 (third letter of that date).

To William Cox Redfield

My dear Mr. Secretary: [The White House] 25 July, 1919.

The trouble about having anybody do informally what the Senate Committee is not willing to have done formally is that it might create a misunderstanding, and I am afraid we had better let matters alone and let the consequences of what the Senate Committee has done presently appear, as they certainly will.

Cordially and faithfully yours,   [Woodrow Wilson]

CCL (WP, DLC).

To Henry White

The White House, 25 July, 1919.

I greatly value and admire the way you have been handling the Italians in the matter of the Adriatic and Asia Minor. This is just a word of sincere appreciation.

May I not urge, in connection with the Greek claims in Thrace, that inasmuch as I think there is a very serious danger of producing bitterness and friction by either choice presented to the Council, it would be wise to urge the alternative suggestion already once made, that the portion of Thrace in question between Greece and Bulgaria should be included in the mandate for Constantinople. This seems a practicable solution and, I believe, would be more likely to promote the peace of the world than either of the others.

Woodrow Wilson

T telegram (WP, DLC).

To James Henry Taylor

My dear Mr. Taylor: The White House 25 July, 1919.
   I sincerely hope I shall be able to get to the church on Sunday for the Communion Service, and thank you for your letter of the twenty-second. I hope that you will have a real rest along with your vacation. You generally use it for business.
   In haste,   Faithfully yours,   Woodrow Wilson

TLS (WP, DLC).

To May Randolph Petty

My dear Mrs. Petty: [The White House] 25 July, 1919.
   Illness and public business combined to have prevented my acknowledging your letter of July 18th enclosing your check for $135.00 in payment of the loan I was so glad to let you have.
   I am so poor a hand at keeping my private papers in order that I find that I cannot put my hand on the note you sent me, and therefore am enclosing a receipt which I think will cover the matter thoroughly, and you may be sure that if I come across the note, I will return it to you to be destroyed.
   In haste, but with the warmest good wishes for you both.
                    Sincerely yours,   Woodrow Wilson

TLS (Letterpress Books, WP, DLC).

To Hugh Campbell Wallace

My dear Wallace: [The White House] 25 July, 1919
   No apologies were needed for sending me your excellent speeches enclosed in your letter of July fifth, and I am glad that

you racked [raked] Walter Berry fore and aft.[1] He is just the sort I have an absolute contempt for.

It was very delightful to see you constantly gaining in influence and approval in Paris, and you may be sure that I follow everything you do with the greatest interest and sympathy.

Things are very much mixed over here, but after we go through a certain distemper, I still feel confident that they will work out all tight [right].

With warmest regards from us both to you both,

Cordially and sincerely yours,   Woodrow Wilson

TLS (Letterpress Books, WP, DLC).
  [1] H. C. Wallace to WW, July 5, 1919, TLS (WP, DLC). Wallace enclosed T MSS (WP, DLC) of addresses he had made on July 4 at the tomb of Lafayette and at a luncheon of the American Chamber of Commerce in Paris. He also enclosed a T MS (WP, DLC) of the speech of Walter Van Rensselaer Berry, the president of the American Chamber of Commerce in Paris, at the latter affair. In his letter, Wallace referred to Berry as "a dirty puppy," who was "anti-Administration."

To William Procter Gould Harding

My dear Mr. Harding: [The White House] 25 July, 1919.

You are very kind to remember my former suggestion that Professor Fine of Princeton should be asked to serve as Secretary of the Federal Reserve Board. I am very much obliged to you for the suggestion you make in your letter of July 21st.[1] Knowing my former colleague's preferences and engagements, I have very little hope that he would be willing to give up University work now. He is, moreover, probably by this time sixty years old or thereabouts, and I doubt whether it would be wise to try to induct even a man of his extraordinary ability into a new place of this sort so near the end of his active career.

I warmly appreciate your own letter and hope that everything goes well with you.

Cordially and sincerely yours,   Woodrow Wilson

TLS (Letterpress Books, WP, DLC).
  [1] W. P. G. Harding to WW, July 21, 1919, ALS (WP, DLC). Harding reminded Wilson that in 1914 the members of the Federal Reserve Board had elected Henry Burchard Fine, Wilson's long-time friend and colleague at Princeton University, to be Secretary of the Board at a salary of $6,000 per annum. Fine had at that time declined on the ground that the salary was "inadequate for his needs," as Harding put it. Since the position was presently vacant, and since its salary was now $10,000 per year, Harding was writing to inquire whether Wilson thought that Fine might now accept the place, and whether his appointment would still be "gratifying" to Wilson. WW to H. B. Fine, Aug. 14, 1914, WWhw telegram, and H. B. Fine to WW, Aug. 18, 1914, ALS, both in WP, DLC, confirm that Wilson had proposed Fine's appointment to members of the Federal Reserve Board in mid-August 1914 and that Fine had declined the position for financial and professional reasons.

From Joseph Patrick Tumulty, with Enclosure

Dear Governor: The White House, July 25, 1919.

I hope you will read this at once. I thought it so important I had it taken stenographically over the telephone. Would it not be a good thing for you to send for Pittman?   J.P.T.

TL (WP, DLC).

E N C L O S U R E

Statement from Senator Pittman over the telephone, July 25, 1919.

We had a field day today. Those who favored the approval of the Treaty without any changes whatever, by reservation or amendment or interpretative clause, gained votes. My speech[1] was listened to carefully. I proved by precedents of the Senate, decisions of the Supreme Court, and quotations from works on the ratification of treaties that any language added to the Treaty in the form of amendment or in the resolution of ratification became a part of the Treaty and necessitated a re-submission of the Treaty to the various Parliaments or other agencies in all of the other countries—parties to the Treaty—for their approval or rejection or further change. I showed that the Parliaments of Great Britain, France and Italy would have to approve any changes, even if only in wording, that might be made by the Senate. I also demonstrated that if any of the other countries added any interpretation or reservation to the Treaty either with regard to the matters that we had changed, or with regard to matters particularly affecting their own interests, each of such changes would not only have to come back to the United States Senate for its consideration and approval, but that it would again have to go to each of the other governments for approval, rejection or final amendment. It was clear that such a procedure being engaged in by 27 nations would be interminable.

I then called attention to conditions in Europe and the chaos that would naturally follow. I stated that while we might not suffer any direct effects by a long postponement of the ratification of the Treaty, conditions in Europe required immediate action; that Bolshevism was the only thing that was growing in Europe. I went on further to state that it was a rank and poisonous weed and that unless we insisted on cutting it down and stamping it into the dust immediately, its seeds would be scattered over the world.

Senator Borah followed me, and after making interrogations he stated that it was impossible for any lawyer to dispute the propositions that I had made—that there was only one alternative, and that was either to defeat the Treaty or approve and ratify it as negotiated by the President. He then criticised Taft and stated that the Ex-President admitted that he was actuated in his recommendation of reservations solely by political expediency; that it was such expediency that was moving most of those who are supporting the plan for interpretative reservations. He said that as far as he was concerned he was going to do all in his power to see that there was an issue between the adopting and the rejection of the Treaty; that he served notice that he would vote against every amendment to the Treaty or reservation in the resolution of approval.

I had a talk with Senator Borah after he had finished speaking. I consider my conversation with him of considerable importance. I do not care to discuss it over the phone.

T MS (WP, DLC).
[1] Pittman's and Borah's speeches are printed in *Cong. Record*, 66th Cong., lst sess., pp. 3130-35, 3141-49.

Two Letters from Joseph Patrick Tumulty

Dear Governor: The White House 25 July 1919.

I am calling your attention to this clipping containing a statement by Cardinal Gibbons favoring the League of Nations.[1]

On the information I have been able to get, there is a tremendous effort being made to line up the Catholic Church against the League of Nations by the Irish Catholic priests led by Cardinal O'Connell of Boston.[2] It is evident from the interviews that have appeared in the last few weeks that Cardinal Gibbons is fighting this. There isn't any doubt that he carries more weight than O'Connell or Archbishop Hayes[3] of New York, and I think we ought to do everything we can to encourage him openly to support the League. If you could write him a letter, personal and confidential, expressing your deep appreciation of the interview which I am calling to your attention and saying how important it is that the League of Nations be speedily adopted and that you count upon all lovers of humanity to support you, I think it would bring results.

This is really more important than I can tell you. If we can get the Cardinal on our side, the attitude of the Irish in the country will have little weight with the Senate.

Sincerely yours,   Tumulty

[1] "Cardinal's Prediction Is League Agreement," clipping from the *Washington Post*, July 25, 1919. This report, datelined "Baltimore, Md., July 24," printed the statement of Cardinal Gibbons as follows: "It is my firm conviction that after thorough and honest discussion in both houses of Congress, both parties will finally arrive at a common

agreement, based upon a just and sincere league of nations that will give us a reasonable guarantee against the horrors of war in the future as well as well-grounded assurance of lasting peace without in any way impairing American sovereignty or surrendering any American right and without involving us in entangling alliances. I am sure that an early adoption of the league of nations will infuse intense joy throughout the United States without distinction of party and will be hailed with satisfaction by the allied powers of Europe."

² That is, William Henry Cardinal O'Connell.

³ The Most Rev. Patrick Joseph Hayes.

Dear Governor: The White House 25 July 1919.

One of the important parts of the New York Times editorial¹ I did not call your attention to.

It is this:

"It is for the President to determine whether he will accept the additions to the Act which they propose or any additions at all. The line between amendments, which would be destructive of a treaty, and merely interpretations, he must draw and he (the President) will draw it sharply."

Incidentally, if you make the statement we discussed yesterday, would not this cut off Taft's and Will Hays' retreat and make the issue we will finally put forth, more definite and certain?

Sincerely yours,   J P Tumulty

In this matter, time is of the essence.

TLS (WP, DLC).

¹ "MR. TAFT'S SUGGESTIONS," *New York Times*, July 25, 1919.

To James Cardinal Gibbons

PERSONAL AND CONFIDENTIAL

My dear Cardinal Gibbons: The White House 25 July, 1919.

It is with the deepest pleasure that I learn from this morning's Washington Post of your statement with regard to the League of Nations. You have perceived, as is habitual with you, the really profound interests of humanity and of Christianity which are involved in the issue of the adoption of the League Covenant, and it is with profound pleasure that I find myself alligned alongside of you in this great cause, to which the anxious and prayerful thought of every Christian man, it seems to me, must turn with hope that will permit no denial.

Even a serious delay in the adoption of the League will do much to institute anxiety throughout the world, not excepting Europe, and I know of what significance it will prove to be that you should lend your great influence to prevent giving even an added opportunity to the forces of disorder and of evil.

Cordially and sincerely yours,   Woodrow Wilson

TLS (Baltimore Cathedral Archives).

From the Desk Diary of Robert Lansing

Friday July 25 [1919]

President arrived and discussed Japan and Siberia. Talked of sending Czecho Slovaks thro Bolshevist Russia. I told him they would be murdered. He abandoned idea. . . .

Japanese Chargé came at request. Told him Prest felt compelled to make public Japan's promises in re Shantung unless Japanese Govt did it. He asked how soon. Told him not later than Tuesday.

Hw bound diary (R. Lansing Papers, DLC).

To Robert Lansing, with Enclosure

My dear Mr. Secretary: [The White House] 25 July, 1919.

I am inclined to agree to the course of action proposed by Polk[1] with regard to this important matter, but do not like to do so without first getting your own reaction in the matter. What do you think of it?

Cordially and faithfully yours,   Woodrow Wilson

TLS (Letterpress Books, WP, DLC).
[1] Wilson meant to say Phillips. At this point, Polk was on his way to France, and there are no radiograms from him to Wilson from the time he left Washington on July 21 and the time of his arrival in Paris on July 29.

ENCLOSURE

From William Phillips

Dear Mr. President: Washington July 23, 1919.

May I call to your attention the enclosed despatch from Paris,[1] the last paragraph of which seems to require an answer? Mr. Miller[2] is of the opinion that the proposed Commission of Inquiry is not a Commission provided for by the Treaty of Peace and is thus not within the decision of the Senate Committee on Foreign Relations yesterday.[3]

If you decide to detail an officer of the Army or the Navy to act on this Commission of Inquiry, the expenses would, I should think, be payable out of the appropriation for the Army or the Navy and would doubtless be very small.[4]

Faithfully yours,   William Phillips

TLS (SDR, RG 59, 763.72/13211, DNA).

[1] H. White to RL, Urgent, No. 3214, July 18, 1919, T telegram (SDR, RG 59, 763.72/13211, DNA). White reported that, at a meeting of the Supreme Council in the morning of July 18, Clemenceau had communicated a message, dated July 15, 1919, from the Acting Grand Vizier of Turkey. This message declared that Greek troops had extended their occupation beyond the vilayet of Smyrna into Muslim territory; that they had been guilty of widespread atrocities against the local population, not sparing women and children; and that thousands of the Turkish inhabitants had perished and more than 144,000 had been forced to flee. White further stated that Balfour had said that these reports were true, and that even Vénisélos had admitted that they were accurate. Clemenceau, White continued, had proposed the immediate dispatch of an inter-Allied commission of inquiry and had said that he would send a French general to investigate on his own if his colleagues did not agree to cooperate. The French, British, and Italian delegates had agreed at a meeting in the afternoon to send the commission of inquiry, and White had agreed to refer the matter to Washington. "I shall be grateful," White concluded, "if you will let me know as soon as possible the President's decision in the matter and beg to point out that it will be necessary to make some provision for the expenses of the American representative, should one be appointed, as this mission is not in a position to furnish the necessary funds."

[2] That is, David Hunter Miller, at this time a special assistant in the Department of State. In a memorandum for the President, dated July 23, 1919 (TS MS, SDR, RG 59, 763.72/13211, DNA), Miller advised that the proposed commission of inquiry was not a commission established by the peace treaty; hence, the President, without the consent of the Foreign Relations Committee, could detail an army or navy officer to serve on the commission of inquiry. The expenses of such detail would be payable out of the appropriation for the army or navy.

[3] See H. C. Lodge to WW, July 22, 1919 (first letter of that date).

[4] Wilson must have given his decision orally to Lansing at their meeting at the State Department on July 25. In any event, Lansing replied at once to White as follows: "President has approved appointment of Admiral Bristol as American Representative on Interallied Commission of Inquiry. Navy Department will give instructions through Admiral Knapp to Admiral Bristol." RL to Ammission, No. 2635, July 25, 1919, T telegram (SDR, RG 59, 763.72/13211, DNA).

To Robert Lansing, with Enclosures

My dear Lansing: [The White House] 25 July, 1919.

Here are two letters, one a letter of resignation from Reinsch. I would be very much obliged to you if you would read them and then let me have any advice you are prepared to give me on the subject of my replies.

Cordially and faithfully yours,   Woodrow Wilson

TLS (Letterpress Books, WP, DLC).

E N C L O S U R E   I

From Paul Samuel Reinsch

Dear Mr. President: Peking China, June 7th, 1919.

I have the honor to place in your hands my resignation as Minister to China and to request that I may be relieved of the duties of this post as soon as convenient to yourself and to the Secretary of State. My reason for this action is that I am wearied after nearly six years of continuous strain, that I feel that the interests of my family demand my return to the United States, and that I should like to re-enter affairs at home without making my absence so long as to break off all of the most important relationships.[1]

I desire to thank you for the confidence you have reposed in me and it shall be my greatest desire to continue in the future to co-operate in helping to realize those great purposes of national and international policy which you have so clearly and strongly put before the American nation and the world.

In making this communication to you I cannot but refer to recent developments with respect to China. The general outlook is indeed most discouraging, and it seems impossible to accomplish anything here at present or until the home governments are willing to face the situation and to act. It is not difficulties that deter me and I should stay at my post if it were necessary and if I did not think that I could be of more use in the United States than in China at the present time. But in fact, the situation requires that the American people should be made to realize what is at stake here for us in order that they may give the necessary backing to the government for support in any action which the developments here may require. Unless the American people realize this and the government feels strong enough to take adequate action, the fruits of one hundred and forty years of American work in China will inevitably be lost. Our people will be permitted to exist here only on the sufferance of others, and the great opportunity which has been held out to us by the Chinese people to assist in the development of education and free institutions will be gone beyond recall. In its stead there will come a sinister situation dominated by the unscrupulous methods of the reactionary military regime centered in Tokyo, absolutist in tendency, cynical of the principles of free government and human progress. If this force with all the methods it is accustomed to apply remains unopposed there will be created in the Far East the greatest engine of military oppression and dom-

---

[1] Noel H. Pugach, *Paul S. Reinsch: Open Door Diplomat in Action* (Millwood, N. Y., 1979), pp. 265-66, says that the Shantung settlement at Paris was an important factor in Reinsch's decision to resign and his later break with Wilson.

inance that the world has yet seen. Nor can we avoid the conclusion that the brunt of evil results will fall on the United States, as is already foreshadowed by the bitter hostility and abnormal vituperativeness of the Japanese press with regard to America.

The United States and Great Britain will have to stand together in this matter; I do not think this is realized as fully by Britishers at home than [as] by those out here. If Russia can become an independent representative government its interests would parallel ours. The forces of public opinion and strength which can thus be mobilized are entirely sufficient to control the situation here and to keep it from assuming the menacing character which is threatened at present; but this can only be done if the situation is clearly seen and if it is realized that the military party of Japan will continue its present methods and purposes which have proved successful until it becomes a dead wall of firm, quiet opposition. There will be a great deal of talk of friendship for China, of restoration of Shantung, of loyalty to the League of Nations, but it will be dangerous to accept this and to stop questioning what are the methods actually applied: as long as they exist the menace is growing all the time. We cannot rest secure on treaties nor even on the League of Nations without this checking up of the facts. Otherwise these instruments would only make the game a little more complicated but not change its essential character. The menace can be avoided only if it is made plain to Japan that her purposes are unmistakable and that the methods utilized to effect them will by no means be tolerated. Such purposes are the stirring up of trouble and revolution, encouragement of bandits and pirates, morphia, financial corruption, misleading of the press, refusal of just satisfaction when Americans are injured in order to gain prestige for absolute power, and chief of all official duplicity, such as the disavowal of knowledge when loans are being made to the Chinese Government by leading Japanese banks and the subsequent statement by the Japanese Minister that these loans were private arrangements by "merchants."

If continuous quiet support could be given not only to the activities of American missionaries and merchants but to the constructive forces in Chinese national life itself these purposes and methods would not have the chance to flourish and succeed which they now enjoy.

During the war our action in the support of constructive forces in China necessarily could not be effective, as our energies were required elsewhere. Yet I believe that a great opportunity was missed when China had broken off relations with Germany. The very least recognition of her sentiments, support and efforts on our part would have changed the entire situation. But while millions upon millions were paid to the least important of the countries of Europe not a cent was forthcoming for China. This lack of support drove Tuan[2] and his followers into the arms of the pro-Japanese agents. Instead of support we gave China the Lansing-Ishii note (as interpreted by Japan).

Throughout this period the Japanese game has still been in the stage of bluff; while Germany seemed at her strongest in the war indeed the Japanese were perhaps making their veiled threats with a feeling that if they should ally themselves with a strong Germany the two would be invincible; but even at that time a portion of the American navy detached could have check-mated Japan. Since the complete breakdown of Germany the case of Japan has been carried through solely on bluff, though perhaps it may be that the Japanese militarists have succeeded in convincing themselves that their establishment is formidable. But it is plain that they would be absolutely powerless in the face of a stoppage of commerce and a navy demonstration on the part of any one of the Great Powers. No one desires to think of this contingency but it is plain that after the breakdown of Germany it was not feasible for Japan to use force nor could she have suffered a greater damage than to exclude herself from the peace conference where she had everything to gain and nothing to lose. In ten years there will be a very different situation. Then also our people having grown wise will be sure to shout, "Why was not this stopped while there was yet time?" It seems to me necessary that someone in the government ought to give attention primarily to China and the Far Eastern situation. It is very difficult to get any attention for China. I mean any continuous attention that results in getting something actually done. Everything else seems to come first because Europe seems so much nearer; and yet the destinies of Serbia, Czecho-Slovakia and Greece are infinitesimal in their importance to the future of America compared with those of China.

During my service here I have constantly suffered from this lack of continuous attention to the Far Eastern situation at home. It has reacted on the consular service; the interpreter service which is absolutely necessary to make our consular corps in China effective has been starved, as no new appointments have been made. In my own case promises of assistance which have been given, repeatedly went unfulfilled. In this matter I have not the least personal

[2] Tuan Ch'i-jui, Chinese Prime Minister on four different occasions between April 1916 and October 1918; also a Chinese war lord who collaborated with the Japanese and who, with his war-lord allies, built up a military establishment known as the Anfu Clique.

feeling. I know the result is not due to the personal neglect or ill-will of any man or group of men, only it seems to me to indicate a general sentiment of the unimportance of Far Eastern affairs, which ought to be remedied. I repeat that these statements are not made in a spirit of complaint; all individual members of the Department of State have shown nothing but consideration and readiness to assist, but there has been lacking a concentrated interest in China, which ought to be represented in some one of the high officials, designated to follow up Far Eastern affairs and, accorded influence commensurate with responsibilities in this matter. I feel very strongly about the importance of the entire Far Eastern situation to the United States and I hope before long to have an opportunity to speak to you personally about it.

With the highest regards and the best wishes for your continued well-being, I remain, dear Mr. President,

Faithfully yours,   Paul S Reinsch.

TLS (SDR, RG 59, 123 R 271/101, DNA).

ENCLOSURE   II

From Paul Samuel Reinsch

Personal

Summer Camp of the 15th Infantry,
China Expedition, Chinwangtao, China,

My Dear Mr. President: June 15th, 1919.

In connection with my letter of June 7th, with the deep interest I now have in China and in American work here, I cannot but think of who will be chosen to carry on this work; and while it is far from my mind to desire to make any suggestions, yet I feel that perhaps, some estimate of what the situation requires might be useful to you. I know that if you already have some one in mind, you will not allow this communication to take up your time.

The men who have any special knowledge of China are few indeed, Mr. J. V. A. MacMurray, is perhaps the best informed man on treaty relations and his work in China has given him a grasp also on practical American interests and their essential needs. He is a man of keen intellectual abilities, fitted to deal with the deeply complicated problems that arise here. He will undoubtedly, as he grows older, develope more of general human sympathy, which will increase his effectiveness. He is a keen tactician, and will not unnecessarily yield any advantage.

Among other men, who to my knowledge have, through experience, or study, or both, acquired a special mastery of Chinese and Far Eastern affairs, and whose personality too would fit them to deal with the Chinese effectively, are Mr. Charles Denby,[1] the two Willoughbys,[2] and David C. Barrows,[3] Dean of the University of California, who served during the war as Chief of the Army Intelligence Department in the Far East and who was formally a member of the Philippine Commission.

Of these, Mr. Denby has had the longest practical experience in China, the Willoughbys have won the confidence of the Chinese and gained valuable experience while acting as advisers here, and Mr. Barrows had an unusual grasp of the entire Far Eastern situation.

From what I know of the Chinese and particularly of their feelings concerning the present situation, I know that they would be greatly encouraged if a man of great personal power and previous high rank were to be sent here. Even without a previous experience in Chinese affairs, such a man, if he had breadth of view and sympathy, would be received by them with a feeling that the importance of their country was fully appreciated. If Mr. MacMurray were Counsellor and Mr. Peck[4] First Chinese Secretary, the special knowledge required and advice on any situation which might arise, would be supplied to the Chief of the Mission. If it were possible to send a member of the Cabinet, a Senator, or Ex-Senator, or, from some other walk in life, the biggest man available, with a sound knowledge of industrial life and commerce, the position of American interests would be greatly favored. During the last five years I have not been in direct touch with the leaders at home so that I do not know to whom this opportunity would appeal. I believe that Senator Salisbury of New Jersey[5] has somewhat interested himself in Far Eastern affairs. I also feel that the sending of a high official from the State Department would give encouragement to the Chinese. Mr. William Phillips has been First Secretary of Legation here; Mr. Breckinridge Long has devoted special attention to the affairs of China and realizes the importance of developing our relations with the Chinese.

I know that the Chinese would be greatly honored and encouraged if the United States would take a step in the direction of having an Ambassador at Peking, either by directly suggesting an exchange of Ambassadors or appointing, temporarily, an Official of Ambassadorial rank, as the Japanese did (in the case of Baron Hayashi).[6] Ambassador Fletcher[7] was in charge of the Legation at Peking, as Secretary, at a time when very important negotiations were going on.

I trust that you may not misjudge the spirit in which the above remarks are made. I am proud to be able to report to you, that not-withstanding great difficulties and adverse activities and circumstances, the treasure of American influence, which was committed into my hands, has not been deminished [diminished]; and I cannot, therefore, but feel a deep interest in the personality of the man to whom I am to turn over this important trust. The constructive work possible here, calls for the great practical abilities and a creative mind, but particularly broad sympathy with the efforts of a worthy people to establish representative institutions in the face of every obstacle that foreign intrigue can conceive.

I am writing this letter from the Summer Camp of the Fifteenth Infantry (China Expedition), where I am spending the week end with the Officers.

With the highest regard and the best wishes for your continued well being, I am, dear Mr. President,

Faithfully Yours,   Paul S Reinsch.

TLS (SDR, RG 59, 123 R 271/106, DNA).
    [1] Long-time Foreign Service officer in China; recently special representative of the Department of State in Japan and China.
    [2] Westel Woodbury Willoughby, Professor of Political Science at The Johns Hopkins University; constitutional adviser to the Chinese government, 1916-1917; and William Franklin Willoughby, Director of the Institute for Governmental Research, Washington, D. C., constitutional adviser to the Chinese Republic, 1914-1916.
    [3] Actually, David Prescott Barrows.
    [4] Willys Ruggles Peck, Consul at Tsingtao, a long-time China hand.
    [5] Actually, Willard Saulsbury, former Democratic senator from Delaware.
    [6] Gonsuke Hayashi (1860-1939), Japanese career diplomat; Japanese Minister, with rank of Ambassador, to China, 1916-1919.
    [7] That is, Henry Prather Fletcher, Ambassador to Mexico.

From Robert Lansing, with Enclosure

My dear Mr. President: Washington July 25, 1919.

I am enclosing copies of two telegrams, one from Mr. Stevens[1] and one from Mr. Smith,[2] the American member of the Inter-Allied Committee for Supervising the Siberian Railways, which I think you may want to note.   Faithfully yours,   Robert Lansing

TLS (WP, DLC).
    [1] J. F. Stevens to RL, July 19, 1919, T telegram (WP, DLC), which reads as follows: "It will be unfortunate if Japanese are utilized to take the place of Czechs guarding railway. Japanese preponderance and domination should be lessened rather than increased."
    [2] Charles Hadden Smith.

E N C L O S U R E

Vladivostock. July 19, 1919.

Important. 416. A telegram was sent to the Omsk government eighteenth July, signed by all members of the inter-Allied Committees except Horvath[1] who agreed but felt he could not sign, as follows: "Since March first the Allied Powers have been endeavoring to restore the Siberian transport system in conformity with the inter-Allied agreement to which the Russian government is a party. Our aim has been to revive Russia and to place her again among leading nations without thought of other reward than that of seeing Russia a united whole and a free, democratic country which her people deserve. And we want no special interests, concessions, territorial advantages, or other selfish emoluments, but desire to have Russia maintain the open door policy to all friendly nations.

To date our efforts have only met with small success. This has been due entirely to the unresponsive actions of certain of the governments own agents, Russian military authorities, especially Semenoff,[2] and the officers in charge of Russian military transportation have continually hindered and obstructed the movement of trains and the disposition of cars. The transport of Russian military supplies has been seriously diminished by their actions. The military are indispensable for their proper task of defending the railway. Their interferences in its operation, however, is nothing but a hindrance to the civil authorities to whose admirable spirit of loyalty and cooperation the committee can testify. The Committee also appreciates the action of Minister Oustroogu[3] in his telegram of recent date relative to shop management and repairs, and feels that analogous action is required in the other departments of the administration.

In view of the above data we the undersigned members of the inter-Allied Committee feel it is our duty to require that the following provisions be fulfilled immediately.

One. That Semenoff must at once stop his interference with the operation of the railway and also all other arbitrary and violent acts.

Two. That all the military officers in charge of military transportation be required to obey the committee's resolution of May 27 which says that only railway officials shall have the right to operate the railway.

Three. That the general supervision, the technical and economic management and the operation of all railways in the zone where the Allied Powers are now operating be trusted to the inter-Allied Committee and its subordinate board in accordance with the terms of the agreement entered into by the Allied Powers.

Four. That no obstacle of whatever kind which would be in contravention to point three be imposed by any Russian governmental agency now existing or which may be created during the term of this agreement.

Five. That an approval to this telegram is required at the very earliest moment.

The committe is anxious to aid Russia and has the requisite funds at hand but does not consider that these can be applied to advantage unless the above requirements are fully complied with."

Copies of the above have been sent to all Allied representatives in Omsk who are asked to present same at once to Government. Ambassador Morris will receive copy. Smith.   Caldwell

T telegram (WP, DLC).
    [1] That is, Dmitrii Leonidovich Horvath or Horvat.
    [2] That is, Grigorii Mikhailovich Semenov.
    [3] That is, Leonid Aleksandrovich Ustrugov.

From Robert Lansing

My dear Mr. President: Washington July 25, 1919.

May I bring to your attention the serious situation which has developed within the past few days in the Republic of Honduras.

As you know the term of office of President Bertrand[1] of Honduras terminates on the 30th of January 1920 and elections should be held, according to the Constitution of that country, in October 1919. It appears that two candidates in opposition to the present Government have presented themselves, one being Doctor Membreno,[2] at present Vice-President of Honduras, and ex-Minister to Washington, now temporarily in the United States, and the other General Lopez Gutierrez,[3] formerly Minister of War and brother of the last Honduran Minister in Washington.[4] President Bertrand, it is understood, is opposed to these two candidates and desires to have elected his brother-in-law, Doctor Soriano,[5] who has lived most of his life in Salvador and is little known in his own country. As so much opposition was aroused by the desire of President Bertrand to impose his candidate, Doctor Soriano, on Honduras, he has apparently decided to take all steps in his power, even though contrary to the Constitution, to have Soriano elected. According to the reports of the American Minister,[6] which are contained in the copies of telegrams attached herewith, it seems that Bertrand has practically assumed a dictatorship and is attempting to intimidate all those opposed to his will by expulsion from the country, imprisonment, etc.

Some months ago upon receipt of information that the country was much aroused over President Bertrand's arbitrary acts which practically forecasted his attitude toward holding a fair election, the Department instructed the American Minister by cable to approach him in a confidential and informal manner and point out to him the friendly interest which the United States Government took in the situation in Honduras and its hope that freedom in elections would be guaranteed by him.[7] This statement on the part of the Government of the United States seems to have had no effect and as Bertrand has placed the police and armed forces of the Government under the command of Corso,[8] a Mexican General, and appears only to confer with the Mexican Minister, the Salvadoran Minister, and is rumored to have conferred with Tinoco's representative in Honduras,[9] it would seem that he has made up his mind not to heed the friendly advices of the United States and is determined to carry out his plans at all hazards in order to perpetuate his family in control of Honduras, the result of which would undoubtedly be the complete domination of that Republic by Mexican and Salvadoran influences.

The Honduran Chargé d'Affaires, Mr. Diaz,[10] who has been in Washington for several years and who is not affiliated with any of the present political parties, has approached the Department on several occasions stating in the strictest confidence that the situation in Honduras is more than serious and has requested that the United States Government take some steps in order that the peace may not be disturbed. He stated that he considered President Bertrand to be proceeding against the provisions of the Constitution and that Doctor Soriano is more of a Salvadoran that a Honduran and if elected would turn over Honduras body and soul to Salvador.

In view of the critical situation as reported in Minister Jones' cable of July 18, and 19, the Department instructed him by cable on July 20[11] again to bring to the attention of President Bertrand the United States interest in seeing Honduras attain her development along lines of freedom in elections and to say that the attitude of the United States towards the present Government of the country must be guided by the actions of those in control. In his reply to the above mentioned cablegram the Minister reports that Bertrand did not appear to desire to receive the Department's friendly advices and made no statement as regards freedom in elections.[12] This would tend to confirm the Department's opinion that he is unwilling to be guided by the United States and turns to Salvador and Mexico.

The latest cable which the Department has received[13] states that General Lopez Gutierrez, one of the presidential candidates, is re-

ported to have started a revolutionary movement some forty miles
from the Capital and that the Government has sent troops in pursuit. The Minister adds that the situation continues "grave in the
extreme." In the light of this cable it would seem, unless some radical step is taken by the Government of the United States in the
immediate future, that Honduras will be plunged into civil war, the
consequences of which would be difficult to forecast.

A situation almost analogous to the present one occurred in 1911
when the Department of State offered its good offices to both the
Government of Honduras, and the leader of a revolution inviting
them on board a United States war vessel, TACOMA with the intention of assisting them to compose, by peaceful means, their controversy and in an endeavor to find a solution of any question connected with the presidency which would best represent the will of
the people of Honduras and the legitimate aspirations of all parties.[14] The United States gunboat MACHIAS, is now at the port of
Amapala, and the United States ship DENVER, with two sister ships
are now steaming from Balboa to that port. It is therefore suggested that an invitation be sent both to President Bertrand and
General Lopez Gutierrez to come on board the flagship, under the
good offices of the United States, with a view to composing their
differences and in an endeavor to come to a settlement of this serious situation. This action would undoubtedly bring forth beneficial results for the tranquility of Central America unless President
Bertrand is so dominated by Salvadoran and Mexican influence
that he may be unwilling to give heed to the good counsel of the
United States. Should this be true it may be necessary for the
United States to proceed in a more forceful manner, in order to
safeguard American lives and property and preserve peace and order in Central America.

Faithfully yours,   Robert Lansing[15]

TLS (WP, DLC).
    [1] Francisco Bertrand.
    [2] Alberto Membreño.
    [3] Gen. Rafael López Gutiérrez.
    [4] J. Antonio López Gutiérrez.
    [5] Nazario Soriano.
    [6] Thomas Sambola Jones. For his reports, see T. S. Jones to FLP, Feb. 17, 1919;
March 18 and 20, 1919; and T. S. Jones to W. Phillips, July 18 and 19, 1919, all printed
in FR 1919, II, 374-79, passim.
    [7] FLP to T. S. Jones, March 15, 1919, ibid., p. 376.
    [8] Gen. Castillo Corso.
    [9] The Mexican Minister to Honduras was Alberto C. Franco; the Salvadoran Minister
was one A. López. The representative of Féderico Tinoco Granados, President of Costa
Rica, cannot be identified.
    [10] R. Camilo Díaz.
    [11] W. Phillips to T. S. Jones, July 20, 1919, ibid., pp. 379-80. The most important
paragraph of this telegram reads as follows:
    "The Department desires that you seek earliest opportunity to call upon President
Bertrand and convey to him orally the substance of the following statement: The Gov-

ernment of the United States, in the light of the past friendly and informal communications to the Government of Honduras relative to its great interest in seeing its sister Republic of Honduras continue to develop its life along those broad lines of freedom in elections and the peace and harmony to which it has been accustomed, cannot but view the present situation with very considerable apprehension. The Government of the United States therefore considers that it is its duty to reiterate its former statements in connection with the hope which it has expressed concerning the freedom of elections and wishes to inform the Government of Honduras that its friendship for the people of that Republic and its desire to see peace prevail in all parts of the Western Hemisphere, necessitate its very close scrutiny of the present conditions and require that its future attitude toward those in control of the political destinies of that country be guided by their actions."

[12] T. S. Jones to W. Phillips, July 23, [21?], 1919, *ibid.*, p. 381. Jones reported as follows: "Immediately after receipt of your cable of July 20, 11 p.m. I requested audience with Bertrand. I called upon him at 8 p.m. and delivered orally the substance of your message to him in a polite but emphatic manner. He replied that unless furnished in writing, formally and officially, he could make no reply, that his eyes and ears were closed to everything not officially presented. He expressed appreciation and thanks for friendly interest of the Government of the United States for peace and harmony in Honduras and said that it has been and will be his endeavor to always maintain very best relations with the Government of the United States but made no reply as to freedom in elections."

[13] T. S. Jones to W. Phillips, July 22, 1919, *ibid.*, pp. 380-81.

[14] About these events, see Dana G. Munro, *Intervention and Dollar Diplomacy in the Caribbean, 1900-1921* (Princeton, N. J., 1964), pp. 225-30, and *FR 1911*, pp. 292-307.

[15] We print this letter, not because Wilson saw and read it (he wrote "Honduras" at the top of it), but because he did not answer it, either because of preoccupation with European affairs, or he forgot it, or he did not have the energy to become involved in Latin American affairs on such an intimate level, a fact which is evident from his correspondence with the State Department during July and August 1919. About the State Department's intervention in Honduran affairs during the summer of 1919, see the documents printed in *FR 1919*, II, 374-95, and Munro, *Intervention and Dollar Diplomacy in the Caribbean, 1900-1921*, pp. 452-55.

From Thomas William Lamont

Dear Mr. President: [New York] July 25th, 1919.
Treaty Situation
Since talking with you that morning in Washington two weeks ago, I have been disturbed and distressed that the situation has seemingly failed to clear up to any extent. I am not in close touch with Washington, and I may be unduly apprehensive, but the opponents to the ratification of the Treaty precisely as it stands today, seem to me still sadly lacking in insight.

The point about the situation that perhaps disturbs me most, is that the public itself, taking its cue from headlines of opposing newspapers, seems, to a certain extent, to have the feeling that information is being with-held from them. Until this public is put in possession of all information necessary, and is therefore convinced that the Treaty is as it should be, it will fail to bring to bear a proper public opinion upon the Senate.

You have, as I take, proposed to meet this view, if it exists, by possibly making a series of public utterances throughout the country. I have ventured to give considerable thought to this plan, and my present conviction is that such a plan may possibly serve to intensify the opposition in the Senate. I believe that the alternate plan, which I am writing in this letter for the purpose of suggesting to you, would not have the disadvantages of a speaking tour, and yet would line up the whole country for the Treaty as it stands to-day.

My suggestion therefore is for you to go direct to the Senate, or to the Foreign Relations Committee, preferably the Senate, and explain by word of mouth, in a series of carefully prepared memoranda, all the chief points of controversy or question; such explanations to be publicly reported. Every word of these utterances will be sent to every hamlet in the United States, and after you had finished the series, the country would feel that it knew everything that you know (except such minor points as could not with compatibility be made public), and would in my judgment back you up to the uttermost.

Of course such a suggestion may be unprecedented, but the whole situation is unprecedented, and in my judgment requires still more active effort. I would have you say in effect to the Senate:

"In my address on July 10th, I expressed a desire to meet the members of the Foreign Relations Committee to discuss the Treaty with them. The Committee has not seen fit to respond favorably to my suggestion. I therefore insist upon the opportunity of addressing in detail, the Senate, which is the co-ordinating treaty making agency of our Government. I purpose during the next week to make six direct written or oral communications to the Senate upon the details of the Treaty; and subsequent to such communications I shall be available to the Senate Foreign Relations Committee to answer specific inquiries."

This of course will sound to you very crude. But some such direct challenge as this would draw instant and enthusiastic response from the public I believe.

Therefore, I am astonished to find this curious feeling that the public is being kept in the dark. Whence this feeling arises I do not know, but it has to be reckoned with. The American people are reasonable and fair, and need only to be given specific reasons for such compromises as it was absolutely necessary to make in Paris, in order to understand and accept them. By some such course as this I believe you would be cutting the ground from under the feet of the opposing Senators.

On the contrary, if you should make the suggested tour, the present spirit of partisanship would, I fear, be greatly augmented. Such a tour would be painted as a campaign against the Senate, and arouse further resentment in many of the senators. Probably a number of them, or of their adherents, would precede or follow you with opposing speeches in different parts of the country.

Such a direct course as I have suggested, would, as I say, rivet the public attention of everybody, and many senators who are now hesitant, would, I believe, be greatly influenced by such a course. The collective judgment of the American people is poised expectantly, awaiting more information upon matters which are not understood or which have been deliberately misrepresented. A series of direct, concise and categorical written or spoken communications from the President of the United States to the Senate upon the principal points of the Treaty which have been under discussion, would furnish in my judgment the foundation for the wisest exercise of that collective judgment.

This morning I had Leffingwell[1] on the telephone, in order to give him this thought, which he said he would get to you, but I am so concerned over the situation that I am following up that conversation with this written letter. Under almost any other circumstances I should consider it an impertinence to proffer a suggestion such as this, or in such a manner. But I am sure, dear Mr. President, that you will not misunder[stand] my motives in addressing you with informality. The issues at stake are too great for me to do otherwise; and fortunately I feel that you have always encouraged me to speak to you so directly that I have ample excuse for writing you.

With great respect, I am,

Sincerely yours,   [Thomas W. Lamont]

TCL (T. W. Lamont Papers, MH-BA).
    [1] That is, Russell Cornell Leffingwell.

ADDENDUM

From Frank Irving Cobb

Dear Mr. President: [New York] June 6, 1917.

After giving the most earnest consideration of which I am capable to your suggestion of Sunday, I am convinced that it would be a great mistake for you to appoint me to such a position.[1]

Whatever help I have been able to give you has owed its effectiveness to its disinterestedness and to The World's independent position in journalism. Both the disinterestedness and the independence would be swept away if I became the official defender and promoter of the Administration's war policies. I might still believe myself disinterested, but nobody else would believe it; nor could The World maintain its journalistic reputation for independence except by showing itself less friendly and helpful to you than in the past. Great newspapers are strange organisms which function according to laws of their own. In order to do the work that you have in mind, it would be necessary for me to sever connection with The World permanently. I should owe that to the paper and the paper would naturally demand it in order to keep itself free. That is a rule of the office to which there are no exceptions and, least of all, to which an exception could be made for the editor himself. However ardently The World might wish to support the Administration, it could not tolerate the suspicion that it was edited by the Administration.

I should be willing enough to leave The World and go to Washington if I could be more useful there than here in this crisis. But would that be the case? The same kind of work that I do on The World in explaining the war policies and purposes of the Administration would lose most of its effectiveness if I were to do this. The public would take a different view of it. The newspapers would take a different view of it. What is now a labor of disinterested patriotism would then appear as paid propaganda, to be discounted as such. If I had an independent income and could serve without salary, it might be different, but to be obliged to accept pay instantly raises public doubts as to the character of the service. So much for the personal aspects of the case.

As for the rest, I am by no means convinced that the need of such a department is as yet vital or even desirable. The American people know more about this war than their critics think. They have responded generously to every appeal that you have made— the war resolution, the selective draft and the Liberty Loan. They will continue to respond—but to you, and to you alone. Events may quicken them, but propaganda will not except as it may be directed toward the accomplishment of a definite thing. The best way to do that, it seems to me, is to leave it to the various departments. The Navy has done superbly under Daniels's direction with the campaign for recruits. Baker has handled the conscription thing admirably. McAdoo's work for the Liberty Loan has been splendid. Hoover's food crusade can be handled in the same way, with all of us turning in and doing our utmost to make it successful. The great mass of the American newspapers will respond at once to an appeal of that kind for support when made by you or by a responsible official of the Government, but they are certain to look askance upon arguments and policies that come from a department devoted wholly to Government propaganda and directed by paid agencies.

I do not think that you can overestimate the necessity for voluntary service even in work of that kind. My own observation has been that every government in this war which has undertaken to subsidize a publicity campaign of any kind has made a mess of it and done itself more harm than good.

In the larger aspects of the war, Lane's speech[2] is a notable example of what can be done. Most of the newspapers printed it in full on their first pages. It was worth ten thousand inspired articles in newspapers and magazines, because it rang with the fervor and sincerity of the man.

In that connection, your note to the Russian Government[3] is one of the great documents of the war, which you should have printed by all means, regardless of the theories of the mandarins of the foreign offices. That one note is worth more than a year's effort on the part of an official bureau of publicity in enlightening the country as to the aims and objects of the war.

The time may come when it will be necessary for the Government to spend money for propaganda purposes, but I doubt it if the Administration will use the voluntary agencies at its command. In that connection, I think the Cabinet ought to be admonished to establish better relations with the correspondents and capitalize their enthusiasm in giving publicity to the Government's plans. Correspondents will eagerly write such information as they obtain personally from the departments, where they would not touch it at all if it came from an official bureau and looked to them like "press agent stuff."

There is one service that I can do for you personally without any change in relationship in respect to The World, and it will have the merit of being done gratuitously. I can watch public opinion closely for you, with all its changes and fluctuations, noting where it sags and when it is halting and hesitant. This I can report to you from week to week, with my best judgment as to how the situation can be met. It is something that can be done here much better than in the official atmosphere of Washington. Somehow, I lose my touch with public opinion when I am long in Washington, and yet my instinct for sensing it is the only talent I have that is of any particular value. If you want me to do this, I shall regard it as a privilege.[4]

I have written to you with the utmost frankness, Mr. President, because there can be nothing but frankness between us. All my desire is to do everything I can to help and, if I could see my way clear to be of real service to you in the work you suggest, I should abandon everything else for it. But I am convinced that, for the present at least, I can help more where I am than I could possibly help as a member of your official family. This opinion has been reached after much perturbation of spirit, but it is my honest conviction and as such I submit it to you.

The compliment you have paid me is one that I shall always remember and treasure, but it is because I sincerely desire to give the best there is in me for the war that I know it would be a mistake for me to undertake a task in which I should find myself hopelessly handicapped through my lack of complete financial independence. If, in time, however, you feel that this work must be done, and done by me, I will make some sort of arrangements, whatever they be, and come, but with the understanding that it is to be without compensation. To accept pay for it would chill and kill the spirit of the service.

With sincere regards,   As ever yours,   [Frank I. Cobb]

CCL (received from Hubbard H. Cobb).
    [1] Wilson had invited Cobb to come to the White House on Sunday, June 3, 1917, "to discuss a very important matter." See WW to F. I. Cobb, June 1, 1917, Vol. 42. Cobb came for lunch at about 12:30 and seems to have left at 2:30. Cobb's letter makes clear for the first time what Wilson had in mind to ask Cobb to do. The letter also reveals that Wilson had not yet realized or known about the vast propaganda organization that George Creel was at this very time fashioning in the Committe on Public Information.
    [2] Cobb was undoubtedly referring to a speech that Lane gave on June 4 to the Home Club of the Interior Department. See the *New York Times*, June 5, 1917.
    [3] Wilson's message to the Russian provisional government, printed as the Enclosure with WW to RL, April 6, 1917, Vol. 41.
    [4] Insofar as the Editors and Hubbard H. Cobb, Cobb's son, know, Cobb did not make such reports to Wilson.

INDEX

NOTE ON THE INDEX

The alphabetically arranged analytical table of contents at the front of the volume eliminates duplication, in both contents and index, of references to certain documents, such as letters. Letters are listed in the contents alphabetically by name, and chronologically within each name by page. The subject matter of all letters is, of course, indexed. The Editorial Notes and Wilson's writings are listed in the contents chronologically by page. In addition, the subject matter of both categories is indexed. The index covers all references to books and articles mentioned in text or notes. Footnotes are indexed. Page references to footnotes which place a comma between the page number and "n" cite both text and footnote, thus: "418,n1." On the other hand, absence of the comma indicates reference to the footnote only, thus: "59n1"—the page number denoting where the footnote appears.

The index supplies the fullest known form of names and, for the Wilson and Axson families, relationships as far down as cousins. Persons referred to by nicknames or shortened forms of names can be identified by reference to entries for these forms of the names.

All entries consisting of page numbers only and which refer to concepts, issues, and opinions (such as democracy, the tariff, and money trust, leadership, and labor problems), are references to Wilson's speeches and writings.

Four cumulative contents-index volumes are now in print: Volume 13, which covers Volumes 1-12, Volume 26, which covers Volumes 14-25, Volume 39, which covers Volumes 27-38, and Volume 52, which covers Volumes 40-49 and 51.

INDEX

Aborigines Protection Society, 276,n4, 277, 314

Abyssinia: *see* Ethiopia

Adalia (now Antalya), Turkey, 221

Addis Ababa, 406,n1

Address of the President of the United States to the Senate . . . July 10, 1919, 436n

Adinkerke, Belgium, 3

Adrianople, Turkey, 159

Adriatic question: Jay on, 109; WW memorandum on, 170-71; D. W. Johnson on, 227-30; White rejects Tittoni's proposal on, 551-54; Italian position on, 575

Africa: Lord Milner on German colonies and mandates, 261, 262-64, 265

Aidin (now Aydin), Turkey, 212, 216

Alabama: and woman suffrage, 464, 479, 537

Albania, 344, 405, 552, 554, 575

Albert I, King of the Belgians, 3n1, 5, 6, 7, 11, 12, 14, 15-16, 25,n2; WW on, 16; WW's toast to, 16,n1; R. S. Baker on, 29-30; WW's thank you to, 33, 35-36; thanks WW, 61, 355; wishes to visit U.S., 609; photographs of, *illustration section*

Albrecht-Carrié, René, 584n2

alcoholism: and American Expeditionary Forces, 531, 532-33

alcohol: *see* prohibition

Allenby, Gen. Sir Edmund Henry Hynman, 8n1, 157

Allied Maritime Transport Council, 151,n5

All Russia Union of Cooperatives, 359

Along the Afric Shore: An historic review of two centuries of U.S.-African relations (Howe), 406n2

Alsberg, Henry Garfield, 243,n7

Ambrosius, Lloyd E., 66n3

American Chamber of Commerce in Paris, 625n1

American Commissioners Plenipotentiary to Negotiate Peace (Wilson, Bliss, House, Lansing, White): Westermann on Near East issues, 128-29

American Commission to Negotiate Peace, 341; WW meets with, 32, 33-34; Hornbeck on China signing treaty with reservations, 176; on international consultation, 520-22, 587; on setting up commissions as provided by peace treaty, 585-87

American Committee for the Independence of Armenia, 486n1

American Expeditionary Forces: psychiatrist's evaluation of men in, 530, 531-33; *see also* United States Army

American Expeditionary Forces University, 361n2

American Federation of Labor: endorses League of Nations, 66, 138, 231; on prohibition, 294; resolution against mob rule and lynchings, 357-59; requests Burleson's removal, 364-65; and railroads, 377; and California telephone workers' strike, 503-504

American Red Cross, *see* Red Cross, American

Anatolia, 128, 212, 216, 240, 344, 345

Anderson, John Crawford: and suffrage amendment, 479,n1

Andrássy, Count Gyula (1823-1890), 94

Andrews, Edward House, 332,n4

Anti-Slavery and Aborigines Protection Society, 276n4

Antivari, Montenegro (now Bar, Yugoslavia), 405

Anxiety in England over League Fight. Maurice Tells of Fear of Its Effect on Anglo-American Friendship. Other Obstacles Serious. General Says Mutual Recognition of Countries' Part in War Would Help Clear Air (Maurice), 182,n1

Arabia, 159

Archiwum Polityczne Ignacego Paderewskiego (Janowska *et al.*, eds.), 271n2

Armenia, 128, 156, 238; WW on mandate for, 240, 246, 253, 424; suggestion of Resident Commissioner to, 314, 339; mission to, 486, 487

Armistice, the: and sinking of German fleet at Scapa Flow, 57n8, 83-84, 85, 102-103, 123, 142-43, 146, 168-70

arms limitation: League of Free Nations Association on, 447; *see also* demobilization; disarmament

Army (U.S.): *see* United States Army

Ars Poetica (Horace), 361n1

Ashurst, Henry Fountain: on WW's address to Senate, 445-46; on Bastille Day reception at French embassy, 492

Asia Minor, 128, 159; Council of Four on Italy and, 211-12, 217, 220, 342n3; WW on Italy and, 307, 309, 346; and Italy's claims in, 553, 554

Asquith, Herbert Henry, 386, 387

Assignment: America. De Valera's Mission to the United States (O'Doherty), 183n2

Assistance to France in the Event of Unprovoked Aggression by Germany. Message from the President of the United States, 66th Cong., 1st sess., 313n

Assling Triangle, 42, 227, 552

Associated Press, 369, 370, 605n1

Atherton, Gertrude Franklin (Mrs. George H. Bowen), 294,n4

Atherton, Ray, 555,n4

Aubert, Louis, 43

Auchincloss, Gordon, 134, 181, 232, 295, 332

Austria, 55, 430; and Klagenfurt Basin, 41-43, 51-56, 57-59; and frontiers, 172, 357, 371; Hoover's proposal for economic reconstruction of, 173-74; and Südbahn, 280; *see also* Paris Peace Conference—Austrian treaty

Austria-Hungary, 56; and railroads of former monarchy (Südbahn), 317-21

Axson, Stockton (Isaac Stockton Keith Axson II), brother-in-law of WW, 31, 78, 397;

WOODROW WILSON

Woodrow Wilson, cont.

ences with American correspondents, 235-38, 240-45, 246-52, 252-54, 417-24; plans for arrival in U.S., 291, 371, 376, 377; statement on signing of peace treaty, 292-93; at treaty-signing ceremony, then departs for U.S., 302-306, 328, 333, 354; signs treaty with EBW's pen, 303; signs autographs at Versailles, 323, 324-25; seal for treaty signing, 324; statement upon leaving France, 350; aboard *George Washington* returning to U.S., 354, 355-56; receives honorary degree from University of Geneva, 356-57; works on message to Senate, 356, 360-61, 362, 363, 369, 370; talk of third term, 374, 506n1, 577; handwriting contrast, 376n1; address to fellow passengers aboard *George Washington*, 378-82, 383; solicits suggestions from advisers on message to Senate, 385-86, 386-88, 388; to address Senate, 397; welcome in New York City, 401; address in Carnegie Hall, 401-404; congratulatory notes to, 407, 410, 411; text of address to Senate, 426-36; comments on address to Senate, 425, 444-45, 445-46, 459; holds reception-discussion after Senate address, 437-38; acknowledges letters on his Senate address, 462-63; new availability to congressmen, 474-75; Whitlock sends Whistler's book to, 489,n1; invitations to and meetings with Republican senators on treaty, 492-93,n2, 516-18, 541, 548,n1, 561-62, 569-70, 593-95, 599-602, 619-22; on increase of Red Cross fund from sale of wool from White House sheep, 505; and payment for bronze wreath in memory of *Otranto* victims, 508,n1; remarks to Czech soldiers, 518-19; and testimonial to wartime volunteers, 540; illness may postpone trip west, 578

APPEARANCE AND IMPRESSIONS

attire on Belgian tour, 5-6; in new straw hat, 34; Ike Hoover on, 112n1; twitch in eye, 112n1; C. T. Thompson on, 246; looks well, 363; photographs, *illustration section*

APPOINTMENT SUGGESTIONS, APPOINTMENTS, AND RESIGNATIONS

Hoover to remain as Food Administrator, 133; Lansing and McCormick discuss appointments, 134; Whitlock named ambassador to Italy, 290; on making Pershing Chief of Staff, 293; H. White on his son in diplomatic service in Siam, 348n3; American Federation of Labor requests Burleson's removal, 364-65; Gibson appointed minister to Poland, 365n1; and first Belgian ambassador to U.S., 385; WW considers Polk for ambassadorial position, 396; Hurley's resignation, 439-40, 440-41; and F. B. Harrison's resignation, 478,n1; and

Woodrow Wilson, cont.

U.S. Court of Claims, 482,n1; no nepotism in appointments, 482; controversy over Reparation Commission appointment, 493, 520-21, 544, 582, 609,n1; Taussig's resignation, 514, 550, 617-18; power to make appointments to international commissions, 519, 520, 522,n2; T. N. Page's resignation, 559-60; T. W. Page appointed to Tariff Commission, 617,n2; Taussig interested in position of ambassador to Germany, 618; H. B. Fine suggested for secretary of Federal Reserve Board, 625,n1; and proposed Interallied Commission of Inquiry, 629-30,n4; Reinsch's resignation, 631-36; Cobb rejects WW's offer of press information position, 644-46

FAMILY AND PERSONAL LIFE

and income tax, 116; makes toast to peace and League of Nations, 135; House on Poincaré invitation episode, 179; WW's signet ring, 179; aides surprise with mechanical toys, 231; hand trembling from excitement when signing treaty, 324; incidents at Princeton, 361-62; R. S. Baker on personal traits of, 383; arrival at the White House, 401; R. S. Baker on WW not praising or commending him, 416; the Pettys repay loan, 543, 624; news to Cousin Lucy, 551; takes two-day cruise aboard *Mayflower*, 562-63; receives autographed book by Canby, 568,n2

HEALTH

fatigue from Belgian trip, 33; Lloyd George on long recovery of, 44; Ike Hoover on changed mental attitude and behavior after illness in Paris, 112n1; tired, 112n1, 231, 543; Montenegro presents Grayson with medal for keeping WW healthy, 239; rests, 356; looks well, 363; and badly written shorthand, 368n5; morning walk aboard ship, 374; indications of lack of proper blood supply to head, 446,n1; noticeable contraction in back of neck, 446,n1; EBW concerned over hot weather and WW's speaking tour, 543; handwriting deterioration, 544n2; appears well when reviewing Czech troops, 569; small stroke on July 19, 1919, 569, 578-79; good wishes from his pastor, 595,n1

OPINIONS AND COMMENTS

on destruction of Ypres, 5,n6; In coming personally I had merely followed my own heart and the heart of the people of America to Belgium, 8; on King Albert, 16; I believe that Belgium and her part in the war is in one sense the key of the whole struggle, because the violation of Belgium was the call to duty which aroused the nations. The enemy committed many outrages in